The All-America
Football Conference

The All-America Football Conference

Players, Coaches, Records, Games and Awards, 1946–1949

Edited by
KENNETH R. CRIPPEN
and MATT REASER

McFarland & Company, Inc., Publishers
Jefferson, North Carolina

Acknowledgments

A work like this could not be accomplished without the efforts of a lot of people. The Professional Football Researchers Association would like to thank the following people (in alphabetical order) for their contributions to this effort: George Bozeka, John Collins, Ken Crippen, Mark L. Ford, John Hogrogian, Sean Lahman, Tod Maher, John Maxymuk, Pete Palmer, Bill Pepperell, Andy Piascik, Ken Pullis, Matt Reaser, Gary Selby, John Turney, Kevin Voorhees, Ron Wolf and Mark Palczewski.

ALSO OF INTEREST

The Original Buffalo Bills: A History of the All-America Football Conference Team, 1946–1949, by Kenneth R. Crippen (McFarland, 2010)

LIBRARY OF CONGRESS CATALOGUING-IN-PUBLICATION DATA

Names: Crippen, Kenneth R., editor. | Reaser, Matt, 1986– editor.
Title: The All-America Football Conference : players, coaches, records, games and awards, 1946–1949 / edited by Kenneth R. Crippen and Matt Reaser.
Description: Jefferson, North Carolina : McFarland & Company, Inc., Publishers, 2018. | Includes bibliographical references and index.
Identifiers: LCCN 2017054919 | ISBN 9781476670959 (softcover : acid free paper) ∞
Subjects: LCSH: All-America Football Conference—History. | Football—United States—Histsory—20th century.
Classification: LCC GV955.5.A43 A55 2018 | DDC 796.33209—dc23
LC record available at https://lccn.loc.gov/2017054919

BRITISH LIBRARY CATALOGUING DATA ARE AVAILABLE

ISBN (print) 978-1-4766-7095-9
ISBN (ebook) 978-1-4766-3107-3

© 2018 Kenneth R. Crippen and Matt Reaser. All rights reserved

No part of this book may be reproduced or transmitted in any form or by any means, electronic or mechanical, including photocopying or recording, or by any information storage and retrieval system, without permission in writing from the publisher.

Front cover: 49ers running back Norm Standlee (72) is tackled high by Cleveland Browns guard Alex Kapter in a game on November 10, 1946, at Kezar Stadium in San Francisco (Acme Telephoto)

Printed in the United States of America

*McFarland & Company, Inc., Publishers
Box 611, Jefferson, North Carolina 28640
www.mcfarlandpub.com*

Table of Contents

ACKNOWLEDGMENTS   iv
PREFACE (by Kenneth R. Crippen)   1

Part 1: A Brief History of the AAFC
(by Kenneth R. Crippen)   3

Part 2: PFRA All-Pro Selections
(by Kenneth R. Crippen, Matt Reaser and Andy Piascik)   10

PFRA's AAFC All-Pro Teams   10
PFRA's All-Time Team   13
PFRA's AAFC All-Time Team Biographies   14
PFRA's AAFC Notables   21

Part 3: Individual Statistics   25

1946   25
1947   33
1948   40
1949   47
Lifetime Leaders   53

Part 4: Awards and Statistical Records   55

All-Conference Teams (by Andy Piascik)   55
Statistical Records   59
Statistical Champions by Season   68

Part 5: Conference Statistics   70

Conference Standings   70
Club versus Club Records   71
Conference Statistics by Season   77
Attendance (by Andy Piascik)   78

v

Part 6: Linescores 83
Exhibition Games 83
Regular and Post-Season Games 84

Part 7: The Draft 147
History of the AAFC Draft (by Kenneth R. Crippen) 147
1947 148
1948 153
1949 158
Allocation Draft 163

Part 8: Player Register 168

Part 9: Coach Register (by John Maxymuk) 342

Sources 353

Index 355

Preface

by Kenneth R. Crippen

The Professional Football Researchers Association (PFRA) is a non-profit educational organization dedicated to preserving pro football history. Incorporated in 1979, the organization has steadily grown to over 400 members in 10 countries, and contains some of the world's foremost historians of the game.

Throughout its history, the PFRA has covered all aspects of pro football history. From teams to players to various major and minor leagues, the PFRA has touched on a variety of topics through publication of its magazine—*The Coffin Corner*—or through its books. The All-America Football Conference (AAFC) is among the topics covered.

I started to organize this project as I was working on my book *The Original Buffalo Bills: The History of the All-America Football Conference Team, 1946–1949* (McFarland, 2010). While researching that book, I had the opportunity to interview the surviving members of the team, as well as members of other AAFC teams. That inspired me to make sure that the story of the AAFC would be told. This book is an attempt to preserve that story.

What makes this book unique is that we wanted to take the knowledge of the PFRA and apply it. For the first time, the PFRA has put together its official All-Pro teams all four years of the AAFC, and an All-Conference team. We also included scouting reports, as well as biographies for the members of the All-Conference team. Beyond that, we also picked notable people from the AAFC that were not included in the All-Conference team. This included members of the Pro Football Hall of Fame that have an affiliation with the AAFC, as well as coaches and owners.

An interesting story is how the PFRA obtained the official AAFC scoresheets. From PFRA member Pete Palmer:

> Around the year 2000, PFRA member Tod Maher ran across an article in *Sporting News* from 1981, which mentioned that a gentleman by the name of Steve Boda had copies of the official AAFC scoresheets. When Tod found him, he was 83 years old, retired and living in Kansas. He had accumulated a ton of stuff over the years, including lots of Notre Dame material. Steve was a long-time NCAA person who spent a lot of time in New York and the NCAA office was across the hall from the AAFC. Steve noticed they had thrown a lot of stuff out when the league folded in 1949, so he scooped it up.
>
> Tod inquired about the AAFC data, but didn't make much progress. He happened to mention it to me, so I thought I would give it a try. I wrote to Steve and sent him a $100 check to cover the cost of making copies, just to get him started. Of course, I was willing to pay more when the data actually arrived. He sent it back, saying he wasn't interested. So I tried again a few months later. I can't remember the details, but I finally talked to him and we made a deal. Unfortunately, 1948 only had the first third of the season, but the other three years were complete. Steve did not know what happened to the other games, although he did look around for them.
>
> During our conversation, he mentioned he also had weekly NBA stats for 1950–51 through 1955–56. The NCAA had kept stats for the NBA during that period. For some reason, the NBA did not keep splits for traded players from 1950–51 through 1963–64. Also, in some years they did not list players in less than 10 games. When the *Sporting News* took over the NBA guide in 1957–58, Bill Mokray tried to recreate the missing data from box scores, but he made a few mistakes. So I was anxious to get that data as well. So, we agreed on a price of $1,200 ($1,000 for the AAFC scoresheets and $200 for the basketball data). This was in 2007. I made two copies, sent one to Ken Crippen at the PFRA and the other to Joe Horrigan at the Pro Football Hall of Fame (the costs were split between Ken Crippen and Joe Horrigan). Bob Carroll (executive Director of the PFRA at the time) had told me that Joe [Horrigan] knew Steve [Boda] had the stuff, but figured he would never give it up. I arranged for the three of us to split the cost. Ken then digitized all of the printouts.

The stats were valuable because the league office had made corrections and almost everything added up correctly to the league stats. Ken Pullis (PFRA member) made up day-to-day charts for everyone, except for the missing games in 1948. Ken was able to find some stats for the missing games in various newspapers. Unfortunately in those days, individual stats were not usually shown in the papers. The *Los Angeles Times* had quite detailed individual stats, as did the *San Francisco Chronicle* and the *Cleveland Press* and *Plain Dealer*, although usually the home games had more coverage than the games away. The *Chicago Tribune* had good team stats, but not much for players. We are still missing over half the games for 1948. In doing so, Ken did find a couple of mistakes. In 1947, Bob Nelson of the [Los Angeles] Dons, a center, was given three catches for 61 yards and a touchdown, which actually belonged to Joe Aguirre. In another case, Bill Daley, a fullback for the [Chicago] Rockets in 1947, was given six pass attempts, three completions, 70 yards, a touchdown and an interception, which really were by Al Dekdebrun. Those were the only passes credited to Daley in three years and 175 rushes.

As a final note to this story, Steve Boda had a large collection of Notre Dame archives. When he passed, it was his wish to have the items donated to Notre Dame. However, in need of money, Boda sold the archives to a collector on consignment in order to pay bills. An attorney, Barry Toone, stepped up to purchase the archives and has said that he will donate them to the school. The missing AAFC scoresheets have never been found, even accidentally in the basketball or Notre Dame archives.

As mentioned by Pete Palmer above, there were a few errors in the official scoresheets. Those errors were published in the official record manuals and have been part of the historical record ever since. However, the PFRA believes in making sure that the record is accurate. To that end, we have made the corrections to the records and have noted the changes. However, for errors that we could not independently verify, the official statistics were used. Notations were made to indicate what statistics could not be independently verified.

Finally, John Maxymuk has done excellent work with coaching registers and has found errors in the records seen in most encyclopedias. We have noted his corrections in our Coaches Register.

The PFRA is proud to present this work. The history of the AAFC has been forgotten by many. It is our hope that this work will help preserve the records of a major competitor to the National Football League.

Part 1: A Brief History of the AAFC

by Kenneth R. Crippen

During World War II, there were several leagues that were looking to compete against the National Football League (NFL). Only one was able to get a foothold in the professional football landscape: the All-America Football Conference (AAFC).

The AAFC grew out of a desire by several people to own professional football franchises. In 1944, there were four groups of financial backers looking to obtain NFL franchises. The first group consisted of singer Bing Crosby, actor Don Ameche, Frank Mandel (cousin of Fred Mandel, the owner of the Detroit Lions), Graham Smith and A.G. Atwater (brother-in-law of Philip K. Wrigley of the Chicago Cubs). The second group was headed by Anthony J. Morabito, co-owner of the Lumber Terminal Company. He wanted a franchise in San Francisco. Finally, there were two groups looking to start a franchise in Buffalo: One group led by sports promoter Charles Murray and the other led by Globe Construction Company president Sam Cordovano. However, Murray did not have the financial backing that Cordovano did, and Cordovano became the only Buffalo application considered.

Buffalo was considered to have the best shot at getting a franchise. The league worried about having teams on the west coast as travel expenses would play a large factor in the success of the league as it was trying to get through the war. The final decision was to be made at the spring meeting in April of that year. However, at a meeting on January 14, 1944, the NFL tabled the applications for all three cities, but only returned the deposit money of $25,000 to Los Angeles and San Francisco. The league stated that Buffalo still had a chance at the April meeting. Unfortunately for Buffalo, on April 21, 1944, the NFL owners voted to table all expansion applications until after the war.

That is when *Chicago Tribune* sports editor Arch Ward entered the picture. He had visions of forming a rival professional football league and this was his chance. He immediately contacted the rejected groups from Los Angeles, San Francisco and Buffalo. In June of 1944 in St. Louis, the AAFC held its first organizational meeting, albeit in secret. At that meeting, charter franchises were awarded to Buffalo, Chicago, Cleveland, Los Angeles, New York and San Francisco.

Another secret meeting was held in September to accept the franchise application for Baltimore. This brought the league to seven teams, but they still needed one more to even out the divisions. Applications were accepted from Detroit, Boston and Philadelphia, but none were granted franchises at that meeting. At that point, the league publically announced their formation and named the franchise owners:

Baltimore: Gene Tunney (former heavyweight boxing champion);
Buffalo: James F. Breuil (president of Frontier Oil Refining Corporation), Sam Cordovano (president of Globe Construction Company), William Bennett (treasurer of Frontier Oil Refining Corporation);
Chicago: John L. Keeshin (president of Keeshin Freight Lines);
Cleveland: Arthur McBride (owner of a taxicab company);
Los Angeles: Don Ameche (actor) and Christy Walsh (former newspaper syndicate director);
New York: Eleanor Gehrig (widow of Lou Gehrig) and Ray J. Ryan (president of Ryan Oil Company);
San Francisco: Anthony J. Morabito and Allen E. Sorrell (co-owners of Lumber Terminal Company), Ernest J. Turre (general manager of Del E. Webb Construction Company of Phoenix, Arizona).

Also announced were two resolutions from the owners: The conference forbade any franchise from trying to steal players from the NFL, and no player would be accepted into the Conference as long as they still had college eligibility remaining.

Finally, the AAFC announced that if the Conference had a franchise in the same city as the NFL, all efforts would be made to avoid conflicts in game dates and playing sites.

At a December meeting, Lt. Commander James Crowley was named as the commissioner of the con-

---

Parts of this conference history first appeared in Kenneth R. Crippen, *The Original Buffalo Bills: A History of the All-America Football Conference Team, 1946–1949*, McFarland, 2010).

ference. Crowley gained fame as part of the famous Four Horsemen backfield at Notre Dame. Interestingly, his backfield teammate Elmer Layden was commissioner of the NFL. Also at that meeting, Christy Walsh was named vice-president, Eleanor Gehrig was named secretary and Sam Cordovano was named treasurer. Ray Miller (Cleveland), Anthony Morabito and John Keeshin were appointed to draw up a constitution and bylaws.

The conference experienced a setback shortly after this meeting. Ray Ryan withdrew his New York franchise from the league. Baltimore owner Gene Tunney agreed to move his franchise to New York, but soon after, he was called to military duty and had to withdraw his franchise. To partially make up for this deficit, a group headed by Harvey Hester was awarded a franchise for Miami.

In April of 1945, the conference met to try and award a final franchise. Kansas City was considered, but tabled. There was interest from Dan Topping, owner of the Brooklyn Tigers of the NFL, to move his franchise from the NFL to the AAFC. A representative of the Tigers was at the meeting. This solved two problems for the AAFC. First, it would give the Conference their eighth franchise to even out the divisions. Second, it would put a team back in the New York market.

It was decided that each AAFC team would pay Dan Topping $75,000, plus an additional $25,000 out of the first year's gate receipts. The new team became the New York Yankees. However, Topping could not just transfer his franchise to the rival league. He needed to fold it and start with a new franchise in the AAFC. When Topping folded his franchise in the NFL, all of his player contracts were given to the Boston Yanks, who merged with the Tigers for the 1945 season. However, Topping was able to sign away the bulk of the Tigers' players and essentially had the same team in the AAFC.

Initially, the AAFC had no intentions of competing with the NFL. They felt that they could peacefully coexist and went to work to hammer out an agreement between the two leagues. The NFL, however, did not see things the same way. In September of 1945, Cleveland coach Paul Brown and Chicago owner John Keeshin were appointed to confer with NFL Commissioner Elmer Layden regarding a working agreement between the two major leagues. They were unsuccessful in their efforts to meet with Layden and later attempts to discuss such agreements also failed.

The NFL wanted nothing to do with the AAFC. Since they did not want to peacefully coexist, the AAFC started to play for keeps. In August of 1945, AAFC Commissioner Jim Crowley announced the signing of 150 players, including two NFL stalwarts: Bob Steuber of the Chicago Bears and Lou Rymkus of the Washington Redskins. Both became the newest members of the Cleveland franchise. According to Crowley, "We originally resolved not to tamper with National league players, but since the N.F.L. snubbed us we see no reason why we can't hire their players." The theft continued as Miami signed Hampton Pool of the Chicago Bears and Jim Poole of the New York Giants.

Of course, the battles were not strictly between leagues, but also intra-league. In November of 1945, the league saw a battle between the college ranks, the NFL, and the Chicago and Buffalo franchises in the AAFC. Halfback Elroy "Crazy Legs" Hirsch was claimed by Wisconsin, the Cleveland Rams of the NFL and the Chicago Rockets of the AAFC. Hirsh was on the Wisconsin team in 1942 before heading off to Michigan as a V-12 trainee in 1943. While in the Marine Corps, Hirsch played on the star-studded El Toro Flying Tigers team. Chicago claimed that they had signed Hirsch, but Badger coach Harry Struhldeher and Hirsch both denied that assertion. In 1945, Hirsch was drafted by the Cleveland Rams. To make things more complicated, Buffalo claimed that Hirsch made a "verbal commitment to play with Buffalo" and filed a claim with commissioner Crowley. According to Sam Cordovano, "I have no doubt that Crowley will recognize our claim." Cordovano was wrong and Hirsch started the 1946 season with the Chicago Rockets. Hirsch played three years with Chicago before going to the Los Angeles Rams (formerly the Cleveland Rams) to end his Hall of Fame career.

The Conference was under way. Throughout 1944 and 1945, there were six leagues competing on the professional gridiron circuit (Pan America, United States, National, American and Trans-America football leagues, as well as the All-America Football Conference). By 1946, all that remained were the National Football League (NFL) and the All-America Football Conference (AAFC).

It was at that point where the war really began. Comparisons were being made between the two leagues in order to determine who would come out on top. The most outstanding of the comparisons dealt with stadium rights. Most of the NFL teams played in baseball stadiums. The previous year, the baseball owners declared that football teams could not use the baseball stadiums until the baseball season was over. With the AAFC having only one team using a baseball stadium (the Brooklyn Dodgers using Ebbets Field), this gave a clear advantage to the upstart conference, as they gained fan support before the NFL started their season. The only way the NFL could compete with this was to play on neutral fields, but this would not generate the necessary fan interest in their home towns. This also impacted revenue, as each team needed to pay 15 percent off the top for park rental. The Green Bay Packers were the only NFL team immune from these fees, as they were the only team not playing in a baseball stadium. That was a factor in the battle, as there had only been four money-making teams in the NFL prior to the inter-circuit war.

The struggle between the two leagues only got worse and neither league would be immune.

The beginning of 1946 saw continued turmoil surrounding franchises in the AAFC. At a three-day organizational meeting to kick off the new year, Edwin Nielsen (New York oilman and Baltimore representative at the meeting) stated that there were delays in securing a lease to play at Baltimore Municipal Stadium. Nielsen also expressed doubts about his franchise's ability to get enough players to field a team in 1946. As a result, the owners agreed to the delay and stated that Baltimore could enter the league in 1947.

In the end, this made things easier for the league, as now there was an even number of teams (eight), which were broken up into two divisions. The Eastern Division included Brooklyn, Buffalo, Miami and New York, while the Western Division was made up of Chicago, Cleveland, Los Angeles and San Francisco. The teams would play a fourteen game home-and-home season, with the winners of each division playing for the championship.

It was also decided at the organizational meeting that the clubs would contribute seven players to Dan Topping's New York team. Each club would allow New York their choice of a player from their roster, after scratching three of their best players from the list. This essentially gave Topping seven free players.

The most interesting development to come out of the organizational meeting in January was the institution of a draft for college players. The NFL had been holding college drafts since 1936, so the concept was not new. The AAFC, however, decided to take a different approach with their "secret" draft: They only drafted players with no college eligibility remaining and who showed a desire to play professional football. In past years, the NFL drafted college all-stars who really had no desire to play professionally or who still had a year or two left in the collegiate ranks. Dr. Mal Stevens, former Yale and American University coach who was with the Brooklyn franchise, stated at the time that "the National League puts college seniors on the block like pieces of property with 500 or more names listed for hire. That practice has irked college athletic directors and coaches.... There is no sense in publicizing a list of players who have no intentions of entering the professional field. The National League has conducted this draft system mainly to advance its own game by flaunting names of college stars before the public eye."

The AAFC decided to write to the National Collegiate Coaches Association asking for a list of college players known to be interested in continuing football as a professional. They only approached interested players after receiving the approval of their coaches. This definitely made an impact with college coaches, as can be seen in a letter from Cornell University to Buffalo scout Fiore Cesare. In it, Cornell head coach Ed McKeever stated, "I think your idea of not drafting anyone eligible for college ball will get more cooperation for your league, as I had a bitter taste last year of the Cleveland Rams taking our best player." Additional letters from collegiate coaches mirrored similar sentiments, as the coaches were more than happy to assist with requests for information. The draft was held December 20th and 21st of 1946.

Heading into 1946, the NFL changed commissioners. Out was Elmer Layden and in came Bert Bell. Bell, in association with Lud Wray, bought an NFL franchise in 1933 and named it the Philadelphia Eagles. The Eagles struggled and were put up for auction in 1934. Bell paid $4,500 and obtained sole ownership of the team. Pittsburgh owner Art Rooney sold the Steelers to Alexis Thompson and Rooney joined Bell as co-owner of the Eagles at the end of 1940 season. Thompson wanted to move his team to Boston, but the NFL owners refused. Fearing that Pittsburgh would be without an NFL franchise, Bell and Rooney decided to move their franchise to Pittsburgh (to be the new Steelers) and Thompson moved his franchise to Philadelphia to become the new Eagles. This placated Thompson as it allowed him to move his franchise closer to his hometown of Boston and allowed Rooney to keep a team in Pittsburgh. Bell gave up his interests in the Steelers when he was named commissioner.

In his first test as NFL commissioner, Bell had to address a franchise relocation situation. On January 12, Dan Reeves announced that he was moving his Cleveland Rams franchise to Los Angeles. This was an interesting move, as the Cleveland Browns would have been fighting the Rams for supremacy of the city. By leaving, the NFL abandoned the town and allowed the AAFC sole possession. With the Rams being the NFL Champion in 1945, this seemed like an unwise move. Other NFL owners agreed and voted 6–4 against the relocation. Reeves was determined and worked out deals with the Los Angeles Memorial Coliseum and the Cotton Bowl in Dallas to play games. In the end, the owners relented and agreed to allow Reeves to move to Los Angeles, where he went head-to-head with the Los Angeles Dons of the AAFC. Only time would tell as to whether this was a good move.

The AAFC had a firm foothold on the west coast, with franchises in both San Francisco and Los Angeles. The NFL was just getting started with Reeves' Rams, but had no other presence out west. The NFL felt that more still needed to be done in order to compete. In stepped the Pacific Coast Football League (PCFL), a minor league consisting namely of teams in California. Three owners of the league, J. Howard Sullivan (attorney from Los Angeles), Frank Ciraolo (owner of Dugan's Café in San Francisco) and Clyde Mowdy (printer from Oakland), signed a working agreement with the NFL, and "immediately proclaimed themselves the instruments which will break the rival millionaire-supported All-America football conference." In the agreement, four PCFL teams would work with four NFL teams to hurt the AAFC: the Los Angeles Bulldogs would work with the Los Angeles Rams, the San Francisco Clippers with the New York Giants, San Diego Bombers with the Green Bay Packers and the Hollywood Bears with the Washington Redskins. It was agreed that the PCFL would not play in the same city as the NFL on the same day. Additionally, when the NFL was not playing a game on the West Coast, the PCFL would schedule a game to rival the AAFC. This forced the AAFC to take on both the NFL and the PCFL at the gate, while the NFL just battled the AAFC. The PCFL also agreed not to employ any AAFC players on their roster. In return for their help, the PCFL was promised two future franchises in the NFL, presumably Los Angeles and San Francisco. According to J. Howard Sullivan of the Los Angeles Bulldogs, "This fall will be tough on us, but we don't have to worry too much. The NFL has guaranteed to make up the deficit which we will suffer. No, we aren't worried. But what we want to do is start taking in money by the wheelbarrow full instead of the bucket full." According to an article in the *Syracuse Herald Journal*, "In the National-A.A. battle, it figures close to $30,000 in expenses to take a club to the west coast under the new transcontinental setup. Every buck at the gate is going to count terrifically and the PCFL through its schedule maneuvering is going to chisel away at the A.A. gate while leaving the N.F.L. a clear path."

Why would the NFL help out the PCFL? After all, the PCFL was just a minor league and had no impact on the NFL. None of the teams were at the same talent level as the NFL, so bringing in a PCFL team did not make sense. Since the NFL was not keen on expansion, it also did not make sense to promise a franchise or two to the PCFL. The PCFL had to have known this from the beginning. The only explanation that was plausible was that the PCFL rosters were being raided by both the NFL and AAFC, and the deal was probably made to stop the hemorrhaging and to keep the PCFL somewhat intact.

While that was transpiring, the Boston Yanks of the NFL announced the signing of Notre Dame quarterback Angelo Bertelli, who had previously agreed to a contract with the Los Angeles Dons. Bertelli was a Heisman Trophy winner and was a major signing for the team. After signing with the Yanks, Bertelli reportedly returned the bonus money he was paid by the Dons. Los Angeles, obviously, was furious and filed a lawsuit against both Bertelli and the Yanks. This lawsuit was not just about a player, but about the competition between the NFL and AAFC. Failure to win this lawsuit could prove to be disastrous to the upstart league and it was imperative for Los Angeles to win. After the Dons filed suit, they obtained a restraining order, preventing Bertelli from playing for any team other than the Dons. Bertelli counter-sued for fraud and misrepresentation. It was shortly after the start of the season, but the legal battle was won by the Dons and Bertelli reported to Los Angeles to play for the team. Superior Court Judge Felix Forte upheld the equity of AAFC player contracts when he ruled that Angelo Bertelli was prohibited from playing for any professional team other than the Los Angeles Dons.

A week after Boston signed Bertelli, they also outbid Buffalo for the services of quarterback Paul Governali. Buffalo was willing to take the battle to the courtroom, but later decided to relinquish Governali to the Yanks. Governali was Boston's insurance policy, in case the courts gave Bertelli back to the Dons. With the courts ruling in favor of Los Angeles, this was a wise decision. The Governali signing was also another blow in the already bitter inter-league war.

The All-America Football Conference had finished its first year with the Cleveland Browns defeating the New York Yankees 14–9 for the conference championship, but the league office saw continued turnover as Harvey Hester and John Keeshin resigned from their posts on the Executive Committee. Jim Crowley resigned as conference commissioner in order to take charge of the Chicago Rockets, accepting the positions of executive vice-president, general manager and coach of the team. According to the *1947 All-America Football Conference Record Manual*,

> The confidence of one individual who has never been accused of stupidity was shown in the decision of James H. (Sleepy Jim) Crowley to leave the commissionership with nearly four years to run on his $25,000 a year contract, in order to become general manager and head coach of the Chicago Rockets. There are two well-established National League clubs in that city, and the Rockets did only fairly well in 1946. Crowley had enough faith in the AAFC and in the ability of that lusty city to support a third major league team to cast his future with the Rockets.

The Miami Seahawks were in trouble as the AAFC filed charges against the Seahawks for violating the conference's indebtedness clause. Throughout the 1946 season, clubs within the conference made attempts to help Miami stay financially sound, but attendance was just not there. In the end, they were expelled from the AAFC for failure to meet their financial obligations.

With the Seahawks finished for good, Baltimore stepped up to the plate, in the person of Robert Ridgway Rodenberg. Rodenberg—the son of an Illinois congressman—was a reporter for the Washington *Herald* and *Capital Daily* and served in Burma during World War II. With the help of Charlie McCormick, J.C. Herbert Bryant, Maurice (Maury) L. Nee and William R. Rodenberg (brother of Robert), Robert purchased the Seahawks franchise for $50,000 and moved them to Baltimore. This angered Washington Redskins owner George Preston Marshall, but since he could not exercise territorial rights on a team from a different league, there was not much he could do.

Despite the failure of the Miami Seahawks, the NFL was on notice that the All-America Football Conference was not a minor league. There were 110 former NFL players on AAFC rosters. Of those, only three made the official All-Conference first team and only eight were on the combined first and second team lists.

The conference had talent and they proved it by the end of the first season. Not only could you look at the All-Conference teams, but the AAFC also set 64 major league records. Some of those records could be explained by the AAFC playing a 14-game schedule, versus the ten or eleven game schedules in which the original records were set. Others could not be explained away as easily. A field goal efficiency of 48.5 percent, a point after touchdown efficiency of 92.9 percent and an average punt return of 13.7 yards were more impressive with the increased number of games.

Regardless of records and All-Conference teams, the AAFC still wanted to tweak their system. Throughout the 1946 season, games were played on practically any night. This loose scheduling of games made it more difficult for fans. As a result, the conference decided to play strictly on Sunday afternoons and Friday nights, except for Thanksgiving Day, which saw two games. They also needed to deal with the Cleveland and New York situation, where both teams clinched the division title early in the season. These two teams were obviously far superior to the rest of the conference, so the AAFC decided to implement a player distribution system. In this system, the stronger squads each gave up players in order to help the other teams. It was hoped that this could keep fan interest alive throughout the season as teams would be more evenly matched.

Over the course of two days, the All-America Football Conference held its first college draft. Similar to the system used by the NFL, the AAFC teams drafted in reverse order of finish from the 1946 season. Since Miami was no longer in the league, its draft picks were sent to the new Baltimore franchise which replaced it. One difference in the AAFC draft was the special selections, which occurred before the start of the draft. Each team was given two picks, but Los Angeles and San Francisco each traded one of their picks to the Buffalo Bills. The first fifteen rounds of the draft went as expected. In additional rounds after the draft, certain teams did not select. For example, in rounds 16 through 20, Cleveland and New York did not select. From rounds 21 through 25, Cleveland, New York, San Francisco and Los Angeles did not select. This was designed to achieve parity in the league. The weaker teams had more draft selections.

Once Jim Crowley's resignation was officially accepted, Los Angeles Dons' owner Benjamin Lindheimer—the chairman of the conference's new Executive Committee—was appointed acting Commissioner and Dan Topping of the New York Yankees was named the Acting President of the conference. These positions were only temporary and by February of 1947, they were permanently filled. Admiral Jonas H. Ingram was named the Conference's new Commissioner and O.O. Kessing was appointed the Deputy Commissioner.

Ingram was a four-star Commander-in-Chief of the Atlantic Fleet during World War II. Oliver Owen "Scrappy" Kessing operated the first Navy Pre-Flight School at Chapel Hill, North Carolina, and was later the Commodore of the Navy, directing base operations in the Pacific.

The Cleveland Browns again beat the New York Yankees to take the 1947 AAFC Championship. The Browns repeated in 1948, beating the Buffalo Bills to take the title.

As 1948 came to a close, merger talks between the All-America Football Conference and the National Football League became more serious. In a 14-hour secret meeting between owners, no agreement was produced; however, it became more apparent that a merger would eventually take place. The major sticking point at that meeting was raised by Washington Redskins owner George Preston Marshall. He opposed any merger that included the Baltimore Colts, as they infringed on his 75-mile territorial rights. He wanted Baltimore to pay $250,000 in order to agree to the merger. Any merger required unanimous consent of all of the owners, so resolution of this issue was paramount.

On December 20, AAFC officials met with NFL officials to discuss mutual concerns and attempted to end the war between the leagues. Again, no permanent solution was reached, but that marked the first time that the NFL publicly recognized the AAFC. Since April 20, 1945, the AAFC had worked to obtain mutual agreements with the NFL to ensure the stability and solvency of major league football. After all of that time, the NFL finally relented, knowing that it was necessary for the survival of their league. Salaries took off and teams of both leagues needed to find a solution.

Before the 1949 season, the AAFC needed to make a change in order to stay viable, so rosters were cut from 35 to 32 players and the regular season schedule was reduced from 14 games to 12 games. Also, the Brooklyn Dodgers and the New York Yankees merged to form the Brooklyn–New York Dodgers-Yankees. With the conference down to seven teams, the divisional format was eliminated. As a result, a new playoff system was adopted. In the first round, the first- and fourth-place teams competed, while the second- and third-place teams battled it out. The winners of each of those games faced each other for the championship.

The Chicago Rockets were in turmoil from the beginning. In what seemed like a yearly occurrence, the team was sold. The Chicago Rockets were purchased for $300,000 by James C. Thompson, owner of the Chicago Opera building. With this change, the Rockets were renamed the Hornets and were stocked with players from the former Brooklyn club. Six players from the original Brooklyn team went to the new Brooklyn–New York squad, while the remaining players were sent to Chicago. It was hoped that the influx of talent would help the struggling franchise.

Also, Admiral Ingram resigned as commissioner and was replaced by Deputy Commissioner O.O. Kessing.

The Cleveland Browns won their fourth straight championship in 1949. Over the four years of the conference's existence, the Cleveland Browns were the best team. They accumulated a record of 47–4–3, won four championships and were also the first team to go through a season undefeated and win a championship. This pre-dated the undefeated Miami Dolphins by almost 25 years.

On December 9, 1949, the All-America Football Conference and the National Football League announced a merger. It was not so much a merger as the dissolution of the AAFC, with three of its teams being admitted into the NFL. After five and a half years of bitter rivalry and contention, the war was over. New York Bulldogs owner Ted Collins was reported to have lost over one million dollars in the fight, and the Green Bay Packers and Pittsburgh Steelers were on the verge of bankruptcy from the conflict. The NFL needed this agreement to stay alive and the AAFC owners could not financially continue the skirmish.

The "merging" of the leagues took effect in 1950 and the new effort was called the National-American Football League (NAFL). The Cleveland Browns, San Francisco 49ers and Baltimore Colts were the only AAFC franchises to continue to play in 1950. According to author and historian Mark L. Ford:

> As part of the merger agreement, New York Bulldogs owner Ted Collins had purchased the rights to all but six of the 32 players on the AAFC's New York Yankees, gaining the right to play the 1950 season at Yankee Stadium. The Giants would have their choice of six players and keep playing at the Polo Grounds. Collins and Giants' owner Tim Mara couldn't reach an agreement on players, so Bell ordered both men to appear before him at 4:00 to determine which six players would be allotted to Mara. Unhappy with Bell's solution, Collins declined to appear.... Though the Colts, Browns and 49ers were the only 3 AAFC clubs officially included in the merger agreement, the AAFC Yankees replaced the NFL Bulldogs for all practical purposes, surviving the merger nearly intact and becoming the New York Yanks.

The remaining AAFC franchises were disbanded and players were allocated through a dispersal draft. The addition of the Colts was an interesting story. Washington Redskins owner George Preston Marshall consistently refused to include Baltimore in any merger talks, citing his exclusive territorial rights to the region. It was not until Baltimore paid him $50,000 that he saw the error of his ways and realized that a Baltimore franchise created a natural rivalry with his Washington team. As part of Marshall's agreement to allow Baltimore into the NAFL, Baltimore needed to show a profit after their first year.

The Buffalo Bills attempted to get into the NFL, but their efforts were rebuffed. Owner Jim Breuil dropped his franchise and took a partial ownership stake in the Cleveland Browns. A civic group petitioned the NFL to be included in the merger, but in the end, the NFL voted against Buffalo's admission.

This left the NAFL with a 13-team league, which was divided up into two divisions of six teams each. The 13th team floated between the divisions. Originally, the Cleveland Browns were designated as this floating team, but coach Paul Brown threatened to withdraw if that were the case. As a result, Baltimore was given that dubious title. After a few months, the league took steps to minimize the AAFC by removing the "American" part of their new name, which reverted the name back to the National Football League (NFL).

The Buffalo Bills, Chicago Rockets and Los Angeles Rams were officially disbanded and the players from those teams were put into a dispersal draft. The draft order was determined by the order of finish of the 1949 season. Therefore, the draft order was as follows: Baltimore, New York Yanks, Green Bay, Detroit, Washington, New York Giants, Pittsburgh, Chicago Cardinals (tied with Pittsburgh), Chicago Bears, San Francisco 49ers (tied with the Chicago Bears), Los Angeles, Cleveland and Philadelphia. Since Baltimore and Green Bay were the weakest teams, they were given five extra draft picks each.

Any doubt as to the strength of the top teams in the AAFC was quickly put to rest, as the Cleveland Browns sent a message early and often: "We are the best." They won not once, but twice against the two-time defending NFL champion Philadelphia Eagles in the 1950 season.

The NFL was scared of the AAFC. They knew that the talent was strong, namely because they tried to sign the very same players. Sometimes, they were successful. Sometimes, they were not. The strength of the talent can be assessed by the number of All-Pros and Hall of Famers that came out of the AAFC. Over the same time period, the NFL and AAFC produced relatively the same number of All-Pros and Hall of Famers.

The NFL refused to settle their disputes with the AAFC on the gridiron. Why? Because they knew that there was a realistic chance that the NFL would lose. Then, their argument that the AAFC was an inferior league was moot.

The downfall of the AAFC was in the way that the conference was run. According to Paul Brown, the AAFC "had no direction from the top then, and it didn't help that the players and financial resources were always being used to help poorly run teams." Brown was referring to the AAFC forcing the better teams to simply give players to the weaker teams without compensation. Combine that with relatively weak bottom franchises, and the AAFC just could not continue. Of course, the NFL also had weak franchises, but the owners were involved with the league for a much longer time and therefore were in a better position to absorb losses.

Part 2: PFRA All-Pro Selections

by Kenneth R. Crippen, Matt Reaser and Andy Piascik

It is always difficult to pick all-pro teams when pro football is in flux with offensive and defensive schemes, as well as switching from a one-platoon system to a two-platoon system. With that in mind, we wanted to pick the best players in the conference, and then adjusted the schemes based off of those players. For example, in 1946 we went with a 6–2–3 defense, whereas in other years we used a 5–3–3 scheme. That was to pick the best defensive team in the conference for that particular year.

The same went for offense, namely the backfield. We picked a quarterback and a fullback. We did not pick two quarterbacks or two fullbacks, but if two tailbacks were better than a tailback and a halfback, we went with two tailbacks.

Through careful research and extensive film study, here are our picks for the AAFC All-Pro teams from 1946–49, as well as our AAFC All-Time team.

PFRA's AAFC All-Pro Teams

1946

OFFENSE

Dante Lavelli was clearly the best end in the conference in 1946. However, there was some discussion on whether Alyn Beals or Mac Speedie should take the second offensive end spot. Beals won out as we felt that he had a greater impact on the offense. He ranked first in receptions (tied with Lavelli), second in receiving yards and first in receiving touchdowns. Beals also beat Speedie in yards-per-reception and yards-per-game.

Almost all of the offensive line positions were unanimous decisions, as was Otto Graham at quarterback and Marion Motley at fullback. There was some debate between Lou Rymkus and Lee Artoe for the tackle position, but Rymkus had the edge based on his excellent technique.

The discussion for the best single-wing tailback came down to Glenn Dobbs and Spec Sanders. Dobbs was the league leader in passing attempts, completions, yards, but also interceptions. Sanders was the league leader in rushing attempts, yards and touchdowns. In the end, Dobbs was determined to have more of an impact on the offense than Sanders, which is why he won the league's Most Valuable Player award. But, we selected Sanders for the final back position as he was the second best back in the Conference that year.

End: Dante Lavelli (Cleveland Browns)
End: Alyn Beals (San Francisco 49ers)
Tackle: Lou Rymkus (Cleveland Browns)
Tackle: Bob Reinhard (Los Angeles Dons)
Guard: Bruno Banducci (San Francisco 49ers)
Guard: Ed Ulinski (Cleveland Browns)
Center: Bob Nelson (Los Angeles Dons)
Quarterback: Otto Graham (Cleveland Browns)
Tailback: Glenn Dobbs (Brooklyn Dodgers)
Fullback: Marion Motley (Cleveland Browns)
Back (Tailback): Spec Sanders (New York Yankees)

DEFENSE

New York Yankee Jack Russell was an easy selection at defensive end. The debate came down to the second defensive end as either Dale Gentry or Bruce Alford. Ultimately, Gentry had more of an impact on the defense, so he was chosen for the position.

Martin Ruby, "Bruiser" Kinard and Bill Willis were unanimous choices for the two defensive tackle positions and the middle guard, respectively. Bill Radovich had an excellent year at middle guard and defensive guard. Since we felt that he had a better year than the top three linebackers, we went with a 6–2–3 alignment to give Radovich the honor.

Tom Colella and Ken Casanega were relatively easy choices for defensive back. The final defensive back position came down to Cliff Lewis and Steve Juzwik. Either one would have been a good choice, but Juzwik edged Lewis on the combination of ability and statistics.

End: Jack Russell (New York Yankees)
End: Dale Gentry (Los Angeles Dons)

Tackle: Martin Ruby (Brooklyn Dodgers)
Tackle: "Bruiser" Kinard (New York Yankees)
Middle Guard: Bill Willis (Cleveland Browns)
Defensive Guard: Bill Radovich (Los Angeles Dons)
Linebacker: Lou Saban (Cleveland Browns)
Linebacker: Norm Standlee (San Francisco 49ers)
Defensive Back: Tom Colella (Cleveland Browns)
Defensive Back: Ken Casanega (San Francisco 49ers)
Defensive Back: Steve Juzwiik (Buffalo Bisons)

Special Teams

For place kicker, it came down to Steve Nemeth or Lou Groza. Nemeth won out based on field goal percentage and extra point percentage. Granted, Groza had more attempts, but there was definitely a wide disparity between Nemeth and Groza in field goal percentage.

Nemeth: Field Goals: 9–12 (75%); Extra Points: 23–33 (97%)
Groza: Field Goals: 13–29 (44.8%); Extra Points: 45–47 (95.7%)

Chuck Fenenbock and Spec Sanders were close decisions for both the punt returner and kick returner positions. In the end, Fenenbock took the punt returner position and Sanders took the kick returner position, based on their respective overall statistics.

Place Kicker: Steve Nemeth (Chicago Rockets)
Punter: Glenn Dobbs (Brooklyn Dodgers)
Punt Returner: Chuck Fenenbock (Los Angeles Dons)
Kick Returner: Spec Sanders (New York Yankees)

1947

Offense

Mac Speedie was a clear choice for the first offensive end position, as was Dante Lavelli for the second offensive end position. They were first and second in the league respectively for receptions, receiving yards, receiving touchdowns and receiving yards per game.

The offensive line was unanimous among the selectors.

For the backfield, Otto Graham led the league in almost every passing category. For the categories where he did not lead the league, he was second. The combination of his rushing and passing gave Spec Sanders the edge over Glenn Dobbs for the single-wing tailback position. It came down to Chet Mutryn and Glenn Dobbs for the final back position. Mutryn was determined to have a bigger impact on the offense and took the fourth backfield position.

End: Mac Speedie (Cleveland Browns)
End: Dante Lavelli (Cleveland Browns)
Tackle: Lou Rymkus (Cleveland Browns)
Tackle: Nate Johnson (New York Yankees)
Guard: Dick Barwegan (New York Yankees)
Guard: Bruno Banducci (San Francisco 49ers)
Center: Bob Nelson (Los Angeles Dons)
Quarterback: Otto Graham (Cleveland Browns)
Tailback: Spec Sanders (New York Yankees)
Fullback: Marion Motley (Cleveland Browns)
Back (Halfback): Chet Mutryn (Buffalo Bills)

Defense

The defensive back position came down to four players: Tom Colella, Len Eshmont, Harmon Rowe, and Bill Kellagher. All four were relatively close, but Rowe beat out Kellagher for the final position. Kellagher was on a bad pass defense and his abilities were not on par with the other three defensive backs.

End: Jack Russell (New York Yankees)
End: Bruce Alford (New York Yankees)
Tackle: Martin Ruby (Brooklyn Dodgers)
Tackle: John Woudenberg (San Francisco 49ers)
Middle Guard: Bill Willis (Cleveland Browns)
Linebacker: Alex Agase (Chicago/Los Angeles)
Linebacker: Lou Saban (Cleveland Browns)
Linebacker: Norm Standlee (San Francisco 49ers)
Defensive Back: Tom Colella (Cleveland Browns)
Defensive Back: Len Eshmont (San Francisco 49ers)
Defensive Back: Harmon Rowe (New York Yankees)

Special Teams

Ben Agajanian was the clear choice at place kicker, as was Monk Gafford and Chet Mutryn at the punt returner and kick returner positions respectively.

The punter position came down to Horace Gillom and Mickey Colmer. Yards per punt were almost identical between the two, but Gillom won out on his infamous hang time.

Place Kicker: Ben Agajanian (Los Angeles Dons)
Punter: Horace Gillom (Cleveland Browns)
Punt Returner: Monk Gafford (Brooklyn Dodgers)
Kick Returner: Chet Mutryn (Buffalo Bills)

1948

Offense

The largest debate in this process surrounded the offensive end position for 1948. Al Baldwin was the clear choice for first position, but the second position came down to Alyn Beals or Mac Speedie. Looking at statistics, both were close. Speedie had more yards per game, but Beals had more touchdowns. Looking at the scouting reports for both players in 1948, Beals had better adjustment to the ball, better blocking and better competitiveness. Speedie had better hands, was better at separation and overall athleticism. In the end, we thought it was best to honor both players.

For the single-wing tailback position, it came down to Billy Hillenbrand and Glenn Dobbs. While Dobbs was a better passer, Hillenbrand was a better receiver. Combining passing, rushing and receiving, Hillenbrand had the edge.

End: Al Baldwin (Buffalo Bills)
(TIE) End: Alyn Beals (San Francisco 49ers)
(TIE) End: Mac Speedie (Cleveland Browns)
Tackle: Lou Rymkus (Cleveland Browns)
Tackle: Bob Reinhard (Los Angeles Dons)
Guard: Dick Barwegan (New York Yankees)
Guard: Ed Ulinksi (Cleveland Browns)
Center: Bob Nelson (Los Angeles Dons)
Quarterback: Frankie Albert (San Francisco 49ers)
Tailback: Billy Hillenbrand (Baltimore Colts)
Fullback: Marion Motley (Cleveland Browns)
Back (Halfback): Chet Mutryn (Buffalo Bills)

Defense

Choices were relatively straightforward for the defensive positions. We decided to go with a middle guard and three linebackers for this season. Jack Russell was a clear choice as the best defensive end in 1948. The same was true for Lou Saban at linebacker and Otto Schnellbacher at defensive back.

End: Jack Russell (New York Yankees)
End: John North (Baltimore Colts)
Tackle: Martin Ruby (Brooklyn Dodgers)
Tackle: Chet Adams (Cleveland Browns)
Middle Guard: Bill Willis (Cleveland Browns)
Linebacker: "Buckets" Hirsch (Buffalo Bills)
Linebacker: Lou Saban (Cleveland Browns)
Linebacker: Weldon Humble (Cleveland Browns)
Defensive Back: Otto Schnellbacher (New York Yankees)
Defensive Back: Eddie Carr (San Francisco 49ers)
Defensive Back: Tommy James (Cleveland Browns)

Special Teams

Rex Grossman beat out Lou Groza for the place kicker position. His field goal percentage was much higher (55.6% to 42.1%) on only one less field goal attempt. Grossman also had a slightly higher extra point percentage than did Groza.

Glenn Dobbs led the league in punts, punting yards and yards per punt for the easy choice at punter.

Rex Bumgardner was a relatively easy choice for punt returner. He had more yards on less returns, and led the league in returns for touchdowns.

Chet Mutryn beat out Monk Gafford for the kick returner position. He had a better kick return average with only a few less returns.

Place Kicker: Rex Grossman (Baltimore Colts)
Punter: Glenn Dobbs (Los Angeles Dons)
Punt Returner: Rex Bumgardner (Buffalo Bills)
Kick Returner: Forrest Hall (San Francisco 49ers)

1949

Offense

Mac Speedie and Alyn Beals easily had the best seasons of the offensive ends. The offensive line positions were unanimous. The discussion for offense came down to the single-wing tailback position. Bob Hoernschemeyer got the nod based on his overall abilities, namely his passing.

End: Mac Speedie (Cleveland Browns)
End: Alyn Beals (San Francisco 49ers)
Tackle: Lou Rymkus (Cleveland Browns)
Tackle: Bob Reinhard (Los Angeles Dons)
Guard: Dick Barwegan (New York Yankees)
Guard: Joe Signaigo (New York Yankees)
Center: Bob Nelson (Los Angeles Dons)
Quarterback: Otto Graham (Cleveland Browns)
Tailback: Bob Hoernschemeyer (Chicago Hornets)
Fullback: Joe Perry (San Francisco 49ers)
Back (Halfback): Chet Mutryn (Buffalo Bills)

Defense

Visco Grgich had an excellent season and was picked at the second defensive guard position over a third linebacker.

End: Jack Russell (New York Yankees)
End: Hal Shoener (San Francisco 49ers)
Tackle: Arnie Weinmeister (New York Yankees)
Tackle: John Kissell (Buffalo Bills)
Middle Guard: Bill Willis (Cleveland Browns)
Defensive Guard: Visco Grgich (San Francisco 49ers)
Linebacker: Lou Saban (Cleveland Browns)
Linebacker: Tony Adamle (Cleveland Browns)
Defensive Back: Jim Cason (San Francisco 49ers)
Defensive Back: Len Eshmont (San Francisco 49ers)
Defensive Back: Otto Schnellbacher (New York Yankees)

Special Teams

Rex Grossman led the league in field goal percentage and made every extra point attempted in 1947.

Frankie Albert led the league in yards per punt to take the punter position. Tom Landry was also considered.

Bob Livingstone had 17.1 yards per return and a punt return for touchdown to lead the league in both categories. Jim Cason was also considered.

Ray Ramsey had the best kick return average in the league and took the kick returner position. Herm Wedemeyer was also considered.

Place Kicker: Rex Grossman (Baltimore Colts)
Punter: Frankie Albert (San Francisco 49ers)
Punt Returner: Bob Livingstone (Chicago/Buffalo)
Kick Returner: Ray Ramsey (Chicago Hornets)

PFRA's AAFC All-Time Team

Offense

Mac Speedie and Alyn Beals were the clear choices for offensive ends. The same went for the offensive line positions, as well as Otto Graham for the t-formation quarterback and Marion Motley for the fullback position.

Spec Sanders took the single-wing tailback position over Glenn Dobbs, based on overall play throughout the conference. The same went for Chet Mutryn for the final back position.

End: Mac Speedie (Cleveland Browns)
End: Alyn Beals (San Francisco 49ers)
Tackle: Lou Rymkus (Cleveland Browns)
Tackle: Bob Reinhard (Los Angeles Dons)
Guard: Dick Barwegan (New York/Baltimore)
Guard: Bruno Banducci (San Francisco 49ers)
Center: Bob Nelson (Los Angeles Dons)
Quarterback: Otto Graham (Cleveland Browns)
Tailback: Spec Sanders (New York Yankees)
Fullback: Marion Motley (Cleveland Browns)
Back (Halfback): Chet Mutryn (Buffalo Bills)

Defense

Jack Russell, Martin Ruby, Bill Willis, and Lou Saban were easy choices for the all-time conference team, as all of them made the all-pro teams each of the four years in the conference. Tom Colella, Len Eshmont and Otto Schnellbacher each made two all-pro teams.

For the second defensive tackle position, we considered Arnie Weinmeister and John Woudenberg. Even though Weinmeister only played two years in the conference, film study showed him to be a better player overall, and therefore, he received the nod.

Tony Adamle edged out Norm Standlee for the final linebacker position, based on his overall play in the conference. The same went for Visco Grgich getting the second defensive guard position over Radovich or a third linebacker.

Even though John Yonakor did not make any of the individual all-pro teams, he was selected to the all-time team based on his solid play throughout his time in the conference.

End: Jack Russell (New York Yankees)
End: John Yonakor (Cleveland Browns)
Tackle: Martin Ruby (Brooklyn/New York)
Tackle: Arnie Weinmeister (New York Yankees)
Middle Guard: Bill Willis (Cleveland Browns)
Defensive Guard: Visco Grgich (San Francisco 49ers)
Linebacker: Lou Saban (Cleveland Browns)
Linebacker: Tony Adamle (Cleveland Browns)
Defensive Back: Tom Colella (Cleveland/Buffalo)
Defensive Back: Len Eshmont (San Francisco 49ers)
Defensive Back: Otto Schnellbacher (New York Yankees)

Special Teams

Even though Spec Sanders was not picked for any of the seasonal punt returner positions, his overall play throughout the four years gave him the nod.

Place Kicker: Rex Grossman (Baltimore Colts)
Punter: Glenn Dobbs (Brooklyn/Los Angeles)
Punt Returner: Spec Sanders (New York Yankees)
Kick Returner: Chet Mutryn (Buffalo Bills)

PFRA's AAFC All-Time Team Biographies

Mac Speedie
Position: End
Years: 1946–49 Cleveland Browns

Speedie was drafted by the Detroit Lions in 1942, but the owner of the Lions decided to wait until after the war to attempt to sign him. After four years in the military, Speedie signed a pro football contract, but it was with the Cleveland Browns. There, he led the AAFC in receiving yards twice and receptions three times on his way to helping the team win four AAFC championships. After the 1952 season, Speedie left the Browns to join the Canadian Football League. In 1960, he was hired as an assistant coach with the Houston Oilers. Later, he joined the staff of the Denver Broncos, before being elevated to the head coach position with the Broncos. He resigned in 1966, but stayed with the team as a scout until he retired in 1982.

Scouting Report: Very good overall athleticism; however, balance was an issue while blocking. Balance was not an issue on sideline passes. He did well to shed defenders to release into his route. His speed was definitely an asset as he was able to get excellent separation from the defenders. Because of this, Speedie was able to get excellent yards after the catch. He also showed very good to excellent hands. Competitiveness was an issue as he did not always show effort with downfield blocking, as well as blocking on the line. He also made poor decisions on blocking downfield.

Alyn Beals
Position: End
Years: 1946–49 San Francisco 49ers

Beals was drafted by the Chicago Bears in 1942. However, after serving three years in the military, he decided to sign with his hometown team: the San Francisco 49ers. During his time in the AAFC, Beals led the league in receptions his rookie year and led the league in touchdowns all four years of the Conference's existence.

Scouting Report: Beals showed excellent strength and explosiveness off the ball. He got into his routes quickly and showed good to very good separation from the defender. He also got into his stance quickly while blocking. Excellent competitiveness in fighting for the ball and getting yards after the catch. Very good to excellent competitiveness as he always looked for downfield blocks when he was not the receiver.

Lou Rymkus
Position: Tackle
Years: 1946–49 Cleveland Browns

Drafted by the Washington Redskins in 1943, Rymkus only played one season with the team. After the 1943 campaign, Rymkus joined the Marine Corps and was stationed at the Great Lakes Naval Training Station. There, he met Paul Brown, who signed him to a contract before the 1946 season. Known as an excellent defensive tackle, Brown decided to move Rymkus primarily to offensive tackle during most of his AAFC years. During that time and into his time with the Browns in the NFL, Rymkus was the prototypical offensive tackle who showed excellent technique. After retiring from his playing career, Rymkus went into coaching. He held assistant coaching positions with the Green Bay Packers and Los Angeles Rams, before accepting the head coaching job with the Houston Oilers. While with Houston, he led the team to the 1960 AFL Championship. After his firing in Houston, Rymkus held assistant coaching positions with the Detroit Lions and Baltimore Colts.

Scouting Report: Overall, Rymkus showed excellent abilities on offense and very good abilities on defense. Very competitive. On offense, Rymkus showed excellent technique for the most part. There were times when he was slow off the ball and struggled to get into position. However, he made up for it with strength. It was not often that the defender was able to impact the play. The Browns also used him to block on the opposite side of the field on sweeps and screens. He was not quick, but he was able to cross the field in time to make a block. He rarely gave up on a play on offense. On defense, he was not as aggressive. There were times when he was blocked away from the play and did not fight to get in on the play. However, when he did show competitiveness on defense, he was able to get good pressure into the backfield and to make tackles.

Bob Reinhard
Position: Tackle
Years: 1946–49 Los Angeles Dons

Bob Reinhard played for the University of California from 1939–41. He earned All-American honors the last two years. In 1943, Reinhard entered the Navy and served three years. When he returned, he joined the Los Angeles Dons and played all four years of their existence. After the AAFC merged with the NFL, Reinhard played a season for the Los Angeles Rams before retiring from football.

Scouting Report: Overall, Reinhard showed very good speed for someone his size. He also showed excellent strength and was very competitive. His pad level was a little high at times, which allowed his opponent to get leverage and move him around. On offense, he displayed excellent blocking abilities. He was very good blocking downfield and made very good blocking decisions. On defense, his did face a lot of double-teams. However, when one-on-one, he was able to easily shed blocks. His pursuit angles were not always the best, and at times he could be easily blocked away from the play. He was quick off the ball and quickly engaged the offensive lineman.

Dick Barwegan
Position: Guard
Years: 1947 New York Yankees, 1948–49 Baltimore Colts

Barwegan started his professional career after serving in the military. He played one season for the New York Yankees before being sent to the Baltimore Colts. He was part of the AAFC's attempt to balance the teams; sending players from the stronger teams to the weaker teams. In 1950, Baltimore traded Barwegan and Dub Garrett to the Chicago Bears for five players: George Blanda, Bob Perina, Ernie Zalejski, Jimmy Crawford and Bob Jensen. Barwegan played three years for the Chicago Bears before finishing the last two years of his playing career with the newest version of the Baltimore Colts.

Scouting Report: Barwegan showed better abilities on offense than defense. On offense, he was a solid run blocker and effective in pass blocking. He kept his balance and positioning against the defender. An effective trap blocker. He showed very good quickness and agility while pulling, but did not always complete the block. On defense, he played multiple positions. While on the line, he was very good in run defense and was able to get some pressure into the backfield. While playing linebacker, he was quick to read and react to the play. He was disciplined in the zone. However, he struggled in pass coverage and had a habit of getting knocked around by offensive linemen.

Bruno Banducci
Position: Guard
Years: 1946–49 San Francisco 49ers

While at Stanford, Banducci played tackle as the team won the 1941 Rose Bowl. However, he switched to guard when he went to the NFL. Banducci started his professional football career with the Philadelphia Eagles. After two seasons, he left to join the San Francisco 49ers. There, he played nine seasons for the team. He was named to the Pro Bowl in 1954 and was named to the Pro Football Hall of Fame's All-Decade team on the 1940s. He played one season in the Canadian Football League before he retired and went into coaching. He was an assistant coach for the 49ers and Eagles before coaching high school football.

Scouting Report: Banducci was a very good run blocker. He showed ability to pull and trap block. He showed excellent instincts, but was not always quick enough to get into position to make the block. Had a tendency to get high in his pass blocking, which allowed the defender to knock him off balance or toss him aside. Competitiveness could not be questioned. He always fought throughout the play. Even when knocked down, he would still get up and run to finish the play. Had a tendency to over-pursue on his downfield blocks, which put him out of position. Overall, he lacked strength and was pushed around.

Bob Nelson
Position: Center
Years: 1946–49 Los Angeles Dons

Bob Nelson was drafted by the Detroit Lions in 1941. After playing a season for the team, he left to join the military. After returning from service, he rejoined the Lions for a season before going to the Los Angeles Dons. After four years with the team, he played a final season with the Baltimore Colts in 1950. Nelson was named first-team all-conference three of his four years in the AAFC.

Scouting Report: On offense, he was a very good blocker. At times, he was a little slow to get into his stance and could get knocked off balance. But, he was able to disrupt the defender to keep him away from the play. On defense, he showed good down-the-line pursuit of plays going to the opposite side of the field. However, he was a poor tackler.

Otto Graham
Position: Quarterback
Years: 1946–49 Cleveland Browns

After playing at Northwestern, Otto Graham enlisted in the Navy. He served until 1945, when he signed to play with the Cleveland Browns. His career consisted of leading his team to ten straight championship games, seven championships, leading the league in passing yards five times, and being nominated to five Pro Bowls in his Hall of Fame career. Also, Graham is one of only two people (Gene Conley is the other) to win championships in two of the four major sports in North America. He won football championships in the AAFC and NFL, as well as winning a championship with the Rochester Royals of the National Basketball League, the predecessor to the NBA. After retiring from football, Graham went on to coach the Coast Guard Academy and the Washington Redskins.

Scouting Report: Extremely accurate. Accurate when his feet are set, accurate when he threw off his back foot, accurate off balance, accurate when the defender is hanging on him, accurate under pressure and accurate on the move. Specifically impressive with intermediate accuracy. The ball was on the money on deep outs and anything inside. Very good ball handling. Very good to excellent pocket presence, with good escapability, especially from the front side. However, he did play it safe on occasion and took too many sacks. Very good footwork. He does have a hop at the top of his drop, but it is consistent and was in rhythm. Quick through his progressions. Keeps his eyes downfield when outside of the pocket. Had an excellent feel for back side pressure. Not a huge arm, but could make all of the throws. He had touch on the ball, but was also able to throw with velocity when needed. Good runner. On defense, he stayed close to receivers and could tackle. However, he did not have form tackling and some were able to break through his grasp and attempted arm tackles.

Spec Sanders
Position: Tailback
Years: 1946–48 New York Yankees

Spec Sanders was drafted by the Washington Redskins in the first round of the 1942 NFL draft. He did not sign with the team. Instead, he joined the Navy. After serving in the Pacific, he returned and finished his education at the University of Texas. He signed with the New York Yankees in 1946 and played for the team for three years. During that time, he led the league in rushing attempts three times, rushing yards twice and touchdowns twice. However, knee injuries in 1948 forced him to retire. At the time, he was the conference's second-leading rusher and led the conference in rushing touchdowns. He tried to make a comeback in 1950 with the New York Yanks. He only played defense, but was named to the Pro Bowl and tied an NFL record with 13 interceptions. After he retired, he returned to Oklahoma to run his sporting goods business.

Scouting Report: Spec Sanders was an effective single-wing tailback. In the running game, he showed ability to run both inside and outside effectively. Quick to turn up field. Very good downhill runner. Can run through arm tackles and had good speed. Vision, balance and footwork were very good. There were times when his pad level was a little high, making him easier to tackle. In the passing game, he had mixed results. There were times when his ball was crisp and perfectly on target. Other times, he was off. He did not always make the best decisions, as he would occasionally throw into double and triple coverage. He stood flat-footed and was not very elusive against the pass rush. For the most part, he showed half-field progression in his reads and did have a tendency to stare down his receivers. With short passing, Sanders was pretty accurate. He was decisive, accurate and had a quick release. The mid-range game was mixed and he was average with the long ball. He changed his throwing motion with long passes, which caused him to be inaccurate. His receivers did not help him as many passes that were on target were dropped. Very good velocity on the ball on short and mid-range passes. He showed good ball handling on the fake.

Marion Motley
Position: Fullback
Years: 1946–49 Cleveland Browns

Marion Motley joined the Navy in 1944 and was stationed at the Great Lakes Naval Training Station. There, he played football for Paul Brown. After leaving the service in 1945, Motley returned to Nevada to finish his education. In 1946, he signed to play with the Cleveland Browns. Over his eight year career with the team, he led the league in rushing yards twice and was named to the Pro Bowl in 1950. He retired from football after the 1953 season due to injuries. In 1955, he came back and played seven games for the Pittsburgh Steelers, but was released part way through the season. Motley tried to get into coaching, but was turned away from all opportunities in the NFL. He was inducted into the Pro Football Hall of Fame in 1968. In 1994, Motley was named to the NFL's 75th Anniversary All-Time Team.

Scouting Report: Tough, downhill runner. Fast through the hole. Able to run through defenders, drag defenders, and fight for extra yards. Good balance, except on tosses and sweeps. When he was running sideways, it was easier to get him down, but you still needed to tackle him low or he would shake off the defender. Very good hands. He was an excellent option on screens, swing passes and backside passes. He struggled on pass protection. Only about a third of the time was he able to hold his ground. The rest of the time, the defender either pushed him back or easily slid off of him or around him to pressure Graham. Run blocking and lead blocking was similar. If he was straight-on with the defender, he did well. However, If the defender was not in front of him, he would either not block anyone or he made a weak block. On defense, he was quick while chasing or pursuing. He got off of blocks well. However, there were times he missed making the play because he got turned around and was not fast enough to recover. Violent tackler. Ripped the ball carrier to the ground.

Chet Mutryn
Position: Back
Years: 1946–49 Buffalo Bisons/Bills

At Cathedral Latin High School (Cleveland, Ohio), Chet Mutryn earned All-Scholastic honors. Moving on to Xavier, Mutryn was a two-time Little All-American selection and was the leading scorer for his team each year. In 1942, he set records for the most touchdowns (12) and most points (96) in a season. He received Xavier's highest award, the Legion of Honor Medal, which is given for accomplishments in both athletics and academics. He was drafted by the "Steagles" in 1943 (20th round), but was serving in the Navy at the time. Upon his return from two years of military duty, he joined the Cleveland Browns but was sent to Buffalo before the inaugural season of the franchise. He went on to become a three-time first team All-Conference player while in the AAFC. When the AAFC folded, Mutryn played a season for the Baltimore Colts before retiring from his playing career. After retiring from football, Mutryn went to work for the City of Cleveland doing real estate assessments. In Dr. David Shapiro's book: *The 135 Greatest Pro Running Backs: How They Stack Up Against Each Other*, Mutryn was rated number one of the pre-1950 group, putting him ahead of backs Steve Van Buren, Bronco Nagurski, Spec Sanders and Beattie Feathers. Mutryn was honored as Outstanding Athlete by the *Polish Everybody's Daily* and the Quarterback Club of Buffalo and is a member of the Cathedral Latin School, Greater Cleveland, and Xavier Athletic Halls of Fame. He also received the Good Joe of 1988 award, as well as the Cleveland Society Heritage Award, which is given to members who foster the cultural heritage of Poland and promote the principles of American citizenship.

Scouting Report: Very good agility, athleticism and competitiveness. He was physical when he had the ball, but was not physical when he did not have the ball (offense and defense). He was a north/south runner who ran tough. He didn't really drag anyone for extra yards, but pounded the ball to get the available yards. He gained consistent yardage between the tackles. On sweeps and tosses, he would get outside, plant his foot and get upfield. Quick feet when avoiding the defense through the holes and between the tackles. Elusive in the open field without running sideways. He got upfield. He didn't break tackles, but he fought for extra yardage. He ran through arms in the hole. As a receiver, he did not run great routes, but did get himself open. Not great hands, but dependable. He didn't fight for jump balls downfield. Run after the catch was the same as with running the ball. He didn't break tackles, but would get upfield and if he had space, he could make a guy miss. On defense, he did not let receivers get behind him. Not a good tackler, but was quick to come up in run support. As a returner, he would get upfield. If he had to go sideways, he would stick his foot in the ground and get upfield. Very good speed and elusiveness.

Jack Russell
Position: Defensive End
Years: 1946–49 New York Yankees

At Baylor, Russell was All-American in 1940 and 1941. During his time in the military, he played for the Eastern Army All-Stars, Blackland Army Air Field and the Hawaiian Flyers.

Scouting Report: On offense, he showed good leverage with his blocks. He didn't always finish his blocks and didn't always seem interested in blocking. He took plays off. However, he did excel in down blocking. His route-running was mixed. He seemed to coast into his route and rarely went full speed. However, on quick outs, he used his speed to beat the defender towards the sideline. He did seem to find a way to get open, even while he lacked effort. Good hands, but catching did not seem natural for him as it looked like he fought to catch the ball. He seemed like a different player on defense, as if he were saving himself for that side of the ball. He showed full effort/motor on defense. He stood in both a two-point and three-point stance. On the pass rush, he applied consistent pressure. He was quick off the snap and quick to the passer. He didn't have to loop past the blocker, he just went right by him. He did get caught inside a few times, which allowed the passer to get outside of him. In pass coverage, he was good, but he had a habit of looking into the backfield and losing his man. Good agility and didn't miss tackles.

John Yonakor
Position: Defensive End
Years: 1946–49 Cleveland Browns

John Yonakor started his college career in 1942 at the University of Notre Dame and won a national championship the following year. At the end of the season, he joined the Marine Corps and served until 1945. That year, Yonakor was drafted by the Philadelphia Eagles, but decided to sign with the Cleveland Browns and played all four years in the AAFC with the team. In 1950, he played for the New York Yanks before going to the Canadian Football League to play for the Montreal Allouettes. He returned to the NFL to play a season with the Washington Redskins before retiring from football. After football, Yonakor held several jobs in Boston before returning to Cleveland.

Scouting Report: Very good run blocking on offense. Excellent when straight ahead and very good in pass protection. He was slow in his routes and his routes were not crisp. Very good hands, although he always let the ball come to him. He didn't high point or attack the ball, which allowed defenders to knock away should-be receptions. On defense, he was positionally sound. Very good base and strong at the point of attack. He did have a habit of letting quarterbacks and running backs get outside of him too often, but on a play-to-play basis, he set the edge well. Got good push. He frequently pressured the passer, although he was a step too late to get to the passer before they were able to throw. However, he did force quick throws. Not real quick. He was an arm tackler, but was still able to make the tackles. He was good when he dropped into coverage.

Martin Ruby
Position: Tackle
Years: 1946–48 Brooklyn Dodgers,
       1949 New York Yankees

Martin Ruby enlisted in the Army Air Force during halftime of the 1942 Cotton Bowl Classic. After serving over four years in the military, Ruby signed with the Brooklyn Dodgers and played four years for the team (the fourth year was when the Dodgers merged with the New York Yankees for the 1949 season). In 1950, Ruby played for the New York Yanks of the NFL. In 1951, he went to Canada to play seven years for the Saskatchewan Roughriders. He was inducted into the Canadian Football Hall of Fame in 1974. After retiring from playing football, Ruby coached at Baylor University, Texas A&M University and the University of Tulsa.

Scouting Report: Known more for his defensive abilities than for his offensive abilities, but he performed very well on both sides of the ball. On defense, he was able to quickly shed blocks and go down the line to pursue the play. On the pass rush, he was able to get good penetration into the backfield to pressure the passer. On offense, he showed very good to excellent blocking ability and was able to quickly get leverage on the defender. Overall, he was not very fast, but made up for it with excellent strength. Very good hand placement, as well as competitiveness. He was able to use his strength to make up for any deficiencies.

Arnie Weinmeister
Position: Defensive Tackle
Years: New York Yankees, 1948–49

After four years at the University of Washington, Weinmeister left to join the Army. When he returned, he played for the New York Yankees for the last two years of their existence in the AAFC. When the Conference merged with the NFL, Weinmeister played for the New York Giants before he finished his playing career with the British Columbia Lions of the Canadian Football League. During his tenure with the Giants, he earned four Pro Bowl berths. After he retired from football, Weinmeister became heavily involved with the International Brotherhood of Teamsters.

Scouting Report: On offense, Weinmeister was a better run blocker than in pass protection. He was best when straight ahead drive blocking. However, he did end up on his knees often. He showed very good strength and leverage. He finished blocks. However, he did get high a few times, which resulted in him getting knocked off balance or pushed back. On defense, he was almost always high off the snap, but it did not hurt him due to his size and strength. He only got turned or blocked out of a play a few times. He had poor play recognition and was hesitant on misdirection or fakes. Excellent competitiveness. He did not give up on a play, but lacked speed and quickness in pursuit to the opposite side of the field. He was excellent coming off the edge and when the run was up the middle. On those plays, he was quick down the line to make a tackle.

Bill Willis
Position: Middle Guard
Years: 1946–49 Cleveland Browns

Bill Willis graduated from Ohio State University in 1945. Willis was about to play for the Montreal Allouettes of the Canadian Football League, but received a call from the Browns to attend their training camp. Willis made the team and played for the Browns for eight seasons. During that time, he was named to the Pro Bowl three times and was eventually named to the Pro Football Hall of Fame's All-Decade team of the 1940s. After retiring from football, Willis dedicated himself to working with kids in the community. He was inducted into the Pro Football Hall of Fame in 1977.

Scouting Report: On offense he showed great leverage. Very good in pass protection and straight-ahead run blocking. He struggled when pulling as he was hesitant, which put him behind the paly. He did not always find someone to block when pulling. On defense, he showed great leverage and agility. He could pop up off the ground back to his feet and get to speed quickly. Extremely quick and quick off the snap. Could split double teams, as well as fight through and fight off double teams. Very good hands in throwing aside defenders and getting off blocks. Quick to get to the passer. Quick through the line to be there just as the back was getting the ball. Quick in pursuit to make plays in the backfield and behind the line of scrimmage. Very disruptive. Excellent tackler. He got low and wrapped up.

Visco Grgich
Position: Defensive Guard
Years: 1946–49 San Francisco 49ers

Visco Grgich went to Santa Clara University before enlisting in the Air Force. During his time of service, he played for the Second Air Force Superbombers

(1944) and the Fourth Air Force Fliers (1945). Grgich was drafted by the Chicago Bears in 1946, but decided to sign with the San Francisco 49ers. He played seven years for the team before a knee injury ended his career in 1952. Grgich was a car salesman before becoming a coach at Oakdale High School in California.

Scouting Report: On both sides of the ball, he was quick. No wasted movement and he was very competitive. He played snap-to-whistle. Excellent leverage both on blocking and defensively. On offense, he was excellent in run blocking, although only adequate in pass protection. Excellent pulling guard, quick when pulling and was out of his stance quickly. On defense, he was quick off the snap and very quick shooting the gaps. Very good play recognition. Decisive. He saw the ball and went in a straight line to the ball with no wasted movements or false steps. He was always in pursuit and quick in pursuit. Also dropped into coverage from the middle guard position. However, he did have a tendency to keep his head down, which caused him to run by plays.

Lou Saban
Position: Linebacker
Years: 1946–49 Cleveland Browns

Lou Saban played four years for the Cleveland Browns before starting his coaching career. His first position was at Case Institute in Cleveland in 1950. From there, he went to Northwestern and Western Illinois before entering the pro ranks. In 1960, he became the head coach of the Boston Patriots of the American Football League. From there, he had stints with the Buffalo Bills (where he won two AFL championships), the Denver Broncos and then back to the Buffalo Bills. He then went back to the college ranks with coaching jobs at the University of Miami, Army, the University of Central Florida and Penn State, as well as some high school coaching jobs. He then coached in the arena league with the Tampa Bay Storm and the Milwaukee Mustangs. He also spent two years as the president of baseball's New York Yankees (1981–82).

Scouting Report: Great form tackler. He was always around the ball. Very good in coverage, but occasionally got beat when in man coverage. Receivers could get behind him, but he was very good in underneath coverage. Very good speed and quick in pursuit. Very good play recognition. Competitive and athletic for his size. Very consistent in his play.

Tony Adamle
Position: Linebacker
Years: 1947–49 Cleveland Browns

Tony Adamle attended Ohio State University and played on the 1942 freshman team. After the season, he enlisted in the Air Force, and then returned to play for Ohio State in 1946. Adamle left school early to sign with the Cleveland Browns in 1947. After the 1951 season, he left the team to enter medical school. He returned for a season to play for the Browns in 1954, but again retired after the season. During his six seasons with the Browns, Adamle was named to two Pro Bowls. He graduated from medical school in 1956 and ran a practice until his death in 2000.

Scouting Report: On offense, he lacked speed. Similar pass blocking as Marion Motley: defenders would slide off, especially when he tried to cut the rushing defender. On defense, he always played to the whistle. Very good tackling. Very good in coverage. He lacked speed, but it did not seem to hurt his play. He usually was in position, got in position, or got to where he needed to be to make the tackle. Very good sideline-to-sideline pursuit. Not easily blocked, especially in pursuit. He would just run through attempted blocks or cuts. Very good at shedding blocks. He didn't get caught up in traffic, while always being focused on the ball carrier. Had great instincts to avoid players on the ground and attempted blocks. When he had pulling guards in front of him, he would either split the blockers or shed the block to make the play. Great play recognition.

Tom Colella
Position: Defensive Back
Years: 1946–48 Cleveland Browns, 1949 Buffalo Bills

As a three-sport athlete at Albion High School, Colella set the tone for his college career. While at Canisius, Colella earned Little All-American honors (twice). Because of his spectacular college career, Colella was inducted into the inaugural class of the Golden Griffin Sports Hall of Fame. Drafted by the Detroit Lions in 1942, Colella started his professional football career there. After playing the 1942 and 1943 seasons for Detroit, he was traded to the Cleveland Rams, where he spent the next two years of his career. Colella joined the Cleveland Browns in 1946 and won championships all three years that he was with the team. In 1949, Colella came home and played for the Buffalo Bills. Colella was inducted into the Greater Buffalo Sports Hall of Fame in 2002.

Scouting Report: On offense, he mostly went in motion and was away from the play or carried out a fake. On defense, he had very good awareness. He showed very good athleticism, agility and speed. Excellent ball skills. He was tight in downfield coverage. He made the tackle on anything short in front of him. He did struggle on intermediate routes both outside and inside, and got beat on occasion. He looked to play the passer and not the receiver. He kept his eyes in the backfield. He always went after the ball in the air and played the ball and not the man. Very good in run support as he was quick to come up against the run. Very good tackling. He got low and wrapped up. He rarely missed tackles.

Len Eshmont
Position: Defensive Back
Years: 1946–49 San Francisco 49ers

Len Eshmont was drafted by the New York Giants in 1941 and played for the team for a year. After returning from service in the Navy, he joined the San Francisco 49ers and played the 1946–49 seasons. He is credited with scoring the first touchdown in 49ers history. It was a 40-yard pass from Frankie Albert in the first quarter of their first game (their opponent was the New York Yankees). After he retired from his playing career, he coached at the Naval Academy and at the University of Virginia. Eshmont passed away at the age of 39 from hepatitis. Every year, the 49ers give out the Eshmont Award to the player who most exemplified the inspirational and courageous play of Len Eshmont.

Scouting Report: Overall, he was athletic, competitive and had good speed. On offense, he was a very good receiver out of the backfield. Very good hands and run after the catch. He was a willing and a very good blocker. He was a lead blocker and blocked the end to open the outside for the ball carrier. On defense, he was not a great tackler, but a willing tackler. He was willing to take on blocks. He would run across the field to make a tackle. He would come up in run support, although he usually lined up deep so he rarely got there. In coverage, he stuck to his man. He stayed on his hip and contested the pass and fought for the ball. Was excellent in coverage. However, he did have a few plays where he was burned. Overall, an excellent defensive back.

Otto Schnellbacher
Position: Defensive Back
Years: 1948–49 New York Yankees

Otto Schnellbacher was drafted by the Chicago Cardinals in 1947, but signed to play with the New York Yankees starting in 1948. After the AAFC merged with the NFL, Schnellbacher played two years for the New York Giants. Both years, he was named to the Pro Bowl and in 1951 he led the league in interceptions with 11. He also played professional basketball for the Providence Steamrollers of the Basketball Association of America and played in the NBA for the St. Louis Bombers.

Scouting Report: On offense, he was a very willing blocker and would run downfield in a straight line to make a block. Poor in pass routes. On defense, he was a very good tackler. Anything caught in front of him, he would come up and make the tackle. If he got both hands on the ball carrier, he would make the tackle. Was physical and could hit. He wasn't fast, but could close the gap quickly. However, he was a little stiff in coverage. He did not have good lateral movement and receivers could get a step on him, especially to the corners. He had good ball skills.

Rex Grossman
Position: Kicker
Years: 1948–49 Baltimore Colts

At Indiana University, Rex Grossman played quarterback and fullback. He left college to join the Army and helped his team to the Air Force Championship of England. During his military service, he earned the Purple Heart, the Combat Infantryman's Badge and four battle stars. When he returned, he joined the Baltimore Colts. When the AAFC merged with the NFL, Grossman played with the Colts for eight games before going to the Detroit Lions for four games to end his playing career. His grandson, Rex Grossman, played for the Chicago Bears, Houston Texans and Washington Redskins.

Scouting Report: From the fullback position, he was excellent in pass protection/blocking/picking up the blitz/picking up the free rusher/etc. Similarly, he was very good as a lead blocker, although better in pass protection. As a runner, he had no real power or moves. He was slower with the ball in his hands than as a blocker. On defense, he had impressive hustle. Had good play recognition. He was a good tackler, except when the ball carrier cut back on him. He did not have the agility to make the tackle. He was aggressive to the ball at times, but was more deliberate other times. He got in front of the ball and made the tackle. He was easily blocked when the offensive line got to him. He was pushed back and he had trouble shedding blocks. He also tripped over bodies downfield. He was a one-step straight-on kicker. Good distance on kickoffs. He showed control and aim on his kickoffs. Accurate kicker.

Glenn Dobbs
Position: Back, Punter
Years: 1946–47 Brooklyn Dodgers, 1947–49 Los Angeles Dons

Glenn Dobbs was drafted by the Chicago Cardinals in 1943. Failing to agree to a contract, Dobbs enlisted in the Army Air Force. When he returned from military service, he signed with the Brooklyn Dodgers. He played with the team for two years before going to the Los Angeles Dons for two seasons. In 1951, he started a three-year stint with the Saskatchewan Roughriders, before playing a season with the Hamilton Tiger-Cats to end his playing career. After retirement, he became the athletic director at the University of Tulsa and coached the team from 1961 through 1968. He also spent three years as the president of a minor league baseball team.

Scouting Report: On offense, his passing was accurate with good ball location. He could throw on the move. When scrambling, he kept his eyes downfield and found the open receiver. Not a huge arm, but he threw with velocity. His footwork was choppy. He bounced and hopped, which made him slow to accelerate away from the rush. While rushing, he ran upright with swiveling hips. He wasn't fast, but he had a burst through the hole and could weave through the defense. He always fell forward. On defense, he was slow to change direction and had a natural hesitation when the runner cut back. He was flat-footed. His punts had good distance.

PFRA's AAFC Notables

We have covered the players on the All-Conference team. Now, we will focus on the notable people from the AAFC who were not part of the All-Conference team. This includes players, coaches, owners and commissioners.

Frankie Albert
Quarterback, 1946–49 San Francisco 49ers

After guiding Stanford University to a Rose Bowl victory in 1940, Frankie Albert joined the Navy. After returning from the war, Albert played for St. Mary's—as well as the Los Angeles Bulldogs of the Pacific Coast League—before joining the San Francisco 49ers. While in the AAFC, he led the league in completion percentage once and touchdowns twice. In 1948, he was named the conference's co-MVP along with Cleveland's Otto Graham. He finished his playing career with one season in the Canadian Football League. After retiring as a player, Albert joined the 49ers as head coach for three seasons. After retiring from football for good, Albert went into real estate.

Paul Brown
Head Coach, Cleveland Browns, 1946–49
Pro Football Hall of Fame, Class of 1967

Paul Brown started his coaching career at Severn School in Severna Park, Maryland. After two years, he went to Massillon Washington High School before taking the head coaching job at Ohio State. There, he won the first national championship in school history (1942). Over his first three coaching jobs, he amassed a 110–18–4 record, including a 35-game winning streak while at Massillon. During the war, Brown coached at the Great Lakes Naval Training Station. In 1945, Brown accepted the head coaching job with the Cleveland Browns. During his tenure, the Browns won seven championships and coached the first major-league professional football team to go undefeated and win a championship game (1948). After a conflict with team ownership, Brown was fired in 1963. In 1968, Brown became coach, general manager and part owner of the Cincinnati Bengals. He coached the team for eight years before retiring.

Jim Crowley
AAFC Commissioner, 1944–46
Head Coach, Chicago Rockets, 1947

Jim Crowley was famous as one quarter of the legendary "Four Horsemen" backfield at Notre Dame (along with Elmer Layden, Don Miller and Harry Stuhldreher). After leaving Notre Dame, Crowley played professional football for the Waterbury Blues, Green Bay Packers and Providence Steamroller (all were members of the NFL). After playing, Crowley was the assistant coach at the University of Georgia before becoming the head coach at Michigan State, Fordham and the North Carolina Pre-Flight of the Navy. Crowley joined the AAFC as the first commissioner, but stepped down after the 1946 season to become the head coach of the Chicago Rockets, as well as a partial owner. After one season, Crowley retired from football. Between his retirement and his passing in 1986, Crowley was an insurance salesman, worked at a television station and was the chairman of the Pennsylvania State Athletic Commission. He was inducted into the College Football Hall of Fame in 1966.

Ray Flaherty
Head Coach, New York Yankees, 1946–48
Head Coach, Chicago Hornets, 1949
Pro Football Hall of Fame, Class of 1976

Ray Flaherty started his playing career with the Los Angeles Wildcats of the American Football League. After a single season with the team, Flaherty joined the New York Yankees of the NFL. In 1928, he moved over to the New York Giants and stayed there until he retired from playing in 1935. However, he did take a year off in 1930 to coach Gonzaga. In 1936, he became the head coach of the Boston Redskins, winning a championship the following year. He won a second championship in 1942, with the team now playing out of Washington. In 1946, he became the head coach of the New York Yankees of the AAFC. After three years with the team, he went to the Chicago Hornets before retiring for good from football. After he retired, he ran a beverage distribution business and was a columnist for the *Spokane Daily Chronicle*.

Len Ford
Defensive End, Los Angeles Dons, 1948–49
Pro Football Hall of Fame, Class of 1976

Len Ford played one year of football for Morgan State University before he enlisted in the Navy. After returning from service, he transferred to the University of Michigan and played for the Wolverines for three seasons, including the famed 1947 undefeated team. In 1948, Ford started his professional career with the Los Angeles Dons after being passed over by the NFL. When the AAFC merged with the NFL, Ford became a member of the Cleveland Browns. In his eight seasons with the team, Ford was named to four Pro Bowls and was selected to the Pro Football Hall of Fame's All-Decade team of the 1950s. He finished his career with a single season with the Green Bay Packers. After he retired from football, Ford pursued his law degree, but never graduated. He died of a heart attack at the age of 46.

Frank Gatski
Center, Cleveland Browns, 1946–49
Pro Football Hall of Fame, Class of 1985

Frank Gatski attended Marshall, but his Army reserve unit was activated during his senior year and he served overseas. When he returned in 1945, Marshall still had suspended their football program. Gatski decided to transfer to Auburn for his senior year. After graduation, Gatski tried out and made the squad for the Cleveland Browns. He stayed with the team until 1956, earning a Pro Bowl nod and several all-pro selections. He finished his playing career with a single season with the Detroit Lions. A few years after he retired, he joined the Boston Patriots as a scout for two years. He coached the West Virginia Industrial School for Boys until he retired in 1982.

Lou Groza
Tackle, Place Kicker, Cleveland Browns, 1946–49
Pro Football Hall of Fame, Class of 1974

Lou Groza attended Ohio State University. After a single season with the team, he enlisted in the Army and served in the Pacific. When he returned, he joined the Cleveland Browns for their inaugural season. He stayed with the Browns his entire career (1946–59 and 1961–67). He took the 1960 season off and started an insurance business. He was also a scout for the Browns. He was persuaded to come out of retirement in 1961 and played until 1967. After his playing career, he focused on his insurance business. Groza made the Pro Bowl nine times, was named to the Pro Football Hall of Fame's All-Decade team of the 1950s and was selected to the NFL's 75th Anniversary All-Time team.

Elroy "Crazy Legs" Hirsch
Halfback, End, Chicago Rockets, 1946–48
Pro Football Hall of Fame, Class of 1968

Elroy Hirsch played college football for both the University of Wisconsin and the University of Michigan. He was drafted by the Cleveland Rams in 1945, but said that he wanted to return to the University of Wisconsin after he finished serving in the Marine Corps. However, he signed with the Chicago Rockets in 1946 and played three seasons for the team. After a contractual disagreement, Hirsch wanted to be released to play for the Green Bay Packers. However, since the Rams had drafted him in 1945, they still retained his rights and he signed with the Rams. While with the team, Hirsch earned three Pro Bowl nods and was eventually selected to the Pro Football Hall of Fame's All-Decade team of the 1950s. After his retirement from his playing career, Hirsch got into broadcasting, appeared in a few films, was general manager of the Los Angeles Rams and was athletic director at the University of Wisconsin.

Jonas Ingram
AAFC Commissioner, 1947–49

Jonas Ingram joined the United States Naval Academy in 1903. While there, he played football for the Midshipmen and was eventually inducted into the College Football Hall of Fame. In 1915, he became the head coach of the Midshipmen and amassed a 9–8–2 record in his two seasons leading the team. From 1926 through 1930, Ingram served as the athletic director at the Naval Academy. He retired from active duty in 1947, after achieving the rank of Admiral and having won numerous medals. At that point, he was named the second AAFC commissioner, taking over for Jim Crowley. After he resigned from the AAFC in 1949, he joined the Reynolds Metals Company as vice-president.

Oliver Kessing
AAFC Commissioner, 1949

Oliver Kessing entered the United States Naval Academy in 1910 and was a multi-sport athlete. In 1926, he was named the Navy's first graduate manager of athletics. He held that title until 1929. After heading the North Carolina Navy Pre-Flight School, Kessing went back to sea for three and a half years. He then joined General Douglas MacArthur's staff until he retired from active military service in 1947. That same year, Kessing was named the deputy commissioner of the AAFC under Jonas Ingram. When Ingram resigned in 1949, Kessing became the third and final commissioner of the Conference.

Frank "Bruiser" Kinard
Tackle, New York Yankees, 1946–47
Pro Football Hall of Fame, Class of 1971

Frank Kinard played college football for the University of Mississippi. During that time, he earned the school's first All-American honors. He was drafted by the Brooklyn Dodgers in 1938 and played for the team from 1938 through 1944. He joined the New York Yankees in 1946 and played two seasons for the team. After retiring from pro football, Kinard was the offensive line coach for the University of Mississippi until 1970. He then became the school's athletic director from 1971 to 1973. He was inducted into the College Football Hall of Fame in 1961 and the Pro Football Hall of Fame in 1971.

Tom Landry
Back, New York Yankees, 1949
Pro Football Hall of Fame, Class of 1990

Tom Landry is best known as the Hall of Fame coach for the Dallas Cowboys from their inaugural season in 1960 through 1988. But, he started his pro football career as a player for the New York Yankees. After the AAFC merged with the NFL, Landry went to the New York Giants and played through the 1955 season. In 1954, he also added coaching duties for the Giants as the defensive coordinator. The offensive coordinator was Hall of Fame coach Vince Lombardi. During his coaching career, he has been credited with creating both the 4–3 defense and the Flex Defense. He finished his coaching career with a 250–162–6 record with two Super Bowl championships.

Dante Lavelli
End, Cleveland Browns, 1946–49
Pro Football Hall of Fame, Class of 1975

Dante Lavelli played running back in high school, but changed to end when he entered Ohio State University. However, due to injuries, Lavelli saw limited action with the Buckeyes. In 1942, Lavelli was drafted into the Army and served in Europe during the war. When he returned, the Detroit Tigers of Major League Baseball again tried to recruit him (their first offer came when he was in high school). He opted again to concentrate on football and signed with the Cleveland Browns. Over his eleven seasons with the team, he was named to three Pro Bowls, was named to several all-pro teams and was eventually named to the Pro Football Hall of Fame's All-Decade team of the 1940s, as well as the NFL's 50th Anniversary All-Time team. After he retired from football, Lavelli held several jobs, including owning an appliance business, owning a furniture store, and helped found both the NFL Alumni Organization and the NFL Players Association.

Benjamin Lindheimer
Owner, Los Angeles Dons, 1946–49

Benjamin Lindheimer was a stakeholder in the Los Angeles Dons, but his primary focus was horse racing. He owned Washington Park Race Track in Chicago, as well as Arlington Park Race Track, also in Chicago. Earlier in life, he was in real estate and development. He was president of the Chicago Board of Local Improvements, chairman of the Illinois Commerce Commission and a member of the South Park Commissioners. He also helped to organize the Association of Jewish Charities.

Anthony Morabito
Owner, San Francisco 49ers, 1946–49

Tony Morabito played football at St. Ignatiius High School and the University of Santa Clara. However, his football career was cut short due to a shoulder injury. After graduating from Santa Clara, Morabito ran a lumber hauling business in the 1930s and 1940s. After failing to secure a franchise in the NFL, Morabito joined the AAFC as majority owner of the San Francisco 49ers. He held the team until the day he died—while watching the 49ers play the Chicago Bears, in 1957. Team ownership eventually went to his wife, Josephine, who became the first woman to hold a majority ownership in a professional sports franchise.

Arthur McBride
Owner, Cleveland Browns, 1946–49

Arthur McBride started his career in the newspaper business at an early age: around six years old, he was a newsboy. By 1913, he worked his way to being the circulation manager of the *Cleveland News*. In 1930, he got into the taxi business, as well as continued investing in real estate. McBride's first attempt to get into professional football was when he tried to purchase the Cleveland Rams in 1942. He was denied and eventually joined the AAFC as the owner of the Cleveland Browns. He held the team until he sold it in 1953. After he sold the Browns, he continued to work in the taxi and real estate businesses.

Clarence "Ace" Parker
Back, New York Yankees, 1946
Pro Football Hall of Fame, Class of 1972

Ace Parker was a five-sport athlete in high school. He intended to go to Virginia Tech, but after a visit to

Duke University, he decided to become a Blue Devil. Parker was drafted by the Brooklyn Dodgers in 1937, but he chose to play baseball for the Philadelphia Athletics. After one season with the team, he decided that he also wanted to play football. He played baseball for the Athletics and football for the Dodgers. In 1938, he focused solely on football and just played for the Dodgers. In 1942, he joined the Navy. When he returned in 1945, he joined the Boston Yanks of the NFL for a season, before swapping leagues and playing a season for the New York Yankees of the AAFC. After he retired from playing, he became an assistant football coach at Duke until 1966. He was also the head baseball coach from 1953 through 1966. Over the next 30 years, he went on to scout for the San Francisco 49ers and the Arizona Cardinals.

Joe Perry
Fullback, San Francisco 49ers, 1948–49
Pro Football Hall of Fame, Class of 1969

After being rejected to attend UCLA, Joe Perry started his collegiate football career at Compton Junior College. After having an outstanding year, UCLA came calling, but he rejected them and instead joined the Navy. In 1948, he was offered a contract with the Los Angeles Rams, but decided instead to play for the San Francisco 49ers. He led the Conference in rushing touchdowns in 1948 and 1949, as well as led the Conference in rushing yards in 1949. He continued with the 49ers until 1960, when he was traded to the Baltimore Colts. He was traded back to the 49ers for the 1963 season before he retired from professional football. After he retired, he became a professional bowler, worked as a scout for the 49ers and worked as a sales representative for a winery.

Lawrence T. "Buck" Shaw
Head Coach, San Francisco 49ers, 1946–49

Buck Shaw started his collegiate career at Creighton University. After a single game, the flu epidemic cancelled the remainder of the season. He transferred to the University of Notre Dame and played three seasons for the Fighting Irish. He started his coaching career at North Carolina State. He was there for a year before heading to the University of Nevada. From 1929 to 1935, he was the line coach at Santa Clara University and then became the head coach for the next seven seasons. After a single season with the University of California, Shaw joined the San Francisco 49ers. From 1946 through 1954, he had a record of 71–39–4. After leaving the 49ers, he coached Air Force (1956–57) and the Philadelphia Eagles (1958–60), winning a championship in his final season as a head coach.

Y.A. Tittle
Quarterback, Baltimore Colts, 1948–49
Pro Football Hall of Fame, Class of 1971

Y.A. Tittle started his professional career in 1948 with the Baltimore Colts, where UPI named him Rookie of the Year. After the Colts folded in 1950, Tittle was selected by the San Francisco 49ers. He played 10 seasons for the 49ers, at which point he was traded to the New York Giants. He retired after the 1964 season. Throughout his career, he was named to seven Pro Bowls and won Most Valuable Player or Player of the Year honors three times. After he retired, he started an insurance business and served as an assistant coach for the 49ers and Giants.

Arch Ward
AAFC Founder

Along with being the founder of the AAFC, Arch Ward is credited with creating both the Major League All-Star Game and the College All-Star game. He also created the Golden Gloves boxing tournament. His primary occupation was as a sportswriter and sports editor. He started in 1920 as Notre Dame's sports publicity director. In 1921, he joined the staff of the *Rockford Star* as a sports editor. He stayed at the *Star* until he moved to the *Chicago Tribune* in 1925 as a sports writer. In 1930, he was elevated to the sports editor, a position he held until he passed away in 1955. He was inducted into the National Sportscasters and Sportswriters Hall of Fame in 1973.

Part 3: Individual Statistics

1946

Players are ranked based on total yards, except in pass receiving, interception returns, points after touchdown and field goals. Those are ranked based on total number. Punting is based on averages. Scoring is based on points.

There are a few discrepancies between the actual statistics and the official records in 1946. The total receiving yards for the season for Len Eshmont, Joe Vetrano, Ed Balatti and Ken Roskie were not consistent. Eshmont had an extra six receiving yards, while Vetrano was missing six yards. Balatti had an extra seven receiving yards and Roskie was missing seven yards. Since the numbers could not be verified, the official statistics are listed.

Total Offense Leaders (Net Yards Gained)

	# of Plays	Rush	Pass	Total	Avg Gain
Glenn Dobbs, Brooklyn	364	208	1,886	2,094	5.75
Otto Graham, Cleveland	204	−125	1,834	1,709	8.38
Bob Hoernschemeyer, Chi	304	375	1,266	1,641	5.40
Frankie Albert, SF	266	−10	1,404	1,394	5.24
Charlie O'Rourke, LA	229	50	1,250	1,300	5.68
Spec Sanders, New York	219	709	411	1,120	5.11
Ace Parker, New York	190	184	763	947	4.98
Angelo Bertelli, LA	138	−16	917	901	6.53
Norm Standlee, SF	134	651	0	651	4.86
Vic Kulbitski, Buffalo	97	605	0	605	6.24
George Terlep, Buffalo	159	29	574	603	3.79
Marion Motley, Cleveland	73	601	0	601	8.23
Edgar Jones, Cleveland	81	539	4	543	6.70
Marion Pugh, Miami	147	−125	608	483	3.36
John Kimbrough, LA	122	473	0	473	3.88
Al Dekdebrun, Buffalo	91	−55	517	462	5.08
Steve Juzwik, Buffalo	71	455	0	455	6.41
Cotton Price, Miami	89	−55	484	429	4.82
Walt Clay, Chicago	92	283	140	423	4.60
Chuck Fenenbock, LA	51	420	0	420	8.24
Bob Perina, New York	93	135	279	414	4.45
Lew Mayne, Brooklyn	95	191	219	410	4.32
Harry Hopp, Buffalo–Miami	83	218	190	408	4.92
Len Eshmont, SF	75	340	42	382	5.09
Elroy Hirsch, Chicago	107	226	156	382	3.57

Rushing

	Rush	Yds	Avg Gain	TD
Spec Sanders, New York	140	709	5.06	6
Norm Standlee, San Francisco	134	651	4.86	2
Vic Kulbitski, Buffalo	97	605	6.24	2
Marion Motley, Cleveland	73	601	8.23	5
Edgar Jones, Cleveland	77	539	7.00	4
John Kimbrough, Los Angeles	122	473	3.88	6
Steve Juzwik, Buffalo	71	455	6.41	3
Chuck Fenenbock, Los Angeles	50	420	8.40	3
Bob Hoernschemeyer, Chicago	111	375	3.38	0
Earle Parsons, San Francisco	74	362	4.89	2
John Strzykalski, San Francisco	79	346	4.38	2
Len Eshmont, San Francisco	73	340	4.66	6
Chet Mutryn, Buffalo	57	289	5.07	1
Walt Clay, Chicago	65	283	4.35	1
Don Greenwood, Cleveland	77	274	3.56	6
Harry Clarke, Los Angeles	62	250	4.03	0
Gaylon Smith, Cleveland	62	240	3.87	5
Eddie Prokop, New York	65	236	3.63	1
Elroy Hirsch, Chicago	87	226	2.60	1
Pres Johnston, Miami–Buffalo	45	218	4.84	2
Harry Hopp, Buffalo–Miami	61	218	3.57	3
Glenn Dobbs, Brooklyn	95	208	2.19	4
Lew Mayne, Brooklyn	70	191	2.73	1
Ace Parker, New York	75	184	2.45	3
Bob H. Kennedy, New York	58	179	3.09	2
Bill Kellagher, Chicago	49	178	3.63	3
Billy Hillenbrand, Chicago	50	175	3.50	2
Pug Manders, New York	49	168	3.43	3
Bob Seymour, Los Angeles	37	165	4.46	0
Earl Elsey, Los Angeles	47	165	3.51	0
Dub Jones, Miami–Brooklyn	43	164	3.81	0
Ernie Lewis, Chicago	57	164	2.88	1
Jimmy Nelson, Miami	39	163	4.18	2
Mickey Colmer, Brooklyn	46	155	3.37	0
Dom Principe, Brooklyn	39	139	3.56	2
Lou Tomasetti, Buffalo	43	139	3.23	1
Bob Perina, New York	45	135	3.00	1
Don Durdan, San Francisco	32	132	4.13	0
Frank Trigilio, Los Angeles–Miami	41	126	3.07	1
Tom Colella, Cleveland	30	118	3.93	2
Ray Terrell, Cleveland	39	117	3.00	0
Bernie Nygren, Los Angeles	26	111	4.27	0
Bus Mertes, Los Angeles	40	111	2.78	0
Don Reece, Miami	30	109	3.63	2
Ned Mathews, Chicago–SF	30	109	3.63	1
Gene Fekete, Cleveland	26	106	4.08	1
Andy Dudish, Buffalo	30	106	3.53	0
Bob Paffrath, Brooklyn–Miami	31	100	3.23	2
Jim Reynolds, Miami	32	96	3.00	0
Andy Marefos, Los Angeles	30	93	3.10	4
Ken Casanega, San Francisco	29	90	3.10	1
Dick Renfro, San Francisco	18	85	4.72	3
Charlie Armstrong, Brooklyn	22	78	3.55	0
John Polanski, Los Angeles	28	77	2.71	1

Part 3: Individual Statistics

	Rush	Yds	Avg Gain	TD
Dewey Proctor, New York	23	76	3.30	1
Bill Lund, Cleveland	23	72	3.13	1
Joe Vetrano, San Francisco	23	69	3.00	1
Monk Gafford, Miami–Brooklyn	24	66	2.75	1
Charlie Timmons, Brooklyn	23	65	2.83	0
Lamar Davis, Miami	14	64	4.57	0
Bill Daley, Brooklyn–Miami	14	63	4.50	0
Harvey Johnson, New York	16	63	3.94	0
Stan Kozlowski, Miami	18	61	3.39	0
Bob Morrow, New York	8	54	6.75	0
Curt Sandig, Buffalo	22	52	2.36	1
Charlie O'Rourke, Los Angeles	47	50	1.06	1
Jim Thibaut, Buffalo	10	48	4.80	1
Al Akins, Cleveland	5	42	8.40	1
Bill Schroeder, Chicago	12	42	3.50	0
Dick Erdlitz, Miami	26	38	1.46	1
Lou Zontini, Buffalo	13	36	2.77	0
Ken Stofer, Buffalo	16	36	2.25	0
Paul Vinnola, Los Angeles	23	36	1.57	0
Parker Hall, San Francisco	17	31	1.82	0
Dale Gentry, Los Angeles	5	29	5.80	1
Lowell Wagner, New York	15	29	1.93	0
George Terlep, Buffalo	36	29	0.81	1
Fred Evans, Cleveland	8	27	3.38	0
Terry Fox, Miami	12	26	2.17	0
Fred Gloden, Miami	13	24	1.85	1
Bob Sweiger, New York	7	22	3.14	0
Russ Morrow, Brooklyn	0	22	—	1
Pete Lamana, Chicago	6	21	3.50	0
Rhoten Shetley, Brooklyn	9	21	2.33	0
Max Morris, Chicago	1	20	20.00	0
Frankie Sinkwich, New York	7	20	2.86	0
Bob Steuber, Cleveland	8	19	2.38	0
Walt Williams, Chicago	21	19	0.90	1
Harry Connolly, Brooklyn	8	18	2.25	0
Fondren Mitchell, Miami	5	17	3.40	0
Ken Roskie, San Francisco	9	16	1.78	0
Dante Lavelli, Cleveland	1	14	14.00	0
Bob Nowaskey, Los Angeles	3	14	4.67	0
Don Griffin, Chicago	28	13	0.46	0
Norm Cox, Chicago	1	12	12.00	0
Cal Purdin, Brooklyn–Miami	10	12	1.20	0
Blondy Black, Buffalo	1	10	10.00	0
Bill Kerr, Los Angeles	1	10	10.00	0
Steve Nemeth, Chicago	4	10	2.50	0
Art Van Tone, Brooklyn	4	10	2.50	0
Bill Boedeker, Chicago	6	8	1.33	0
Bob Sneddon, Los Angeles	3	6	2.00	0
Harry Burrus, New York	1	3	3.00	0
Daryl Cato, Miami	0	3	—	0
Bob Titchenal, San Francisco	1	2	2.00	0
Ed Ulinski, Cleveland	1	2	2.00	0
Lloyd Cheatham, New York	3	2	0.67	0
Bob Thurbon, Buffalo	3	2	0.67	0
Herb Nelson, Buffalo	1	1	1.00	0
Bud Schwenk, Cleveland	6	−1	−0.17	1
John Fekete, Buffalo	1	−1	−1.00	0
Pat Lahey, Chicago	1	−2	−2.00	0
Lou Saban, Cleveland	4	−4	−1.00	0
Pete Franceschi, San Francisco	8	−5	−0.63	1
Joe Aguirre, Los Angeles	2	−5	−2.50	0
Doyle Tackett, Brooklyn	11	−6	−0.55	0
Alyn Beals, San Francisco	2	−7	−3.50	0
Johnny Vardian, Miami	5	−8	−1.60	0
Frankie Albert, San Francisco	69	−10	−0.14	4
Walt McDonald, Miami–Brooklyn	4	−11	−2.75	0
Bob Mitchell, Los Angeles	8	−12	−1.50	0
Angelo Bertelli, Los Angeles	11	−16	−1.45	1
Jess Freitas, San Francisco	6	−21	−3.50	0
Ken Holley, Miami	2	−22	−11.00	0
Bob Reinhard, Los Angeles	1	−30	−30.00	0
Cliff Lewis, Cleveland	24	−34	−1.42	0
Kay Eakin, Miami	15	−41	−2.73	0
Jim Tarrant, Miami	5	−46	−9.20	0
Al Dekdebrun, Buffalo	25	−55	−2.20	0
Cotton Price, Miami	15	−55	−3.67	0
Otto Graham, Cleveland	30	−125	−4.17	1
Marion Pugh, Miami	29	−125	−4.31	2

Passing

	Comp	Att	Yds	TD	Int
Glenn Dobbs, Brooklyn	135	269	1,886	13	15
Otto Graham, Cleveland	95	174	1,834	17	5
Frankie Albert, San Francisco	104	197	1,404	14	14
Bob Hoernschemeyer, Chicago	95	193	1,266	14	14
Charlie O'Rourke, Los Angeles	105	182	1,250	12	14
Angelo Bertelli, Los Angeles	67	127	917	7	14
Ace Parker, New York	62	115	763	8	3
Marion Pugh, Miami	55	118	608	5	12
George Terlep, Buffalo	48	123	574	7	14
Al Dekdebrun, Buffalo	28	66	517	8	8
Cotton Price, Miami	36	74	484	2	5
Spec Sanders, New York	33	79	411	4	9
Kay Eakin, Miami	19	45	331	2	5
Bob Perina, New York	21	48	279	1	4
Bud Schwenk, Cleveland	15	23	276	4	0
Jess Freitas, San Francisco	22	44	234	3	7
Walt Williams, Chicago	13	30	226	1	5
Lew Mayne, Brooklyn	14	25	219	3	4
Harry Hopp, Buffalo	11	22	190	0	0
Elroy Hirsch, Chicago	12	20	156	1	2
Walt Clay, Chicago	12	27	140	2	3
Jimmy Nelson, Miami	8	24	135	0	4
Charlie Armstrong, Brooklyn	9	21	126	1	2
Cliff Lewis, Cleveland	11	30	125	1	1
Jim Tarrant, Miami	5	12	95	1	0
Ken Stofer, Buffalo	9	26	86	1	1
Eddie Prokop, New York	4	11	72	0	0
Steve Nemeth, Chicago	5	23	68	0	0
Frankie Sinkwich, New York	5	12	61	0	2
Bob H. Kennedy, New York	2	6	45	0	3
Len Eshmont, San Francisco	1	2	42	1	0
Ken Holley, Miami	3	11	36	0	4
Harry Connolly, Brooklyn	2	8	29	0	1
Don Greenwood, Cleveland	1	1	27	0	0
Ned Mathews, San Francisco	1	1	26	0	0
Walt McDonald, Miami	1	3	24	0	1
Bob Mitchell, Los Angeles	3	10	19	0	2
Ernie Lewis, Chicago	4	8	17	0	1
Bill Kellagher, Chicago	2	3	15	0	1
Parker Hall, San Francisco	2	8	15	0	0
Pug Manders, New York	2	3	14	0	0
Dick Erdlitz, Miami	1	1	10	0	0
Bill Schroeder, Chicago	1	2	10	0	0
Pres Johnston, Miami	1	1	9	0	0
Bob Reinhard, Los Angeles	1	1	7	0	0
Edgar Jones, Cleveland	1	4	4	0	0

	Comp	Att	Yds	TD	Int
Dub Jones, Brooklyn	1	2	0	0	1
Joe Aguirre, Los Angeles	0	1	0	0	0
Chuck Fenenbock, Los Angeles	0	1	0	0	0
Bob Paffrath, Brooklyn	0	1	0	0	0
Lou Zontini, Buffalo	0	1	0	0	0
Don Griffin, Chicago	0	1	0	0	1
Ray Terrell, Cleveland	0	2	0	0	0
Lou Saban, Cleveland	0	3	0	0	1
Billy Hillenbrand, Chicago	0	3	0	0	2
Cal Purdin, Brooklyn	1	1	-2	0	0
Monk Gafford, Miami	1	5	-3	0	2
Johnny Vardian, Miami	1	1	-4	0	0

Receiving

	Rec	Yds	Avg Gain	TD
Dante Lavelli, Cleveland	40	843	21.8	8
Alyn Beals, San Francisco	40	586	14.7	10
Saxon Judd, Brooklyn	34	443	13.0	4
Fay King, Buffalo	30	466	15.5	6
Elroy Hirsch, Chicago	27	347	12.9	3
Mac Speedie, Cleveland	24	564	23.5	7
Dale Gentry, Los Angeles	24	341	14.2	3
Steve Juzwik, Buffalo	23	357	15.5	3
Jack Russell, New York	23	223	9.7	4
Joe Davis, Brooklyn	22	337	15.3	1
Mickey Colmer, Brooklyn	22	327	14.9	1
Lamar Davis, Miami	22	275	12.5	2
Billy Hillenbrand, Chicago	21	315	15.0	4
Ralph Heywood, Chicago	20	287	14.4	4
Al Krueger, Los Angeles	19	213	11.2	1
Bob Nowaskey, Los Angeles	19	198	10.4	3
Bill Fisk, San Francisco	19	186	9.8	1
Len Eshmont, San Francisco	17	287	16.9	2
Spec Sanders, New York	17	259	15.2	3
Pat Lahey, Chicago	17	203	11.9	0
Bob Seymour, Los Angeles	17	188	11.1	3
Neal Adams, Brooklyn	15	225	15.0	2
Monk Gafford, Miami	14	270	19.3	4
Joe Aguirre, Los Angeles	14	246	17.6	2
Earl Elsey, Los Angeles	14	179	12.8	0
Lamar Blount, Miami	13	218	16.8	1
Prince Scott, Miami	13	180	13.8	2
Bruce Alford, New York	13	173	13.3	0
Bernie Nygren, Los Angeles	13	170	13.1	1
Frank Quillen, Chicago	13	143	11.0	2
Walt McDonald, Miami–Brooklyn	12	126	10.5	0
Cal Purdin, Brooklyn-Miami	12	108	9.0	0
Jim McCarthy, Brooklyn	11	296	26.9	3
Chuck Fenenbock, Los Angeles	11	67	6.1	0
Bob H. Kennedy, New York	11	59	5.4	0
Harry Burrus, New York	10	251	25.1	1
Doyle Tackett, Brooklyn	10	191	19.1	2
Marion Motley, Cleveland	10	188	18.8	1
Harry Clarke, Los Angeles	10	123	12.3	2
Bob Masterson, New York	10	119	11.9	0
John Kimbrough, Los Angeles	9	162	18.0	1
Lowell Wagner, New York	9	126	14.0	1
Bob Motl, Chicago	9	124	13.8	1
John Stryzkalski, San Francisco	9	80	8.9	0
John Harrington, Cleveland	8	136	17.0	0
Fondren Mitchell, Miami	8	131	16.4	0
Bob Sweiger, New York	8	55	6.9	1
Earle Parsons, San Francisco	8	52	6.5	0
Chet Mutryn, Buffalo	7	168	24.0	3
Bob Titchenal, San Francisco	7	160	22.9	2
Art Van Tone, Brooklyn	7	152	21.7	3
Bill Kerr, Los Angeles	7	122	17.4	0
Johnny Vardian, Miami	7	108	15.4	0
John Yonakor, Cleveland	7	98	14.0	2
Gaylon Smith, Cleveland	7	73	10.4	0
Bob Dove, Chicago	7	67	9.6	1
Dick Erdlitz, Miami	7	31	4.4	0
Ned Mathews, Chicago	6	100	16.7	2
Lou Tomasetti, Buffalo	6	81	13.5	1
Al Vandeweghe, Buffalo	6	67	11.2	1
Kay Eakin, Miami	6	67	11.2	0
Pres Johnston, Miami-Buffalo	6	54	9.0	1
Ken Casanega, San Francisco	5	102	20.4	1
Nick Susoeff, San Francisco	5	98	19.6	0
Bill Boedeker, Chicago	5	82	16.4	1
Perry Schwartz, New York	5	82	16.4	0
Bus Mertes, Los Angeles	5	61	12.2	1
Eddie Prokop, New York	5	52	10.4	1
Dick Horne, Miami	5	48	9.6	0
Don Griffin, Chicago	5	28	5.6	0
Lew Mayne, Brooklyn	5	9	1.8	0
Edgar Jones, Cleveland	4	120	30.0	1
Hub Ulrich, Miami	4	75	18.8	1
Bill Lund, Cleveland	4	64	16.0	2
Lloyd Cheatham, New York	4	54	13.5	1
Walt Clay, Chicago	4	48	12.0	0
Herb Nelson, Buffalo	4	47	11.8	0
Jack Morton, Los Angeles	4	44	11.0	1
Marion Pugh, Miami	4	43	10.8	0
Paul Vinnola, Los Angeles	4	39	9.8	0
Joe Vetrano, San Francisco	4	37	9.3	0
Ray Terrell, Cleveland	4	21	5.3	0
Jimmy Nelson, Miami	4	20	5.0	0
Ed Balatti, San Francisco	4	15	3.8	0
Don Greenwood, Cleveland	4	0	0.0	0
Bob Paffrath, Brooklyn-Miami	4	-6	-1.5	0
Max Morris, Chicago	3	66	22.0	0
Hampton Pool, Miami	3	63	21.0	0
Mel Conger, New York	3	61	20.3	0
Pug Manders, New York	3	49	16.3	0
George Young, Cleveland	3	37	12.3	0
Pete Franceschi, San Francisco	3	35	11.7	1
Dewey Proctor, New York	3	32	10.7	1
Hank Norberg, San Francisco	3	29	9.7	0
Terry Fox, Miami	3	27	9.0	0
Bob McCain, Brooklyn	3	27	9.0	0
Dom Principe, Brooklyn	3	25	8.3	0
Bill Kellagher, Chicago	2	36	18.0	0
Al Coppage, Cleveland	2	34	17.0	0
Andy Dudish, Buffalo	2	33	16.5	0
Don Durdan, San Francisco	2	27	13.5	1
John Batorski, Buffalo	2	27	13.5	0
Stan Kozlowski, Miami	2	27	13.5	0
Ernie Lewis, Chicago	2	26	13.0	0
Parker Hall, San Francisco	2	25	12.5	0
Henry Stanton, New York	2	25	12.5	0
Nick Daukas, Brooklyn	2	19	9.5	0
Harvey Johnson, New York	2	19	9.5	0
Marty Comer, Buffalo	2	17	8.5	0
Cotton Price, Miami	2	17	8.5	0
Ray Ebli, Buffalo	2	15	7.5	1
John Polanski, Los Angeles	2	15	7.5	1

28 Part 3: Individual Statistics

	Rec	Yds	Avg Gain	TD
Curt Sandig, Buffalo	2	15	7.5	0
Bob Sneddon, Los Angeles	2	11	5.5	0
Harry Hopp, Buffalo	2	−1	−0.5	0
Norm Standlee, San Francisco	2	−5	−2.5	0
Bill Daley, Brooklyn	2	−5	−2.5	0
Lou Saban, Cleveland	1	45	45.0	0
Jim Reynolds, Miami	1	32	32.0	0
Blondy Black, Buffalo	1	21	21.0	0
Frank Hrabetin, Brooklyn	1	17	17.0	0
Jack Dugger, Buffalo	1	15	15.0	0
Ken Stofer, Buffalo	1	14	14.0	0
Andy Marefos, Los Angeles	1	13	13.0	0
John Rokisky, Cleveland	1	13	13.0	0
Tom Colella, Cleveland	1	12	12.0	1
Bob Hoernschemeyer, Chicago	1	11	11.0	0
Rhoten Shetley, Brooklyn	1	10	10.0	0
Nick Klutka, Buffalo	1	9	9.0	0
Bill Schroeder, Chicago	1	9	9.0	0
Bob Steuber, Cleveland	1	9	9.0	0
Russ Morrow, Brooklyn	1	8	8.0	1
Fred Evans, Cleveland	1	7	7.0	1
Bob Morrow, New York	1	6	6.0	0
Don Reece, Miami	1	5	5.0	0
Charlie Timmons, Brooklyn	1	4	4.0	0
Martin Ruby, Brooklyn	1	3	3.0	0
Walt Williams, Chicago	1	3	3.0	0
Gene Fekete, Cleveland	1	2	2.0	0
Bob Mitchell, Los Angeles	1	1	1.0	0
Vic Kulbitski, Buffalo	1	0	0.0	0
Bob Thurbon, Buffalo	1	−3	−3.0	0
Glenn Dobbs, Brooklyn	1	−5	−5.0	0
Ken Roskie, San Francisco	0	7	—	0
Willie Wilkin, Chicago	0	3	—	0

Punting

	Punts	Avg	Had Blocked
Glenn Dobbs, Brooklyn	80	47.8	2
Frankie Albert, San Francisco	54	41.0	0
Ernie Lewis, Chicago	50	41.7	1
Tom Colella, Cleveland	47	40.3	0
Bob Reinhard, Los Angeles	44	45.4	1
Lou Zontini, Buffalo	44	36.3	0
Kay Eakin, Miami	37	41.4	1
Spec Sanders, New York	33	36.6	2
Pres Johnston, Miami–Buffalo	28	39.7	1
Ace Parker, New York	27	33.7	2
Walt Williams, Chicago	24	41.6	1
Jimmy Nelson, Miami	16	39.7	0
Harry Hopp, Buffalo	15	30.7	2
Monk Gafford, Miami–Brooklyn	13	40.3	0
Bob Hoernschemeyer, Chicago	11	44.0	0
Bob Perina, New York	11	37.5	0
Charlie O'Rourke, Los Angeles	8	39.0	0
Fred Evans, Cleveland	8	37.0	0
Bob H. Kennedy, New York	7	37.0	1
Don Durdan, San Francisco	6	39.8	0
Joe Vetrano, San Francisco	6	39.3	0
Charlie Armstrong, Brooklyn	6	38.5	0
Curt Sandig, Buffalo	4	38.8	0
Cotton Price, Miami	4	26.3	1
Ken Stofer, Buffalo	3	36.0	0
Mac Speedie, Cleveland	3	28.0	0

	Punts	Avg	Had Blocked
Lew Mayne, Brooklyn	3	26.3	0
Steve Nemeth, Chicago	2	46.0	0
Joe Aguirre, Los Angeles	2	45.5	0
Terry Fox, Miami	2	44.0	0
Angelo Bertelli, Los Angeles	2	38.0	0
Ralph Heywood, Chicago	2	28.5	0
Bill Kellagher, Chicago	1	56.0	0
Bob Sweiger, New York	1	52.0	0
Bob Paffrath, Miami	1	50.0	0
Walt Clay, Chicago	1	45.0	0
Bob Mitchell, Los Angeles	1	44.0	0
Jim Reynolds, Miami	1	39.0	0
Norm Standlee, San Francisco	1	34.0	0
George Terlep, Buffalo	1	31.0	0

Interceptions

	Int	Yds	Avg Ret	TD
Tom Colella, Cleveland	10	110	11.0	0
Ken Casanega, San Francisco	8	146	18.3	0
Elroy Hirsch, Chicago	6	97	16.2	0
Walt Clay, Chicago	6	72	12.0	0
Steve Juzwik, Buffalo	5	108	21.6	1
Otto Graham, Cleveland	5	102	20.4	1
Cliff Lewis, Cleveland	5	41	8.2	0
Felto Prewitt, Buffalo	4	89	22.3	0
Monk Gafford, Miami-Brooklyn	4	88	22.0	0
Bob Sweiger, New York	4	82	20.5	0
Bill Davis, Miami	4	40	10.0	0
Bob Seymour, Los Angeles	4	34	8.5	0
Lou Saban, Cleveland	4	32	8.0	0
Ray Terrell, Cleveland	3	101	33.7	1
John Stryzkalski, San Francisco	3	55	18.3	0
Billy Hillenbrand, Chicago	3	37	12.3	0
Bob Kennedy, New York	3	35	11.7	0
Joe Vetrano, San Francisco	3	32	10.7	0
Al Dekdebrun, Buffalo	3	19	6.3	0
Walt Williams, Chicago	2	148	74.0	1
Spec Sanders, New York	2	71	35.5	1
Don Greenwood, Cleveland	2	56	28.0	0
Charlie Armstrong, Brooklyn	2	54	27.0	0
Glenn Dobbs, Brooklyn	2	44	22.0	0
Jesse Freitas, San Francisco	2	40	20.0	0
Don Durdan, San Francisco	2	38	19.0	0
Harry Burrus, New York	2	37	18.5	0
Jim Reynolds, Miami	2	33	16.5	0
Kay Eakin, Miami	2	31	15.5	0
Walt McDonald, Brooklyn	2	31	15.5	0
Bernie Nygren, Los Angeles	2	30	15.0	0
Al Wukits, Miami	2	26	13.0	0
Bob Perina, New York	2	24	12.0	0
Ken Whitlow, Miami	2	20	10.0	0
Edgar Jones, Cleveland	2	16	8.0	0
Joe Ruetz, Chicago	2	13	6.5	0
Ned Mathews, Chicago	2	8	4.0	0
Jimmy Nelson, Miami	2	8	4.0	0
Sam Brazinsky, Buffalo	2	7	3.5	0
Harry Clarke, Los Angeles	2	7	3.5	0
Elmer Jones, Buffalo	2	7	3.5	0
Earl Elsey, Los Angeles	2	2	1.0	0
Mike Scarry, Cleveland	2	0	0.0	0
Bob Steuber, Cleveland	1	52	52.0	0
John Polanski, Los Angeles	1	50	50.0	0

	Int	Yds	Avg Ret	TD
Frank Gatski, Cleveland	1	35	35.0	1
Bob Nowaskey, Los Angeles	1	35	35.0	1
Dutch Elston, San Francisco	1	34	34.0	0
Bill Kerr, Los Angeles	1	34	34.0	0
Bob Mitchell, Los Angeles	1	32	32.0	0
Daryl Cato, Miami	1	29	29.0	0
Bill Boedeker, Chicago	1	26	26.0	0
Herb Coleman, Chicago	1	25	25.0	0
Hank Norberg, San Francisco	1	22	22.0	0
Fred Evans, Cleveland	1	21	21.0	0
Buddy Jungmichel, Miami	1	21	21.0	0
Vic Kulbitski, Buffalo	1	20	20.0	0
Don Griffin, Chicago	1	19	19.0	0
Blondy Black, Buffalo	1	18	18.0	0
Don Reece, Miami	1	17	17.0	0
Pete Lamana, Chicago	1	16	16.0	0
Doyle Tackett, Brooklyn	1	16	16.0	0
Pres Johnston, Buffalo	1	15	15.0	0
Bob Sneddon, Los Angeles	1	15	15.0	0
Bus Mertes, Los Angeles	1	14	14.0	0
Eddie Prokop, New York	1	14	14.0	0
Don Nolander, Los Angeles	1	13	13.0	0
Dick Erdlitz, Miami	1	12	12.0	0
Bill Lund, Cleveland	1	12	12.0	0
Patsy Martinelli, Buffalo	1	12	12.0	0
Jack Morton, Los Angeles	1	11	11.0	0
Bob Hoernschemeyer, Chicago	1	10	10.0	0
Ernie Lewis, Chicago	1	10	10.0	0
Frank Quillen, Chicago	1	9	9.0	0
Al Akins, Cleveland	1	7	7.0	0
Nick Daukas, Brooklyn	1	5	5.0	0
Bob Nelson, Los Angeles	1	5	5.0	0
Art Van Tone, Brooklyn	1	5	5.0	0
Chet Adams, Cleveland	1	4	4.0	1
Pat Lahey, Chicago	1	4	4.0	0
Bill Schroeder, Chicago	1	4	4.0	0
Paul Vinnola, Los Angeles	1	4	4.0	0
Lloyd Cheatham, New York	1	3	3.0	0
Jim McCarthy, Brooklyn	1	3	3.0	0
Tex Williams, Miami	1	3	3.0	0
Dick Bassi, San Francisco	1	2	2.0	0
Fondren Mitchell, Miami	1	2	2.0	0
Lou Zontini, Buffalo	1	2	2.0	0
Mickey Colmer, Brooklyn	1	0	0.0	0
Bob Masterson, New York	1	0	0.0	0
Marion Motley, Cleveland	1	0	0.0	0
Prince Scott, Miami	1	0	0.0	0
Gaylon Smith, Cleveland	1	0	0.0	0
Lou Tomasetti, Buffalo	1	0	0.0	0
Lloyd Wasserbach, Chicago	1	0	0.0	0
Ed Balatti, San Francisco	0	22	—	1
Willie Wilkin, Chicago	0	18	—	0
Charlie O'Rourke, Los Angeles	0	7	—	0

Punt Returns

	Ret	Yds	Avg Ret	TD
Chuck Fenenbock, Los Angeles	16	299	18.7	0
Spec Sanders, New York	17	257	15.1	1
Ken Casanega, San Francisco	18	248	13.8	0
Elroy Hirsch, Chicago	17	235	13.8	1
Bob Seymour, Los Angeles	18	211	11.7	0
Bob Perina, New York	15	205	13.7	0
Earle Parsons, San Francisco	15	198	13.2	0
Billy Hillenbrand, Chicago	13	180	13.8	1
Tom Colella, Cleveland	8	172	21.5	0
Earl Elsey, Los Angeles	9	147	16.3	0
Glenn Dobbs, Brooklyn	7	146	20.9	1
Lou Tomasetti, Buffalo	7	138	19.7	0
Steve Juzwik, Buffalo	11	135	12.3	0
Cliff Lewis, Cleveland	8	133	16.6	0
Otto Graham, Cleveland	12	129	10.8	0
Monk Gafford, Miami	9	117	13.0	0
Eddie Prokop, New York	4	116	29.0	1
Charlie Armstrong, Brooklyn	6	97	16.2	0
Bob Hoernschemeyer, Chicago	6	91	15.2	0
Ace Parker, New York	8	85	10.6	0
Joe Vetrano, San Francisco	7	84	12.0	0
Andy Dudish, Buffalo	5	73	14.6	0
Edgar Jones, Cleveland	7	73	10.4	0
Jimmy Nelson, Miami	7	71	10.1	0
Walt Clay, Chicago	8	70	8.8	0
Blondy Black, Buffalo	2	58	29.0	0
Chet Mutryn, Buffalo	5	57	11.4	0
Lowell Wagner, New York	2	55	27.5	1
Lamar Davis, Miami	4	54	13.5	0
Ken Stofer, Buffalo	5	53	10.6	0
Cal Purdin, Brooklyn	4	52	13.0	0
Lew Mayne, Brooklyn	6	47	7.8	0
Don Durdan, San Francisco	3	37	12.3	0
Bill Lund, Cleveland	2	30	15.0	0
Kay Eakin, Miami	3	30	10.0	0
Bill Boedeker, Chicago	2	29	14.5	0
Lloyd Cheatham, New York	1	26	26.0	0
John Stryzkalski, San Francisco	3	26	8.7	0
Len Eshmont, San Francisco	2	25	12.5	0
Harry Clarke, Los Angeles	2	24	12.0	0
Paul Vinnola, Los Angeles	2	24	12.0	0
Curt Sandig, Buffalo	2	20	10.0	0
Bob Kennedy, New York	3	20	6.7	0
Pete Lamana, Chicago	0	20	—	1
George Zorich, Miami	1	18	18.0	0
George Perpich, Brooklyn	1	16	16.0	0
Dale Gentry, Los Angeles	1	14	14.0	0
Steve Nemeth, Chicago	1	14	14.0	0
Bob Sweiger, New York	1	14	14.0	0
Jesse Freitas, San Francisco	1	10	10.0	0
Mickey Colmer, Brooklyn	1	9	9.0	0
Bill Schroeder, Chicago	0	7	—	0
Frankie Albert, San Francisco	1	6	6.0	0
Harry Connolly, Brooklyn	1	6	6.0	0
Pete Franceschi, San Francisco	1	6	6.0	0
Dub Jones, Brooklyn	1	6	6.0	0
Prince Scott, Miami	1	6	6.0	0
Walt Williams, Chicago	1	6	6.0	0
Bob Nowaskey, Los Angeles	1	5	5.0	0
Art Van Tone, Brooklyn	1	5	5.0	0
Stan Kozlowski, Miami	1	4	4.0	0
Vic Obeck, Brooklyn	1	3	3.0	0
Doyle Tackett, Brooklyn	1	3	3.0	0
Bob Paffrath, Miami	1	1	1.0	0
Fred Evans, Cleveland	1	0	0.0	0
Marion Motley, Cleveland	1	0	0.0	0

*Received lateral from punt receiver.

Kick Returns

	Ret	Yds	Avg Ret	TD
Chuck Fenenbock, Los Angeles	17	479	28.2	1
Steve Juzwik, Buffalo	21	452	21.5	0
Spec Sanders, New York	13	395	30.4	1
Elroy Hirsch, Chicago	14	384	27.4	1
Monk Gafford, Miami–Brooklyn	11	345	31.4	0
Earl Elsey, Los Angeles	15	335	22.3	0
Edgar Jones, Cleveland	12	307	25.6	1
Bob Hoernschemeyer, Chicago	9	275	30.6	0
Len Eshmont, San Francisco	10	264	26.4	0
Lamar Davis, Miami	5	235	47.0	0
Billy Hillenbrand, Chicago	8	220	27.5	1
Glenn Dobbs, Brooklyn	12	214	17.8	0
Andy Dudish, Buffalo	7	196	28.0	0
Jimmy Nelson, Miami	10	192	19.2	0
John Stryzkalski, San Francisco	7	142	20.3	0
Lowell Wagner, New York	4	119	29.8	0
Ned Mathews, Chicago–SF	6	118	19.7	0
Dom Principe, Brooklyn	6	117	19.5	0
Al Dekdebrun, Buffalo	6	116	19.3	0
Harry Hopp, Buffalo–Miami	6	113	18.8	0
John Kimbrough, Los Angeles	5	111	22.2	0
Bob H. Kennedy, New York	4	105	26.3	0
Don Greenwood, Cleveland	5	105	21.0	0
Dick Erdlitz, Miami	6	104	17.3	0
Bob Sweiger, New York	5	103	20.6	0
Earle Parsons, San Francisco	4	94	23.5	0
Charlie Armstrong, Brooklyn	3	93	31.0	0
Dub Jones, Brooklyn	6	91	15.2	0
Lew Mayne, Brooklyn	4	90	22.5	0
Bernie Nygren, Los Angeles	4	88	22.0	0
Bob Seymour, Los Angeles	4	87	21.8	0
Lou Tomasetti, Buffalo	2	85	42.5	0
Bill Boedeker, Chicago	2	84	42.0	0
Paul Vinnola, Los Angeles	5	83	16.6	0
Ken Stofer, Buffalo	2	81	40.5	0
Bob Perina, New York	4	81	20.3	0
Vic Kulbitski, Buffalo	5	81	16.2	0
Ray Terrell, Cleveland	3	80	26.7	0
Chet Mutryn, Buffalo	4	79	19.8	0
Cal Purdin, Brooklyn–Miami	4	77	19.3	0
Bob Paffrath, Miami	4	76	19.0	0
Doyle Tackett, Brooklyn	5	76	15.2	0
Al Akins, Cleveland	2	74	37.0	0
Frankie Albert, San Francisco	4	74	18.5	0
Stan Kozlowski, Miami	3	72	24.0	0
Cliff Lewis, Cleveland	3	70	23.3	0
Bruce Alford, New York	1	62	62.0	0
Ken Casanega, San Francisco	3	61	20.3	0
Bob Masterson, New York	5	55	11.0	0
Saxon Judd, Brooklyn	3	54	18.0	0
Bob Steuber, Cleveland	2	53	26.5	0
Marion Motley, Cleveland	3	53	17.7	0
Fondren Mitchell, Miami	4	52	13.0	0
Kay Eakin, Miami	4	51	12.8	0
Joe Vetrano, San Francisco	3	49	16.3	0
Harry Clarke, Los Angeles	2	48	24.0	0
Bill Kellagher, Chicago	3	48	16.0	0
Eddie Prokop, New York	2	47	23.5	0
Walt Clay, Chicago	2	43	21.5	0
Curt Sandig, Buffalo	2	43	21.5	0
Harry Connolly, Brooklyn	2	41	20.5	0
Bus Mertes, Los Angeles	2	35	17.5	0
Norm Standlee, San Francisco	1	33	33.0	0
Bill Lund, Cleveland	1	32	32.0	0
Joe Davis, Brooklyn	2	32	16.0	0
Cotton Price, Miami	2	32	16.0	0
Walt McDonald, Miami–Brooklyn	3	32	10.7	0
Don Griffin, Chicago	2	31	15.5	0
Tom Colella, Cleveland	1	29	29.0	0
Charlie O'Rourke, Los Angeles	1	28	28.0	0
Prince Scott, Miami	2	28	14.0	0
Ace Parker, New York	2	27	13.5	0
Pug Manders, New York	1	26	26.0	0
Art Van Tone, Brooklyn	2	25	12.5	0
Terry Fox, Miami	1	24	24.0	0
Marion Pugh, Miami	1	24	24.0	0
George Terlep, Buffalo	1	23	23.0	0
Johnny Vardian, Miami	1	23	23.0	0
Perry Schwartz, New York	2	23	11.5	0
Parker Hall, San Francisco	1	22	22.0	0
Ernie Lewis, Chicago	2	22	11.0	0
Gene Fekete, Cleveland	1	21	21.0	0
Pres Johnston, Buffalo	2	21	10.5	0
Herb Coleman, Chicago	1	20	20.0	0
Fred Gloden, Miami	1	20	20.0	0
Dick Renfro, San Francisco	1	20	20.0	0
Bill Schroeder, Chicago	1	19	19.0	0
Lou Zontini, Buffalo	1	19	19.0	0
Pete Lamana, Chicago	1	18	18.0	0
Walt Williams, Chicago	1	18	18.0	0
John Harrington, Cleveland	2	16	8.0	0
Bob Thurbon, Buffalo	1	15	15.0	0
Al Vandeweghe, Buffalo	1	15	15.0	0
Lee Artoe, Los Angeles	1	13	13.0	0
George Bernhardt, Brooklyn	1	13	13.0	0
Frank Quillen, Chicago	1	13	13.0	0
Jim Reynolds, Miami	1	13	13.0	0
Lloyd Wasserbach, Chicago	1	13	13.0	0
Bill Daley, Brooklyn	1	10	10.0	0
Nick Susoeff, San Francisco	1	10	10.0	0
Mickey Colmer, Brooklyn	1	9	9.0	0
Jim McCarthy, Brooklyn	1	8	8.0	0
Lloyd Cheatham, New York	1	7	7.0	0
Pat Lahey, Chicago	1	5	5.0	0
Mitch Olenski, Miami	1	2	2.0	0
Mac Speedie, Cleveland	1	1	1.0	0
George Doherty, Buffalo	1	0	0.0	0
Garland Gregory, San Francisco	1	0	0.0	0
Bob Nelson, Los Angeles	1	0	0.0	0

Total Returns (Punt and Kick)

	Ret	Yds	Avg Ret	TD
Chuck Fenenbock, Los Angeles	33	778	23.6	1
Spec Sanders, New York	30	652	21.7	2
Elroy Hirsch, Chicago	31	619	20.0	2
Steve Juzwik, Buffalo	32	587	18.3	0
Earl Elsey, Los Angeles	24	482	20.1	0
Monk Gafford, Miami–Brooklyn	20	462	23.1	0
Billy Hillenbrand, Chicago	21	400	19.0	2
Edgar Jones, Cleveland	19	380	20.0	1
Bob Hoernschemeyer, Chicago	15	366	24.4	0
Glenn Dobbs, Brooklyn	19	360	18.9	1
Ken Casanega, San Francisco	21	309	14.7	0
Bob Seymour, Los Angeles	22	298	13.5	0

	Ret	Yds	Avg Ret	TD
Earle Parsons, San Francisco	19	292	15.4	0
Lamar Davis, Miami	9	289	32.1	0
Len Eshmont, San Francisco	12	289	24.1	0
Bob Perina, New York	19	286	15.1	0
Andy Dudish, Buffalo	12	269	22.4	0
Jimmy Nelson, Miami	17	263	15.5	0
Lou Tomasetti, Buffalo	9	223	24.8	0
Cliff Lewis, Cleveland	11	203	18.5	0
Tom Colella, Cleveland	9	201	22.3	0
Charlie Armstrong, Brooklyn	9	190	21.1	0
Ken Stofer, Buffalo	7	187	26.7	0
Lowell Wagner, New York	6	174	29.0	1
John Stryzkalski, San Francisco	10	168	16.8	0
Eddie Prokop, New York	6	163	27.2	1
Lew Mayne, Brooklyn	10	137	13.7	0
Chet Mutryn, Buffalo	9	136	15.1	0
Joe Vetrano, San Francisco	10	133	13.3	0
Cal Purdin, Brooklyn-Miami	8	129	16.1	0
Otto Graham, Cleveland	12	129	10.8	0
Bob Kennedy, New York	7	125	17.9	0
Ned Mathews, Chicago-SF	6	118	19.7	0
Dom Principe, Brooklyn	6	117	19.5	0
Bob Sweiger, New York	6	117	19.5	0
Al Dekdebrun, Buffalo	6	116	19.3	0
Bill Boedeker, Chicago	4	113	28.3	0
Harry Hopp, Buffalo-Miami	6	113	18.8	0
Walt Clay, Chicago	10	113	11.3	0
Ace Parker, New York	10	112	11.2	0
John Kimbrough, Los Angeles	5	111	22.2	0
Paul Vinnola, Los Angeles	7	107	15.3	0
Don Greenwood, Cleveland	5	105	21.0	0
Dick Erdlitz, Miami	6	104	17.3	0
Dub Jones, Brooklyn	7	97	13.9	0
Bernie Nygren, Los Angeles	4	88	22.0	0
Vic Kulbitski, Buffalo	5	81	16.2	0
Kay Eakin, Miami	7	81	11.6	0
Ray Terrell, Cleveland	3	80	26.7	0
Frankie Albert, San Francisco	5	80	16.0	0
Doyle Tackett, Brooklyn	6	79	13.2	0
Bob Paffrath, Miami	5	77	15.4	0
Stan Kozlowski, Miami	4	76	19.0	0
Al Akins, Cleveland	2	74	37.0	0
Harry Clarke, Los Angeles	4	72	18.0	0
Curt Sandig, Buffalo	4	63	15.8	0
Bruce Alford, New York	1	62	62.0	0
Bill Lund, Cleveland	3	62	20.7	0
Blondy Black, Buffalo	2	58	29.0	0
Bob Masterson, New York	5	55	11.0	0
Saxon Judd, Brooklyn	3	54	18.0	0
Bob Steuber, Cleveland	2	53	26.5	0
Marion Motley, Cleveland	4	53	13.3	0
Fondren Mitchell, Miami	4	52	13.0	0
Bill Kellagher, Chicago	3	48	16.0	0
Harry Connolly, Brooklyn	3	47	15.7	0
Pete Lamana, Chicago	1	38	18.0	1
Don Durdan, San Francisco	3	37	12.3	0
Bus Mertes, Los Angeles	2	35	17.5	0
Prince Scott, Miami	3	34	11.3	0
Norm Standlee, San Francisco	1	33	33.0	0
Lloyd Cheatham, New York	2	33	16.5	0
Joe Davis, Brooklyn	2	32	16.0	0
Cotton Price, Miami	2	32	16.0	0
Walt McDonald, Miami-Brooklyn	3	32	10.7	0
Don Griffin, Chicago	2	31	15.5	0
Art Van Tone, Brooklyn	3	30	10.0	0
Charlie O'Rourke, Los Angeles	1	28	28.0	0
Pug Manders, New York	1	26	26.0	0
Bill Schroeder, Chicago	1	26	19.0	0
Terry Fox, Miami	1	24	24.0	0
Marion Pugh, Miami	1	24	24.0	0
Walt Williams, Chicago	2	24	12.0	0
George Terlep, Buffalo	1	23	23.0	0
Johnny Vardian, Miami	1	23	23.0	0
Perry Schwartz, New York	2	23	11.5	0
Parker Hall, San Francisco	1	22	22.0	0
Ernie Lewis, Chicago	2	22	11.0	0
Gene Fekete, Cleveland	1	21	21.0	0
Pres Johnston, Buffalo	2	21	10.5	0
Herb Coleman, Chicago	1	20	20.0	0
Fred Gloden, Miami	1	20	20.0	0
Dick Renfro, San Francisco	1	20	20.0	0
Lou Zontini, Buffalo	1	19	19.0	0
George Zorich, Miami	1	18	18.0	0
Mickey Colmer, Brooklyn	2	18	9.0	0
George Perpich, Brooklyn	1	16	16.0	0
John Harrington, Cleveland	2	16	8.0	0
Bob Thurbon, Buffalo	1	15	15.0	0
Al Vandeweghe, Buffalo	1	15	15.0	0
Dale Gentry, Los Angeles	1	14	14.0	0
Steve Nemeth, Chicago	1	14	14.0	0
Lee Artoe, Los Angeles	1	13	13.0	0
George Bernhardt, Brooklyn	1	13	13.0	0
Frank Quillen, Chicago	1	13	13.0	0
Jim Reynolds, Miami	1	13	13.0	0
Lloyd Wasserbach, Chicago	1	13	13.0	0
Bill Daley, Brooklyn	1	10	10.0	0
Jesse Freitas, San Francisco	1	10	10.0	0
Nick Susoeff, San Francisco	1	10	10.0	0
Jim McCarthy, Brooklyn	1	8	8.0	0
Pete Franceschi, San Francisco	1	6	6.0	0
Pat Lahey, Chicago	1	5	5.0	0
Bob Nowaskey, Los Angeles	1	5	5.0	0
Vic Obeck, Brooklyn	1	3	3.0	0
Mitch Olenski, Miami	1	2	2.0	0
Mac Speedie, Cleveland	1	1	1.0	0
George Doherty, Buffalo	1	0	0.0	0
Fred Evans, Cleveland	1	0	0.0	0
Garland Gregory, San Francisco	1	0	0.0	0
Bob Nelson, Los Angeles	1	0	0.0	0

Point After Touchdowns

	Made	Att	%
Lou Groza, Cleveland	45	47	95.7
Harvey Johnson, New York	36	36	100.0
Steve Nemeth, Chicago	32	33	97.0
Joe Aguirre, Los Angeles	31	32	96.9
Joe Vetrano, San Francisco	31	38	81.6
Lou Zontini, Buffalo	30	31	96.8
Dick Erdlitz, Miami	22	22	100.0
Phil Martinovich, Brooklyn	21	22	95.5
Chet Adams, Cleveland	5	5	100.0
Jim McCarthy, Brooklyn	5	7	71.4
Bill Daddio, Buffalo	3	3	100.0
Bob Nelson, Los Angeles	3	5	60.0
Ed Balatti, San Francisco	2	2	100.0
Andy Marefos, Los Angeles	2	2	100.0
Alyn Beals, San Francisco	1	1	100.0

Part 3: Individual Statistics

	Made	Att	%
Joe Davis, Brooklyn	1	1	100.0
Pres Johnston, Miami	1	1	100.0
John Rokisky, Cleveland	1	1	100.0
Mac Speedie, Cleveland	1	1	100.0
Lee Artoe, Los Angeles	1	2	50.0
John Mellus, San Francisco	1	2	50.0
Elroy Hirsch, Chicago	0	1	0.0

Field Goals

	Made	Att	%
Lou Groza, Cleveland	13	29	44.8
Steve Nemeth, Chicago	9	12	75.0
Harvey Johnson, New York	6	8	75.0
Phil Martinovich, Brooklyn	5	10	50.0
Joe Vetrano, San Francisco	4	7	57.1
Lou Zontini, Buffalo	4	8	50.0
Joe Aguirre, Los Angeles	4	11	36.4
Bob Nelson, Los Angeles	2	6	33.3
Dick Erdlitz, Miami	2	7	28.6
Bob Masterson, New York	0	1	0.0
Jim McCarthy, Brooklyn	0	1	0.0
John Mellus, San Francisco	0	1	0.0

Scoring

	TD Rush	TD Pass	Pts After TD	FG	Tot Pts
Lou Groza, Cleveland	0	0	45–47	13–29	84
Spec Sanders, New York	9	3	0–0	0–0	72
Alyn Beals, San Francisco	0	10	1–1	0–0	61
Steve Nemeth, Chicago	0	0	32–33	9–12	59
Joe Aguirre, Los Angeles	0	2	31–32	4–11	55
Len Eshmont, San Francisco	7	2	0–0	0–0	54
Harvey Johnson, New York	0	0	36–36	6–8	54
Joe Vetrano, San Francisco	1	0	31–38	4–7	49
Dante Lavelli, Cleveland	0	8	0–0	0–0	48
Billy Hillenbrand, Chicago	4	4	0–0	0–0	48
Mac Speedie, Cleveland	0	7	1–1	0–0	43
John Kimbrough, Los Angeles	6	1	0–0	0–0	42
Lou Zontini, Buffalo	0	0	30–31	4–8	42
Steve Juzwik, Buffalo	4	3	0–0	0–0	42
Fay King, Buffalo	0	6	0–0	0–0	36
Don Greenwood, Cleveland	6	0	0–0	0–0	36
Elroy Hirsch, Chicago	3	3	0–1	0–0	36
Glenn Dobbs, Brooklyn	6	0	0–0	0–0	36
Edgar Jones, Cleveland	5	1	0–0	0–0	36
Marion Motley, Cleveland	5	1	0–0	0–0	36
Phil Martinovich, Brooklyn	0	0	21–22	5–10	36
Dick Erdlitz, Miami	1	0	22–22	2–7	34
Gaylon Smith, Cleveland	5	0	0–0	0–0	30
Saxon Judd, Brooklyn	1	4	0–0	0–0	30
Monk Gafford, Miami	1	4	0–0	0–0	30
Chet Mutryn, Buffalo	2	3	0–0	0–0	30
Dale Gentry, Los Angeles	2	3	0–0	0–0	30
Andy Marefos, Los Angeles	4	0	2–2	0–0	26
Ralph Heywood, Chicago	0	4	0–0	0–0	24
Jack Russell, New York	0	4	0–0	0–0	24
Chuck Fenenbock, Los Angeles	4	0	0–0	0–0	24
Ace Parker, New York	4	0	0–0	0–0	24
Frankie Albert, San Francisco	4	0	0–0	0–0	24
Bob Nowaskey, Los Angeles	1	3	0–0	0–0	24
Jim McCarthy, Brooklyn	0	3	5–7	0–1	23
Pres Johnston, Miami–Buffalo	2	1	1–1	0–0	19
Ned Mathews, Chicago	1	2	0–0	0–0	18
Bill Kellagher, Chicago	3	0	0–0	0–0	18
Pug Manders, New York	3	0	0–0	0–0	18
Dick Renfro, San Francisco	3	0	0–0	0–0	18
Bob Seymour, Los Angeles	0	3	0–0	0–0	18
Tom Colella, Cleveland	2	1	0–0	0–0	18
Eddie Prokop, New York	2	1	0–0	0–0	18
Bill Lund, Cleveland	1	2	0–0	0–0	18
Art Van Tone, Brooklyn	0	3	0–0	0–0	18
Harry Hopp, Buffalo–Miami	3	0	0–0	0–0	18
Chet Adams, Cleveland	2	0	5–5	0–0	17
Neal Adams, Brooklyn	0	2	0–0	0–0	12
Bob Tichenal, San Francisco	0	2	0–0	0–0	12
Russ Morrow, Brooklyn	1	1	0–0	0–0	12
John Yonakor, Cleveland	0	2	0–0	0–0	12
Dewey Proctor, New York	1	1	0–0	0–0	12
John Polanski, Los Angeles	1	1	0–0	0–0	12
Don Reece, Miami	2	0	0–0	0–0	12
Dom Principe, Brooklyn	2	0	0–0	0–0	12
Vic Kulbitski, Buffalo	2	0	0–0	0–0	12
Norm Standlee, San Francisco	2	0	0–0	0–0	12
Marion Pugh, Miami	2	0	0–0	0–0	12
Al Vandeweghe, Buffalo	1	1	0–0	0–0	12
Frank Quillen, Chicago	0	2	0–0	0–0	12
Ken Casanega, San Francisco	1	1	0–0	0–0	12
Earle Parsons, San Francisco	2	0	0–0	0–0	12
Lew Mayne, Brooklyn	2	0	0–0	0–0	12
Lou Tomasetti, Buffalo	1	1	0–0	0–0	12
Otto Graham, Cleveland	2	0	0–0	0–0	12
Jimmy Nelson, Miami	2	0	0–0	0–0	12
Lowell Wagner, New York	1	1	0–0	0–0	12
Lamar Davis, Miami	0	2	0–0	0–0	12
John Stryzkalski, San Francisco	2	0	0–0	0–0	12
Harry Clarke, Los Angeles	0	2	0–0	0–0	12
Bob H. Kennedy, New York	2	0	0–0	0–0	12
Pete Franceschi, San Francisco	1	1	0–0	0–0	12
Prince Scott, Miami	0	2	0–0	0–0	12
Walt Williams, Chicago	2	0	0–0	0–0	12
Doyle Tackett, Brooklyn	0	2	0–0	0–0	12
Bob Paffrath, Brooklyn–Miami	2	0	0–0	0–0	12
Bob Nelson, Los Angeles	0	0	3–5	2–6	9
Ed Balatti, San Francisco	1	0	2–2	0–0	8
Joe Davis, Brooklyn	0	1	1–1	0–0	7
Bud Schwenk, Cleveland	1	0	0–0	0–0	6
Ray Ebli, Buffalo	0	1	0–0	0–0	6
Bob Motl, Chicago	0	1	0–0	0–0	6
Angelo Bertelli, Los Angeles	1	0	0–0	0–0	6
Lamar Blount, Miami	1	0	0–0	0–0	6
Frank Trigilio, Miami	0	1	0–0	0–0	6
Al Krueger, Los Angeles	1	0	0–0	0–0	6
Jim Thibaut, Buffalo	0	1	0–0	0–0	6
Hub Ulrich, Miami	1	0	0–0	0–0	6
Bill Fisk, San Francisco	0	1	0–0	0–0	6
Bob Reinhard, Los Angeles	0	1	0–0	0–0	6
Harry Burrus, New York	1	0	0–0	0–0	6
Ray Frankowski, Los Angeles	0	1	0–0	0–0	6
Marty Comer, Buffalo	1	0	0–0	0–0	6
Frank Gatski, Cleveland	1	0	0–0	0–0	6
Jack Dugger, Buffalo	1	0	0–0	0–0	6
Jack Morton, Los Angeles	1	0	0–0	0–0	6
Bernie Nygren, Los Angeles	0	1	0–0	0–0	6
Ray Terrell, Cleveland	0	1	0–0	0–0	6
Al Akins, Cleveland	1	0	0–0	0–0	6
Bus Mertes, Los Angeles	1	0	0–0	0–0	6

	TD Rush	TD Pass	Pts After TD	FG	Tot Pts		TD Rush	TD Pass	Pts After TD	FG	Tot Pts
Charlie O'Rourke, Los Angeles	1	0	0–0	0–0	6	Bob Sweiger, New York	0	1	0–0	0–0	6
George Terlep, Buffalo	1	0	0–0	0–0	6	Mickey Colmer, Brooklyn	0	1	0–0	0–0	6
Ernie Lewis, Chicago	1	0	0–0	0–0	6	Bob Dove, Chicago	0	1	0–0	0–0	6
Gene Fekete, Cleveland	1	0	0–0	0–0	6	Brooklyn Safeties (2)	0	0	0–0	0–0	4
Fred Gloden, Miami	1	0	0–0	0–0	6	Los Angeles Safeties (2)	0	0	0–0	0–0	4
John Kuzman, San Francisco	1	0	0–0	0–0	6	Bill Daddio, Buffalo	0	0	3–3	0–0	3
Bob Perina, New York	1	0	0–0	0–0	6	Cleveland Safety	0	0	0–0	0–0	2
Walt Clay, Chicago	1	0	0–0	0–0	6	San Francisco Safety	0	0	0–0	0–0	2
Don Durdan, San Francisco	0	1	0–0	0–0	6	John Rokisky, Cleveland	0	0	1–1	0–0	1
Bill Boedeker, Chicago	0	1	0–0	0–0	6	John Mellus, San Francisco	0	0	1–2	0–1	1
Lloyd Cheatham, New York	0	1	0–0	0–0	6	Lee Artoe, Los Angeles	0	0	1–2	0–0	1
Curt Sandig, Buffalo	1	0	0–0	0–0	6	Bob Masterson, New York	0	0	0–0	0–1	0
Pete Lamana, Chicago	1	0	0–0	0–0	6						

1947

Players are ranked based on total yards, except in pass receiving, interception returns, punting, points after touchdown and field goals. Those are ranked based on total number. Scoring is based on points.

There are a few discrepancies between actual statistics and the official records. George Ratterman was credited with a rushing attempt for zero yards and a touchdown in the first game of the season. For Cleveland, the rushing totals were off for three games (missing two yards for week one, there were an extra five yards for week five, and missing three yards for week 14). John Strzykalski was credited with a receiving touchdown, but had zero receptions for zero yards. This happened in game one of the season. For the Chicago Rockets, John Harrington had an extra two receiving yards and Pat Lahey was missing two receiving yards for the season. Since these statistics could not be verified, the official statistics were listed. However, there were two instances where the statistics could be verified and the official statistics were modified: Joe Aguirre and Bob Nelson had receiving yards for game one swapped; and Bill Daley and Al Dekdebrun had passing statistics swapped for game seven. These changes are detailed below.

Total Offense Leaders (Net Yards Gained)

	# of Plays	Rush	Pass	Total	Avg Gain
Spec Sanders, New York	402	1,432	1,442	2,874	7.15
Otto Graham, Cleveland	288	72	2,753	2,825	9.81
Bud Schwenk, Baltimore	352	58	2,236	2,294	6.52
Frankie Albert, SF	288	179	1,692	1,871	6.50
George Ratterman, Buffalo	261	–49	1,840	1,791	6.86
Bob Hoernschemeyer, Chicago–Brooklyn	325	704	926	1,630	5.02
Sam Vacanti, Chicago	236	–9	1,571	1,562	6.62
Charlie O'Rourke, LA	202	55	1,449	1,504	7.45

	# of Plays	Rush	Pass	Total	Avg Gain
John Strzykalski, SF	147	906	38	944	6.42
Glenn Dobbs, Brklyn–LA	185	131	762	893	4.83
Marion Motley, Cleveland	146	889	0	889	6.09
Chet Mutryn, Buffalo	140	868	0	868	6.20
Buddy Young, New York	118	712	13	725	6.14
Al Dekdebrun, Chicago	98	71	626	697	7.11
Mickey Colmer, Brooklyn	155	578	20	598	3.86
Norm Standlee, SF	145	585	0	585	4.03
John Kimbrough, LA	131	562	0	562	4.29
Edgar Jones, Cleveland	72	443	79	522	7.25
Bill Daley, Chicago	127	447	70	517	4.07
Eddie Prokop, New York	84	324	137	461	5.49
Ray Ramsey, Chicago	70	433	0	433	6.19
Julie Rykovich, Buffalo	92	414	0	414	4.50
Len Eshmont, San Francisco	84	381	0	381	4.54
Frankie Sinkwich, NY–Balt	86	241	93	334	3.88
Lou Tomasetti, Buffalo	92	326	0	326	3.54

Bill Daley had three pass completions out of six pass attempts for 70 yards, a touchdown and an interception in the official records. These statistics should have been for Al Dekdebrun. This reflects the corrected statistics. The error occurred in game seven of the season.

Rushing

	Rush	Yds	Avg Gain	TD
Spec Sanders, New York	231	1,432	6.20	18
John Strzykalski, San Francisco	143	906	6.34	5
Marion Motley, Cleveland	146	889	6.09	8
Chet Mutryn, Buffalo	140	868	6.20	9
Buddy Young, New York	116	712	6.14	3
Bob Hoernschemeyer, Chi–Brkln	152	704	4.63	5
Norm Standlee, San Francisco	145	585	4.03	8
Mickey Colmer, Brooklyn	152	578	3.80	9
John Kimbrough, Los Angeles	131	562	4.29	8
Bill Daley, Chicago	121	447	3.69	4
Edgar Jones, Cleveland	69	443	6.42	5
Ray Ramsey, Chicago	70	433	6.19	2
Julie Rykovich, Buffalo	92	414	4.50	4

Part 3: Individual Statistics

	Rush	Yds	Avg Gain	TD
Len Eshmont, San Francisco	84	381	4.54	0
Lou Tomasetti, Buffalo	92	326	3.54	2
Eddie Prokop, New York	76	324	4.26	4
Bus Mertes, Baltimore	95	321	5.86	1
Bob H. Kennedy, New York	44	258	5.86	1
Vic Kulbitski, Buffalo	56	249	4.45	1
Bill Kellagher, Chicago	42	243	5.79	0
Frankie Sinkwich, NY–Baltimore	71	241	3.39	0
Ned Mathews, San Francisco	39	238	6.10	2
Monk Gafford, Brooklyn	46	232	5.04	1
Bob Kelly, Los Angeles	51	205	4.02	2
Billy Hillenbrand, Baltimore	66	204	3.09	2
Bill Boedeker, Cleveland	31	194	6.26	4
Chuck Fenenbock, Los Angeles	58	185	3.19	3
Bob Cowan, Cleveland	38	181	4.76	2
Frankie Albert, San Francisco	46	179	3.89	5
Spiro Dellerba, Cleveland	29	176	6.07	0
Harry Clarke, Los Angeles	44	173	3.93	2
Len Masini, San Francisco	38	167	4.39	2
Bert Piggott, Los Angeles	46	161	3.50	0
Bob Reinhard, Los Angeles	41	150	3.66	0
George Koch, Buffalo	37	149	4.03	1
Dub Jones, Brooklyn	43	136	3.16	1
Glenn Dobbs, Brooklyn–LA	42	131	3.12	1
Steve Juzwik, Buffalo	26	130	5.00	0
Earle Parsons, San Francisco	33	125	3.79	0
Fred Evans, Buffalo–Chicago	31	124	4.00	1
Bob Perina, Brooklyn	67	116	1.73	3
John Wright, Baltimore	38	113	2.97	0
Bill Lund, Cleveland	14	105	7.50	1
John Sylvester, New York	17	101	5.94	0
Tony Adamle, Cleveland	23	95	4.13	1
Don Greenwood, Cleveland	18	94	5.22	0
Rudy Mobley, Baltimore	26	90	3.46	1
Bob Mitchell, Los Angeles	32	85	2.66	0
Al Akins, Brooklyn	15	79	5.27	1
Tom Colella, Cleveland	11	77	7.00	1
Lew Mayne, Cleveland	41	75	1.83	0
Wally Yonamine, San Francisco	19	74	3.89	0
Otto Graham, Cleveland	19	72	3.79	1
Al Dekdebrun, Chicago	20	71	3.55	0
Cliff Lewis, Cleveland	11	66	6.00	0
Jim Dewar, Cleveland	14	64	4.57	1
Bud Schwenk, Baltimore	25	58	2.32	1
Johnny Vardian, Baltimore	35	57	1.63	0
Charlie O'Rourke, Los Angeles	24	55	2.29	1
Harry Hopp, Los Angeles	10	52	5.20	0
Elroy Hirsch, Chicago	23	51	2.22	1
Alyn Beals, San Francisco	5	48	9.60	0
Ray Terrell, Baltimore–Cleveland	26	48	1.85	0
Ernie Lewis, Chicago	13	47	3.62	0
Bill Schroeder, Chicago	11	45	4.09	0
Lee Tevis, Brooklyn	4	44	11.00	0
Bob Sweiger, New York	9	44	4.89	0
Alex Wizbicki, Buffalo	9	44	4.89	0
Bill Bass, Chicago	28	44	1.57	0
Walt Clay, Los Angeles	9	42	4.67	0
Eddie Carr, San Francisco	11	42	3.82	0
Blondy Black, Baltimore	5	39	7.80	0
Ted Scalissi, Chicago	35	37	1.06	0
Albie Reisz, Buffalo	2	32	16.00	0
Andy Dudish, Baltimore	28	30	1.07	1
Sugarfoot Anderson, LA	3	24	8.00	0
Ed Robnett, San Francisco	7	18	2.57	0
Jim Castiglia, Baltimore	9	18	2.00	0
Pug Manders, Buffalo	3	15	5.00	0
Dewey Proctor, New York	15	15	1.00	1
Lamar Davis, Baltimore	3	14	4.67	0
George Terlep, Buffalo	4	11	2.75	0
Ben Raimondi, New York	6	11	1.83	0
Ermal Allen, Cleveland	7	11	1.57	0
Joe Vetrano, San Francisco	10	11	1.10	0
Buckets Hirsch, Buffalo	4	7	1.75	0
Harry Burrus, New York	1	5	5.00	0
George Benson, Brooklyn	2	5	2.50	0
Lamar Blount, Buffalo–Baltimore	4	5	1.25	0
Hal Thompson, Brooklyn	1	4	4.00	0
Walt Heap, Los Angeles	5	3	0.60	0
Bill Reinhard, Los Angeles	1	2	2.00	1
Angelo Bertelli, Chicago	1	2	2.00	0
Don Durdan, San Francisco	1	2	2.00	0
Bob Steuber, Los Angeles	1	2	2.00	0
Walt McDonald, Brooklyn	1	1	1.00	0
Steve Nemeth, Baltimore	1	1	1.00	0
Ernie Case, Baltimore	1	0	0.00	0
Weldon Humble, Cleveland	1	0	0.00	0
Bob Titchenal, Los Angeles	1	0	0.00	0
Hub Bechtol, Baltimore	2	−1	−0.50	0
Armand Cure, Baltimore	2	−1	−0.50	0
Elmore Harris, Brooklyn	3	−2	−0.67	0
Lloyd Cheatham, New York	1	−2	−2.00	0
Harmon Rowe, New York	2	−3	−1.50	0
Norm Cox, Chicago	1	−3	−3.00	0
Buzz Trebotich, Baltimore	3	−4	−1.33	0
John Galvin, Baltimore	1	−4	−4.00	0
Ernie Blandin, Cleveland	1	−6	−6.00	0
Mac Speedie, Cleveland	1	−7	−7.00	0
Sam Vacanti, Chicago	11	−9	−0.82	1
Jesse Freitas, San Francisco	6	−9	−1.50	0
Mort Landsberg, Los Angeles	2	−11	−5.50	0
George Ratterman, Buffalo	17	−49	−2.88	1

Passing

	Comp	Att	Yds	TD	Int
Otto Graham, Cleveland	163	269	2,753	25	11
Bud Schwenk, Baltimore	168	327	2,236	13	20
George Ratterman, Buffalo	124	244	1,840	22	20
Frankie Albert, San Francisco	128	242	1,692	18	15
Sam Vacanti, Chicago	96	225	1,571	16	16
Charlie O'Rourke, Los Angeles	89	178	1,449	13	16
Spec Sanders, New York	93	171	1,442	14	17
Bob Hoernschemeyer, Chi–Brklyn	73	173	926	4	11
Glenn Dobbs, Brooklyn–LA	61	143	762	7	8
Al Dekdebrun, Chicago	48	81	626	6	8
Jesse Freitas, San Francisco	13	33	215	4	2
Eddie Prokop, New York	4	8	137	2	1
Frankie Sinkwich, NY–Baltimore	8	15	93	0	0
Bob Perina, Brooklyn	11	24	91	0	2
Ermal Allen, Cleveland	4	13	88	0	0
Edgar Jones, Cleveland	2	3	79	0	0
Cliff Lewis, Cleveland	5	11	70	1	1
Bob H. Kennedy, New York	2	3	56	0	0
Ben Raimondi, New York	3	15	54	0	0
George Terlep, Buffalo	5	23	51	2	3
Ernie Case, Baltimore	4	11	49	0	1
Bev Wallace, San Francisco	5	16	48	0	2
John Strzykalski, San Francisco	1	4	38	0	0

1947

	Comp	Att	Yds	TD	Int
Dub Jones, Brooklyn	3	15	37	0	2
John Galvin, Baltimore	3	6	34	0	0
Bob Reinhard, Los Angeles	2	4	21	0	0
Mickey Colmer, Brooklyn	1	3	20	0	0
Steve Nemeth, Baltimore	2	6	18	0	2
Jim McCarthy, Brooklyn	1	2	17	0	1
Bill Bass, Chicago	1	1	14	0	0
Buddy Young, New York	1	2	13	0	0
Norm Cox, Chicago	1	2	9	0	0
Chuck Fenenbock, Los Angeles	1	7	7	0	2
Lamar Davis, Baltimore	0	1	0	0	0
Elroy Hirsch, Chicago	0	1	0	0	0
Dewey Proctor, New York	0	1	0	0	0
John Sylvester, New York	0	1	0	0	0
Billy Hillenbrand, Baltimore	0	1	0	0	1
Fred Evans, Buffalo-Chicago	0	2	0	0	0
Ned Mathews, San Francisco	0	2	0	0	0
Bill Reinhard, Los Angeles	0	2	0	0	0
Lee Tevis, Brooklyn	0	3	0	0	0
Angelo Bertelli, Chicago	2	7	-5	0	2

*Bill Daley had three pass completions out of six pass attempts for 70 yards, a touchdown and an interception in the official records. These statistics should have been for Al Dekdebrun. This reflects the corrected statistics. This occurred in game seven of the season.

Receiving

	Rec	Yds	Avg Gain	TD
Mac Speedie, Cleveland	67	1,146	17.1	6
Dante Lavelli, Cleveland	49	799	16.3	9
Alyn Beals, San Francisco	47	655	13.9	10
Lamar Davis, Baltimore	46	515	11.2	2
Billy Hillenbrand, Baltimore	39	702	18.0	7
Ray Ramsey, Chicago	35	768	21.9	8
Buddy Young, New York	27	303	11.2	2
Fay King, Buffalo	26	382	14.7	6
Al Baldwin, Buffalo	25	468	18.7	7
Nick Susoeff, San Francisco	24	223	9.3	2
Dale Gentry, Los Angeles	22	352	16.0	2
Max Morris, Chicago	22	239	10.9	1
Jack Russell, New York	20	368	18.4	2
Bruce Alford, New York	20	298	14.9	5
Chuck Fenenbock, Los Angeles	20	276	13.8	2
Al Coppage, Buffalo	20	226	11.3	2
Len Eshmont, San Francisco	19	303	15.9	2
Saxon Judd, Brooklyn	18	204	11.3	1
Mickey Colmer, Brooklyn	18	190	10.6	1
John Harrington, Chicago	17	233	13.7	3
Hub Bechtol, Baltimore	17	167	9.8	1
John Kimbrough, Los Angeles	16	281	17.6	3
Johnny Vardian, Baltimore	16	280	17.5	1
John Strzykalski, San Francisco	15	258	17.1	3
Hal Thompson, Brooklyn	15	148	9.9	0
Pat Lahey, Chicago	13	148	11.4	0
Lou Tomasetti, Buffalo	13	125	9.6	0
Burr Baldwin, Los Angeles	12	275	22.9	1
Bill Daley, Chicago	12	116	9.7	0
Joe Aguirre, Los Angeles	11	219	19.9	5
Sugarfoot Anderson, Los Angeles	11	126	11.5	1
Rudy Mobley, Baltimore	11	121	11.0	1
Bob Sweiger, New York	11	108	9.8	1
Elroy Hirsch, Chicago	10	282	28.2	3
Chet Mutryn, Buffalo	10	176	17.6	2
Jim McCarthy, Brooklyn	10	147	14.7	0
Earle Parsons, San Fransisco	9	163	18.1	2
Vic Kulbitski, Buffalo	9	117	13.0	4
Bob Kelly, Los Angeles	9	68	7.6	1
Bob Perina, Brooklyn	9	67	7.4	1
Harry Burrus, New York	8	192	24.0	2
Van Davis, New York	8	179	22.4	0
Bill Boedeker, Cleveland	8	175	21.9	1
Paul Gibson, Buffalo	8	154	19.3	0
Lamar Blount, Buffalo–Baltimore	8	148	18.5	0
Monk Gafford, Brooklyn	8	113	14.1	0
Bob Nowaskey, Los Angeles	8	106	13.3	0
Sig Sigurdson, Baltimore	8	104	13.0	0
Ed Balatti, San Francisco	8	98	12.3	1
Bill Bass, Chicago	8	79	9.9	1
Elmer Madar, Baltimore	8	53	6.6	0
Andy Dudish, Baltimore	7	130	18.6	1
Frank Quillen, Chicago	7	113	16.1	1
Jerry Mulready, Chicago	7	108	15.4	0
Marion Motley, Cleveland	7	73	10.4	1
Bob Titchenal, Los Angeles	7	97	13.9	0
Bert Piggott, Los Angeles	7	63	9.0	1
Lew Mayne, Cleveland	6	238	39.7	3
Bill Lund, Cleveland	6	110	18.3	0
Al Akins, Brooklyn	6	101	16.8	1
John Yonakor, Cleveland	6	95	15.8	2
Bob Dove, Chicago	6	61	10.2	1
Ned Mathews, San Francisco	6	51	8.5	2
Ray Terrell, Baltimore–Cleveland	6	21	3.5	0
Edgar Jones, Cleveland	5	92	18.4	1
Fred Evans, Buffalo-Chicago	5	84	16.8	1
Ted Scalissi, Chicago	5	67	13.4	2
Bob Cowan, Cleveland	5	60	12.0	1
Don Greenwood, Cleveland	5	49	9.8	0
Bill Fisk, San Francisco	5	39	7.8	0
Steve Juzwik, Buffalo	5	35	7.0	1
Lloyd Cheatham, New York	4	124	31.0	2
Tom Colella, Cleveland	4	63	15.8	1
Lowell Wagner, New York	4	50	12.5	1
Julie Rykovich, Buffalo	4	44	11.0	0
Eddie Carr, San Francisco	4	41	10.3	0
Ray Ebli, Chicago	4	38	9.5	1
Eddie Prokop, New York	3	79	26.3	1
Dick Horne, San Francisco	3	69	23.0	0
Harry Hopp, Los Angeles	3	59	19.7	0
Harry Clarke, Los Angeles	3	54	18.0	0
Wally Yonamine, San Francisco	3	40	13.3	0
Ray Kuffel, Buffalo	3	37	12.3	0
Bob Mitchell, Los Angeles	3	36	12.0	1
Bob Reinhard, Los Angeles	3	34	11.3	1
Walt McDonald, Brooklyn	3	30	10.0	0
Ralph Jones, Baltimore	3	23	7.7	0
Bill Kellagher, Chicago	3	22	7.3	0
Marty Comer, Buffalo	2	75	37.5	1
Roy Kurrasch, New York	2	53	26.5	0
Hank Norberg, San Francisco	2	31	15.5	0
Marshall Shurnas, Cleveland	2	30	15.0	0
Bus Mertes, Baltimore	2	28	14.0	0
Horace Gillom, Cleveland	2	24	12.0	0
Norm Standlee, San Francisco	2	22	11.0	0
Glenn Dobbs, Los Angeles	2	21	10.5	0
Bill Schroeder, Chicago	2	19	9.5	1
Gorham Getchell, Baltimore	2	17	8.5	0
Herb Nelson, Brooklyn	2	17	8.5	0
Vince Mazza, Buffalo	2	11	5.5	0

Part 3: Individual Statistics

	Rec	Yds	Avg Gain	TD
Ted Sruggs, Brooklyn	2	9	4.5	0
Walt Heap, Los Angeles	2	0	0.0	1
Walt Clay, Los Angeles	1	52	52.0	0
Tony Adamle, Cleveland	1	22	22.0	0
Ollie Poole, New York	1	19	19.0	0
Spiro Dellerba, Cleveland	1	14	14.0	0
Spec Sanders, New York	1	13	13.0	0
Jim Castiglia, Baltimore	1	10	10.0	0
George Koch, Buffalo	1	10	10.0	0
John Rokisky, Chicago	1	8	8.0	0
Blondy Black, Baltimore	1	7	7.0	0
Bob Hein, Brooklyn	1	7	7.0	0
John Sylvester, New York	1	5	5.0	0
Bob Hoernschemeyer, Chi–Brklyn	1	4	4.0	1
Dewey Proctor, New York	1	4	4.0	0
Gil Meyers, Baltimore	1	3	3.0	0
Frankie Sinkwich, NY–Baltimore	1	3	3.0	0
Mort Landsberg, Los Angeles	1	0	0.0	0
Doyle Tackett, Brooklyn	0	25	—	0
Dick Danehe, Los Angeles	0	8	—	0
John Mellus, Baltimore	0	5	—	0
Tex Warrington, Brooklyn	0	2	—	0

*Joe Aguirre had three receptions for 61 yards and a touchdown credited to Bob Nelson in the official records. This reflects the corrected statistics. The error occurred in game one of the season.

Punting

	Punts	Avg	Had Blocked
John Galvin, Baltimore	66	36.0	2
Ernie Lewis, Chicago	65	39.2	4
Albie Reisz, Buffalo	57	37.0	0
Mickey Colmer, Brooklyn	56	44.7	0
Horace Gillom, Cleveland	47	44.6	0
Spec Sanders, New York	46	42.1	2
Glenn Dobbs, Brooklyn–LA	44	43.4	2
Frankie Albert, San Francisco	40	44.0	1
Bob Reinhard, Los Angeles	28	45.7	1
Jesse Freitas, San Francisco	8	42.0	0
Frankie Sinkwich, NY–Baltimore	7	37.1	1
Bob Perina, Brooklyn	7	29.9	2
Lee Tevis, Brooklyn	5	49.2	0
Ernie Case, Baltimore	5	30.4	1
Bob H. Kennedy, New York	5	25.2	3
Ermal Allen, Cleveland	4	33.8	0
Steve Nemeth, Baltimore	3	42.0	0
Bev Wallace, San Francisco	2	39.0	0
Fred Evans, Chicago	2	36.5	0
Bob Hoernschemeyer, Chi–Brklyn	2	28.0	1
John Sylvester, New York	1	42.0	0
Tom Colella, Cleveland	1	36.0	0

Interceptions

	Int	Yds	Avg Ret	TD
Tom Colella, Cleveland	6	130	21.7	1
Bill Kellagher, Chicago	6	77	12.8	0
Len Eshmont, San Francisco	6	72	12.0	0
Walt Heap, Los Angeles	5	107	21.4	1
Ray Ramsey, Chicago	5	66	13.2	0
Glenn Dobbs, Brooklyn–LA	5	44	8.8	0
Ned Mathews, San Francisco	4	149	37.3	1
Bill Schroeder, Chicago	4	148	37.0	2
Ermal Allen, Cleveland	4	63	15.8	0
Bob Perina, Brooklyn	4	40	10.0	0
Don Greenwood, Cleveland	4	19	4.8	0
Cliff Lewis, Cleveland	4	19	4.8	0
Buckets Hirsch, Buffalo	3	73	24.3	1
Spec Sanders, New York	3	63	21.0	0
Eddie Prokop, New York	3	57	19.0	0
Johnny Vardian, Baltimore	3	48	16.0	0
George Koch, Buffalo	3	24	8.0	0
Monk Gafford, Brooklyn	3	16	5.3	0
Bill Bass, Chicago	2	104	52.0	1
Al Baldwin, Buffalo	2	90	45.0	0
Bob H. Kennedy, New York	2	66	33.0	0
Julie Rykovich, Buffalo	2	61	30.5	0
Eddie Carr, San Francisco	2	59	29.5	0
Ernie Case, Baltimore	2	56	28.0	0
Bob Nelson, Los Angeles	2	52	26.0	1
Bob Sweiger, New York	2	51	25.5	1
Bob Kelly, Los Angeles	2	47	23.5	0
John Schiechl, San Francisco	2	45	22.5	0
Bill Lund, Cleveland	2	36	18.0	1
Dub Jones, Brooklyn	2	35	17.5	0
Weldon Humble, Cleveland	2	31	15.5	0
John Strzykalski, San Francisco	2	25	12.5	0
Bob Mitchell, Los Angeles	2	24	12.0	0
Felto Prewitt, Buffalo	2	20	10.0	0
Harmon Rowe, New York	2	20	10.0	0
Bob Nowaskey, Los Angeles	2	15	7.5	0
Dutch Elston, San Francisco	2	13	6.5	0
Lee Tevis, Brooklyn	2	9	4.5	0
Rudy Mobley, Baltimore	2	8	4.0	0
Lou Saban, Cleveland	2	2	1.0	0
Frank Gatski, Cleveland	2	0	0.0	0
Jim Dewar, Cleveland	1	50	50.0	0
Billy Hillenbrand, Baltimore	1	48	48.0	0
Marion Motley, Cleveland	1	48	48.0	1
Lou Tomasetti, Buffalo	1	44	44.0	1
Bert Corley, Buffalo	1	41	41.0	0
Jack Russell, New York	1	33	33.0	0
Dewey Proctor, New York	1	32	32.0	0
Al Akins, Brooklyn	1	31	31.0	0
Horace Gillom, Cleveland	1	29	29.0	0
Vince Mazza, Buffalo	1	26	26.0	0
Tony Adamle, Cleveland	1	25	25.0	0
Lenny Simonetti, Cleveland	1	22	22.0	0
Walt Clay, Los Angeles	1	20	20.0	0
Wally Yonamine, San Francisco	1	20	20.0	0
Doyle Tackett, Brooklyn	1	17	17.0	0
Harry Hopp, Los Angeles	1	16	16.0	0
Floyd Konetsky, Baltimore	1	15	15.0	0
Vic Kulbitski, Buffalo	1	14	14.0	0
Lamar Davis, Baltimore	1	12	12.0	0
Ray Terrell, Baltimore–Cleveland	1	12	12.0	0
Harry Burrus, New York	1	11	11.0	0
Jesse Freitas, San Francisco	1	11	11.0	0
Chet Mutryn, Buffalo	1	11	11.0	0
George Smith, San Francisco	1	10	10.0	0
Bert Piggott, Los Angeles	1	9	9.0	0
Bob Hoernschemeyer, Chi–Brklyn	1	8	8.0	0
Roy Ruskusky, New York	1	8	8.0	0
Hub Bechtol, Baltimore	1	7	7.0	0
Bill Reinhard, Los Angeles	1	7	7.0	0
John Wright, Baltimore	1	5	5.0	0

	Int	Yds	Avg Ret	TD
Alex Agase, Chicago	1	4	4.0	0
John Brown, Los Angeles	1	4	4.0	0
Tony Calvelli, San Francisco	1	2	2.0	0
Joe Kodba, Baltimore	1	2	2.0	0
Bruce Alford, New York	1	1	1.0	0
Lou Daukas, Brooklyn	1	1	1.0	0
Fran Mattingly, Chicago	1	1	1.0	0
Alyn Beals, San Francisco	1	0	0.0	0
Joe Gibson, Brooklyn	1	0	0.0	0
Otto Graham, Cleveland	1	0	0.0	0
Len Masini, San Francisco	1	0	0.0	0
Bob Reinhard, Los Angeles	1	0	0.0	0
George Terlep, Buffalo	1	0	0.0	0
Bob Hoernschemeyer, Chicago–Brooklyn	1	19	19.0	0
Walt McDonald, Brooklyn	1	19	19.0	0
Ray Terrell, Baltimore–Cleveland	1	18	18.0	0
Ernie Case, Baltimore	2	18	9.0	0
Al Akins, Brooklyn	1	17	17.0	0
George Terlep, Buffalo	1	17	17.0	0
Frankie Sinkwich, NY–Baltimore	1	15	15.0	0
Vic Kulbitski, Buffalo	1	13	13.0	0
Ed Balatti, San Francisco	2	8	4.0	1
Bert Piggott, Los Angeles	1	7	7.0	0
Ollie Poole, New York	1	5	5.0	0
Bill Daley, Chicago	1	3	3.0	0
Len Eshmont, San Francisco	1	3	3.0	0
Jim Dewar, Cleveland	1	2	2.0	0
Gerry Conlee, San Francisco	1	1	1.0	0

Punt Returns

	Ret	Yds	Avg Ret	TD
Glenn Dobbs, Brooklyn–LAs	19	215	11.3	0
Chuck Fenenbock, Los Angeles	17	210	12.4	0
Billy Hillenbrand, Baltimore	13	201	15.5	0
Chet Mutryn, Buffalo	13	187	14.4	0
Monk Gafford, Brooklyn	11	186	16.9	0
Spec Sanders, New York	6	164	27.3	0
Dub Jones, Brooklyn	14	157	11.2	0
Joe Vetrano, San Francisco	12	137	11.4	0
Ray Ramsey, Chicago	11	131	11.9	0
Buddy Young, New York	8	127	15.9	1
Andy Dudish, Baltimore	5	121	24.2	0
Otto Graham, Cleveland	10	121	12.1	0
Tom Colella, Cleveland	5	113	22.6	1
Earle Parsons, San Francisco	10	106	10.6	0
Alex Wizbicki, Buffalo	9	105	11.7	0
Julie Rykovich, Buffalo	7	93	13.3	0
Bill Bass, Chicago	10	85	8.5	0
George Koch, Buffalo	4	84	21.0	0
Cliff Lewis, Cleveland	7	84	12.0	0
Bill Boedeker, Cleveland	3	82	27.3	0
Eddie Prokop, New York	7	78	11.1	0
Rudy Mobley, Baltimore	5	74	14.8	0
John Strzykalski, San Francisco	8	70	8.8	0
Bob Kelly, Los Angeles	4	69	17.3	0
Johnny Vardian, Baltimore	5	66	13.2	0
Ned Mathews, San Francisco	4	44	11.0	0
Bob H. Kennedy, New York	6	44	7.3	0
Harry Clarke, Los Angeles	3	38	12.7	0
Edgar Jones, Cleveland	2	37	18.5	0
John Sylvester, New York	3	37	12.3	0
Steve Juzwik, Buffalo	4	36	9.0	0
Tony Adamle, Cleveland	0	36	—	0
Bruce Alford, New York	1	34	34.0	1
Lamar Davis, Baltimore	1	33	33.0	0
Rupe Thornton, San Francisco	1	32	32.0	0
Garland Gregory, San Francisco	1	31	31.0	0
Fred Evans, Buffalo–Chicago	5	30	6.0	0
Wally Yonamine, San Francisco	2	29	14.5	0
Ermal Allen, Cleveland	4	28	7.0	0
Bob Perina, Brooklyn	4	27	6.8	0
Ted Scalissi, Chicago	2	26	13.0	0
Elroy Hirsch, Chicago	2	24	12.0	0
Bob Nowaskey, Los Angeles	1	22	22.0	0
Bill Reinhard, Los Angeles	2	22	11.0	0
Eddie Carr, San Francisco	1	20	20.0	0
Bruno Banducci, San Francisco	1	19	19.0	0

Kick Returns

	Ret	Yds	Avg Ret	TD
Chet Mutryn, Buffalo	21	691	32.9	1
Spec Sanders, New York	22	593	27.0	1
Monk Gafford, Brooklyn	21	565	26.9	0
Billy Hillenbrand, Baltimore	18	466	25.9	1
Chuck Fenenbock, Los Angeles	18	452	25.1	0
Ray Ramsey, Chicago	16	406	25.4	0
Buddy Young, New York	12	332	27.7	1
Elmore Harris, Brooklyn	14	329	23.5	0
Marion Motley, Cleveland	13	322	24.8	0
Bill Bass, Chicago	12	264	22.0	0
Julie Rykovich, Buffalo	12	257	21.4	0
Harry Clarke, Los Angeles	8	225	28.1	0
Ray Terrell, Baltimore–Cleveland	9	204	22.7	0
Eddie Prokop, New York	7	188	26.9	0
Andy Dudish, Baltimore	8	184	23.0	0
Len Eshmont, San Francisco	9	177	19.7	0
Elroy Hirsch, Chicago	6	172	28.7	0
Ted Scalissi, Chicago	8	171	21.4	0
Alex Wizbicki, Buffalo	5	164	32.8	1
Fred Evans, Buffalo–Chicago	9	159	17.7	0
Bill Daley, Chicago	7	145	20.7	0
Bill Boedeker, Cleveland	6	133	22.2	0
Al Akins, Brooklyn	5	131	26.2	0
Johnny Vardian, Baltimore	6	128	21.3	0
Wally Yonamine, San Francisco	7	127	18.1	0
John Strzykalski, San Francisco	6	124	20.7	0
Dub Jones, Brooklyn	7	121	17.3	0
Bert Piggott, Los Angeles	5	120	24.0	0
Glenn Dobbs, Brooklyn–LA	5	119	23.8	0
Bob Mitchell, Los Angeles	6	119	19.8	0
Frankie Sinkwich, NY–Baltimore	5	118	23.6	0
Joe Vetrano, San Francisco	5	117	23.4	0
Ernie Case, Baltimore	4	104	26.0	0
Lew Mayne, Cleveland	5	102	20.4	0
Earle Parsons, San Francisco	4	99	24.8	0
John Kimbrough, Los Angeles	4	96	24.0	0
Bill Schroder, Chicago	5	92	18.4	0
Bruce Alford, New York	2	90	45.0	1
Mickey Colmer, Brooklyn	3	77	25.7	0
Lou Tomasetti, Buffalo	4	74	18.5	0
Cliff Lewis, Cleveland	4	71	17.8	0
Bob Perina, Brooklyn	3	67	22.3	0
Jack Russell, New York	4	66	16.5	0

Part 3: Individual Statistics

	Ret	Yds	Avg Ret	TD
Bob Kelly, Los Angeles	3	61	20.3	0
Bob Cowan, Cleveland	3	55	18.3	0
Edgar Jones, Cleveland	2	48	24.0	0
Ned Mathews, San Francisco	2	46	23.0	0
Lamar Davis, Baltimore	2	44	22.0	0
Eddie Carr, San Francisco	2	42	21.0	0
Bob Reinhard, Los Angeles	3	42	14.0	0
John Galvin, Baltimore	2	38	19.0	0
Bill Lund, Cleveland	2	37	18.5	0
Spiro Dellerba, Cleveland	1	34	34.0	0
Al Coppage, Buffalo	2	28	14.0	0
Bruno Banducci, San Francisco	1	27	27.0	0
Jim Dewar, Cleveland	1	25	25.0	0
John Sylvester, New York	1	25	25.0	0
Charlie O'Rourke, Los Angeles	1	24	24.0	0
Norm Standlee, San Francisco	3	24	8.0	0
Frankie Albert, San Francisco	1	23	23.0	0
Tony Adamle, Cleveland	1	22	22.0	0
Visco Grgich, San Francisco	1	21	21.0	0
Steve Juzwik, Buffalo	1	20	20.0	0
Vic Kulbitski, Buffalo	1	19	19.0	0
Rudy Mobley, Baltimore	1	18	18.0	0
Harmon Rowe, New York	1	18	18.0	0
Pat Lahey, Chicago	2	18	9.0	0
Frank Gatski, Cleveland	1	17	17.0	0
Buzz Trebotich, Baltimore	1	17	17.0	0
Lee Artoe, Los Angeles	1	16	16.0	0
Ed Balatti, San Francisco	1	16	16.0	0
Bob Dove, Chicago	1	16	16.0	0
Dewey Proctor, New York	1	15	15.0	0
Elmer Madar, Baltimore	1	14	14.0	0
Hub Bechtol, Baltimore	1	13	13.0	0
Tom Colella, Cleveland	1	13	13.0	0
Harry Hopp, Los Angeles	1	13	13.0	0
Max Morris, Chicago	1	13	13.0	0
George Koch, Buffalo	1	12	12.0	0
Bob Sweiger, New York	1	12	12.0	0
Bob Hoernschemeyer, Chicago–Brooklyn	1	11	11.0	0
Chet Kozel, Buffalo	1	11	11.0	0
Dante Lavelli, Cleveland	1	10	10.0	0
Van Davis, New York	1	9	9.0	0
Harley McCollum, Chicago	1	9	9.0	0
Barry French, Baltimore	1	8	8.0	0
John Kuzman, Chicago	1	7	7.0	0
Al Baldwin, Buffalo	1	6	6.0	0
Saxon Judd, Brooklyn	2	5	2.5	0
Jack Durishan, New York	1	3	3.0	0
John Woudenberg, San Francisco	1	2	2.0	0
Nick Daukas, Brooklyn	1	1	1.0	0
John Yonakor, Cleveland	1	0	0.0	0

Total Returns (Punt and Kick)

	Ret	Yds	Avg Ret	TD
Chet Mutryn, Buffalo	34	878	25.8	1
Spec Sanders, New York	28	757	27.0	1
Monk Gafford, Brooklyn	32	751	23.5	0
Billy Hillenbrand, Baltimore	31	667	21.5	1
Chuck Fenenbock, Los Angeles	35	662	18.9	0
Ray Ramsey, Chicago	27	537	19.9	0
Buddy Young, New York	20	459	22.9	2
Julie Rykovich, Buffalo	19	350	18.4	0

	Ret	Yds	Avg Ret	TD
Bill Bass, Chicago	22	349	15.9	0
Glenn Dobbs, Brooklyn–LA	24	334	13.9	0
Elmore Harris, Brooklyn	14	329	23.5	0
Marion Motley, Cleveland	13	322	24.8	0
Andy Dudish, Baltimore	13	305	23.5	0
Dub Jones, Brooklyn	21	278	13.2	0
Alex Wizbicki, Buffalo	14	269	19.2	1
Eddie Prokop, New York	14	266	19.0	0
Harry Clarke, Los Angeles	11	263	23.9	0
Joe Vetrano, San Francisco	17	254	14.9	0
Ray Terrell, Baltimore–Cleveland	10	222	22.2	0
Bill Boedeker, Cleveland	9	215	23.9	0
Earle Parsons, San Francisco	14	205	14.6	0
Ted Scalissi, Chicago	10	197	19.7	0
Elroy Hirsch, Chicago	8	196	24.5	0
Johnny Vardian, Baltimore	11	194	17.6	0
John Strzykalski, San Francisco	14	194	13.9	0
Fred Evans, Buffalo–Chicago	14	189	13.5	0
Len Eshmont, San Francisco	10	180	18.0	0
Wally Yonamine, San Francisco	9	156	17.3	0
Cliff Lewis, Cleveland	11	155	14.1	0
Al Akins, Brooklyn	6	148	24.7	0
Bill Daley, Chicago	8	148	18.5	0
Frankie Sinkwich, NY–Baltimore	6	133	22.2	0
Bob Kelly, Los Angeles	7	130	18.6	0
Bert Piggott, Los Angeles	6	127	21.2	0
Tom Colella, Cleveland	6	126	21.0	1
Bruce Alford, New York	3	124	41.3	2
Ernie Case, Baltimore	6	122	20.3	0
Otto Graham, Cleveland	10	121	12.1	0
Bob Mitchell, Los Angeles	6	119	19.8	0
Lew Mayne, Cleveland	5	102	20.4	0
John Kimbrough, Los Angeles	4	96	24.0	0
George Koch, Buffalo	5	96	19.2	0
Bob Perina, Brooklyn	7	94	13.4	0
Bill Schroder, Chicago	5	92	18.4	0
Rudy Mobley, Baltimore	6	92	15.3	0
Ned Mathews, San Francisco	6	90	15.0	0
Edgar Jones, Cleveland	4	85	21.3	0
Mickey Colmer, Brooklyn	3	77	25.7	0
Lamar Davis, Baltimore	3	77	25.7	0
Lou Tomasetti, Buffalo	4	74	18.5	0
Jack Russell, New York	4	66	16.5	0
Eddie Carr, San Francisco	3	62	20.7	0
John Sylvester, New York	4	62	15.5	0
Tony Adamle, Cleveland	1	58	22.0	0
Steve Juzwik, Buffalo	5	56	11.2	0
Bob Cowan, Cleveland	3	55	18.3	0
Bruno Banducci, San Francisco	2	46	23.0	0
Bob H. Kennedy, New York	6	44	7.3	0
Bob Reinhard, Los Angeles	3	42	14.0	0
John Galvin, Baltimore	2	38	19.0	0
Bill Lund, Cleveland	2	37	18.5	0
Spiro Dellerba, Cleveland	1	34	34.0	0
Rupe Thornton, San Francisco	1	32	32.0	0
Vic Kulbitski, Buffalo	2	32	16.0	0
Garland Gregory, San Francisco	1	31	31.0	0
Bob Hoernschemeyer, Chicago–Brooklyn	2	30	15.0	0
Al Coppage, Buffalo	2	28	14.0	0
Ermal Allen, Cleveland	4	28	7.0	0
Jim Dewar, Cleveland	2	27	13.5	0
Charlie O'Rourke, Los Angeles	1	24	24.0	0
Ed Balatti, San Francisco	3	24	8.0	1

	Ret	Yds	Avg Ret	TD
Norm Standlee, San Francisco	3	24	8.0	0
Frankie Albert, San Francisco	1	23	23.0	0
Bob Nowaskey, Los Angeles	1	22	22.0	0
Bill Reinhard, Los Angeles	2	22	11.0	0
Visco Grgich, San Francisco	1	21	21.0	0
Walt McDonald, Brooklyn	1	19	19.0	0
Harmon Rowe, New York	1	18	18.0	0
Pat Lahey, Chicago	2	18	9.0	0
Frank Gatski, Cleveland	1	17	17.0	0
George Terlep, Buffalo	1	17	17.0	0
Buzz Trebotich, Baltimore	1	17	17.0	0
Lee Artoe, Los Angeles	1	16	16.0	0
Bob Dove, Chicago	1	16	16.0	0
Dewey Proctor, New York	1	15	15.0	0
Elmer Madar, Baltimore	1	14	14.0	0
Hub Bechtol, Baltimore	1	13	13.0	0
Harry Hopp, Los Angeles	1	13	13.0	0
Max Morris, Chicago	1	13	13.0	0
Bob Sweiger, New York	1	12	12.0	0
Chet Kozel, Buffalo	1	11	11.0	0
Dante Lavelli, Cleveland	1	10	10.0	0
Van Davis, New York	1	9	9.0	0
Harley McCollum, Chicago	1	9	9.0	0
Barry French, Baltimore	1	8	8.0	0
John Kuzman, Chicago	1	7	7.0	0
Al Baldwin, Buffalo	1	6	6.0	0
Ollie Poole, New York	1	5	5.0	0
Saxon Judd, Brooklyn	2	5	2.5	0
Jack Durishan, New York	1	3	3.0	0
John Woudenberg, San Francisco	1	2	2.0	0
Gerry Conlee, San Francisco	1	1	1.0	0
Nick Daukas, Brooklyn	1	1	1.0	0
John Yonakor, Cleveland	1	0	0.0	0

Point After Touchdowns

	Made	Att	%
Harvey Johnson, New York	49	51	96.1
Ben Agajanian, Los Angeles	39	40	97.5
Lou Groza, Cleveland	39	42	92.9
Joe Vetrano, San Francisco	38	43	88.4
John Rokisky, Chicago	33	35	94.3
Steve Juzwik, Buffalo	28	32	87.5
Phil Martinovich, Brooklyn	22	25	88.0
Augie Lio, Baltimore	19	20	95.0
Lou Saban, Cleveland	10	11	90.9
Graham Armstrong, Buffalo	8	10	80.0
Ed Balatti, San Francisco	1	1	100.0
Ernie Case, Baltimore	1	1	100.0
Vic Kulbitski, Buffalo	1	1	100.0
Steve Nemeth, Baltimore	1	1	100.0
Chet Adams, Cleveland	1	2	50.0
Chet Mutryn, Buffalo	1	2	50.0
George Ratterman, Buffalo	0	1	0.0
Frankie Albert, San Francisco	0	2	0.0

Field Goals

	Made	Att	%
Ben Agajanian, Los Angeles	15	24	62.5
Harvey Johnson, New York	7	8	87.5
Lou Groza, Cleveland	7	19	36.8
John Rokisky, Chicago	4	8	50.0
Joe Vetrano, San Francisco	4	12	33.3
Augie Lio, Baltimore	3	8	37.5
Phil Martinovich, Brooklyn	3	20	15.0
Steve Juzwik, Buffalo	2	3	66.7
Chet Adams, Cleveland	1	1	100.0
Ernie Case, Baltimore	1	1	100.0
Graham Armstrong, Buffalo	0	1	0.0
Angelo Bertelli, Chicago	0	1	0.0
Steve Nemeth, Baltimore	0	1	0.0

Scoring

	TD Rush	TD Pass	Pts After TD	FG	Tot Pts
Spec Sanders, New York	19	0	0-0	0-0	114
Ben Agajanian, LA	0	0	39-40	15-24	84
Chet Mutryn, Buffalo	10	2	1-2	0-0	73
Harvey Johnson, NY	0	0	49-51	7-8	70
John Kimbrough, LA	8	3	0-0	0-0	66
Lou Groza, Cleveland	0	0	39-42	7-19	60
Alyn Beals, SF	0	10	0-0	0-0	60
Billy Hillenbrand, Balt	3	7	0-0	0-0	60
Ray Ramsey, Chicago	2	8	0-0	0-0	60
Marion Motley, Cleve	9	1	0-0	0-0	60
Mickey Colmer, Brklyn	9	1	0-0	0-0	60
Dante Lavelli, Cleve	0	9	0-0	0-0	54
Joe Vetrano, SF	0	0	38-43	4-12	50
John Strzykalski, SF	5	3	0-0	0-0	48
Norm Standlee, SF	8	0	0-0	0-0	48
John Rokisky, Chi	0	0	33-35	4-8	45
Mac Speedie, Cleve	1	6	0-0	0-0	42
Buddy Young, NY	5	2	0-0	0-0	42
Bruce Alford, NY	2	5	0-0	0-0	42
Al Baldwin, Buffalo	0	7	0-0	0-0	42
Steve Juzwik, Buffalo	0	1	28-32	2-3	40
Fay King, Buffalo	0	6	0-0	0-0	36
Chuck Fenenbock, LA	4	2	0-0	0-0	36
Edgar Jones, Cleveland	5	1	0-0	0-0	36
Bob Hoernschemeyer, Chicago–Brooklyn	5	1	0-0	0-0	36
Phil Martinovich, Brooklyn	0	0	22-25	3-20	31
Vic Kulbitski, Buffalo	1	4	1-1	0-0	31
Eddie Prokop, New York	4	1	0-0	0-0	30
Bill Boedeker, Cleveland	4	1	0-0	0-0	30
Ned Mathews, SF	3	2	0-0	0-0	30
Frankie Albert, SF	5	0	0-2	0-0	30
Joe Aguirre, Los Angeles	0	5	0-0	0-0	30
Augie Lio, Baltimore	0	0	19-20	3-8	28
Julie Rykovich, Buffalo	4	0	0-0	0-0	24
Elroy Hirsch, Chicago	1	3	0-0	0-0	24
Bob Perina, Brooklyn	3	1	0-0	0-0	24
Tom Colella, Cleveland	3	1	0-0	0-0	24
John Harrington, Chicago	0	3	0-0	0-0	18
Bill Daley, Chicago*	3	0	0-0	0-0	18
Lew Mayne, Cleveland	0	3	0-0	0-0	18
Bill Schroder, Chicago	2	1	0-0	0-0	18
Lou Tomasetti, Buffalo	3	0	0-0	0-0	18
Jack Russell, New York	1	2	0-0	0-0	18
Bob Kelly, Los Angeles	2	1	0-0	0-0	18
Bob Cowan, Cleveland	2	1	0-0	0-0	18
Bill Lund, Cleveland	2	1	0-0	0-0	18
Ed Balatti, San Francisco	1	1	1-1	0-0	13
Bus Mertes, Baltimore	2	0	0-0	0-0	12
Dale Gentry, Los Angeles	0	2	0-0	0-0	12
Lloyd Cheatham, New York	0	2	0-0	0-0	12
Nick Susoeff, San Francisco	0	2	0-0	0-0	12

Part 3: Individual Statistics

	TD Rush	TD Pass	Pts After TD	FG	Tot Pts
Walt Heap, Los Angeles	1	1	0–0	0–0	12
Bob Nelson, Los Angeles	1	1	0–0	0–0	12
Harry Burrus, New York	0	2	0–0	0–0	12
Len Masini, San Francisco	2	0	0–0	0–0	12
Bill Bass, Chicago	1	1	0–0	0–0	12
Harry Clarke, Los Angeles	2	0	0–0	0–0	12
Andy Dudish, Baltimore	1	1	0–0	0–0	12
Len Eshmont, San Francisco	0	2	0–0	0–0	12
Ted Scalissi, Chicago	0	2	0–0	0–0	12
Al Akins, Brooklyn	1	1	0–0	0–0	12
Glenn Dobbs, Brooklyn–LA	2	0	0–0	0–0	12
Earle Parsons, San Francisco	0	2	0–0	0–0	12
Lamar Davis, Baltimore	0	2	0–0	0–0	12
Al Coppage, Buffalo	0	2	0–0	0–0	12
Rudy Mobley, Baltimore	1	1	0–0	0–0	12
Max Morris, Chicago	1	1	0–0	0–0	12
Bob Sweiger, New York	1	1	0–0	0–0	12
John Yonakor, Cleveland	0	2	0–0	0–0	12
Fred Evans, Buffalo–Chicago	1	1	0–0	0–0	12
Lou Saban, Cleveland	0	0	10–11	0–0	10
Graham Armstrong, Buffalo	0	0	8–10	0–1	8
Jim Castiglia, Baltimore	1	0	0–0	0–0	6
Bud Schwenk, Baltimore	1	0	0–0	0–0	6
Marty Comer, Buffalo	0	1	0–0	0–0	6
George Ratterman, Buffalo	1	0	0–1	0–0	6
Ray Ebli, Chicago	0	1	0–0	0–0	6
Frank Quillen, Chicago	0	1	0–0	0–0	6
Sam Vacanti, Chicago	1	0	0–0	0–0	6
Sugarfoot Anderson, LA	0	1	0–0	0–0	6
Burr Baldwin, Los Angeles	0	1	0–0	0–0	6
Lou Sossamon, New York	1	0	0–0	0–0	6
Lowell Wagner, New York	0	1	0–0	0–0	6
Buckets Hirsch, Buffalo	1	0	0–0	0–0	6
Otto Graham, Cleveland	1	0	0–0	0–0	6
Bob H. Kennedy, New York	1	0	0–0	0–0	6
Bill Reinhard, Los Angeles	1	0	0–0	0–0	6
Monk Gafford, Brooklyn	1	0	0–0	0–0	6
Alex Wizbicki, Buffalo	1	0	0–0	0–0	6
Johnny Vardian, Baltimore	0	1	0–0	0–0	6
Dub Jones, Brooklyn	1	0	0–0	0–0	6
Bert Piggott, Los Angeles	0	1	0–0	0–0	6
Paul Mitchell, Los Angeles	0	1	0–0	0–0	6
Bob Reinhard, Los Angeles	0	1	0–0	0–0	6
Spiro Dellerba, Cleveland	1	0	0–0	0–0	6
Jim Dewar, Cleveland	1	0	0–0	0–0	6
Charlie O'Rourke, LA	1	0	0–0	0–0	6
Tony Adamle, Cleveland	1	0	0–0	0–0	6
Bob Dove, Chicago	0	1	0–0	0–0	6
Dewey Proctor, New York	1	0	0–0	0–0	6
Hub Bechtol, Baltimore	0	1	0–0	0–0	6
George Koch, Buffalo	1	0	0–0	0–0	6
Saxon Judd, Brooklyn	0	1	0–0	0–0	6
Chet Adams, Cleveland	0	0	1–2	1–1	4
Los Angeles Safeties (2)	0	0	0–0	0–0	4
Ernie Case, Baltimore	0	0	1–1	1–1	4
Baltimore Safety	0	0	0–0	0–0	2
Chicago Safety	0	0	0–0	0–0	2
New York Safety	0	0	0–0	0–0	2
Steve Nemeth, Baltimore	0	0	1–1	0–1	1
Angelo Bertelli, Chicago	0	0	0–0	0–1	0

*Joe Aguirre had three receptions for 61 yards and a touchdown credited to Bob Nelson in the official records. This reflects the corrected statistics. This happened in game one of the season.

**Bill Daley had three pass completions out of six pass attempts for 70 yards, a touchdown and an interception in the official records. These statistics should have been for Al Dekdebrun. This reflects the corrected statistics. This happened in game seven of the season. This occurred in game seven of the season.

1948

Players are ranked based on total yards, except in pass receiving, interception returns, punting, points after touchdown and field goals. Those are ranked based on total number. Scoring is based on points.

Total Offense Leaders

	# of Plays	Rush	Pass	Tot	Avg Gain
		(Net Yards Gained)			
Glenn Dobbs, Los Angeles	460	539	2,403	2,942	6.40
Otto Graham, Cleveland	356	146	2,713	2,859	8.03
Y.A. Tittle, Baltimore	341	157	2,522	2,679	7.86
George Ratterman, Buffalo	347	–18	2,577	2,559	7.37
Frankie Albert, SF	333	349	1,990	2,339	7.02
Bob Chappuis, Brooklyn	265	310	1,402	1,712	6.46
Spec Sanders, New York	337	759	918	1,677	4.98
Jesse Freitas, Chicago	191	25	1,425	1,450	7.59
Bob Hoernschemeyer, Brooklyn	265	574	854	1,428	5.39
Pete Layden, New York	200	576	816	1,392	6.96
Marion Motley, Cleveland	158	964	0	964	6.10
John Strzykalski, SF	142	915	0	915	6.44
Chet Mutryn, Buffalo	153	823	21	844	5.52
Lou Tomasetti, Buffalo	134	716	0	716	5.34
Mickey Colmer, Brooklyn	165	704	0	704	4.27
Bus Mertes, Baltimore	155	680	0	680	4.39
Sam Vacanti, Chicago	123	7	633	640	5.20
Joe Perry, San Francisco	77	562	0	562	7.30
Billy Hillenbrand, Baltimore	100	510	0	510	5.10
Bob Pfohl, Baltimore	107	455	0	455	4.25
Julie Rykovich, Buffalo–Chi	97	425	12	437	4.51
Bob Steuber, Buffalo	71	437	–4	433	6.10
Forrest Hall, San Francisco	66	413	0	413	6.26
Edgar Jones, Cleveland	100	400	0	400	4.00
Charlie O'Rourke, Baltimore	58	15	377	392	6.76

Rushing

	Rush	Yds	Avg Gain	TD
Marion Motley, Cleveland	157	964	6.14	5
John Strzykalski, San Francisco	141	915	6.49	4
Chet Mutryn, Buffalo	147	823	5.60	10
Spec Sanders, New York	169	759	4.49	9
Lou Tomasetti, Buffalo	134	716	5.34	7
Mickey Colmer, Brooklyn	164	704	4.29	6
Bus Mertes, Baltimore	155	680	4.39	4
Pete Layden, New York	95	576	6.06	3
Bob Hoernschemeyer, Brooklyn	110	574	5.22	3
Joe Perry, San Francisco	77	562	7.30	10
Glenn Dobbs, Los Angeles	91	539	5.92	4
Billy Hillenbrand, Baltimore	100	510	5.10	7
Bob Pfohl, Baltimore	107	455	4.25	4
Bob Steuber, Buffalo	69	437	6.33	3
Julie Rykovich, Buffalo–Chicago	96	425	4.43	6
Forrest Hall, San Francisco	66	413	6.26	2
Edgar Jones, Cleveland	100	400	4.00	5
Frankie Albert, San Francisco	69	349	5.06	8
Verl Lillywhite, San Francisco	53	340	6.42	3
Bob Chappuis, Brooklyn	52	310	5.96	1
Len Eshmont, San Francisco	50	296	5.92	1
Walt Clay, Los Angeles	86	293	3.41	3
Eddie Prokop, Chicago	54	266	4.93	1
Norm Standlee, San Francisco	52	261	5.02	3
Bill Boedeker, Cleveland	78	254	3.26	3
Herm Wedemeyer, Los Angeles	79	249	3.15	0
Buddy Young, New York	70	245	3.50	1
Jim Mello, Chicago	50	243	4.86	1
Bill Gompers, Buffalo	48	219	4.56	1
Lu Gambino, Baltimore	54	194	3.59	1
Dewey Proctor, Chicago	47	190	4.04	1
John Kimbrough, Los Angeles	76	189	2.49	3
Chuck Fenenbock, Chicago	43	174	4.05	0
Bob Livingstone, Chicago	55	174	3.16	0
Y.A. Tittle, Baltimore	52	157	3.02	4
Vic Kulbitski, Buffalo	40	152	3.80	0
Dub Jones, Cleveland	33	149	4.52	1
Jim Cason, San Francisco	20	146	7.30	2
Otto Graham, Cleveland	23	146	6.35	6
Ara Parseghian, Cleveland	32	135	4.22	1
Ollie Cline, Cleveland	29	129	4.45	0
Eddie Carr, San Francisco	14	121	8.64	1
Bob Sullivan, San Francisco	33	121	3.67	0
Floyd Simmons, Chicago	36	121	3.36	1
Bill Daley, New York	40	102	2.55	1
Bob Cowan, Cleveland	33	99	3.00	1
Bill Kellagher, Chicago	33	97	2.94	1
Lowell Tew, New York	24	95	3.96	5
Elroy Hirsch, Chicago	23	93	4.04	0
Bob H. Kennedy, New York	33	90	2.73	1
Tony Adamle, Cleveland	17	88	5.18	1
Jake Leicht, Baltimore	20	88	4.40	1
Rex Bumgardner, Buffalo	14	82	5.86	0
Harry Clarke, LA–Chicago	22	79	3.59	0
Tom Casey, New York	18	75	4.17	0
Joe Vetrano, San Francisco	12	71	5.92	1
Don Schneider, Buffalo	15	70	4.67	0
Mike Graham, Los Angeles	19	69	3.63	1
Jeff Durkota, Los Angeles	14	66	4.71	0
Paul Crowe, San Francisco	12	65	5.42	0
Tom Colella, Cleveland	14	60	4.29	1
Dean Sensanbaugher, Cleveland	18	59	3.28	1
Ernie Lewis, Chicago	13	54	4.15	0
Monk Gafford, Brooklyn	30	51	1.70	1
Ray Ramsey, Brooklyn	22	48	2.18	0
Cliff Lewis, Cleveland	5	44	8.80	0
Jim Camp, Brooklyn	8	43	5.38	0
Lin Sexton, Los Angeles	7	39	5.57	0
Bill Reinhard, Los Angeles	6	31	5.17	0
Aubrey Fowler, Baltimore	6	30	5.00	0
Chick Maggioli, Buffalo	11	27	2.45	0
Lew Mayne, Baltimore	14	26	1.86	0
Jesse Freitas, Chicago	24	25	1.04	0
Al Dekdebrun, New York	7	24	3.43	0
Hardy Brown, Brooklyn	6	23	3.83	1
Bob Reinhard, Los Angeles	1	21	21.00	0
Steve Juzwik, Chicago	13	19	1.46	0
Walt McDonald, Brooklyn	6	15	2.50	0
Charlie O'Rourke, Baltimore	7	15	2.14	1
Johnny Vardian, Baltimore	6	13	2.17	0
John Wozniak, Brooklyn	10	13	—	0
Walt Heap, Los Angeles	3	12	4.00	0
Len Masini, Los Angeles	3	12	4.00	0
Dick Ottele, Los Angeles	2	11	5.50	0
Hugo Marcolini, Brooklyn	5	11	2.20	0
Bob Kelly, Los Angeles	3	10	3.33	0
Carl Allen, Brooklyn	1	9	9.00	0
Dante Lavelli, Cleveland	1	9	9.00	0
Tommy James, Cleveland	1	8	8.00	0
Ed Gustafson, Brooklyn	1	7	7.00	0
Bob Smith, Buffalo	1	7	7.00	0
Mac Speedie, Cleveland	1	7	7.00	0
Sam Vacanti, Chicago	7	7	1.00	2
Bud Schwenk, New York	3	6	2.00	0
Ralph Sazio, Brooklyn	0	5	—	0
Tom Farris, Chicago	4	5	1.25	0
Nick Forkovitch, Brooklyn	1	4	4.00	0
George Terlep, Cleveland	1	4	4.00	0
Bob Sweiger, New York	3	4	1.33	0
Bob Gaudio, Cleveland	1	2	2.00	0
Bev Wallace, San Francisco	3	2	0.67	0
Gail Bruce, San Francisco	1	1	1.00	0
Joe Smith, Baltimore	1	1	1.00	0
Morrie Warren, Brooklyn	1	1	1.00	0
Lloyd Cheatham, New York	2	1	0.50	0
Bob Perina, Chicago	6	1	0.17	0
Johnny Naumu, Los Angeles	1	0	0.00	0
Spiro Dellerba, Baltimore	2	0	0.00	0
Angelo Bertelli, Chicago	2	-1	-0.50	0
Bob Sullivan, Brooklyn	2	-1	-0.50	0
Bob Mitchell, Los Angeles	2	-2	-1.00	0
Rex Grossman, Baltimore	8	-3	-0.38	0
Harry Burrus, Brooklyn	1	-3	-3.00	0
Bob Nelson, Los Angeles	1	-7	-7.00	0
Al Akins, Brooklyn	4	-9	-2.25	0
George Ratterman, Buffalo	12	-18	-1.50	3
Jim Still, Buffalo	5	-26	-5.20	0

Passing

	Comp	Att	Yds	TD	Int
Otto Graham, Cleveland	173	333	2,713	25	15
George Ratterman, Buffalo	168	335	2,577	16	22
Y.A. Tittle, Baltimore	161	289	2,522	16	9
Glenn Dobbs, Los Angeles	185	369	2,403	21	20
Frankie Albert, San Francisco	154	246	1,990	29	10

Part 3: Individual Statistics

	Comp	Att	Yds	TD	Int
Jesse Freitas, Chicago	84	167	1,425	14	16
Bob Chappuis, Brooklyn	100	213	1,402	8	15
Spec Sanders, New York	78	168	918	5	11
Bob Hoernschemeyer, Brklyn	71	155	854	8	15
Pete Layden, New York	43	105	816	9	8
Sam Vacanti, Chicago	47	116	633	2	15
Charlie O'Rourke, Baltimore	24	51	377	3	4
Monk Gafford, Brooklyn	17	39	268	4	2
Al Dekdebrun, New York	10	20	149	0	2
Chuck Fenenbock, Chicago	4	15	136	2	1
Bev Wallace, San Francisco	8	22	114	1	3
Jim Still, Buffalo	5	14	89	1	3
Herm Wedemeyer, Los Angeles	9	30	79	0	3
Cliff Lewis, Cleveland	4	8	69	1	0
Angelo Bertelli, Chicago	7	32	60	1	3
Bud Schwenk, New York	6	17	52	0	3
Tom Casey, New York	2	5	31	1	0
George Terlep, Buffalo–Cleve	1	4	27	0	2
Tom Farris, Chicago	3	9	24	0	3
Chet Mutryn, Buffalo	2	6	21	0	0
Bob Mitchell, Los Angeles	1	2	15	0	1
Julie Rykovich, Chicago	1	1	12	0	0
Mickey Colmer, Brooklyn	0	1	0	0	0
Bob H. Kennedy, New York	0	1	0	0	0
Chick Maggioli, Buffalo	1	1	0	0	0
Marion Motley, Cleveland	0	1	0	0	0
Eddie Prokop, Chicago	0	1	0	0	0
Ray Ramsey, Brooklyn	0	1	0	0	0
John Strzykalski, San Francisco	0	1	0	0	0
Lee Tevis, Brooklyn	0	1	0	0	0
Verl Lillywhite, San Francisco	0	1	0	0	1
Bill Reinhard, Los Angeles	0	5	0	0	0
Bob Steuber, Buffalo	1	2	−4	0	0

Receiving

	Rec	Yds	Avg Gain	TD
Mac Speedie, Cleveland	58	816	14.1	4
Al Baldwin, Buffalo	54	916	17.0	8
Billy Hillenbrand, Baltimore	50	970	19.4	6
Fay King, Chicago	50	647	12.9	7
Alyn Beals, San Francisco	45	591	12.8	14
Lamar Davis, Baltimore	41	765	18.7	7
Chet Mutryn, Buffalo	39	794	20.4	5
Joe Aguirre, Los Angeles	38	599	15.8	9
Herm Wedemeyer, Los Angeles	36	330	9.2	2
Bruce Alford, New York	32	578	18.1	3
Windell Williams, Baltimore	32	360	11.3	2
Saxon Judd, Brooklyn	32	350	10.9	2
Len Ford, Los Angeles	31	598	19.3	7
Zeke O'Connor, Buffalo	31	301	9.7	2
Max Morris, Brooklyn	28	372	13.3	1
Dale Gentry, Los Angeles	28	308	11.0	0
Nick Susoeff, San Francisco	27	237	8.8	1
John Strzykalski, San Francisco	26	485	18.7	7
Dante Lavelli, Cleveland	25	463	18.5	5
Jack Russell, New York	23	433	18.8	6
Dan Edwards, Brooklyn	23	176	7.7	0
Lou Tomasetti, Buffalo	22	213	9.7	1
Mickey Colmer, Brooklyn	21	372	17.7	4
Buddy Young, New York	21	259	12.3	4
Horace Gillom, Cleveland	20	295	14.8	1
Bob Jensen, Chicago	20	276	13.8	1
Ray Kuffel, Chicago	19	365	19.2	3
Hank Foldberg, Brooklyn	16	129	8.1	0
Monk Gafford, Brooklyn	15	274	18.3	4
Bob Cowan, Cleveland	15	265	17.7	4
Bob Livingstone, Chicago	15	240	16.0	2
Hal Shoener, San Francisco	15	76	5.1	3
Edgar Jones, Cleveland	14	293	20.9	5
Len Eshmont, San Francisco	14	214	15.3	0
Ray Ramsey, Brooklyn	13	315	24.2	2
Bill Boedeker, Cleveland	13	237	18.2	2
Marion Motley, Cleveland	13	192	14.8	2
Bob Pfohl, Baltimore	13	134	10.3	1
Jake Leicht, Baltimore	12	134	11.2	1
Bob Sweiger, New York	12	129	10.8	0
Paul Gibson, Buffalo	11	216	19.6	0
Bob Hoernschemeyer, Brooklyn	11	173	15.7	3
Harry Burrus, Brooklyn	10	227	22.7	1
John Kimbrough, Los Angeles	10	131	13.1	2
Walt Clay, Los Angeles	10	118	11.8	1
Burr Baldwin, Los Angeles	10	96	9.6	0
Dub Jones, Cleveland	9	119	13.2	2
Bill Fisk, Los Angeles	9	102	11.3	0
John North, Baltimore	8	204	25.5	1
Joe Smith, Baltimore	8	131	16.4	1
Chuck Fenenbock, Chicago	8	111	13.9	1
Joe Perry, San Francisco	8	79	9.9	1
Eddie Prokop, Chicago	7	223	31.9	3
Elroy Hirsch, Chicago	7	101	14.4	1
Lowell Tew, New York	7	97	13.9	0
Lloyd Cheatham, New York	7	76	10.9	0
Walt McDonald, Brooklyn	7	41	5.9	1
Lowell Wagner, New York	6	99	16.5	1
Bus Mertes, Baltimore	6	56	9.3	0
Lu Gambino, Baltimore	6	28	4.7	0
Otto Schnellbacher, New York	5	72	14.4	0
Julie Rykovich, Buffalo–Chicago	5	71	14.2	0
Marty Comer, Buffalo	5	66	13.2	1
Gail Bruce, San Francisco	5	49	9.8	0
Bill Reinhard, Los Angeles	5	48	9.6	0
John Yonakor, Cleveland	5	27	5.4	0
Bob H. Kennedy, New York	5	23	4.6	0
Jim Cason, San Francisco	4	99	24.8	1
Forrest Hall, San Francisco	4	87	21.8	0
Bob Sullivan, San Francisco	4	58	14.5	1
Bob Reinhard, Los Angeles	4	54	13.5	0
Van Davis, New York	4	49	12.3	1
Lou Mihajlovich, Los Angeles	4	42	10.5	0
Harry Clarke, Los Angeles–Chicago	4	38	9.5	0
Hal Thompson, Brooklyn	4	37	9.3	1
Paul Cleary, New York	4	37	9.3	0
Bill Daley, New York	4	31	7.8	0
Duke Iverson, New York	4	30	7.5	0
Eddie Carr, San Francisco	3	40	13.3	0
Jim Mello, Chicago	3	38	12.7	0
Vic Kulbitski, Buffalo	3	37	12.3	0
Hardy Brown, Brooklyn	3	36	12.0	1
Jim McCarthy, Chicago	3	30	10.0	0
Walt McDonald, New York	3	30	10.0	0
Johnny Vardian, Baltimore	3	26	8.7	0
Chick Maggioli, Buffalo	3	23	7.7	0
Al Akins, Brooklyn–Buffalo	3	12	4.0	0
Floyd Simmons, Chicago	2	60	30.0	1
Hugo Marcolini, Brooklyn	2	38	19.0	0
Lew Mayne, Baltimore	2	33	16.5	0
Ara Parseghian, Cleveland	2	31	15.5	1

	Rec	Yds	Avg Gain	TD
Hub Bechtol, Baltimore	2	25	12.5	0
George Young, Cleveland	2	20	10.0	0
Dewey Proctor, Chicago	2	18	9.0	0
Bob Steuber, Buffalo	2	14	7.0	0
Bob Perina, Chicago	2	13	6.5	0
Jeff Durkota, Los Angeles	2	12	6.0	0
Glenn Dobbs, Los Angeles	2	11	5.5	0
Walt Heap, Los Angeles	2	9	4.5	0
Rex Bumgardner, Buffalo	1	63	63.0	0
Tommy James, Cleveland	1	44	44.0	0
Jim Camp, Brooklyn	1	43	43.0	0
Joe Vetrano, San Francisco	1	34	34.0	0
Bob Nowaskey, Baltimore	1	31	31.0	0
Ned Maloney, San Francisco	1	29	29.0	1
George Kisiday, Buffalo	1	20	20.0	0
Howie Parker, New York	1	17	17.0	0
Don Schneider, Buffalo	1	14	14.0	0
Clarence Howell, San Francisco	1	9	9.0	0
Ted Scruggs, Brooklyn	1	8	8.0	0
Tom Colella, Cleveland	1	7	7.0	0
Harvey Johnson, New York	1	6	6.0	0
Ernie Lewis, Chicago	1	6	6.0	0
Steve Juzwik, Chicago	1	5	5.0	0
Ollie Poole, Baltimore	1	2	2.0	0
Frankie Albert, San Francisco	1	1	1.0	0
Norm Standlee, San Francisco	1	1	1.0	0
Graham Armstrong, Buffalo	1	0	0.0	0
Verl Lillywhite, San Francisco	1	-1	-1.0	0
Len Masini, Los Angeles	1	-1	-1.0	0
Lee Tevis, Brooklyn	1	-8	-8.0	0
Paul Crowe, San Francisco	0	16	—	1
Mike Perrotti, Los Angeles	0	7	—	0
Jack Flagerman, Los Angeles	0	6	—	0
Hank Rockwell, Los Angeles	0	6	—	0
Mike Graham, Los Angeles	0	2	—	0
Art Statuto, Buffalo	0	2	—	0

Punting

	Punts	Avg	Had Blocked
Glenn Dobbs, Los Angeles	68	49.1	3
Charlie O'Rourke, Baltimore	66	38.6	1
Ernie Lewis, Chicago	60	44.7	0
Mickey Colmer, Brooklyn	56	42.5	2
Tom Colella, Cleveland	49	35.0	0
Jim Still, Buffalo	47	38.8	0
Spec Sanders, New York	42	40.6	0
Frankie Albert, San Francisco	35	44.8	0
Pete Layden, New York	21	42.1	0
Bob Smith, Buffalo-Brooklyn	14	38.4	1
Bob H. Kennedy, New York	7	33.9	0
Tom Casey, New York	6	40.3	0
Horace Gillom, Cleveland	6	37.8	0
Bob Reinhard, Los Angeles	6	34.0	0
Lee Tevis, Brooklyn	5	42.8	0
Bev Wallace, San Francisco	5	38.4	0
Verl Lillywhite, San Francisco	3	25.3	0
Chick Maggioli, Buffalo	2	47.5	0
Bill Daley, New York	1	41.0	0
Bob Hoernschemeyer, Brooklyn	1	40.0	0
Bob Steuber, Buffalo	1	40.0	0
Joe Vetrano, San Francisco	1	38.0	0
Johnny Naumu, Los Angeles	1	34.0	0
Cliff Lewis, Cleveland	1	18.0	0
Herm Wedemeyer, Los Angeles	1	10.0	0

Interceptions

	Int	Yds	Avg Return	TD
Otto Schnellbacher, New York	11	239	21.7	1
Cliff Lewis, Cleveland	9	103	11.4	0
Eddie Carr, San Francisco	7	144	20.6	1
Ray Ramsey, Brooklyn	7	124	17.7	0
Bob Perina, Chicago	6	87	14.5	0
Lamar Davis, Baltimore	5	110	22.0	0
Walt Heap, Los Angeles	5	94	18.8	1
Jake Leicht, Baltimore	5	91	18.2	0
Paul Crowe, San Francisco	5	69	13.8	1
Jim Cason, San Francisco	5	46	9.2	0
Lou Saban, Cleveland	5	41	8.2	0
Fred Negus, Chicago	5	30	6.0	0
Carl Schuette, Buffalo	4	97	24.3	1
George Strohmeyer, Brooklyn	4	79	19.8	0
Bill Reinhard, Los Angeles	4	52	13.0	1
Bob H. Kennedy, New York	4	49	12.3	0
Tommy James, Cleveland	4	37	9.3	0
Bob Smith, Buffalo-Brooklyn	4	29	7.3	0
Harry Burrus, Brooklyn	3	82	27.3	0
Julie Rykovich, Chicago	3	65	21.7	0
Pete Layden, New York	3	63	21.0	0
Alex Wizbicki, Buffalo	3	49	16.3	0
Verl Lillywhite, San Francisco	3	26	8.7	0
Walt McDonald, Brooklyn	3	21	7.0	0
John Strzykalski, San Francisco	3	21	7.0	0
Bob Kelly, Los Angeles	3	14	4.7	0
Bob Mitchell, Los Angeles	3	1	0.3	0
Aubrey Fowler, Baltimore	3	0	0.0	0
Bill Gompers, Buffalo	2	74	37.0	0
Elroy Hirsch, Chicago	2	59	29.5	0
Carl Allen, Brooklyn	2	45	22.5	1
Tom Colella, Cleveland	2	34	17.0	0
Walt Clay, Los Angeles	2	33	16.5	0
Spiro Dellerba, Baltimore	2	18	9.0	0
Rex Grossman, Baltimore	2	13	6.5	0
Rex Bumgardner, Buffalo	2	7	3.5	0
Riley Matheson, San Francisco	2	4	2.0	0
Jim Camp, Brooklyn	1	69	69.0	0
Ara Parseghian, Cleveland	1	56	56.0	0
Jim Still, Buffalo	1	37	37.0	0
Glenn Dobbs, Los Angeles	1	32	32.0	0
Lowell Wagner, New York	1	31	31.0	0
Lin Sexton, Los Angeles	1	30	30.0	0
John North, Baltimore	1	25	25.0	0
Joe Perry, San Francisco	1	24	24.0	0
Spec Sanders, New York	1	24	24.0	0
Mike Graham, Los Angeles	1	20	20.0	0
Jeff Durkota, Los Angeles	1	18	18.0	0
Al Dekdebrun, New York	1	16	16.0	0
Don Clark, San Francisco	1	12	12.0	0
Joe Magliolo, New York	1	12	12.0	0
Weldon Humble, Cleveland	1	11	11.0	0
Charley Riffle, New York	1	11	11.0	0
Roland Nabors, New York	1	10	10.0	0
Chick Maggioli, Buffalo	1	7	7.0	0
John Wozniak, Brooklyn	1	7	7.0	0
Bob Sullivan, San Francisco	1	6	6.0	0

Part 3: Individual Statistics

	Int	Yds	Avg Return	TD
Van Davis, New York	1	5	5.0	0
Clarence Howell, San Francisco	1	5	5.0	0
Len McCormick, Baltimore	1	5	5.0	0
Gasper Urban, Chicago	1	5	5.0	0
John Brown, Los Angeles	1	1	1.0	0
Duke Iverson, New York	1	1	1.0	0
Emil Uremovich, Chicago	1	1	1.0	0
John Yonakor, Cleveland	1	1	1.0	0
Dick Barwegan, Baltimore	1	0	0.0	0
Hardy Brown, Brooklyn	1	0	0.0	0
Dutch Elston, San Francisco	1	0	0.0	0
Len Eshmont, San Francisco	1	0	0.0	0
Len Ford, Los Angeles	1	0	0.0	0
Otto Graham, Cleveland	1	0	0.0	0
Bill Johnson, San Francisco	1	0	0.0	0
Pete Lamana, Chicago	1	0	0.0	0
Bob Nelson, Los Angeles	1	0	0.0	0
Jack Russell, New York	1	0	0.0	0
Joe Smith, Baltimore	1	0	0.0	0
John Sylvester, Baltimore	1	0	0.0	0
Vince Mazza, Buffalo	0	5	—	0
Bob Perina, Chicago	2	14	7.0	0
Al Dekdebrun, New York	1	12	12.0	0
Otto Graham, Cleveland	1	12	12.0	0
Harmon Rowe, New York	1	12	12.0	0
Buddy Young, New York	2	11	5.5	0
Lamar Davis, Baltimore	1	10	10.0	0
Bill Gompers, Buffalo	1	10	10.0	0
Doyle Tackett, Brooklyn	1	10	10.0	0
Bob Chappuis, Brooklyn	1	8	8.0	0
Bill Boedeker, Cleveland	2	8	4.0	0
George Strohmeyer, Brooklyn	1	5	5.0	0
Don Schneider, Buffalo	1	4	4.0	0
Bob Hoernschemeyer, Brooklyn	1	3	3.0	0
John Kerns, Buffalo	0	2	—	0
Bob Smith, Buffalo	1	1	1.0	0
Chick Maggioli, Buffalo	1	0	0.0	0

Punt Returns

	Ret	Yds	Avg Ret	TD
Herm Wedemeyer, Los Angeles	23	368	16.0	0
Rex Bumgardner, Buffalo	16	336	21.0	2
Jim Cason, San Francisco	22	309	14.0	0
Bill Reinhard, Los Angeles	16	276	17.3	1
Cliff Lewis, Cleveland	26	258	9.9	0
Billy Hillenbrand, Baltimore	18	231	12.8	0
Tom Casey, New York	9	229	25.4	1
John Strzykalski, San Francisco	13	201	15.5	0
Chet Mutryn, Buffalo	10	171	17.1	1
Chuck Fenenbock, Chicago	17	169	9.9	0
Jake Leicht, Baltimore	8	139	17.4	0
Monk Gafford, Brooklyn	14	130	9.3	0
Spec Sanders, New York	13	128	9.8	0
Bob Pfohl, Baltimore	2	102	51.0	1
Forrest Hall, San Francisco	3	97	32.3	0
Ray Ramsey, Brooklyn	5	82	16.4	1
Eddie Prokop, Chicago	6	80	13.3	0
Pete Layden, New York	7	64	9.1	0
Tom Colella, Cleveland	5	60	12.0	0
Lee Tevis, Brooklyn	6	59	9.8	0
Lin Sexton, Los Angeles	3	47	15.7	0
Tommy James, Cleveland	5	47	9.4	0
Otto Schnellbacher, New York	5	45	9.0	0
Verl Lillywhite, San Francisco	3	41	13.7	0
Aubrey Fowler, Baltimore	4	41	10.3	0
Johnny Vardian, Baltimore	3	34	11.3	0
Alex Wizbicki, Buffalo	3	33	11.0	0
Harry Clarke, LA–Chicago	2	27	13.5	0
Elroy Hirsch, Chicago	2	27	13.5	0
Lew Mayne, Baltimore	2	24	12.0	0
Bob Livingstone, Chicago	3	24	8.0	0
Bob Reinhard, Los Angeles	1	23	23.0	0
Julie Rykovich, Chicago	1	23	23.0	0
Carl Allen, Brooklyn	1	17	17.0	0
John Sylvester, Baltimore	2	16	8.0	0
Bob Bryant, San Francisco	1	14	14.0	0
Bob H. Kennedy, New York	1	14	14.0	0
Paul Crowe, San Francisco	2	14	7.0	0

Kick Returns

	Ret	Yds	Avg Ret	TD
Monk Gafford, Brooklyn	23	559	24.3	0
Chet Mutryn, Buffalo	19	500	26.3	0
Forrest Hall, San Francisco	13	369	28.4	0
Bob Pfohl, Baltimore	17	366	21.5	0
Billy Hillenbrand, Baltimore	16	356	22.3	0
Marion Motley, Cleveland	14	337	24.1	0
Eddie Prokop, Chicago	15	323	21.5	0
Chuck Fenenbock, Chicago	14	311	22.2	0
Buddy Young, New York	12	303	25.3	0
Herm Wedemeyer, Los Angeles	11	240	21.8	0
Ray Ramsey, Brooklyn	10	233	23.3	0
Spec Sanders, New York	9	217	24.1	0
Jim Cason, San Francisco	10	212	21.2	0
Pete Layden, New York	8	211	26.4	0
Bob Livingstone, Chicago	9	211	23.4	0
Jeff Durkota, Los Angeles	9	198	22.0	0
John Strzykalski, San Francisco	9	185	20.6	0
Tom Casey, New York	7	170	24.3	0
Mickey Colmer, Brooklyn	8	163	20.4	0
Cliff Lewis, Cleveland	7	147	21.0	0
Joe Perry, San Francisco	4	145	36.3	1
Mike Graham, Los Angeles	6	145	24.2	0
Rex Bumgardner, Buffalo	9	141	15.7	0
Bob Hoernschemeyer, Brooklyn	6	138	23.0	0
Johnny Naumu, Los Angeles	6	131	21.8	0
Julie Rykovich, Buffalo–Chicago	7	129	18.4	0
Bob Steuber, Buffalo	6	123	20.5	0
Harry Clarke, LA–Chicago	4	96	24.0	0
Bill Daley, New York	4	88	22.0	0
Jake Leicht, Baltimore	4	83	20.8	0
Floyd Simmons, Chicago	3	77	25.7	0
Don Schneider, Buffalo	4	77	19.3	0
Lowell Tew, New York	3	75	25.0	0
Johnny Vardian, Baltimore	3	66	22.0	0
Bill Gompers, Buffalo	4	62	15.5	0
Lew Mayne, Baltimore	3	61	20.3	0
Bill Boedeker, Cleveland	4	61	15.3	0
Lu Gambino, Baltimore	3	57	19.0	0
Bob Chappuis, Brooklyn	3	55	18.3	0
Ollie Cline, Cleveland	3	55	18.3	0
Bill Kellagher, Chicago	3	54	18.0	0
John Kimbrough, Los Angeles	4	54	13.5	0
Bob Cowan, Cleveland	3	53	17.7	0

	Ret	Yds	Avg Ret	TD
Bob Perina, Chicago	3	52	17.3	0
Bob Reinhard, Los Angeles	3	51	17.0	0
Lin Sexton, Los Angeles	3	49	16.3	0
Walt Clay, Los Angeles	4	48	12.0	0
Dick Ottele, Los Angeles	3	47	15.7	0
Ara Parseghian, Cleveland	2	41	20.5	0
Bill Reinhard, Los Angeles	2	41	20.5	0
Bob Sullivan, San Francisco	2	40	20.0	0
Lee Tevis, Brooklyn	2	40	20.0	0
Joe Vetrano, San Francisco	1	38	38.0	0
Glenn Dobbs, Los Angeles	2	38	19.0	0
Chick Maggioli, Buffalo	2	38	19.0	0
Morrie Warren, Brooklyn	1	36	36.0	0
Dub Jones, Cleveland	2	35	17.5	0
Hugo Marcolini, Brooklyn	2	33	16.5	0
Len Eshmont, San Francisco	1	32	32.0	0
Norm Standlee, San Francisco	1	31	31.0	0
Jim Mello, Chicago	2	30	15.0	0
Len Ford, Los Angeles	1	24	24.0	0
Bob Sullivan, Brooklyn	1	22	22.0	0
Dan Edwards, Brooklyn	1	21	21.0	0
Windell Williams, Baltimore	1	20	20.0	0
Bob H. Kennedy, New York	2	20	10.0	0
Lloyd Cheatham, New York	1	18	18.0	0
Vic Kulbitski, Buffalo	1	18	18.0	0
Paul Crowe, San Francisco	2	18	9.0	0
Eddie Carr, San Francisco	1	16	16.0	0
Ray Kuffel, Chicago	1	16	16.0	0
Aubrey Fowler, Baltimore	2	16	8.0	0
Al Dekdebrun, New York	1	15	15.0	0
Bus Mertes, Baltimore	1	15	15.0	0
Max Morris, Brooklyn	1	14	14.0	0
Lou Tomasetti, Buffalo	2	14	7.0	0
Mac Speedie, Cleveland	1	13	13.0	0
Jim Camp, Brooklyn	1	12	12.0	0
Spiro Dellerba, Baltimore	1	12	12.0	0
Nick Susoeff, San Francisco	1	12	12.0	0
Fay King, Chicago	1	11	11.0	0
Joe Aguirre, Los Angeles	1	10	10.0	0
Amos Harris, Brooklyn	1	10	10.0	0
Elroy Hirsch, Chicago	1	10	10.0	0
Bob Jensen, Chicago	1	10	10.0	0
Horace Gillom, Cleveland	3	10	3.3	0
Graham Armstrong, Buffalo	1	9	9.0	0
Paul Cleary, New York	1	8	8.0	0
Dub Garrett, Baltimore	1	6	6.0	0
Hub Bechtol, Baltimore	0	4	—	0
John Kerns, Buffalo	1	3	3.0	0
Bob Sweiger, New York	1	3	3.0	0
Dante Lavelli, Cleveland	1	0	0.0	0
Zeke O'Connor, Buffalo	1	0	0.0	0

Total Returns (Punt and Kick)

	Ret	Yds	Avg Ret	TD
Monk Gafford, Brooklyn	37	689	18.6	0
Chet Mutryn, Buffalo	29	671	23.1	1
Herm Wedemeyer, Los Angeles	34	608	17.9	0
Billy Hillenbrand, Baltimore	34	587	17.3	0
Jim Cason, San Francisco	32	521	16.3	0
Chuck Fenenbock, Chicago	31	480	15.5	0
Rex Bumgardner, Buffalo	25	477	19.1	2
Bob Pfohl, Baltimore	19	468	24.6	1

	Ret	Yds	Avg Ret	TD
Forrest Hall, San Francisco	16	466	29.1	0
Cliff Lewis, Cleveland	33	405	12.3	0
Eddie Prokop, Chicago	21	403	19.2	0
Tom Casey, New York	16	399	24.9	1
John Strzykalski, San Francisco	22	386	17.5	0
Spec Sanders, New York	22	345	15.7	0
Marion Motley, Cleveland	14	337	24.1	0
Bill Reinhard, Los Angeles	18	317	17.6	1
Ray Ramsey, Brooklyn	15	315	21.0	1
Buddy Young, New York	14	314	22.4	0
Pete Layden, New York	15	275	18.3	0
Bob Livingstone, Chicago	12	235	19.6	0
Jake Leicht, Baltimore	12	222	18.5	0
Jeff Durkota, Los Angeles	9	198	22.0	0
Mickey Colmer, Brooklyn	8	163	20.4	0
Julie Rykovich, Buffalo-Chicago	8	152	19.0	0
Joe Perry, San Francisco	4	145	36.3	1
Mike Graham, Los Angeles	6	145	24.2	0
Bob Hoernschemeyer, Brooklyn	7	141	20.1	0
Johnny Naumu, Los Angeles	6	131	21.8	0
Harry Clarke, Los Angeles-Chicago	6	123	20.5	0
Bob Steuber, Buffalo	6	123	20.5	0
Johnny Vardian, Baltimore	6	100	16.7	0
Lee Tevis, Brooklyn	8	99	12.4	0
Lin Sexton, Los Angeles	6	96	16.0	0
Bill Daley, New York	4	88	22.0	0
Lew Mayne, Baltimore	5	85	17.0	0
Don Schneider, Buffalo	5	81	16.2	0
Floyd Simmons, Chicago	3	77	25.7	0
Lowell Tew, New York	3	75	25.0	0
Bob Reinhard, Los Angeles	4	74	18.5	0
Bill Gompers, Buffalo	5	72	14.4	0
Bill Boedeker, Cleveland	6	69	11.5	0
Bob Perina, Chicago	5	66	13.2	0
Bob Chappuis, Brooklyn	4	63	15.8	0
Tom Colella, Cleveland	5	60	12.0	0
Lu Gambino, Baltimore	3	57	19.0	0
Aubrey Fowler, Baltimore	6	57	9.5	0
Ollie Cline, Cleveland	3	55	18.3	0
Bill Kellagher, Chicago	3	54	18.0	0
John Kimbrough, Los Angeles	4	54	13.5	0
Bob Cowan, Cleveland	3	53	17.7	0
Walt Clay, Los Angeles	4	48	12.0	0
Dick Ottele, Los Angeles	3	47	15.7	0
Tommy James, Cleveland	5	47	9.4	0
Otto Schnellbacher, New York	5	45	9.0	0
Ara Parseghian, Cleveland	2	41	20.5	0
Verl Lillywhite, San Francisco	3	41	13.7	0
Bob Sullivan, San Francisco	2	40	20.0	0
Joe Vetrano, San Francisco	1	38	38.0	0
Glenn Dobbs, Los Angeles	2	38	19.0	0
Chick Maggioli, Buffalo	3	38	12.7	0
Elroy Hirsch, Chicago	3	37	12.3	0
Morrie Warren, Brooklyn	1	36	36.0	0
Dub Jones, Cleveland	2	35	17.5	0
Bob H. Kennedy, New York	3	34	11.3	0
Hugo Marcolini, Brooklyn	2	33	16.5	0
Alex Wizbicki, Buffalo	3	33	11.0	0
Len Eshmont, San Francisco	1	32	32.0	0
Paul Crowe, San Francisco	4	32	8.0	0
Norm Standlee, San Francisco	1	31	31.0	0
Jim Mello, Chicago	2	30	15.0	0
Al Dekdebrun, New York	2	27	13.5	0
Len Ford, Los Angeles	1	24	24.0	0

Part 3: Individual Statistics

	Ret	Yds	Avg Ret	TD
Bob Sullivan, Brooklyn	1	22	22.0	0
Dan Edwards, Brooklyn	1	21	21.0	0
Windell Williams, Baltimore	1	20	20.0	0
Lloyd Cheatham, New York	1	18	18.0	0
Vic Kulbitski, Buffalo	1	18	18.0	0
Carl Allen, Brooklyn	1	17	17.0	0
Eddie Carr, San Francisco	1	16	16.0	0
Ray Kuffel, Chicago	1	16	16.0	0
John Sylvester, Baltimore	2	16	8.0	0
Bus Mertes, Baltimore	1	15	15.0	0
Bob Bryant, San Francisco	1	14	14.0	0
Max Morris, Brooklyn	1	14	14.0	0
Lou Tomasetti, Buffalo	2	14	7.0	0
Mac Speedie, Cleveland	1	13	13.0	0
Jim Camp, Brooklyn	1	12	12.0	0
Spiro Dellerba, Baltimore	1	12	12.0	0
Otto Graham, Cleveland	1	12	12.0	0
Harmon Rowe, New York	1	12	12.0	0
Nick Susoeff, San Francisco	1	12	12.0	0
Fay King, Chicago	1	11	11.0	0
Joe Aguirre, Los Angeles	1	10	10.0	0
Lamar Davis, Baltimore	1	10	10.0	0
Amos Harris, Brooklyn	1	10	10.0	0
Bob Jensen, Chicago	1	10	10.0	0
Doyle Tackett, Brooklyn	1	10	10.0	0
Horace Gillom, Cleveland	3	10	3.3	0
Graham Armstrong, Buffalo	1	9	9.0	0
Paul Cleary, New York	1	8	8.0	0
Dub Garrett, Baltimore	1	6	6.0	0
George Strohmeyer, Brooklyn	1	5	5.0	0
John Kerns, Buffalo	1	5	3.0	0
Hub Bechtol, Baltimore	0	4	—	0
Bob Sweiger, New York	1	3	3.0	0
Bob Smith, Buffalo	1	1	1.0	0
Dante Lavelli, Cleveland	1	0	0.0	0
Zeke O'Connor, Buffalo	1	0	0.0	0

Point After Touchdowns

	Made	Att	%
Joe Vetrano, San Francisco	62	66	93.9
Lou Groza, Cleveland	51	52	98.1
Rex Grossman, Baltimore	43	43	100.0
Harvey Johnson, New York	37	37	100.0
Ben Agajanian, Los Angeles	31	32	96.9
Hardy Brown, Brooklyn	25	29	86.2
Jim McCarthy, Chicago	21	21	100.0
Bob Steuber, Buffalo	20	23	87.0
Graham Armstrong, Buffalo	15	17	88.2
Vic Kulbitski, Buffalo	8	10	80.0
Steve Juzwik, Chicago	5	5	100.0
Lee Tevis, Brooklyn	4	4	100.0
Farnham Johnson, Chicago	2	2	100.0
Joe Aguirre, Los Angeles	2	3	66.7
Harry Burrus, Brooklyn	2	3	66.7
Ned Maloney, San Francisco	1	1	100.0
Frankie Albert, San Francisco	1	2	50.0
Al Baldwin, Buffalo	0	1	0.0
Bob Stefik, Buffalo	0	1	0.0

Field Goals

	Made	Att	%
Rex Grossman, Baltimore	10	18	55.6
Lou Groza, Cleveland	8	19	42.1
Joe Vetrano, San Francisco	5	8	62.5
Ben Agajanian, Los Angeles	5	15	33.3
Jim McCarthy, Chicago	2	3	66.7
Harvey Johnson, New York	2	7	28.6
Lee Tevis, Brooklyn	2	7	28.6
Bob Steuber, Buffalo	1	2	50.0
Graham Armstrong, Buffalo	0	1	0.0
Hardy Brown, Brooklyn	0	1	0.0
Julie Rykovich, Chicago	0	1	0.0

Scoring

	TD Rush	TD Pass	Pts After TD	FG	Tot Pts
Chet Mutryn, Buffalo	11	5	0–0	0–0	96
Alyn Beals, San Francisco	0	14	0–0	0–0	84
Joe Vetrano, San Francisco	1	0	62–66	5–8	83
Billy Hillenbrand, Baltimore	7	6	0–0	0–0	78
Lou Groza, Cleveland	0	0	51–52	8–19	75
Rex Grossman, Baltimore	0	0	43–43	10–18	73
Joe Perry, San Francisco	11	1	0–0	0–0	72
John Strzykalski, SF	4	7	0–0	0–0	66
Edgar Jones, Cleveland	5	5	0–0	0–0	60
Mickey Colmer, Brooklyn	6	4	0–0	0–0	60
Joe Aguirre, Los Angeles	0	9	2–3	0–0	56
Spec Sanders, New York	9	0	0–0	0–0	54
Frankie Albert, SF	8	0	1–2	0–0	49
Al Baldwin, Buffalo	0	8	0–1	0–0	48
Lou Tomasetti, Buffalo	7	1	0–0	0–0	48
Ben Agajanian, Los Angeles	0	0	31–32	5–15	46
Harvey Johnson, New York	0	0	37–37	2–7	43
Lamar Davis, Baltimore	0	7	0–0	0–0	42
Marion Motley, Cleveland	5	2	0–0	0–0	42
Bob Hoernschemeyer, Brklyn	4	3	0–0	0–0	42
Len Ford, Los Angeles	0	7	0–0	0–0	42
Fay King, Chicago	0	7	0–0	0–0	42
Bob Steuber, Buffalo	3	0	20–23	1–2	41
Hardy Brown, Brooklyn	1	1	25–29	0–1	37
Jack Russell, New York	0	6	0–0	0–0	36
Otto Graham, Cleveland	6	0	0–0	0–0	36
Bob Pfohl, Baltimore	5	1	0–0	0–0	36
Julie Rykovich, Buf–Chi	6	0	0–0	0–1	36
Monk Gafford, Brooklyn	1	4	0–0	0–0	30
Buddy Young, New York	1	4	0–0	0–0	30
Lowell Tew, New York	5	0	0–0	0–0	30
Bill Boedeker, Cleveland	3	2	0–0	0–0	30
John Kimbrough, LA	3	2	0–0	0–0	30
Bob Cowan, Cleveland	1	4	0–0	0–0	30
Dante Lavelli, Cleveland	0	5	0–0	0–0	30
Jim McCarthy, Chicago	0	0	21–21	2–3	27
Y.A. Tittle, Baltimore	4	0	0–0	0–0	24
Eddie Prokop, Chicago	1	3	0–0	0–0	24
Walt Clay, Los Angeles	3	1	0–0	0–0	24
Glenn Dobbs, Los Angeles	4	0	0–0	0–0	24
Bus Mertes, Baltimore	4	0	0–0	0–0	24
Mac Speedie, Cleveland	0	4	0–0	0–0	24
George Ratterman, Buffalo	3	0	0–0	0–0	18
Bruce Alford, New York	0	3	0–0	0–0	18
Hal Shoener, San Francisco	0	3	0–0	0–0	18
Verl Lillywhite, SF	3	0	0–0	0–0	18
Ray Ramsey, Brooklyn	1	2	0–0	0–0	18
Jim Cason, San Francisco	2	1	0–0	0–0	18
Pete Layden, New York	3	0	0–0	0–0	18
Dub Jones, Cleveland	1	2	0–0	0–0	18

	TD Rush	TD Pass	Pts After TD	FG	Tot Pts
Norm Standlee, SF	3	0	0–0	0–0	18
Ray Kuffel, Chicago	0	3	0–0	0–0	18
Graham Armstrong, Buffalo	0	0	15–17	0–1	15
Vic Kulbitski, Buffalo	1	0	8–10	0–0	14
Sam Vacanti, Chicago	2	0	0–0	0–0	12
Saxon Judd, Brooklyn	0	2	0–0	0–0	12
John North, Baltimore	1	1	0–0	0–0	12
Forrest Hall, San Francisco	2	0	0–0	0–0	12
Herm Wedemeyer, LA	0	2	0–0	0–0	12
Bob Livingstone, Chicago	0	2	0–0	0–0	12
Rex Bumgardner, Buffalo	2	0	0–0	0–0	12
Jake Leicht, Baltimore	1	1	0–0	0–0	12
Floyd Simmons, Chicago	1	1	0–0	0–0	12
Ara Parseghian, Cleveland	1	1	0–0	0–0	12
Bill Reinhard, Los Angeles	2	0	0–0	0–0	12
Len Eshmont, San Francisco	2	0	0–0	0–0	12
Windell Williams, Baltimore	0	2	0–0	0–0	12
Paul Crowe, San Francisco	1	1	0–0	0–0	12
Eddie Carr, San Francisco	2	0	0–0	0–0	12
Zeke O'Connor, Buffalo	0	2	0–0	0–0	12
Lee Tevis, Brooklyn	0	0	4–4	2–7	10
Harry Burrus, Brooklyn	0	1	2–3	0–0	8
Ned Maloney, San Francisco	0	1	1–1	0–0	7
Tony Adamle, Cleveland	1	0	0–0	0–0	6
Dean Sensanbaugher, Cleve	1	0	0–0	0–0	6
Hank Foldberg, Brooklyn	1	0	0–0	0–0	6
Marty Comer, Buffalo	0	1	0–0	0–0	6
Hal Thompson, Brooklyn	0	1	0–0	0–0	6
George Young, Cleveland	1	0	0–0	0–0	6
Dewey Proctor, Chicago	1	0	0–0	0–0	6
Charlie O'Rourke, Baltimore	1	0	0–0	0–0	6
Walt Heap, Los Angeles	1	0	0–0	0–0	6
Fred Negus, Chicago	1	0	0–0	0–0	6
Carl Schuette, Buffalo	1	0	0–0	0–0	6
Walt McDonald, Brooklyn	0	1	0–0	0–0	6
Lowell Wagner, New York	0	1	0–0	0–0	6
Van Davis, New York	0	1	0–0	0–0	6
Joe Smith, Baltimore	0	1	0–0	0–0	6
Vince Mazza, Buffalo	1	0	0–0	0–0	6
Tom Colella, Cleveland	1	0	0–0	0–0	6
Otto Schnellbacher, NY	1	0	0–0	0–0	6
Carl Allen, Brooklyn	1	0	0–0	0–0	6
Chuck Fenenbock, Chicago	0	1	0–0	0–0	6
Tom Casey, New York	1	0	0–0	0–0	6
Mike Graham, Los Angeles	1	0	0–0	0–0	6
Bill Daley, New York	1	0	0–0	0–0	6
Bill Gompers, Buffalo	1	0	0–0	0–0	6
Lu Gambino, Baltimore	1	0	0–0	0–0	6
Bob Chappuis, Brooklyn	1	0	0–0	0–0	6
Bill Kellagher, Chicago	1	0	0–0	0–0	6
Bob Sullivan, San Francisco	0	1	0–0	0–0	6
Jim Mello, Chicago	1	0	0–0	0–0	6
Bob H. Kennedy, New York	1	0	0–0	0–0	6
Max Morris, Brooklyn	0	1	0–0	0–0	6
Nick Susoeff, San Francisco	0	1	0–0	0–0	6
Bob Jensen, Chicago	0	1	0–0	0–0	6
Horace Gillom, Cleveland	0	1	0–0	0–0	6
Elroy Hirsch, Chicago	0	1	0–0	0–0	6
Steve Juzwik, Chicago	0	0	5–5	0–0	5
Farnham Johnson, Chicago	0	0	2–2	0–0	2
Baltimore Safety	0	0	0–0	0–0	2
Buffalo Safety	0	0	0–0	0–0	2
Cleveland Safety	0	0	0–0	0–0	2
San Francisco Safety	0	0	0–0	0–0	2
Bob Stefik, Buffalo	0	0	0–1	0–0	0

1949

Note: Players are ranked based on total yards, except in pass receiving, interception returns, punting, points after touchdown and field goals. Those are ranked based on total number. Scoring is based on points.

Total Offense Leaders

	# of Plays	Rush	Pass	Tot	Avg Gain
Otto Graham, Cleveland	312	107	2,785	2,892	9.27
Y.A. Tittle, Baltimore	318	89	2,209	2,298	7.23
Frankie Albert, SF	295	249	1,862	2,111	7.16
George Ratterman, Buffalo	288	85	1,777	1,862	6.47
Bob Hoernschemeyer, Chi	300	456	1,063	1,519	5.06
Johnny Clement, Chicago	220	388	906	1,294	5.88
George Taliaferro, LA	219	472	790	1,262	5.76
Glenn Dobbs, Los Angeles	187	161	825	986	5.27
Don Panciera, New York	160	–4	801	797	4.98
Joe Perry, San Francisco	117	783	0	783	6.69
Chet Mutryn, Buffalo	131	696	0	696	5.31
Marion Motley, Cleveland	113	570	0	570	5.04
Billy Grimes, Los Angeles	86	429	105	534	6.21
Ollie Cline, Buffalo	125	518	0	518	4.14
Bob H. Kennedy, New York	119	490	27	517	4.34
Buddy Young, New York	76	495	0	495	6.51
Hosea Rodgers, Los Angeles	132	494	0	494	3.74
Sherman Howard, NY	117	459	0	459	3.92
Sam Cathcart, SF	69	412	0	412	5.97
Rex Bumgardner, Buffalo	101	391	0	391	3.87
Dub Jones, Cleveland	77	312	0	312	4.05
Herm Wedemeyer, Baltimore	65	291	0	291	4.48
John Strzykalski, SF	66	287	0	287	4.35
Bill Boedeker, Cleveland	50	269	0	269	5.38
Verl Lillywhite, SF	69	263	0	263	3.81

Rushing

	Rush	Yds	Avg Gain	TD
Joe Perry, San Francisco	115	783	6.81	8
Chet Mutryn, Buffalo	131	696	5.31	5

Part 3: Individual Statistics

	Rush	Yds	Avg Gain	TD
Marion Motley, Cleveland	113	570	5.04	8
Ollie Cline, Buffalo	125	518	4.14	3
Buddy Young, New York	76	495	6.51	5
Hosea Rodgers, Los Angeles	131	494	3.77	5
Bob H. Kennedy, New York	118	490	4.15	5
George Taliaferro, Los Angeles	95	472	4.97	5
Sherman Howard, New York	117	459	3.92	3
Bob Hoernschemeyer, Chicago	133	456	3.43	2
Billy Grimes, Los Angeles	83	429	5.17	4
Sam Cathcart, San Francisco	69	412	5.97	1
Rex Bumgardner, Buffalo	101	391	3.87	1
Johnny Clement, Chicago	106	388	3.66	5
Dub Jones, Cleveland	77	312	4.05	4
Herm Wedemeyer, Baltimore	64	291	4.55	0
John Strzykalski, San Francisco	66	287	4.35	3
Bill Boedeker, Cleveland	50	269	5.38	1
Verl Lillywhite, San Francisco	69	263	3.81	2
Frankie Albert, San Francisco	35	249	7.11	3
Lou Tomasetti, Buffalo	54	249	4.61	2
Norm Standlee, San Francisco	44	237	5.39	4
Lu Gambino, Baltimore	56	208	3.71	0
Billy Stone, Baltimore	51	205	4.02	2
Bob Pfohl, Baltimore	67	205	3.06	2
Chick Jagade, Baltimore	33	174	5.27	2
Len Eshmont, San Francisco	25	164	6.56	0
Glenn Dobbs, Los Angeles	34	161	4.74	3
Lou Kusserow, New York	39	136	3.49	0
Edgar Jones, Cleveland	43	127	2.95	4
Eddie Carr, San Francisco	19	120	6.32	2
Earl Howell, Los Angeles	31	116	3.74	1
Ed Susteric, Cleveland	23	114	4.96	1
Don Garlin, San Francisco	21	113	5.38	1
Eddie Prokop, New York	31	109	3.52	2
Otto Graham, Cleveland	27	107	3.96	3
Mickey Colmer, New York	36	100	2.78	0
Pete Layden, New York	19	96	5.05	0
Tom Landry, New York	29	91	3.14	0
Y.A. Tittle, Baltimore	29	89	3.07	2
Rip Collins, Chicago	28	88	3.14	0
George Ratterman, Buffalo	36	85	2.36	4
Paul Page, Baltimore	25	81	3.24	0
Jim Cason, San Fransisco	21	70	3.33	1
Lowell Tew, New York	14	65	4.64	1
Tony Adamle, Cleveland	17	64	3.76	0
Joe Sutton, Buffalo	9	63	7.00	0
Duke Iverson, New York	6	50	8.33	0
Joe Vetrano, San Francisco	11	50	4.55	0
Jim Spavital, Los Angeles	15	44	2.93	0
Ernie Lewis, Chicago	11	43	3.91	1
Ray Ramsey, Chicago	32	43	1.34	0
Warren Lahr, Cleveland	9	36	4.00	1
Les Horvath, Cleveland	10	35	3.50	1
Walt Clay, Los Angeles	9	34	3.78	0
Harper Davis, Los Angeles	13	33	2.54	1
Alyn Beals, San Francisco	4	32	8.00	0
Ara Parseghian, Cleveland	12	31	2.58	0
Dick Wilkins, Los Angeles	8	28	3.50	0
Tommy James, Cleveland	10	28	2.80	0
Gil Johnson, New York	3	21	7.00	0
Harmon Rowe, New York	6	21	3.50	0
Vito Kissell, Buffalo	10	19	1.90	0
Larry Joe, Buffalo	2	18	9.00	0
Bob Sweiger, Chicago	3	17	5.67	0
Lowell Wagner, San Francisco	3	17	5.67	0
Bob Kelly, Baltimore	9	17	1.89	0
George Buksar, Chicago	13	16	1.23	1
Shorty McWilliams, Los Angeles	3	15	5.00	0
Noble Doss, New York	5	15	3.00	0
Bob M. Kennedy, Los Angeles	2	14	7.00	0
Frank Aschenbrenner, Chicago	8	14	1.75	0
Jesse Freitas, Buffalo	3	13	4.33	0
Bob Chappuis, Chicago	4	13	3.25	0
Sam Vacanti, Baltimore	7	10	1.43	0
Horace Gillom, Cleveland	2	8	4.00	0
Bus Mertes, Baltimore	11	8	0.73	0
Wilbur Volz, Buffalo	4	7	1.75	1
Jim Still, Buffalo	2	6	3.00	0
Wayne Kingery, Baltimore	3	3	1.00	0
Hardy Brown, Chicago	1	2	2.00	0
Bev Wallace, San Francisco	2	2	1.00	1
Paul Crowe, SF–Los Angeles	3	2	0.67	0
Burr Baldwin, Los Angeles	1	1	1.00	0
Al Baldwin, Buffalo	2	1	0.50	0
Bob Cowan, Baltimore	1	0	0.00	0
Bob Livingstone, Chicago–Buffalo	1	0	0.00	0
Walt McDonald, Chicago	1	0	0.00	0
George Murphy, Los Angeles	1	0	0.00	0
Paul Patterson, Chicago	2	0	0.00	0
Joe Morgan, San Francisco	0	−1	—	0
Lew Holder, Los Angeles	1	−1	−1.00	0
Dewey Proctor, New York	1	−1	−1.00	0
John Donaldson, LA–Chicago	1	−2	−2.00	0
Bob Gaudio, Cleveland	1	−2	−2.00	0
Ed Kelley, Los Angeles	1	−2	−2.00	0
Don Panciera, New York	10	−4	−0.40	0
Jake Leicht, Baltimore	6	−7	−1.17	0
Tom Colella, Buffalo	7	−9	−1.29	0
Alex Wizbicki, Buffalo	5	−10	−2.00	0
Cliff Lewis, Cleveland	9	−12	−1.89	1

Passing

	Comp	Att	Yds	TD	Int
Otto Graham, Cleveland	161	285	2,785	19	10
Y.A. Tittle, Baltimore	148	289	2,209	14	18
Frankie Albert, San Francisco	129	260	1,862	27	16
George Ratterman, Buffalo	146	252	1,777	14	13
Bob Hoernschemeyer, Chicago	69	167	1,063	6	11
Johnny Clement, Chicago	58	114	906	6	13
Glenn Dobbs, Los Angeles	65	153	825	4	9
Don Panciera, New York	51	150	801	5	16
George Taliaferro, Los Angeles	45	124	790	4	14
Gil Johnson, New York	12	36	179	0	5
Cliff Lewis, Cleveland	5	10	144	5	2
Sam Vacanti, Baltimore	11	27	134	0	1
Billy Grimes, Los Angeles	3	3	105	1	0
Bev Wallace, San Francisco	9	23	95	0	4
Jim Still, Buffalo	6	12	86	1	1
Bob Chappuis, Chicago	2	14	40	0	4
Jim Cason, San Francisco	1	2	38	1	0
Bob H. Kennedy, New York	1	1	27	0	0
Pete Layden, New York	2	10	25	0	1
Charlie O'Rourke, Baltimore	1	7	12	0	1
Jesse Freitas, Buffalo	4	9	10	0	2
Walt Clay, Los Angeles	1	1	8	0	0
George Buksar, Chicago	0	1	0	0	0
Rip Collins, Chicago	0	1	0	0	0
Mickey Colmer, New York	0	1	0	0	0

	Comp	Att	Yds	TD	Int
John Donaldson, LA–Chicago	0	1	0	0	0
Edgar Jones, Cleveland	0	1	0	0	0
Lou Kusserow, New York	0	1	0	0	0
Hosea Rodgers, Los Angeles	0	1	0	0	0
Dick Wilkins, Los Angeles	0	1	0	0	0
Rex Grossman, Baltimore	0	1	0	0	1
Herm Wedemeyer, Baltimore	0	1	0	0	1
Shorty McWilliams, Los Angeles	0	2	0	0	0
Joe Perry, San Francisco	0	2	0	0	0

Receiving

	Rec	Yds	Avg Gain	TD
Mac Speedie, Cleveland	62	1,028	16.6	7
Al Baldwin, Buffalo	53	719	13.6	7
Alyn Beals, San Francisco	44	678	15.4	12
Dan Edwards, Chicago	42	573	13.6	3
Lamar Davis, Baltimore	38	548	14.4	1
Len Ford, Los Angeles	36	577	16.0	1
Dick Wilkins, Los Angeles	32	589	18.4	3
Billy Stone, Baltimore	31	621	20.0	6
Chet Mutryn, Buffalo	29	333	11.5	0
Dante Lavelli, Cleveland	28	475	17.0	7
John North, Baltimore	25	490	19.6	4
Paul Salata, San Francisco	24	289	12.0	4
Jim Lukens, Buffalo	24	249	10.4	2
Horace Gillom, Cleveland	23	359	15.6	0
Windell Williams, Baltimore	20	266	13.3	1
Ray Ramsey, Chicago	17	366	21.5	4
Paul Patterson, Chicago	16	304	19.0	4
Hank Foldberg, Chicago	15	202	13.5	0
Marion Motley, Cleveland	15	191	12.7	0
Ollie Cline, Buffalo	15	110	7.3	0
Billy Grimes, Los Angeles	13	189	14.5	2
Dub Jones, Cleveland	12	241	20.1	1
Sam Cathcart, San Francisco	12	182	15.2	0
Buddy Young, New York	12	171	14.3	2
Bill Boedeker, Cleveland	11	371	33.7	2
Bruce Alford, New York	11	213	19.4	1
Joe Perry, San Francisco	11	146	13.3	3
Bob Sweiger, Chicago	11	126	11.5	0
Herm Wedemeyer, Baltimore	10	112	11.2	0
Lu Gambino, Baltimore	10	67	6.7	1
Dan Garza, New York	9	193	21.4	0
Edgar Jones, Cleveland	9	130	14.4	3
Fay King, Chicago	9	88	9.8	1
Lou Tomasetti, Buffalo	9	56	6.2	1
Verl Lillywhite, San Francisco	8	82	10.3	2
Chick Jagade, Baltimore	8	44	5.5	0
Rex Bumgardner, Buffalo	7	168	24.0	4
Eddie Carr, San Francisco	7	165	23.6	3
Jack Russell, New York	7	130	18.6	1
Hosea Rodgers, Los Angeles	7	97	13.9	0
Hal Shoener, San Francisco	7	84	12.0	0
Bob Pfohl, Baltimore	7	62	8.9	0
Bob H. Kennedy, New York	7	55	7.9	1
Rip Collins, Chicago	6	161	26.8	0
Tom Landry, New York	6	109	18.2	0
John Strzykalski, San Francisco	6	99	16.5	1
Barney Poole, New York	6	83	13.8	0
Don Garlin, San Francisco	6	64	10.7	0
Lew Holder, Los Angeles	5	71	14.2	0
Joe Sutton, Buffalo	5	63	12.6	1
Nick Susoeff, San Francisco	5	52	10.4	1
Jim Cason, San Francisco	5	38	7.6	0
Earl Howell, Los Angeles	5	11	2.2	1
Paul Page, Baltimore	4	62	15.5	0
Jim McCarthy, Chicago	4	58	14.5	0
Len Eshmont, San Francisco	3	107	35.7	2
Bob Livingstone, Chicago–Buffalo	3	80	26.7	0
Joe Aguirre, Los Angeles	3	37	12.3	1
Vito Kissell, Buffalo	3	37	12.3	0
Paul Gibson, Buffalo	3	32	10.7	0
Ab Wimberly, Los Angeles	3	22	7.3	0
Les Horvath, Cleveland	2	71	35.5	1
Larry Joe, Buffalo	2	52	26.0	0
Burr Baldwin, Los Angeles	2	26	13.0	0
Van Davis, New York	2	26	13.0	0
Bob Kelly, Baltimore	2	25	12.5	0
Bus Mertes, Baltimore	2	22	11.0	1
Bob Hoffman, Los Angeles	2	21	10.5	0
Jack Carpenter, Buffalo–SF	2	20	10.0	0
Bob Jensen, Chicago	2	14	7.0	0
Harper Davis, Los Angeles	2	13	6.5	0
Mickey Colmer, New York	2	10	5.0	0
Tom Colella, Buffalo	2	6	3.0	0
Frank Aschenbrenner, Chicago	2	−4	−2.0	0
Bob Smith, Chicago	1	31	31.0	0
Bob Cowan, Baltimore	1	26	26.0	0
Sherman Howard, New York	1	24	24.0	0
Warren Lahr, Cleveland	1	20	20.0	0
George Murphy, Los Angeles	1	17	17.0	0
Ed Henke, Los Angeles	1	15	15.0	0
Bob Oristaglio, Buffalo	1	14	14.0	0
Tony Adamle, Cleveland	1	13	13.0	0
Jake Leicht, Baltimore	1	12	12.0	0
Otto Schnellbacher, New York	1	11	11.0	0
Hardy Brown, Chicago	1	10	10.0	0
Gail Bruce, San Francisco	1	9	9.0	0
Eddie Prokop, New York	1	7	7.0	0
Ed Susteric, Cleveland	1	7	7.0	0
Wilbur Volz, Buffalo	1	6	6.0	0
Ara Parseghian, Cleveland	1	2	2.0	0
Bob Reinhard, Los Angeles	1	2	2.0	0
Jim Spavital, Los Angeles	1	−1	−1.0	0
Wayne Kingery, Baltimore	1	−2	−2.0	0
Pete Layden, New York	1	0	0.0	0
George Taliaferro, Los Angeles	0	42	—	1
Lin Houston, Cleveland	0	19	—	0
Vic Vasicek, Buffalo	0	5	—	0
Abe Gibron, Buffalo	0	3	—	0
Chubby Grigg, Cleveland	0	2	—	0

Punting

	Punts	Avg	Had Blocked
Horace Gillom, Cleveland	54	37.2	1
Tom Landry, New York	51	44.1	2
Tom Colella, Buffalo	44	35.3	1
Rip Collins, Chicago	41	42.1	0
Glenn Dobbs, Los Angeles	39	42.3	0
Frankie Albert, San Francisco	31	48.2	0
Charlie O'Rourke, Baltimore	28	39.2	0
Rex Grossman, Baltimore	28	38.8	0
George Taliaferro, Los Angeles	27	36.4	2
Ernie Lewis, Chicago	16	42.5	1
Jim Still, Buffalo	16	38.4	0

Part 3: Individual Statistics

	Punts	Avg	Had Blocked
Pete Layden, New York	15	41.7	0
Hardy Brown, Chicago	10	39.7	0
Norm Standlee, San Francisco	8	34.5	1
Mickey Colmer, New York	5	46.4	0
Verl Lillywhite, San Francisco	4	50.5	0
Bob Hoernschemeyer, Chicago	4	48.8	0
Warren Lahr, Cleveland	4	31.3	1
Wayne Kingery, Baltimore	3	36.3	0
Herm Wedemeyer, Baltimore	3	18.0	0
Bev Wallace, San Francisco	1	30.0	0

Interceptions

	Int	Yds	Avg Return	TD
Jim Cason, San Francisco	9	152	16.9	0
Pete Layden, New York	7	137	19.6	1
Eddie Carr, San Francisco	7	87	12.4	1
Lowell Wagner, San Francisco	6	121	20.2	1
Cliff Lewis, Cleveland	6	53	8.8	0
Tommy James, Cleveland	4	64	16.0	1
Jim Spavital, Los Angeles	4	58	14.5	0
Tony Adamle, Cleveland	4	42	10.5	0
Warren Lahr, Cleveland	4	32	8.0	0
Otto Schnellbacher, New York	4	26	6.5	0
Paul Patterson, Chicago	3	104	34.7	0
Hardy Brown, Chicago	3	59	19.7	0
Len Eshmont, San Francisco	3	56	18.7	0
Harmon Rowe, New York	3	53	17.7	0
Tom Colella, Buffalo	3	49	16.3	0
John Brown, Los Angeles	3	46	15.3	0
Alex Agase, Cleveland	3	31	10.3	0
Bob Kelly, Baltimore	3	24	8.0	0
Bob Cowan, Baltimore	3	17	5.7	0
George Strohmeyer, Chicago	3	9	3.0	0
Ray Ramsey, Chicago	2	79	39.5	0
Weldon Humble, Cleveland	2	55	27.5	0
Dick Woodard, Los Angeles	2	39	19.5	1
Shorty McWilliams, Los Angeles	2	35	17.5	0
Lou Saban, Cleveland	2	35	17.5	1
Fred Negus, Chicago	2	28	14.0	0
Harper Davis, Los Angeles	2	5	2.5	0
Burr Baldwin, Los Angeles	2	4	2.0	0
Les Horvath, Cleveland	2	4	2.0	0
Bob H. Kennedy, New York	2	2	1.0	0
Len Ford, Los Angeles	1	45	45.0	0
Tom Landry, New York	1	44	44.0	0
Lamar Davis, Baltimore	1	35	35.0	0
Bob M. Kennedy, Los Angeles	1	33	33.0	0
Sherman Howard, New York	1	26	26.0	0
Paul Crowe, SF–LA	1	25	25.0	0
Bob Sweiger, Chicago	1	21	21.0	0
Martin Ruby, New York	1	19	19.0	1
Don Clark, San Francisco	1	16	16.0	0
Bill Johnson, San Francisco	1	16	16.0	1
Ab Wimberly, Los Angeles	1	16	16.0	1
Ralph Ruthstrom, Baltimore	1	15	15.0	0
Vito Kissell, Buffalo	1	14	14.0	0
Pete Wissman, San Francisco	1	12	12.0	0
Paul Gibson, Buffalo	1	9	9.0	0
Verl Lillywhite, San Francisco	1	9	9.0	0
Bob Nowaskey, Baltimore	1	9	9.0	0
Tommy Thompson, Cleveland	1	9	9.0	0
Duke Iverson, New York	1	8	8.0	0
Bob Hoffman, Los Angeles	1	7	7.0	0
Bill Leonard, Baltimore	1	7	7.0	0
Hub Bechtol, Baltimore	1	6	6.0	0
Bob Livingstone, Chicago–Buffalo	1	6	6.0	0
Bill Willis, Cleveland	1	6	6.0	0
Gail Bruce, San Francisco	1	5	5.0	0
Jack Russell, New York	1	5	5.0	0
Bill Schroll, Buffalo	1	4	4.0	0
Dan Dworsky, Los Angeles	1	3	3.0	0
Hal Herring, Buffalo	1	1	1.0	0
Harvey Johnson, New York	1	1	1.0	0
Alex Wizbicki, Buffalo	1	1	1.0	0
Sam Cathcart, San Francisco	1	0	0.0	0
Rip Collins, Chicago	1	0	0.0	0
Don Garlin, San Francisco	1	0	0.0	0
Wayne Kingery, Baltimore	1	0	0.0	0
Barney Poole, New York	1	0	0.0	0
Ed Sharkey, New York	1	0	0.0	0
John Donaldson, LA–Chicago	0	23	—	0

Punt Returns

	Ret	Yds	Avg Ret	TD
Jim Cason, San Francisco	21	351	16.7	0
Sam Cathcart, San Francisco	18	306	17.0	0
Bob Livingstone, Chicago–Buf	17	292	17.2	1
Pete Layden, New York	29	287	9.9	0
Herm Wedemeyer, Baltimore	16	221	13.8	0
Cliff Lewis, Cleveland	20	174	8.7	0
Buddy Young, New York	9	171	19.0	0
Shorty McWilliams, Los Angeles	8	112	14.0	0
Jake Leicht, Baltimore	9	109	12.1	0
Paul Crowe, SF–Los Angeles	6	96	16.0	0
Warren Lahr, Cleveland	6	83	13.8	0
Chet Mutryn, Buffalo	7	77	11.0	0
Billy Grimes, Los Angeles	5	67	13.4	0
Ray Ramsey, Chicago	8	64	8.0	0
Joe Sutton, Buffalo	6	62	10.3	0
Jim Spavital, Los Angeles	6	58	9.7	0
George Taliaferro, Los Angeles	2	53	26.5	1
Tom Landry, New York	3	52	17.3	0
Tom Colella, Buffalo	5	42	8.4	0
Harper Davis, Los Angeles	2	37	18.5	0
Rex Bumgardner, Buffalo	4	35	8.8	0
Paul Patterson, Chicago	4	33	8.3	0
Otto Schnellbacher, New York	4	31	7.8	0
Wayne Kingery, Baltimore	2	19	9.5	0
John Strzykalski, San Francisco	2	19	9.5	0
Les Horvath, Cleveland	3	19	6.3	0
John Donaldson, LA–Chicago	1	18	18.0	0
Paul Page, Baltimore	1	16	16.0	0
Joe Vetrano, San Francisco	1	16	16.0	0
Paul Mitchell, New York	1	15	15.0	0
Lou Tomasetti, Buffalo	2	13	6.5	0
Hal Shoener, San Francisco	1	8	8.0	0
Earl Howell, Los Angeles	1	7	7.0	0
Eddie Carr, San Francisco	1	6	6.0	0
Barney Poole, New York	1	6	6.0	0
Ned Maloney, San Francisco	1	5	5.0	0
Bob Hoernschemeyer, Chicago	1	4	4.0	0
Lowell Wagner, San Francisco	1	2	2.0	0
John Yonakor, Cleveland	1	1	1.0	0

Kick Returns

	Ret	Yds	Avg Ret	TD
Herm Wedemeyer, Baltimore	30	602	20.1	0
Billy Grimes, Los Angeles	16	411	25.7	0
Ray Ramsey, Chicago	14	407	29.1	0
Bob Hoernschemeyer, Chicago	14	373	26.6	0
Joe Perry, San Francisco	14	337	24.1	0
Buddy Young, New York	11	316	28.7	1
George Taliaferro, Los Angeles	13	313	24.1	0
Marion Motley, Cleveland	12	262	21.8	0
Jim Cason, San Francisco	11	247	22.5	0
Chet Mutryn, Buffalo	10	224	22.4	0
Dub Jones, Cleveland	8	204	25.5	0
Bill Boedeker, Cleveland	9	189	21.0	0
Jake Leicht, Baltimore	8	171	21.4	0
Rex Bumgardner, Buffalo	9	163	18.1	0
Sam Cathcart, San Francisco	7	138	19.7	0
Lou Kusserow, New York	6	136	22.7	0
Paul Page, Baltimore	4	108	27.0	0
Tom Colella, Buffalo	7	107	15.3	0
Bob Pfohl, Baltimore	4	98	24.5	0
Sherman Howard, New York	4	95	23.8	0
Harper Davis, Los Angeles	4	87	21.8	0
Bob Livingstone, Chicago–Buffalo	6	85	14.2	0
Joe Sutton, Buffalo	4	82	20.5	0
Chick Jagade, Baltimore	6	75	12.5	0
Earl Howell, Los Angeles	4	74	18.5	0
Eddie Prokop, New York	3	62	20.7	0
Bob Sweiger, Chicago	3	59	19.7	0
John Strzykalski, San Francisco	2	57	28.5	0
Wilbur Volz, Buffalo	3	43	14.3	0
Tom Landry, New York	2	39	19.5	0
Ed Susteric, Cleveland	2	39	19.5	0
Frank Aschenbrenner, Chicago	2	35	17.5	0
Jim Spavital, Los Angeles	1	32	32.0	0
Bruce Alford, New York	2	31	15.5	0
Bob Kelly, Baltimore	2	31	15.5	0
Dan Edwards, Chicago	2	29	14.5	1
Pete Layden, New York	1	28	28.0	0
John Donaldson, LA–Chicago	1	27	27.0	0
Bill Leonard, Baltimore	1	25	25.0	0
Billy Stone, Baltimore	1	25	25.0	0
Rip Collins, Chicago	2	23	11.5	0
Noble Doss, New York	1	22	22.0	0
Alex Wizbicki, Buffalo	1	22	22.0	0
Ollie Cline, Buffalo	1	21	21.0	0
Don Garlin, San Francisco	1	21	21.0	0
Dan Garza, New York	1	21	21.0	0
Lou Tomasetti, Buffalo	1	19	19.0	0
Duke Iverson, New York	2	18	9.0	0
Hal Shoener, San Francisco	1	17	17.0	0
Lowell Tew, New York	1	17	17.0	0
Mickey Colmer, New York	1	16	16.0	0
Verl Lillywhite, San Francisco	1	16	16.0	0
Lou Rymkus, Cleveland	1	16	16.0	0
Edgar Jones, Cleveland	1	15	15.0	0
Bob H. Kennedy, New York	1	15	15.0	0
Dan Dworsky, Los Angeles	1	14	14.0	0
Bob Hoffman, Los Angeles	1	14	14.0	0
Lamar Davis, Baltimore	1	13	13.0	0
Len Eshmont, San Francisco	1	13	13.0	0
Fay King, Chicago	1	13	13.0	0
Larry Joe, Buffalo	1	12	12.0	0
Sam Vacanti, Baltimore	1	10	10.0	0
Gail Bruce, San Francisco	1	8	8.0	0
Lou Groza, Cleveland	1	2	2.0	0
Vito Kissell, Buffalo	1	1	1.0	0
Ray Richeson, Chicago	1	0	0.0	0

Total Returns (Punt and Kick)

	Ret	Yds	Avg Ret	TD
Herm Wedemeyer, Baltimore	46	823	17.9	0
Jim Cason, San Francisco	32	598	18.7	0
Buddy Young, New York	20	487	24.4	1
Billy Grimes, Los Angeles	21	478	22.8	0
Ray Ramsey, Chicago	22	471	21.4	0
Sam Cathcart, San Francisco	25	444	17.8	0
Bob Hoernschemeyer, Chicago	15	377	25.1	0
Bob Livingstone, Chi–Buffalo	23	377	16.4	1
George Taliaferro, Los Angeles	15	366	24.4	1
Joe Perry, San Francisco	14	337	24.1	0
Pete Layden, New York	30	315	10.5	0
Chet Mutryn, Buffalo	17	301	17.7	0
Jake Leicht, Baltimore	17	280	16.5	0
Marion Motley, Cleveland	12	262	21.8	0
Dub Jones, Cleveland	8	204	25.5	0
Rex Bumgardner, Buffalo	13	198	15.2	0
Bill Boedeker, Cleveland	9	189	21.0	0
Cliff Lewis, Cleveland	20	174	8.7	0
Tom Colella, Buffalo	12	149	12.4	0
Joe Sutton, Buffalo	10	144	14.4	0
Lou Kusserow, New York	6	136	22.7	0
Paul Page, Baltimore	5	124	24.8	0
Harper Davis, Los Angeles	6	124	20.7	0
Shorty McWilliams, Los Angeles	8	112	14.0	0
Bob Pfohl, Baltimore	4	98	24.5	0
Paul Crowe, SF–Los Angeles	6	96	16.0	0
Sherman Howard, New York	4	95	23.8	0
Tom Landry, New York	5	91	18.2	0
Jim Spavital, Los Angeles	7	90	12.9	0
Warren Lahr, Cleveland	6	83	13.8	0
Earl Howell, Los Angeles	5	81	16.2	0
John Strzykalski, San Francisco	4	76	19.0	0
Chick Jagade, Baltimore	6	75	12.5	0
Eddie Prokop, New York	3	62	20.7	0
Bob Sweiger, Chicago	3	59	19.7	0
John Donaldson, LA–Chicago	2	45	22.5	0
Wilbur Volz, Buffalo	3	43	14.3	0
Ed Susteric, Cleveland	2	39	19.5	0
Frank Aschenbrenner, Chicago	2	35	17.5	0
Paul Patterson, Chicago	4	33	8.3	0
Lou Tomasetti, Buffalo	3	32	10.7	0
Bruce Alford, New York	2	31	15.5	0
Bob Kelly, Baltimore	2	31	15.5	0
Otto Schnellbacher, New York	4	31	7.8	0
Dan Edwards, Chicago	2	29	14.5	1
Bill Leonard, Baltimore	1	25	25.0	0
Billy Stone, Baltimore	1	25	25.0	0
Hal Shoener, San Francisco	2	25	12.5	0
Rip Collins, Chicago	2	23	11.5	0
Noble Doss, New York	1	22	22.0	0
Alex Wizbicki, Buffalo	1	22	22.0	0
Ollie Cline, Buffalo	1	21	21.0	0
Don Garlin, San Francisco	1	21	21.0	0
Dan Garza, New York	1	21	21.0	0
Wayne Kingery, Baltimore	2	19	9.5	0

Part 3: Individual Statistics

	Ret	Yds	Avg Ret	TD
Les Horvath, Cleveland	3	19	6.3	0
Duke Iverson, New York	2	18	9.0	0
Lowell Tew, New York	1	17	17.0	0
Mickey Colmer, New York	1	16	16.0	0
Verl Lillywhite, San Francisco	1	16	16.0	0
Lou Rymkus, Cleveland	1	16	16.0	0
Joe Vetrano, San Francisco	1	16	16.0	0
Edgar Jones, Cleveland	1	15	15.0	0
Bob H. Kennedy, New York	1	15	15.0	0
Paul Mitchell, New York	1	15	15.0	0
Dan Dworsky, Los Angeles	1	14	14.0	0
Bob Hoffman, Los Angeles	1	14	14.0	0
Lamar Davis, Baltimore	1	13	13.0	0
Len Eshmont, San Francisco	1	13	13.0	0
Fay King, Chicago	1	13	13.0	0
Larry Joe, Buffalo	1	12	12.0	0
Sam Vacanti, Baltimore	1	10	10.0	0
Gail Bruce, San Francisco	1	8	8.0	0
Eddie Carr, San Francisco	1	6	6.0	0
Barney Poole, New York	1	6	6.0	0
Ned Maloney, San Francisco	1	5	5.0	0
Lou Groza, Cleveland	1	2	2.0	0
Lowell Wagner, San Francisco	1	2	2.0	0
Vito Kissell, Buffalo	1	1	1.0	0
John Yonakor, Cleveland	1	1	1.0	0
Ray Richeson, Chicago	1	0	0.0	0

Point After Touchdowns

	Made	Att	%
Joe Vetrano, San Francisco	56	56	100.0
Lou Groza, Cleveland	34	35	97.1
Bob Nelson, Los Angeles	34	35	97.1
Chet Adams, Buffalo	32	32	100.0
Harvey Johnson, New York	25	25	100.0
Jim McCarthy, Chicago	21	23	91.3
Rex Grossman, Baltimore	19	19	100.0
Lou Saban, Cleveland	11	11	100.0
Sam Vacanti, Baltimore	3	3	100.0
Alyn Beals, San Francisco	1	1	100.0
Frankie Albert, San Francisco	0	1	0.0

Field Goals

	Made	Att	%
Harvey Johnson, New York	7	15	46.7
Rex Grossman, Baltimore	6	11	54.5
Jim McCarthy, Chicago	6	13	46.2
Chet Adams, Buffalo	4	11	36.4
Bob Nelson, Los Angeles	3	6	50.0
Joe Vetrano, San Francisco	3	7	49.2
Lou Groza, Cleveland	2	9	22.2
Lou Saban, Cleveland	0	2	0.0
Sam Vacanti, Baltimore	0	2	0.0

Scoring

	TD Rush	TD Pass	Pts After TD	FG	Tot Pts
Alyn Beals, San Francisco	0	12	1–1	0–0	73
Joe Perry, San Francisco	8	3	0–0	0–0	66
Joe Vetrano, San Francisco	0	0	56–56	3–7	65
Marion Motley, Cleveland	8	0	0–0	0–0	48
Billy Stone, Baltimore	2	6	0–0	0–0	48
Buddy Young, New York	6	2	0–0	0–0	48
Harvey Johnson, New York	0	0	25–25	7–15	46
Chet Adams, Buffalo	0	0	32–32	4–11	44
Bob Nelson, Los Angeles	0	0	34–35	3–6	43
Al Baldwin, Buffalo	0	7	0–0	0–0	42
Eddie Carr, San Francisco	4	3	0–0	0–0	42
Edgar Jones, Cleveland	4	3	0–0	0–0	42
Dante Lavelli, Cleveland	0	7	0–0	0–0	42
Mac Speedie, Cleveland	0	7	0–0	0–0	42
George Taliaferro, LA	6	1	0–0	0–0	42
Lou Groza, Cleveland	0	0	34–35	2–9	40
Jim McCarthy, Chicago	0	0	21–23	6–13	39
Rex Grossman, Baltimore	0	0	19–19	6–11	37
Billy Grimes, Los Angeles	4	2	0–0	0–0	36
Bob H. Kennedy, New York	5	1	0–0	0–0	36
Rex Bumgardner, Buffalo	1	4	0–0	0–0	30
Johnny Clement, Chicago	5	0	0–0	0–0	30
Dub Jones, Cleveland	4	1	0–0	0–0	30
Chet Mutryn, Buffalo	5	0	0–0	0–0	30
Hosea Rodgers, Los Angeles	5	0	0–0	0–0	30
Dan Edwards, Chicago	1	3	0–0	0–0	24
Verl Lillywhite, SF	2	2	0–0	0–0	24
John North, Baltimore	0	4	0–0	0–0	24
Paul Patterson, Chicago	0	4	0–0	0–0	24
Ray Ramsey, Chicago	0	4	0–0	0–0	24
George Ratterman, Buffalo	4	0	0–0	0–0	24
Paul Salata, San Francisco	0	4	0–0	0–0	24
Norm Standlee, SF	4	0	0–0	0–0	24
John Strzykalski, SF	3	1	0–0	0–0	24
Frankie Albert, SF	3	0	0–1	0–0	18
Bill Boedeker, Cleveland	1	2	0–0	0–0	18
Ollie Cline, Buffalo	3	0	0–0	0–0	18
Glenn Dobbs, Los Angeles	3	0	0–0	0–0	18
Otto Graham, Cleveland	3	0	0–0	0–0	18
Les Horvath, Cleveland	2	1	0–0	0–0	18
Sherman Howard, New York	3	0	0–0	0–0	18
Lou Tomasetti, Buffalo	2	1	0–0	0–0	18
Dick Wilkins, Los Angeles	0	3	0–0	0–0	18
Lou Saban, Cleveland	1	0	11–11	0–2	17
John Brown, Los Angeles	2	0	0–0	0–0	12
Len Eshmont, San Francisco	0	2	0–0	0–0	12
Bob Hoernschemeyer, Chi	2	0	0–0	0–0	12
Earl Howell, Los Angeles	1	1	0–0	0–0	12
Chick Jagade, Baltimore	2	0	0–0	0–0	12
Jim Lukens, Buffalo	0	2	0–0	0–0	12
Bob Pfohl, Baltimore	2	0	0–0	0–0	12
Eddie Prokop, New York	2	0	0–0	0–0	12
Jack Russell, New York	1	1	0–0	0–0	12
Y.A. Tittle, Baltimore	2	0	0–0	0–0	12
Ab Wimberly, Los Angeles	2	0	0–0	0–0	12
Joe Aguirre, Los Angeles	0	1	0–0	0–0	6
Bruce Alford, New York	0	1	0–0	0–0	6
George Buksar, Chicago	1	0	0–0	0–0	6
Jim Cason, San Francisco	1	0	0–0	0–0	6
Sam Cathcart, San Francisco	1	0	0–0	0–0	6
Paul Crowe, SF–LA	1	0	0–0	0–0	6
Lamar Davis, Baltimore	0	1	0–0	0–0	6
Harper Davis, Los Angeles	1	0	0–0	0–0	6
Len Ford, Los Angeles	0	1	0–0	0–0	6
Lu Gambino, Baltimore	0	1	0–0	0–0	6
Don Garlin, San Francisco	1	0	0–0	0–0	6
Tommy James, Cleveland	1	0	0–0	0–0	6
Bill Johnson, San Francisco	1	0	0–0	0–0	6

	TD Rush	TD Pass	Pts After TD	FG	Tot Pts
Fay King, Chicago	0	1	0-0	0-0	6
Warren Lahr, Cleveland	1	0	0-0	0-0	6
Pete Layden, New York	1	0	0-0	0-0	6
Cliff Lewis, Cleveland	1	0	0-0	0-0	6
Ernie Lewis, Chicago	1	0	0-0	0-0	6
Bob Livingstone, Chi-Buf	1	0	0-0	0-0	6
Bus Mertes, Baltimore	0	1	0-0	0-0	6
Fred Negus, Chicago	1	0	0-0	0-0	6
Martin Ruby, New York	1	0	0-0	0-0	6
Nick Susoeff, San Francisco	0	1	0-0	0-0	6
Ed Susteric, Cleveland	1	0	0-0	0-0	6
Joe Sutton, Buffalo	0	1	0-0	0-0	6
Lowell Tew, New York	1	0	0-0	0-0	6
Wilbur Volz, Buffalo	1	0	0-0	0-0	6
Lowell Wagner, SF	1	0	0-0	0-0	6
Bev Wallace, San Francisco	1	0	0-0	0-0	6
Windell Williams, Baltimore	0	1	0-0	0-0	6
Dick Woodard, Los Angeles	1	0	0-0	0-0	6
Sam Vacanti, Baltimore	0	0	3-3	0-2	3
Chicago Safety	0	0	0-0	0-0	2
San Francisco Safety	0	0	0-0	0-0	2

Lifetime Leaders

Players are ranked based on total yards, except in pass receiving, interception returns, points after touchdown and field goals. Those are ranked based on total number. Punting is based on averages. Scoring is based on points.

Total Offense
(Net Yards Gained)

	# of Plays	Rush	Pass	Tot	Avg Gain
Otto Graham, Cleveland	1,160	200	10,085	10,285	8.87
Frankie Albert, SF	1,182	767	6,948	7,715	6.53
Glenn Dobbs, Brklyn-LA	1,196	1,039	5,876	6,915	5.78
Bob Hoernschemeyer, Chicago-Brooklyn	1,194	2,109	4,109	6,218	5.21
George Ratterman, Buffalo	896	18	6,194	6,212	6.93
Spec Sanders, New York	958	2,900	2,771	5,671	5.92
Y.A. Tittle, Baltimore	659	246	4,731	4,977	7.55

Rushing

	Rush	Yds	Avg Gain	TD
Marion Motley, Cleveland	489	3,024	6.18	26
Spec Sanders, New York	540	2,900	5.37	33
Chet Mutryn, Buffalo	475	2,676	5.63	25
John Strzykalski, San Francisco	429	2,454	5.72	14
Bob Hoernschemeyer, Chi-Brklyn	506	2,109	4.17	10
Norm Standlee, San Francisco	375	1,734	4.62	17
Mickey Colmer, Brklyn-NY	398	1,537	3.86	15
Edgar Jones, Cleveland	289	1,509	5.22	18
Buddy Young, New York	262	1,452	5.54	9
Lou Tomasetti, Buffalo	323	1,430	4.43	12
Joe Perry, San Francisco	192	1,345	7.01	18

Others over 1,000 yards: John Kimbrough, Los Angeles (1,224); Len Eshmont, San Francisco (1,181); Bus Mertes, Los Angeles-Baltimore (1,120); Glenn Dobbs, Brooklyn-Los Angeles (1,039); Bob Kennedy, New York (1,017); Vic Kulbitski, Buffalo (1,006).

Note: Kimbrough and Kennedy performed this in three seasons, the rest in four seasons.

Passing

	Comp	Att	Yds	TD	Int
Otto Graham, Cleveland	592	1,061	10,085	86	41
Frankie Albert, San Francisco	515	963	6,948	88	55
George Ratterman, Buffalo	438	831	6,194	52	55
Glenn Dobbs, Brooklyn-LA	446	934	5,876	45	52
Y.A. Tittle, Baltimore	309	578	4,731	30	27
Bob Hoernschemeyer, Chicago-Brooklyn	308	688	4,109	32	51

Receiving

	Rec	Yds	Avg Gain	TD
Mac Speedie, Cleveland	211	3,554	16.8	24
Alyn Beals, San Francisco	177	2,510	14.2	46
Lamar Davis, Miami-Baltimore	147	2,103	14.3	12
Dante Lavelli, Cleveland	142	2,580	18.2	29
Al Baldwin, Buffalo	132	2,103	15.9	22
Fay King, Buffalo-Chicago	115	1,583	13.8	20
Billy Hillenbrand, Chi-Baltimore	110	1,987	18.1	17

Punting

	Punts	Avg	Had Blocked
Glenn Dobbs, Brooklyn-LA	231	46.4	7
Bob Reinhard, Los Angeles	78	44.6	2
Frankie Albert, San Francisco	160	44.0	1
Mickey Colmer, Brooklyn-NY	120	43.8	2
Ernie Lewis, Chicago	191	41.9	6
Horace Gillom, Cleveland	107	40.5	1
Spec Sanders, New York	121	40.1	4

Interceptions

	Int	Yds	Avg Return	TD
Cliff Lewis, Cleveland	24	216	9.0	1
Tom Colella, Cleveland-Buffalo	21	323	15.4	0
Eddie Carr, San Francisco	16	290	18.1	1
Otto Schnellbacher, New York	15	265	17.7	1
Ray Ramsey, Chicago-Brooklyn	14	269	19.2	0
Jim Cason, San Francisco	14	198	14.1	0
Lou Saban, Cleveland	13	110	8.5	1

Part 3: Individual Statistics

	Int	Yds	Avg Return	TD
Bob Perina, NY–Brklyn–Chi	12	171	14.3	0
Bob H. Kennedy, New York	11	152	13.8	0
Pete Layden, New York	10	200	20.0	1
Len Eshmont, San Francisco	10	128	12.8	0

Punt Returns

	Ret	Yds	Avg Ret	TD
Chuck Fenenbock, LA–Chicago	50	678	13.6	0
Jim Cason, San Francisco	43	660	15.3	0
Cliff Lewis, Cleveland	61	649	10.6	0
Billy Hillenbrand, Chi–Balt	44	612	13.9	1
Herman Wedemeyer, LA–Balt	39	589	15.1	0
Spec Sanders, New York	36	349	15.3	0
Chet Mutryn, Buffalo	35	492	14.1	1
Monk Gafford, Miami–Brooklyn	34	433	12.7	0
Tom Colella, Cleveland–Buffalo	23	397	17.3	1
Rex Bumgardner, Buffalo	20	371	18.6	2
Glenn Dobbs, Brooklyn–LA	26	361	13.9	1
Pete Layden, New York	36	351	9.8	0
Bob Livingstone, Chicago–Buf	20	316	15.8	1
John Strzykalski, San Francisco	26	316	12.2	0

Kick Returns

	Ret	Yds	Avg Ret	TD
Chet Mutryn, Buffalo	54	1,494	27.7	0
Monk Gafford, Miami–Brooklyn	55	1,469	26.7	0
Chuck Fenenbock, LA–Chicago	49	1,252	25.6	1
Spec Sanders, New York	44	1,205	27.4	2
Ray Ramsey, Chicago–Brooklyn	40	1,046	26.2	0
Billy Hillenbrand, Chicago–Balt	42	1,042	24.8	2
Marion Motley, Cleveland	42	974	23.2	0
Buddy Young, New York	35	951	27.2	2
Herman Wedemeyer, LA–Balt	41	842	20.5	0
Bob Hoernschemeyer, Chi–Brklyn	30	797	26.6	0

Total Returns (Punt and Kick)

	Ret	Yds	Avg Ret	TD
Chet Mutryn, Buffalo	89	1,986	22.3	1
Chuck Fenenbock, LA–Chicago	99	1,930	19.5	1
Monk Gafford, Miami–Brooklyn	89	1,902	21.4	0
Spec Sanders, New York	80	1,754	21.9	3
Billy Hillenbrand, Chi–Baltimore	86	1,654	19.2	3
Herman Wedemeyer, LA–Balt	80	1,431	17.9	0

	Ret	Yds	Avg Ret	TD
Ray Ramsey, Chicago–Brooklyn	64	1,323	20.7	1
Buddy Young, New York	54	1,260	23.3	3
Jim Cason, San Francisco	64	1,119	17.5	0

Point After Touchdowns

	Made	Att	%
Joe Vetrano, San Francisco	187	203	92.1
Lou Groza, Cleveland	165	182	90.7
Harvey Johnson, New York	147	149	98.7
Ben Agajanian, Los Angeles	70	72	97.2
Rex Grossman, Baltimore	62	62	100.0
Jim McCarthy, Chicago–Brooklyn	47	51	92.2

Field Goals

	Made	Att	%
Lou Groza, Cleveland	30	76	39.5
Harvey Johnson, New York	22	38	57.9
Ben Agajanian, Los Angeles	20	39	51.3
Rex Grossman, Baltimore	16	29	55.2
Joe Vetrano, San Francisco	16	33	48.5

Scoring

	TD Rush	TD Pass	Pts After TD	FG	Tot Pts
Alyn Beals, San Francisco	0	46	2–2	0–0	278
Lou Groza, Cleveland	0	0	169–176	30–76	259
Joe Vetrano, San Francisco	2	0	187–203	16–33	247
Spec Sanders, New York	37	3	0–0	0–0	240
Chet Mutryn, Buffalo	28	10	1–2	0–0	229
Harvey Johnson, New York	0	0	147–149	22–38	213
Billy Hillenbrand, Chi–Balt	14	17	0–0	0–0	186
Marion Motley, Cleveland	27	4	0–0	0–0	186
Edgar Jones, Cleveland	19	10	0–0	0–0	174
Dante Lavelli, Cleveland	0	29	0–0	0–0	174
Mac Speedie, Cleveland	1	24	1–1	0–0	151
John Strzykalski, SF	14	11	0–0	0–0	150
Joe Aguirre, Los Angeles	0	16	33–35	4–11	141
John Kimbrough, LA	17	6	0–0	0–0	138
Joe Perry, San Francisco	19	4	0–0	0–0	138
Al Baldwin, Buffalo	0	22	0–1	0–0	132
Ben Agajanian, Los Angeles	0	0	70–72	20–39	130
Mickey Colmer, Brklyn–NY	15	6	0–0	0–0	126
Frankie Albert, SF	20	0	1–5	0–0	121
Fay King, Buffalo–Chicago	0	20	0–0	0–0	120
Buddy Young, New York	12	8	0–0	0–0	120

Part 4: Awards and Statistical Records

All-Conference Teams *(by Andy Piascik)*

National wire services like the Associated Press (AP) and major daily newspapers like the New York *Daily News* were among the media outlets that selected all-conference teams for the All-America Football Conference. Several outlets selected combined all–AAFC/NFL teams and some selected separate all-conference teams for both leagues. The AAFC league office also selected its own team in all four years of its existence.

With only a handful of exceptions, the teams included both first and second team selections. Some also listed honorable mentions. The transition in pro football at the time from the use of one platoon to looser substitution rules that allowed for the regular use of two platoons was reflected in the fact that most of the all-conference teams consisted of only one first team: 11 players, with an additional 11 on the second team. A smaller number selected separate units of 11 offensive and 11 defensive players, with another 22 on the second team if a second team was included. Football historians generally recognize that when it came to the selection of the teams players who played mostly or exclusively on offense in the early years of the two-platoon era had an advantage over those who played mostly or exclusively on defense.

Additional all-conference teams, especially selections by large circulation daily newspapers in cities with AAFC clubs (the *Cleveland Plain Dealer*, *Buffalo News*, *Baltimore Sun*, etc.), may eventually be unearthed. Either way, those all-pro teams that were selected give us a vivid picture of those players who were regarded at the time as the best in the AAFC.

At the end of the 1946 season, the AAFC's first, the United Press (UP), later known as United Press International after its merger with the International News Service (INS), the New York *Daily News* and the AAFC league office selected all-pro teams while the AP selected a combined all–AAFC/NFL team.

In 1947, the *Daily News* and AAFC office continued with their all–AAFC selections and the AP again selected a combined all–AAFC/NFL team. Sportswriters, Inc., a group of nine prominent sportswriters from around the country, according to football historian John Hogrogian, selected a combined team. Hogrogian also speculates that an entity known as "Coaches and Officials," which selected an all–AAFC team, was actually the UP team, just under a different name. Cliff Battles, head coach of the AAFC Brooklyn Dodgers and a former star back with the Washington Redskins, selected his own all–AAFC team, though he presumably would have submitted a ballot for the Coaches and Officials team as well.

The Sporting News joined the AP and Sportswriters, Inc. in selecting a combined team in 1948. A new football magazine, *Pro Football Illustrated*, and the *Chicago Herald-American* joined the UP, the *Daily News* and the AAFC league office in selecting an all–AAFC team. According to Hogrogian, the *Herald-American*'s team was selected by Roger Treat, a columnist for the paper who later authored what is widely recognized as the first encyclopedia of pro football.

In the AAFC's final season, 1949, the AP and INS were joined by *Sport* magazine in selecting combined all–AAFC/NFL teams. The UP, *Daily News* and AAFC league office, meanwhile, selected an all–AAFC team. Hogrogian notes that a group of coaches and scouts selected an all–AAFC team that was also published nationally by the UP, though for some reason it was done in early November, perhaps as a kind of mid-season all-star team.

Of the AAFC players who were selected at some point during the league's four years, many are well-known to fans of pro football history: Otto Graham, Frankie Albert, Marion Motley, Bruiser Kinard, Buddy Young, Ace Parker, Y.A. Tittle, Joe Perry and Bill Willis, to name just a few. Some, like Hall of Famer Elroy Hirsch, who played three years, are notable for their complete absence. Then there are a handful who were regulars and often made every team selected in a given year—Mac Speedie, Dick Barwegan, Bruno Banducci, Lou Rymkus, Martin Ruby, Bob Nelson, Alyn Beals, Bob Reinhard—who have been somewhat underrated and overlooked historically.

Also striking is how well the AAFC players did in earning spots on the combined all–AAFC/NFL teams. For example, in 1947, just the AAFC's second year, five of the 11 players selected to both the AP's and Sportswriters, Inc.'s first teams were AAFCers while six were from the NFL. The totals were essentially the same on the combined teams selected in 1948 and 1949, with an approximate 6–5 advantage for the NFL. For a brand new league to achieve virtual parity with the NFL, at least as reflected in all-pro selections, at a point when the NFL was approaching its 30th anniversary was quite an accomplishment. That the AAFC was able to do so while always fielding fewer teams (8 as opposed to 10 from 1946–48 and 7 to 10 in 1949), and thus significantly fewer total players, makes that accomplishment even more impressive.

John Hogrogian and John Turney, football historians and long-time members of the Pro Football Researchers Association, have done a masterful job of researching and documenting the history of all-pro teams for the PFRA.

1946

First Team (Official Conference Selection)

E—Dante Lavelli (Cleveland Browns)
E—Alyn Beals (San Francisco 49ers)
T—Frank Kinard (New York Yankees)
T—Martin Ruby (Brooklyn Dodgers)
G—Bruno Banducci (San Francisco 49ers)
G—Bill Willis (Cleveland Browns)
C—Bob Nelson (Los Angeles Dons)
Q—Otto Graham (Cleveland Browns)
H—Glenn Dobbs (Brooklyn Dodgers)
H—Spec Sanders (New York Yankees)
F—Marion Motley (Cleveland Browns)

Second Team (Official Conference Selection)

E—Jack Russell (New York Yankees)
E—Mac Speedie (Cleveland Browns)
T—Bob Reinhard (Los Angeles Dons)
T—Lee Artoe (Los Angeles Dons)
G—Bill Radovich (Los Angeles Dons)
G—Harold Jungmichel (Miami Seahawks)
C—Mike Scarry (Cleveland Browns)
Q—Frankie Albert (San Francisco 49ers)
H—Bob Hoernschemeyer (Chicago Rockets)
H—Steve Juzwik (Buffalo Bisons)
F—Norm Standlee (San Francisco 49ers)

1947

First Team (Official Conference Selection)

E—Mac Speedie (Cleveland Browns)
E—Dante Lavelli (Cleveland Browns)
T—Lou Rymkus (Cleveland Browns)
T—Nate Johnson (New York Yankees)
G—Bruno Banducci (San Francisco 49ers)
G—Bill Willis (Cleveland Browns)
C—Bob Nelson (Los Angeles Dons)
Q—Otto Graham (Cleveland Browns)
H—Spec Sanders (New York Yankees)
H—Chet Mutryn (Buffalo Bills)
F—Marion Motley (Cleveland Browns)

Second Team (Official Conference Selection)

E—Jack Russell (New York Yankees)
E—Alyn Beals (San Francisco 49ers)
T—Martin Ruby (Brooklyn Dodgers)
T—John Woudenberg (San Francisco 49ers)
G—Dick Barwegan (New York Yankees)
G—Leonard Levy (Los Angeles Dons)
C—Lou Sossamon (New York Yankees)
Q—George Ratterman (Buffalo Bills)
H—John Strzykalski (San Francisco 49ers)
H—Buddy Young (New York Yankees)
F—Norm Standlee (San Francisco 49ers)

1948

First Team (Official Conference Selection)

E—Mac Speedie (Cleveland Browns)
E—Alyn Beals (San Francisco 49ers)
T—Lou Rymkus (Cleveland Browns)
T—Bob Reinhard (Los Angeles Dons)
G—Dick Barwegan (Baltimore Colts)
G—Bill Willis (Cleveland Browns)
C—Bob Nelson (Los Angeles Dons)
Q—Otto Graham (Cleveland Browns)
H—John Strzykalski (San Francisco 49ers)
H—Chet Mutryn (Buffalo Bills)
F—Marion Motley (Cleveland Browns)

Second Team (Official Conference Selection)

E—Dante Lavelli (Cleveland Browns)
E—Al Baldwin (Buffalo Bills)
T—John Woudenberg (San Francisco 49ers)
T—Martin Ruby (Brooklyn Dodgers)
G—Riley Matheson (San Francisco 49ers)
G—Ed Ulinski (Cleveland Browns)
C—Lou Saban (Cleveland Browns)
Q—Frankie Albert (San Francisco 49ers)
H—Glenn Dobbs (Los Angeles Dons)
H—Billy Hillenbrand (Baltimore Colts)
F—John Colmer (Brooklyn Dodgers)

1949

First Team (Official Conference Selection)

E—Mac Speedie (Cleveland Browns)
E—Alyn Beals (San Francisco 49ers)
T—Arnie Weinmeister (Brooklyn–New York Yankees)

All-Conference Teams   57

T—Bob Reinhard (Los Angeles Dons)
G—Visco Grgich (San Francisco 49ers)
G—Dick Barwegan (Baltimore Colts)
C—Lou Saban (Cleveland Browns)
B—Joe Perry (San Francisco 49ers)
B—Chet Mutryn (Buffalo Bills)
B—Otto Graham (Cleveland Browns)
B—Frankie Albert (San Francisco 49ers)

Second Team (Official Conference Selection)

E—Al Baldwin (Buffalo Bills)
E—Dante Lavelli (Cleveland Browns)
T—Martin Ruby (Brooklyn–New York Yankees)
T—Lou Rymkus (Cleveland Browns)
G—Joe Signaigo (Brooklyn–New York Yankees)
G—Bill Willis (Cleveland Browns)
C—John Rapacz (Chicago Hornets)
B—Buddy Young (Brooklyn–New York Yankees)
B—Marion Motley (Cleveland Browns)
B—George Taliaferro (Los Angeles Dons)
B—Bob Hoernschemeyer (Chicago Hornets)

Most Valuable Players

1946: Glenn Dobbs—Brooklyn Dodgers
1947: Otto Graham—Cleveland Browns
1948: Otto Graham—Cleveland Browns
     Frankie Albert—San Francisco 49ers
1949: (None Selected)

1946 Press-Selected All-Pros
(Compiled by John Hogrogian)

P	Player	AP	SP	UP	NY	PR
E	Jack Russell (NY Yankees)	2	1	—	—	1d
E	Alyn Beals (SF 49ers)	—	—	1	2	1o
E	Mac Speedie (Clev Browns)	—	—	1	1	—
E	Dante Lavelli (Clev Browns)	2	—	2	2	1o
E	Joe Aguirre (LA Dons)	—	—	2	1	—
E	Dale Gentry (LA Dons)	—	—	—	—	1d
T	Bruiser Kinard (NY Yankees)	1	—	1	1	1d
T	Lou Rymkus (Clev Browns)	—	1	—	—	1o
T	Martin Ruby (Brklyn Dodgers)	2	—	1	1	1d
T	Lou Groza (Cleveland Browns)	—	—	2	—	1o
T	Lee Artoe (Los Angeles Dons)	—	—	2	2	—
T	Bob Reinhard (LA Dons)	—	—	—	2	—
G	Bill Radovich (LA Dons)	1	—	1	1	1d
G	Bill Willis (Cleve Browns)	—	1	—	—	1d
G	Bruno Banducci (SF 49ers)	2	—	1	1	1o
G	Charley Riffle (NY Yankees)	—	—	—	—	1o
G	Buddy Jungmichael (Miami Seahawks)	—	—	2	—	—
G	Ed Ulinski (Cleve Browns)	—	—	2	2	—
G	Garland Gregory (SF 49ers)	—	—	2	—	—
C	Bob Nelson (LA Dons)	2	—	1	2	1d
C	Mike Scarry (Clev Browns)	—	—	2	1	1o
QB	Frankie Albert (SF 49ers)	2	—	2	1	—
QB	Otto Graham (Cleve Browns)	—	—	1	2	1od
P	Player	AP	SP	UP	NY	PR
HB	Glenn Dobbs (Brklyn Dodgers)	1	1	1	1	1o
HB	Spec Sanders (NY Yankees)	1	—	1	1	1od
HB	Lou Saban (Cleve Browns)	—	—	—	—	1d
HB	Bob Hoernschemeyer (Chicago Rockets)	—	—	2	2	—
HB	Steve Juzwik (Buffalo Bills)	—	—	—	2	—
HB	Ace Parker (NY Yankees)	—	—	2	—	—
FB	Marion Motley (Cleve Browns)	2	—	1	1	1o
FB	Norm Standlee (SF 49ers)	—	—	2	2	1d

H denotes "Honorable Mention"; AP—Associated Press; SP—Sportswriters, Inc.; UP—United Press; NY—New York News; PR—Cleveland Press

1947 Press-Selected All-Pros
(Compiled by John Hogrogian)

P	Player	AP	SP	NY	MD	CB
E	Mac Speedie (Cleve Browns)	1	1	1	1	1
E	Bruce Alford (NY Yankees)	1	—	—	1	—
E	Jack Russell (NY Yankees)	—	—	1	2	1
E	Dante Lavelli (Cleve Browns)	H	—	—	2	2
E	Alyn Beals (SF 49ers)	H	—	—	—	2
E	Lamar Davis (Balti Colts)	H	—	—	—	—
T	Lou Rymkus (Cleve Browns)	H	1	1	1	1
T	Martin Ruby (Brklyn Dodgers)	2	—	—	2	—
T	John Woudenberg (SF 49ers)	2	—	—	2	—
T	Nate Johnson (NY Yankees)	—	1	1	—	—
T	Bob Bryant (SF 49ers)	—	—	—	—	1
T	Bruiser Kinard (NY Yankees)	H	—	—	—	2
T	Lee Artoe (LA Dons)	—	—	—	—	2
G	Dick Barwegan (NY Yankees)	2	1	1	1	1
G	Bruno Banducci (SF 49ers)	1	—	1	1	—
G	Bill Willis (Cleve Browns)	—	—	—	2	—
G	Alex Agase (Chicago Rockets)	—	—	—	—	1
G	Weldon Humble (Cleve Browns)	—	—	—	—	2
G	Garland Gregory (SF 49ers)	—	—	—	—	2
G	Al Lolotai (LA Dons)	—	—	—	2	—
G	Bill Radovich (LA Dons)	H	—	—	—	—
G	Harold Lahar (Buffalo Bills)	H	—	—	—	—
C	Bob Nelson (LA Dons)	2	—	1	2	—
C	Lou Sossamon (NY Yankees)	H	—	—	—	1
C	Mike Scarry (Cleve Browns)	—	—	—	1	—
C	Ed Gustafson (Brklyn Dodgers)	—	—	—	—	2
C	Fred Negus (Chicago Rockets)	H	—	—	—	—
QB	Otto Graham (Cleve Browns)	1	1	1	1	1
QB	Frankie Albert (SF 49ers)	2	—	—	—	—
QB	George Ratterman (Buf Bills)	H	—	—	2	2
QB	Bob Sweiger (NY Yankees)	—	—	—	2	—
QB	Bud Schwenk (Baltimore Colts)	H	—	—	—	—
HB	Spec Sanders (NY Yankees)	1	1	1	1	1
HB	Chet Mutryn (Buffalo Bills)	H	—	1	1	—
HB	Billy Hillenbrand (Balt Colts)	—	—	—	—	1
HB	Buddy Young (NY Yankees)	H	—	—	—	2
HB	Bob Hoernschemeyer (Chicago–Brooklyn)	H	—	—	—	2
FB	Marion Motley (Cleve Browns)	2	—	1	1	2
FB	Mickey Colmer (Brklyn Dodgers)	—	—	—	—	1
FB	Norm Standlee (SF 49ers)	H	—	—	—	—
FB	John Kimbrough (LA Dons)	H	—	—	—	—

Note: "H" means Honorable Mention; AP—Associated Press; SP—Sportswriters, Inc.; NY—New York News; MD—Mid-Season United Press; CB—Cliff Battles

1948 Press-Selected All-Pros
(Compiled by John Hogrogian)

P	Player	AP	SN	SG	UP	NY	MD
E	Mac Speedie (Clev Browns)	1	1	1	1	1	1o
E	Alyn Beals (SF 49ers)	2	2	—	1	1	2o
E	Dante Lavelli (Clev Browns)	—	—	—	2	2	1o
E	Jack Russell (NY Yankees)	H	—	—	—	—	1d
E	John Yonakor (Clev Browns)	—	—	—	—	—	1d
E	Al Baldwin (Buffalo Bills)	H	—	—	2	2	2o
E	Len Ford (Los Angeles Dons)	H	—	—	—	—	2d
E	Ted Scruggs (Brooklyn Dodgers)	—	—	—	—	—	2d
E	Lamar Davis (Baltimore Colts)	H	H	—	—	—	—
T	Bob Reinhard (LA Dons)	1	2	1	1	1	1o
T	Lou Rymkus (Clev Browns)	2	H	—	1	2	1o
T	John Woudenberg (SF 49ers)	H	H	—	2	1	2o
T	Martin Ruby (Brooklyn Dodgers)	—	—	—	2	—	1d
T	Arnie Weinmeister (New York Yankees)	H	—	—	—	2	1d
T	Chet Adams (Clev Browns)	—	—	—	—	—	2d
T	Ernie Blandin (Balt Colts)	—	—	—	—	—	2o
T	Lee Artoe (Baltimore Colts)	—	—	—	—	—	2d
T	John Kissell (Buffalo Bills)	H	H	—	—	—	—
T	Nate Johnson (Chi Rockets)	H	—	—	—	—	—
G	Dick Barwegan (Balt Colts)	1	1	1	1	1	1o
G	Bill Willis (Clev Browns)	2	2	—	1	1	—
G	Riley Matheson (SF 49ers)	H	H	—	—	2	1d
G	Weldon Humble (Cleveland Browns)	—	—	—	2	2	1d
G	Ed Ulinski (Cleveland Browns)	—	—	—	2	—	1d
G	Bruno Banducci (SF 49ers)	H	H	—	—	—	2o
G	Knox Ramsey (LA Dons)	—	—	—	—	—	2o
G	Len Levy (Los Angeles Dons)	—	—	—	—	—	2d
G	Tex Warrington (Brooklyn Dodgers)	H	—	—	—	—	2d
G	Jim Pearcy (Chicago Rockets)	H	—	—	—	—	—
G	Joe Signaigo (NY Yankees)	H	—	—	—	—	—
C	George Strohmeyer (Brooklyn Dodgers)	2	—	—	—	—	2d
C	Lou Saban (Cleveland Browns)	—	H	—	1	1	1d
C	Bob Nelson (LA Dons)	H	—	—	2	2	1o
C	Lou Sossamon (NY Yankees)	H	—	—	—	—	2o
QB	Frankie Albert (SF 49ers)	H	1	1	2	1	1o
QB	Otto Graham (Clev Browns)	1	2	—	1	2	2o
QB	Jim Cason (SF 49ers)	—	—	—	—	—	1d
QB	Otto Schnellbacher (New York Yankees)	—	—	—	—	—	2d
QB	George Ratterman (Buf Bills)	H	—	—	—	—	—
QB	Y.A. Tittle (Baltimore Colts)	H	—	—	—	—	—
HB	Chet Mutryn (Buffalo Bills)	2	H	—	1	1	1o
HB	John Strzykalski (SF 49ers)	2	H	—	1	1	2o
HB	Glenn Dobbs (LA Dons)	H	2	—	2	2	2o
HB	Billy Hillenbrand (Balt Colts)	H	2	—	2	2	1o
HB	Tom Colella (Clev Browns)	—	—	—	—	—	1o
HB	Paul Crowe (SF 49ers)	—	—	—	—	—	1d
HB	Spec Sanders (NY Yankees)	H	—	—	—	2	—
HB	Ray Ramsey (Brklyn Dodgers)	—	—	—	—	—	2d
HB	Tommy James (Clev Browns)	—	—	—	—	—	2d
HB	Buddy Young (NY Yankees)	H	—	—	—	—	—
FB	Marion Motley (Cleveland Browns)	1	1	1	1	1	1o
FB	Norm Standlee (SF 49ers)	—	—	—	—	—	1d
FB	Mickey Colmer (Brooklyn Dodgers)	H	—	—	2	—	2o
FB	Walt McDonald (Brooklyn Dodgers)	—	—	—	—	—	2d

AP—Associated Press; SN—The Sporting News; SG—Sport Magazine (published in 1949 Sports Annual); UP—United Press; NY—New York News; MD—Mid-Season United Press

1949 Press-Selected All-Pros
(Compiled by John Hogrogian)

P	Player	AP	SG	IN	UP	NY	MD
E	Mac Speedie (Clev Browns)	1	1	1o	1	1	1
E	Alyn Beals (SF 49ers)	2	—	1o	1	1	2
E	Dante Lavelli (Clev Browns)	H	—	—	2	2	1
E	Jack Russell (NY Yankees)	H	—	—	H	2	2
E	Al Baldwin (Buffalo Bills)	H	—	—	2	—	—
E	Len Ford (Los Angeles Dons)	—	—	—	H	—	—
E	Bob Nowaskey (Balt Colts)	H	—	—	—	—	—
E	Dan Edwards (Chi Hornets)	H	—	—	—	—	—
T	Arnie Weinmeister (New York Yankees)	1	1	—	1	1	1
T	John Kissell (Buffalo Bills)	H	—	1d	2	1	2
T	Lou Rymkus (Clev Browns)	—	—	1o	1	—	2
T	Bob Reinhard (LA Dons)	2	—	—	—	2	—
T	Martin Ruby (NY Yankees)	H	—	—	2	2	1
T	Lou Groza (Clev Browns)	—	—	—	H	—	—
T	John Woudenberg (SF 49ers)	—	—	—	H	—	—
T	Chubby Grigg (Clev Browns)	—	—	—	H	—	—
G	Dick Barwegan (Balt Colts)	1	1	—	1	1	2
G	Joe Signaigo (NY Yankees)	H	—	1o	2	2	1
G	Visco Grgich (SF 49ers)	2	—	—	1	1	—
G	Bill Willis (Clev Browns)	HT	—	—	2	2	1
G	John Mastrangelo (New York Yankees)	—	—	—	H	—	2
G	Lin Houston (Clev Browns)	—	—	—	H	—	—
G	Weldon Humble (Clev Browns)	—	—	—	H	—	—
G	John Wozniak (NY Yankees)	H	—	—	—	—	—
G	Bruno Banducci (SF 49ers)	—	—	—	H	—	—
G	Martin Wendell (Chi Hornets)	—	—	—	H	—	—
C	Lou Saban (Cleveland Browns)	2	—	1d	1	1	1
C	Bob Nelson (LA Dons)	H	—	—	2	2	—
C	John Rapacz (Chi Hornets)	H	—	—	—	—	—
C	Bill Johnson (SF 49ers)	—	—	—	H	—	2
C	Brad Ecklund (NY Yankees)	H	—	—	—	—	—
C	George Strohmeyer (Chicago Hornets)	H	—	—	—	—	—
QB	Otto Graham (Clev Browns)	1	1	1o	1	1	1
QB	Frankie Albert (SF 49ers)	2	—	—	2	2	2
QB	George Ratterman (Buf Bills)	H	—	—	—	—	—
QB	Glenn Dobbs (LA Dons)	H	—	—	—	—	—
QB	Y.A. Tittle (Baltimore Colts)	H	—	—	—	—	—
HB	Chet Mutryn (Buffalo Bills)	1	1	1o	1	2	1
HB	Herman Wedemeyer (Baltimore Colts)	—	—	1d	—	—	—
HB	Jim Cason (SF 49ers)	—	—	1d	—	—	—
HB	Buddy Young (NY Yankees)	H	—	—	—	1	2
HB	Johnny Clement (Chicago Hornets)	H	—	—	—	2	1
HB	George Taliaferro (New York Yankees)	H	—	—	—	2	2
HB	Bob Hoernschemeyer (Chicago Hornets)	H	—	—	—	2	—
HB	Sherman Howard (New York Yankees)	—	—	—	—	—	2

P	Player	AP	SG	IN	UP	NY	MD
HB	Dub Jones (Clev Browns)	—	—	—	H	—	—
HB	Billy Stone (Baltimore Colts)	H	—	—	—	—	—
HB	John Strzykalski (SF 49ers)	—	—	—	H	—	—
HB	Ray Ramsey (Chi Hornets)	H	—	—	—	—	—
HB	Otto Schnellbacher (New York Yankees)	—	—	—	H	—	—
HB	Edgar Jones (Clev Browns)	—	—	—	H	—	—
FB	Joe Perry (SF 49ers)	2	—	—	1	1	1
FB	Marion Motley (Clev Browns)	H	—	—	2	1	2
FB	Ollie Cline (Buffalo Bills)	—	—	—	H	—	—

AP—Associated Press; SG—Sport Magazine (published in 1950 Sport Annual); IN—International News Service; UP—United Press; NY—New York News; MD—Mid-Season United Press

Statistical Records

Note: There were 14 games in 1946, 1947 and 1948. There were 12 games in 1949.

Consecutive

Individual Records

- Most Consecutive Forward Passes Completed: 14, Glenn Dobbs, Brooklyn. Gained 222 yards. Record started October 19, 1946, vs. New York, and ended October 25, 1946, vs. Miami.
- Most Consecutive Pass Attempts without Interception: 118, Otto Graham, Cleveland. Record started October 9, 1949, vs. San Francisco and ended November 20, 1949, vs. Yankees.
- Most Pass Completions without Interception: 69, Otto Graham, Cleveland. Record started October 9, 1949, vs. San Francisco, and ended November 20, 1949, vs. Yankees.
- Most Forward Pass Yards Gained without Interception: 1,372, Otto Graham, Cleveland. Record started October 9, 1949, vs. San Francisco, and ended November 20, 1949, vs. Yankees.
- Most Consecutive Games Throwing Touchdown Passes: 16, Frankie Albert, San Francisco. Record Started November 2, 1947, vs. Los Angeles, and ended November 7, 1948, vs. Chicago.
- Most Consecutive Games with Pass Reception: 45, Alyn Beals, San Francisco. Record started November 24, 1946, and continued through the end of the 1949 season.
- Most Consecutive Games with Touchdown Reception: 7, Al Baldwin, Buffalo. Record started November 14, 1948, vs. Los Angeles, and ended August 26, 1949, vs. Chicago.
- Most Consecutive Games with Interception: 7, Otto Schnellbacher, New York. Record started October 24, 1948, and ended December 4, 1948, vs. Chicago.
- Most Consecutive Games with a Score: 56, Joe Vetrano, San Francisco. Record started September 8, 1946, and continued to the end of the 1949 season.
- Most Consecutive Games Scoring Touchdowns: 9, John Strzykalski, San Francisco. Record started August 29, 1948, vs. Buffalo, and ended October 24, 1948, vs. Baltimore. Record tied by Joe Perry, San Francisco. Record started October 1, 1948, vs. Chicago, and ended December 5, 1948, vs. Los Angeles.
- Most Consecutive Points After Touchdown Scored: 107, Joe Vetrano, San Francisco. Record Started September 19, 1948, vs. Los Angeles, and continued to the end of the 1949 season. Of note, Harvey Johnson of the Yankees had a streak of 103 at the end of the 1949 season.
- Most Consecutive Field Goals Scored: 9, Harvey Johnson, New York. Record started October 27, 1946, vs. Los Angeles, and ended October 12, 1947, vs. Brooklyn.
- Most Consecutive Games Scoring Field Goals: 6, Harvey Johnson, Yankees. Record started September 11, 1949, vs. Buffalo, and ended October 23, 1949, vs. San Francisco.
- Most Consecutive Games Started: 56, John Woudenberg, San Francisco. Record started September 8, 1946, and lasted to the end of the 1949 season.
- Most Consecutive Games Played: 59, Otto Graham, Lou Saban and John Yonakor, Cleveland.

Team Records

- Most Consecutive Victories: 18, Cleveland. Record started November 27, 1947, vs. Los Angeles, and ended December 19, 1948, vs. Buffalo (championship game).
- Most Consecutive Games without a Defeat: 29,

Cleveland. Record started October 19, 1947, vs. Chicago, and ended October 2, 1949, vs. Los Angeles.
- Most Consecutive Losses: 11, Chicago. Record started September 17, 1948, vs. Cleveland, and ended December 4, 1948, vs. New York.
- Most Consecutive Games without a Victory: 12, Chicago. Record started November 30, 1946, vs. San Francisco, and ended October 31, 1947, vs. Brooklyn.
- Most Consecutive Games Shutout by Opponent: 2, Miami. Record started December 3, 1946, vs. Cleveland and ended December 9, 1946, vs. New York.

Single Game–Individual

Rushing

- Number of Rushes: 32, Spec Sanders, New York. Record set November 23, 1947, vs. Cleveland.
- Most Yards Gained (Net): 250, Spec Sanders, New York. Record set October 24, 1947, vs. Chicago.
- Most Yards Lost: 48, Glenn Dobbs, Brooklyn. Record set November 10, 1946, vs. Buffalo.
- Best Average Gain per Rush (minimum 7 rushes): 17.9 yards, Marion Motley, Cleveland. Record set October 20, 1946, vs. Los Angeles (8 rushes for 143 yards).
- Most Rushing Touchdowns: 3, Dick Renfro, San Francisco. Record set September 15, 1946, vs. Miami. Tied by six other players: Spec Sanders (twice), New York; Frankie Albert, San Francisco; John Colmer, Brooklyn; Julie Rykovich, Buffalo; Buddy Young, Yankees; Joe Perry, San Francisco.

Passing

- Most Pass Attempts: 55, Glenn Dobbs, Los Angeles. Record set December 5, 1948, vs. San Francisco (27–55 for 405 yards, with 3 touchdowns and 7 interceptions).
- Most Pass Completions: 27, Glenn Dobbs, Los Angeles. Record set December 5, 1948, vs. San Francisco (27–55 for 405 yards, with 3 touchdowns and 7 interceptions). Record tied by Otto Graham, Cleveland, September 5, 1949, vs. Buffalo.
- Most Passing Yards: 405, Glenn Dobbs, Los Angeles. Record set December 5, 1948, vs. San Francisco (27–55 for 405 yards, with 3 touchdowns and 7 interceptions).
- Most Passes Intercepted: 7, Glenn Dobbs, Los Angeles. Record set December 5, 1948, vs. San Francisco (27–55 for 405 yards, with 3 touchdowns and 7 interceptions).
- Best Completion Percentage (minimum 10 attempts): 86.7 percent, Frankie Albert, San Francisco. Record set October 10, 1948, vs. Baltimore (completed 13 of 15 passes).
- Best Average Gain per Pass Completion (minimum 5 completions): 34.8 yards, Bob Hoernschemeyer, Chicago. Record set September 30, 1949, vs. San Francisco (Completed 6 of 15 attempts for 209 yards).
- Best Average Gain per Pass Attempt (minimum 10 attempts): 16.6 yards, Pete Layden, New York. Record set October 31, 1948, vs. Chicago (completed 9 of 13 attempts for 213 yards).
- Most Touchdown Passes: 9, Otto Graham, Cleveland. Record set October 14, 1949, vs. Los Angeles.
- Most Passes Attempted without Interception: 40, Glenn Dobbs, Brooklyn. Record set September 22, 1946, vs. San Francisco (completed 23 for 198 yards).
- Most Passes Completed without Interception: 23, Glenn Dobbs, Brooklyn Record set September 22, 1946, vs. San Francisco (attempted 40).
- Most Passing Yards Gained without Interception: 362, Otto Graham, Cleveland. Record set October 14, 1949, vs. Los Angeles (completed 15 of 24 attempts).

Total Offense

- Most Plays Attempted (Rushing and Passing): 63, Glenn Dobbs, Los Angeles. Record set December 5, 1948, vs. San Francisco (gained 431 yards and scored 3 touchdowns).
- Most Yards Gained (Rushing and Passing): 431, Glenn Dobbs, Los Angeles. Record set December 5, 1948, vs. San Francisco (63 Plays).
- Best Average Gain per Play (Rushing and Passing, minimum 15 plays): 15.3 yards, Bob Chappuis, Brooklyn. Record set November 21, 1948, vs. San Francisco (Gaines 367 yards on 24 plays).
- Most Touchdowns: 6, Frankie Albert, San Francisco. Record set November 21, 1948, vs. Brooklyn (4 touchdown passes and 2 other touchdowns). Tied by Otto Graham, Cleveland on October 14, 1949, vs. Los Angeles (threw 6 touchdown passes).

Receiving

- Most Receptions: 11, Mac Speedie, Cleveland. Record set November 20, 1949, vs. Yankees (gained 228 yards).
- Most Receiving Yards: 228, Mac Speedie, Cleveland. Record set November 20, 1949, vs. Yankees (11 Receptions).
- Best Average Gain per Reception (minimum 4 receptions): 37.3 yards, Ray Ramsey, Brooklyn. Record set November 21, 1948, vs. San Francisco (4 receptions for 149 yards and 1 touchdown).
- Most Touchdown Receptions: 4, Dante Lavelli, Cleveland. Record set October 14, 1949, vs. Los Angeles (7 receptions for 209 yards).

Interceptions and Returns

- Most Interceptions: 3, Bob Sweiger, New York. Record set October 27, 1946, vs. Los Angeles. Record tied by Tom Colella, Cleveland; Eddie Prokop, New York; Harry Burrus, Brooklyn; Jim Cason, San Francisco.
- Most Interception Return Yards: 148, Walter Williams, Chicago. Record set November 24, 1946, vs. New York (2 Interceptions, 1 returned for a touchdown).

Punting

- Most Punts: 11, Glenn Dobbs, Los Angeles. Record set September 22, 1949, vs. Yankees.
- Most Punting Yards: 507, Glenn Dobbs, Brooklyn. Record set November 28, 1946, vs. New York (10 Punts for 50.7 yard average).
- Best Punting Average: 58 yards, Glenn Dobbs, Brooklyn. Record set December 13, 1946, vs. Miami (Punted 4 times for 232 yards).

Punt and Kick Returns

- Most Punt Returns: 6, Roy Gafford, Brooklyn. Record set October 31, 1948, vs. Los Angeles (returned 59 yards). Note: Jim Cason returned 7 punts for 98 yards on December 4, 1949, vs. Yankees in a playoff game.
- Most Punt Return Yards: 148, Tom Casey, New York. Record set August 27, 1948, vs. Brooklyn (4 punt returns).
- Best Punt Return Average (minimum 3 returns): 40.7 yards, Rex Bumgardner, Buffalo. Record set October 24, 1948, vs. Los Angeles (returned 3 punts for 122 yards).
- Most Kick Returns: 5, Dub Jones, Brooklyn. Record set December 8, 1946, vs. Cleveland. Record tied by Chuck Fenenbock, Los Angeles; Ray Ramsey, Brooklyn; Roy Gafford, Brooklyn; Marion Motley, Cleveland.
- Most Kick Return Yards: 158, Roy Gafford, Brooklyn. Record set November 23, 1947, vs. Los Angeles (returned 4 kicks).
- Best Kick Return Average (minimum 3 returns): 46.3 yards, Chuck Fenenbock, Los Angeles. Record set December 8, 1946, vs. San Francisco (returned 3 kicks for 139 yards).
- Most Returns (Punts and Kicks): 9, Roy Gafford, Brooklyn. Record set October 31, 1948, vs. Los Angeles (Returned 6 punts and 3 kicks for 119 yards). Record tied by Herman Wedemeyer, Baltimore on November 20, 1949, vs. Los Angeles (returned 5 punts and 4 kicks for 90 yards).
- Most Return Yards (Punts and Kicks): 181, Billy Hillenbrand, Baltimore. Record set September 7, 1947, vs. Brooklyn (returned 3 kicks).
- Best Return Average (Punts and Kicks, minimum 5 returns): 26.4 yards, Glenn Dobbs, Los Angeles. Record set September 19, 1947, vs. Brooklyn (returned 5 kicks for 132 yards).

Single Game–Team (Offense)

Rushing

- Most Rushing Attempts: 61, New York. Record set November 23, 1947, vs. Cleveland (gained 269 yards). Record tied by Buffalo on October 23, 1949, vs. Los Angeles (gained 325 yards).
- Most Yards Gained (Gross): 418, Buffalo. Record set November 7, 1948, vs. Brooklyn (lost 4 yards).
- Most Yards Gained (Net): 414, Buffalo. Record set November 7, 1948, vs. Brooklyn (in 53 rushes).
- Most Yards Lost: 80, Miami. Record set October 18, 1946, vs. Chicago (netted minus 25 yards).
- Best Average Gain per Rush: 9.45 yards, Cleveland. Record set November 24, 1946, vs. Buffalo (gained 274 yards on 29 rushes).
- Most Rushing Touchdowns: 5, New York. Record set September 5, 1947, vs. Chicago. Record tied twice by San Francisco (against Buffalo and Chicago), once by Brooklyn (against Chicago), and Buffalo (against Chicago).

Passing

- Most Pass Attempts: 56, Los Angeles. Record set December 5, 1948, vs. San Francisco (completed 27 for 405 yards with 3 touchdowns and 7 interceptions).
- Most Pass Completions: 27, Los Angeles.

Record set December 5, 1948, vs. San Francisco (attempted 56 passes for 405 yards with 3 touchdowns and 7 interceptions).
- Most Passing Yards: 423, Cleveland. Record set October 14, 1949, vs. Los Angeles (completes 17 of 28 for 7 touchdowns and 1 interception).
- Most Passes Intercepted: 8, Miami. Record set December 3, 1946, vs. Cleveland (completed 7 of 23 attempts for 38 yards).
- Best Completion Percentage (minimum 10 attempts): 90 percent, Los Angeles. Record set December 1, 1946, vs. Buffalo (completed 18 of 20 attempts for 344 yards with 5 touchdowns and 1 interception).
- Best Average Gain per Pass Completion (minimum 5 completions): 35 yards, New York. Record set December 7, 1947, vs. Brooklyn (completed 5 of 13 attempts for 175 yards).
- Best Average Gain per Pass Attempt (minimum 10 attempts): 17.2 yards, Los Angeles. Record set December 1, 1946, vs. Buffalo (gained 344 yards on 20 attempts).
- Most Touchdown Passes: 7, Cleveland. Record set October 14, 1949, vs. Los Angeles.
- Most Passes Attempted without Interception: 45, Brooklyn. Record set September 22, 1946, vs. San Francisco.
- Most Passes Completed without Interception: 25, Brooklyn. Record set September 22, 1946, vs. San Francisco.
- Most Passing Yards Gained without Interception: 358, Cleveland. Record set December 8, 1946, vs. Brooklyn.

Total Offense
- Most Plays Attempted (Rushing and Passing): 83, San Francisco. Record set September 28, 1947, vs. Buffalo (gained 408 yards). Record tied by Buffalo December 5, 1948, vs. Baltimore (gained 295 yards).
- Most Yards Gained (Rushing and Passing): 607, Los Angeles. Record set December 1, 1946, vs. Buffalo. Record tied by Cleveland October 14, 1949, vs. Los Angeles.
- Best Average Gain per Play (Rushing and Passing): 9.79 yards, Los Angeles. Record set December 1, 1946, vs. Buffalo (gained 607 yards on 62 plays).
- Most Touchdowns: 9, Cleveland. Record set October 14, 1949, vs. Los Angeles.

Interceptions and Returns
- Most Interceptions: 8, Cleveland. Record set December 3, 1946, vs. Miami (95 return yards).
- Most Interception Return Yards: 174, Chicago. Record set November 24, 1946, vs. New York (intercepted 4).

Punting
- Most Punts: 11, Los Angeles. Record set September 22, 1949, vs. New York.
- Most Punting Yards: 507, Brooklyn. Record set November 28, 1946, vs. New York (10 punts).
- Best Punting Average (minimum 4 punts): 58 yards, Brooklyn. Record set December 13, 1946, vs. Miami (punted 4 times for 232 yards).

Punt and Kick Returns
- Most Punt Returns: 7, New York. Record set October 12, 1946, vs. Cleveland. Record tied twice each by New York, Los Angeles and San Francisco. Tied once each by Chicago and Brooklyn. Note: San Francisco returned 10 punts on December 4, 1949, vs. Yankees in playoff game.
- Most Punt Return Yards: 169, New York. Record set August 27, 1948, vs. Brooklyn (Returned 6 punts).
- Best Punt Return Average (minimum 3 returns): 53 yards, Los Angeles. Record set October 8, 1948, vs. Chicago (returned 3 punts for 159 yards).
- Most Kick Returns: 9, Chicago. Record set November 17, 1946, vs. Cleveland. Record tied by Buffalo and Brooklyn.
- Most Kick Return Yards: 232, Los Angeles. Record set December 8, 1946, vs. San Francisco (returned 8 kicks).
- Best Kick Return Average (minimum 3 returns): 57.7 yards, Buffalo. Record set October 17, 1947, vs. Brooklyn (returned 3 kicks for 173 yards).
- Most Returns (Punts and Kicks): 14, Chicago. Record set November 17, 1946, vs. Cleveland (returned 280 yards).
- Most Return Yards (Punts and Kicks): 301, New York. Record set November 2, 1947, vs. Baltimore (returned 9 kicks).
- Best Return Average (Punts and Kicks, minimum 5 returns): 43.2 yards, Baltimore. Record set September 7, 1947, vs. Brooklyn (Returned 5 kicks for 216 yards).

Single Game–Team (Defense)

Rushing
- Fewest Rushes Allowed: 13, San Francisco. Record set November 24, 1946, vs. Brooklyn (allowed 65 yards).

- Fewest Yards Allowed (Gross): 18, Los Angeles. Record set September 20, 1946, vs. Miami (allowed minus 14 yards net).
- Fewest Yards Allowed (Net): Minus 25, Chicago. Record set October 18, 1946, vs. Miami.
- Most Yards Lost by Opponents: 80, Chicago. Record set October 18, 1946, vs. Miami.
- Lowest Average Yards per Rush Allowed: Minus 1.25 yards, New York. Record set October 24, 1947, vs. Chicago (allowed minus 20 yards in 16 attempts).

Passing
- Fewest Pass Attempts Allowed: 4, Chicago. Record set November 20, 1949, vs. Buffalo.
- Fewest Pass Completions Allowed: 1, Buffalo. Record set October 17, 1947, vs. Brooklyn (Brooklyn attempted 7 for 12 yards with 2 interceptions). Record tied by Chicago on November 20, 1949, vs. Buffalo (Buffalo attempted 4 for 20 yards and 1 interception).
- Fewest Pass Yards Allowed: 12, Buffalo. Record set October 17, 1947, vs. Brooklyn (allowed 1 completion in 7 attempts).
- Most Passes Intercepted By: 8, Cleveland. Record set December 3, 1946, vs. Miami (Miami attempted 23 passes).
- Lowest Completion Percentage Allowed (minimum 10 attempts): 16.7%, New York. Record set September 14, 1946, vs. Buffalo (allowed 2 completions in 12 attempts).
- Lowest Average Gain per Completion Allowed (minimum 5 completions): 5.17 yards, Chicago. Record set September 13, 1946, vs. Cleveland (allowed 31 yards on 6 completions and 13 attempts).
- Lowest Average Gain per Attempts Allowed (minimum 10 attempts): 1.36 yards, San Francisco. Record set October 23, 1949, vs. Brooklyn-New York (allowed 15 yards on 11 attempts and 2 completions).

Total Defense
- Fewest Plays Allowed (Rushing and Passing): 33, Chicago. Record set October 11, 1946, vs. Brooklyn (allowed 161 yards).
- Fewest Yards Allowed (Rushing and Passing): 27, Cleveland. Record set September 6, 1946, vs. Miami.
- Lowest Average Gain per Play Allowed (Rushing and Passing): 0.61 yards, Cleveland. Record set September 6, 1946, vs. Miami (allowed 27 yards on 44 plays).

Punting
- Fewest Punts by Opponents: 1, Los Angeles. Record set September 7, 1947, vs. San Francisco. Record tied nine times.
- Fewest Yards Punted By Opponents: 14, Los Angeles. Record set September 7, 1947, vs. San Francisco (Opponent punted once).
- Lowest Average Punt by Opponents (minimum 4 punts): 25.3 yards, Chicago. Record set October 27, 1946, vs. Buffalo (opponents punted 4 times for 101 yards).

Punt and Kick Returns
- Lowest Average per Punt Return Allowed (minimum 3 returns): 2.33 yards, New York. Record set November 21, 1948, vs. Cleveland (allowed 7 yards on 3 punt returns).
- Lowest Average per Kick Return Allowed (minimum 3 returns): 9.33 yards, Los Angeles. Record set September 20, 1946, vs. Miami (allowed 56 yards on 6 returns).
- Lowest Average per Kick Return Allowed (All Kicks, minimum 5 returns): 5.2 yards, Chicago. Record set October 31, 1948, vs. New York (allowed 26 yards on 5 returns).
- Fewest Returns Allowed (All Kicks): 1, Miami. Record set December 8, 1946, vs. Miami (for 62 yards).
- Fewest Yards Kick Returns Allowed: 12, Los Angeles. Record set October 23, 1949, vs. Buffalo (on 2 returns).

Single Season–Individual

Rushing
- Number of Rushes: 231, Spec Sanders, New York. Record set 1947 (Gained 1,432 yards).
- Most Yards Gained (Net): 1,432 yards, Spec Sanders, New York. Record set 1947.
- Most Yards Lost: 233, Glenn Dobbs, Brooklyn. Record set 1946.
- Best Average Gain per Rush (minimum 30 rushes): 8.4 yards, Chuck Fenenbock, Los Angeles. Record set 1946 (gained 420 yards on 50 rushes).
- Most Rushing Touchdowns: 18, Spec Sanders, New York. Record set 1947.

Passing
- Most Pass Attempts: 369, Glenn Dobbs, Los Angeles. Record set 1948 (completed 185 for 2,403 yards with 21 touchdowns and 20 interceptions).

- Most Pass Completions: 185, Glenn Dobbs, Los Angeles. Record set 1948 (attempted 369 for 2,403 yards with 21 touchdowns and 20 interceptions).
- Most Passing Yards: 2,785 yards, Otto Graham, Cleveland. Record set 1949 (completed 161 of 285 passes).
- Most Passes Intercepted: 22, George Ratterman, Buffalo. Record set 1948 (attempted 335 passes).
- Fewest Passes Intercepted (minimum 100 attempts): 3, Ace Parker, Brooklyn. Record set 1946 (attempted 115 passes).
- Best Completion Percentage (minimum 40 attempts): 60.6%, Otto Graham, Cleveland. Record set 1947 (completed 163 of 269 passes).
- Best Average Gain per Pass Completion (minimum 20 attempts): 19.3 yards, Otto Graham, Cleveland. Record set 1946 (completed 95 for 1,834 yards).
- Best Average Gain per Pass Attempt (minimum 40 attempts): 10.5 yards, Otto Graham, Cleveland. Record set 1946 (attempted 174 for 1,834 yards).
- Most Touchdown Passes: 29, Frankie Albert, San Francisco. Record set 1948.

Total Offense

- Most Plays Attempted (Rushing and Passing): 460, Glenn Dobbs, Los Angeles. Record set 1948 (gained 2,942 yards and responsible for 25 touchdowns).
- Most Yards Gained (Rushing and Passing): 2,942 yards, Glenn Dobbs, Los Angeles. Record set 1948 (in 460 plays).
- Best Average Gain per Play (Rushing and Passing, minimum 50 plays): 9.81 yards, Otto Graham, Cleveland. Record set 1947 (gained 2,825 yards on 288 plays and responsible for 26 touchdowns).
- Most Touchdowns: 37, Frankie Albert, San Francisco. Record set 1948 (8 touchdowns and 29 touchdown passes).

Receiving

- Most Receptions: 67, Mac Speedie, Cleveland. Record set 1947 (gained 1,146 yards).
- Most Receiving Yards: 1,146, Mac Speedie, Cleveland. Record set 1947 (67 receptions).
- Best Average Gain per Reception (minimum 8 receptions): 33.7 yards, Bill Boedeker, Cleveland. Record set 1949 (caught 11 passes for 371 yards).
- Most Touchdown Receptions: 14, Alyn Beals, San Francisco. Record set 1948 (Caught 46 passes for 591 yards).

Interceptions and Returns

- Most Interceptions: 11, Otto Schnellbacher, New York. Record set 1948 (returned 239 yards).
- Most Interception Return Yards: 239, Otto Schnellbacher, New York (on 11 interceptions).

Punting

- Most Punts: 80, Glenn Dobbs, Brooklyn. Record set 1946 (punted 3,824 yards for 47.8-yard average).
- Most Punting Yards: 3,824 yards, Glenn Dobbs, Brooklyn. Record set 1946 (80 punts for 47.8-yard average).
- Best Punting Average (minimum 14 punts): 49.1 yards, Glenn Dobbs, Los Angeles. Record set 1948 (punted 68 times for 3,336 yards).

Punt and Kick Returns

- Most Punt Returns: 29, Peter Layden, Yankees. Record set 1949 (returned 287 yards).
- Most Punt Return Yards: 368, Herman Wedemeyer, Los Angeles. Record set 1948 (returned 23 punts).
- Best Punt Return Average (minimum 5 returns): 27.3 yards, Spec Sanders, New York. Record set 1947 (returned 6 punts for 164 yards).
- Most Kick Returns: 30, Herman Wedemeyer, Baltimore. Record set 1949 (returned 602 yards).
- Most Kick Return Yards: 691, Chet Mutryn, Buffalo. Record set 1947 (returned 21 kicks).
- Best Kick Return Average (minimum 10 returns): 32.9 yards, Chet Mutryn, Buffalo. Record set 1947 (returned 21 kicks for 691 yards).
- Most Returns (Punts and Kicks): 46, Herman Wedemeyer, Baltimore. Record set 1949 (returned 16 punts and 30 kicks for 823 yards).
- Most Return Yards (Punts and Kicks): 878, Chet Mutryn, Buffalo. Record set 1947 (returned 34 kicks—13 punts and 21 kicks).
- Best Return Average (Punts and Kicks, minimum 5 returns): 32.1 yards, Lamar Davis, Miami. Record set 1946 (returned 9 kicks for 289 yards).

Single Season–Team (Offense)

Rushing

- Most Rushing Attempts: 603, San Francisco. Record set 1948 (gained 3,663 yards).

- Most Yards Gained (Gross): 3,844, San Francisco. Record set 1948 (lost 181 yards).
- Most Yards Gained (Net): 3,663, San Francisco. Record set 1948 (in 603 rushes).
- Most Yards Lost: 603, Miami. Record set 1946 (netted 848 yards).
- Best Average Gain per Rush: 6.07 yards, San Francisco. Record set 1948 (603 rushes for 3,663 yards).
- Most Rushing Touchdowns: 35, San Francisco. Record set 1948.

Passing

- Most Pass Attempts: 410, Brooklyn. Record set 1948 (completed 188 for 2,524 yards).
- Most Pass Completions: 195, Los Angeles. Record set 1948 (attempted 406 passes and gained 2,497 yards).
- Most Passing Yards: 2,990, Cleveland. Record set 1947 (completed 174 of 296 passes with 26 touchdowns and 12 interceptions).
- Most Passes Intercepted: 38, Chicago. Record set 1948 (attempted 341 passes).
- Best Completion Percentage: 58.8 percent, Cleveland. Record set 1847 (completed 174 of 296 passes).
- Best Average Gain per Pass Completion: 18.4 yards, Cleveland. Record set 1946 (completed 123 of 237 passes for 2,266 yards).
- Best Average Gain per Pass Attempt: 10.1 yards, Cleveland. Record set 1947 (completed 174 of 296 passes for 2,990 yards).
- Most Touchdown Passes: 30, San Francisco. Record set 1948.

Total Offense

- Most Plays Attempted (Rushing and Passing): 899, Buffalo. Record set 1948 (gained 5,421 yards).
- Most Yards Gained (Rushing and Passing): 5,767 yards, San Francisco. Record set 1948 (in 891 plays).
- Best Average Gain per Play (Rushing and Passing): 7.16 yards, Cleveland. Record set 1947 (Gained 5,547 yards on 775 plays).
- Most Touchdowns: 65, San Francisco. Record set 1948.

Interceptions and Returns

- Most Interceptions: 41, Cleveland. Record set 1946 (returned 589 yards).
- Most Interception Return Yards: 589, Cleveland. Record set 1946 (intercepted 41 passes).

Punting

- Most Punts: 91, Chicago. Record set 1946 (punted 3,817 yards for 41.9-yard average).
- Most Punting Yards: 4,185 yards, Brooklyn. Record set 1946 (punted 90 times).
- Best Punting Average: 47.2 yards, Los Angeles. Record set 1948 (punted 76 times for 3,584 yards).

Punt and Kick Returns

- Most Punt Returns: 51, New York and San Francisco. Record set 1946 (New York returned 778 yards and San Francisco returned 640 yards).
- Most Punt Return Yards: 778, New York. Record set 1946 (returned 51 punts).
- Best Punt Return Average: 16.9 yards, Buffalo. Record set 1948 (returned 33 punts for 557 yards).
- Most Kick Returns: 69, Chicago. Record set 1947 (returned 1,483 yards).
- Most Kick Return Yards: 1,483 yards, Chicago. Record set 1947 (returned 69 kicks).
- Best Kick Return Average: 25.6 yards, Buffalo. Record set 1947 (returned 50 kicks for 1,282 yards).
- Most Returns (Punts and Kicks): 106, Los Angeles. Record set 1946 (returned 49 punts and 57 kicks).
- Most Return Yards (Punts and Kicks): 2,031 yards, Los Angeles. Record set 1946 (returned 106 kicks).
- Best Return Average (Punts and Kicks): 21.6 yards, New York. Record set 1947 (returned 85 kicks for 1,840 yards).

Single Season–Team (Defense)

Rushing

- Fewest Rushes Allowed: 360, Brooklyn–New York. Record set 1949 (allowed 1,134 yards).
- Fewest Yards Allowed (Gross): 1,322, Brooklyn–New York. Record set 1949.
- Fewest Yards Allowed (Net): 873, San Francisco. Record set 1946 (in 425 rushes).
- Fewest Touchdowns Allowed: 7, San Francisco. Record set 1946.
- Lowest Average Yards per Rush Allowed: 2.05 yards, San Francisco. Record set 1946 (allowed 873 yards on 425 rushes).

Passing

- Fewest Pass Attempts Allowed: 197, Chicago. Record set 1949 (allowed 107 completions for 1,677 yards).
- Fewest Pass Completions Allowed: 107, Chicago. Record set 1949.
- Fewest Passing Yards Allowed: 1,317 yards, Cleveland. Record set 1946 (Allowed 125 completions of 299 attempts with 41 interceptions).
- Most Passes Intercepted By: 41, Cleveland. Record set 1946 (Allowed 299 attempts).
- Lowest Completion Percentage Allowed: 39.5 percentage, Cleveland. Record set 1949 (allowed 120 completions of 304 attempts by opponent).
- Lowest Average Gain per Completion Allowed: 10.5 yards, Cleveland. Record set 1946 (allowed 1,317 yards on 125 completions by opponents).
- Lowest Average Gain per Attempt Allowed: 4.4 yards, Cleveland. Record set 1946 (allowed 1,317 yards on 299 attempts).
- Fewest Touchdowns Allowed Passing: 8, Cleveland. Record set 1946.

Total Defense

- Fewest Plays Allowed (Rushing and Passing): 664, Chicago. Record set 1949 (allowed 4,041 yards).
- Fewest Yards Allowed (Rushing and Passing): 2,619, New York. Record set 1946 (in 701 plays).
- Lowest Average Gain per Play Allowed (Rushing and Passing): 3.47 yards, Cleveland. Record set 1946 (allowed 2,933 yards in 845 plays).
- Fewest Touchdowns Allowed (Rushing and Passing): 16, Cleveland. Record set 1946.

Punting

- Fewest Punts by Opponents: 50, Baltimore. Record set 1949.
- Fewest Yards Punted by Opponents: 2,029 yards, Brooklyn. Record set 1948 (opponents punted 51 times for a 39.7-yard average).
- Lowest Average per Punt by Opponents: 37.1 yards, San Francisco. Record set 1947 (opponents punted 62 times for 2,300 yards).

Punt and Kick Returns

- Fewest Punt Returns Allowed: 23, San Francisco. Record set 1949.
- Fewest Yards Allowed on Punt Returns: 261, San Francisco. Record set 1949 (opponents returned 23 punts).
- Lowest Average per Punt Return Allowed: 10.3 yards, Baltimore. Record set 1948 (allowed 318 yards on 31 returns).
- Fewest Kick Returns Allowed: 34, Baltimore. Record set 1949 (opponents returned 691 yards).
- Fewest Yards Allowed on Kick Returns: 645, Baltimore. Record set 1947 (opponents returned 38 kicks).
- Lowest Average per Kick Return Allowed: 15.1 yards, Baltimore. Record set 1947 (opponents returned 84 kicks for 1,272 yards).

Rookie Single Season–Individual

Rushing

- Number of Rushes: 140, Spec Sanders, New York. Record set 1946 (gained 709 yards).
- Most Yards Gained (Net): 712, Buddy Young, New York. Record set 1947 (in 116 rushes).
- Best Average Gain per Rush (minimum 30 rushes): 8.23 yards, Marion Motley, Cleveland. Record set 1946 (gained 601 yards in 73 rushes).
- Most Rushing Touchdowns: 10, Joe Perry, San Francisco. Record set 1948.

Passing

- Most Pass Attempts: 289, Y.A. Tittle, Baltimore. Record set 1948.
- Most Pass Completions: 161, Y.A. Tittle, Baltimore. Record set 1948.
- Most Passing Yards: 2,522 yards, Y.A. Tittle, Baltimore. Record set 1948.
- Most Passes Intercepted: 20, George Ratterman, Buffalo. Record set 1947.
- Best Completion Percentage (minimum 40 attempts): 55.7 percent, Y.A. Tittle, Baltimore. Record set 1948.
- Best Average Gain per Pass Completion (minimum 20 completions): 19.3 yards, Otto Graham, Cleveland. Record set 1946 (completed 95 for 1,834 yards).
- Best Average Gain per Pass Attempt (minimum 40 attempts): 10.5 yards, Otto Graham, Cleveland. Record set 1946 (attempted 174 for 1,834 yards).
- Most Touchdown Passes: 22, George Ratterman, Buffalo. Record set 1947.

Total Offense
- Most Plays Attempted (Rushing and Passing): 364, Glenn Dobbs, Brooklyn. Record set 1946 (2,094 yards with 17 touchdowns).
- Most Yards Gained (Rushing and Passing): 2,679 yards, Y.A. Tittle, Baltimore. Record set 1948 (in 341 plays with 20 touchdowns).
- Best Average Gain per Play (Rushing and Passing): 8.38 yards, Otto Graham, Cleveland. Record set 1946 (gained 1,709 yards in 204 plays).
- Most Touchdowns: 23, George Ratterman, Buffalo. Record set 1947 (22 touchdown passes, 1 touchdown).

Receiving
- Most Receptions: 40, Alyn Beals, San Francisco and Dante Lavelli, Cleveland. Record set 1946 (Beals gained 586 yards and Lavelli gained 843 yards).
- Most Receiving Yards: 843, Dante Lavelli, Cleveland. Record set 1946 (on 40 receptions).
- Best Average Gain per Reception (8 or more receptions): 26.9 yards, Jim McCarthy, Brooklyn. Record set 1946 (caught 11 passes for 296 yards).
- Most Touchdown Receptions: 10, Alyn Beals, San Francisco. Record set 1946.

Interceptions and Returns
- Most Interceptions: 11, Otto Schnellbacher, New York. Record set 1948.
- Most Interception Return Yards: 239, Otto Schnellbacher, New York. Record set 1948.

Punting
- Most Punts: 80, Glenn Dobbs, Brooklyn. Record set 1946.
- Most Punting Yards: 3,824 yards, Glenn Dobbs, Brooklyn. Record set 1946.
- Best Punting Average: 47.8 yards, Glenn Dobbs, Brooklyn. Record set 1946 (80 punts for 3,824 yards).

Punt and Kick Returns
- Most Punt Returns: 23, Herman Wedemeyer, Los Angeles. Record set 1948.
- Most Punt Return Yards: 368, Herman Wedemeyer, Los Angeles. Record set 1948.
- Best Punt Return Average (minimum 5 returns): 25.4 yards, Tom Casey, New York. Record set 1948 (returned 9 punts for 229 yards).
- Most Kick Returns: 17, Stormy Pfohl, Baltimore. Record set 1948.
- Most Kick Return Yards: 411, Billy Grimes, Los Angeles. Record set 1949.
- Best Kick Return Average (minimum 4 returns): 47 yards, Lamar Davis, Miami. Record set 1946 (returned 5 kicks for 235 yards).
- Most Returns (Punts and Kicks): 34, Herman Wedemeyer, Los Angeles. Record set 1948 (returned 23 punts and 11 kicks for 608 yards).
- Most Return Yards (Punts and Kicks): 652, Spec Sanders, New York. Record set 1946 (returned 30 kicks).
- Best Return Average (Punts and Kicks, minimum 5 returns): 32.1 yards, Lamar Davis, Miami. Record set 1946 (returned 9 for 289 yards).

Longest Play

- Longest Run from Scrimmage: 84 Yards, Bob Hoernschemeyer, Brooklyn. Record set October 17, 1947, vs. Buffalo. Touchdown.
- Longest Forward Pass: 99 Yards, Otto Graham to Mac Speedie, Cleveland. Record set November 2, 1947, vs. Buffalo. Touchdown.
- Longest Lateral Pass: 58 Yards, Glenn Dobbs (36 yards)—Rob Morrow (22 yards), Brooklyn. Record set September 8, 1946, vs. Buffalo. Touchdown.
- Longest Multiple Pass Play: 66 Yards, Frankie Albert to John Strzykalski to Len Eshmont, San Francisco. Record set September 8, 1946, vs. New York. Touchdown.
- Longest Interception Return: 97 yards, Walter Williams, Chicago. Record set November 24, 1946, vs. New York. Touchdown.
- Longest Fumble Return: 97 yards, Al Vandeweghe, Buffalo. Record set September 14, 1946, vs. New York. Touchdown. Record tied by Fred Negus, Chicago on October 8, 1948, vs. Los Angeles. Touchdown.
- Longest Punt: 84 yards, Spec Sanders, New York. Record set October 5, 1947, vs. Cleveland.
- Longest Punt Return: 94 yards, Tom Casey, New York. Record set August 27, 1948, vs. Brooklyn. Touchdown.
- Longest Kick Return: 103 yards, Spec Sanders, New York. Record set October 27, 1946, vs. Los Angeles. Touchdown.
- Longest Field Goal Attempt: 100 yards, Lew Mayne, Brooklyn. Record set September 8, 1946, vs. Buffalo. Touchdown.
- Longest Field Goal: 53 yards, Ben Agajanian, Los Angeles. Record set October 19, 1947, vs. Baltimore. Record tied by Lou Groza, Cleveland on October 19, 1948, vs. Brooklyn.

Statistical Champions by Season

Individual

Total Offense

- 1946: Glenn Dobbs, Brooklyn (364 plays; 208 rush yards; 1,886 passing yards; 2,094 total yards)
- 1947: Spec Sanders, New York (402 plays; 1,432 rush yards; 1,442 passing yards; 2,874 total yards)
- 1948: Glenn Dobbs, Los Angeles (460 plays; 539 rush yards; 2,403 passing yards; 2,942 total yards)
- 1949: Otto Graham, Cleveland (312 plays; 107 rush yards; 2,785 passing yards; 2,892 total yards)

Rushing

- 1946: Spec Sanders, New York (140 for 709 yards)
- 1947: Spec Sanders, New York (231 for 1,432 yards)
- 1948: Marion Motley, Cleveland (157 for 967 yards)
- 1949: Joe Perry, San Francisco (115 for 783 yards)

Passing

- 1946: Glenn Dobbs, Brooklyn (135–269 for 1,886 yards) and Otto Graham, Cleveland (95–174 for 1,834 yards)
- 1947: Otto Graham, Cleveland (163–269 for 2,753 yards)
- 1948: Otto Graham, Cleveland (173–333 for 2,713 yards)
- 1949: Otto Graham, Cleveland (161–285 for 2,785 yards)

Receiving

- 1946: Dante Lavelli, Cleveland (40 for 843 yards) and Alyn Beals, San Francisco (40 for 586 yards)
- 1947: Mac Speedie, Cleveland (67 for 1,146 yards)
- 1948: Mac Speedie, Cleveland (58 for 816 yards)
- 1949: Mac Speedie, Cleveland (62 for 1,028 yards)

Interception Returns

- 1946: Tom Colella, Cleveland (10 for 110 yards)
- 1947: Tom Colella, Cleveland (6 for 130 yards)
- 1948: Otto Schnellbacher, New York (11 for 239 yards)
- 1949: Jim Cason, San Francisco (9 for 152 yards)

Punting

- 1946: Glenn Dobbs, Brooklyn (80 for 47.8 average)
- 1947: John Colmer, Brooklyn (56 for 44.7 average)
- 1948: Glenn Dobbs, Los Angeles (68 for 49.1 average)
- 1949: Frankie Albert, San Francisco (31 for 48.2 average)

Punt Returns

- 1946: Chuck Fenenbock, Los Angeles (16 for 299 yards)
- 1947: Glenn Dobbs, Los Angeles (19 for 215 yards)
- 1948: Herman Wedemeyer, Los Angeles (23 for 368 yards)
- 1949: Jim Cason, San Francisco (21 for 351 yards)

Kick Returns

- 1946: Chuck Fenenbock, Los Angeles (17 for 479 yards)
- 1947: Chet Mutryn, Buffalo (21 for 691 yards)
- 1948: Roy Gafford, Brooklyn (23 for 559 yards)
- 1949: Herman Wedemeyer, Brooklyn (30 for 602 yards)

Field Goals

- 1946: Lou Groza, Cleveland (13)
- 1947: Ben Agajanian, Los Angeles (15)
- 1948: Rex Grossman, Baltimore (10)
- 1949: Harvey Johnson, Yankees (7)

Points After Touchdowns

- 1946: Lou Groza, Cleveland (45)
- 1947: Harvey Johnson (49)
- 1948: Joe Vetrano, San Francisco (62)
- 1949: Joe Vetrano, San Francisco (56)

Team Records

Total Offense

- 1946: Cleveland (733 plays; 1,978 rush yards; 2,266 passing yards; 4,244 total yards)

- 1947: Cleveland (775 plays; 2,557 rush yards; 2,990 passing yards; 5,547 total yards)
- 1948: San Francisco (891 plays; 3,663 rush yards; 2,104 passing yards; 5,767 total yards)
- 1949: San Francisco (793 plays; 2,798 rush yards; 1,995 passing yards; 4,793 total yards)

Rushing

- 1946: San Francisco (592 for 2,175 yards)
- 1947: New York (534 for 2,930 yards)
- 1948: San Francisco (603 for 3,663 yards)
- 1949: San Francisco (506 for 2,798 yards)

Passing

- 1946: Cleveland (123–237 for 2,266 yards)
- 1947: Cleveland (174–296 for 2,990 yards)
- 1948: Baltimore (185–340 for 2,899 yards)
- 1949: Cleveland (166–296 for 2,929 yards)

Interception Returns

- 1946: Cleveland (41 for 589 yards)
- 1947: Cleveland (32 for 474 yards)
- 1948: San Francisco (32 for 357 yards)
- 1949: San Francisco (32 for 474 yards)

Punting

- 1946: Brooklyn (90 for 46.5 average)
- 1947: Los Angeles (58 for 45.0 average)
- 1948: Los Angeles (76 for 47.2 average)
- 1949: San Francisco (44 for 45.5 average)

Punt Returns

- 1946: New York (51 for 778 yards)
- 1947: Baltimore (33 for 546 yards)
- 1948: Buffalo (33 for 557 yards)
- 1949: San Francisco (46 for 713 yards)

Kick Returns

- 1946: Chicago (54 for 1,323 yards)
- 1947: Buffalo (50 for 1,282 yards)
- 1948: San Francisco (45 for 1,098 yards)
- 1949: Los Angeles (41 for 972 yards)

Field Goals (Based on Percentage)

- 1946: Chicago (9–12)
- 1947: New York (7–8)
- 1948: San Francisco (5–8)
- 1949: Los Angeles (3–6)

Points After Touchdowns (Based on Percentage)

- 1946: New York (36–36)
- 1947: Los Angeles (39–40)
- 1948: Baltimore (43–43)
- 1949: Brooklyn–New York (25–25)

Part 5: Conference Statistics

Conference Standings

1946

Eastern Division

	W	L	T	PF	PA
New York Yankees	10	3	1	270	192
Brooklyn Dodgers	3	10	1	226	339
Buffalo Bills	3	10	1	249	370
Miami Seahawks	3	11	0	167	378

Western Division

	W	L	T	PF	PA
Cleveland Browns	12	2	0	423	137
San Francisco 49ers	9	5	0	307	189
Los Angeles Dons	7	5	2	305	290
Chicago Rockets	5	6	3	263	315

Championship Game: Cleveland 14, New York 9

1947

Eastern Division

	W	L	T	PF	PA
New York Yankees	11	2	1	378	239
Buffalo Bills	8	4	2	320	288
Brooklyn Dodgers	3	10	1	181	310
Baltimore Colts	2	11	1	167	377

Western Division

	W	L	T	PF	PA
Cleveland Browns	12	1	1	410	185
San Francisco 49ers	8	4	2	327	264
Los Angeles Dons	7	7	0	328	256
Chicago Rockets	1	13	0	263	425

Championship Game: Cleveland 14, New York 3

1948

Eastern Division

	W	L	T	PF	PA
Buffalo Bills	8	7	0	388	375
Baltimore Colts	7	8	0	350	355
New York Yankees	6	8	0	263	301
Brooklyn Dodgers	2	12	0	253	387

*Includes Divisional Playoff Game

Western Division

	W	L	T	PF	PA
Cleveland Browns	14	0	0	389	190
San Francisco 49ers	12	2	0	495	248
Los Angeles Dons	7	7	0	258	305
Chicago Rockets	1	13	0	202	439

Championship Game: Cleveland 49, Buffalo 7

1949

	W	L	T	PF	PA
Cleveland Browns	9	1	2	339	171
San Francisco 49ers	9	3	0	416	227
Brooklyn-New York	8	4	0	196	206
Buffalo Bills	5	5	2	236	256
Chicago Hornets	4	8	0	179	268
Los Angeles Dons	4	8	0	253	322
Baltimore Colts	1	11	0	172	341

Playoffs: Cleveland 31, Buffalo 21
San Francisco 17, Brooklyn–New York 7
Championship Game: Cleveland 21, San Francisco 7

Composite Standings

	Cleveland	San Francisco	Yankees	Los Angeles	Buffalo	Baltimore	Chicago	Miami	Brooklyn	W	L	T	Pct
Cleveland	—	6	7	6	6	6	8	2	6	47	4	3	.922
SF	2	—	3	8	5	5	7	2	6	38	14	2	.731
Yankees	0	5	—	7	5	4	6	2	6	35	17	2	.673
Los Angeles	2	0	1	—	3	5	6	2	6	25	27	2	.481
Buffalo	0	2	3	4	—	5	6	0	4	24*	26	5	.480
Baltimore	0	0	2	1	2	—	2	0	3	10	30*	1	.250
Chicago	0	1	1	1	2	4	—	2	0	11	40	3	.216
Miami	0	0	0	0	2	0	0	—	1	3	11	0	.214
Brooklyn	0	0	0	0	1	1	5	1	—	8	32	2	.200

Club versus Club Records

Baltimore Colts

Against Brooklyn
Year	Score	Team	Opp.	W/L/T
1947	16	Brooklyn	7	W
	14	Brooklyn	21	L
1948	35	Brooklyn	20	W
	38	Brooklyn	20	W
	103		68	3-1-0

Against Buffalo
Year	Score	Team	Opp.	W/L/T
1947	15	Buffalo	20	L
	14	Buffalo	33	L
1948	17	Buffalo	35	L
	35	Buffalo	15	W
	17	Buffalo	28	L
1949	35	Buffalo	28	W
	14	Buffalo	38	L
	147		197	2-5-0

Against Chicago
Year	Score	Team	Opp.	W/L/T
1947	21	Chicago	27	L
	14	Chicago	7	W
1948	14	Chicago	21	L
	38	Chicago	24	W
1949	7	Chicago	35	L
	7	Chicago	17	L
	101		131	2-4-0

Against Cleveland
Year	Score	Team	Opp.	W/L/T
1947	0	Cleveland	28	L
	0	Cleveland	42	L
1948	10	Cleveland	14	L
	7	Cleveland	28	L
1949	0	Cleveland	21	L
	20	Cleveland	28	L
	37		161	0-6-0

Against Los Angeles
Year	Score	Team	Opp.	W/L/T
1947	10	Los Angeles	38	L
	0	Los Angeles	56	L
1948	29	Los Angeles	14	W
	14	Los Angeles	17	L
1949	17	Los Angeles	49	L
	10	Los Angeles	21	L
	80		195	1-5-0

Against New York
Year	Score	Team	Opp.	W/L/T
1947	7	New York	21	L
	21	New York	35	L
1948	45	New York	28	W
	27	New York	14	W
1949	21	New York	24	L
	14	New York	21	L
	135		143	2-4-0

Against San Francisco
Year	Score	Team	Opp.	W/L/T
1947	7	San Francisco	14	L
	28	San Francisco	28	T
1948	14	San Francisco	56	L
	10	San Francisco	21	L
1949	17	San Francisco	31	L
	10	San Francisco	28	L
	86		178	0-5-1

Baltimore Won 10, Lost 30*, Tied 1
Baltimore 689; Opponents 1,073
*Includes 1948 Divisional Playoff Game

Brooklyn Dodgers

Against Baltimore
Year	Score	Team	Opp.	W/L/T
1947	7	Baltimore	16	L
	21	Baltimore	14	W
1948	20	Baltimore	35	L
	20	Baltimore	38	L
	68		103	1-3-0

Against Buffalo
Year	Score	Team	Opp.	W/L/T
1946	27	Buffalo	14	W
	14	Buffalo	17	L
1947	14	Buffalo	14	T
	7	Buffalo	35	L
1948	21	Buffalo	31	L
	21	Buffalo	26	L
	104		137	1-4-1

Against Chicago
Year	Score	Team	Opp.	W/L/T
1946	21	Chicago	21	T
	21	Chicago	14	W
1947	35	Chicago	31	W
	7	Chicago	3	W
1948	21	Chicago	7	W
	35	Chicago	14	W
	140		90	5-0-1

Against Cleveland
Year	Score	Team	Opp.	W/L/T
1946	7	Cleveland	26	L
	14	Cleveland	66	L
1947	7	Cleveland	55	L
	12	Cleveland	13	L
1948	17	Cleveland	30	L
	21	Cleveland	31	L
	78		221	0-6-0

Against Los Angeles
Year	Score	Team	Opp.	W/L/T
1946	14	Los Angeles	20	L
	14	Los Angeles	19	L
1947	21	Los Angeles	48	L
	12	Los Angeles	16	L
1948	7	Los Angeles	17	L
	0	Los Angeles	17	L
	68		137	0-6-0

Part 5: Conference Statistics

Against Miami

Year	Score	Team	Opp.	W/L/T
1946	30	Miami	7	W
	20	Miami	31	L
	50		38	1-1-0

Against New York

Year	Score	Team	Opp.	W/L/T
1946	10	New York	21	L
	7	New York	21	L
1947	7	New York	31	L
	17	New York	20	L
1948	3	New York	21	L
	7	New York	21	L
	51		135	0-6-0

Against San Francisco

Year	Score	Team	Opp.	W/L/T
1946	13	San Francisco	32	L
	14	San Francisco	30	L
1947	7	San Francisco	23	L
	7	San Francisco	21	L
1948	20	San Francisco	36	L
	40	San Francisco	63	L
	101		205	0-6-0

Brooklyn Won 8, Lost 32, Tied 2
Brooklyn 660; Opponents 1,066

Buffalo Bisons/Bills

Against Baltimore

Year	Score	Team	Opp.	W/L/T
1947	20	Baltimore	15	W
	33	Baltimore	14	W
1948	35	Baltimore	17	W
	15	Baltimore	35	L
	28	Baltimore	17	W
1949	28	Baltimore	35	L
	38	Baltimore	14	W
	197		147	5-2-0

Against Brooklyn

Year	Score	Team	Opp.	W/L/T
1946	14	Brooklyn	27	L
	17	Brooklyn	14	W
1947	14	Brooklyn	14	T
	35	Brooklyn	7	W
1948	31	Brooklyn	21	W
	26	Brooklyn	21	W
	137		104	4-1-1

Against Chicago

Year	Score	Team	Opp.	W/L/T
1946	35	Chicago	38	L
	49	Chicago	17	W
1947	28	Chicago	20	W
	31	Chicago	14	W
1948	42	Chicago	7	W
	39	Chicago	35	W
1949	14	Chicago	17	L
	10	Chicago	0	W
	248		148	6-2-0

Against Cleveland

Year	Score	Team	Opp.	W/L/T
1946	0	Cleveland	28	L
	17	Cleveland	42	L
1947	14	Cleveland	30	L
	7	Cleveland	28	L
1948	13	Cleveland	42	L
	14	Cleveland	31	L
1949	28	Cleveland	28	T
	7	Cleveland	7	T
	100		236	0-6-2

Against Los Angeles

Year	Score	Team	Opp.	W/L/T
1946	21	Los Angeles	21	T
	14	Los Angeles	62	L
1947	27	Los Angeles	25	W
	25	Los Angeles	0	W
1948	35	Los Angeles	21	W
	20	Los Angeles	27	L
1949	28	Los Angeles	42	L
	17	Los Angeles	14	W
	187		212	4-3-1

Against Miami

Year	Score	Team	Opp.	W/L/T
1946	14	Miami	17	L
	14	Miami	21	L
	28		38	0-2-0

Against New York

Year	Score	Team	Opp.	W/L/T
1946	10	New York	21	L
	13	New York	21	L
1947	28	New York	24	W
	13	New York	35	L
1948	13	New York	14	L
	35	New York	14	W
1949	14	New York	17	L
	17	New York	14	W
	143		160	3-5-0

Against San Francisco

Year	Score	Team	Opp.	W/L/T
1946	17	San Francisco	14	W
	14	San Francisco	27	L
1947	24	San Francisco	41	L
	21	San Francisco	21	T
1948	14	San Francisco	35	L
	28	San Francisco	38	L
1949	28	San Francisco	17	W
	7	San Francisco	51	L
	153		244	2-5-1

Buffalo Won 24*, Lost 26, Tied 5
Buffalo 1,193; Opponents 1,289
*Includes 1948 Divisional Playoff Game

Club versus Club Records 73

Chicago Rockets/Hornets

Against Baltimore

Year	Score	Team	Opp.	W/L/T
1947	27	Baltimore	21	W
	7	Baltimore	14	L
1948	21	Baltimore	14	W
	24	Baltimore	38	L
1949	35	Baltimore	7	W
	17	Baltimore	7	W
	131		101	4–2–0

Against Brooklyn

Year	Score	Team	Opp.	W/L/T
1946	21	Brooklyn	21	T
	14	Brooklyn	21	L
1947	31	Brooklyn	35	L
	3	Brooklyn	7	L
1948	7	Brooklyn	21	L
	14	Brooklyn	35	L
	90		140	0–5–1

Against Buffalo

Year	Score	Team	Opp.	W/L/T
1946	38	Buffalo	35	W
	17	Buffalo	49	L
1947	20	Buffalo	28	L
	14	Buffalo	31	L
1948	7	Buffalo	42	L
	35	Buffalo	39	L
1949	17	Buffalo	14	W
	0	Buffalo	10	L
	148		248	2–6–0

Against Cleveland

Year	Score	Team	Opp.	W/L/T
1946	6	Cleveland	20	L
	14	Cleveland	51	L
1947	21	Cleveland	41	L
	28	Cleveland	31	L
1948	7	Cleveland	28	L
	10	Cleveland	21	L
1949	2	Cleveland	35	L
	6	Cleveland	14	L
	94		241	0–8–0

Against Los Angeles

Year	Score	Team	Opp.	W/L/T
1946	9	Los Angeles	21	L
	17	Los Angeles	17	T
1947	21	Los Angeles	24	L
	14	Los Angeles	34	L
1948	0	Los Angeles	7	L
	28	Los Angeles	49	L
1949	23	Los Angeles	21	W
	14	Los Angeles	24	L
	126		197	1–6–1

Against Miami

Year	Score	Team	Opp.	W/L/T
1946	28	Miami	7	W
	20	Miami	7	W
	48		14	2–0–0

Against New York

Year	Score	Team	Opp.	W/L/T
1946	17	New York	17	T
	38	New York	28	W
1947	26	New York	48	L
	7	New York	28	L
1948	7	New York	42	L
	7	New York	28	L
1949	24	New York	38	L
	10	New York	14	L
	136		243	1–6–1

Against San Francisco

Year	Score	Team	Opp.	W/L/T
1946	21	San Francisco	7	W
	0	San Francisco	14	L
1947	28	San Francisco	42	L
	16	San Francisco	41	L
1948	14	San Francisco	31	L
	21	San Francisco	44	L
1949	7	San Francisco	42	L
	24	San Francisco	42	L
	131		263	1–7–0

Chicago Won 11, Lost 40, Tied 3
Chicago 904; Opponents 1,447

Cleveland Browns

Against Baltimore

Year	Score	Team	Opp.	W/L/T
1947	28	Baltimore	0	W
	42	Baltimore	0	W
1948	14	Baltimore	10	W
	28	Baltimore	7	W
1949	21	Baltimore	0	W
	28	Baltimore	20	W
	161		37	6–0–0

Against Brooklyn

Year	Score	Team	Opp.	W/L/T
1946	26	Brooklyn	7	W
	66	Brooklyn	14	W
1947	55	Brooklyn	7	W
	13	Brooklyn	12	W
1948	30	Brooklyn	17	W
	31	Brooklyn	21	W
	221		78	6–0–0

Against Buffalo

Year	Score	Team	Opp.	W/L/T
1946	28	Buffalo	0	W
	42	Buffalo	17	W
1947	30	Buffalo	14	W
	28	Buffalo	7	W
1948	42	Buffalo	13	W
	31	Buffalo	14	W
1949	28	Buffalo	28	T
	7	Buffalo	7	T
	236		100	6–0–2

74   Part 5: Conference Statistics

Against Chicago

Year	Score	Team	Opp.	W/L/T
1946	20	Chicago	6	W
	51	Chicago	14	W
1947	41	Chicago	21	W
	31	Chicago	28	W
1948	28	Chicago	7	W
	21	Chicago	10	W
1949	35	Chicago	2	W
	14	Chicago	6	W
	241		94	8–0–0

Against Los Angeles

Year	Score	Team	Opp.	W/L/T
1946	31	Los Angeles	14	W
	16	Los Angeles	17	L
1947	10	Los Angeles	13	L
	27	Los Angeles	17	W
1948	19	Los Angeles	14	W
	31	Los Angeles	14	W
1949	42	Los Angeles	7	W
	61	Los Angeles	14	W
	237		110	6–2–0

Against Miami

Year	Score	Team	Opp.	W/L/T
1946	44	Miami	0	W
	34	Miami	0	W
	78		0	2–0–0

Against New York

Year	Score	Team	Opp.	W/L/T
1946	24	New York	7	W
	7	New York	0	W
1947	26	New York	17	W
	28	New York	28	T
1948	35	New York	7	W
	34	New York	21	W
1949	14	New York	3	W
	31	New York	0	W
	199		83	7–0–1

Against San Francisco

Year	Score	Team	Opp.	W/L/T
1946	20	San Francisco	34	L
	14	San Francisco	7	W
1947	14	San Francisco	7	W
	37	San Francisco	14	W
1948	14	San Francisco	7	W
	31	San Francisco	28	W
1949	28	San Francisco	56	L
	30	San Francisco	28	W
	188		181	6–2–0

Cleveland Won 47, Lost 4, Tied 3
Cleveland 1,561; Opponents 683

Los Angeles Dons

Against Baltimore

Year	Score	Team	Opp.	W/L/T
1947	38	Baltimore	10	W
	56	Baltimore	0	W
1948	14	Baltimore	29	L
	17	Baltimore	14	W
1949	49	Baltimore	17	W
	21	Baltimore	10	W
	195		80	5–1–0

Against Brooklyn

Year	Score	Team	Opp.	W/L/T
1946	20	Brooklyn	14	W
	19	Brooklyn	14	W
1947	48	Brooklyn	21	W
	16	Brooklyn	12	W
1948	17	Brooklyn	7	W
	17	Brooklyn	0	W
	137		68	6–0

Against Buffalo

Year	Score	Team	Opp.	W/L/T
1946	21	Buffalo	21	T
	62	Buffalo	14	W
1947	25	Buffalo	27	L
	0	Buffalo	25	L
1948	21	Buffalo	35	L
	27	Buffalo	20	W
1949	42	Buffalo	28	W
	14	Buffalo	17	L
	212		187	3–4–1

Against Chicago

Year	Score	Team	Opp.	W/L/T
1946	21	Chicago	9	W
	17	Chicago	17	T
1947	24	Chicago	21	W
	34	Chicago	14	W
1948	7	Chicago	0	W
	49	Chicago	28	W
1949	21	Chicago	23	L
	24	Chicago	14	W
	197		126	6–1–1

Against Cleveland

Year	Score	Team	Opp.	W/L/T
1946	14	Cleveland	31	L
	17	Cleveland	16	W
1947	13	Cleveland	10	W
	17	Cleveland	27	L
1948	14	Cleveland	19	L
	14	Cleveland	31	L
1949	7	Cleveland	42	L
	14	Cleveland	61	L
	110		237	2–6–0

Against Miami

Year	Score	Team	Opp.	W/L/T
1946	30	Miami	14	W
	34	Miami	21	W
	64		35	2–0–0

Against New York

Year	Score	Team	Opp.	W/L/T
1946	17	New York	31	L
	12	New York	17	L
1947	14	New York	30	L
	13	New York	16	L
1948	20	New York	10	W
	6	New York	38	L
1949	7	New York	10	L
	16	New York	17	L
	105		169	1–7–0

Club versus Club Records

Against San Francisco

Year	Score	Team	Opp.	W/L/T
1946	14	San Francisco	23	L
	7	San Francisco	48	L
1947	14	San Francisco	17	L
	16	San Francisco	26	L
1948	14	San Francisco	36	L
	21	San Francisco	38	L
1949	14	San Francisco	42	L
	24	San Francisco	41	L
	124		271	0–8–0

Los Angeles Won 25, Lost 27, Tied 2
Los Angeles 1,144; Opponents 1,173

Miami Seahawks

Against Brooklyn

Year	Score	Team	Opp.	W/L/T
1946	7	Brooklyn	30	L
	31	Brooklyn	20	W
	38		50	1–1–0

Against Buffalo

Year	Score	Team	Opp.	W/L/T
1946	17	Buffalo	14	W
	21	Buffalo	14	W
	38		28	2–0–0

Against Chicago

Year	Score	Team	Opp.	W/L/T
1946	7	Chicago	28	L
	7	Chicago	20	L
	14		48	0–2–0

Against Cleveland

Year	Score	Team	Opp.	W/L/T
1946	0	Cleveland	44	L
	0	Cleveland	34	L
	0		78	0–2–0

Against Los Angeles

Year	Score	Team	Opp.	W/L/T
1946	14	Los Angeles	30	L
	21	Los Angeles	34	L
	35		64	0–2–0

Against New York

Year	Score	Team	Opp.	W/L/T
1946	21	New York	24	L
	0	New York	31	L
	21		55	0–2–0

Against San Francisco

Year	Score	Team	Opp.	W/L/T
1946	14	San Francisco	21	L
	7	San Francisco	34	L
	21		55	0–2–0

Miami Won 3, Lost 11, Tied 0
Miami 167; Opponents 378

New York Yankees

Note: Brooklyn–New York for 1949

Against Baltimore

Year	Score	Team	Opp.	W/L/T
1947	21	Baltimore	7	W
	35	Baltimore	21	W
1948	28	Baltimore	45	L
	14	Baltimore	27	L
1949	24	Baltimore	21	W
	21	Baltimore	14	W
	143		135	4–2–0

Against Brooklyn

Year	Score	Team	Opp.	W/L/T
1946	21	Brooklyn	10	W
	21	Brooklyn	7	W
1947	31	Brooklyn	7	W
	20	Brooklyn	17	W
1948	21	Brooklyn	3	W
	21	Brooklyn	7	W
	135		51	6–0–0

Against Buffalo

Year	Score	Team	Opp.	W/L/T
1946	21	Buffalo	10	W
	21	Buffalo	13	W
1947	24	Buffalo	28	L
	35	Buffalo	13	W
1948	14	Buffalo	13	W
	14	Buffalo	35	L
1949	17	Buffalo	14	W
	14	Buffalo	17	L
	160		143	5–3–0

Against Chicago

Year	Score	Team	Opp.	W/L/T
1946	17	Chicago	17	T
	28	Chicago	38	L
1947	48	Chicago	26	W
	28	Chicago	7	W
1948	42	Chicago	7	W
	28	Chicago	7	W
1949	38	Chicago	24	W
	14	Chicago	10	W
	243		136	6–1–1

Against Cleveland

Year	Score	Team	Opp.	W/L/T
1946	7	Cleveland	24	L
	0	Cleveland	7	L
1947	17	Cleveland	26	L
	28	Cleveland	28	T
1948	7	Cleveland	35	L
	21	Cleveland	34	L
1949	3	Cleveland	14	L
	0	Cleveland	31	L
	83		199	0–7–1

Against Los Angeles

Year	Score	Team	Opp.	W/L/T
1946	31	Los Angeles	17	W
	17	Los Angeles	12	W
1947	30	Los Angeles	14	W
	16	Los Angeles	13	W
1948	10	Los Angeles	20	L
	38	Los Angeles	6	W
1949	10	Los Angeles	7	W
	17	Los Angeles	16	W
	169		105	7–1–0

Part 5: Conference Statistics

Against Miami
Year	Score	Team	Opp.	W/L/T
1946	24	Miami	21	W
	31	Miami	0	W
	55		21	2–0–0

Against San Francisco
Year	Score	Team	Opp.	W/L/T
1946	21	San Francisco	7	W
	10	San Francisco	9	W
1947	21	San Francisco	16	W
	24	San Francisco	16	W
1948	0	San Francisco	41	L
	7	San Francisco	21	L
1949	24	San Francisco	3	W
	14	San Francisco	35	L
	121		148	5–3–0

New York Won 35, Lost 17, Tied 2
New York 1,109; Opponents 938

San Francisco 49ers

Against Baltimore
Year	Score	Team	Opp.	W/L/T
1947	14	Baltimore	7	W
	28	Baltimore	28	T
1948	56	Baltimore	14	W
	21	Baltimore	10	W
1949	31	Baltimore	17	W
	28	Baltimore	10	W
	178		86	5–0–1

Against Brooklyn
Year	Score	Team	Opp.	W/L/T
1946	32	Brooklyn	13	W
	30	Brooklyn	14	W
1947	23	Brooklyn	7	W
	21	Brooklyn	7	W
1948	36	Brooklyn	20	W
	63	Brooklyn	40	W
	205		101	6–0–0

Against Buffalo
Year	Score	Team	Opp.	W/L/T
1946	14	Buffalo	17	L
	27	Buffalo	14	W
1947	41	Buffalo	24	W
	21	Buffalo	21	T
1948	35	Buffalo	14	W
	38	Buffalo	28	W
1949	17	Buffalo	28	L
	51	Buffalo	7	W
	244		153	5–2–1

Against Chicago
Year	Score	Team	Opp.	W/L/T
1946	7	Chicago	21	L
	14	Chicago	0	W
1947	42	Chicago	28	W
	41	Chicago	16	W
1948	31	Chicago	14	W
	44	Chicago	21	W
1949	42	Chicago	7	W
	42	Chicago	24	W
	263		131	7–1–0

Against Cleveland
Year	Score	Team	Opp.	W/L/T
1946	34	Cleveland	20	W
	7	Cleveland	14	L
1947	7	Cleveland	14	L
	14	Cleveland	37	L
1948	7	Cleveland	14	L
	28	Cleveland	31	L
1949	56	Cleveland	28	W
	28	Cleveland	30	L
	181		188	2–6–0

Against Los Angeles
Year	Score	Team	Opp.	W/L/T
1946	23	Los Angeles	14	W
	48	Los Angeles	7	W
1947	17	Los Angeles	14	W
	26	Los Angeles	16	W
1948	36	Los Angeles	14	W
	38	Los Angeles	21	W
1949	42	Los Angeles	14	W
	41	Los Angeles	24	W
	271		124	8–0–0

Against Miami
Year	Score	Team	Opp.	W/L/T
1946	21	Miami	14	W
	34	Miami	7	W
	55		21	2–0–0

Against New York
Year	Score	Team	Opp.	W/L/T
1946	7	New York	21	L
	9	New York	10	L
1947	16	New York	21	L
	16	New York	24	L
1948	41	New York	0	W
	21	New York	7	W
1949	3	New York	24	L
	35	New York	14	W
	148		121	3–5–0

San Francisco Won 38, Lost 14, Tied 2
San Francisco 1,545; Opponents 925

Conference Statistics by Season

Note: All averages are per game, unless otherwise noted.

	1946	1947	1948	1949
Average First Downs	21.6	25.2	29.4	26.2
Average by Rushing	11.6	14.1	15.9	13.7
Average by Passing	8.7	9.6	11.6	10.8
Average by Penalty	1.3	1.5	1.9	1.7
Average Yards Gained	508.4	596.8	677.4	637.9
Average Yards Rushing	239.3	301.2	324.3	306.5
Average Yards Passing	269.2	295.6	353.1	331.5
Average Number Offensive Plays	110.7	110.7	121.1	119.2
Average per Offensive Play	4.59	5.39	5.59	5.35
Average Number of Rushes	70.5	69.6	71.0	72.5
Average per Rushing Play	3.40	4.33	4.57	4.23
Average Number of Passes Attempted	40.3	41.1	50.1	46.7
Average Number Passes Completed	19.5	20.1	24.5	22.1
Percent Passes Completed	0.484	0.490	0.488	0.474
Average Yards per Pass Attempt	6.68	7.19	7.05	7.09
Average Yards per Pass Completed	13.8	14.7	14.4	15.0
Percent Passes Intercepted	0.083	0.071	0.067	0.073
Number Passes Intercepted	187	164	187	143
Average Number of Passes Intercepted	3.3	2.9	3.3	3.4
Average Yards per Interception Return	50.7	48.9	47.1	46.7
Number of Returns for Touchdowns	9	12	8	9
Average Number of Punts	10.9	8.9	9.0	10.3
Average Yards per Punt	40.6	40.7	41.4	40.3
Net Gain per Punt	33.1	32.9	33.2	33.3
Number of Punts Blocked	15	20	7	9
Average Number of Punt Returns	5.9	5.2	5.4	5.6
Average Yards per Punt Return	13.7	13.4	13.7	12.7
Average Return per Punt	7.5	7.7	8.2	6.9
Number Returns for Touchdowns	7	4	7	2
Average Number of Kickoff Returns	7.2	7.6	7.4	6.9
Average Yards per Kickoff Return	22.1	22.9	21.1	21.5
Number of Kickoff Returns for Touchdowns	5	6	1	2
Average Number of Penalties	8.3	7.9	11.3	10.0
Average Yards Penalized	65.0	62.6	96.7	79.9
Average Number of Fumbles	6.6	5.5	5.2	5.7
Average Number of Fumbles Lost	3.2	2.6	2.5	3.3
Number Fumbles Returned for Touchdowns	11	8	6	8
Average Number of Touchdowns	5.3	5.8	6.3	5.8
Number of Touchdowns Rushing	163	175	185	139
Average Number of Touchdowns Rushing	2.9	3.1	3.3	3.3
Number of Touchdowns Passing	133	147	167	104
Average Number of Touchdowns Passing	2.4	2.6	3.0	2.5
Average Number of Points After Touchdowns	4.9	5.2	5.9	5.6
Percent of Points After Touchdowns Made	0.929	0.904	0.938	0.971
Number of Field Goals Scored	49	47	35	31
Number of Field Goals Attempted	101	107	82	76
Percent Field Goals Made	0.485	0.439	0.427	0.408
Average Number of Points Scored	39.5	42.4	45.6	42.6

Attendance *(by Andy Piascik)*

Originally published in The Coffin Corner, *Volume 29, Number 3 (2007)*

When the All-America Football Conference was formed in 1944, its founders adopted a two-pronged strategy regarding franchise location. One part of that strategy was to establish teams in Miami, Los Angeles, and San Francisco, cities where the NFL had never ventured. In so doing, the AAFC became the first major sports league to locate in the South and on the West Coast, the first league indeed to be truly national. (The NFL had briefly had a team called the Los Angeles Buccaneers in 1926, but the franchise actually operated out of Chicago and played all of its games east of the Mississippi).

At the time, the prevailing wisdom was that the South was college football country and would not go for a pro team. As for the West Coast, travel costs had been too prohibitive to make locating franchises there economically viable. That was less of a concern by 1946, however, as air travel became more feasible financially.

The AAFC had the foresight to put teams in both Los Angeles and San Francisco, which enabled visiting teams to stay over for a two-game road trip. When the Rams moved, by contrast, they were the only NFL team west of Chicago and they had to agree to share a larger percentage of gate proceeds to defray travel costs.

Attendance-wise, the AAFC venture into California proved a rousing success. The Dons did very well in their battle with the Rams even though they played in the same division as the powerhouse Browns and 49ers and never finished better than third. In San Francisco, meanwhile, the 49ers drew well enough that they were one of only a few teams in either league to show a profit during the four years of AAFC-NFL competition. Over the 1946–49 period, only the Browns, Rams, and Bears outdrew San Francisco.

The second part of the AAFC strategy was to challenge the NFL in Chicago, Cleveland, and New York City. Initially the sole New York entry was the Brooklyn Dodgers, but the AAFC got a big boost when Dan Topping brought his NFL franchise over to the new league and took up residence in Yankee Stadium as the New York Yankees. That Yankee Stadium was larger and newer than the Polo Grounds was undoubtedly a cause for concern to Giants' owner Tim Mara and the rest of the NFL.

AAFC founder Arch Ward was the sports editor of the *Chicago Tribune* and he was determined to establish the AAFC there. However, it is not surprising that Chicago turned out to be a trouble spot for the new league. By 1945, Chicago was the only city with two NFL franchises, one of which was the powerhouse Bears. Ward did all he could to promote the AAFC, and the Rockets were successful in securing Soldier Field, not an insignificant fact both because it was newer than Wrigley Field and Comiskey Park and larger than the other two combined. In the end, although the Rockets were not as much of a disaster at the gate as they were on the field, they finished behind the Bears and Cardinals in attendance all four years.

The battle in Cleveland never came off. Despite the opposition of all of the NFL's other owners, Dan Reeves moved the Rams to Los Angeles in January of 1946. Even more than in Chicago and New York, stadium venue was an important issue in Cleveland. The Browns signed a lease to play in Cleveland Stadium, then less than 15 years old and with a seating capacity of over 80,000. The Rams, on the other hand, had played all but a handful of their games in League Park in nine years in the NFL. Like the Yankees and Rockets, the Browns would play in a stadium that was both larger and newer than their would-have-been rivals.

Reeves was also likely somewhat alarmed by the steamroller that the Browns had become in their first year of operation. Owner Mickey McBride vigorously promoted the new team and coach Paul Brown was an Ohio legend who consciously tapped into the strong interest in the game in the state. Brown signed a significant number of players who had played at Ohio State, others who were Ohio natives and/or had played at other Ohio colleges, and some from other Big Ten schools with whom Ohioans were very familiar.

Reeves took his team to Los Angeles knowing he would still have to face AAFC competition. Ben Lindheimer and a group of Hollywood producers and movie stars had been awarded the AAFC Dons, and both teams signed leases to play in the Los Angeles Coliseum. Lindheimer was at least as wealthy as Reeves and he proved himself willing to both spend money on his team and share it with struggling AAFC franchises.

The AAFC also brought major league football back to Buffalo. The city had been an original entrant when the NFL was formed as the American Professional Football Association in 1920 but had been without a team since 1929. Although things did not turn out well for Buffalo fans when the AAFC ended in 1949, for a three-year period beginning in 1947 they proved themselves to be among the best fans in either league.

As dismissive as they had been of the AAFC at the time of its founding, people in the NFL hierarchy certainly must have taken notice during the new league's first week of play in September of 1946. In the AAFC's first-ever game, the Browns and the Miami Seahawks established a new attendance record for a regularly scheduled game when 60,135 fans attended their game in Cleveland. Then a week later, the Browns played the Rockets before 51,962, the largest crowd ever for a pro game in Chicago.

1946 marked the beginning of a short-lived sports attendance boom, a boom that would benefit both the AAFC and NFL. By year's end, the NFL established its highest per game attendance mark, while the AAFC drew more fans per game than the NFL had in every one of its seasons except 1945 and 1946.

1946

	Games	Attendance	Average
NFL	55	1,732,135	31,493
AAFC	56	1,376,998	24,589

The Browns and Giants were the individual winners. Cleveland established a new pro record by averaging 57,138 per home date, while the Giants set a new record for all games by averaging 44,213, a mark that just topped Cleveland's 43,783. Three times the leagues played in the same city on the same day and the NFL came out ahead each time (occasions where the Giants and AAFC Dodgers went head to head are not included):

11/10/46

Eagles at Giants	Dons at Yankees
60,874	30,765

11/17/46

Yanks at Giants	49ers at Yankees
35,583	18,695

11/24/46

Steelers at Giants	Rockets at Yankees
45,347	21,270

The NFL also won the head to head competition for the season in Los Angeles, New York, and Chicago:

	Games	Attendance	Average
Rams	5	211,916	42,383
Dons	7	139,294	19,899
Giants	7	362,437	51,777
Yankees	7	194,140	27,734
Bears	6	253,748	42,291
Cardinals	4	134,966	33,741
Rockets	7	195,627	27,947

In 1947, the AAFC scored a major victory by turning the tables on all accounts except for the race in Chicago. The new league won the overall attendance battle by establishing a record for per game average that stood until 1955. Both the Dons and Yankees outdrew their NFL rivals, while the Browns again finished first at 55,848 and also topped the Giants' 1946 record by averaging 47,573 for all games, home and away.

The AAFC also prevailed on all three occasions when the leagues played in the same city on the same day. Perhaps most impressive of all, the AAFC had three of the four best team marks, as the Browns, Dons, and Yankees ranked 1, 2, and 4, with the Bears finishing third.

1947

	Games	Attendance	Average
AAFC	56	1,828,480	32,651
NFL	60	1,837,437	30,624
Dons	7	304,177	43,454
Rams	6	200,103	33,351
Yankees	7	264,412	37,773
Giants	6	190,173	31,696
Bears	6	229,399	38,233
Cardinals	5	163,955	32,791
Rockets	7	135,274	19,325

11/9/47

49ers at Yankees	Eagles at Giants
37,342	29,016

11/23/47

Browns at Yankees	Packers at Giants
70,060	27,939

11/30/47

Bills at Yankees	Cardinals at Giants
39,012	28,744

There is no question that the AAFC was playing a high caliber, exciting game that appealed both to fans in cities like New York and Cleveland with pro football traditions and cities like San Francisco and Los Angeles where major league football was new. Success at the gate was uneven but that was just as true in the NFL. One factor in the AAFC's success is the pioneering role the league played in the integration of pro sports.

It is difficult if not impossible to calculate precisely how much of an impact black players had on attendance 60 years after the fact, but it's clear from accounts at the time that tens of thousands of black fans who had probably not previously attended pro games turned out to watch the AAFC in action. That was especially true in Cleveland, New York, and Los Angeles as the Browns, Yankees, and Dons all featured black players sooner than most other teams. The Yankees had been just as good in 1946 as in 1947, yet their attendance improved by over 10,000 per home date. Part of the reason, perhaps the main reason, was the addition of the electrifying Buddy Young and the black fans he drew to the team's games.

As the following charts indicate, the AAFC was far ahead of the NFL in signing black players beginning in 1947 even though in every year the AAFC had fewer teams and fewer roster spots:

Black Players in Pro Football

	1947	1948	1949
AAFC	9	11	13
NFL	1	4	5

Cumulative Number of Integrated Teams

	1947	1948	1949
AAFC	5 (out of 8)	6	6
NFL	1 (out of 10)	3	3

Perhaps the best illustration of the attendance boost black fans gave the AAFC in 1947 were the crowds for the three games between the Browns and Yankees. In those games, the teams drew 80,067 in Cleveland, 70,060 in New York, and 61,879 in the league title game, also in New York, an average of over 70,000. Each game set some kind of attendance record: the crowd for the first was the largest ever in Cleveland, the turnout for the second was the largest ever in New York (a record that lasted until 1958), and the 61,879 was the largest ever for a Championship Game, a record that stood until 1955.

The total of 212,006 was also the most for games between two teams in a season until the Colts and Dolphins topped it in 1971. Estimates at the time indicate that a quarter to a third of the fans for the three games were African-Americans.

The AAFC again won the battle in 1948. The Giants slipped past the Yankees but the Dons again bested the Rams. AAFC teams again accounted for three of the top four spots with Browns 1st, the Dons 3rd, and the 49ers 4th, while the Bears were 2nd. Considering how bad they were, it's surprising the Rockets did as well as they did, although they were outdrawn decisively by both the Bears and Cardinals.

Attendance in Cleveland slipped, but the Browns again set an all-time pro mark of 82,769 for their game against the 49ers to go along with their number one finish at 45,517 per home date. By the end of 1948, the AAFC had attracted the seven largest crowds in the history of pro football in just three years, a remarkable feat for a new league to have accomplished so quickly.

1948

	Games	Attendance	Average
AAFC	56	1,618,626	28,904
NFL	60	1,525,243	25,421
Dons	7	287,676	41,097
Rams	6	194,408	32,401
Giants	6	139,568	23,261
Yankees	7	166,864	22,793
Bears	6	262,435	43,739
Cardinals	6	181,217	30,203
Rockets	7	103,481	14,783

There were head-to-head games in Chicago for the first time in 1948, and not surprisingly the NFL was the winner each time, as it was in the four head-to-head battles in New York:

10/17/48	
Cardinals at Giants	49ers at Yankees
35,584	29,743

10/24/48	
Yanks at Cardinals	Dodgers at Rockets
23,423	5,964

10/31/48	
Giants at Bears	Yankees at Rockets
41,608	13,239

11/7/48	
Eagles at Giants	Dons at Yankees
24,983	17,386

11/14/48	
Rams at Giants	Dodgers at Yankees
22,766	17,642

11/28/48	
Yanks at Giants	Bills at Yankees
19,636	18,376

Virtually every team in both leagues was losing money and 1949 turned out to be the last year for the AAFC. However, the upstart league closed on a successful note as it won the attendance battle for the third year in a row. The Rams shot past the Dons in Los Angeles and also went past Cleveland for overall supremacy, but the Yankees rebounded to top the Giants in New York. The Rockets were re-named the Hornets but they were worse than ever, the clear attendance loser in Chicago.

The 49ers were probably the most exciting team in either league and it showed as they wrested the AAFC attendance crown from the Browns by drawing 39,032. The fact that the Rams and Bears ranked first and second among all teams while the NFL was losing the league-wide battle serves to partially refute the common perception that the NFL was less top-heavy than the AAFC.

1949

	Games	Attendance	Average
AAFC	42	1,122,811	26,734
NFL	60	1,391,735	23,196
Rams	6	299,128	49,855
Dons	6	134,980	22,497
Yankees	6	144,659	24,110
Giants	6	43,489	23,915
Bears	6	262,946	43,824
Cardinals	6	172,444	28,740
Hornets	6	107,222	17,870

The AAFC won five of the six head to head matchups in 1949, all of which occurred in New York:

9/22/49

Dons at Yankees	Eagles at Bulldogs
14,437	8,426

10/23/49

49ers at Yankees	Bears at Giants
38,187	30,587

10/30/49

Colts at Yankees	Redskins at Bulldogs
10,692	3,678

11/6/49

Bulldogs at Giants	Bills at Yankees
23,222	16,758

11/13/49

Hornets at Yankees	Cardinals at Bulldogs
9,091	9,072

11/20/49

Browns at Yankees	Lions at Giants
50,711	21,338

For the four years, the NFL won ten of the same day, same city battles, the AAFC eight. NFL teams also won the cumulative battles in New York, Los Angeles, and Chicago. However, the AAFC's average attendance for the four years was higher. Again, that is a remarkable accomplishment for a new league engaged in a battle with a much older rival.

The AAFC won the four-year attendance battle despite an NFL policy in 1946 and 1947 of granting some stronger and better-drawing teams more home games than others. The Giants, for example, played seven home games and only four road games in 1946, while the Eagles played seven of twelve games at home in 1947. All AAFC teams, by contrast, played the same number of home games. Had the league copied the NFL and put more games in Cleveland, Los Angeles, and San Francisco and fewer in Chicago and Brooklyn, its overall numbers and margin of victory would have been larger.

1946-49

	Games	Attendance	Average
AAFC	210	5,946,915	28,319
NFL	235	6,486,550	27,600
Rams	23	905,555	39,372
Dons	27	866,127	32,079
Giants	25	835,667	33,427
Yankees	27	770,075	28,521
Bears	24	1,008,528	42,022
Cardinals	21	652,582	31,075
Rockets	27	541,604	20,059

Stadium size naturally favored teams with the largest seating capacities like the Rams and Browns. Playing its games in a stadium that was far smaller but with a succession of excellent teams, the Bears consistently drew crowds that were at or near capacity. It's possible the Bears might have drawn the kinds of crowds the Browns did had they played in a stadium of comparable size, as might the 1946 Giants.

However, AAFC attendance was also held down somewhat for the same reason. Given that they all played at least occasionally in front of full houses, the 49ers, Bills, Yankees, and even the Browns might have drawn more had they played in larger stadiums. One counter-argument to the notion that the Browns dominated in attendance because of the size of their stadium is the case of the Rams. Despite having a string of good teams and playing in a stadium with 15,000 more seats, the Rams did not approach the overall attendance accomplishments of the Browns.

The Bills and Colts, while not among the attendance leaders, did quite well in percentage of tickets sold. Buffalo in particular was a success story considering that it was the smallest city in either league except for Green Bay, although the Packers played half of their home games in Milwaukee, which was larger than Buffalo. Given that the Bills were one of the few teams in either league whose attendance was higher in 1949 than 1948, it was especially unfortunate that the NFL refused to include the Bills in the 1950 merger.

When the AAFC came to an end, eight of the ten largest crowds of all time were for AAFC games (six in Cleveland, one in Los Angeles, and one in New York) while only two were in the NFL (both in Los Angeles).

The AAFC accomplished that feat despite having played only 210 games, compared to 1,910 for the NFL:

10 Largest Crowds, 1920–49

1. 86,080 (Bears at Rams 10/30/49)
2. 82,769 (49ers at Browns 11/14/48)
3. 82,675 (Yankees at Dons 9/12/47)
4. 80,067 (Yankees at Browns 10/5/47)
5. 76,504 (49ers at Browns 11/16/47)
6. 74,673 (Cardinals at Rams 12/4/49)
7. 72,189 (49ers at Browns 10/30/49)
8. 71,134 (Dons at Browns 10/20/46)
9. 70,385 (49ers at Browns 10/27/46)
10. 70,060 (Browns at Yankees 11/23/47)

Almost three seasons after its demise, the AAFC still accounted for seven of the ten largest crowds in pro football history. The one change in that time to the list above was a notable one: on September 16, 1950, 71,237 fans in Philadelphia saw the Browns destroy the Eagles 35–10 in the better-late-than-never AAFC-NFL Super Bowl.

As far as quality of play goes for a comparable period of time, the AAFC was the best insurgent league in the history of pro sports. That is the main reason the NFL has pretended and continues to pretend that it never existed. The historical record tells a different tale, however, and a big part of that tale is this: the negotiating table is about the only place the NFL got the better of the AAFC. It never did so on the playing field and it certainly didn't do so at the turnstile.

Home

Team	1946	1947	1948	1949	Total
Cleveland Browns	399,963	390,939	318,619	188,947	1,298,468
San Francisco 49ers	182,198	239,217	287,183	234,192	942,790
Los Angeles Dons	139,294	304,177	287,676	134,980	866,127
New York Yankees	194,140	264,412	166,864	144,659	770,075
Buffalo Bisons/Bills	117,954	217,699	176,197	160,430	672,280
Baltimore Colts	—	199,661	206,109	152,381	558,151
Chicago Rockets/Hornets	195,627	135,274	103,481	107,222	541,604
Brooklyn Dodgers	97,671	77,101	72,497	—	247,269
Miami Seahawks	50,151	—	—	—	50,151
TOTAL	1,376,998	1,828,480	1,618,626	1,122,811	5,946,915

Away

Team	1946	1947	1948	1949	Total
Cleveland Browns	212,999	275,078	270,980	212,526	971,583
New York Yankees	173,915	334,005	216,557	171,515	895,922
San Francisco 49ers	157,278	248,855	256,161	213,628	875,922
Los Angeles Dons	193,625	243,240	211,256	132,061	780,182
Buffalo Bisons/Bills	151,472	211,554	157,060	134,559	654,645
Chicago Rockets/Hornets	155,649	166,892	164,262	127,924	614,727
Brooklyn Dodgers	165,633	190,876	175,869	—	532,378
Baltimore Colts	—	157,980	166,481	130,598	455,059
Miami Seahawks	166,427	—	—	—	166,427
TOTAL	1,376,998	1,828,480	1,618,626	1,122,811	5,946,915

Other

	1946	1947	1948	1949	Total
Exhibitions		161,070	138,128	209,114	299,125	807,437
Championships		41,181	61,879	22,981	22,550	148,591
Playoffs		—	—	27,327	58,563	85,890
GRAND TOTAL						6,988,833

Part 6: Linescores

Exhibition Games

1946

August 18, Brooklyn 14 vs. Chicago 14 (Portland, OR)
August 24, New York 21 vs. Brooklyn 14 (Spokane, WA)
August 24, San Francisco 17 vs. Los Angeles 7 (San Diego, CA)
August 30, Buffalo 23 vs. Miami 21 (Baltimore, MD)
August 30, Brooklyn 20 vs. Cleveland 35 (Akron, OH)
August 30, New York 21 vs. Los Angeles 7 (Los Angeles, CA)
September 1, Chicago 14 vs. San Francisco 14 (San Francisco, CA)

1947

August 17, Brooklyn 16 vs. Los Angeles 17 (Portland, OR)
August 18, Buffalo 7 vs. New York 29 (Newark, NJ)
August 22, Buffalo 29 vs. Baltimore 20 (Hershey, PA)
August 23, Brooklyn 20 vs. Chicago 17 (Salt Lake City, UT)
August 24, Los Angeles 14 vs. San Francisco 7 (San Francisco, CA)
August 29, Baltimore 0 vs. Cleveland 28 (Akron, OH)

1948

August 8, Baltimore 21 vs. Los Angeles 27 (Portland, OR)
August 13, Buffalo 28 vs. New York 28 (Newark, NJ)
August 17, Brooklyn 19 vs. Buffalo 21 (Buffalo, NY)
August 18, Chicago 27 vs. New York 35 (Freeport, NY)
August 18, Los Angeles 24 vs. San Francisco 42 (Pasadena, CA)
August 21, Brooklyn 7 vs. New York 14 (Boston, MA)
August 22, Baltimore 14 vs. San Francisco 42 (San Francisco, CA)
August 22, Buffalo 21 vs. Cleveland 35 (Akron, OH)
August 27, Baltimore 21 vs. Cleveland 17 (Toledo, OH)

1949

August 5, Buffalo 79 vs. Jersey City Giants 0 (Buffalo, NY)
August 10, Baltimore 28 vs. Buffalo 12 (Wilmington, DE)
August 10, Los Angeles 7 vs. San Francisco 28 (San Francisco, CA)
August 14, Chicago 0 vs. Cleveland 21 (Toledo, OH)
August 14, Buffalo 10 vs. San Francisco 21 (San Francisco, CA)
August 16, New York 28 vs. Baltimore 14 (Baltimore, MD)
August 18, Chicago 48 vs. Bay City All-Stars 2 (Bay City, MI)
August 19, Baltimore 14 vs. New York 28 (Allentown, PA)
August 19, San Francisco 21 vs. Cleveland 21 (Cleveland, OH)
August 19, Bethlehem Bulldogs 0 vs. Buffalo 48 (Buffalo, NY)
August 21, Baltimore vs. Chicago (Des Moines, IA) (Cancelled)
August 26, New York 21 vs. Cleveland 28 (Akron, OH)
September 3, New York 24 vs. Charlotte Clippers 7 (Charlotte, NC)
October 9, Baltimore 31 vs. Charlotte Clippers 0 (Charlotte, NC)
October 16, Chicago 28 vs. Knoxville Rebels 3 (Knoxville, TN)
October 30, Buffalo vs. Charlotte Clippers (Charlotte, NC)(Cancelled)

Regular and Post-Season Games

1946

By the Professional Football Researchers Association's Linescore Committee. Chaired by Gary Selby

WEEK ONE
Bye: Chicago, Los Angeles
Friday Night, September 6, at Cleveland Municipal Stadium. Attendance—60,135

The Cleveland Browns and the Miami Seahawks launched the All-America Football Conference campaign before the largest crowd ever to see a regularly scheduled pro football game. The previous record was reported at 57,000 when the New York Giants and the Washington Redskins of the NFL met at the Polo Grounds several years ago.

Paul Brown's Cleveland squad used a balanced attack to dominate the weak Miami squad, building a huge halftime lead. Seventeen points in the final period buried the Seahawks. A quintet of Browns provided most of the scoring. Ends Dante Lavelli and Mac Speedie along with halfbacks Tom Colella, Don Greenwood and Ray Terrell each added touchdowns. But the game's scoring star was Browns tackle Lou Groza. The Martins Ferry, Ohio native booted five extra points and three field goals for a total of 14 points.

Miami Seahawks	0	0	0	0–0
Cleveland Browns	10	17	0	17–44

1 Cle—Speedie 19 pass from Lewis (Groza kick)
   Cle—FG Groza 22
2 Cle—Lavelli 39 pass from Graham (Groza kick)
   Cle—Colella 50 run (Groza kick)
   Cle—FG Groza 27
4 Cle—Greenwood 3 fumble return (Groza kick)
   Cle—FG Groza 21
   Cle—Terrell 76 interception return (Groza kick)

Sunday, September 8, at San Francisco Kezar Stadium. Attendance—35,000

In the season opener for both teams, the Yankees combined crushing ground power with a clever passing attack to defeat the 49ers. Buck Shaw's 49ers began the scoring when southpaw quarterback Frank Albert passed to right half John Strzykalski, who then lateraled to halfback Len Eshmont. Eshmont raced 40 yards for the home team's only touchdown.

The tide turned however in the second period when Yankee halfback Lowell Wagner caught a partially blocked 49er punt, taking it 40 yards to tie the score at 7–7. Led by tailbacks Ace Parker and Spec Sanders, the Yankees tore the 49ers to shreds in the second half with long touchdown marches. A 52-yard drive in the third quarter preceded a 72-yard thrust in the final period to seal the victory. Yankee reserve power told in the second half. Strong substitutes allowed New York Coach Ray Flaherty to parade practically three different elevens onto the field.

New York Yankees	0	7	7	7–21
San Francisco 49ers	7	0	0	0–7

1 SF—Eshmont 40 lateral from Strzykalski after 26 pass from Albert (Vetrano kick)
2 NY—Wagner 40 blocked punt return (Johnson kick)
3 NY—Parker 7 run (Johnson kick)
4 NY—Proctor 3 run (Johnson kick)

Sunday, September 8, at Buffalo Civic Stadium. Attendance—25,489

Glenn Dobbs, his injured right hand taped, passed the Dodgers to two fourth-period touchdowns and a victory over the Bisons in the Eastern Conference opener for both teams. In a scoreless first period the Dodgers held the Bisons just inches short of a touchdown after Steve Juzwik's 68-yard run. Then Brooklyn took the lead when Mickey Mayne returned a missed field goal by Buffalo's Lou Zontini. In the third period Brooklyn took a 14–0 lead when Tex Warrington recovered a fumble by Buffalo's Harry Hopp at the Bison's 27. Mayne then passed to Saxon Judd for the score.

An exciting fourth period began with the Bisons driving 70 yards in 10 plays, with Juzwik scoring on a Statue of Liberty play. Buffalo's Ken Stofer recovered Mayne's fumble to set up the second score less than 4 minutes later. Curt Sandig whipped through the line to tie the score 14–14. That's when Dobbs, who suffered a chipped bone in his right hand in an exhibition game, took charge. He hit Joe Davis for a 50-yard gain. On the next play he threw to Saxon Judd for the tie-breaking touchdown. Later Dobbs recovered a fumble at the Dodger 27. Dom Principe crashed for 15 yards. Dobbs then ran for 32 yards and lateraled to Russell Morrow, who ran the remaining 26 yards for the final score. Admiral William F. Halsey and Jim Crowley, AAFC Commissioner, were among the spectators.

Brooklyn Dodgers	0	7	7	13–27
Buffalo Bisons	0	0	0	14–14

2 Bkln—Mayne 104 missed field goal return (Davis kick)
3 Bkln—Judd 28 pass from Mayne (McCarthy kick)
4 Buff—Juzwik 5 run (Daddio kick)
   Buff—Sandig 9 run (Daddio kick)
   Bkln—Judd 31 pass from Dobbs (kick failed)
   Bkln—Morrow 26 lateral from Dobbs after 32 run (McCarthy kick)

Week Two

Friday Night, September 13, at Chicago
Soldier Field. Attendance—51,962

Touchdown runs of 20 and 41 yards, plus two field goals by Lou Groza, powered the Browns to a victory over the Rockets before the largest crowd ever to watch a professional football contest in Chicago. The Browns scored in the first period when fullback Marion Motley (12 carries for 122 yards), after galloping 24 yards and gaining 12 more on a pass from Otto Graham, drilled 20 yards for a touchdown.

After a scoreless second period, Groza added his field goals. With two minutes left in the third, Don Greenwood dashed 41 yards on a fake reverse and criss-crossed through the Rocket's defense for Cleveland's second touchdown. Billy Hillenbrand posted the Rockets only score on the first play of the fourth period when he sprinted in from 35 yards. Aided by Walter Clay's line smashing and passing, the new Chicago pros drove to the Brown's 2-yard line just as the game ended.

Cleveland Browns	7	0	13	0–20
Chicago Rockets	0	0	0	6–6

1 Cle—Motley 20 run (Groza kick)
3 Cle—FG Groza 21
   Cle—FG Groza 37
   Cle—Greenwood 41 run (Groza kick)
4 Chi—Hillenbrand 35 run (kick failed)

Friday Night, September 13, at Los Angeles
Memorial Coliseum. Attendance—19,500

The Dons made their AAFC opening an artistic, if not financial, success by lacing the Dodgers. The Dons, paced by the passing of Charlie O'Rourke and the running of Charley Fenenbock and John Kimbrough, showed a fair balance of power, plus a rugged enough defense to withstand Brooklyn's second-half bid, which was sparked by the whiplash pitching arm of rookie Glenn Dobbs.

Doug DeGroot's Los Angeles squad snapped into high gear for 14 points before the Dodgers could get untracked. A pass play from O'Rourke to Bernie Nygren tallied the first touchdown. Andy Marefos notched the second touchdown on a short buck in the second period. Brooklyn scored after marches of 67 and 72 yards, with Dobbs passing to Saxon Judd for one score in the second quarter and Bob Paffrath plunging a yard for the other in the closing minutes. The Dons sewed it up with an 80-yard drive early in the fourth quarter when Fenenbock went over on a sweep.

Brooklyn Dodgers	0	7	0	7–14
Los Angeles Dons	7	7	0	6–20

1 LA—Nygren 55 pass from O'Rourke (Nelson kick)
2 LA—Marefos 2 run (Nelson kick)
   Bkln—Judd 23 pass from Dobbs (McCarthy kick)
4 LA—Fenenbock 21 run (kick failed)
   Bkln—Paffrath 1 run (McCarthy kick)

Saturday Night, September 14, at Bronx, NY
Yankee Stadium. Attendance—40,606

The Yankees beat the Bisons in a game decided by turnovers. Despite outgaining Buffalo in total yardage 286–102, the Yankees needed a fourth quarter surge to stop the Bisons. New York scored first with the recovery of a Buffalo fumble by Harry Hopp at the Bison 12. Clarence (Pug) Manders, carrying four consecutive times, crashed over from the two. A few minutes later the Bisons struck back. The Yankees were headed for a second touchdown, but Dewey Proctor fumbled and Buffalo's Al Vandeweghe scooped it up and ran 95 yards to tie the score. In the second period Buffalo's Pat Martinelli stole an errant Yankee pass to set up a field goal by Lou Zontini.

This 10–7 halftime deficit did not demoralize the Yankees, who continued to outplay the visitors and then made the most of a blocked kick. New York's Roman Bentz turned the trick as Zontini attempted a punt. Lloyd Cheatham recovered for the Yankees and was downed at the 8. On the first play the brilliant newcomer, Spec Sanders (16 carries for 105 yards), skirted wide around left end for the tally. The last Yankee touchdown was the result of a 59-yard drive that ended with Sanders going over for his second score, this time on a sweep around the left flank.

Buffalo Bisons	7	3	0	0–10
New York Yankees	7	0	0	14–21

1 NY—Manders 2 run (Johnson kick)
   Buff—Vandeweghe 95 fumble return (Daddio kick)
2 Buff—FG Zontini 26
4 NY—Sanders 8 run (Johnson kick)
   NY—Sanders 1 run (Johnson kick)

Sunday, September 15, at San Francisco
Kezar Stadium. Attendance—25,000

The 49ers gained their first home victory with a decision over the Seahawks. The winless Seahawks dropped their second league game in as many weeks. The 49ers scored in the opening period on a plunge by Dick Renfro. Miami tied the score when Marion Pugh passed to Hamp Pool, who then lateraled to Lamar Davis for the final 22 yards. In the second quarter Renfro put the 49ers ahead for good with a touchdown run.

In the third period Renfro found the end zone again with a 3-yard run. The Seahawks concluded the scoring in the fourth period when Cotton Price passed to halfback Monk Gafford, who lateraled to Prince Scott for the last 30 yards. With a minute left San Francisco's Frankie Albert gambled on fourth-and-10, but was dropped for a 5-yard loss. However four Miami passes fell incomplete.

Miami Seahawks	7	0	0	7–14
San Francisco 49ers	7	7	7	0–21

1 SF—Renfro 8 run (Vetrano kick)
　Mia—Davis 22 lateral from Pool after 22 pass from Pugh (Erdlitz kick)
2 SF—Renfro 5 run (Vetrano kick)
3 SF—Renfro 3 run (Vetrano kick)
4 Mia—Scott 30 lateral from Gafford after pass from Price (Erdlitz kick)

Week Three

Friday Night, September 20, at Chicago Soldier Field. Attendance—25,000

A last minute touchdown pass from Walt Williams to fellow rookie Bill Boedeker enabled the Rockets to salvage a tie with the Yankees. The desperation pass spoiled the Yankees' bid for their third consecutive win and minimized a sparkling one-man show by New York rookie Spec Sanders, who tossed two touchdown passes. After a first period field goal by Chicago's Steve Nemeth, Sanders connected with end Harry Burrus for a touchdown aerial in the second quarter. Harvey Johnson then added a field goal to give the Yanks a 10–3 halftime edge. The Rockets knotted the score at 10–10 in the third quarter on a touchdown flip from Walt Clay to Bob Motl.

The Yankees seemed in control when Sanders broke loose for a 59-yard run in the fourth period. He followed this with a touchdown pass to Dewey Proctor, and New York led 17–10. But penalties shoved the Yankees deep into their own territory and the Rockets, with the clock running out, pressed to the New York 36. Then, with 0:55 left, Williams fired the payoff pass to Boedeker, who grabbed the ball on the 10 and scampered across for the score. Nemeth added the extra point and the game ended a few seconds later.

New York Yankees	0	10	0	7–17
Chicago Rockets	3	0	7	7–17

1 Chi—FG Nemeth 13
2 NY—Burrus 19 pass from Sanders (Johnson kick)
　NY—FG Johnson 19
3 Chi—Motl 36 pass from Clay (Nemeth kick)
4 NY—Proctor 16 pass from Sanders (Johnson kick)
　Chi—Boedeker 36 pass from Williams (Nemeth kick)

Friday Night, September 20, at Los Angeles Memorial Coliseum. Attendance—23,000

Using a balanced offensive attack and a sparkling defensive effort, the Dons whipped the Seahawks to keep pace with the Browns atop the AAFC's Western Division. While Angelo Bertelli was sidelined on the bench, teammate Charlie O'Rourke completed 9 of 17 passes for 128 yards and three touchdowns for the Dons. Los Angeles built a 10–0 first half lead on a Bob Nelson field goal and a touchdown pass from O'Rourke to Bus Mertes. Miami rebounded in the second quarter with Marion Pugh powering in and Kay Eakins flipping a 10-yarder over the goal line to Lamar Davis, giving the Seahawks a promising 14–10 halftime lead.

But the Dons controlled the second half with 20 unanswered points. Al Krueger made a brilliant leaping catch of an O'Rourke toss for a score. Then ex-Bear Harry Clarke reeled off 50 yards in four carries in a 75-yard march, culminated by a touchdown run by John Kimbrough. The final score was an O'Rourke pass to Bob Nowaskey. Los Angeles' only blemish was a serious leg injury to Nelson in the third period. The Seahawks were hampered by six turnovers and a feeble running attack (minus 17 yards). They completed 12 of 36 passes for 250 yards. The Dons had 108 yards rushing.

Miami Seahawks	0	14	0	0–14
Los Angeles Dons	3	7	13	7–30

1 LA—FG Nelson 36
2 LA—Mertes 32 pass from O'Rourke (Nelson kick)
　Mia—Pugh 3 run (Erdlitz kick)
　Mia—Davis 10 pass from Eakin (Johnston pass from Eakin)
3 LA—Krueger 22 pass from O'Rourke (kick blocked)
　LA—Kimbrough 1 run (Aguirre kick)
4 LA—Nowaskey 11 pass from O'Rourke (Aguirre kick)

Sunday, September 22, at Buffalo Civic Stadium. Attendance—30,302

The Browns scored their third straight victory by exploding for three first-period touchdowns and cruising to a triumph over the Bisons. The defeat was the third for the Bisons against no wins. The Browns scored the first time they laid hands on the ball, with Otto Graham pitching over Chet Mutryn's head to John Yonakor, who made the catch on the Bison 18 and ran over the goal line to complete the 52-yard touchdown. Tom Colella stopped a Bison march by intercepting a George Terlep pass. Otto Graham's pinpoint passing drove Cleveland to its second score, Graham hitting Marion Motley down the sideline for the touchdown. Late in the first quarter Gaylon Smith's sweep gave Cleveland a 21–0 lead.

The Bisons, playing without their injured ace Steve Juzwik, made four threats in the second half on the running of Vic Kulbitski and Harry Hopp, but were halted short of a score on each occasion. Then in the fourth period Chet Adams picked up a fumble and romped 25 yards for Cleveland's final touchdown. Despite 95 yards in penalties, the Browns dominated Buffalo in total yardage, 329 to 164. Groza, Cleveland's star kicker, has made good on all 16 of his extra points this season.

Cleveland Browns	21	0	0	7–28
Buffalo Bisons	0	0	0	0–0

1 Cle—Yonakor 52 pass from Graham (Groza)
Cle—Motley 33 pass from Graham (Groza kick)
Cle—Smith 12 run (Groza kick)
4 Cle—Adams 25 fumble return (Groza kick)

**Sunday, September 22, at San Francisco
Kezar Stadium. Attendance—35,000**

The 49ers, behind the clever quarterbacking of Frank Albert, passed and charged their way to a one-sided win over the Dodgers. Albert passed for two touchdowns and ran for another. After both teams missed 36-yard field goal tries, Brooklyn took a 7–0 lead when halfback Lewis Mayne hit John Colmer on a touchdown pass in the opening period. The 49ers then ran off 32 unanswered points. Len Eshmont began with a touchdown run around right end to make it 7–7. Albert then threw touchdown tosses to Eshmont and to end Alyn Beals in the second stanza. But both extra points were blocked and the halftime score was 19–7.

In the third period Albert slipped the ball to Eshmont, who passed to end Bob Titchenal for the touchdown. Albert tallied the final San Francisco touchdown on a "sneak play" around right end. Brooklyn's second touchdown climaxed an 81-yard fourth quarter drive with Glenn Dobbs completing 7 passes for 54 yards. Dobbs threw the scoring pass to O'Neale Adams. Except for their two touchdown splurges, the Dodgers had little to offer except the passes of halfback Glenn Dobbs. Even these, in a majority of cases, proved too fast for his receivers to handle. Brooklyn also lost big in the running game, mustering only 33 yards to San Francisco's 141.

Brooklyn Dodgers	7	0	0	6–13
San Francisco 49ers	7	12	13	0–32

1 Bkln—Colmer 27 pass from Mayne (McCarthy kick)
SF—Eshmont 5 run (Mellus kick)
2 SF—Eshmont 35 pass from Albert (kick blocked)
SF—Beals 43 pass from Albert (kick blocked)
3 SF—Titchenal 42 pass from Eshmont (kick failed)
SF—Albert 10 run (Vetrano kick)
4 Bkln—Adams 5 pass from Dobbs (kick blocked)

Week Four

**Bye: Brooklyn, Miami
Wednesday Night, September 25, at Chicago
Soldier Field. Attendance—20,768**

Coach Dick Hanley severed relations with the Rockets in a row with the owner, John L. Keeshin, over coaching policies. Hanley, who viewed the game as a spectator in the stands, claimed he was fired. Keeshin, in a halftime statement, said, "Within the past several weeks Dick Hanley has repeatedly submitted his resignation. On the last occasion, today, I accepted it. I am sorry that Dick's relationship with the Rockets terminated in this fashion. As far as I am concerned, we part as friends."

Hanley, who had signed a 3-year contract, told reporters it was "simply a case of incompatible personalities" and that he had never encountered so much front office advice. "For somebody who knows nothing about football, Keeshin had more coaching advice than anybody I ever knew," said Hanley. He also said that Keeshin told him that if the Rockets failed to win tonight's game with Buffalo, he and the team "might as well jump in the lake."

As it turned out the Rockets didn't need their swimsuits. Chicago rallied with 17 fourth quarter points to beat the Bisons. Both teams featured big-play touchdowns in this wild, seesaw affair. Of the game's 10 touchdowns, six were at least 40 yards in length. Buffalo's George Terlep threw three touchdown passes while Billy Hillenbrand posted three scores for the Rockets, the third being a 68-yard punt return. Later a touchdown reception by Ralph Heywood knotted the score at 35–35. Then, with 0:05 left, Steve Nemeth hit the winning field goal. Chicago's Elroy Hirsch had five catches for 136 yards. The teams combined for 798 yards of total offense, 402 for Chicago and 396 for Buffalo. The 73 points represented the AAFC's highest scoring game to date.

Buffalo Bisons	7	7	14	7–35
Chicago Rockets	7	7	7	17–38

1 Buff—Kulbitski 47 run (Zontini kick)
Chi—Hirsch 68 pass from Hoernschemeyer (Nemeth kick)
2 Chi—Hillenbrand 51 pass from Hoernschemeyer (Nemeth kick)
Buff—Tomasetti 28 pass from Terlep (Zontini kick)
3 Chi—Hillenbrand 34 run (Nemeth kick)
Buff—King 52 pass from Dekdebrun (Zontini kick)
Buff—Juzwik 40 pass from Terlep (Zontini kick)
4 Buff—Juzwik 24 pass from Terlep (Zontini kick)
Chi—Hillenbrand 68 punt return (Nemeth kick)
Chi—Heywood 5 pass from Hoernschemeyer (Nemeth kick)
Chi—FG Nemeth 13

**Sunday, September 29, at Buffalo
Civic Stadium. Attendance—18,163**

The favored Dons and the hard luck Bisons battled to a tie. Buffalo, losers of four previous games, led 21–14 with only four minutes before the final gun. But the Don's Charlie O'Rourke threw a 67-yard touchdown pass to Joe Aguirre to gain the tie. Just three days earlier, Buffalo blew a 35–21 lead at Chicago, losing 38–35 to the Rockets. The Bisons scored first on Chet Mutryn's slash, capping a 59-yard drive. The Dons marched 80 yards on 10 plays to tie after taking the second-half kickoff. Bob Seymour's 40-yard run was the big gainer. Johnny Polanski bowled in for the touchdown.

The Dons went ahead late in the third quarter when Bob Reinhard blocked Harry Hopp's punt, Bill (Bud) Kerr recovering in the end zone. In the fourth quarter the Bisons went 73 yards to tie again. Vic Kulbitski's 48-yard run set up the touchdown, which was scored on George Terlep's flip to Al Vandeweghe. A few minutes later, Buffalo took over on the Don's 12 when a punt snap sailed over the head of Reinhard. Lou Tomasetti smashed the final four yards. The Bisons pilfered three passes for interceptions. The Dons won the total yardage battle, 240–168. The game was brilliantly contested, despite intermittent rain that made the field treacherous.

Los Angeles Dons	0	0	14	7–21
Buffalo Bisons	7	0	0	14–21

1 Buff—Mutryn 25 run (Zontini kick)
3 LA—Polanski 5 run (Aguirre kick)
   LA—Kerr blocked punt recovery in end zone (Aguirre kick)
4 Buff—Vanderweghe 8 pass from Terlep (Zontini kick)
   Buff—Tomasetti 4 run (Zontini kick)
   LA—Aguirre 67 pass from O'Rourke (Aguirre kick)

Sunday, September 29, at Chicago Soldier Field. Attendance—26,875

Bob Hoernschemeyer threw for two touchdowns and contributed runs of 71 and 56 yards to lead the Rockets to a upset of the 49ers. The rejuvenated Rockets, getting their second win in a row against a loss and a tie, romped under the combined coaching of Willie Wilken, Ned Mathews and Bob Dove, while their ousted coach Dick Hanley watched from the grandstands.

After Steve Nemeth booted a field goal against a brisk wind, Hoernschemeyer spearheaded two quick touchdowns at the start of the third quarter. He took the 49ers' kickoff on his own 5, dropped the ball, then picked it up and rambled 71 yards. After four plays Hoernschemeyer tossed to Elroy Hirsch for the score. Eight minutes later Hoernschemeyer raced 56 yards to the San Francisco 18. Bill Kellagher then smashed through center to give the Rockets a commanding 17–0 lead.

Frankie Albert's toss to Nick Susoeff was good for 59 yards as the 49ers pressed to the Rocket's 2-yard line at the close of the third period. To begin the fourth period Len Eshmont drilled the touchdown for the 49ers only score. After Ernie Lewis intercepted an Albert toss, Hoernschemeyer drove the Rockets to their final score, a toss to Ralph Heywood. When the victorious Rockets streamed into the dressing room after the game, they collected around a blackboard while one of them wrote: "This game is for our boss, Mr. J. L. Keeshin." It was signed: "The boys."

San Francisco 49ers	0	0	0	7–7
Chicago Rockets	0	3	14	7–24

2 Chi—FG Nemeth 20
3 Chi—Hirsch 8 pass from Hoernschemeyer (Nemeth kick)
   Chi—Kellagher 3 run (Nemeth kick)
4 SF—Eshmont 2 run (Vetrano kick)
   Chi—Heywood 15 pass from Hoernschemeyer (Nemeth kick)

Sunday, September 29, 1946, at Cleveland Municipal Stadium. Attendance—57,084

The mistake-prone Yankees were no match for the Browns in their encounter at a muddy, rain-swept Municipal Stadium. Ray Flaherty's crippled squad, suffering its first loss against two wins and a tie, fell before the superior forces of Paul Brown to the delight of a partisan crowd. The Browns struck twice in the first period. Don Greenwood stole a New York pass and raced to the Yankee 16. Three plays later Otto Graham (10 of 15 for 144 yards) pitched to Dante Lavelli for the first touchdown. Then Cleveland's Mike Scarry picked off another Bob Kennedy toss, putting the Browns at the New York 30. Greenwood followed with a touchdown plunge, being set up by a Graham to Mac Speedie 28-yard flip. New York's Spec Sanders, playing with a damaged shoulder, completed a touchdown pass to end Jack Russell before the first period ended.

As the game progressed, the Yankees had several chances to score, but their attack bogged down in the mud whenever they reached scoring territory. Cleveland assured victory with 10 fourth quarter points, a Lou Groza field goal and a 43-yard bolt from Edgar Jones. Cleveland outrushed New York 151 yards to 36. The sloppy weather caused 15 fumbles by both teams (a new AAFC single game record), 10 by the Yankees. The Browns also tallied four interceptions.

New York Yankees	7	0	0	0–7
Cleveland Browns	14	0	0	10–24

1 Cle—Lavelli 7 pass from Graham (Groza kick)
   Cle—Greenwood 2 run (Groza kick)
   NY—Russell 14 pass from Sanders (Johnson kick)
4 Cle—FG Groza 22
   Cle—Jones 43 run (Groza kick)

WEEK FIVE

Friday Night, October 4, at Buffalo Civic Stadium. Attendance—17,101

Sensational rookie Spec Sanders, the AAFC's leader in total offense, threw a touchdown pass and scored on a punt return to lead the Yankees to a win over the Bisons. Through three periods of play the only score came from a New York 9-play drive in the second quarter, with Bob Kennedy going in from 8 yards out. The Bisons stole a Bob Perina pass late in the third, which led to George Terlep's touchdown sweep around end early in the fourth quarter. But George (Bruiser) Kinard blocked the extra point try, preserving New York's slim 7–6 lead.

On the ensuing kickoff, Sanders returned the ball 57 yards, and then threw a touchdown pass to Lowell Wagner. Less than two minutes later, Sanders fielded a Lou Zontini punt and spun 76 yards behind marvelous blocking for the score. Buffalo added a late score on a pass from Al Dekdebrun to Chet Mutryn. Buffalo had a slight edge in total yardage, 223 to 193. But the Yankees won the turnover battle 5–2. New York improved its record to 3–1–1 while Buffalo slipped to 1–4–1.

New York Yankees	0	7	0	14–21
Buffalo Bisons	0	0	0	13–13

2 NY—Kennedy 8 run (Johnson kick)
4 Buff—Terlep 2 run (kick blocked)
   NY—Wagner 47 pass from Sanders (Johnson kick)
   NY—Sanders 76 punt return (Johnson kick)
   Buff—Mutryn 54 pass from Dekdebrun (Zontini kick)

Friday Night, October 4, at Chicago Soldier Field. Attendance—31,076

The Dons, thoroughly outplayed in the first half, bounced back with three touchdowns in the second stanza to defeat the Rockets. In the first half most of the action was contributed by the Rockets, including an exciting touchdown run by Billy Hillenbrand on the opening kickoff. The Rocket's Steve Nemeth added a field goal in the second quarter, extending the Chicago lead to 9–0.

In the second half the Dons were more aggressive and got their first break with nine minutes gone when Dale Gentry blocked a punt by Walt Williams of the Rockets on the 6-yard line. Gentry scooped up the bouncing ball and went across for the score. In the opening minutes of the fourth period the Dons took the lead for good on a plunge by Andy Marefos. The final Los Angeles touchdown came on a pass from Charlie O'Rourke to Jack Morton, who snagged it at the 6-yard line and went across unmolested. The Rocket's record fell to 2–2–1. The Dons improved to three wins and a tie.

Los Angeles Dons	0	0	7	14–21
Chicago Rockets	6	3	0	0–9

1 Chi—Hillenbrand 88 kickoff return (kick failed)
2 Chi—FG Nemeth 28
3 LA—Gentry 3 blocked punt return (Aguirre kick)
4 LA—Marefos 1 run (Aguirre kick)
   LA—Morton 19 pass from O'Rourke (Aguirre kick)

Sunday, October 6, at Cleveland Municipal Stadium. Attendance–43,713

The Browns notched their fifth triumph, swamping the Dodgers. Mixing accurate passing with long runs, the Browns built a 19–0 first-half lead. The Dodgers relied on the passing of Glenn Dobbs, but early fumbles put them in a hole from which they could not climb out. The Browns scored early in the first period when defensive end Alton Coppage recovered Dobb's fumble on the Brooklyn 20. Lou Groza then kicked a field goal from a difficult angle. A few minutes, later Cleveland added a safety when Dobbs fumbled again and was nailed in his own end zone.

Cleveland's first touchdown was set up when Cliff Lewis and Marion Motley combined for a 60-yard punt return to the Dodger 5. Don Greenwood then scored midway through the first period. Greenwood scored another touchdown in the second after Mac Speedie made a sensational catch, taking it to the Brooklyn 7. The Dodger's score came in the third when tackle Martin Ruby recovered Lewis' fumble on the Cleveland 6 and Lewis Mayne skirted right end for the touchdown. Tom Colella went over in the final period for the Brown's last tally. Cleveland won the turnover battle 6–1 and prevailed in total yardage, 259–177.

Brooklyn Dodgers	0	0	7	0–7
Cleveland Browns	12	7	0	7–26

1 Cle—FG Groza 15
   Cle—Safety, Coppage and Rymkus tackled Dobbs in end zone
   Cle—Greenwood 1 run (Groza kick)
2 Cle—Greenwood 1 run (Groza kick)
3 Bkln—Mayne 4 run (Martinovich kick)
4 Cle—Colella 4 run (Groza kick)

Tuesday Night, October 8, at Miami Orange Bowl. Attendance—7,621

The Seahawks and the 49ers inaugurated professional football in the Deep South tonight before a slim crowd. The game was originally scheduled for October 7, but got postponed one day due to a hurricane. The winless Seahawks must have felt like hurricane victims as the impressive 49ers stormed to a 34–7 win. San Francisco's Len Eshmont crashed over line in the opening period for the first score. This was followed by a touchdown pass in the second quarter from Jesse Freitas to Alyn Beals to make the halftime score 14–0. Late in the third quarter Earle Parsons scored the third 49er touchdown.

The Seahawks finally scored following a 56-yard reception by Monk Gafford, downed at the San Francisco 4. Quarterback Jimmy Tarrant then passed to Prince Scott for the Miami touchdown. Eshmont paced another 49er advance that led to a touchdown run by Pete Franceshi. Then Miami's Tarrant fumbled on the San Francisco 28, where 49er tackle John Kuzman recovered and experienced the defensive lineman's dream, running 72 yards for the final touchdown. San Francisco prevailed in the rushing statistics, gaining 204 yards against only 41 for Miami.

San Francisco 49ers	7	7	7	13–34
Miami Seahawks	0	0	0	7–7

1 SF—Eshmont 2 run (Vetrano kick)
2 SF—Beals 12 pass from Freitas (Vetrano kick)
3 SF—Parsons 24 run (Vetrano kick)
4 Mia—Scott 4 pass from Tarrant (Erdlitz kick)
  SF—Franceshi 8 run (kick failed)
  SF—Kuzman 72 fumble return (Vetrano kick)

Week Six

Friday Night, October 11, at Brooklyn, NY
Ebbets Field. Attendance—16,211

If a tie in football is like kissing your sister, Brooklyn and Chicago gave each other a big smooch tonight. The Dodgers could not hold a promising 16–0 first quarter lead and the Rockets, despite piling up an amazing 500 yards of total offense, could not secure victory. Brooklyn's early lead stemmed from a touchdown run by Dom Principe, a touchdown pass from Glenn Dobbs to Jerry McCarthy and a safety when Chicago's Walt Williams fumbled a quick kick from Dobbs out of the end zone.

Chicago scored in the second on a plunge by Ned Mathews to cap a 62-yard march. Chicago's Williams suffered another safety in the third period when Joe Davis sacked him in the end zone. Chicago responded with a touchdown pass to Ralph Heywood (5 catches for 103 yards) to end the third quarter scoring. In the fourth period Martinovich added a field goal, giving Brooklyn a 21–14 lead. With 1:10 left, Chicago's Bob Hoernschemeyer whipped a pass to Heywood, who lateraled to Mathews to complete the 66-yard touchdown for the tie. Although clearly out-played, the Dodger's trump card was the punting of Dobbs, who averaged 53.2 yards per punt, including a 75-yarder. Brooklyn's total offense was just 157 yards.

| Chicago Rockets | 0 | 7 | 7 | 7–21 |
| Brooklyn Dodgers | 16 | 0 | 2 | 3–21 |

1 Bkln—Principe 1 run (Martinovich kick)
  Bkln—McCarthy 55 pass from Dobbs (Martinovich kick)
  Bkln—Safety, Williams fumbled out of end zone
2 Chi—Mathews 3 run (Nemeth kick)
3 Bkln—Safety, Davis tackled Williams in end zone
  Chi—Heywood 20 pass from Hoernschemeyer (Nemeth kick)
4 Bkln—FG Martinovich 23
  Chi—Mathews 44 lateral from Heywood after 22 pass from Hoernschemeyer (Nemeth kick)

Friday Night, October 11, at Buffalo
Civic Stadium. Attendance—5,040

Halfback Johnny Vardian's field goal with 1:45 left gave the Seahawks their first AAFC victory as they beat the Bisons before a sparse crowd. It was the first win by either team this season. Buffalo's Steve Juzwik intercepted an early Miami pass and raced 50 yards to the Miami 25-yard line. This set up a 6-inch dive by Harry Hopp five plays later to give the Bisons a 7–0 lead. Miami's Mitch Olenski recovered a Buffalo fumble, which led to a touchdown run by Monk Gafford to tie the score at 7–7. Later in the first period Miami's Fred Gloden bucked through tackle to put the Seahawks ahead 14–7.

After a scoreless second quarter, Buffalo marched 65 yards in the third session to tie the game, with substitute end Fay King nabbing the touchdown pass from Ken Stofer. Then Vardian added the winning kick. Buffalo's record fell to 0–6–1 while Miami improved to 1–4–0.

| Miami Seahawks | 14 | 0 | 0 | 3–17 |
| Buffalo Bisons | 7 | 0 | 7 | 0–14 |

1 Buff—Hopp 1 run (Zontini kick)
  Mia—Gafford 5 run (Erdlitz kick)
  Mia—Gloden 4 run (Erdlitz kick)
3 Buff—King 4 pass from Stofer (Zontini kick)
4 Mia—FG Vardian 20

Saturday Night, October 12, at Bronx, NY
Yankee Stadium. Attendance—34,252

The opportunistic Browns capitalized on turnovers to trip up the Yankees, the contest being played almost entirely in a constant downpour of rain. A scoreless first half saw the Yankees dominate the Browns in every statistic except the one that counts. However the Yankees could only advance as far as the Cleveland 11-yard line, where they had to forfeit possession on downs. Lou Groza, Cleveland's ace kicker, tried two field goals, but the treacherous turf allowed the Yankees to block these attempts easily.

The game-deciding play came early in the third quarter. Tommy Colella punted to New York's Spec Sanders, who was stationed at his 33-yard line. Sanders braced for the reception, but allowed the slippery ball to get away from him. Cleveland guard Ed Ulinski pounced on the miscue. The groans from the Yankee partisans were still in the air as Otto Graham brought his troops to the scrimmage line for the game's only score, launching a beautiful touchdown pass to Dante Lavelli. Once ahead the Browns used a stingy defense and the muddy field to hold off New York's desperate passing attack. The Yankees outgained the Browns 237 to 67 yards in total offense, but lost the turnover battle 4–0.

| Cleveland Browns | 0 | 0 | 7 | 0–7 |
| New York Yankees | 0 | 0 | 0 | 0–0 |

3 Cle—Lavelli 33 pass from Graham (Groza kick)

Saturday Night, October 12, at Los Angeles
Gilmore Stadium. Attendance—12,500

The speedy 49ers, paced by Frank Albert, scored on three quick touchdown plays to upset the Dons. Albert passed for one touchdown and scored another himself. Joe Vetrano kicked a field goal in the opening period for the 49ers. Albert then passed to end Allyn Beals to make it 10–0. The Dons answered with a 75-yard march in the second stanza, fullback Andy Marefos plunging over from the 1-yard line.

In the third quarter Albert tallied a touchdown run. A stray Albert toss was intercepted by the Dons' Bob Nowaskey, who raced 35 yards for the score. The final score was a dash by San Francisco's Earle Parsons, who outran the Dons' secondary. A balanced 49er attack accounted for 229 yards of total offense. The Dons relied strictly on the 178 passing yards of Angelo Bertelli and Charlie O'Rourke. The Dons' rushing attack was nonexistent, registering zero yardage. The game was to be played at Memorial Coliseum, but was moved to Gilmore Stadium because of a scheduling conflict.

San Francisco 49ers	10	0	7	6–23
Los Angeles Dons	0	7	7	0–14

1 SF—FG Vetrano 26
   SF—Beals 5 pass from Albert (Vetrano kick)
2 LA—Marefos 1 run (Aguirre kick)
3 SF—Albert 5 run (Vetrano kick)
   LA—Nowaskey 35 interception return (Aguirre kick)
4 SF—Parsons 66 run (kick failed)

WEEK SEVEN

**Friday Night, October 18, at Chicago
Soldier Field. Attendance—20,172**

The player-coached Rockets bagged their third AAFC victory by trimming the Seahawks. The Seahawks, completely outplayed by the Rockets' line, finished with minus 28 yards rushing compared with Chicago's 210. With two minutes left in the first half, Chicago's Elroy Hirsch zigzagged 17 yards for the first touchdown. Bob Hoernschemeyer flipped two touchdown passes, one to Ned Mathews via a lateral from Ralph Heywood, and another to Frank Quillan. Ernie Lewis battered a touchdown run as the Rockets built a 28–0 fourth quarter lead. The Seahawks scored with only two minutes left on a pass from Kay Eakin to end Monk Gafford. Miami's record fell to 1–5–0 while the Rockets improved to 3–2–2.

Miami Seahawks	0	0	0	7–7
Chicago Rockets	0	7	14	7–28

2 Chi—Hirsch 17 run (Nemeth kick)
3 Chi—Mathews 20 lateral from Heywood after 13 pass from Hoernschemeyer (Nemeth kick)
   Chi—Lewis 4 run (Nemeth kick)
4 Chi—Quillan 9 pass from Hoernschemeyer (Nemeth kick)
   Mia—Gafford 40 pass from Eakin (Erdlitz kick)

**Saturday Night, October 19, at Bronx, NY
Yankee Stadium. Attendance—30,212**

Glenn Dobbs, who has been dubbed the "passmaster" of the AAFC, turned in a dazzling performance in an attempt to lead the Dodgers to an upset victory over their cross-town rival Yankees. But the versatile Yankees rallied in the fourth quarter to secure the win. New York struck first with veteran Ace Parker scoring on a 10-yard jaunt. The score remained 7–0 until the Dodgers posted 10 third quarter points. Phil Martinovich kicked a field goal and Dobbs added a touchdown toss to Russell Morrow.

But the fourth quarter belonged to the Yankees. Led by Bob Perina and Spec Sanders, the Yankees put together a 72-yard touchdown drive, capped by Perina's toss to Sanders. The Yankees then recovered their own kickoff and Perina ran around the right side for the final touchdown. Dobbs accounted for 125 of his team's 150 yards passing. He also averaged 54.3 yards per punt. But the Dodgers could only muster 15 yards rushing. The Yankees had 328 yards of total offense, 179 through the air. The victory gave the Yankees a comfortable lead in the Eastern Division with a mark of 4–2–1.

Brooklyn Dodgers	0	0	10	0–10
New York Yankees	7	0	0	14–21

1 NY—Parker 10 run (Johnson kick)
3 Bkln—FG Martinovich 36
   Bkln—Morrow 8 pass from Dobbs (Martinovich kick)
4 NY—Sanders 27 pass from Perina (Johnson kick)
   NY—Perina 40 run (Johnson kick)

**Saturday Night, October 19, at Buffalo
Civic Stadium. Attendance—6,101**

The Bisons captured their first AAFC victory by upsetting the heavily favored 49ers. A small but spirited crowd saw the home team score the winning touchdown on a 55-yard drive late in the final period. The Bisons opened the scoring with a Lou Zontini field goal. San Francisco countered with a touchdown run from Len Eshmont and a Jess Freitas touchdown pass to Allyn Beals. Just before halftime Buffalo's Allan Dekdebrun passed to Chet Mutryn to make the score 14–10, San Francisco. This 49er lead held until two minutes to go in the game. Then Buffalo mounted the winning 5-play drive with Dekdebrun passing to Lafayette King for the game-winning touchdown. Buffalo improved to 1–6–1 and San Francisco slipped to 4–3–0.

San Francisco 49ers	0	14	0	0–14
Buffalo Bisons	3	7	0	7–17

1 Buff—FG Zontini 45
2 SF—Eshmont 2 run (Vetrano kick)
   SF—Beals 25 pass from Freitas (Vetrano kick)
   Buff—Mutryn 29 pass from Dekdebrun (Zontini kick)
4 Buff—King 2 pass from Dekdebrun (Zontini kick)

**Sunday, October 20, at Cleveland
Municipal Stadium. Attendance—71,134**

The Browns spotted the Dons a 7–0 lead, then roared back to win. It was the Browns' seventh win in the new AAFC loop. The Dons marched 67 yards in the first few minutes to score on an pass from Charlie O'Rourke to Bob Nowaskey. The Browns were helpless in the first half, save a long field goal from Lou Groza. Cleveland took the lead in the third quarter after an 85-yard drive ended with Otto Graham diving over from the 2. The highlight of the drive was a 37-yard pass to Dante Lavelli.

The Dons tried to tie the score early in the fourth period on Joe Aguirre's 40-yard field goal attempt, but the stingy Browns blocked it, recovering on their 34. Three plays later Graham hit Mac Speedie for a touchdown pass. Cleveland tallied again on a Marion Motley (8 carries for 143 yards) dash. The Dons rebounded with a 62-yard drive, O'Rourke scoring from the 6. But on Cleveland's next play from scrimmage, Motley went 68 yards for the game's final score. On paper the Dons should have won. They outgained the Browns 395 to 353, had more than twice as many first downs (21–10) and fewer penalty yards.

Los Angeles Dons	7	0	0	7–14
Cleveland Browns	0	3	7	21–31

1 LA—Nowaskey 18 pass from O'Rourke (Aguirre kick)
2 Cle—FG Groza 48
3 Cle—Graham 2 run (Groza kick)
4 Cle—Speedie 47 pass from Graham (Groza kick)
   Cle—Motley 49 run (Groza kick)
   LA—O'Rourke 6 run (Aguirre kick)
   Cle—Motley 68 run (Groza kick)

Week Eight

Friday Night, October 25, at Brooklyn, NY Ebbets Field. Attendance—15,200

A spectacular performance by Brooklyn's Glenn Dobbs, who set two AAFC records, sparked the Dodgers' thumping of the visiting Seahawks. The former Army Air Force lieutenant's versatile one-man-show also included two interceptions and a punting average of 54 yards. Completing his first 9 passes, along with 5 more against the Yankees last week, brought Dobbs' total to 14 consecutive pass completions, a new conference mark. Dobbs' second record was an electrifying 78-yard punt return, topping the mark of 75 yards set by New York's Spec Sanders on October 4.

The Seahawks, who were never in the contest, didn't score until 2:15 to go in the game. Their only other threat was a drive to the Brooklyn 3 in the second period, where they were pushed back by the Dodger defense. Brooklyn, scoring in every quarter, built a 17–0 halftime lead. Dobbs crushed all Miami hopes in the third stanza with a touchdown pass to Jim McCarthy after faking a reverse. Dobbs' 11 of 15 passing for 222 yards was the dominant statistic. Miami had five turnovers to Brooklyn's two. A prominent spectator was Dr. Marvin (Mal) Stevens, who during the afternoon had resigned as head coach of the Dodgers.

Miami Seahawks	0	0	0	7–7
Brooklyn Dodgers	10	7	7	6–30

1 Bkln—FG Martinovich 38
   Bkln—Principe 3 run (Martinovich kick)
2 Bkln—Davis 23 pass from Mayne (Martinovich kick)
3 Bkln—McCarthy 65 pass from Dobbs (Martinovich kick)
4 Bkln—Dobbs 78 punt return (kick failed)
   Mia—Gloden 1 run (Erdlitz kick)

Sunday, October 27, at Los Angeles Memorial Coliseum. Attendance—15,000

The favored Yankees staged a come-from-behind victory over the Dons, powered by three touchdowns from rookie Spec Sanders. The versatile Sanders tallied scores on a run, a catch and a kickoff return. After New York's Harvey Johnson booted a field goal, the Dons responded with two touchdowns, a run by John Kimbrough and a reception by Joe Aguirre to give Los Angeles a 14–3 lead. Sanders then took the ensuing kickoff and sped 103 yards to close the scoring on an exciting first quarter.

The Yankees scored three more touchdowns, Sanders doing the honors with a catch from Ace Parker and a brilliant 75-yard run. Pug Manders added a plunge in the fourth period. The Dons could only manage a field goal from Bob Nelson after their impressive first period attack. The squads were fairly even in total offense, the Yankees with 285 yards and the Dons with 299. The Yankees stole four Los Angeles passes. New York improved to 5–2–1. Los Angeles, suffering its third straight loss, fell to 3–3–1 as they looked forward to hosting the league-leading Browns.

New York Yankees	10	7	7	7–31
Los Angeles Dons	14	0	3	0–17

1 NY—FG Johnson 27
   LA—Kimbrough 4 run (Aguirre kick)
   LA—Aguirre 26 pass from O'Rourke (Aguirre kick)
   NY—Sanders 103 kickoff return (Johnson kick)
2 NY—Sanders 20 pass from Parker (Johnson kick)
3 LA—FG Nelson 15
   NY—Sanders 75 run (Johnson kick)
4 NY—Manders 1 run (Johnson kick)

Sunday, October 27, at Buffalo Civic Stadium. Attendance—15,758

Most pro football games are decided by 60 minutes of play; this one was over in three minutes and 15 seconds. The Bisons closed their home campaign by setting an AAFC scoring record with a victory over the Rockets. Leading 7–3, Buffalo popped three quick touchdowns in those 3:15 to take a commanding 28–3 halftime advantage. The Bison defense led the way, scoring four touchdowns, three on fumble recoveries, to smother the hapless Rockets. Meanwhile Jim Thibaut, Preston Johnston and Steve Juzwik each added a touchdown run for Buffalo.

Chicago's self-inflicted wounds included six turnovers and 65 yards in penalties. Their only highlight was an 88-yard kickoff return by Elroy Hirsch, which tied an AAFC record ironically held by teammate Billy Hillenbrand. The Bisons outrushed the Rockets 217 to 49. Buffalo's 49 points topped the Cleveland's 44 points against Miami in the league's inaugural contest, September 6. Their 28 points in the second quarter were also a new conference mark.

Chicago Rockets	0	3	7	7–17
Buffalo Bisons	0	28	14	7–49

2 Chi—FG Nemeth 9
 Buff—Thibaut 2 run (Zontini kick)
 Buff—Johnston 1 run (Zontini kick)
 Buff—Comer 50 fumble return (Zontini kick)
 Buff—Juzwik 45 lateral from Mutryn after 3 interception return (Zontini kick)
3 Buff—Juzwik 22 run (Zontini kick)
 Chi—Hirsch 88 kickoff return (Nemeth kick)
 Buff—Mutryn 60 lateral from Lahar after fumble return (Zontini kick)
4 Chi—Williams 1 run (Nemeth kick)
 Buff—Dugger 20 fumble return (Zontini kick)

Sunday, October 27, at Cleveland Municipal Stadium. Attendance—70,385

The 49ers buried the myth that the Browns could not be beaten. Riding the pitching arm of Frankie Albert (14 of 21 for 180 yards), the 49ers rebounded from last week's disappointing loss to Buffalo to put the whammy on the Browns. Albert, who tossed three touchdown passes, led the 49ers to a 27–6 third quarter lead before Cleveland's ace Otto Graham (14 of 19 for 284 yards) could get untracked. Graham tallied a fourth quarter touchdown pass to Dante Lavelli (8 catches for 183 yards), however the Browns were a badly beaten team by then.

Meanwhile Albert and his mates were having a field day. End Allyn Beals hauled in two touchdown passes while Don Durdan caught the third. Len Eshmont added a touchdown run and Joe Vetrano kicked two field goals. The 49er defense forced five fumbles and an interception to stymie the Cleveland attack. Pouring salt on the wound, Cleveland's Lou Groza, the league's leading scorer with 46 points, suffered a back injury in the second period and never returned to the fray. The Browns fell to 7-1-0 while San Francisco advanced to 5-3-0.

San Francisco 49ers	3	17	7	7–34
Cleveland Browns	0	6	0	14–20

1 SF—FG Vetrano 22
2 SF—Beals 16 pass from Albert (Vetrano kick)
 SF—Eshmont 6 run (Vetrano kick)
 Cle—Greenwood 3 run (errant snap from center)
 SF—FG Vetrano 19
3 SF—Durdan 9 pass from Albert (Vetrano kick)
4 Cle—Lavelli 21 pass from Graham (Rokisky kick)
 SF—Beals 15 pass from Albert (Vetrano kick)
 Cle—Smith 3 run (Speedie pass from Graham)

WEEK NINE

Saturday Night, November 2, at Chicago Soldier Field. Attendance—17,924

Playing in a rainstorm, the visiting Dodgers, led by AAFC total offense leader Glenn Dobbs, defeated the Rockets. Dobbs counted for two touchdown runs and a touchdown pass. It appeared that the Dodgers, with their new coach Cliff Battles making his debut, would run away with it early. Dobbs hit Art Van Tone with a pass for the first score to end a 66-yard drive, the key play being a 31-yard flip to Joe Davis. A few minutes later Dobbs added a short touchdown run for the second marker.

But Chicago rebounded following linebacker Pete Lamana's interception of a Dobbs pass. Elroy Hirsch tossed a "sleeper" pass to Billy Hillenbrand for Chicago's first touchdown. Hirsch then tied the score with a punt return. Early in the third period Brooklyn's John "Mickey" Colmer filched a Hirsch pass. Dobbs capitalized by sprinting 42 yards to the endzone. From there on neither team threatened to score on the wet turf. Dobbs completed six of 16 passes for 84 yards and rushed 11 times for 110 yards. In the first period he registered a 75-yard punt.

Brooklyn Dodgers	14	0	7	0–21
Chicago Rockets	0	14	0	0–14

1 Bkln—Van Tone 14 pass from Dobbs (Martinovich kick)
 Bkln—Dobbs 3 run (Martinovich kick)
2 Chi—Hillenbrand 40 pass from Hirsch (Nemeth kick)
 Chi—Hirsch 54 punt return (Nemeth kick)
3 Bkln—Dobbs 42 run (Martinovich kick)

Saturday Night, November 2, at San Francisco Kezar Stadium. Attendance—12,500

The 49ers, ringing up three fourth-quarter touchdowns, rallied to beat Buffalo to avenge a defeat at the hands of the Bisons just two weeks earlier. Halfback Len Eshmont and quarterback Frankie Albert posted two touchdowns each for the victors. In the second period Buffalo resorted to trickery to forge ahead. Driving to the 49er 9-yard line, the Bisons faked a field goal try, instead opting for a touchdown pass from Al Dekdebrun to halfback Steve Juzwik for a 7–0 halftime lead.

Eshmont started the third quarter by stealing the ball from Buffalo fullback Luther "Pres" Johnston and going 15 yards for the tying score. The 49ers controlled the fourth quarter, with Eshmont adding a touchdown run. Then the talented Albert took over with touchdown passes to ends Ken Casanega and Bob Titchenal. Buffalo's backup quarterback George Terlep concluded the scoring with a short toss to end Fay King.

Buffalo Bisons	0	7	0	7–14
San Francisco 49ers	0	0	7	20–27

2 Buff—Juzwik 14 pass from Dekdebrun (Zontini kick)
3 SF—Eshmont 15 fumble return (Vetrano kick)
4 SF—Eshmont 34 run (Vetrano kick)
   SF—Casanega 18 pass from Albert (Vetrano kick)
   SF—Titchenal 54 pass from Albert (kick failed)
   Buff—King 3 pass from Terlep (Zontini kick)

Sunday, November 3, at Los Angeles Memorial Coliseum. Attendance—24,800

Big Joe Aguirre's field goal in the last 0:20 lifted the underdog Dons over the Browns, giving the visitors their second consecutive loss of the season. The win avenged a frustrating loss to the Browns just two weeks earlier. The Dons scored on the first play from scrimmage on a long run by Chuck Fenenbock. Cleveland answered with a Lou Groza field goal, a short touchdown run by Bill Lund and a touchdown pass from Otto Graham (12 of 19 for 241 yards) to Mac Speedie (4 catches for 134 yards). However Groza missed the second conversion, his first miss in 23 tries this season, making the halftime score 16–7 Cleveland.

The Dons' comeback started with some questionable play-calling by the Browns. Electing not to punt, Cleveland's Tom Colella tried a fourth down run, but was thrown back to his own 22. Los Angeles took over and scored quickly on Dale Gentry's end around run. In the final minute John Kimbrough led the Dons to the Cleveland 4, where Aguirre added the game winning field goal. The Dons punished the Cleveland defenders with 220 yards rushing while the Browns rushed for only 43 yards.

Cleveland Browns	3	13	0	0–16
Los Angeles Dons	7	0	0	10–17

1 LA—Fenenbock 75 run (Aguirre kick)
   Cle—FG Groza 25
2 Cle—Lund 5 run (Groza kick)
   Cle—Speedie 79 pass from Graham (kick failed)
4 LA—Gentry 8 run (Aguirre kick)
   LA—FG Aguirre 11

Sunday, November 3, at Bronx, NY Yankee Stadium. Attendance—18,800

Led by veteran Ace Parker, the Yankees slipped past the Seahawks to avoid a major pro football upset. Parker engineered a 71-yard touchdown drive in the closing minutes to defeat the stubborn Seahawks. After trading early touchdowns, the Yankees took the lead on a Harvey Johnson field goal. Then Parker recovered a Miami miscue and raced for a touchdown, giving New York a 17–7 lead. In the next two periods the crowd witnessed staunch defense and some fancy punting. Parker placed a coffin corner kick at the Miami 1. Then Miami's Kay Eakin, from his end zone, punted to the New York 31, nearly 80 yards away.

Early in the fourth quarter Miami's Don Reece scored on a run. Then came the Seahawks big break. Al Wukits stole a pass from New York's Spec Sanders. Three plays later Cotton Price hit Monk Gafford in the end zone and new coach Hampton Pool's Miami squad led 21–17. Five minutes and 18 seconds remained when Parker began the game winning drive. On the eleventh play, he hit Jack Russell for the final touchdown. New York led in total offense, 375 yards to Miami's 214 yards.

Miami Seahawks	7	0	0	14–21
New York Yankees	17	0	0	7–24

1 NY—Cheatham 15 pass from Perina (Johnson kick)
   Mia—Reece 1 run (Erdlitz kick)
   NY—FG Johnson 18
   NY—Parker 22 fumble return (Johnson kick)
4 Mia—Reece 13 run (Erdlitz kick)
   Mia—Gafford 19 pass from Price (Erdlitz kick)
   NY—Russell 11 pass from Parker (Johnson kick)

Week Ten

Sunday, November 10, at San Francisco Kezar Stadium. Attendance—41,061

Avenging their only home loss of the season, the Browns defeated the 49ers, giving Paul Brown's troops a 2-game cushion lead in the AAFC's competitive Western Division. Behind tremendous line power, ace Otto Graham drove the Browns 67 yards to paydirt on the game's opening series. At the 49er 3-yard line, he hit Dante Lavelli with a touchdown pass. Late in the first half, Cleveland's Mike Scarry recovered a 49er fumble at the Browns' 33. Graham promptly flipped a screen pass to Marion Motley who rambled 64 yards before being stopped, again at the 49er 3-yard line. Graham then handed to substitute Gaylon Smith, who smashed over center for the score.

San Francisco finally scored early in the fourth period on a balanced 64-yard advance, the key play being a thrilling 39-yard dash by Norman Standlee. With the ball at the Cleveland 1-yard line, Frank Albert recovered his own fumble and went in for the score. Cleveland held the edge in total offense, 271 yards to the 49ers' 212 yards. The Browns also won the turnover battle 4–2.

Cleveland Browns	7	7	0	0–14
San Francisco 49ers	0	0	0	7–7

1 Cle—Lavelli 3 pass from Graham (Groza kick)
2 Cle—Smith 3 run (Groza kick)
4 SF—Albert 1 fumble return (Vetrano kick)

Sunday, November 10, at Brooklyn, NY Ebbets Field. Attendance—12,820

The Dodger's hopes of catching the Yankees in the Eastern Division were dashed in a bitter loss to the Bisons. In fact only the pitching arm of Glenn Dobbs, who was rushed and harassed for most of the contest, kept the Dodgers close. Buffalo struck early when Felton Prewitt swiped a Dobbs' pass deep in Bison territory, returning it past mid-field. Four plays later Preston Johnston crashed through for the touchdown. A 69-yard run by Vic Kulbitski (15 carries for 134 yards) set up a Lou Zontini field goal. Dobbs answered with a strike to Art Van Tone to cut the Bison lead to 10–7. In the third period Ray Elbi caught a touchdown pass for Buffalo after Steve Juzwik scampered 62 yards.

But Dobbs kept the paying customers in their seats, finding Doyle Tackett on a 40-yard bomb to trim the deficit to 17–14. In the closing seconds he hit O'Neale Adams in-stride on the goal line, only to see the former Arkansas end drop the potential winning touchdown. Then all hopes for a tie sailed away when southpaw kicker Phil Martinovich missed a 31-yard field goal attempt. Despite Dobbs' heroics, 13 of 26 for 280 yards passing, he could not overcome the 316-yard ground assault by the Bisons.

Buffalo Bisons	10	0	7	0–17
Brooklyn Dodgers	0	7	0	7–14

1 Buff—Johnston 6 run (Zontini kick)
  Buff—FG Zontini 15
2 Bkln—Van Tone 20 pass from Dobbs (Martinovich kick)
3 Buff—Ebli 5 pass from Dekdebrun (Zontini kick)
4 Bkln—Tackett 40 pass from Dobbs (Martinovich kick)

Sunday, November 10, at Bronx, NY
Yankee Stadium. Attendance—30,765

Taking another step toward the Eastern Division title, the Yankees toppled the Dons, twice coming from behind, and then winning it with a spectacular punt return. The Dons jumped out front when Bill Radovich blocked a quick kick try by New York's Ace Parker, the ball rolling beyond the end zone for an automatic safety. Then Joe Aguirre added a field goal to give Los Angeles a 5–0 lead. The Yankees scored when Parker hit rookie Spec Sanders with a short toss, Sanders cutting across the field and outrunning the defense for the touchdown.

With 0:31 left in the half, Angelo Bertelli fired a long aerial to Bob Seymour, who was hemmed in by Yankee defenders Parker and Pug Manders. Manders leaped and batted the ball, only to see it carom into to hands of Seymour, who scurried untouched to the endzone. After intermission the Yankees drove deep into Dons territory where Harvey Johnson converted a field goal. Late in the third period, New York speedster Eddie Prokop fielded a Bill Reinhard punt and raced down the sideline for the winning score. Although neither team had impressive statistics, the game was close all the way. Los Angeles did have 149 yards passing, but suffered 55 yards in penalties.

Los Angeles Dons	0	12	0	0—12
New York Yankees	0	7	10	0—17

2 LA—Safety, Radovich blocked punt out of end zone
  LA—FG Aguirre 32
  NY—Sanders 49 pass from Parker (Johnson kick)
  LA—Seymour 47 pass from Bertelli (Aguirre kick)
3 NY—FG Johnson 18
  NY—Prokop 77 punt return (Johnson kick)

Monday Night, November 11, at Miami
Orange Bowl. Attendance—7,438

In a bruising battle the Rockets defeated the Seahawks in the hot, muggy weather of south Florida before a sparse audience. The Rockets were powered by two touchdown runs from Bill Kellagher and the accurate place-kicking of Steve Nemeth. Kellagher tallied his first score to cap a 52-yard Chicago drive, dashing in from the 1-yard line. Cotton Price and Prince Scott drove their Miamians to within inches of the Rocket goal line, only to fail on a fourth-and-goal try just before the half ended. In the third stanza Chicago drove to the Miami 3 but had to settle for a Nemeth field goal, the key play being Bob Hoernschemeyer's 41-yard run.

After an interception by Miami's Jim Reynolds, Marion Pugh passed to Hub Ulrich for the Seahawks' only touchdown. Then Kellagher broke through the Miami defense for his second touchdown to put the game on ice. Nemeth closed the evening with his second field goal. Chicago won the total offense war, 232 to 167, and also in turnovers 4–2. The Rockets improved to 4–4–2 and the struggling Seahawks fell to 1–8–0.

Chicago Rockets	7	0	3	10–20
Miami Seahawks	0	0	0	7–7

1 Chi—Kellagher 1 run (Nemeth kick)
3 Chi—FG Nemeth 10
4 Mia—Ulrich 28 pass from Pugh (Erdlitz kick)
  Chi—Kellagher 53 run (Nemeth kick)
  Chi—FG Nemeth 14

Week Eleven

Sunday, November 17, at Cleveland
Municipal Stadium. Attendance—60,457

Gaining momentum as the game progressed, the Browns flexed their muscles by smothering the Rockets with an avalanche of points, virtually clinching the AAFC's first Western Division crown. The 51 points were the most yet in an AAFC game and ironically Cleveland's Lou Groza set the league's distance mark with a 51-yard field goal. Groza's field goal also tied the pro season record of ten. But the star was Cleveland's Otto Graham, who passed for four touchdowns, two each to Dante Lavelli and Mac Speedie.

Other touchdowns came from Edgar Jones (5 carries for 100 yards) on a run to open the scoring, a pass from Bud Schwenk to Bill Lund and an interception return by Frank Gatski in the fourth quarter. Chicago's Bob Hoernschemeyer figured in both Rocket scores, passing to Elroy Hirsch in the second period and combining with Pete Lamana on a long punt return. Cleveland dominated in total offense, 360–156. The Rockets were victims of eight turnovers, including five interceptions.

| Chicago Rockets | 0 | 7 | 7 | 0–14 |
| Cleveland Browns | 7 | 10 | 14 | 20–51 |

1 Cle—Jones 26 run (Groza kick)
2 Cle—Lavelli 8 pass from Graham (Groza kick)
 Chi—Hirsch 17 pass from Hoernschemeyer (Nemeth kick)
 Cle—FG Groza 51
3 Cle—Lavelli 34 pass from Graham (Groza kick)
 Cle—Speedie 39 pass from Graham (Groza kick)
 Chi—Lamana 20 lateral from Hoernschemeyer after 55 punt return (Nemeth kick)
4 Cle—Speedie 7 pass from Graham (Groza kick)
 Cle—Lund 20 pass from Schwenk (Groza kick)
 Cle—Gatski 36 interception return (kick failed)

Sunday, November 17, at Brooklyn, NY
Ebbets Field. Attendance—7,500

Bad luck continued to follow the Dodgers as they fell to the Dons on a rain-soaked, muddy Ebbets Field. The loss nullified another brilliant display of passing by Brooklyn's Glenn Dobbs, who hit on 21 passes for 263 yards. From the start Brooklyn was playing catch-up as Los Angeles jumped to a 14–0 lead, first with an Angelo Bertelli pass to Bob Seymour and then with a dash by Chuck Fenenbock, who was aided by several devastating blocks.

Dobbs answered with a touchdown pass to Doyle Tackett, then he tallied another score with a short run to tie the score 14–14 at halftime. In the fourth period Los Angeles drove to within inches of a score, but the Dodger defense held. Two plays later Dobbs went back to pass, only to accidentally step out of the end zone for the automatic safety. A few minutes later Joe Aguirre would add a Dons' field goal for a 5-point lead. Dobbs wasn't finished as he drove his offense to the Dons' 12-yard line. He fired the apparent go-ahead touchdown pass to O'Neale Adams in the end zone, but Adams failed to make the difficult grab. A fumble ensued and the Dons ran out the clock. Los Angeles had 199 yards rushing to offset Dobbs' heroics.

| Los Angeles Dons | 7 | 7 | 0 | 5–19 |
| Brooklyn Dodgers | 0 | 14 | 0 | 0–14 |

1 LA—Seymour 24 pass from Bertelli (Artoe kick)
2 LA—Fenenbock 76 run (Nelson kick)
 Bkln—Dobbs 2 run (Martinovich kick)
 Bkln—Tackett 12 pass from Dobbs (Martinovich kick)
4 LA—Safety, Dobbs stepped out of end zone
 LA—FG Aguirre 30

Sunday, November 17, at Bronx, NY
Yankee Stadium. Attendance—18,695

The Yankees clinched the AAFC's first Eastern Division title by defeating the 49ers, riding the arm of Clarence (Ace) Parker. The dark and murky weather couldn't dim the smile of Yankee Owner Dan Topping, who had chased title hopes for 12 futile years in the rival NFL. The 49ers began strong in the rain, building a 9–0 lead on a Joe Vetrano field goal and a John Strzykalski touchdown run. But Vetrano missed the extra point, later to be a costly error. Parker, subbing for Bob Perina who was forced from the game with a nose injury, drove the Yankees to a field goal by Harvey Johnson.

After a scoreless third period Parker, battling the 49er defense and the elements, orchestrated a 76-yard drive to tie the score, flipping a touchdown toss to Eddie Prokop. Johnson's extra point secured victory. The Yankees controlled the statistics, gaining 253 total yards to the 49ers 174. The loss virtually eliminated San Francisco's chances of catching Cleveland in the West. To even tie the Browns, the 49ers had to win their remaining games and hope that the Browns lost all of their games, a possible scenario, but not very likely.

| San Francisco 49ers | 0 | 9 | 0 | 0–9 |
| New York Yankees | 0 | 3 | 0 | 7–10 |

2 SF—FG Vetrano 26
 SF—Strzykalski 7 run (kick failed)
 NY—FG Johnson 23
4 NY—Prokop 25 pass from Parker (Johnson kick)

Monday Night, November 18, at Miami
Orange Bowl. Attendance—5,592

The inspired Seahawks won their second AAFC contest by defeating the Bisons, sparked by the deadeye passing of Marion Pugh and a hard-hitting forward wall. The win stopped a 4-game losing streak for Miami. Seconds into the second period Pugh tallied with a strike to little Monk Gafford. The Bisons retaliated with an Al Dekdebrun pass to Fay King to tie the score at 7–7.

In the third stanza Pugh capped an 80-yard touchdown drive, hitting Lamar (Pappy) Blount with a long touchdown pass. A few minutes later Pugh tacked on a touchdown run, giving Miami a 21–7 lead. Buffalo's second touchdown came from a Steve Juzwik scoot around end. The fourth period saw both squads make a desperate but fruitless aerial bid for another score. Going up and down the field, the teams combined for 643 yards of total offense. Although only 20 yards in penalties were assessed, there were plenty of turnovers, Buffalo with six and Miami with five.

| Buffalo Bisons | 0 | 7 | 7 | 0–14 |
| Miami Seahawks | 0 | 7 | 14 | 0–21 |

2 Mia—Gafford 24 pass from Pugh (Erdlitz kick)
 Buff—King 11 pass from Dekdebrun (Zontini kick)
3 Mia—Blount 35 pass from Pugh (Erdlitz kick)
 Mia—Pugh 1 run (Erdlitz kick)
 Buff—Juzwik 24 run (Zontini kick)

Week Twelve
Sunday, November 24, at Bronx, NY
Yankee Stadium. Attendance—21,270

In a thrill-packed contest, the lowly Rockets stunned the Eastern Division champion Yankees, scoring 21 unanswered points to gain the win. The mistake-prone Yankees could not overcome 10 turnovers, 6 via fumbles. Building a 21–10 halftime lead featuring two Ace Parker touchdown passes, the Yankees seemed to have the Rockets under control. After intermission the teams traded touchdowns, the Rockets Bob Hoernschemeyer hitting Billy Hillenbrand on a bomb and the Yankee's Spec Sanders bolting in from the 1. Trailing 28–17, Chicago suddenly forged ahead, first on a touchdown run by Walt Clay and then on another Hoernschemeyer bomb, this one to Ralph Heywood.

Now behind 31–28, Parker drove his team to Chicago's 15-yard line with three minutes left. Then Parker fired to Jack Russell, who had stationed himself at the 3-yard line with a hook pattern. But Russell bobbled the ball. It caromed to Chicago's Walt Williams, who sped 97 yards for the score to essentially end the game. Williams' interception return set a league record (Ray Terrell, 76, Sep 6). On paper New York dominated Chicago, piling up 314 total yards to just 162 for the Rockets. But the turnovers were too much baggage.

Chicago Rockets	7	3	14	14–38
New York Yankees	7	14	7	0–28

1 NY—Prokop 32 run (Johnson kick)
  Chi—Hillenbrand 27 pass from Hoernschemeyer (Nemeth kick)
2 Chi—FG Nemeth 18
  NY—Sweiger 8 pass from Parker (Johnson kick)
  NY—Russell 5 pass from Parker (Johnson kick)
3 Chi—Hillenbrand 62 pass from Hoernschemeyer (Nemeth kick)
  NY—Sanders 1 run (Johnson kick)
  Chi—Clay 2 run (Nemeth kick)
4 Chi—Heywood 43 pass from Hoernschemeyer (Nemeth kick)
  Chi—Williams 97 interception return (Nemeth kick)

Sunday, November 24, at Brooklyn, NY
Ebbets Field. Attendance—15,100

The 49ers struck gold at Ebbets Field by defeating the Dodgers for the second time this year. Brooklyn's great Glenn Dobbs could not compete with the devastating 265-yard ground attack of the West Coast squad. The 49ers opened a 14–0 lead on a touchdown pass from Frank Albert to Alyn Beals, followed by a short run from Norm Standlee (21 carries for 134 yards). Dobbs was up to the task as he hit O'Neale Adams for a score. Then Albert passed to John Strzykalski, who was hit so hard by Brooklyn's Walt McDonald that he fumbled. Dobbs pounced on the miscue and returned it for the touchdown.

The 49ers rebounded with a touchdown pass from Albert to Bill Fisk. Following a botched kickoff return, Dobbs found himself being chased and dropped in the end zone by a group of 49ers for a safety, his second such demise in as many contests. In the second half the only score came on a short pass from San Francisco's Jesse Freitas to Beals. Dobbs increased his rushing and passing totals to 1,860 yards for the season.

San Francisco 49ers	14	9	0	7–30
Brooklyn Dodgers	0	14	0	0–14

1 SF—Beals 20 pass from Albert (Vetrano kick)
  SF—Standlee 5 run (Vetrano kick)
2 Bkln—Adams 7 pass from Dobbs (Martinovich kick)
  Bkln—Dobbs 40 fumble return (Martinovich kick)
  SF—Fisk 4 pass from Albert (Vetrano kick)
  SF—Safety, Dobbs tackled in end zone
4 SF—Beals 4 pass from Freitas (Vetrano kick)

Sunday, November 24, at Cleveland
Municipal Stadium. Attendance—37,054

The Browns clinched the AAFC's first Western Division crown by routing the Bisons for the second time this year. The Bisons were competitive early, but the Browns reeled off 35 unanswered points to put it away. Buffalo built a 10–7 first-quarter lead on a plunge by Vic Kulbitski, courtesy of a Cleveland fumble, and a Lou Zontini field goal. All this action had followed a touchdown jaunt by the Browns' Edgar Jones (7 carries for 105 yards).

Then Otto Graham took over, the Cleveland ace firing two touchdown passes. Long touchdown runs from Marion Motley and Al Akins followed. The Browns' fifth consecutive touchdown was delivered by Bud Schwenk, following a 58-yard punt return from Tom Colella. Buffalo's final score came primarily from 52 yards of Cleveland penalties, a pass interference and two roughing calls. George Terlep capitalized with a short toss to Fay King to end the scoring. The Browns piled up 455 yards in passing and rushing. Adding the 153 yards in returning kicks, the number soared to 608 yards.

Buffalo Bisons	10	0	0	7–17
Cleveland Browns	7	7	14	14–42

1 Cle—Jones 46 run (Groza kick)
  Buff—Kulbitski 1 run (Zontini kick)
  Buff—FG Zontini 40
2 Cle—Jones 37 lateral from Lavelli after 18 pass from Graham (Groza kick)
3 Cle—Speedie 4 pass from Graham (Groza kick)
  Cle—Motley 76 run (Groza kick)
4 Cle—Akins 50 run (Groza kick)
  Cle—Schwenk 1 run (Groza kick)
  Buff—King 12 pass from Terlep (Zontini kick)

Monday Night, November 25, at Miami Orange Bowl. Attendance—9,987

The Dons rallied to defeat the Seahawks in an exciting game. Taking advantage of turnovers, Miami used some razzle-dazzle to build a 21-14 halftime lead, but could not hold on against the tough visitors from the West Coast. An explosive first quarter began with a plunge by Miami's Dick Erdlitz, courtesy of a Dons' fumble. The Dons took to the air with Angelo Bertelli firing two touchdown passes. Bertelli's second touchdown pass was the result of a fumble by Miami's Frank Trigilio. The Seahawks' Marion Pugh countered with a strike to a wide-open and speedy Monk Gafford for a score. Following Ken Whitlow's fumble recovery, Trigilio redeemed himself with a touchdown run to end the half.

But Los Angeles controlled the second half, scoring 20 unanswered points. First Big John Kimbrough crashed over, and then Charlie O'Rourke hit Harry Clarke with a short touchdown pass to cap a 95-yard drive. Late in the fourth quarter Andy Marefos added a touchdown run after the Dons had recovered a fumble at the Miami 18-yard line. Lee Artoe's try for the extra point was low. The inspired Seahawks staged two goal-line stands in the third period.

Los Angeles Dons	14	0	7	13–34
Miami Seahawks	14	7	0	0–21

1 Mia—Erdlitz 2 run (Erdlitz kick)
  LA—Seymour 7 run after lateral from Aguirre pass from Bertelli (Aguirre kick)
  LA—Nowaskey 17 pass from Bertelli (Aguirre kick)
  Mia—Gafford 63 pass from Pugh (Erdlitz kick)
2 Mia—Trigilio 18 run (Erdlitz kick)
3 LA—Kimbrough 4 run (Aguirre kick)
4 LA—Clarke 5 pass from O'Rourke (Aguirre kick)
  LA—Marefos 2 run (kick failed)

Week Thirteen

Thursday, November 28, at Brooklyn, NY Ebbets Field. Attendance—16,240

Thanksgiving Day at Ebbets Field saw the visiting Yankees, kingpins of the Eastern Division, defeat the undermanned Dodgers. Despite outplaying the Dodgers all day, the Yankees found themselves tied entering the final stanza. A fumble by Brooklyn's Mickey Colmer set up New York's first score, with Ace Parker dashing in from four yards out. The squads battled toe-to-toe, with Glenn Dobbs keeping his Dodger mates competitive with long quick-kicks, until the third quarter. That's when Dobbs forged a drive and skirted around right end for the score and a 7-7 tie.

New York rebounded in the fourth period with Ace Parker finding Jack Russell with a touchdown strike. Following four incomplete Dodger passes, the Yanks took over on downs. With 0:11 left, Spec Sanders bolted around right end for the final New York touchdown. Dobbs had 82 yards passing, but Brooklyn's rushing game was a paltry four yards. New York finished with 171 yards rushing. At halftime the crowd was entertained by comedian Milton Berle, who performed on behalf of the Sister Kenny Foundation.

New York Yankees	7	0	0	14–21
Brooklyn Dodgers	0	0	7	0–7

1 NY—Parker 4 run (Johnson kick)
3 Bkln—Dobbs 12 run (Martinovich kick)
4 NY—Russell 11 pass from Parker (Johnson kick)
  NY—Sanders 42 run (Johnson kick)

Saturday, November 30, at San Francisco Kezar Stadium. Attendance—18,500

The 49ers avenged a previous Saturday loss to Chicago by shutting out the Rockets on this Saturday. The win put San Francisco slightly ahead of their California rivals, the Dons, for second place in the AAFC's tough Western Division. Early on, however, the 49ers were in a bind. In the first period Frank Albert fumbled and the Rockets had possession at the San Francisco 30-yard line. Chicago drove to the 49ers' 4-yard line, where the defense held on downs.

A pass from Albert to halfback Ken Casanega for 21 yards highlighted the first scoring drive, with John Strzykalski smashing through right guard for the score on the first play of the second quarter. Later in the same period, Casanega intercepted an errant Rocket pass, raced 63 yards and, when about to be tackled, lateraled to Ed Balatti who ran the final 22 yards to score. A scoreless second half ensued. The Rockets recovered a fumble after the opening kickoff of the second half, but were held on downs at the San Francisco 5-yard line.

Chicago Rockets	0	0	0	0–0
San Francisco 49ers	0	14	0	0–14

2 SF—Strzykalski 7 run (Vetrano kick)
  SF—Balatti 22 lateral from Casanega after 63 interception return (Vetrano kick)

Sunday, December 1, at Los Angeles Memorial Coliseum. Attendance—27,000

The Dons crushed the Bisons using the passing skills of Angelo Bertelli and Charlie O'Rourke, along with the powerful running of John Kimbrough. The 62 points set a new AAFC scoring mark, topping Cleveland's 51 against Chicago on November 17. The 76 total points were also a new league mark. Kimbrough, who seemed unstoppable, led the way with three scores in the touchdown parade, two on runs and one through the air. Dale Gentry had with two touchdown catches. Bertelli, Harry Clarke, Ray Frankowski and John Polanski each added a touchdown, Frankowski's via a Bisons' fumble.

The stunned Bisons could only muster two touchdown passes, one to Preston Johnston and the other to Chet Mutryn. Bertelli and O'Rourke combined to connect on an amazing 17 of 19 pass attempts. Joe Aguirre's final extra point attempt was missed from the 25-yard line after the Dons were guilty of holding on the first attempt. The Bisons, who suffered their worst loss of the year, ended their season with a dismal record of 3–10–1. Halftime festivities featured a mass initiation of 2,000 American Legion members by Lt. Governor-elect Goodwin J. Knight.

Buffalo Bisons	0	7	7	0–14
Los Angeles Dons	14	14	14	20–62

1 LA—Kimbrough 38 pass from O'Rourke (Aguirre kick)
  LA—Kimbrough 3 run (Aguirre kick)
2 LA—Clark 71 pass from Bertelli (Aguirre kick)
  Buff—Johnston 15 pass from Terlep (Zontini kick)
  LA—Gentry 8 pass from O'Rourke (Aguirre kick)
3 LA—Kimbrough 15 run (Aguirre kick)
  LA—Gentry 15 pass from Bertelli (Aguirre kick)
  Buff—Mutryn 24 pass from Dekdebrun (Zontini kick)
4 LA—Bertelli 1 run (Aguirre kick)
  LA—Frankowski 54 fumble return (Aguirre kick)
  LA—Polanski 7 pass from O'Rourke (kick failed)

Tuesday Night, December 3, at Miami
Orange Bowl. Attendance—9,083

Scoring in every quarter, the Browns staged a great show of speed and precision in blanking the Seahawks in gusty, rainy weather. The struggling Seahawks failed to advance past the Browns' 20-yard line. Cleveland's Otto Graham, usually an offensive star, showed his defensive prowess by intercepting a Marion Pugh pass and returning it for the game's first score behind a wall of blockers. AAFC scoring leader Lou Groza kicked an impressive field goal, and Edgar Jones then added a plunge to score.

Following intermission Gaylon Smith and Gene Fekete added touchdown runs of two and 16 yards respectively, Fekete's being his first of the season. Sandwiched in-between was another Groza field goal. Miami's one highlight was a 71-yard kickoff return by Lamar Davis as the final gun sounded. The Browns intercepted eight passes and outgained the Seahawks 233 to 46 in total yards. Originally scheduled for Monday, the game was rescheduled due to heavy rains.

Cleveland Browns	7	10	7	10–34
Miami Seahawks	0	0	0	0–0

1 Cle—Graham 37 interception return (Groza kick)
2 Cle—FG Groza 50
  Cle—Jones 1 run (Groza kick)
3 Cle—Smith 2 run (Groza kick)
4 Cle—FG Groza 11
  Cle—Fekete 16 run (Groza kick)

Week Fourteen
Bye: Buffalo, Chicago
Sunday, December 8, at San Francisco
Kezar Stadium. Attendance—25,000

The 49ers ended their regular season with an impressive win over the Dons. The victory assured the 49ers of second place in the Western Division. San Francisco's Frank Albert threw the first of his three touchdown passes to start the scoring, a toss to Alyn Beals. Los Angeles countered with a kickoff return by Chuck Fenenbock to tie the score at 7–7. From there on it was all San Francisco.

Albert threw two more touchdown passes and scored another on a short dive. Ken Casanega, Pete Franceschi, Norm Standlee and Joe Vetrano each added a touchdown. Beals finished with two touchdowns. San Francisco had 388 yards of total offense. A weak rushing attack, only 33 yards, and five turnovers plagued the Dons all day. San Francisco finished with a record of 9–5–0. Los Angeles, now at 7–5–1, concluded its regular season next Sunday, hosting Chicago.

Los Angeles Dons	7	0	0	0–7
San Francisco 49ers	21	0	7	20–48

1 SF—Beals 7 pass from Albert (Vetrano kick)
  LA—Fenenbock 97 kickoff return (Aguirre kick)
  SF—Beals 40 pass from Albert (Vetrano kick)
  SF—Casanega 26 run (Vetrano kick)
3 SF—Albert 2 run (Vetrano kick)
4 SF—Franceschi 28 pass from Albert (Balatti pass from Albert)
  SF—Standlee 3 run (Beals pass from Albert)
  SF—Vetrano 30 run (kick failed)

Sunday, December 8, at Brooklyn, NY
Ebbets Field. Attendance—14,600

The Browns ended their season by smashing the Dodgers with a league record 66 points, scoring in just about every conceivable manner. A blistering aerial attack (358 yards) featured three touchdown passes from Otto Graham's understudy Bud Schwenk. Nine different Browns hit paydirt, with Dante Lavelli catching six passes for 140 yards. It was the most points ever in a regular season pro game and the most since the Bears' famous 73–0 win over the Redskins in the 1940 NFL Championship game.

Lou Groza set two pro season marks with 13 field goals (Jack Manders, 10, 1934) and 45 extra points (Bob Snyder, 39, 1943). Groza also set the AAFC season mark with 84 total points. He might have had more, but he was carried from the field with a leg injury in the third quarter. The Dodgers, who were without their star Glenn Dobbs, got two touchdowns from Saxon Judd (4 catches for 108 yards) on a fumble recovery and a reception. Otherwise they were doomed by six turnovers.

| Cleveland Browns | 14 | 14 | 17 | 21–66 |
| Brooklyn Dodgers | 0 | 7 | 0 | 7–14 |

1 Cle—Lund 22 pass from Schwenk (Groza kick)
  Cle—Motley 7 run (Groza kick)
2 Cle—Speedie 11 pass from Graham (Groza kick)
  Bkln—Judd 12 fumble return (Martinovich kick)
  Cle—Jones 96 kickoff return (Groza kick)
3 Cle—FG Groza 31
  Cle—Adams 4 interception return (Adams kick)
  Cle—Smith 2 run (Adams kick)
4 Cle—Yonakor 18 pass from Schwenk (Adams kick)
  Bkln—Judd 52 pass from Armstrong (Martinovich kick)
  Cle—Lavelli 37 pass from Schwenk (Adams kick)
  Cle—Colella 12 pass from Graham (Adams kick)

Monday Night, December 9, at Miami Orange Bowl. Attendance—7,090

The Yankees concluded their regular season with a shutout of the Seahawks. It was the Manders and Sanders show as Pug Manders and Spec Sanders scored three of the four Yankee touchdowns. After a long field goal by Harvey Johnson, the Yankees broke it open in the second quarter. Manders drilled a touchdown run and Bob Kennedy followed with another score. The Seahawks had a chance to climb back into the game when Lamar Davis returned the ensuing kickoff 88 yards to the New York 12. But the New York defense stiffened to preserve the 17–0 halftime lead.

The second half belonged to Sanders, who in the third quarter stole a Marion Pugh pass and returned it for a score. Late in the fourth period New York's Harry Burrus galloped 75 yards to the Miami 8. Sanders proceeded to punch it across from there. Miami didn't offer much offense, just 114 total yards. Meanwhile New York amassed 294 total yards. New York finished with a 10–3–1 record. Miami will host the Brooklyn Dodgers this coming Friday night.

| New York Yankees | 3 | 14 | 7 | 7–31 |
| Miami Seahawks | 0 | 0 | 0 | 0–0 |

1 NY—FG Johnson 40
2 NY—Manders 1 run (Johnson kick)
  NY—Kennedy 21 run (Johnson kick)
3 NY—Sanders 50 interception return (Johnson kick)
4 NY—Sanders 8 run (Johnson kick)

Week Fifteen

Bye: Buffalo, Cleveland, New York, San Francisco

Friday Night, December 13, at Miami Orange Bowl. Attendance—2,340

The Seahawks and Dodgers concluded their regular seasons with a thrill-packed, seesaw affair witnessed by a scant, rain-drenched crowd. The muddy, slimy field favored the offenses as the teams combined for 782 total yards, with almost half, 354, coming from the Miami rushing attack. After a Miami field goal from Dick Erdlitz, the teams swapped a pair of touchdowns. Brooklyn's Glenn Dobbs fired two long touchdown passes and Miami's Harry Hopp (11 carries for 111 yards) and Bob Paffrath each added a score, giving the Seahawks a 17–14 halftime lead.

In the second half Phil Martinovich booted two field goals, the first one to tie and the second to give Brooklyn a slim 20–17 edge. Miami responded with a 67-yard touchdown drive, Hopp going in for his second tally. Later Miami's Jimmy Nelson slipped through the line and went 75 yards to put the game on ice. Dobbs completed 9 of 20 passes for 187 yards, giving him 1,886 passing yards for the season, a new AAFC record, edging Otto Graham's 1,833 yards set this past Sunday. Miami had the league's worst record at 3–11–0. Brooklyn didn't fare much better at 3–10–1.

| Brooklyn Dodgers | 7 | 7 | 3 | 3–20 |
| Miami Seahawks | 10 | 7 | 0 | 14–31 |

1 Mia—FG Erdlitz 21
  Bkln—McCarthy 52 pass from Dobbs (Martinovich kick)
  Mia—Hopp 55 pass from Davis (Erdlitz kick)
2 Bkln—Van Tone 51 pass from Dobbs (Martinovich kick)
  Mia—Paffrath 4 run (Erdlitz kick)
3 Bkln—FG Martinovich 17
4 Bkln—FG Martinovich 20
  Mia—Hopp 3 run (Erdlitz kick)
  Mia—Nelson 75 run (Erdlitz kick)

Sunday, December 15, at Los Angeles Memorial Coliseum. Attendance—22,515

The Rockets and the Dons battled to a tie in the final 1946 AAFC regular season game. The Dons were their own worst enemy, committing 50 yards in penalties and losing the turnover war 5–2. Los Angeles was clicking early though, capping a 34-yard drive with a John Kimbrough plunge. Joe Aguirre's field goal made it 10–0 in the second period. Chicago got on the board with a touchdown strike from Bob Hoernschemeyer to end Frank Quillen. The Rockets took the lead on a neat jump pass from Walt Clay to Bob Dove, the score being set up by Herb Coleman's interception.

Chicago's Steve Nemeth added a field goal early in the fourth stanza for a 17–10 lead. The determined Dons pulled even as Angelo Bertelli fired three quick passes, the last one to Dale Gentry for the touchdown. Aguirre's extra point squared matters. Chicago edged Los Angeles in total yardage, 226 to 197. The tie gave Los Angeles third place in the Western Division at 7–5–2. Chicago, at 5–6–3, wound up in fourth place.

| Chicago Rockets | 0 | 7 | 7 | 3–17 |
| Los Angeles Dons | 7 | 3 | 0 | 7–17 |

1 LA—Kimbrough 1 run (Aguirre kick)
2 LA—FG Aguirre 21
  Chi—Quillen 27 pass from Hoernschemeyer (Nemeth kick)
3 Chi—Dove 3 pass from Clay (Nemeth kick)
4 Chi—FG Nemeth 32
  LA—Gentry 21 pass from Bertelli (Aguirre kick)

AAFC Championship
Sunday, December 22, at Cleveland Municipal Stadium. Attendance—41,181

Otto Graham led the Browns to a come-from-behind victory over the determined Yankees to win the first All-America Football Conference Championship. The Browns' passing ace completed 16 of 27 tosses for 213 yards and stemmed a late Yankees rally with an interception. The Yankees led off the scoring with a first-quarter field goal by Harvey Johnson, which was set up by an Eddie Prokop interception of Graham. The Browns followed with two unsuccessful drives, failing on a fourth down try at the New York 6-yard line and missing a field goal. Late in the second period, Graham's passing fueled a 70-yard drive with Marion Motley scoring the touchdown on a 1-yard smash.

In the third quarter New York drove 80 yards to score. Spec Sanders bolted over from two yards out to register the touchdown. Cleveland tackle Lou Rymkus broke through to block Johnson's try for the conversion. With the fourth quarter draining away, Graham led the Browns downfield again with an aerial attack. There were only about five minutes left when Graham shot a scoring pass to Dante Lavelli to put Cleveland back in front. The Yankees rallied on the passing arm of Ace Parker, but Graham snuffed the threat with an interception at the Cleveland 30-yard line.

New York Yankees	3	0	6	0–9
Cleveland Browns	0	7	0	7–14

1 NY—FG Johnson 12
2 Cle—Motley 1 run (Groza kick)
3 NY—Sanders 2 run (kick blocked)
4 Cle—Lavelli 16 pass from Graham (Groza kick)

Team Statistics	CLE	NYY
First Downs	18	10
Rushing	8	6
Passing	10	4
Penalty	0	0
Total Yards	325	146
Rushing Yards	112	65
Net Passing Yards	213	81
Pass att.–comp.–int	27–16–1	20–8–1
Fumbles Lost	0	1
Punting-Average	2–38.5	5–32.2
Penalty–Yards	5–25	4–20

Individual Statistics

Rushing
Cle—Motley 13 for 98, 1 TD; Jones 10 for 16; Greenwood 5 for 14; Colella 4 for 14; Terrell 1 for -4; Lavelli 1 for -7; Graham 3 for -19
NYY—Sanders 14 for 55, 1 TD; Parker 9 for 5; Prokop 5 for 5; Wagner 1 for 0

Passing
Cle—Graham 16 of 27 for 213, 1 TD, 1 int
NYY—Parker 8 of 18 for 81, 1 int; Sanders 0 of 2 for 0

Receiving
Cle—Lavelli 6 for 87, 1 TD; Speedie 6 for 71; Jones 3 for 45; Yonakor 1 for 8; Greenwood lateral for 2
NYY—Russell 5 for 58; Schwartz 1 for 12; Masterson 1 for 7; Prokop 1 for 4

1947

Week One
Bye: Baltimore, Cleveland
Friday Night, August 29, at Chicago Soldier Field. Attendance—41,182

In a see-saw battle the Dons outlasted the Rockets in the AAFC season opener. The Dons were led by John Kimbrough and Charlie O'Rourke while the Rockets, under the direction of former league Commissioner Jim Crowley, relied on backs Bill Daley and Bob Hoernschemeyer. The Dons struck first with a touchdown reception by Joe Aguirre. The Rockets answered with a Hoernschemeyer touchdown catch. The Dons retaliated as Kimbrough skirted around end for a touchdown. Chicago's Daley then smashed over to knot the score again at halftime.

The Rockets forged ahead on a tricky forward lateral from Al Dekdebrun to Elroy Hirsch to Ray Ramsey. Ben Agajanian added a field goal to cut the Rocket lead to 21–17. Kimbrough then scored the deciding touchdown early in the final period. The Rockets had 129 yards rushing and 175 yards passing. The Dons had 139 yards rushing and 140 yards through the air. Turnovers were even at two each.

Los Angeles Dons	7	7	3	7–24
Chicago Rockets	7	7	7	0–21

1 LA—Aguirre 51 pass from O'Rourke (Agajanian kick)
Chi—Hoernschemeyer 4 pass from Dekdebrun (Rokisky kick)
2 LA—Kimbrough 2 run (Agajanian kick)
Chi—Daley 22 run (Rokisky kick)
3 Chi—Ramsey 22 run lateral from Hirsch (Rokisky kick)
LA—FG Agajanian 40
4 LA—Kimbrough 4 run (Agajanian kick)

Sunday, August 31, at San Francisco Kezar Stadium. Attendance—31,874

The 49ers opened their second AAFC season in impressive fashion by defeating the Dodgers. Frank Albert powered the 49ers with two first-half touchdown passes. The Dodgers, led by their great passer Glenn

Dobbs, scored within the first three minutes, Dobbs finding Mickey Colmer on a touchdown pass after a San Francisco fumble. An interception by 49er center John Schiechl set up Albert's first aerial score, a toss to end Alyn Beals to tie the game. The 49ers took the lead for good when Albert threw a short pass to halfback Len Eshmont, who lateraled to John Strzykalski for the final yardage to paydirt. A failed extra point put the halftime score at 13–7, San Francisco.

The second half belonged to the 49ers. Joe Vetrano booted a field goal in the third stanza. The 49ers then capped a 57-yard drive in the fourth period with substitute Jesse Freitas finding Beals for his second touchdown reception. The 49ers had 275 total yards, with 144 passing. The Dodgers, despite winning the turnover battle 3–1, could only manage 74 yards rushing and 91 yards passing.

Brooklyn Dodgers	7	0	0	0–7
San Francisco 49ers	7	6	3	7–23

1 Bkln—Colmer 9 pass from Dobbs (Martinovich kick)
   SF—Beals 12 pass from Albert (Vetrano kick)
2 SF—Strzykalski 17 lateral from Eshmont after 11 pass from Albert (kick failed)
3 SF—FG Vetrano 35
4 SF—Beals 23 pass from Freitas (Vetrano kick)

**Sunday, August 31, at Buffalo
Civic Stadium. Attendance—32,385**

In a thrilling season opener, the Bills upended the defending Eastern Conference Champion Yankees. George Ratterman starred for the Bills, passing for two scores and running for another. Yankee stars Buddy Young, Frank Sinkwich and Spec Sanders couldn't offset their team's porous pass defense. New York scored first on a run by Eddie Prokop. Ratterman responded with a short touchdown plunge and a scoring toss to Lafayette King for a 14–7 lead. Sanders then skirted around right end to knot the halftime score at 14–14.

A bomb from Sanders to Young put New York ahead 21–14. Ratterman then guided the Bills 76 yards, with George Koch diving in. Another Yankee drive stalled deep in Bills territory, where Harvey Johnson kicked a field goal. The Bills then drove 78 yards, with Ratterman hitting Chet Mutryn on a fourth down toss for the winning score with 8:36 left on the clock. Now desperate, Sanders completed five straight passes, forging to the Bills 26. Two plays later the Yankees had a first and goal at the Buffalo 10, but time ran out. The Yankees had 399 total yards to Buffalo's 258 yards. New York stole one Buffalo pass while the Bills recovered two Yankee fumbles.

New York Yankees	7	7	7	3–24
Buffalo Bills	7	7	7	7–28

1 NY—Prokop 4 run (Johnson kick)
   Buff—Ratterman 1 run (Juzwik kick)
2 Buff—King 39 pass from Ratterman (Juzwik kick)
   NY—Sanders 16 run (Johnson kick)
3 NY—Young 50 pass from Sanders (Johnson kick)
   Buff—Koch 1 run (Juzwik kick)
4 NY—FG Johnson 20
   Buff—Mutryn 4 pass from Ratterman (Juzwik kick)

Week Two

**Friday Night, September 5, at Cleveland
Municipal Stadium. Attendance—62,263**

The Browns opened their 1947 campaign with an impressive win over Buffalo. The Bills, winners last week over the Yankees, were buried by 27 first half Cleveland points. Short touchdown runs by Edgar Jones and Marion Motley paced the Browns in the first quarter. Jones preceded his score with a 43-yard run while Motley's was set up by a 43-yard jaunt by Ermal Allen. To begin the second quarter, Motley stole a George Ratterman toss and romped for the third Brown touchdown. Just before halftime Cleveland's Dante Lavelli hauled in a touchdown pass from Otto Graham.

The Bills rebounded with a 15-play scoring drive to start the third stanza, with Lou Tomasetti plunging in. A 32-yard pass interference penalty against the Browns set up Buffalo's final score, with Ratterman hitting Alton Coppage on a buttonhook pass in the end zone. Cleveland's Mike Scarry recovered a Bills fumble and Lou Groza connected on a short field goal in the final quarter. The Browns balanced attack of 193 yards rushing and 139 yards passing overcame Buffalo's 308 yards rushing, led by Chet Mutryn's 12 carries for 114 yards. The Bills hit just three of 16 passes for 24 yards.

Buffalo Bills	0	0	14	0–14
Cleveland Browns	13	14	0	3–30

1 Cle—Jones 11 run (kick failed)
   Cle—Motley 3 run (Groza kick)
2 Cle—Motley 48 int (Groza kick)
   Cle—Lavelli 51 pass from Graham (Groza kick)
3 Buff—Tomasetti 3 run (Juzwik kick)
   Buff—Coppage 3 pass from Ratterman (Juzwik kick)
4 Cle—FG Groza 17

**Friday Night, September 5, at Bronx, NY
Yankee Stadium. Attendance—36,777**

The Yankees rang up seven touchdowns in a wild, seesaw win over the Rockets, setting a new team scoring mark. In all eleven touchdowns were scored in the contest. Spec Sanders led the Yankees with two touchdown runs and a touchdown toss to build a 27–13 halftime lead. Chicago's first half highlight was a touchdown pass from Bob Hoernschemeyer to Elroy Hirsch. Late in the first half Hirsch left the game after being kicked in the back.

After intermission the Rockets narrowed the Yankee lead to a single point, scoring on a Bill Daley run and an interception return by Bill Schroeder. New York answered with Jack Russell pouncing on a fumble in the Chicago endzone. Then New York's Eddie Prokop and Bob Kennedy iced the game with long touchdown bursts. Kennedy's 78-yarder set a new AAFC record, surpassing the 76-yard mark shared by Cleveland's Marion Motley and Chuck Fenenbock of the Los Angeles Dons. Although he didn't score, New York rookie Buddy Young was a most effective decoy as well as a sensational punt returner.

New York's Harvey Johnson had his AAFC record of 42 consecutive extra points snapped with a miss in the second quarter. The Yankees had 235 yards rushing and 146 passing. The Rockets had 119 yards rushing and 102 passing.

Chicago Rockets	6	7	13	0–26
New York Yankees	14	13	7	14–48

1 NY—Sanders 19 run (Johnson kick)
NY—Sanders 2 run (Johnson kick)
Chi—Hirsch 73 pass from Hoernschemeyer (kick failed)
2 Chi—Daley 9 run (Rokisky kick)
NY—Wagner 21 pass from Sanders (Johnson kick)
NY—Proctor 1 run (kick failed)
3 Chi—Daley 7 run (Rokisky kick)
Chi—Schroeder 30 interception return (kick failed)
NY—Russell fumble recovery in end zone (Johnson kick)
4 NY—Prokop 52 run (Johnson kick)
NY—Kennedy 78 run (Johnson kick)

Sunday, September 7, at Baltimore
Municipal Stadium. Attendance—27,418

Two kickoffs, two disasters. That was the fate that befell the Dodgers in a loss to the Colts. The first disaster was the opening kickoff. Brooklyn rookie Elmore Harris corralled the ball and raced to the 25-yard line where he was slammed by the Colts' Hub Bechtol. Harris fumbled and teammate Harry Buffington scooped up the ball and headed the wrong way—toward his own goal line. Reaching the endzone he realized his error and made a weak attempt to pass the ball, but officials ruled it a free ball. Baltimore's Jim Castiglia pounced on the ball and a touchdown was declared. Both the Dodgers and the crowd were stunned by the event.

But the Dodgers rebounded from Buffington's blunder with a 70-yard drive, capped by Glenn Dobbs scoring a sweep. Then disaster struck again. On the opening kickoff of the second half Baltimore's Billy Hillenbrand recorded an electrifying touchdown return. Now trailing 13–7, Brooklyn's bad luck continued as Bob Perina picked off two Colt tosses, only to fumble them away after substantial returns. Baltimore, coached by former Packer star Cecil Isbell, added an Ernie Case field goal to seal the victory. Both the Colts, successors to the Miami Seahawks and playing their first AAFC game, and the Dodgers struggled for yardage on a muddy field. Baltimore had 59 yards rushing and 111 yards passing. Brooklyn had 99 yards rushing, but only 19 yards through the air. In a game marred by nine turnovers and inclement weather, each team committed just one penalty.

Brooklyn Dodgers	7	0	0	0–7
Baltimore Colts	6	0	7	3–16

1 Balt—Castiglia fumble recovery in end zone (kick failed)
Buff—Dobbs 5 run (Martinovich kick)
3 Balt—Hillenbrand 96 kickoff return (Nemeth kick)
4 Balt—FG Case 16

Sunday, September 7, at San Francisco
Kezar Stadium. Attendance—31,298

Joe Vetrano's fourth quarter field goal canceled a Dons second half comeback and gave the 49ers a victory. The 49ers built a 14–0 lead only to see the Dons convert two turnovers into touchdowns to even the score. San Francisco, sparked by a 55-yard pass from Frankie Albert to Alyn Beals, drove 80 yards for their first touchdown, with Norm Standlee going in. After a George Smith interception, the 49ers then drove 70 yards, finishing with Albert going around right end to begin the second quarter. Momentum shifted in the second quarter when Standlee was thrown so hard that he swallowed his tongue, knocking him out for several minutes. Standlee would sit out the second half, which saw the Dons engineer an 84-yard drive, with Chuck O'Rourke hitting John Kimbrough on a pass to paydirt.

In the fourth quarter Bob Reinhard quick-kicked 80 yards from his own three to San Francisco's Earle Parsons, who fumbled. John Brown recovered for the Dons, which led to a touchdown dive by Bob Kelly. Vetrano then decided the contest. The 49ers pounded out 416 yards of total offense, 262 via the ground game. The Dons only had 71 yards rushing and 123 passing. San Francisco also won the turnover battle 4–2.

Los Angeles Dons	0	0	7	7–14
San Francisco 49ers	7	7	0	3–17

1 SF—Standlee 1 run (Vetrano kick)
2 SF—Albert 8 run (Vetrano kick)
3 LA—Kimbrough 41 pass from O'Rourke (Agajanian kick)
4 LA—Kelly 3 run (Agajanian kick)
SF—FG Vetrano 12

Week Three

Friday Night, September 12, at Brooklyn, NY
Ebbets Field. Attendance—18,876

Capitalizing on five turnovers, including four interceptions, the defending AAFC champion Browns laid waste to the Dodgers in hot humid weather, rolling up eight touchdowns of various types. Brooklyn, without star Glenn Dobbs, was overwhelmed by the Ohio machine and barely avoided the shutout when Bob Hoernschemeyer slashed in to cap an 80-yard march in the second quarter.

Cleveland's big guns were Marion Motley and Otto Graham. The powerful Motley had 111 yards rushing on just five carries, including touchdown bursts of 13 and 51 yards. Graham sliced the Dodgers defense, completing 9 of 11 passes for 146 yards, including touchdown strikes to Dante Lavelli and Mac Speedie. Rubbing salt into the wound, Tom Colella set an AAFC record with an 82-yard punt return for a touchdown, breaking Dobb's 1946 mark of 78 yards against the Miami Seahawks.

Cleveland Browns	20	0	21	14	55
Brooklyn Dodgers	0	7	0	0	7

1 Cle—Motley 13 run (Groza kick)
   Cle—Colella 82 punt return (kick failed)
   Cle—Lavelli 53 pass from Graham (Groza kick)
2 Bkln—Hoernschemeyer 6 run (Martinovich kick)
3 Cle—Motley 51 run (Groza kick)
   Cle—Speedie 19 pass from Graham (Groza kick)
   Cle—Lund 28 interception return (Groza kick)
4 Cle—Boedeker 2 run (Groza kick)
   Cle—Boedeker 8 run (Groza kick)

Friday Night, September 12, at Los Angeles Memorial Coliseum. Attendance—82,675

Spec Sanders led the Yankees to four touchdowns and a victory over the Dons. The record crowd for a regular season pro game witnessed furious first quarter scoring, followed by the Dons succumbing to relentless Yankee power down the stretch. The Dons drew first blood with a touchdown strike from Charlie O'Rourke to Joe Aguirre. Using crushing blocks, Sanders returned the ensuing kickoff 98 yards to score. Los Angeles answered with a 70-yard march, capped by an O'Rourke touchdown pass to Bob Mitchell. Sanders then fired a bomb to Bruce Alford to cut the Dons lead to 1. A Harvey Johnson field goal put New York ahead for good.

The Yankees owned the second half as Sanders, Buddy Young and Eddie Prokop ripped off huge gains in between effective passing. Sanders added touchdown passes to Alford and Harry Burrus to conclude the scoring. Glenn Dobbs made his debut as a Don, but the former Dodger and MVP of 1946 was uneasy in the new formations. He did have effective punts of 57 and 60 yards. The Yankees had 99 yards rushing and 195 yards passing. The Dons managed just 24 yards rushing and 128 yards passing. The Yankees were intercepted once, the only turnover of the game.

New York Yankees	13	3	7	7	30
Los Angeles Dons	14	0	0	0	14

1 LA—Aguirre 30 pass from O'Rourke (Agajanian kick)
   NY—Sanders 98 kickoff return (kick blocked)
   LA—Mitchell 23 pass from O'Rourke (Agajanian kick)
   NY—Alford 52 pass from Sanders (Johnson kick)
2 NY—FG Johnson 31
3 NY—Alford 11 pass from Sanders (Johnson kick)
4 NY—Burrus 33 pass from Sanders (Johnson kick)

Sunday, September 14, at Buffalo Civic Stadium. Attendance—33,648

The Bills, converting two turnovers into touchdowns, won their second AAFC game in three starts, downing the Rockets. Chicago rallied with two touchdowns in the last three minutes, but it was too little too late. After a scoreless first period, Buffalo's Alton Baldwin stole an Angelo Bertelli pass and raced 71 yards to the Chicago 2-yard line, where Vic Kulbitski smashed through for a 7–0 halftime lead. In the third, Rocco Pirro recovered Sam Vacanti's fumble on the Rockets 35-yard line. Two passes from George Ratterman to Lafayette King pushed the Bill's lead to 14 points.

The Rockets rebounded with a 23-yard forward lateral, Vacanti to Ted Scalissi to Bill Schroeder, for their first touchdown. Buffalo's Chet Mutryn, aided by a great block by King, scored following a roughing penalty against the Rockets. Dippy Evans grabbed a George Terlep toss for Buffalo's final score. Vacanti fired two late touchdown aerials, but only 0:11 remained. Despite outgaining the Bills 330 to 265, the Rockets dropped their third straight game. Bertelli left the game with a knee injury in the fourth period.

Chicago Rockets	0	0	6	14	20
Buffalo Bills	0	7	7	14	28

2 Buff—Kulbitski 2 run (Juzwik kick)
3 Buff—King 5 pass from Ratterman (Juzwik kick)
   Chi—Schroeder 15 lateral from Scalissi after 8 pass from Vacanti (kick failed)
4 Buff—Mutryn 13 run (Juzwik kick)
   Buff—Evans 31 pass from Terlep (Juzwik kick)
   Chi—Ramsey 41 pass from Vacanti (Rokisky kick)
   Chi—Morris 6 pass from Vacanti (Rokisky kick)

Sunday, September 14, at San Francisco Kezar Stadium. Attendance—25,787

In foggy weather, the undefeated 49ers used a smothering defense and a strong rushing attack to stymie the Colts. Norm Standlee tallied both San Francisco scores on short plunges. The 49ers scored first following an interception at the Colts 37-yard line. A 4-play drive ensued, featuring an 11-yard toss from Frankie Albert to Len Eshmont. Standlee then cracked the goal line from one yard out. The Colts engineered an impressive 90-yard drive, featuring a 53-yard pass from Bud Schwenk to Lamar Davis. Doc Mobley raced around end for the lone Baltimore score, the first of his pro career.

Forcing the Colts to punt from their 7-yard line, the 49ers moved 40 yards in the third period, with Standlee packing it straight through the line for the final score. San Francisco piled up 259 yards rushing and 84 yards passing. Baltimore was held to minus 35 yards rushing, but 11 completions on 20 attempts netted the Colts 144 yards passing. The 49ers won the first down battle 18–8.

Baltimore Colts	0	7	0	0–7
San Francisco 49ers	7	0	7	0–14

1 SF—Standlee 1 run (Vetrano kick)
2 Balt—Mobley 3 run (Case kick)
3 SF—Standlee 3 run (Vetrano kick)

Week Four

Friday Night, September 19, at Los Angeles Memorial Coliseum. Attendance—38,817

The Dons outscored the winless Dodgers, striking in every period. Leading by 10 after three stanzas, the Dons put the Dodgers away with 17 unanswered points. Six different Dons scored, including ace kicker Ben Agajanian. Chuck Fenenbock paced the Dons in the first half with two scores, one on a bomb from former Brooklyn star Glenn Dobbs. Bob Nelson returned one of the three interceptions pilfered by the Dons defense for a score in the second period.

Bob Hoernschemeyer played a part in all three Brooklyn scores, throwing for two and running for the third. Joe Aguirre, Dale Gentry and John Kimbrough all rang the scoreboard for Los Angeles in the second half. Agajanian contributed 11 points. The pass happy Dodgers connected on 21 of 40 aerials for 221 yards, but gained only 117 yards and suffered five turnovers. The Dons had a more balanced attack with 142 yards rushing and 215 yards passing.

Brooklyn Dodgers	0	7	14	0–21
Los Angeles Dons	3	21	7	17–48

1 LA—FG Agajanian 43
2 LA—Fenenbock 9 run (Agajanian kick)
  LA—Nelson 32 interception return (Agajanian kick)
  Bkln—Perina 17 pass from Hoernschemeyer (Martinovich kick)
  LA—Fenenbock 70 pass from Dobbs (Agajanian kick)
3 Bkln—Judd 22 lateral from Tackett after 25 pass from Hoernschemeyer (Martinovich kick)
  LA—Aguirre 40 pass from O'Rourke (Agajanian kick)
  Bkln—Hoernschemeyer 4 run (Martinovich kick)
4 LA—FG Agajanian 34
  LA—Gentry 54 pass from O'Rourke (Agajanian kick)
  LA—Kimbrough 6 run (Agajanian kick)

Friday Night, September 19, at Chicago Soldier Field. Attendance—22,685

Buffalo's George Ratterman unleashed an air assault against the winless Rockets, setting an AAFC record with 294 yards passing and tying another with four touchdown tosses. The win earned the Bills a first place spot in the Eastern Division. Ratterman surpassed Otto Graham's 284 yards set on Oct 27, 1946 against the 49ers and his four touchdown passes equaled Graham's mark against these same Rockets on Nov 17, 1946.

Buffalo surged to a 17–0 lead, with Ratterman hitting Burr Baldwin and Vic Kulbitski for scores. Elroy Hirsch (4 catches for 120 yards) led a Rockets' comeback, hauling in a 76-yard flip from Sam Vacanti, the longest so far in the 1947 season, and scoring on a short plunge. But Ratterman stayed hot in the second half, finding Chet Mutryn and Lafayette King for scores. Buffalo almost doubled Chicago in total yardage, 448 to 245. Ratterman completed 19 of 33 passes. The struggling Rockets played a clean game, having just one penalty for five yards.

Buffalo Bills	10	7	7	7–31
Chicago Rockets	0	14	0	0–14

1 Buff—Baldwin 5 pass from Ratterman (Juzwik kick)
  Buff—FG Juzwik 29
2 Buff—Kulbitski 2 pass from Ratterman (Juzwik kick)
  Chi—Hirsch 76 pass from Vacanti (Rokisky kick)
  Chi—Hirsch 1 run (Rokisky kick)
3 Buff—Mutryn 58 pass from Ratterman (Juzwik kick)
4 Buff—King 18 pass from Ratterman (Juzwik kick)

Sunday, September 21, at Cleveland Municipal Stadium. Attendance—44,257

On just a dozen plays the powerful Browns rolled up three first quarter touchdowns and cruised to a win over the Colts. Winning their third straight, Coach Paul Brown rested his starters after the first quarter blitz while the subs sent the Colts to their second loss in three games. Otto Graham engineered a 9-play, 67-yard drive, ending with a plunge by Marion Motley, his 5th score of the season. Tommy Colella then picked off the Colts Bud Schwenk, returning it untouched for Cleveland's second score. Graham then combined with teammate Tony Adamle on a 40-yard punt return, setting up a score by Bill Boedeker.

The Browns went 78 yards in just six plays to score in the second period, featuring a 34-yard pass to Mac Speedie, a 21-yard bolt by Motley and a 20-yarder by Spiro Dellerba. The only Colts threat was a 56-yard pass from Schwenk to Billy Hillenbrand to the Browns 4. In four plays however, the Browns hurled the Colts back to the 17, where they regained possession on downs. Total yardage was almost even, 295 for Cleveland and 297 for Baltimore, but the Colts committed six turnovers. Motley had 10 rushes for 68 yards.

Baltimore Colts	0	0	0	0–0
Cleveland Browns	21	7	0	0–28

1 Cle—Motley 2 run (Groza kick)
  Cle—Colella 23 interception return (Groza kick)
  Cle—Boedeker 6 run (Groza kick)
2 Cle—Cowan 1 run (Groza kick)

Sunday, September 21, at San Francisco
Kezar Stadium. Attendance—52,819

Led by the brilliant play of Spec Sanders and Eddie Prokop, the Yankees pounded out a tough win over the 49ers, handing them their first loss of the season. The Yankees scored 21 unanswered points and thwarted two 4th quarter challenges by the local club. Sanders and Prokop tallied two scores on short runs in the second session. Sanders then fired to Bob Sweiger for a 21–3 lead in the third period. Frankie Albert, the 49ers star QB, rallied his troops with two second half touchdown passes. But the Yankees defense made a goal line stand at their 1 and later Prokop intercepted Albert at the 7-yard line.

Prokop tied a Yankees record and an AAFC record with three interceptions, two leading to touchdowns. The team record was set by Sweiger against the Dons on Oct 27, 1946, and was later tied by Cleveland's Tom Colella against the Rockets on Nov 17, 1946. San Francisco had more than double the total yardage of New York, 337 to 166. But four turnovers plagued them at critical times in the contest. Norm Standlee, 49ers fullback, led all rushers with 89 yards on 22 carries.

| New York Yankees | 0 | 14 | 7 | 0 – 21 |
| San Francisco 49ers | 3 | 0 | 7 | 6 – 16 |

1 SF—FG Vetrano 30
2 NY—Sanders 4 run (Johnson kick)
  NY—Prokop 2 run (Johnson kick)
3 NY—Sweiger 25 pass from Sanders (Johnson kick)
  SF—Beals 25 pass from Albert (Vetrano kick)
4 SF—Balatti 30 pass from Albert (kick failed)

Week Five

Bye: Brooklyn, Los Angeles
Friday Night, September 26, at Chicago
Soldier Field. Attendance—23,067

The undefeated Browns, now undisputed leaders of the Western Division, raced to a big halftime lead and trounced the winless Rockets. Five Browns found paydirt while Lou "The Toe" Groza tacked on two field goals in the scoring bonanza. Cleveland featured two touchdown passes from Otto Graham to Mac Speedie and John Yonakor and touchdown runs by Bob Cowan and Bill Boedeker. Spiro Dellerba returned an errant fumble for Cleveland's final score. The Rockets regrouped in the second half, with Sam Vacanti tossing touchdown passes to Frank Quillen, Bob Dove and Bill Bass.

The careless Rockets committed 10 turnovers and were outgained by 395 to 322 yards. The Browns dominated the ground attack, 232 to 127 yards. Cleveland's only blemish was the end of Graham's streak of 91 pass attempts without an interception, an AAFC record. Ironically Graham's streak started against these Rockets on Nov 17, 1946.

| Cleveland Browns | 10 | 17 | 0 | 14 – 41 |
| Chicago Rockets | 0 | 0 | 14 | 7 – 21 |

1 Cle—FG Groza 32
  Cle—Speedie 70 pass from Graham (Groza kick)
2 Cle—Yonakor 8 pass from Graham (Groza kick)
  Cle—Cowan 3 run (Groza kick)
  Cle—FG Groza 20
3 Chi—Quillen 31 pass from Vacanti (Rokisky kick)
  Chi—Dove 9 pass from Vacanti (Rokisky kick)
4 Cle—Boedeker 15 run (Groza kick)
  Cle—Dellerba 10 fumble return (Groza kick)
  Chi—Bass 48 pass from Vacanti (Rokisky kick)

Sunday, September 28, at Buffalo
Civic Stadium. Attendance—36,099

The 49ers staged a remarkable comeback to defeat the Bills before a stunned, record crowd in Buffalo. Trailing by 17, the 49ers, aided by five Buffalo turnovers, ripped off 34 unanswered points to run their record to 4–1. After trading touchdowns, the Bills forged ahead with a touchdown pass from George Ratterman to Alton Baldwin and a Steve Juzwik field goal. When Chet Mutryn (8 carries for 102 yards) sped 87 yards to paydirt with the second half kickoff, the Bills looked invincible.

Then the 49ers Gold Rush began. Jess Freitas flipped to Allyn Beals for a tally. Buffalo fumbles and a Len Eshmont interception of a George Ratterman pass led to four rushing touchdowns, two by Frankie Albert and one each by Norm Standlee and John Strzykalski (18 carries for 115 yards). Albert tied AAFC records with three touchdowns and 18 points scored. San Francisco's 22 first downs tied an AAFC record, set by Chicago against Brooklyn on Oct 11, 1946. The 49ers rushing attack led the way to outgaining the Bills in total yardage, 408 to 279.

| San Francisco 49ers | 0 | 7 | 14 | 20 – 41 |
| Buffalo Bills | 7 | 10 | 7 | 0 – 24 |

1 Buff—Rykovich 14 run (Juzwik kick)
2 SF—Albert 1 run (Vetrano kick)
  Buff—Baldwin 58 pass from Ratterman (Juzwik kick)
  Buff—FG Juzwik 18
3 Buff—Mutryn 87 kickoff return (Juzwik kick)
  SF—Beals 14 pass from Freitas (Vetrano failed)
  SF—Albert 14 run (Vetrano kick)
4 SF—Standlee 3 run (Vetrano kick)
  SF—Albert 2 run (Vetrano kick)
  SF—Strzykalski 2 run (pass failed)

Sunday, September 28, at Baltimore
Municipal Stadium. Attendance—51,583

The Yankees claimed first place of the Eastern Division with a solid win over the Colts. Once again Spec

Sanders, the rangy Texas tailback, played a hand in all of the Yankee scores. Sanders guided the Yankees to two first quarter scores, slashing in on a short run and then firing a perfect strike to a wide open Harry Burrus. Following a fumble recovery, Baltimore's Bus Mertes crashed over from the 5-yard line for their only score. Then Sanders and the mercurial Buddy Young engineered a 65-yard drive, with Sanders covering the last five yards.

A scoreless second half saw the Colts make three threatening bids. Bud Schwenk drove the Colts to New York's 4, 21 and 7-yard lines, but without success. The Colts outgained the Yankees in total yardage, 264 to 231. Although the game featured just five punts and five penalties, it was rife with turnovers, five by each squad. Sanders two touchdowns pushed his league leading total to seven.

New York Yankees	14	7	0	0–21
Baltimore Colts	0	7	0	0–7

1 NY—Sanders 4 run (Johnson kick)
   NY—Burrus 34 pass from Sanders (Johnson kick)
2 Balt—Mertes 5 run (Lio kick)
   NY—Sanders 5 run (Johnson kick)

Week Six

Friday Night, October 3, at Chicago Soldier Field. Attendance—16,844

Although both winless, the Dodgers and the Rockets produced one of the most exciting games of the 1947 AAFC season. The Dodgers rallied with three touchdowns in the fourth quarter to notch a 35–31 win. Chicago suffered its sixth loss in a row. Through three quarters the Rockets, powered by touchdowns from rookie Ted Scalissi and Bill Daley (15 carries for 128 yards), held a modest 17–14 lead. The Dodgers got scores from Bob Perina and Mickey Colmer.

The wild 35-point fourth quarter saw the Brooklyn squad forge ahead for good on two more Colmer tallies. The Rockets struck back with Scalissi's second score, but Perina's second score thwarted Chicago's comeback. Ray Ramsey concluded the scoring, hauling in a pass from Sam Vacanti. Chicago had over 200 yards rushing and receiving and outgained Brooklyn in total yardage, 414 to 318, but lost possession on three fumbles. Brooklyn's Colmer tied AAFC single game records with three touchdowns and 18 points.

Brooklyn Dodgers	0	7	7	21–35
Chicago Rockets	7	10	0	14–31

1 Chi—Scalissi 21 pass from Vacanti (Rokisky kick)
2 Chi—FG Rokisky 20
   Bkln—Perina 1 run (Martinovich kick)
   Chi—Daley 15 run (Rokisky kick)
3 Bkln—Colmer 1 run (Martinovich kick)
4 Bkln—Colmer 1 run (Martinovich kick)
   Bkln—Colmer 17 run (Martinovich kick)
   Chi—Scalissi 22 lateral from Harrington after 17 pass from Dekdebrun (Rokisky kick)
   Bkln—Perina 1 run (Martinovich kick)
   Chi—Ramsey 62 pass from Vacanti (Rokisky kick)

Sunday, October 5, at Los Angeles Memorial Coliseum. Attendance—36,087

Led by rookie George Ratterman's three touchdown passes, the Bills edged the Dons. The Bills stampeded out early. Two 5-play drives of 70 and 78 yards yielded 14 points. Each ended with a Ratterman touchdown toss, the first to Alton Baldwin, and then one to Dolly King. In between the Dons had a laborious 11-play drive covering 65 yards for their first score, with Charlie O'Rourke spinning the last five yards. Then Ed Hirsch scooped up a Los Angeles fumble and raced to the Dons 7, where Chet Mutryn bounced over for the Bills third score.

Ratterman struck again in the third stanza, firing 22 yards to ace kicker Steve Juzwik for a 27–7 Bills lead. The feisty Dons rebounded with two touchdown passes from O'Rourke to Joe Aguirre. Ratterman donated two safeties to the Dons to help run out the clock. The Dons far outgained the Bills in total offense, 356 to 172, but lost the turnover battle 5–2. Mutryn led all rushers with 63 yards on 15 tries. Los Angeles' Chuck Fenenbock tied an AAFC record with five kickoff returns, first set by Cleveland's Dub Jones against Brooklyn on Dec 8, 1946.

Buffalo Bills	20	0	7	0–27
Los Angeles Dons	7	0	14	4–25

1 Buff—Baldwin 32 pass from Ratterman (Juzwik kick)
   LA—O'Rourke 5 run (Agajanian kick)
   Buff—King 61 pass from Ratterman (Juzwik kick)
   Buff—Mutryn 7 run (kick failed)
3 Buff—Juzwik 22 pass from Ratterman (Juzwik kick)
   LA—Aguirre 31 pass from O'Rourke (Agajanian kick)
   LA—Aguirre 4 pass from O'Rourke (Agajanian kick)
4 LA—Safety, Ratterman stepped out of end zone
   LA—Safety, Ratterman stepped out of end zone

Sunday, October 5, at Cleveland Municipal Stadium. Attendance—80,067

For the fourth time, including last year's championship game, the Yankees failed to defeat the Browns. The Yankees only had three penalties all day, but one would be crucial. The Browns found themselves trailing for the first time this season after Harvey Johnson's first quarter field goal. Sparked by Otto Graham and Marion Motley, the Browns got back on track. Touchdowns from Bob Cowan and Tom Colella and a Lou Groza field goal gave the Browns a 17–3 lead at the break. New York fought back. Spec Sanders found Lloyd Cheatham for a score. A minute later Bob Sweiger pilfered a Graham aerial and raced to the endzone. At the 10 minute mark in the third period, Graham found Mac Speedie in the end zone to regain the lead. But Lou Sossamon blocked Groza's extra point try.

Then the penalty came. With four minutes left, Cleveland tried a 42-yard field goal. Groza missed, but New York was ruled off sides, giving Cleveland a first down. The Browns ran two minutes off the clock before Groza's successful field goal. The Browns had 374 total yards, including 212 on the ground, compared to New York's 222 total yards. Neither team fumbled, but Cleveland stole three New York passes. Sanders set an AAFC record with an 84-yard punt, topping Bob Reinhold's 81-yarder against San Francisco on Sep 7, 1947.

New York Yankees	3	0	14	0–	17
Cleveland Browns	0	17	6	3–	26

1 NY—FG Johnson 47
2 Cle—Cowan 42 pass from Graham (Groza kick)
  Cle—Colella 29 run (Groza kick)
  Cle—FG Groza 25
3 NY—Cheatham 7 pass from Sanders (Johnson kick)
  NY—Sweiger 20 interception return (Johnson kick)
  Cle—Speedie 10 pass from Graham (kick blocked)
4 Cle—FG Groza 43

Sunday, October 5, at Baltimore
Municipal Stadium. Attendance—29,556

Saddled with five turnovers, the favored 49ers needed a fourth quarter rally to salvage a tie with the Colts. It was the first tie game in the 1947 AAFC season. Bud Schwenk (18 of 29 for 241 yards) and Billy Hillenbrand (6 catches for 153 yards) were the Colt flies in the 49ers ointment, connecting on two long touchdown passes in the first half. Norm Standlee answered the first Colts score, sliding off the weak side to score. Frankie Albert (12 of 16 for 217 yards) tossed to Earle Parsons for a score to tie the game at halftime.

Schwenk and Hillenbrand continued to vex the Californians. Schwenk flipped a touchdown pass to Lamar Davis. Schwenk then hit Hillenbrand for a 20-yard gain to the 49ers 8. Hillenbrand swept around right end for a 28–14 Colts lead. But Albert threw two touchdown passes to tie the game for the third and final time. Allyn Beals and John Strzykalski combined on a pass-lateral score, and Parsons snagged the tying aerial. Parsons' two touchdowns were his only receptions. Davis set a single game AAFC record with 10 receptions, breaking Dante Lavelli's mark of 8 against San Francisco on Oct 27, 1946.

San Francisco 49ers	7	7	0	14–28
Baltimore Colts	7	7	14	0–28

1 Balt—Hillenbrand 51 pass from Schwenk (Lio kick)
  SF—Standlee 4 run (Vetrano kick)
2 Balt—Hillenbrand 64 pass from Schwenk (Lio kick)
  SF—Parsons 36 pass from Albert (Vetrano kick)
3 Balt—Davis 3 pass from Schwenk (Lio kick)
  Balt—Hillenbrand 8 run (Lio kick)
4 SF—Strzykalski 45 lateral from Beals after 8 pass from Albert (Vetrano kick)
  SF—Parsons 62 pass from Albert (Vetrano kick)

Week Seven
Sunday, October 12, at Buffalo
Civic Stadium. Attendance—27,345

The Bills nipped the Colts in a game that ended with players, officials and fans swarming the field, and a Colts announcement that they would protest to Commissioner Jonas Ingram. With 0:07 left, the Colts' Bud Schwenk (15 of 24 for 197 yards) fired deep to Lamar Davis, who caught it at the Bills 20 and headed for paydirt. But field judge Eddie Tryon ruled that he was forced out at the 2-foot line. Davis continued into the endzone, believing he had the winning score. A few seconds later umpire George Simpson fired the game-ending gun, giving many the impression that the game wasn't over (AAFC rules don't permit the gun to be fired while a play is in motion; it must be fired after a play is completed).

Seeing Tryon's call, Colts Coach Cecil Isbell stormed the field, followed by players and many fans. Officials finally controlled the situation, but Baltimore President Robert Rodenberg protested. In a telegram to Ingram, he suggested that the referees be summoned to New York to view films of the game. Colts players were adamant that Davis stayed inbounds, but the final score stood. The Colts had leads of 12–0 and 15–7 before two Bills touchdowns gave them their win. A 32-yard reverse by Julius Rykovich sparked the last Bills score. Buffalo had 239 yards rushing. Alton Baldwin tied an AAFC record with a touchdown catch in four consecutive games.

Baltimore Colts	3	12	0	0–15
Buffalo Bills	0	7	7	6–20

1 Balt—FG Lio 22
2 Balt—Safety, Phillips tackled Ratterman in end zone
  Balt—Schwenk 6 run (Lio kick)
  Buff—Mutryn 2 run (Juzwik kick)
  Balt—FG Lio 19
3 Buff—Baldwin 31 pass from Ratterman (Mutryn kick)
4 Buff—Mutryn 8 run (kick failed)

Sunday, October 12, at Cleveland
Municipal Stadium. Attendance—63,124

Ben Agajanian nailed a short field goal to snap the Browns winning streak at 11 games. Critical turnovers and a late penalty stymied the champions from Ohio. The Browns started in whirlwind fashion. A Lou Groza field goal preceded a 7-play, 66-yard drive, capped by Marion Motley's sixth touchdown of the season. But a Motley fumble was grabbed on the fly by Chuck Fenenbock, who tore down the sidelines to reduce the Los Angeles deficit to three by halftime.

Another Motley fumble led to Agajanian's long field goal to tie the game. Turnovers were traded, with Bob Kelly stealing an Otto Graham (19 of 29 for 233 yards) pass for the Dons and Weldon Humble falling on a John Kimbrough fumble for the Browns at the Cleveland 13. With 5 minutes left, the Dons Joe Aguirre scooped up a Bill Lund fumble and raced to the Cleveland 9. After an unsuccessful shot at the endzone, Agajanian tried a field goal. It was wide, but Cleveland was penalized for being offsides. Agajanian then booted the winning points. Cleveland dominated Los Angeles in total yardage (395–161) and first downs (22–10). Cleveland's Mac Speedie caught 8 passes for 110 yards.

Los Angeles Dons	0	7	3	3–13
Cleveland Browns	10	0	0	0–10

1 Cle—FG Groza 28
   Cle—Motley 14 run (Groza kick)
2 LA—Fenenbock 28 fumble return (Agajanian kick)
3 LA—FG Agajanian 46
4 LA—FG Agajanian 17

Sunday, October 12, at Bronx, NY
Yankee Stadium. Attendance—21,882

The Yankees rebounded from a tough loss at Cleveland with an easy, and almost expected, victory over the listless Dodgers in sunny weather. The Yankees confidence was expressed in Coach Ray Flaherty's decision to start his second string backfield on offense. New York took just five minutes to score on Eddie Prokop's toss to Jack Russell. Their next scoring drive went 68 yards on nine consecutive running plays, highlighted by 18 and 25-yard spurts by Buddy Young. Ed Mieszkowski recovered an Spec Sanders fumble that led to Brooklyn's only score, with Mickey Colmer going over the middle of the line from a yard out.

Less than a minute into the third stanza, Sanders faked a reverse to Young and bolted up the middle for New York's third score. Later Young found the endzone, weaving 8 yards through the right side of the strong New York line. Harvey Johnson's field goal was his ninth consecutive over a 2-year span. The Yankees had 339 total yards, with 239 rushing. Brooklyn mustered only 86 total yards and four first downs. The final score could have been even more lopsided had New York not committed three turnovers.

Brooklyn Dodgers	0	7	0	0–7
New York Yankees	14	0	14	3–31

1 NY—Russell 30 pass from Prokop (Johnson kick)
   NY—Prokop 3 run (Johnson kick)
2 Bkln—Colmer 1 run (Martinovich kick)
3 NY—Sanders 52 run (Johnson kick)
   NY—Young 8 run (Johnson kick)
4 NY—FG Johnson 31

Sunday, October 12, at San Francisco
Kezar Stadium. Attendance—23,300

The 49ers hammered the Rockets to gain a first place tie with the Browns in the Western Division. It was the third game this season that the struggling Chicagoans have allowed at least 40 points. Five different 49ers found the end zone en route to a comfortable 42–7 lead, with Allyn Beals making two visits. Despite being hopelessly beaten for three quarters, the Rockets rallied with three touchdowns to keep the fans entertained. The 42 points were the 49ers second highest ever, just six shy of their total against the Los Angeles Dons on Dec 8, 1946.

San Francisco had 366 total yards, including 250 rushing. Chicago had 338 total yards, with 273 passing, but committed 10 turnovers, including an AAFC record-tying six fumbles (San Francisco vs. Buffalo, Nov 2, 1946; New York vs. Chicago, Nov 24, 1946). Their only bright spot was halfback Ray Ramsey, who had 229 combined net yards, with 137 yards receiving on six catches.

Chicago Rockets	0	7	0	21–28
San Francisco 49ers	21	7	14	0–42

1 SF—Beals 14 pass from Albert (Vetrano kick)
   SF—Strzykalski 4 run (Vetrano kick)
   SF—Mathews 4 run (Vetrano kick)
2 SF—Beals 14 pass from Freitas (Vetrano kick)
   Chi—Ramsey 61 pass from Dekdebrun (Rokisky kick)
3 SF—Standlee 1 run (Vetrano kick)
   SF—Masini 9 run (Vetrano kick)
4 Chi—Harrington 47 pass from Vacanti (Rokisky kick)
   Chi—Schroeder 50 interception return (Rokisky kick)
   Chi—Harrington 5 pass from Vacanti (Rokisky kick)

Week Eight
Bye: New York, San Francisco
Friday Night, October 17, at Brooklyn, NY
Ebbets Field. Attendance—9,792

Coming off their terrible showing against New York and led by a record-setting performance by Bob Hoernschemeyer, the Dodgers achieved a tie with the Bills. Hoernschemeyer set two AAFC records, and the Brooklyn offense set two others and tied a third, all three being nothing to brag about. Following a goal line stand, Brooklyn scored in six plays, the touchdown coming on an Al Akins reverse. But Brooklyn native Alex Wizbicki returned the ensuing kickoff 91 yards to score. Phil Martinovich missed a 49-yard field goal attempt for the Dodgers in the second period, followed by an 8-play scoring drive by Buffalo. Chet Mutryn, the AAFC's leading rusher and scorer, tallied on a quick opener up the middle.

Two minutes into the final period, Hoernschemeyer ran a sweep around the right end and sped an AAFC record 84 yards (Bob Kennedy 78, Sep 5, 1947). Hoernschemeyer also had 179 yards rushing on 19 attempts, erasing Marion Motley's 143 yards against Los Angeles on Oct 20, 1946. Perhaps because of Brooklyn's prolific ground game (274 yards), their passing "attack" consisted of one completion for 12 yards, both new AAFC single game lows. Their seven pass attempts tied an AAFC low as well (Miami, Nov 11, 1946). Buffalo's Julie Rykovich had 13 carries for 110 yards.

Buffalo Bills	7	7	0	0–14
Brooklyn Dodgers	7	0	0	7–14

1 Bkln—Akins 18 run (Martinovich kick)
   Buff—Wizbicki 91 kickoff return (Armstrong kick)
2 Buff—Mutryn 14 run (Armstrong kick)
4 Bkln—Hoernschemeyer 84 run (Martinovich kick)

Sunday, October 19, at Cleveland Municipal Stadium. Attendance—35,266

The Browns, perhaps looking forward to their big showdown with San Francisco next week, escaped with a win over the aroused Rockets. The Browns had hoped to rest many of their starters, but the Rockets forced them to go all out. The Browns built a seemingly cushy 24–7 lead early into the fourth period on touchdowns by Marion Motley, Mac Speedie (5 catches for 166 yards) and Edgar Jones, and a Lou Groza field goal. Speedie's score was thrilling. Snaring an Otto Graham pass, he went to his knees, scrambled up, faked a lateral and broke free from three Chicago defenders.

Then the Ray Ramsey show began. Scoring three times in the final period, the former Bradley Tech speedster gave all of the Ohio faithful the jitters. Fortunately for them, his last touchdown came with just 0:20 left. If not for a second Jones touchdown, an upset by the Rockets over the defending champions would have rivaled the Redskins upset of the Bears in the 1942 NFL championship. Cleveland had 456 total yards, with 297 passing. Chicago had 365 total yards, with 260 passing.

Chicago Rockets	0	7	0	21–28
Cleveland Browns	3	7	7	14–31

1 Cle—FG Groza 21
2 Chi—Hirsch 37 pass from Vacanti (Rokisky kick)
   Cle—Motley 22 run (Groza kick)
3 Cle—Speedie 49 pass from Graham (Groza kick)
4 Cle—Jones 2 run (Groza kick)
   Chi—Ramsey 11 run (Rokisky kick)
   Cle—Jones 3 run (Groza kick)
   Chi—Ramsey 7 pass from Vacanti (Rokisky kick)
   Chi—Ramsey 20 pass from Vacanti (Rokisky kick)

Sunday, October 19, at Baltimore Municipal Stadium. Attendance—36,852

Erasing a 10-point deficit, the Dons romped to a win over the Colts. Ben Agajanian's record setting field goal was the highlight of the game. A Bud Schwenk to Billy Hillenbrand pass and an Augio Lio field goal put the Colts ahead 10–0. Then the Dons line, heaviest in the AAFC, gradually wore down the Colts. Los Angeles reeled off four touchdowns, including two by Big John Kimbrough, the former Texas A & M Aggie.

Then Agajanian, who lost the toes of his right foot in a college accident, booted a 53-yard field goal. It struck the crossbar and bounced over. The kick bettered the 51-yarder by Lou Groza against Chicago on Nov 17, 1946 and was just a yard short of the NFL record, held by Glenn Presnell of the Detroit Lions in 1934. Walter Heap concluded the scoring, pilfering a Schwenk pass and galloping 55 yards to paydirt. The Dons picked off four Colt passes in all, and outgained the Colts in total yardage, 245 to 184.

Los Angeles Dons	0	14	7	17–38
Baltimore Colts	10	0	0	0–10

1 Balt—Hillenbrand 58 pass from Schwenk (Lio kick)
   Balt—FG Lio 24
2 LA—Kimbrough 23 pass from O'Rourke (Agajanian kick)
   LA—Fenenbock 13 run (Agajanian kick)
3 LA—Kimbrough 2 run (Agajanian kick)
4 LA—Reinhard 7 pass from O'Rourke (Agajanian kick)
   LA—FG Agajanian 53
   LA—Heap 55 interception return (Agajanian kick)

Week Nine

Friday Night, October 24, at Chicago Soldier Field. Attendance—20,310

Spec Sanders turned in an incredible performance, leading the Yankees to a win over the Rockets, who suffered their 9th consecutive loss. Sanders rushed for a pro football record 250 yards, shattering both Bob Hoernschemeyer's AAFC record 179 yards set just last week and Cliff Battle's NFL record 215 yards vs. the New York Giants on Oct 8, 1933. Sanders, the first round pick of the Washington Redskins in 1942, scored twice and threw for a third score to Bruce Alford. Buddy Young returned the second half opening kickoff 95 yards for New York's second touchdown. The Rockets averted a shutout when Sam Vacanti scored on a sneak late in the game.

Sanders set another AAFC record with 24 rushing attempts, erasing Norm Standlee's 21 against Brooklyn on Nov 24, 1946. New York set an AAFC team record with 395 yards rushing, breaking Miami's record of 353 against Brooklyn on Dec 13, 1946. Chicago's anemic running game yielded minus 20 yards. The Yankees were penalized for 105 yards.

New York Yankees	7	0	21	0–28
Chicago Rockets	0	0	0	7–7

1 NY—Sanders 8 run (Johnson kick)
3 NY—Young 95 kickoff return (Johnson kick)
   NY—Alford 20 pass from Sanders (Johnson kick)
   NY—Sanders 70 run (Johnson kick)
4 Chi—Vacanti 1 run (Rokisky kick)

Sunday, October 26, at Los Angeles Memorial Coliseum. Attendance—27,007

After corralling the Colts last week on the East coast, the Dons inflicted even more damage by smashing Baltimore on the West coast. Including last week's game, the Dons had scored 94 unanswered points against the Colts. Bruising line play, along with the passing of Glenn Dobbs, produced the most lopsided score in AAFC history, pushing Cleveland's 66–14 thrashing of Brooklyn out of the record book. Dobbs threw an AAFC record tying four touchdown passes (Otto Graham, George Ratterman), one each to John Kimbrough, Ezzret Anderson, Burr Baldwin and Walter Heap.

Kimbrough had three touchdowns and Harry Clarke another. The Dons punted only once, tying an AAFC low, and forced 10 punts out of the Colts, tying an AAFC record high. Ben Agajanian's eight extra points also tied an AAFC record, held by Joe Aguirre against Buffalo on Dec 1, 1946. The Dons had 467 total yards, with 275 passing. The Colts had 95 total yards and only five first downs.

Baltimore Colts	0	0	0	0–0
Los Angeles Dons	7	14	14	21–56

1 LA—Fenenbock 19 run (Agajanian kick)
2 LA—Clark 10 run (Agajanian kick)
  LA—Kimbrough 12 run (Agajanian kick)
3 LA—Kimbrough 8 pass from Dobbs (Agajanian kick)
  LA—Anderson 14 pass from Dobbs (Agajanian kick)
4 LA—Baldwin 4 pass from Dobbs (Agajanian kick)
  LA—Heap 8 pass from Dobbs (Agajanian kick)
  LA—Kimbrough 1 run (Agajanian kick)

Sunday, October 26, at Buffalo Civic Stadium. Attendance—23,762

Rookie George Ratterman led the Bills to a thumping of the Dodgers, avenging last week's tie with Brooklyn and keeping pace with New York in the Eastern Division title race. Brooklyn struck first though, with Mickey Colmer dashing down the side line for the initial score. Julius Rykovich then cracked over guard to tie the score. Ratterman tossed two touchdown passes and Lou Tomasetti scored twice on a short run and an interception return.

In the second period Brooklyn lineman Tex Warrington was ejected from the game after a tiff with head linesman Bill Ohrenberger. After Brooklyn was flagged for unnecessary roughness, Ohrenberger reported that Warrington shoved him, and then slugged him after being ruled out of the game. Later, Deputy Commissioner O. O. Kessing, who was in attendance, suspended Warrington for the rest of the season and fined him $500. Ratterman completed 11 of 22 passes for 171 yards. The Bills had 426 total yards and tied an AAFC record with 22 first downs. Brooklyn had 140 total yards and completed only two of 10 passes.

Brooklyn Dodgers	7	0	0	0–7
Buffalo Bills	0	14	21	0–35

1 Bkln—Colmer 41 run (Martinovich kick)
2 Buff—Rykovich 5 run (Armstrong kick)
  Buff—Kulbitski 38 pass from Ratterman (Armstrong kick)
3 Buff—Tomasetti 2 run (Armstrong kick)
  Buff—Kulbitski 20 lateral from King after 14 pass from Ratterman (Armstrong kick)
  Buff—Tomasetti 44 interception return (Armstrong kick)

Sunday, October 26, at San Francisco Kezar Stadium. Attendance—54,325

In one of the most anticipated games of the season, Otto Graham brilliantly led the Browns to a tough win over the 49ers. The game, played in gloomy weather, tightened Cleveland's grip on the Western Division title. Graham, who completed 19 of 25 passes for 278 yards, fired long touchdown passes to Dante Lavelli and Mac Speedie (10 catches for 141 yards) for a 14–0 halftime lead. The 49ers marched 80 yards in the third quarter, with Norm Standlee ramming over from the 1-foot line to cut their deficit to 7.

Cleveland had other scoring opportunities. Lou Groza missed two field goal attempts, a 38-yarder in the second period and a 48-yarder in the third. Early in the fourth period, Marion Motley was poised for a third Cleveland touchdown, but defensive tackle Bob Bryant ripped the ball away from the big fullback as he was plunging over the goal line. The Browns tied an AAFC record with 22 first downs, and the teams combined for an AAFC record 37 first downs, surpassing the 35 by Los Angeles and Buffalo on Dec 1, 1946. The 49ers' John Strzykalski was the game's leading rusher, with 68 yards on 12 carries.

Cleveland Browns	7	7	0	0–14
San Francisco 49ers	0	0	7	0–7

1 Cle—Lavelli 22 pass from Graham (Groza kick)
2 Cle—Speedie 42 pass from Graham (Groza kick)
3 SF—Standlee 1 run (Vetrano kick)

WEEK TEN

Friday Night, October 31, at Brooklyn, NY Ebbets Field. Attendance—2,960

A sparse but ardent crowd endured the rain and mud to witness two of the AAFC's worst squads square off. The result was a Dodgers win over the Rockets, in a game almost as miserable as the weather. Chicago managed a short drive that led to a 20-yard field goal by Johnny Rokisky, the key play being a 22-yard burst up the middle by Bill Daley. That slim lead looked like it would give the Midwesterners their first win of the season. But with five minutes to play, Brooklyn standout Bob Hoernschemeyer engineered an 8-play touchdown drive, the big play being his 21-yard pass to

Mickey Colmer. Bob Perina dashed around left end for the winning points.

Despite the bad weather, only one fumble was made. In fact, the backs of both teams seemed to have better control of the ball than of themselves. Slides of five and even 10 yards were commonplace when the players hit the slippery gridiron. Brooklyn had 200 total yards and Chicago had 207. Each team punted seven times. Brooklyn picked off two Chicago passes, and only three penalties were committed.

Chicago Rockets	0	3	0	0–3
Brooklyn Dodgers	0	0	7	0–7

2 Chi—FG Rokisky 20
3 Bkln—Perina 2 run (Martinovich kick)

Sunday, November 2, at Bronx, NY
Yankee Stadium. Attendance—21,714

In a clash of contrasting styles, the Yankees defeated the Colts to take undisputed first place in the Eastern Division. New York's rushing attack was countered by Baltimore's aerial attack, but the big factor deciding this game was special teams. The opening kickoff was a bad omen for the Colts as Bruce Alford took it to the house for the first score. Spec Sanders (14 carries for 140 yards) and Buddy Young tormented the Colts on punt returns the entire game. Young's touchdown punt return was the play of the game. Dodging and circling would-be tacklers, he retreated to his 40, slipped to all fours, got up and lit out for the left sideline and—whoosh!—he was gone.

The Colts special teams were so porous that the Yankees set AAFC records with 165 punt return yards and 301 combined kick return yards. Bud Schwenk tossed three touchdown passes to keep the Colts competitive and Johnny Vardian had three catches for 136 yards. New York had 286 yards rushing and Baltimore had 236 yards passing. Sanders tallied three scores and had 97 yards on two punt returns. New York was penalized for 82 yards.

Baltimore Colts	0	7	7	7–21
New York Yankees	14	0	7	14–35

1 NY—Alford 79 kickoff return (Johnson kick)
  NY—Sanders 3 run (Johnson kick)
2 Balt—Hillenbrand 21 pass from Schwenk (Lio kick)
3 NY—Sanders 5 run (Johnson kick)
  Balt—Vardian 72 pass from Schwenk (Lio kick)
4 NY—Sanders 56 run (Johnson kick)
  NY—Young 53 punt return (Johnson kick)
  Balt—Hillenbrand 13 pass from Schwenk (Lio kick)

Sunday, November 2, at Buffalo
Civic Stadium. Attendance—43,167

Otto Graham engineered three long drives and set an unbreakable passing record as the Browns whipped the Bills before a record Buffalo football crowd. He completed 13 of 16 passes for 256 yards and three touchdowns. Graham orchestrated 82 and 76-yard drives for a 14–0 lead. Edgar Jones cut off left tackle for his touchdown and Dante Lavelli's touchdown was a diving catch on the goal line, where he fell across. The Bills drove 85 yards in the third period, the big play being George Ratterman's 39-yard shot to Al Coppage, but were stopped on downs at the Cleveland 1-yard line.

Graham then crossed up the Bills defense. From his end zone, he tossed to Mac Speedie (7 catches for 147 yards), who caught the ball on the goal line, picked up blockers down the sideline and raced 99 yards. The play set an AAFC record and tied the NFL record, a Frank Filchock pass to Andy Farkas of the Redskins against the Pittsburgh Pirates on Oct 15, 1939. John Yonakor's touchdown capped a 76-yard drive. Buffalo's score was sparked by Chet Mutryn's 28-yard punt return and ended with a Ratterman pass to Burr Baldwin. First downs were even at 13, but Cleveland had 402 total yards to Buffalo's 252.

Cleveland Browns	7	7	7	7–28
Buffalo Bills	0	0	0	7–7

1 Cle—Jones 12 run (Groza kick)
2 Cle—Speedie 99 pass from Graham (Groza kick)
3 Cle—Lavelli 11 pass from Graham (Groza kick)
4 Cle—Yonakor 39 pass from Graham (Groza kick)
  Buff—Baldwin 11 pass from Ratterman (Armstrong kick)

Sunday, November 2, at Los Angeles
Memorial Coliseum. Attendance—53,726

Frankie Albert completed 14 of 23 passes for 202 yards to power the 49ers past the Dons. Albert's four touchdown passes tied an AAFC record, held jointly by Otto Graham and Glenn Dobbs. Nick Susoeff, John Strzykalski (7 catches for 100 yards), Ned Mathews and Allyn Beals all rang the scoreboard for San Francisco, courtesy of Albert's sharpshooting. Strzykalski led all rushers with 79 yards on 16 carries.

Charlie O'Rourke pitched two touchdown passes for Los Angeles, the first to Bert Piggott and the second to Bob Kelly, just before the final gun sounded. Agajanian's tremendous 51-yard field goal, just two yards shy of his AAFC record, was tempered by a missed extra point, which hit the upright. The 49ers had 205 yards rushing to complement Albert's passing. The Dons had 196 total yards. The 49ers had 21 first downs to 10 for the Dons. Each team intercepted two passes.

San Francisco 49ers	7	7	6	6–26
Los Angeles Dons	0	10	0	6–16

1 SF—Susoeff 11 pass from Albert (Vetrano kick)
2 SF—Strzykalski 27 pass from Albert (Vetrano kick)
  LA—Pigott 19 pass from O'Rourke (kick failed)
  LA—FG Agajanian 51
3 SF—Mathews 25 pass from Albert (kick failed)
4 SF—Beals 37 pass from Albert (kick failed)
  LA—Kelly 9 pass from O'Rourke (kick failed)

Week Eleven
Friday Night, November 7, at Chicago
Soldier Field. Attendance—5,395

Before a small, frigid crowd, the Rockets ended months of misery by beating the Colts for their first AAFC win in 11 tries. A series of Colt turnovers allowed Chicago to explode for a club record 24 second quarter points. The Colts drew first blood, capitalizing on a Ray Ramsey fumble, with Bud Schwenk finding Lamar Davis for the initial score. But Chicago responded with Dippy Evans dashing around end to score. Colt turnovers then led to a Johnny Rokisky field goal and touchdowns by Max Morris and Bill Bass. The Colts added two touchdowns in the fourth period, but it was too little too late. Schwenk completed 22 of 40 passes for 274 yards. Baltimore had 17 first downs to 7 for Chicago. They outgained the Rockets in total yardage, 348 to 201.

Baltimore Colts	7	0	0	14–21
Chicago Rockets	0	24	0	3–27

1 Balt—Davis 5 pass from Schwenk (Lio kick)
2 Chi—Evans 13 run (Rokisky kick)
   Chi—FG Rokisky 31
   Chi—Morris 1 fumble return (Rokisky kick)
   Chi—Bass 82 interception return (Rokisky kick)
4 Chi—FG Rokisky 35
   Balt—Hillenbrand 31 run (Lio kick)
   Balt—Mobley 29 pass from Schwenk (Lio kick)

Sunday, November 9, at Cleveland
Municipal Stadium. Attendance—30,279

If not for the misfortunes of kicker Phil Martinovich, Brooklyn might have pulled off one of the major upsets in all of pro football. One of the AAFC's favorite doormats, the inspired Dodgers fell to the champion Browns by one point. Brooklyn surprised Cleveland, going 80 yards to score on the opening drive. Brilliant running by Monk Gafford (8 carries for 110 yards), Bob Hoernschemeyer and Mickey Colmer sparked the drive. But Martinovich's extra point was blocked. Otto Graham tied the score, hurling a bomb to Dante Lavelli. Another Brooklyn drive led to a 43-yard field goal attempt by Martinovich, but it was short.

Cleveland's second score was a Graham to Lew Mayne pass, but a bad snap spoiled Lou Groza's extra point try. Gafford returned a punt 37 yards in the second period, but Martinovich's 29-yard field goal was wide. Martinovich got another shot in the fourth period from the 45, but it was short. With seven minutes left, Gafford broke loose for a long score, but Martinovich missed the extra point. Cleveland had 261 total yards and Brooklyn had 273. Cleveland had three turnovers, but committed no penalties.

Brooklyn Dodgers	6	0	0	6–12
Cleveland Browns	7	6	0	0–13

1 Bkln—Colmer 4 run (kick blocked)
   Cle—Lavelli 72 pass from Graham (Groza kick)
2 Cle—Mayne 15 pass from Graham (kick failed)
4 Bkln—Gafford 79 run (kick failed)

Sunday, November 9, at Buffalo
Civic Stadium. Attendance—21,293

The Bills concluded their home season with a shutout of the Dons. The southern Californians seemingly couldn't adjust to a snow-covered, muddy field and the frigid air. George Ratterman led the Bills to their first score, a toss to Alton Baldwin. But Graham Armstrong's extra point kick was low. It was Ratterman's 17th touchdown pass of the season, tying the AAFC record set last year by Otto Graham.

In the second half, Buffalo's stingy defense led to three more scores, all set up by interceptions. Felto Prewitt, Julius Rykovich and Vince Mazza stole Charlie O'Rourke passes to produce 19 points. O'Rourke finished his frustrating day with four completions on 19 attempts for 42 yards. Marty Comer and John Kerns recovered fumbles to halt late Los Angeles marches. Los Angeles never got inside Buffalo's 20-yard line. The teams combined for just 14 first downs.

Los Angeles Dons	0	0	0	0–0
Buffalo Bills	6	0	13	6–25

1 Buff—Baldwin 27 pass from Ratterman (kick failed)
3 Buff—Mutryn 11 run (pass failed)
   Buff—Mutryn 6 run (Kulbitski run)
4 Buff—Kulbitski 16 pass from Terlep (kick failed)

Sunday, November 9, at Bronx, NY
Yankee Stadium. Attendance—37,342

In a game rife with fumbles and blocked punts, the Yankees stage a thrilling rally to defeat the 49ers. And for the first time, they outdrew the Giants of the NFL. A New York fumble led to a Joe Vetrano field goal, and another stopped a Yanks drive at the 49ers 3-yard line. Spec Sanders (20 carries for 160 yards) drove New York to their first score, a touchdown toss to Jack Russell early in the second. Then San Francisco blocked two of Sanders' punts, each resulting in a touchdown pass by Frankie Albert of the visitors.

A Sanders aerial to Bruce Alford brought New York another score in the third. Harvey Johnson's talented toe regained the lead, popping a 27-yard field goal. With five minutes left, Jack Russell blocked Albert's punt and Alford scooped it up and scampered for the clinching touchdown. Sanders put on a tremendous show, netting a staggering 437 yards in runs, passes and kick returns. New York had 411 total yards to San Francisco's 139. The teams combined for eight fumbles, with New York losing four of their six to the 49ers.

San Francisco 49ers	3	13	0	0–16
New York Yankees	0	7	7	10–24

1 SF—FG Vetrano 14
2 NY—Russell 14 pass from Sanders (Johnson kick)
  SF—Mathews 8 pass from Albert (Vetrano kick)
  SF—Beals 9 pass from Albert (kick failed)
3 NY—Alford 34 pass from Sanders (Johnson kick)
4 NY—FG Johnson 27
  NY—Alford 18 fumble return (Johnson kick)

Week Twelve
Bye: Buffalo, Chicago
Sunday, November 16, at Brooklyn, NY
Ebbets Field. Attendance—9,604

Spearheaded by the powerful running of Bob Hoernschemeyer (19 carries for 136 yards) and Mickey Colmer, the Dodgers prevailed over the Colts. Hoernschemeyer rushed for 136 yards on 19 carries to offset the passing wizardry of Baltimore's Bud Schwenk. A 27-yard punt return by Monk Gafford led to Brooklyn's first touchdown, with Colmer crashing through to score. In two plays, Schwenk knotted the score, with Bill Dudish making a circus catch of his pass.

Saxon Judd blocked a punt, which the Dodgers recovered at the Colts 11. Colmer bulled across for Brooklyn's final tally. With less than a minute to play, the Colts recovered a fumble. Baltimore swept 70 yards on 3 Schwenk passes. He hit Billy Hillenbrand (4 catches for 103 yards) twice for 58 yards, then pegged Hub Bechtol in the end zone as the final gun sounded. Brooklyn had 280 total yards, with 228 rushing. Baltimore had 330 total yards, with 255 passing. Schwenk set two AAFC season marks. Through 11 games, he had 147 completions on 280 attempts, exceeding the 1946 marks of Glenn Dobbs (134 on 273)

| Baltimore Colts | 0 | 7 | 0 | 7–14 |
| Brooklyn Dodgers | 0 | 7 | 7 | 7–21 |

2 Bkln—Colmer 4 run (Martinovich kick)
  Balt—Dudish 70 pass from Schwenk (Lio kick)
3 Bkln—Hoernschemeyer 28 run (Martinovich kick)
4 Bkln—Colmer 3 run (Martinovich kick)
  Balt—Bechtol 12 pass from Schwenk (Lio kick)

Sunday, November 16, at Bronx, NY
Yankee Stadium. Attendance—37,625

Perhaps looking forward to next week's clash with defending champion Cleveland, the Yankees barely beat the Dons. Once again, Spec Sanders (22 carries for 159 yards) was the star, driving the Yankees closer to another Eastern Division title and setting a pro football record. Derrell Palmer blocked a Glenn Dobbs punt, scoring a safety. A pass interception set up Eddie Prokop's score for a 9–0 Yanks lead. A hard tackle of Sanders by Wally Heap, both former Texas Longhorns, caused a fumble. Dobbs pounced on it and raced to paydirt. A Ben Agajanian field goal gave the Dons a 1-point lead at intermission.

Mercurial rookie Buddy Young snared a Sanders aerial near the sideline and dodged his way through the Dons defense to score standing up in the third. Despite the hard running of John Kimbrough and the eye-popping punts of Dobbs, the Dons were repeatedly offsides and could only produce three second half points. Sanders established a new pro single season rushing record with 1,093 yards. The previous mark was 1,004 yards by Beattie Feathers of the Chicago Bears in 1934. The Yankees had 378 total yards and the Dons only had 103. Dobbs had punts of 67 and 73 yards.

| Los Angeles Dons | 0 | 10 | 3 | 0–13 |
| New York Yankees | 2 | 7 | 7 | 0–16 |

1 NY—Safety, Palmer blocked punt out of end zone
2 NY—Prokop 40 pass from Sanders (Johnson kick)
  LA—Dobbs 67 fumble return (Agajanian kick)
  LA—FG Agajanian 35
3 NY—Young 33 pass from Sanders (Johnson kick)
  LA—FG Agajanian 33

Sunday, November 16, at Cleveland
Municipal Stadium. Attendance—76,504

The Browns clinched their second Western Division title, smothering the 49ers. A red hot Otto Graham and crucial turnovers by the 49ers decide this game. Following a field goal by big Chet Adams, subbing for an injured Lou Groza, the 49ers fumbled in Cleveland territory. Graham then marched the Browns to their first touchdown, pitching to Dante Lavelli (7 catches for 127 yards). A more frustrating fumble, this one by Norm Standlee, was recovered in the end zone by Marion Motley for Cleveland. This spoiled a 49ers 73-yard drive.

Graham found Lavelli again for another score, capping an 81-yard drive just before halftime. Tom Colella picked off a Frankie Albert pass and took it to the San Francisco 2, where Graham snuck over from the half yard line. Graham's third scoring toss to Lavelli increased the lead to 30–7. Short runs by John Strzykalski and Tony Adamle concluded the scoring. Except for San Francisco's four turnovers, the teams were quite even statistically. Graham completed 15 of 22 passes for 222 yards, setting a new AAFC season mark with 18 touchdown passes.

| San Francisco 49ers | 0 | 7 | 0 | 7–14 |
| Cleveland Browns | 9 | 7 | 14 | 7–37 |

1 Cle—FG Adams 44
  Cle—Lavelli 23 pass from Graham (kick failed)
2 SF—Eshmont 8 pass from Albert (Vetrano kick)
  Cle—Lavelli 15 pass from Graham (Adams kick)
3 Cle—Graham 1 run (Saban kick)
  Cle—Lavelli 64 pass from Graham (Saban kick)
4 SF—Strzykalski 5 run (Vetrano kick)
  Cle—Adamle 1 run (Saban kick)

Week Thirteen
Friday Night, November 21, at Chicago Soldier Field. Attendance—5,791

The 49ers, still smarting from their defeat in Cleveland, travelled 300 miles west and took their frustration out on the lowly Rockets. It was Chicago's 11th loss in 12 games. The 49ers raced to a 34–0 lead on touchdown runs by Frankie Albert and John Strzykalski, two touchdown catches by Alyn Beals and a blocked punt return by Ed Balatti, teammate Rupe Thornton making the block.

Chicago's only bright spot occurred on consecutive plays, with halftime between them. Ray Ramsey snared an Allen Dekdebrun pass on the last play of the first half to score. On the opening kickoff of the second half, Visco Grgich fielded the kick and lateraled to Ed Carr, who was promptly tackled in the end zone by Chicago center Fred Negus for a safety. Len Asini scored the 49ers final touchdown in the third. Ramsey's second score was a long scamper in the fourth period. San Francisco piled up 432 total yards, with 219 rushing. Chicago had 287 total yards, with 170 passing. The 49ers picked off three Chicago passes and the Rockets recovered three 49er fumbles.

San Francisco 49ers	14	20	7	0–41
Chicago Rockets	0	7	2	7–16

1 SF—Albert 2 run (Vetrano kick)
  SF—Beals 46 pass from Albert (Vetrano kick)
2 SF—Strzykalski 2 run (kick blocked)
  SF—Balatti 4 blocked punt return (Balatti pass from Albert)
  SF—Beals 15 pass from Freitas (Vetrano kick)
  Chi—Ramsey 24 pass from Dekdebrun (Rokisky kick)
3 Chi—Safety, Negus tackled Carr in end zone
  SF—Masini 1 run (Vetrano kick)
4 Chi—Ramsey 40 run (Rokisky kick)

Sunday, November 23, at Baltimore Municipal Stadium. Attendance—19,593

The Bills climbed to within a game of New York in the Eastern Division by defeating the Colts in a rough contest. Fists flew on several occasions, so much so that Buffalo tackle Jack Carpenter and Baltimore end Hub Bechtol were sent to the showers early for fighting in the third period. Chet Mutryn and linebacker Buckets Hirsch gave Buffalo a 13–0 lead on a run and an interception return. The Colts then drove 80 yards, with Billy Hillenbrand catching the pay-off pass from Bud Schwenk.

Touchdowns by Marty Comer and Julius Rykovich in the third swelled Buffalo's lead to 26–7. Another long Baltimore drive finished with Andy Dudish plowing in from the 1. Mutryn then scored again, crashing over from three yards out. Buffalo had 325 total yards, with 232 rushing. Baltimore had 240 total yards, with 143 passing. Mutryn led all rushers with 10 carries for 79 yards. Each team intercepted three passes.

Buffalo Bills	7	6	13	7–33
Baltimore Colts	0	7	0	7–14

1 Buff—Mutryn 3 run (Juzwik kick)
2 Buff—Hirsch 45 interception return (kick failed)
  Balt—Hillenbrand 17 pass from Schwenk (Lio kick)
3 Buff—Comer 58 pass from Ratterman (kick failed)
  Buff—Rykovich 2 run (Juzwik kick)
4 Balt—Dudish 1 run (Lio kick)
  Buff—Mutryn 3 run (Juzwik kick)

Sunday, November 23, at Bronx, NY Yankee Stadium. Attendance—70,060

Finally, the Yankees were going to beat their Midwestern nemesis, the Browns. The Yankees knew it and the record crowd knew it; but someone forget to tell the Browns. In a game replete with vicious blocking, jarring tackles and dynamic running and passing, the Browns erased a 4-touchdown deficit to forge a thrill-packed tie. Nearly flawless in the first half, the Yankees scored on their first four possessions. Spec Sanders and Buddy Young ran roughshod through the Browns defense. In less than 23 minutes of play, they had a 28–0 lead, as Sanders scored three times. Otto Graham's touchdown pass to Bill Boedeker late in the first half went almost unnoticed by the delirious crowd.

The turning point came late in the third period. With New York poised to go up 35–7, the Browns made a miraculous goal line stand at their 1. Graham then shocked the Yankees, connecting on an 82-yard pass to Mac Speedie (6 catches for 154 yards). Two plays later Marion Motley scored on a Graham toss. Some three minutes later, Motley bulled in from 10 yards out. Late in a tense fourth quarter, Graham engineered a 14-play 90-yard drive, with Jimmy Dewar going the final four yards. Sanders and Young drove New York furiously to Cleveland's 30, but the threat fizzled as time ran out. Cleveland had 424 total yards, with 325 passing. New York had 331 total yards, with 269 rushing. Graham completed 15 of 28 passes for an AAFC record 325 yards. Sanders had 147 yards rushing on an AAFC record 32 carries. The teams set an AAFC record with 38 combined first downs.

Cleveland Browns	0	7	14	7–28
New York Yankees	14	14	0	0–28

1 NY—Sanders 1 run (Johnson kick)
  NY—Sanders 3 run (Johnson kick)
2 NY—Sanders 27 run (Johnson kick)
  NY—Young 5 run (Johnson kick)
  Cle—Boedeker 34 pass from Graham (Saban kick)
3 Cle—Motley 12 pass from Graham (Saban kick)
  Cle—Motley 10 run (Saban kick)
4 Cle—Dewar 5 run (Saban kick)

Sunday, November 23, at Brooklyn, NY
Ebbets Field. Attendance—11,866

The Dons rallied in the fourth quarter to beat the Dodgers, as former Dodgers ace Glenn Dobbs returned to his old stomping grounds. Operating on a muddy field, Ben Agajanian's pinpoint kicking contributed 10 points. The Dons scored on the opening drive on an Agajanian field goal. Bob Hoernschemeyer then fired a long pass to Al Akins for Brooklyn's lone touchdown, but Dobbs blocked Phil Martinovich's extra point try. Doyle Tackett's interception of a Dobbs pass set up a Martinovich field goal with 0:03 left in the first half.

Monk Gafford returned the opening kickoff of the second half 86 yards, but Brooklyn had to settle for another Martinovich field goal for a 12–3 lead. After Agajanian's second field goal, the Dons drove to the go-ahead touchdown, led by John Kimbrough and Charlie O'Rourke. After Agajanian's third field goal, Brooklyn drove to the Los Angeles 11, where a fumble ended the final threat. Los Angeles had 358 total yards and Brooklyn had 282. Agajanian and Martinovich set an AAFC record with five successful field goals. The Dons Chuck Fenenbock saw his AAFC record of 139 kickoff return yards get broken, as Brooklyn's Gafford went for 158. At halftime, two youth teams, Frank Sinatra's Cyclones and Milton Berle's Bombers, battled to a stalemate. The kids got muddy and Berle posed for several photographs. Sinatra wasn't present to "coach" his team.

Los Angeles Dons	3	0	3	10–16
Brooklyn Dodgers	0	9	3	0–12

1 LA—FG Agajanian 26
2 Bkln—Akins 60 pass from Hoernschemeyer (kick blocked)
  Bkln—FG Martinovich 18
3 Bkln—FG Martinovich 24
  LA—FG Agajanian 15
4 LA—Kimbrough 3 run (Agajanian kick)
  LA—FG Agajanian 32

Week Fourteen

Thursday, November 27, at Los Angeles
Memorial Coliseum. Attendance—45,009

The Browns celebrated Thanksgiving by avenging their only loss of the season, conquering the Dons. Otto Graham paced the winners, now 11–1–0, as the Dons fell to 6–7–0. The Dons led early on a Ben Agajanian field goal and a Harry Clarke run, which was set up by Bill Reinhard's interception of a Graham toss. Then Marion Motley broke loose for the first Cleveland score, followed by a Graham aerial to halfback Tom Colella for the second.

On the first play of the third period, Graham stunned the Dons with a touchdown bomb to a wide-open Mickey Mayne (2 catches for 123 yards). Three times Glenn Dobbs drove the Dons inside Cleveland's 10, but a fumble and the stout Cleveland line threw them back. Their 4th drive went 82 yards in seven plays, with Chuck Fenenbock catching a Dobbs' toss to score. Later an errant Fenenbock lateral was snapped out of the air by Mac Speedie, who easily stepped across the goal line. Los Angeles had 19 first downs and 492 total yards, compared to Cleveland's 9 and 330 total yards. But the Dons committed five turnovers and couldn't match Graham and his mates in the pinches. Agajanian's field goal was his 13th of the season, tying the mark of Cleveland's Lou Groza, who was out with an injury. Burr Baldwin had four catches for 118 yards for the Dons.

Cleveland Browns	7	7	6	7–27
Los Angeles Dons	10	0	0	7–17

1 LA—FG Agajanian 43
  LA—Clark 8 run (Agajanian kick)
  Cle—Motley 43 run (Saban kick)
2 Cle—Colella 18 pass from Graham (Saban kick)
3 Cle—Mayne 69 pass from Graham (kick failed)
4 LA—Fenenbock 35 pass from Dobbs (Agajanian kick)
  Cle—Speedie 8 fumble return (Saban kick)

Thursday, November 27, at Brooklyn, NY
Ebbets Field. Attendance—9,837

Thanksgiving Day at Ebbets Field saw the 49ers thoroughly dominate the Dodgers. The brilliant backfield combination of Frankie Albert, Len Eshmont, John Strzykalski (11 carries for 114 yards) and Norm Standlee functioned with clocklike precision against the locals. The 49ers made three long drives for a 21–0 halftime lead. Standlee scored on a sweep to climax a 71 yard march. Albert fired 60 yards to Eshmont to complete a 70 yard drive. Strzykalski's plunge finished a 66-yard advance.

Mickey Colmer made Brooklyn's lone tally, slicing over to conclude an arduous 9-play 96 yard drive. Interceptions and fumbles sabotaged several Brooklyn advances. Two goal line stands by Brooklyn's defense, both at their 3, and the final whistle stopped three more San Francisco drives, keeping the score respectable. San Francisco had 415 total yards, with 295 rushing. Brooklyn had 225 total yards, with 129 passing. Brooklyn threw three interceptions and lost two fumbles.

San Francisco 49ers	7	14	0	0–21
Brooklyn Dodgers	0	0	0	7–7

1 SF—Standlee 9 run (Vetrano kick)
2 SF—Eshmont 60 pass from Albert (Vetrano kick)
  SF—Strzykalski 1 run (Vetrano kick)
4 Bkln—Colmer 5 run (Martinovich kick)

Sunday, November 30, at Bronx, NY
Yankee Stadium. Attendance—39,012

Avenging an earlier loss, the Yankees walloped the Bills to clinch their second consecutive Eastern Division title. Spec Sanders (23 carries for 144 yards) scored three touchdowns and Buddy Young, rookie and former Illinois speedster, tallied once to power the Yankees. The Yankees went 72 yards in nine plays, with Young accounting for 46 yards and the score. Later a George Ratterman fumble was scooped up by Lou Sossamon, who raced 60 yards untouched.

The second half star was Sanders, sparking two long drives and a long run around left end to generate 21 New York points. Some trickeration by Ratterman yielded a bomb to Alton Baldwin in the first minute of the fourth quarter for the Bills second touchdown. New York had 360 total yards, with 254 rushing. Buffalo had 202 total yards and committed five turnovers. New York's Harvey Johnson set an AAFC season record with 47 successful extra points, topping Lou Groza's mark of 45 set last season.

Buffalo Bills	0	6	0	7–13
New York Yankees	14	0	7	14–35

1 NY—Young 1 run (Johnson kick)
   NY—Sossamon 60 fumble return (Johnson kick)
2 Buff—Rykovich 2 run (kick failed)
3 NY—Sanders 1 run (Johnson kick)
4 Buff—Baldwin 59 pass from Ratterman (Juzwik kick)
   NY—Sanders 1 run (Johnson kick)
   NY—Sanders 56 run (Johnson kick)

Sunday, November 30, at Baltimore
Municipal Stadium. Attendance—14,085

In a rematch of the AAFC's cellar dwellers, the Colts defeated the Rockets before chilled fans. A surprisingly entertaining game produced a razzle-dazzle finish. Baltimore struck first, driving 56 yards to score on Bus Mertes (27 carries for 125 yards) 13-yard scamper. A Colts threat in the second ended with a missed field goal by Augie Lio, tried from a difficult angle. Just before halftime, a Chicago drive was thwarted when Doc Mobley picked off a Sam Vacanti pass at the goal line.

After a Colts fumble, Chicago scored when John Harrington (8 catches for 109 yards) took a Vacanti pass and tumbled into the endzone. Chicago's Ray Ramsey intercepted a Bud Schwenk pass, only to fumble. Billy Hillenbrand recovered it, and then caught Schwenk's pay-off pass for the final touchdown. The final minute resembled a circus. Billy Schroeder picked off a Colts pass at his 5, and, three laterals later, teammate Dippy Evans was dropped at the Chicago 31. Ted Scalissi then took a long Vacanti pass and headed for paydirt. But Baltimore's Lamar Blount somehow came up with the ball at the 12. Then, after recovering his own fumble, Blount scrambled away from everyone as the final gun ended the merry-go-round. Baltimore had 318 total yards to Chicago's 315. Each team committed five turnovers.

Chicago Rockets	0	0	7	0–7
Baltimore Colts	7	0	0	7–14

1 Balt—Mertes 13 run (Lio kick)
3 Chi—Harrington 10 pass from Vacanti (Rokisky kick)
4 Balt—Hillenbrand 16 pass from Schwenk (Lio kick)

Week Fifteen

Sunday, December 7, at San Francisco
Kezar Stadium. Attendance—22,943

The 49ers and Bills concluded their regular seasons with a thrill-packed fourth quarter and a tie. Because of heavy rain, a relatively small crowd witnessed the back-and-forth contest. San Francisco's Nick Susoeff caught a Frankie Albert pass in the end zone for the opening salvo. Buffalo countered with a George Ratterman pass to Alton Coppage, capping a 70-yard drive.

Ratterman passed to Dolly King for a 14–7 Bills lead. The 49ers' Ned Mathews then tallied twice, first going around left end and later pilfering a Ratterman pass. Late in the fourth, Ratterman engineered an 80-yard drive to tie, finding King in the end zone. San Francisco had 229 total yards, with 131 rushing. Buffalo had 297 total yards, with 176 passing. The 49ers picked off four Buffalo passes. San Francisco's Alyn Beals set an AAFC record with 17 consecutive games with a pass reception, while teammate Joe Vetrano scored in 28 consecutive games, also an AAFC record. Buffalo's Paul Gibson had five catches for 127 yards.

Buffalo Bills	0	7	0	14–21
San Francisco 49ers	0	7	0	14–21

2 SF—Susoeff 7 pass from Albert (Vetrano kick)
   Buff—Coppage 7 pass from Ratterman (Juzwik kick)
4 Buff—King 12 pass from Ratterman (Juzwik kick)
   SF—Mathews 2 run (Vetrano kick)
   SF—Mathews 35 interception return (Vetrano kick)
   Buff—King 13 pass from Ratterman (Juzwik kick)

Sunday, December 7, at Los Angeles
Memorial Coliseum. Attendance—20,856

The Dons finished their season by pasting the hapless Rockets. Before the game, a dispirited Jim Crowley announced his resignation as Coach of the Rockets to enter business in New York. The Dons rang the scoreboard six times in the first three quarters, with Bob Kelly, Dale Gentry, John Kimbrough (17 carries for 106 yards) and Billy Reinhard registering touchdowns and Ben Agajanian booting two field goals. Late in the game, Agajanian barely missed a 40-yard field goal try.

The Rockets sizzled only twice, on an 80-yard bomb from Sam Vacanti to Ray Ramsey (3 catches for 102 yards) and a 10-yard toss from Al Dekdebrun to Ray Ebli. Otherwise Chicago's offense fired duds. The Dons had 314 total yards, with 183 rushing. Chicago had 213 total yards, 137 passing. Each team committed four turnovers. Agajanian set a new pro season record with 15 successful field goals, topping Lou Groza's AAFC mark of 13 in 1946 and Paddy Driscoll's 12, set in 1926 with the Chicago Bears.

Chicago Rockets	0	7	0	7–14
Los Angeles Dons	7	7	20	0–34

1 LA—Kelly 3 run (Agajanian kick)
2 Chi—Ramsey 80 pass from Vacanti (Rokisky kick)
  LA—Gentry 16 pass from O'Rourke (Agajanian kick)
3 LA—Kimbrough 40 run (Agajanian kick)
  LA—Reinhard 2 run (Agajanian kick)
  LA—FG Agajanian 20
  LA—FG Agajanian 25
4 Chi—Ebli 10 pass from Dekdebrun (Rokisky kick)

Sunday, December 7, at Baltimore Municipal Stadium. Attendance—20,574

The Browns finished their second AAFC campaign by laying waste to a disinterested group of Colts. The Browns will face the New York Yankees in a rematch of last year's championship game. Edgar Jones and Bill Lund scored two touchdowns apiece, while Dante Lavelli and Lewis Mayne accounted for the other two touchdowns. Lou Groza, returning from injury, did his usual neat job on extra points. The Colts threatened only once, driving to the Cleveland 12-yard line, but ceded possession on downs.

The Browns had 559 total yards, with 334 rushing. The Colts had 186 total yards and committed four turnovers. Cleveland's Otto Graham completed 12 of 16 passes for 207 yards and three touchdowns. Graham set an AAFC record by throwing a touchdown pass in eight consecutive games. He also set season marks for passing yards (2,753), touchdown passes (25) and completion percentage (60.3). Cleveland's Mac Speedie set season marks for receptions (67) and receiving yards (1,146). Baltimore's Bud Schwenk set season marks for pass attempts (327) and completions (168).

Cleveland Browns	14	7	14	7–42
Baltimore Colts	0	0	0	0–0

1 Cle—Jones 11 pass from Graham (Groza kick)
  Cle—Lavelli 8 pass from Graham (Groza kick)
2 Cle—Jones 1 run (Groza kick)
3 Cle—Mayne 36 pass from Graham (Groza kick)
  Cle—Lund 18 pass from Lewis (Groza kick)
4 Cle—Lund 63 run (Groza kick)

Sunday, December 7, at Brooklyn, NY Ebbets Field. Attendance—14,166

Harvey Johnson's field goal with 0:32 left saved the Yankees from an embarrassing tie with the lowly Dodgers. The decision by New York Coach Ray Flaherty to use his starters sparingly in the first half nearly came back to bite him. Spec Sanders passed to Bruce Alford for a 7–0 New York lead. A Phil Martinovich field goal made it 7–3. Eddie Prokop's long aerial to Lloyd Cheatham and Johnson's first field goal gave New York a 17–3 lead. With nothing to lose, Brooklyn faked a punt, and punter Lee Tevis raced 44 yards. This led to Dub Jones crashing over to cut the deficit in half.

Late in the third, Brooklyn's Bob Hoernschemeyer skirted around right end to score and tie the game at 17. The Yankees then fumbled on their 22, but Jack Russell blocked Martinovich's field goal try. Late in the fourth, Sanders and Buddy Young drove New York 65 yards to set up Johnson's deciding kick. New York had 357 total yards, with 182 rushing. Brooklyn had 186 total yards, with 156 rushing. Sanders, although held to just 48 yards rushing, set season marks for rushing attempts (231), rushing yards (1,432), touchdown runs (18), total touchdowns (19), points (114) and kickoff returns (22). Johnson set season marks for extra point attempts (51), extra points made (49) and consecutive extra points made (42).

New York Yankees	7	10	0	3–20
Brooklyn Dodgers	3	7	7	0–17

1 NY—Alford 19 pass from Sanders (Johnson kick)
  Bkln—FG Martinovich 17
2 NY—Cheatham 70 pass from Prokop (Johnson kick)
  NY—FG Johnson 19
  Bkln—Jones 3 run (Martinovich kick)
3 Bkln—Hoernschemeyer 5 run (Martinovich kick)
4 NY—FG Johnson 11

AAFC Championship
Sunday, December 14, at Bronx, NY Yankee Stadium. Attendance–60,103

The Browns captured their second consecutive AAFC Championship, beating the Yankees. A treacherous field, frozen solid on one end and slippery with mud on the other, slowed both teams and made footwork an adventure. Turnovers and penalties at critical times hurt the Yankees. The Browns scored late in the first, with Otto Graham's sneak culminating a 66-yard drive. The drive, which featured a spectacular 51-yard burst by Marion Motley, was nearly ended when Bruce Alford intercepted a Graham toss near the New York goal line. But the Yankees were penalized for clipping, which nullified the interception.

Early in the second, New York's star backs, Spec Sanders and Buddy Young, guided the Yankees to the Cleveland 5. There the icy field came into play. Sanders, the league's rushing king, swept the right side and was dropped for no gain. A reverse by the fleet-footed

Young lost a yard on third down. New York had to settle for a Harvey Johnson field goal. In the third, Cleveland's Tom Colella picked off a Sanders pass and the Browns scored their second touchdown on a 6-play 41 yard drive. On 1st and goal from the 4, Graham faked to Motley up the middle, faked a pitch to the motion man and handed off to Edgar Jones, who bulled around right end for the clinching score.

Then two New York drives deep into Browns' territory were foiled, first by Young's fumble of a pitch-out and then by an unnecessary roughness penalty against Harmon Rowe, who took a healthy punch at Colella. Asked about using sneakers on the poor field, Coaches Paul Brown and Ray Flaherty stated that they had agreed before the game to wear only regulation cleats. Flaherty added "Anyway, sneakers would not have done much good—the field was that bad."

New York Yankees	0	3	0	0–3
Cleveland Browns	7	0	7	0–14

1 Cle—Graham 1 run (Groza kick)
2 NY—FG Johnson 12
3 Cle—Jones 4 run (Groza kick)

Team Statistics	CLE	NYY
First Downs	15	13
Rushing	10	8
Passing	4	5
Penalty	1	0
Total Yards	284	212
Rushing Yards	172	123
Net Passing Yards	112	89
Pass att.-comp.-int	21–14–0	18–7–1
Fumbles Lost	1	2
Punting-Average	5–45.0	6–36.0
Penalty-Yards	7–45	3–21

Individual Statistics

Rushing

Cle—Motley 13 for 109; Jones 10 for 27, 1 TD; Graham 4 for 21, 1 TD; Lewis 1 for 9; Colella 1 for 6; Mayne 4 for 0
NYY—Young 16 for 69; Sanders 12 for 40; Prokop 5 for 14

Passing

Cle—Graham 14 of 21 for 112
NYY—Sanders 7 of 17 for 89, 1 int.; Prokop 0 of 1 for 0

Receiving

Cle—Speedie 4 for 25; Lavelli 3 for 37; Jones 3 for 31; Colella 2 for 7; Mayne 1 for 8; Lewis 1 for 4
NYY—Young 2 for 25; Sweiger 2 for 12; Kurrasch 1 for 20; Davis 1 for 18; Russell 1 for 14

1948

Week One
Bye: Baltimore, Cleveland
Friday Night, August 27, at Chicago
Soldier Field. Attendance—26,479

Interceptions and the punting of Glenn Dobbs led the Dons to victory over the Rockets on a wet field. Late in the second quarter Bob Kelly intercepted a Tom Farris pass and returned it to the Chicago 38-yard line. From there the Dons drove steadily until John Kimbrough plunged over for the touchdown. Twice the Rockets drove inside the Dons' 15-yard line in the first half, but Los Angeles took over on downs both times. In the fourth quarter Dobbs, who averaged 51.6 yards punting, had a punt blocked. It was recovered by Chicago's Bob Perina at the Dons' 30-yard line. But Bob Mitchell stole Angelo Bertelli's pass to snuff the Rockets' final chance. The Rockets outgained the Dons 242–97 in total yards. Rain began falling midway through the second period and continued until the end.

Los Angeles Dons	0	7	0	0–7
Chicago Rockets	0	0	0	0–0

2 LA—Kimbrough 1 run (Agajanian kick)

Friday Night, August 27, at Brooklyn, NY
Ebbets Field. Attendance—16,411

In sweltering 90-degree weather the Yankees struck for three touchdowns in rapid succession to spoil the coaching debut of Brooklyn's Carl Voyles. The passing of Bob Chappuis and Bob Hoernschemeyer set up a field goal by Lee Tevis as the Dodgers forged only lead. Early in the third period New York's Charley Riffle blocked a field goal attempt which led the Spec Sanders' (11 carries for 147 yards) first touchdown. Moments later Sanders sprinted to his second touchdown. Rookie Tom Casey then fielded a Mickey Colmer punt and raced an AAFC record 94 yards (Tom Collela, 82, 1947) to ice the game. Casey also set a league single game record with 148 punt return yards. The Yankees outgained the Dodgers 333 to 233 in total yards.

New York Yankees	0	0	21	0–21
Brooklyn Dodgers	0	3	0	0–3

2 Bkln—FG Tevis 17
3 NY—Sanders 8 run (Johnson kick)
NY—Sanders 60 run (Johnson kick)
NY—Casey 94 punt return (Johnson kick)

Sunday, August 29, at San Francisco
Kezar Stadium. Attendance—33,946

Coach Buck Shaw's 49ers, behind a smart aerial game and tremendous ground power, beat the Bills in sunny weather. Frankie Albert (13 of 18 for 136 yards) passed for two touchdowns, and touchdown jaunts by John Strzykalski (7 carries for 76 yards) and Joe Perry helped San Francisco build a commanding 28–7 halftime lead. Threatening to score again in the third stanza, the 49ers' Norm Standlee fumbled at Buffalo's 8-yard line. From there George Ratterman (17 of 36 for 196 yards) led the Bills on a 92-yard touchdown drive, which featured a 49-yard reception by Al Baldwin (4 catches for 92 yards). Buffalo's Chet Mutryn had 14 carries for 114 yards. The teams combined to set a league record with 880 total yards of offense (Dons–Bills, 871, 12/1/1946).

| Buffalo Bills | 0 | 7 | 7 | 0–14 |
| San Francisco 49ers | 7 | 21 | 0 | 7–35 |

1 SF—Schoener 2 pass from Albert (Vetrano kick)
2 SF—Cason 2 run (Vetrano kick)
  Buff—Mutryn 5 run (Armstrong kick)
  SF—Strzykalski 48 run (Vetrano kick)
  SF—Perry 57 run (Vetrano kick)
3 Buff—O'Connor 5 pass from Ratterman (Armstrong kick)
4 SF—Cason 36 pass from Albert (Vetrano kick)

Week Two

Friday Night, September 3, at Cleveland Municipal Stadium. Attendance—60,193

The Browns opened their 1948 season with a workmanlike victory over the Dons. Leading 3–0, Otto Graham (9 of 17 for 122 yards) capped a 70-yard drive with a touchdown pass to Ara Parseghian. In the third period Horace Gillom's punt rolled out at the Los Angeles 1-yard line. Trying to pass, the Dons' Glenn Dobbs (15 of 24 for 134 yards) accidently stepped out of the end zone. After the free kick Graham hit three passes for 35 yards to set up Bill Boedeker's touchdown. The Dons scored twice in the last 0:33, with Joe Aguirre recovering an onside kick to set up his touchdown catch. The Dons had two interceptions and two fumbles deep in Cleveland territory. The Browns set a league record with 125 penalty yards and the teams combined for a league record 185 penalty yards.

| Los Angeles Dons | 0 | 0 | 0 | 14–14 |
| Cleveland Browns | 3 | 7 | 9 | 0–19 |

1 Cle—FG Groza 51
2 Cle—Parseghian 17 pass from Graham (Groza kick)
3 Cle—Safety, Dobbs stepped out of end zone
  Cle—Boedeker 6 run (Groza kick)
4 LA—Kimbrough 2 run (Agajanian kick)
  LA—Aguirre 9 pass from Dobbs (Agajanian kick)

Sunday, September 5, at San Francisco Kezar Stadium. Attendance—32,606

Southpaw Frankie Albert (19 of 29 for 269 yards) passed for three touchdowns and ran for another as the 49ers rolled past the Dodgers. After a San Francisco fumble, Bob Chappuis (7 carries for 62 yards) tallied for Brooklyn. Albert answered that opening salvo with two scoring passes to Hal Shoener, the first one ending an 80-yard drive, and a third one to Alyn Beals. Joe Vetrano's field goal pushed the halftime lead to 22–7. John Strzykalski scored on a third-quarter plunge and Albert dashed around right end to conclude San Francisco's scoring. Brooklyn's Mickey Colmer scored twice, on a reception from Bob Hoernschemeyer and on a run in the final three minutes. The 49ers outgained the Dodgers 485–242 in total yards.

| Brooklyn Dodgers | 7 | 0 | 7 | 6–20 |
| San Francisco 49ers | 6 | 16 | 7 | 7–36 |

1 Bkln—Chappuis 7 run (Brown kick)
  SF—Shoener 2 pass from Albert (kick failed)
2 SF—Shoener 8 pass from Albert (kick blocked)
  SF—Beals 49 pass from Albert (Vetrano kick)
  SF—FG Vetrano 25
3 SF—Strzykalski 4 run (Vetrano kick)
  Bkln—Colmer 40 pass from Hoernschemeyer (Brown kick)
4 SF—Albert 25 run (Vetrano kick)
  Bkln—Colmer 1 run (kick blocked)

Sunday, September 5, at Baltimore Municipal Stadium. Attendance—31,800

Rookie Y. A. Tittle, Otto Graham's understudy at Cleveland last season, hit 11 of 21 passes for a league record 346 yards (Graham, 325, 11/23/1947) as the restructured Colts upset the Yankees. Tittle pitched scoring tosses to Billy Hillenbrand (4 catches for 102 yards) and Lamar Davis, while New York's Spec Sanders (175 yards from scrimmage) scored twice, as the teams battled to a 21–21 tie midway in the third period. Then Tittle hit John North and Hillenbrand with touchdown passes, and scored on a run, to put the game away. Tittle tied the league record with four touchdown passes. Nelson Greene blocked a punt to set up Sanders' second touchdown. New York's Buddy Young suffered a fractured rib in the first quarter.

| New York Yankees | 0 | 7 | 14 | 7–28 |
| Baltimore Colts | 14 | 7 | 14 | 10–45 |

1 Balt—Hillenbrand 13 pass from Tittle (Grossman kick)
  Balt—Tittle 1 run (Grossman kick)
2 NY—Sanders 1 run (Johnson kick)
  Balt—Davis 60 pass from Tittle (Grossman kick)
3 NY—Daley 4 run (Johnson kick)
  NY—Sanders 1 run (Johnson kick)
  Balt—North 80 pass from Tittle (Grossman kick)
  Balt—Hillenbrand 5 run (Grossman kick)
4 Balt—Hillenbrand 49 pass from Tittle (Grossman kick)
  NY—Alford 15 pass from Sanders (Johnson kick)
  Balt—FG Grossman 51

Monday Night, September 6, at Buffalo Civic Stadium. Attendance—25,816

Carl Schuette scored on an interception return and recovered Bob Livingstone's fumble at Chicago's

36-yard line to set up Julie Rykovich's third touchdown as the Bills drubbed the pass-happy Rockets. Paul Gibson's (4 catches for 102 yards) 30-yard catch led to Rykovich's first score and George Ratterman's (10 of 14 for 185 yards) 25-yard pass to Al Baldwin set up Rykovich's second touchdown. The Bills recovered five fumbles and held Chicago to 32 rushing yards. Unable to run, the Rockets attempted a league record 49 passes. Sam Vacanti hit 20 of a league record 42 pass attempts (Glenn Dobbs, 40, 9/22/1946) for 241 yards. Chicago avoided the shutout when Dewey Proctor plunged over with 0:05 left, climaxing an 80-yard march.

| Chicago Rockets | 0 | 0 | 0 | 7–7 |
| Buffalo Bills | 14 | 14 | 14 | 0–42 |

1 Buff—Mutryn 1 run (Armstrong kick)
  Buff—Rykovich 8 run (Armstrong kick)
2 Buff—Schuette 26 interception return (Armstrong kick)
  Buff—Rykovich 7 run (Armstrong kick)
3 Buff—Tomasetti 1 run (Armstrong kick)
  Buff—Rykovich 1 run (Armstrong kick)
4 Chi—Proctor 1 run (Juzwik kick)

Week Three

**Friday Night, September 10, at Chicago
Soldier Field. Attendance—14,642**

Sam Vacanti threw a touchdown pass and scored with 3:13 left as the Rockets captured their first victory of the season, upsetting the Colts. Vacanti's scoring toss to Lafayette King capped an 86-yard drive, and Eddie Prokop (15 carries for 103 yards) scored midway through the second session. The Colts' Y. A. Tittle capped a 77-yard drive with a touchdown plunge. Tittle followed that with a touchdown pass to Lamar Davis. Aided by Dewey Proctor's (10 carries for 106 yards) 50-yard run, the Rockets went to Baltimore's 5-yard line. But Spiro Dellerba recovered Prokop's fumble. A short punt out to Baltimore's 30-yard line helped set up Vacanti's game-winning score. Prokop and Proctor became the first teammates with 100 rushing yards in the same game in AAFC history.

| Baltimore Colts | 0 | 0 | 7 | 7–14 |
| Chicago Rockets | 7 | 7 | 0 | 7–21 |

1 Chi—King 20 pass from Vacanti (Juzwik kick)
2 Chi—Prokop 21 run (Juzwik kick)
3 Balt—Tittle 1 run (Grossman kick)
4 Balt—Davis 47 pass from Tittle (Grossman kick)
  Chi—Vacanti 1 run (Juzwik kick)

**Friday Night, September 10, at Los Angeles
Memorial Coliseum. Attendance—35,246**

Bill Reinhard registered two of Los Angeles' four interceptions to help the Dons defeat the Dodgers in their home season opener. Herman Wedemeyer had a 26-yard run and a 27-yard reception to set up Glenn Dobbs' (9 carries for 97 yards; 11 of 14 for 103 yards) touchdown pass to Len Ford. Ben Agajanian added a field goal for a 10–0 halftime lead. Reinhard stole a pass at Brooklyn's 22-yard line and two plays later Dobbs scored standing up. The Dodgers scored when Bob Hoernschemeyer (12 carries for 65 yards; 10 of 19 for 145 yards) flipped a pass to Walt McDonald. Late in game the Dodgers recovered a fumble. With the ball at the Dons' 10-yard line Reinhard intercepted Hoernschemeyer to seal victory. Brooklyn outgained Los Angeles 321–275 in total yards.

| Brooklyn Dodgers | 0 | 0 | 0 | 7–7 |
| Los Angeles Dons | 7 | 3 | 0 | 7–17 |

1 LA—Ford 27 pass from Dobbs (Agajanian kick)
2 LA—FG Agajanian 27
4 LA—Dobbs 18 run (Agajanian kick)
  Bkln—McDonald 1 pass from Hoernschemeyer (Brown kick)

**Sunday, September 12, at Buffalo
Civic Stadium. Attendance—35,340**

Otto Graham (11 of 21 for 197 yards) accounted for three touchdowns and Mac Speedie tied a league record with 10 receptions (Lamar Davis, 10/5/1947; Speedie, 10/26/1947) for 151 yards as the Browns whipped the Bills. Graham's scoring tosses to Bob Cowan and Speedie, and Marion Motley's (17 carries for 136 yards) touchdown burst, built a 21–6 lead. The second half was all Cleveland as Graham, Tom Collela and Dean Sensenbaugher scored on runs to complete the rout. The Bills' Julie Rykovich had 13 carries for 122 yards. The Browns harried George Ratterman and Jim Still so successfully that they completed just three of 12 pass attempts for a meager 20 yards. Cleveland outgained Buffalo 504–236 in total yards.

| Cleveland Browns | 14 | 7 | 7 | 14–42 |
| Buffalo Bills | 0 | 13 | 0 | 0–13 |

1 Cle—Cowan 11 pass from Graham (Groza kick)
  Cle—Motley 18 run (Groza kick)
2 Buff—Rykovich 25 run (kick blocked)
  Cle—Speedie 10 pass from Graham (Groza kick)
  Buff—Mutryn 12 run (Armstrong kick)
3 Cle—Graham 1 run (Groza kick)
4 Cle—Colella 23 run (Groza kick)
  Cle—Sensenbaugher 3 run (Groza kick)

**Sunday, September 12, at San Francisco
Kezar Stadium. Attendance—60,927**

Frankie Albert (8 of 13 for 135 yards) accounted for four touchdowns as the 49ers handed the Yankees their worst loss in AAFC play before a record San Francisco crowd. Bob Kennedy fumbled the opening kickoff and Len Eshmont recovered for the first touchdown. John Strzykalski pilfered a desperation pass by Spec Sanders' (20 carries for 88 yards) and Norman Maloney recovered a fumble to set up Albert's second and third touchdown passes respectively. Early in the third quarter Albert scored on a reverse. Paul Crowe scored on a lateral from Eshmont and an interception, and intercepted a Sanders' pass in the second quarter to stop New York's most serious threat. The 49ers forced six turnovers in their first win ever against the Yankees.

New York Yankees	0	0	0	0–0
San Francisco 49ers	13	14	7	7–41

1 SF—Eshmont fumble recovery in end zone (Vetrano kick)
   SF—Crowe 18 lateral from Eshmont after 17 pass from Albert (kick failed)
2 SF—Beals 14 pass from Albert (Vetrano kick)
   SF—Strzykalski 22 pass from Albert (Vetrano kick)
3 SF—Albert 17 run (Vetrano kick)
4 SF—Crowe 39 interception return (Vetrano kick)

Week Four

Bye: Brooklyn, Buffalo
Thursday Night, September 16, at Bronx, NY
Yankee Stadium. Attendance—18,959

Y. A. Tittle completed 10 of 17 passes for 241 yards and one touchdown as Coach Cecil Isbell's Colts captured their first road victory ever. Spec Sanders (18 carries for 86 yards) capped a 64-yard drive with a touchdown as the Yankees grabbed their only lead. In an 86-yard advance Tittle hit five passes for 75 yards to set up Bob Pfohl's plunge. Tittle then hit Billy Hillenbrand (9 carries for 72 yards; 5 catches for 143 yards) with a screen pass for the Colts' second touchdown, ending an 80-yard drive. John North scooped up Sanders' fumble for the next touchdown, and Spiro Dellerba recovered Tom Casey's fumble to set up Rex Grossman's second field goal. The Colts won despite a league record 130 penalty yards (Browns, 125, 9/3/1947).

Baltimore Colts	0	7	7	13–27
New York Yankees	7	0	0	7–14

1 NY—Sanders 4 run (Johnson kick)
2 Balt—Pfohl 1 run (Grossman kick)
3 Balt—Hillenbrand 43 pass from Tittle (Grossman kick)
4 Balt—FG Grossman 15
   Balt—North 47 fumble return (Grossman kick)
   Balt—FG Grossman 35
   NY—Sanders 3 run (Johnson kick)

Friday Night, September 17, at Chicago
Soldier Field. Attendance—30,874

Otto Graham (12 of 20 for 157 yards) passed for three touchdowns and ran for another as the undefeated Browns overwhelmed the Rockets. Graham, back to pass, circled his right end and scored standing up to cap a 63-yard drive. Midway in the second period Alex Agase recovered Elroy Hirsch's fumble at the Chicago 20-yard line to set up Graham's scoring toss to Bill Boedeker. Cliff Lewis' interception at the Rockets' 14-yard line set up Graham's first touchdown pass to Bob Cowan, whose second touchdown grab concluded a 61-yard advance. Angelo Bertelli's touchdown pass to Hirsch ended a 63-yard drive to avoid the shutout. The Browns forced six turnovers.

Cleveland Browns	7	7	14	0–28
Chicago Rockets	0	7	0	0–7

1 Cle—Graham 12 run (Groza kick)
2 Cle—Boedeker 4 pass from Graham (Groza kick)
   Chi—Hirsch 13 pass from Bertelli (Juzwik kick)
3 Cle—Cowan 2 pass from Graham (Groza kick)
   Cle—Cowan 40 pass from Graham (Groza kick)

Sunday, September 19, at San Francisco
Kezar Stadium. Attendance—45,420

On a fog-shrouded field Frankie Albert (15 of 22 for 213 yards) pitched three touchdown passes and ran for another as the 49ers took their fourth victory of the season in a hard-fought contest. Albert capped 64, 71 and 79-yard drives with scoring passes to Alyn Beals, John Strzykalski (11 carries for 86 yards) and Bob Sullivan, respectively. Glenn Dobbs' touchdown pass to Herman Wedemeyer cut the Dons' deficit to six points, but Bob Bryant burst through to block Dobb's punt for a safety. Albert then fooled the Los Angeles defense to score on a bootleg play early in the fourth quarter. Dobbs' touchdown pass to Joe Aguirre was set up by the recovery of a fumbled punt. The 49ers outgained the Dons 508–184 in total yards.

Los Angeles Dons	0	7	7	0–14
San Francisco 49ers	7	13	2	14–36

1 SF—Beals 19 pass from Albert (Vetrano kick)
2 SF—Perry 4 run (kick failed)
   LA—Aguirre 17 pass from Dobbs (Agajanian kick)
   SF—Strzykalski 49 pass from Albert (Vetrano kick)
3 LA—Wedemeyer 5 pass from Dobbs (Agajanian kick)
   SF—Safety, Dobbs punt blocked out of end zone
4 SF—Albert 9 run (Maloney pass from Albert)
   SF—Sullivan 14 pass from Albert (Vetrano kick)

Week Five

Sunday, September 26, at Baltimore
Municipal Stadium. Attendance—34,554

Bob "Stormy" Pfohl registered three touchdowns as the upstart Colts smeared the Dodgers and tightened their grip on first place in the Eastern Division. Pfohl climaxed 70 and 42-yard drives with touchdown plunges and scored on a brilliant punt return. Y. A. Tittle completed two passes to Lamar Davis for 40 yards to set up Billy Hillenbrand's touchdown, capping a 59-yard march. Charlie O'Rourke's scoring toss to Joe Smith pushed Baltimore's lead to 35–7. Bob Hoernschemeyer was the workhorse of the Dodger attack, passing for three touchdowns and doing a good bit of running. Operating primarily against Colt substitutes in the fourth quarter, Hoernschemeyer fired his second touchdown pass to Monk Gafford and ended the scoring with a toss to Hal Thompson.

Brooklyn Dodgers	0	7	0	13–20
Baltimore Colts	14	7	14	0–35

1 Balt—Pfohl 5 run (Grossman kick)
  Balt—Hillenbrand 15 run (Grossman kick)
2 Bkln—Gafford 2 pass from Hoernschemeyer (Brown kick)
  Balt—Pfohl 92 punt return (Grossman kick)
3 Balt—Pfohl 1 run (Grossman kick)
  Balt—Smith 14 pass from O'Rourke (Grossman kick)
4 Bkln—Gafford 7 pass from Hoernschemeyer (Brown kick)
  Bkln—Thompson 5 pass from Hoernschemeyer (kick failed)

Sunday, September 26, at Cleveland Municipal Stadium. Attendance—37,190

The Browns spotted the lowly Rockets a 10-point lead and then rallied with a second-half splurge for their fourth victory of the season. Jesse Freitas (9 of 17 for 159 yards) threw a touchdown bomb to ex-Brown Eddie Prokop on the first play from scrimmage to surprise the Browns. Jim McCarthy booted a field goal just before halftime. Weldon Humble stole a Freitas pass at the Browns' 40-yard line, and Otto Graham (11 of 22 for 216) capped the 60-yard drive with a touchdown pass to Bill Boedeker. On a fake trap play Graham fired a scoring pass to Dub Jones. Graham's 23-yard pass to Mac Speedie (5 catches for 103 yards) was the feature play in a 62-yard advance, ending in Boedeker's second score. The Browns got inside Chicago's 10-yard line three times in the first half.

Chicago Rockets	7	3	0	0–10
Cleveland Browns	0	0	14	7–21

1 Chi—Prokop 74 pass from Freitas (McCarthy kick)
2 Chi—FG McCarthy 18
3 Cle—Boedeker 37 pass from Graham (Groza kick)
  Cle—D. Jones 43 pass from Graham (Groza kick)
4 Cle—Boedeker 2 run (Groza kick)

Sunday, September 26, at Buffalo Civic Stadium. Attendance—31,103

Jim Cason and Verl Lillywhite each scored on a run and intercepted a pass to set up touchdowns as the 49ers beat the Bills in a wide-open game. Cason's 31-yard interception return set up John Strzykalski's touchdown plunge and Lillywhite's theft led to a scoring run by Frankie Albert, who in the first quarter capped a 98-yard drive with a touchdown pass to Alyn Beals. The Bills rode the arm of George Ratterman (23 of 35 for 299 yards), who capped a 52-yard drive with a touchdown plunge and threw a touchdown pass to Chet Mutryn for a 21–14 Buffalo lead. Ratterman's scoring toss to Al Baldwin cut the San Francisco lead to three points, but Albert's run sealed the victory. The 49ers outgained the Bills 536–404 in total yards.

San Francisco 49ers	7	10	14	7–38
Buffalo Bills	7	14	0	7–28

1 Buff—Ratterman 1 run (Kulbitski kick)
  SF—Beals 29 pass from Albert (Vetrano kick)
2 Buff—Steuber 47 run (Kulbitski kick)
  SF—Cason 59 run (Vetrano kick)
  Buff—Mutryn 30 pass from Ratterman (Kulbitski kick)
  SF—FG Vetrano 28
3 SF—Strzykalski 1 run (Vetrano kick)
  SF—Lillywhite 4 run (Vetrano kick)
4 Buff—Baldwin 14 pass from Ratterman (Armstrong kick)
  SF—Albert 20 run (Vetrano kick)

Wednesday Night, September 29, at Los Angeles Memorial Coliseum. Attendance—35,655

Glenn Dobbs and the Dons caught fire in the final five minutes to upset the Yankees in a rough game. Dobbs covered 99 yards in seven passes, the last to Joe Aguirre for the touchdown. Dobbs then capped a 71-yard drive with a scoring toss to Len Ford. In the final minute Dobbs faked a pass and scooted down the sideline for the clinching touchdown. For New York, Pete Layden's 15-yard interception return set up his scoring plunge and Duke Iverson's interception led to Harvey Johnson's field goal. In the first half the Dons' Herman Wedemeyer was ejected for fighting. Three plays later New York's Marion Shirley was tossed for punching Dobbs. For three quarters the Dons frittered away several scoring opportunities with six turnovers.

New York Yankees	0	0	7	3–10
Los Angeles Dons	0	0	0	20–20

3 NY—Layden 1 run (Johnson kick)
4 NY—FG Johnson 41
  LA—Aguirre 31 pass from Dobbs (Aguirre kick)
  LA—Ford 4 pass from Dobbs (Aguirre kick)
  LA—Dobbs 33 run (kick failed)

Week Six

Friday Night, October 1, at Chicago Soldier Field. Attendance—14,553

Frankie Albert (12 of 25 for 157 yards) passed for a pair of touchdowns and the 49ers converted two fumbles into two more touchdowns as the 49ers captured their sixth victory of the season, handing the Rockets their fifth loss in six starts. Late in the first quarter Albert concluded a 53-yard drive with a touchdown pass to Alyn Beals. John Strzykalski recovered a Chicago fumble to set up Norm Standlee's touchdown. Moments later another Rocket fumble led to Joe Perry's touchdown. Albert's touchdown pass to Strzykalski and a Joe Vetrano field goal put the game out of reach. Chicago's Bob Perina intercepted a San Francisco aerial to begin a 61-yard drive, capped by Floyd Simmons' touchdown plunge.

| San Francisco 49ers | 7 | 14 | 10 | 0–31 |
| Chicago Rockets | 0 | 7 | 0 | 7–14 |

1 SF—Beals 15 pass from Albert (Vetrano kick)
2 SF—Standlee 10 run (Vetrano kick)
   SF—Perry 14 run (Vetrano kick)
   Chi—Kuffel 46 pass from Fenenbock (McCarthy kick)
3 SF—Strzykalski 45 pass from Albert (Vetrano kick)
   SF—FG Vetrano 16
4 Chi—Simmons 1 run (McCarthy kick)

Sunday, October 3, at Buffalo Civic Stadium. Attendance—17,694

The Bills handed the victory-starved Dodgers their fifth defeat before the smallest football crowd in Civic Stadium in two seasons. Buffalo jumped to a 10–0 lead on Bob Steuber's field goal and Lou Tomasetti's run. Brooklyn's Bob Chappuis hit four passes to set up Hardy Browns' touchdown. George Ratterman and Bob Hoernschemeyer then staged a touchdown pass contest. Ratterman passed twice to Chet Mutryn while Hoernschemeyer found Brown and Monk Gafford for scores. The outcome was still in doubt until Mickey Colmer's 35-yard punt return set up Julie Rykovich's touchdown plunge with 0:16 left. Garland Williams recovered a fumble to set up Hoernschemeyer's first touchdown pass. The Dodgers were held to nine rushing yards.

| Brooklyn Dodgers | 0 | 7 | 7 | 7–21 |
| Buffalo Bills | 3 | 14 | 7 | 7–31 |

1 Buff—FG Steuber 24
2 Buff—Tomasetti 15 run (Steuber kick)
   Bkln—Brown 2 run (Brown kick)
   Buff—Mutryn 43 pass from Ratterman (Steuber kick)
3 Bkln—Brown 7 pass from Hoernschemeyer (Brown kick)
   Buff—Mutryn 9 pass from Ratterman (Steuber kick)
4 Bkln—Gafford 27 pass from Hoernschemeyer (Brown kick)
   Buff—Rykovich 1 run (Steuber kick)

Tuesday Night, October 5, at Baltimore Municipal Stadium. Attendance—22,359

Fans braved a cold drizzle to watch the Browns win a grueling battle with the Colts in the mud. The Colts scored on their second play from scrimmage as Y. A. Tittle threw a screen pass to Billy Hillenbrand, who dashed all the way to paydirt. Otto Graham threw a 44-yard pass to Tommy James, and Edgar Jones crashed over three plays later. With a strong wind at his back, Rex Grossman easily kicked a field goal. The wind also helped set up the winning touchdown. The Colts' Charlie O'Rourke punted from his 9-yard line and the ball flew out of bounds at the 27. Graham found Jones in the end zone four plays later. From then on Baltimore was busy fighting off Cleveland attempts to score. The Browns' Marion Motley had 130 rushing yards.

| Cleveland Browns | 7 | 0 | 7 | 0–14 |
| Baltimore Colts | 7 | 3 | 0 | 0–10 |

1 Balt—Hillenbrand 77 pass from Tittle (Grossman kick)
   Cle—E. Jones 2 run (Groza kick)
2 Balt—FG Grossman 40
3 Cle—E. Jones 12 pass from Graham (Groza kick)

Week Seven
Friday Night, October 8, at Los Angeles Memorial Coliseum. Attendance—31,119

Glenn Dobbs hit 19 of 33 passes for a league record 356 yards (Y. A. Tittle, 346, 9/5/1948) and tied the league record with four touchdown passes as the Dons used a fourth-period burst to fizzle the Rockets. Dobbs' second touchdown pass to Len Ford (5 catches for 126 yards), Bill Reinhard's punt return and Walt Heap's interception return broke the game open. For Chicago, Eddie Prokop (3 catches for 109 yards) scored two touchdowns and Fred Negus set a league record with a 97-yard fumble return. The Dons' John Kimbrough (13 carries for 58 yards) capped a 90-yard drive with his touchdown catch. Los Angeles forced seven turnovers, and the 77 total points were the second most in AAFC history (80: Browns-Dodgers, 12/8/1946). The teams combined for a league record 627 passing yards.

| Chicago Rockets | 7 | 0 | 14 | 7–28 |
| Los Angeles Dons | 7 | 14 | 7 | 21–49 |

1 Chi—King 37 pass from Freitas (McCarthy kick)
   LA—Ford 8 pass from Dobbs (Agajanian kick)
2 LA—Wedemeyer 10 pass from Dobbs (Agajanian kick)
   LA—Kimbrough 3 run (Agajanian kick)
3 Chi—Prokop 26 pass from Freitas (McCarthy kick)
   Chi—Negus 97 fumble return (McCarthy kick)
   LA—Kimbrough 22 pass from Dobbs (Agajanian kick)
4 LA—Ford 40 pass from Dobbs (Agajanian kick)
   LA—W. Reinhard 87 punt return (Agajanian kick)
   Chi—Prokop 60 pass from Fenenbock (McCarthy kick)
   LA—Heap 18 interception return (Agajanian kick)

Sunday, October 10, at Buffalo Civic Stadium. Attendance—18,825

Fans groaned when Harvey Johnson's 52nd consecutive extra point kick split the uprights as the Yankees rallied to nip to Bills. Passing brilliantly, Buffalo's George Ratterman capped an 83-yard drive with a touchdown pass to Marty Comer. Ratterman's 41-yard pass to Vic Kulbitski set up Chet Mutryn's touchdown, but Bruce Alford crashed through to block Bob Steuber's extra point attempt. In the third period New York's Spec Sanders set up his touchdown run around right end with a 41-yard pass to Alford. In the fourth quarter Sanders hit Lowell Wagner with a touchdown pass to tie the game. The Yankees' Buddy Young, who played briefly, had a 54-yard touchdown run nullified in the first half by a man-in-motion penalty. The Bills suffered three turnovers.

New York Yankees	0	0	7	7	–14
Buffalo Bills	7	6	0	0	–13

1 Buff—Comer 8 pass from Ratterman (Steuber kick)
2 Buff—Mutryn 1 run (kick blocked)
3 NY—Sanders 5 run (Johnson kick)
4 NY—Wagner 54 pass from Sanders (Johnson kick)

Sunday, October 10, at Baltimore Municipal Stadium. Attendance—37,209

In a dazzling display of T-quarterback wizardry, southpaw Frankie Albert passed for two touchdowns, ran for a touchdown and an extra point, and set up Joe Perry's touchdown with the moth-eaten Statue of Liberty play as the 49ers laid waste to the Colts in a club-record point total. Albert, who threw scoring passes to John Strzykalski and Alyn Beals, hit 13 of 15 passes to set an AAFC single game record of 86.7 completion percentage. Eddie Carr scored on a run right down the middle of Baltimore's defense and an interception return to help complete the rout. After the third quarter Albert gave way to Bev Wallace, who rifled a touchdown pass to Norm Maloney. Forrest Hall gained 33 yards on the Statue of Liberty play. Y. A. Tittle's touchdown pass capped a 40-yard drive.

San Francisco 49ers	7	21	14	14	–56
Baltimore Colts	7	0	0	7	–14

1 SF—Strzykalski 8 pass from Albert (Vetrano kick)
   Balt—Pfohl 7 pass from Tittle (Grossman kick)
2 SF—Lillywhite 28 run (Vetrano kick)
   SF—Beals 18 pass from Albert (Albert run)
   SF—Albert 1 run (Vetrano kick)
3 SF—Perry 3 run (Vetrano kick)
   SF—Carr 54 run (Vetrano kick)
4 SF—Maloney 29 pass from Wallace (Vetrano kick)
   SF—Carr 30 interception return (Vetrano kick)
   Balt—Gambino 39 run (Grossman kick)

Sunday Night, October 10, at Cleveland Municipal Stadium. Attendance—31,187

The Browns pushed across two fourth-quarter touchdowns to gain their sixth win of the season, handing the feisty Dodgers their sixth loss of the season. George Young tallied on a fumble return and Marion Motley (110 rushing yards) capped a 73-yard drive with a touchdown plunge for the clinching points. Passes by Otto Graham set up touchdown runs by Edgar Jones and Bill Boedeker. In the early minutes Cleveland's Lou Groza missed a 56-yard field goal attempt, as the ball hit the crossbar and bounced back. Late in the first period Groza tied the league record with a 53-yarder (Ben Agajanian, 10/19/1947). The game was moved to the evening to avoid a conflict with the Indians–Braves World Series game during the afternoon.

Brooklyn Dodgers	0	10	7	0	–17
Cleveland Browns	10	0	7	13	–30

1 Cle—E. Jones 3 run (Groza kick)
   Cle—FG Groza 53
2 Bkln—Colmer 2 run (Tevis kick)
   Bkln—FG Tevis 36
3 Cle—Boedeker 10 run (Groza kick)
   Bkln—Foldberg 51 blocked field goal return (Brown kick)
4 Cle—Young 9 fumble return (kick failed)
   Cle—Motley 3 run (Groza kick)

WEEK EIGHT

Friday Night, October 15, at Los Angeles Memorial Coliseum. Attendance—40,019

The Colts finally broke their Western Division jinx by gradually wearing down the Dons, and then crushing them in the fourth quarter. Los Angeles built a 14–0 lead on Bill Reinhard's interception return and Glenn Dobbs' touchdown pass. Y. A. Tittle capped an 81-yard drive with a scoring toss to Lamar Davis. Then ex-Don Charlie O'Rourke tied the game with a touchdown toss to Windell Williams. In the final stanza a touchdown burst by Billy Hillenbrand, two field goals by Rex Grossman and a safety buried Los Angeles. The Colts' Bus Mertes ran 16 times for 87 yards. The Dons' Herman Wedemeyer and John Kimbrough went out with injuries, and Dobbs' passing was erratic at best. At one point it was third down and 73 to go for Los Angeles, after a series of losses and penalties.

Baltimore Colts	0	7	7	15	–29
Los Angeles Dons	7	7	0	0	–14

1 LA—W. Reinhard 10 interception return (Agajanian kick)
2 LA—Aguirre 1 pass from Dobbs (Agajanian kick)
   Balt—Davis 40 pass from Tittle (Grossman kick)
3 Balt—Williams 26 pass from O'Rourke (Grossman kick)
4 Balt—Hillenbrand 1 run (Grossman kick)
   Balt—FG Grossman 23
   Balt—Safety, Dobbs tackled in end zone
   Balt—FG Grossman 20

Friday Night, October 15, at Brooklyn, NY Ebbets Field. Attendance—8,671

In a battle of cellar dwellers, Bob Hoernschemeyer (16 carries for 109 yards; 8 of 19 for 73 yards) capitalized on a pair of Chicago miscues as the Dodgers snapped a 9-game losing streak. Ray Ramsey pilfered a Jesse Freitas pass and eight plays later Hoernschemeyer cashed in Brooklyn's first touchdown. In the third period a Chicago lateral went astray and Walt McDonald recovered on the Rocket 23-yard line. Three plays later Hoernschemeyer scored again. Chicago's Dewey Proctor returned the ensuing kickoff 37 yards, and Freitas capped the 58-yard drive with a touchdown pass to Lafayette King. Mickey Colmer (19 carries for 114 yards), who had a 72-yard quick-kick in the second quarter, ended a 60-yard march with a touchdown catch from Bob Chappuis.

Chicago Rockets	0	0	7	0–7
Brooklyn Dodgers	7	0	7	7–21

1 Bkln—Hoernschemeyer 7 run (Brown kick)
3 Bkln—Hoernschemeyer 16 run (Brown kick)
Chi—King 25 pass from Freitas (McCarthy kick)
4 Bkln—Colmer 28 pass from Chappuis (Brown kick)

Sunday, October 17, at Cleveland
Municipal Stadium. Attendance—28,054

On a dull rainy afternoon, the smallest home crowd in Browns' history witnessed Otto Graham lead Cleveland past Buffalo. Graham pitched touchdown passes to Edgar Jones and Mac Speedie (7 catches for 142 yards), and used more aerials to set up Marion Motley's (13 carries for 99 yards) touchdown plunge in a busy first quarter. Trailing 24–7, George Ratterman's 44-yard pass to Chet Mutryn (4 catches for 128 yards) set up his scoring toss to Lou Tomasetti. In the final minute Speedie capped a 70-yard drive with his second touchdown reception. The Bills threatened twice in the second half, but lost the ball on downs and an interception. The teams combined for a league record 63 pass attempts (49ers–Dodgers, 62, 9/22/12946).

Buffalo Bills	7	0	0	7–14
Cleveland Browns	17	0	7	7–31

1 Cle—E. Jones 44 pass from Graham (Groza kick)
Buff—Baldwin 22 pass from Still (Steuber kick)
Cle—FG Groza 45
Cle—Motley 3 run (Groza kick)
3 Cle—Speedie 15 pass from Graham (Groza kick)
4 Buff—Tomasetti 9 pass from Ratterman (Steuber kick)
Cle—Speedie 30 pass from Lewis (Groza kick)

Sunday, October 17, at Bronx, NY
Yankee Stadium. Attendance—29,743

The fleet-footed 49ers rode a 229-yard rushing attack to their eighth consecutive triumph. A fumble set up Frankie Albert's (6 of 13 for 79 yards) touchdown pass to John Strzykalski, and Forrest Hall's 56-yard punt return led to Albert's touchdown on a sneak. In a 72-yard drive, Spec Sanders set up his touchdown with a 28-yard pass to Bruce Alford. Joe Perry iced the game with a touchdown in the final minutes. The Yankees threatened in the second quarter, but a pass ricocheted off the head of New York's Otto Schnellbacher and into the arms of the 49ers' Paul Crowe in the end zone. The Yankees rebuffed three San Francisco advances, as Jack Russell blocked a field goal, Schnellbacher recovered a fumble and Bob Kennedy intercepted a pass.

San Francisco 49ers	0	14	0	7–21
New York Yankees	0	0	0	7–7

2 SF—Strzykalski 25 pass from Albert (Vetrano kick)
SF—Albert 1 run (Vetrano kick)
4 NY—Sanders 3 run (Johnson kick)
SF—Perry 1 run (Vetrano kick)

Week Nine

Sunday, October 24, at San Francisco
Kezar Stadium. Attendance—27,978

John Strzykalski (14 carries for 144 yards) led a blistering 390-yard rushing attack as the 49ers rallied to their ninth consecutive victory. The Colts struck first on Rex Grossman's field goal, capping an 86-yard drive. Aubrey Fowler stole a Frankie Albert pass at the Colt 10-yard line, and Baltimore swept 90 yards to Y. A. Tittle's touchdown pass to Billy Hillenbrand. Strzykalski and Joe Perry climaxed 72 and 63-yard drives with scoring sprints as the 49ers surged ahead. Late in the game Albert drove the 49ers 92 yards, capped by his touchdown pass to Nick Susoeff. Strzykalski set a league record by scoring a touchdown in his ninth consecutive game. San Francisco outgained Baltimore 494–308 in total yards, but committed four turnovers.

Baltimore Colts	0	10	0	0–10
San Francisco 49ers	0	0	7	14–21

2 Balt—FG Grossman 20
Balt—Hillenbrand 17 pass from Tittle (Grossman kick)
3 SF—Strzykalski 29 run (Vetrano kick)
4 SF—Perry 19 run (Vetrano kick)
SF—Susoeff 43 pass from Albert (Vetrano kick)

Sunday, October 24, at Chicago
Soldier Field. Attendance—5,964

Bob Hoernschemeyer's passing and a pair of interceptions led the Dodgers to their second win over the Rockets in successive games. Hoernschemeyer's aerials set up both of Mickey Colmer's (21 carries for 113 yards) touchdown plunges. George Strohmeyer intercepted a Sam Vacanti pass to set up Monk Gafford's touchdown, and Carl Allen intercepted another Vacanti pass for Brooklyn's fourth touchdown. Gafford concluded the scoring with a toss to Max Morris. Vacanti capped a 3-play, 69-yard march with a pass to Ray Kuffel for Chicago's first touchdown. Chuck Fenenbock's 59-yard dash was the feature play in an 80-yard drive that ended with Vacanti's touchdown run. The Dodgers forced five turnovers.

Brooklyn Dodgers	0	14	7	14–35
Chicago Rockets	0	0	7	7–14

2 Bkln—Colmer 2 run (Brown kick)
Bkln—Colmer 2 run (Brown kick)
3 Chi—Kuffel 49 pass from Vacanti (McCarthy kick)
Bkln—Gafford 10 run (Brown kick)
4 Chi—Vacanti 3 run (McCarthy kick)

Bkln—Allen 17 interception return (Brown kick)
Bkln—Morris 24 pass from Gafford (Brown kick)

Sunday, October 24, at Los Angeles Memorial Coliseum. Attendance—26,818

Buffalo's George Ratterman (17 of 27 for 310 yards) and Los Angeles' Glenn Dobbs (21 of 36 for 219 yards) staged an air war as the Bills rallied to defeat the Dons. Dobbs' passing staked the Dons to a 14–0 lead with two scoring strikes to Joe Aguirre. Rex Bumgardner began the rally with a punt return for a touchdown. The Bills then rattled off 28 additional points, capped by Ratterman's touchdown pass to Al Baldwin (4 catches for 154 yards) and Chet Mutryn's second touchdown run. Dobbs added a touchdown pass to Len Ford, but left shortly thereafter with injured ribs. The game produced league records with 69 pass attempts (Browns-Bills, 63, 10/17/1948) and 38 pass completions (35: 49ers-Dodgers, 9/22/1946; 49ers-Dons, 12/8/1946).

Buffalo Bills	0	14	14	7–35
Los Angeles Dons	7	7	0	7–21

1 LA—Aguirre 12 pass from Dobbs (Agajanian kick)
2 LA—Aguirre 25 pass from Dobbs (Agajanian kick)
   Buff—Bumgardner 91 punt return (Steuber kick)
   Buff—Mutryn 2 run (Steuber kick)
3 Buff—Steuber 1 run (Steuber kick)
   Buff—Baldwin 59 pass from Ratterman (Steuber kick)
4 Buff—Mutryn 21 run (Steuber kick)
   LA—Ford 26 pass from Dobbs (Agajanian kick)

Sunday, October 24, at Cleveland Municipal Stadium. Attendance—46,912

In a brilliant performance, Otto Graham (21 of 30 for 310 yards) tied the league record with four touchdown passes and scored another as the Browns laid waste to the Yankees. Graham capped 99 and 75-yard drives with touchdown passes to Dante Lavelli (5 catches for 89 yards) and ended a 45-yard drive with a scoring toss to Mac Speedie (8 catches for 84 yards). New York's Otto Schnellbacher stole a George Terlep pass and returned it 51 yards to set up Elmer Layden's touchdown pass to Buddy Young in the final minute. Cleveland's line gave Graham all the time in the world to get off his throws. After his touchdown run around left end, Graham threw the ball into the packed bleachers and retired to the bench. The Browns outgained the Yankees 486–235 in total yards.

New York Yankees	0	0	0	7–7
Cleveland Browns	7	14	7	7–35

1 Cle—Lavelli 29 pass from Graham (Groza kick)
2 Cle—Cowan 63 pass from Graham (Groza kick)
   Cle—Speedie 9 pass from Graham (Groza kick)
3 Cle—Lavelli 18 pass from Graham (Groza kick)
4 Cle—Graham 22 run (Groza kick)
   NY—Young 34 pass from Layden (Johnson kick)

Week Ten
Bye: Cleveland, San Francisco
Sunday, October 31, at Buffalo Civic Stadium. Attendance—23,694

The Bills shook off Y. A. Tittle's haymaker touchdown bomb on the first play from scrimmage to trim the Colts and gain a first place tie with Baltimore in the Eastern Division. Deadlocked 14–14 at halftime, the Colts took their second lead on Rex Grossman's field goal early in the third quarter. Long passes from George Ratterman to Bill O'Conner moved the ball 69 yards to set up Chet Mutryn's second touchdown. Ratterman followed that with scoring tosses to Mutryn and O'Conner to ice the game, the latter capping an 89-yard drive. Aubrey Fowler's interception set up Charlie O'Rourke's touchdown. Tittle sat out the second half with a knee injury. The teams combined to set a league record with 893 total yards of offense (49ers-Bills, 880, 8/29/1948).

Baltimore Colts	7	7	3	0–17
Buffalo Bills	7	7	7	14–35

1 Balt—Hillenbrand 64 pass from Tittle (Grossman kick)
   Buff—Mutryn 3 run (Steuber kick)
2 Buff—Gompers 43 run (Steuber kick)
   Balt—O'Rourke 1 run (Grossman kick)
3 Balt—FG Grossman 30
   Buff—Mutryn 1 run (Steuber kick)
4 Buff—Mutryn 49 pass from Ratterman (Steuber kick)
   Buff—O'Connor 35 pass from Ratterman (Steuber kick)

Sunday, October 31, at Brooklyn, NY Ebbets Field. Attendance—12,825

Florida Governor Millard Caldwell and 125 members of the Orange Bowl Committee were among those who witnessed Glenn Dobbs complete five passes to generate 10 points as the Dons handed the Dodgers their first shutout loss in league play. Late in the first half Dobbs hit three passes to set up Ben Agajanian's field goal. Bob Reinhard blocked Mickey Colmer's punt and Dobbs completed two passes, the second being Joe Aguirre's touchdown catch. Lin Sexton's 28-yard interception return set up Walter Clay's touchdown midway through the fourth period. Brooklyn's Lee Tevis missed a 26-yard field goal in the first quarter, and late in the game the Dodgers lost the ball on downs deep in Los Angeles territory. Brooklyn's Monk Gafford set a league record with six punt returns.

Los Angeles Dons	0	3	7	7–17
Brooklyn Dodgers	0	0	0	0–0

2 LA—FG Agajanian 50
3 LA—Aguirre 4 pass from Dobbs (Agajanian kick)
4 LA—Clay 1 run (Agajanian kick)

Sunday, October 31, at Bronx, NY
Yankee Stadium. Attendance—13,239

Pete Layden (14 carries for 118 yards) completed 9 of 13 passes for 216 yards and Otto Schnellbacher had two interceptions to set up scores as the Yankees handed the injury-ridden Rockets their seventh consecutive loss. Schnellbacher's interceptions set up Layden's touchdown passes to Buddy Young, which were sandwiched around a pair of touchdown plunges by Lowell Tew, as the Yankees built a 35–0 lead. A flashy forward-lateral play involving Jesse Freitas, ex–Yankee Bob Perina and Floyd Simmons produced Chicago's touchdown. On the final play Tom Casey flipped to Van Davis for the final touchdown. Julie Rykovich missed a 33-yard field goal try on Chicago's initial drive, and the Rockets were stopped on New York's 6-yard line in the fourth period.

Chicago Rockets	0	0	0	7–7
New York Yankees	0	21	7	14–42

2 NY—Russell 59 pass from Layden (Johnson kick)
  NY—Young 26 pass from Layden (Johnson kick)
  NY—Tew 2 run (Johnson kick)
3 NY—Tew 2 run (Johnson kick)
4 NY—Young 41 pass from Layden (Johnson kick)
  Chi—Simmons 57 lateral from Perina after 8 pass from Freitas (McCarthy kick)
  NY—Davis 7 pass from Casey (Johnson kick)

Week Eleven

Sunday, November 7, at Cleveland
Municipal Stadium. Attendance—32,314

The Browns spanked the Colts to set a league record with their 12th consecutive victory. An early Baltimore gamble backfired when the Browns stuffed the Colts' Lucien Gambino on fourth down at the Baltimore 28-yard line. Two plays later Edgar Jones had his first touchdown. Otto Graham led the Browns 72 yards, capped by Marion Motley's dash through the middle of the Colt defense. Graham passed 37 yards to Mac Speedie to set up Jones' second score, and Lin Houston recovered Bus Mertes' fumble at the Colt 20-yard line to set up Ara Parseghian's touchdown. The Colts finally dented the scoreboard with seven minutes left as Billy Hillenbrand took Y. A. Tittle's pass and did a tight-rope act down the sideline for the touchdown.

Baltimore Colts	0	0	0	7–7
Cleveland Browns	7	7	7	7–28

1 Cle—E. Jones 4 run (Groza kick)
2 Cle—Motley 22 run (Groza kick)
3 Cle—E. Jones 4 pass from Graham (Groza kick)
4 Cle—Parseghian 15 run (Groza kick)
  Balt—Hillenbrand 69 pass from Tittle (Grossman kick)

Sunday, November 7, at Brooklyn, NY
Ebbets Field. Attendance—7,805

Chet Mutryn (17 carries for 185 yards) and Lou Tomasetti (15 carries for 141 yards) led a league-record 414-yard rushing attack to overshadow a record-setting performance by Brooklyn's Bob Chappuis as the Bills edged the Dodgers. Mutryn scored two touchdowns, and Rex Bumgardner's 22-yard punt return set up Tomasetti's touchdown. In the fourth period Carl Schuette stole a Chappuis pass and lateraled near Brooklyn's goal line, but the ball rolled into the end zone, where teammate Vince Mazza fell on it for the score. Chappuis, who set records with 51 pass attempts and 26 completions (Glenn Dobbs, 23 of 40, 9/22/1946), threw a touchdown pass to Saxon Judd. Ray Ramsey scored on a punt return in the final minute, but the Bills recovered the onside kick and ran out the clock.

Buffalo Bills	13	0	6	7–26
Brooklyn Dodgers	0	7	0	14–21

1 Buff—Mutryn 68 run (kick failed)
  Buff—Tomasetti 15 run (Steuber kick)
2 Bkln—Colmer 2 run (Tevis kick)
3 Buff—Mutryn 9 run (kick failed)
4 Buff—Mazza fumble recovery in end zone (Steuber kick)
  Bkln—Judd 43 pass from Chappuis (Tevis kick)
  Bkln—Ramsey 70 punt return (Tevis kick)

Sunday, November 7, at San Francisco
Kezar Stadium. Attendance—25,306

The powerful 49ers registered their tenth consecutive victory of the season by crushing the hapless Rockets. Six different 49ers scored touchdowns and Frankie Albert set a league record by throwing a touchdown pass in 16 consecutive games (Otto Graham, 13). Forrest Hall and Norm Standlee tallied on long runs. A partially blocked punt set up Albert's scoring toss to Alyn Beals and Paul Crowe's interception led to Len Eshmont's touchdown. Coach Buck Shaw cleared his bench of substitutes for the fourth quarter which allowed the Rockets to score their touchdowns, all on passes from Jesse Freitas. The 49ers outgained the Rockets 566–288 in total yards. Note: the sequence of the final three scores is in doubt.

Chicago Rockets	0	0	0	21–21
San Francisco 49ers	10	20	7	7–44

1 SF—Hall 65 run (Vetrano kick)
  SF—FG Vetrano 41
2 SF—Perry 3 run (Vetrano kick)
  SF—Beals 18 pass from Albert (pass failed)
  SF—Eshmont 1 run (Vetrano kick)
3 SF—Standlee 57 run (Vetrano kick)
4 Chi—Jensen 12 pass from Freitas (McCarthy kick)
  Chi—King 14 pass from Freitas (McCarthy kick)
  SF—Lillywhite 27 run (Vetrano kick)
  Chi—King 12 pass from Freitas (McCarthy kick)

Sunday, November 7, at Bronx, NY
Yankee Stadium. Attendance—17,386

Pete Layden (16 carries for 132 yards; 7 of 22 for 139 yards) pitched three touchdown passes as the improving Yankees thumped the Dons and gained a tie with the Colts for second place in the Eastern Division. Layden capped 80 and 45-yard drives with touchdown passes to Jack Russell, and ended a 91-yard advance with a scoring toss to Bruce Alford. An interception led to Harvey Johnson's field goal. Glenn Dobbs, hobbled by injured ribs, completed a 50-yard pass to Len Ford to set up Mike Graham's touchdown to get the Dons on the board. Spec Sanders came in for just two plays, both of which clicked for scores in the fourth quarter. Tempers flared in the final stanza, and New York's Nelson Greene and Los Angeles' Walt Clay were ejected for fighting.

Los Angeles Dons	0	0	0	6–6
New York Yankees	7	14	3	14–38

1 NY—Russell 70 pass from Layden (Johnson kick)
2 NY—Russell 7 pass from Layden (Johnson kick)
   NY—Alford 19 pass from Layden (Johnson kick)
3 NY—FG Johnson 20
4 LA—Graham 1 run (kick failed)
   NY—Sanders 6 run (Johnson kick)
   NY—Young 35 pass from Sanders (Johnson kick)

WEEK TWELVE

Sunday, November 14, at Bronx, NY
Yankee Stadium. Attendance—17,642

The Yankees pushed across three touchdowns and repulsed several Dodger advances to move into a 3-way tie for first place with the Bills and the Colts in the East. Bob Kennedy stole a Bob Chappuis aerial and returned it 24 yards to set up Buddy Young's touchdown. Pete Layden (15 carries for 74 yards) cut back through the Dodger defense for the second touchdown. Spec Sanders sprinted 50 yards to set up Lowell Tew's touchdown. George Strohmeyer's 15-yard interception return set up Chappuis' scoring toss to Bob Hoernschemeyer in the final minute. The Dodgers lost the ball on downs three times in Yankee territory, and Otto Schnellbacher's interception stopped a Brooklyn drive late in the first half. The King's Point Merchant Marine Academy band performed at halftime.

Brooklyn Dodgers	0	0	0	7–7
New York Yankees	7	7	0	7–21

1 NY—Young 4 run (Johnson kick)
2 NY—Layden 15 run (Johnson kick)
4 NY—Tew 1 run (Johnson kick)
   Bkln—Hoernschemeyer 20 pass from Chappuis (Tevis kick)

Sunday, November 14, at Baltimore
Municipal Stadium. Attendance—21,899

The Colts broke a 10–10 halftime tie with 28 second-half points to whip the Rockets and gain a 3-way tie for first place in the East with the Yankees and the Bills. A 15-yard interception return by Jake Leicht set up Bus Mertes' (19 carries for 118 yards) second touchdown. Y. A. Tittle then got his throwing arm warmed up and pitched touchdown passes to Windell Williams and Lamar Davis as Baltimore built a 31–17 lead. Jesse Freitas kept the Rockets in the fray with three touchdown passes, including two to Bob Livingstone (3 catches for 100 yards). Fred Negus recovered Mertes' fumble two plays after the opening kickoff to set up Jim McCarthy's field goal. The Colts outgained the Rockets 452–316 in total yards, but committed four turnovers.

Chicago Rockets	3	7	0	14–24
Baltimore Colts	0	10	14	14–38

1 Chi—FG McCarthy 29
2 Chi—Livingstone 55 pass from Freitas (McCarthy kick)
   Balt—Mertes 9 run (Grossman kick)
   Balt—FG Grossman 35
3 Balt—Mertes 10 run (Grossman kick)
   Balt—Williams 38 pass from Tittle (Grossman kick)
4 Chi—Livingstone 34 pass from Freitas (F. Johnson kick)
   Balt—Davis 46 pass from Tittle (Grossman kick)
   Chi—Kuffel 70 pass from Freitas (F. Johnson kick)
   Balt—Hillenbrand 1 run (Grossman kick)

Sunday, November 14, at Buffalo
Civic Stadium. Attendance—23,725

Walt Heap's 17-yard interception return in the final minute set up Glenn Dobbs' (8 carries for 66 yards) game-winning touchdown pass to Joe Aguirre as the inspired Dons threw a monkey wrench into the Bills' Eastern Division title hopes. Despite sore ribs, Dobbs capped a 72-yard drive with his first touchdown run and completed passes to Aguirre and Walt Clay for 47 yards to set up his second touchdown. The Bills rode the arm of George Ratterman (14 of 35 for 208 yards), who pitched three touchdown passes, including two to Al Baldwin. Buffalo threatened late in the game, but Dobbs took the pressure off with an interception. The Bills outgained the Dons 397–282 in total yards, but had three turnovers. The Dons' Ben Agajanian set a league record with five field goal attempts.

Los Angeles Dons	0	6	14	7–27
Buffalo Bills	6	0	7	7–20

1 Buff—Baldwin 30 pass from Ratterman (kick failed)
2 LA—FG Agajanian 51
   LA—FG Agajanian 34
3 LA—Dobbs 26 run (Agajanian kick)
   Buff—Mutryn 36 pass from Ratterman (Kulbitski kick)
   LA—Dobbs 6 run (Agajanian kick)
4 Buff—Baldwin 38 pass from Ratterman (Kulbitski kick)
   LA—Aguirre 3 pass from Dobbs (Agajanian kick)

Sunday, November 14, at Cleveland
Municipal Stadium. Attendance—82,769

Billed as the gridiron battle of the century, a record pro football crowd witnessed the Browns snap the

49ers' 10-game winning streak in a game that was, for the greater part, a rather duff affair. Cleveland's Lou Saban recovered Forrest Hall's fumble on the opening kickoff to set up Otto Graham's touchdown two plays later. The 49ers then swept 80 yards, capped by Joe Perry's touchdown plunge. Edgar Jones cracked over left tackle on a quick-opener for the winning touchdown to cap an 84-yard drive. The Browns threatened twice in the second quarter, but a fumble and a missed field goal by Lou Groza stopped them. The 49ers threatened three times in the final quarter, but interceptions by Cliff Lewis and Tom Colella, and a Bill Willis fumble recovery, halted them. The Browns held the 49ers to 32 passing yards and forced six turnovers.

San Francisco 49ers	7	0	0	0–7
Cleveland Browns	7	0	7	0–14

1 Cle—Graham 14 run (Groza kick)
   SF—Perry 1 run (Vetrano kick)
3 Cle—E. Jones 4 run (Groza kick)

Week Thirteen
Bye: Buffalo, Chicago
Sunday, November 21, at Bronx, NY
Yankee Stadium. Attendance—52,518

Otto Graham (9 of 23 for 211 yards) and Marion Motley (10 carries for 75 yards) paced the Browns as Cleveland took its seventh victory over New York in eight attempts, blemished only by last year's tie in November. Motley took a screen pass from Graham for the first score, and capped a 68-yard drive with his second touchdown for a 34–14 lead. Ara Parseghian's 57-yard interception return set up Edgar Jones' touchdown. The Yankees' biggest crowd of the season discerned a ray of hope when they scored twice in less than 90 seconds in the second period, but two Lou Groza field goals sandwiched around Bob Cowan's touchdown brought them back to reality. With the game in hand, Coach Paul Brown cleared his bench of substitutes for fourth-quarter action.

Cleveland Browns	14	13	7	0–34
New York Yankees	0	14	0	7–21

1 Cle—Motley 78 pass from Graham (Groza kick)
   Cle—E. Jones 1 run (Groza kick)
2 NY—Alford 29 pass from Layden (Johnson kick)
   NY—Schnellbacher 40 interception return (Johnson kick)
   Cle—FG Groza 34
   Cle—Cowan 9 run (Groza kick)
   Cle—FG Groza 18
3 Cle—Motley 12 run (Groza kick)
4 NY—Kennedy 1 run (Johnson kick)

Sunday, November 21, at Baltimore
Municipal Stadium. Attendance—25,228

Bill Reinhard recovered Lou Gambino's fumble at the Colt 6-yard line to set up Ben Agajanian's field goal with 0:35 left as the Dons continued to vex members of the Eastern Division. Knox Ramsey blocked Rex Grossman's field goal attempt and recovered Y. A. Tittle's fumble to set up both of Glenn Dobbs' touchdown passes as Los Angeles took a 14–7 lead at the intermission. Billy Hillenbrand took a screen pass from Tittle and raced 58 yards to set up Bob Pfohl's touchdown run. In the third quarter Tittle ended an 80-yard drive with a touchdown pass to Lamar Davis, who sidestepped the last Don defender at the 10-yard line. Agajanian had missed from the 37 and 45-yard lines, and had a third attempt blocked. The Colts outgained the Dons 406–188 in total yards.

Los Angeles Dons	0	14	0	3–17
Baltimore Colts	7	0	7	0–14

1 Balt—Pfohl 25 run (Grossman kick)
2 LA—Clay 32 pass from Dobbs (Agajanian kick)
   LA—Aguirre 19 pass from Dobbs (Agajanian kick)
3 Balt—Davis 46 pass from Tittle (Grossman kick)
4 LA—FG Agajanian 17

Sunday, November 21, at Brooklyn, NY
Ebbets Field. Attendance—9,336

Frankie Albert (16 of 23 for 219 yards) ran for two scores and tied a league record with four touchdown passes as the 49ers and Dodgers staged the highest scoring game in pro football history. Albert threw three scoring passes to Alyn Beals, while John Strzykalski, Joe Perry, Norm Standlee and Forrest Hall each registered a touchdown. For Brooklyn, Bob Chappuis (11 of 19 for 308 yards) pitched for three touchdowns, including two to Mickey Colmer (2 catches for 118 yards), and Ray Ramsey had four catches for 149 yards. The teams combined to set records for total offense (1,030 yards), total touchdowns (15), touchdown passes (8) and points (103). The 49ers' Joe Vetrano set a league record with nine successful extra points. After the game Brooklyn's Tex Warrington and San Francisco's Don Clark got into a fight in the runway under the stands.

San Francisco 49ers	14	14	21	14–63
Brooklyn Dodgers	7	7	7	19–40

1 SF—Albert 4 run (Vetrano kick)
   Bkln—Judd 4 pass from Hoernschemeyer (Brown kick)
   SF—Strzykalski 21 pass from Albert (Vetrano kick)
2 SF—Albert 1 run (Vetrano kick)
   SF—Beals 15 pass from Albert (Vetrano kick)
   Bkln—Ramsey 50 pass from Chappuis (Brown kick)
3 SF—Beals 6 pass from Albert (Vetrano kick)
   SF—Beals 4 pass from Albert (Vetrano kick)
   Bkln—Colmer 37 pass from Chappuis (Brown kick)
   SF—Perry 87 kickoff return (Vetrano kick)
4 Bkln—Hoernschemeyer 10 fumble return (kick blocked)
   Bkln—Colmer 1 run (kick failed)
   SF—Standlee 3 run (Vetrano kick)
   Bkln—Colmer 81 pass from Chappuis (Brown kick)
   SF—Hall 63 run (Vetrano kick)

Week Fourteen

Thursday, November 25, at Chicago
Soldier Field. Attendance—6,305

The Bills scored two touchdowns on returns in the final four minutes to take a free-scoring decision over the stubborn Rockets in a sloppy game. Chet Mutryn fielded Ernie Lewis' punt and handed off to Rex Bumgardner, who raced down the sideline for the score. Minutes later Vic Kulbitski scooped up Chuck Fenenbock's fumble and rumbled to paydirt. Lou Tomasetti capped 75, 61 and 80-yard drives with touchdown runs to give Buffalo a 26–21 edge in the third quarter. Chicago's Jesse Freitas rifled three touchdown passes, including two to Lafayette King. The first one to King capped a 95-yard drive and the second one came in the final minute. Chicago's Jim Mello had 19 carries for 136 yards. The Bills forced seven turnovers and the Rockets forced five.

Buffalo Bills	6	13	7	13–39
Chicago Rockets	14	7	7	7–35

1 Chi—Rykovich 1 run (McCarthy kick)
   Buff—Tomasetti 5 run (kick failed)
   Chi—Fenenbock 53 pass from Freitas (McCarthy kick)
2 Buff—Baldwin 33 pass from Ratterman (Kulbitski kick)
   Chi—Kellagher 5 run (McCarthy kick)
   Buff—Tomasetti 7 run (kick blocked)
3 Buff—Tomasetti 8 run (Kulbitski kick)
   Chi—King 17 pass from Freitas (McCarthy kick)
4 Buff—Bumgardner 90 punt return (Kulbitski kick)
   Buff—Kulbitski 64 fumble return (kick failed)
   Chi—King 25 pass from Freitas (McCarthy kick)

Thursday, November 25, at Los Angeles
Memorial Coliseum. Attendance—60,031

Otto Graham (16 of 32 for 239 yards) and the Browns took to the air to subdue the feisty Dons before their largest home crowd of the season. Graham found Dante Lavelli for a touchdown bomb in the second quarter. Late in the first half a roughing penalty and two Graham passes set up his touchdown throw to Bob Cowan. More Graham aerials in the third quarter led to his touchdown on a sneak and Lou Groza's field goal. Led by the brilliant Glenn Dobbs, the Dons played the defending champions toe-to-toe in the first half. Dobbs ran and passed Los Angeles to 75- and 80-yard scoring drives, both capped by Walt Clay touchdown plunges. Cliff Lewis' interception off of Dobbs, the only turnover of the game, set up Tony Adamle's touchdown sprint.

Cleveland Browns	0	14	17	0–31
Los Angeles Dons	7	7	0	0–14

1 LA—Clay 1 run (Agajanian kick)
2 Cle—Lavelli 49 pass from Graham (Groza kick)
   LA—Clay 1 run (Agajanian kick)
   Cle—Cowan 17 pass from Graham (Groza kick)
3 Cle—Graham 1 run (Groza kick)
   Cle—FG Groza 36
   Cle—Adamle 19 run (Groza kick)

Sunday, November 28, at Brooklyn, NY
Ebbets Field. Attendance—7,629

The running of Billy Hillenbrand (12 carries for 112 yards) and the passing of Y. A. Tittle (20 of 26 for 249 yards) rallied the Colts past the Dodgers before a slim crowd that included some 2,000 Baltimore fans, who had followed their team to Brooklyn in two special trains. Hillenbrand's 36-yard run set up Bus Mertes' first touchdown, and Hillenbrand capped a 68-yard drive with a touchdown dash around right end. Tittle ended a 70-yard drive with a touchdown pass to Lamar Davis, and an interception set up Tittle's scoring toss to Jake Leicht with 0:20 left. The victory overshadowed the efforts of Brooklyn's Monk Gafford, who subbed for an injured Bob Chappuis and threw three touchdown passes to help the Dodgers to a 20–17 halftime lead.

Baltimore Colts	14	3	7	14–38
Brooklyn Dodgers	13	7	0	0–20

1 Balt—Mertes 1 run (Grossman kick)
   Bkln—Ramsey 36 pass from Gafford (Brown kick)
   Bkln—Burrus 60 pass from Gafford (kick failed)
   Balt—Davis 50 pass from Tittle (Grossman kick)
2 Balt—FG Grossman 27
   Bkln—Hoernschemeyer 42 pass from Gafford (Brown kick)
3 Balt—Mertes 3 run (Grossman kick)
4 Balt—Hillenbrand 8 run (Grossman kick)
   Balt—Leicht 35 pass from Tittle (Grossman kick)

Sunday, November 28, at Bronx, NY
Yankee Stadium. Attendance—18,376

Paced by George Ratterman (12 of 22 for 200 yards) and an ill Chet Mutryn, the Bills blasted the Yankees out of the race for the Eastern Division title, eliminating their chance for a third divisional crown. Ratterman capped 40, 80 and 55-yard drives with a touchdown pass to Al Baldwin and two touchdown plunges, respectively. Mutryn crawled out of his sick bed to torment the Yankees, rushing nine times for 67 yards, catching four passes for 65 yards and returning two punts for 99 yards, including one for a touchdown for a 28–7 Buffalo lead. For New York, Spec Sanders ended 38 and 63-yard drives with touchdown passes to Jack Russell and Harvey Johnson set a pro football record with 73 consecutive extra points, exceeding Jack Manders' NFL record of 72.

Buffalo Bills	7	14	14	0–35
New York Yankees	0	7	0	7–14

1 Buff—Baldwin 12 pass from Ratterman (Armstrong kick)
2 Buff—Ratterman 1 run (Armstrong kick)

Buff—Ratterman 4 run (Armstrong kick)
NY—Russell 6 pass from Sanders (Johnson kick)
3 Buff—Mutryn 88 punt return (Armstrong kick)
Buff—Tomasetti 2 run (Armstrong kick)
4 NY—Russell 8 pass from Sanders (Johnson kick)

1 NY—Layden 3 run (Johnson kick)
2 NY—Tew 2 run (Johnson kick)
NY—Tew 5 run (Johnson kick)
3 NY—Russell 63 pass from Layden (Johnson kick)
4 Chi—Mello 1 run (McCarthy kick)

Sunday, November 28, at San Francisco
Kezar Stadium. Attendance—59,785

Despite a severely wrenched knee, Otto Graham (11 of 23 for 234 yards) tied a league record with four touchdown passes as the Browns clinched the Western Division title in a bruising contest. Fumble recoveries by Tony Adamle and Forrest Grigg set up Graham's scoring toss to Dante Lavelli and Lou Groza's field goal. The 49ers responded with Joe Perry's first touchdown and two touchdown passes from Frankie Albert (10 of 21 for 117 YARDS) to Alyn Beals, the first one being set up by a fumble. Graham responded by capping 73 and 61-yard drives with touchdown passes to Marion Motley and Dub Jones. Moments later an interception set up Graham's touchdown pass to Edgar Jones. Perry's touchdown catch capped a 77-yard drive. The 49ers' John Strzykalski had 15 carries for 108 yards.

Cleveland Browns	10	0	21	0–31
San Francisco 49ers	0	14	7	7–28

1 Cle—Lavelli 40 pass from Graham (Groza kick)
Cle—FG Groza 24
2 SF—Perry 2 run (Vetrano kick)
SF—Beals 4 pass from Albert (Vetrano kick)
3 SF—Beals 29 pass from Albert (Vetrano kick)
Cle—Motley 6 pass from Graham (Groza kick)
Cle—D. Jones 20 pass from Graham (Groza kick)
Cle—E. Jones 33 pass from Graham (Groza kick)
4 SF—Perry 14 pass from Albert (Vetrano kick)

Week Fifteen

Saturday, December 4, at Chicago
Soldier Field. Attendance—4,930

The Yankees converted four of their six forced turnovers into an equal number of touchdowns to trounce the Rockets. Bob Kennedy's interception off of Jesse Freitas (11 of 23 for 198 yards) set up Pete Layden's (9 of 19 for 190 yards) touchdown. Fumble recoveries by Bruce Alford and Luke Iverson led to touchdown plunges by Lowell Tew. In the third period the Rockets went to New York's 1-foot line, but Kennedy stole another Freitas pass. Four plays later Layden capped an 80-yard drive with a touchdown bomb to Jack Russell (4 catches for 106 yards). Chicago's Jim Mello (12 carries for 74 yards) scored early in the fourth quarter to avoid the shutout. New York's Otto Schnellbacher set a league record with his 11th interception of the season (Tom Colella, 10, 1946).

New York Yankees	7	14	7	0–28
Chicago Rockets	0	0	0	7–7

Sunday, December 5, at Baltimore
Municipal Stadium. Attendance—33,090

Y. A. Tittle scored two touchdowns and passed for another as the Colts forced a divisional playoff game with the Bills. After Chet Mutryn's touchdown capped a 55-yard march, Billy Hillenbrand skirted around left end to score, capping a 59-yard drive. Hillenbrand's 30-yard punt return and two passes to Lamar Davis (3 catches for 109 yards) set up Tittle's first touchdown. Late in the third quarter Tittle hit Davis with a touchdown pass. After Tittle's second touchdown, George Ratterman threw a scoring toss to Al Baldwin to end an 80-yard drive with three minutes left. In the final minute Davis stole a Ratterman pass and returned it to Buffalo's 1-yard line, where Jake Leicht battered his way into the end zone on the next play.

Buffalo Bills	6	2	0	7–15
Baltimore Colts	7	7	7	14–35

1 Buff—Mutryn 1 run (kick failed)
Balt—Hillenbrand 10 run (Grossman kick)
2 Balt—Tittle 1 run (Grossman kick)
Buff—Safety, Mazza tackled Tittle in end zone
3 Balt—Davis 80 pass from Tittle (Grossman kick)
4 Balt—Tittle 1 run (Grossman kick)
Buff—Baldwin 4 pass from Ratterman (Armstrong kick)
Balt—Leicht 1 run (Grossman kick)

Sunday, December 5, at Brooklyn, NY
Ebbets Field. Attendance—9,821

Otto Graham (10 of 17 for 194 yards) passed for two touchdowns and ran for another as the Browns engaged in a little light exercise at the expense of the hapless Dodgers in the final major pro football game in Brooklyn. Dub Jones' score capped an 80-yard drive, and Graham ended 76 and 91-yard drives with a scoring toss to Dante Lavelli and a touchdown plunge. After Graham's touchdown pass to Horace Gillom, Coach Paul Brown emptied his bench of substitutes. The Dodgers responded with three touchdowns, including two scoring passes by Bob Chappuis (14 of 29 for 318 yards). Brooklyn's Harry Burrus tied a league record with three interceptions (Bob Sweiger, 10/27/1946; Tom Colella, 11/17/1946; Eddie Prokop, 9/21/1947).

Cleveland Browns	7	14	10	0–31
Brooklyn Dodgers	0	0	7	14–21

1 Cle—D. Jones 1 run (Groza kick)
2 Cle—Lavelli 54 pass from Graham (Groza kick)
Cle—Graham 1 run (Groza kick)
3 Cle—FG Groza 37
Cle—Gillom 25 pass from Graham (Groza kick)

Bkln—Hoernschemeyer 38 pass from Chappuis (Brown kick)
4 Bkln—Hoernschemeyer 3 run (Brown kick)
Bkln—Gafford 60 pass from Chappuis (Brown kick)

Sunday, December 5, at Los Angeles Memorial Coliseum. Attendance—51,460

The 49ers ended their bittersweet season with a convincing victory over the Dons and yet another second-place finish in the Western Division. Interceptions set up Joe Vetrano's touchdown and Frankie Albert's first touchdown pass to Alyn Beals. Joe Perry's (9 carries for 160 yards) touchdown run capped a 73-yard drive, and Vetrano's field goal built a formidable 31–7 San Francisco lead. With no rushing attack, the Dons' Glenn Dobbs threw three touchdown passes, including two to Len Ford, and set league records for pass attempts (55), completions (27), passing yards (405) and, unfortunately interceptions (7). Joe Aguirre had 124 receiving yards for Los Angeles. The 49ers had 369 rushing yards and won despite 112 penalty yards.

| San Francisco 49ers | 21 | 0 | 10 | 7–38 |
| Los Angeles Dons | 0 | 7 | 7 | 7–21 |

1 SF—Vetrano 30 run (Vetrano kick)
SF—Strzykalski 59 pass from Albert (Vetrano kick)
SF—Beals 7 pass from Albert (Vetrano kick)
2 LA—Ford 7 pass from Dobbs (Agajanian kick)
3 SF—Perry 7 run (Vetrano kick)
SF—FG Vetrano 47
LA—Ford 11 pass from Dobbs (Agajanian kick)
4 SF—Beals 35 pass from Albert (Vetrano kick)
LA—Kimbrough 18 pass from Dobbs (Agajanian kick)

Eastern Division Playoff

Sunday, December 12, at Baltimore Municipal Stadium. Attendance—27,325

George Ratterman rallied his Bills to three fourth-quarter touchdowns to win the AAFC's Eastern Division title and break the hearts of angry Baltimore fans. The Colts took a 3-point lead in the opening quarter on Rex Grossman's field goal. But Buffalo came back in the second period to go in front on a touchdown pass from Ratterman to Bill O'Conner. The third quarter saw the Colts build a 17–7 lead on the passing arm of Y. A. Tittle and the running of Bus Mertes, who scored both touchdowns. The Bills narrowed the gap early in the fourth quarter on a pass from Ratterman to Bill Gompers, with Gompers racing the final 40 yards. With a little over five minutes left, the Bills began a drive from their 25-yard line. Ratterman's passes brought them to the Baltimore 25-yard line where the Bills' ace passed to Al Baldwin for the score. During the drive a controversial call resulted in Buffalo retaining possession. After the game, officials had to be protected by players from both sides and the police. Ed Hirsch intercepted a Tittle pass for the clinching touchdown as time ran down.

| Buffalo Bills | 0 | 7 | 0 | 21–28 |
| Baltimore Colts | 3 | 0 | 14 | 0–17 |

1 Balt—FG Grossman 16
2 Buff—O'Connor 8 pass from Ratterman (Armstrong kick)
3 Balt—Mertes 8 run (Grossman kick)
Balt—Mertes 1 run (Grossman kick)
4 Buff—Gompers 66 pass from Ratterman (Armstrong kick)
Buff—Baldwin 25 pass from Ratterman (Armstrong kick)
Buff—E. Hirsch 18 interception return (Armstrong kick)

Team Statistics	Balt	Buff
First Downs	11	24
Rush Yards	162	177
Pass Yards	135	217
Passes	10–18–1	17–37–1
Fumbles Lost	1	2
Punts	3–40	5–42
Penalty	25	60

AAFC Championship

Sunday, December 19, at Cleveland Municipal Stadium. Attendance—22,981

The Browns completed a perfect season with a thrashing of the Bills before a disappointing, but hardly disappointed, crowd at Municipal Stadium. The Browns thus became the first professional football team in a major league to win every game of the regular season and then continue victorious through the championship game. The rout of the Bills was fully expected. That anticipation no doubt held down the crowd. The first half was played on comparatively even terms, but Cleveland scored once in each quarter. First, Edgar Jones went three yards to a touchdown with only 0:10 left in the opening quarter. Early in the second quarter, Cleveland's George Young returned Rex Bumgardner's fumble 18 yards for the Browns' second touchdown. The second half was all Cleveland. Barely two minutes into the session, Otto Graham passed nine yards to Edgar Jones to make the score 21–0. Marion Motley, Cleveland's 238-pound fullback, took over from there and scored three touchdowns on runs to bury the Bills.

| Buffalo Bills | 0 | 0 | 7 | 0–7 |
| Cleveland Browns | 7 | 7 | 14 | 21–49 |

1 Cle—E. Jones 3 run (Groza kick)
2 Cle—Young 18 fumble return (Groza kick)
3 Cle—E. Jones 9 pass from Graham (Groza kick)
Cle—Motley 29 run (Groza kick)
Buff—Baldwin 10 pass from Still (Armstrong kick)
4 Cle—Motley 31 run (Groza kick)
Cle—Motley 5 run (Groza kick)
Cle—Saban 39 interception return (Groza kick)

Team Statistics	Cle	Buff
First Downs	20	13
Rushing	10	4
Passing	8	7
Penalty	2	2
Total Yardage	333	167
Net Rushing Yardage	215	118
Net Passing Yardage	118	104
Passes att.-comp.-had int.	26-11-1	36-11-5

Rushing

Cle—Motley 14 for 133, 3 TDs; E. Jones 8 for 29, 1 TD; D. Jones 5 for 22; Cline 1 for 20; Parseghian 4 for 14; Sensenbaugher 2 for 2; Colella 1 for 1; Graham 1 for 0; Adamle 2 for -1; Terlep 2 for -5

Buff—Bumgardner 11 for 34; Tomasetti 11 for 20; Mutryn 8 for 8; Kulbitski 2 for 1; Still 1 for 0

Passing

Cle—Graham 11 of 24 for 118, 1 TD, 1 int.; E. Jones 0 of 2

Buff—Still 6 of 18 for 80, 1 TD, 2 int.; Ratterman 5 of 18 for 104, 3 int

Receiving

Cle—E. Jones 3 for 39, 1 TD; Speedie 2 for 22; Lavelli 2 for 16; D. Jones 2 for 13; Gillom 1 for 15; Motley 1 for 13

Buff—O'Connor 3 for 41; Mutryn 2 for 5; Bumgardner 1 for 25; Kulbitski 1 for 14; A. Baldwin 1 for 10, 1TD; Gibson 1 for 7; Snyder 1 for 4; Tomasetti 1 for -2

1949

Week One

Bye: Cleveland, Los Angeles, New York
Friday Night, August 26, at Chicago
Soldier Field. Attendance—23,800

George Strohmeyer intercepted a pass to set up Jim McCarthy's field goal in the final minutes as the renovated Hornets beat the Bills to equal their victory total of last season. Buffalo recovered a fumble to set up Jim Still's touchdown pass to Al Baldwin (2 catches for 88 yards). The Rockets answered with Bob Hoernschemeyer's (7 of 17 for 150 yards) scoring bomb to Ray Ramsey. Rip Collins recovered a fumble to set up John Clement's touchdown pass to Paul Patterson. The Bills pulled even when a blocked punt led to Chet Mutryn's touchdown. Buffalo's Chet Adams missed a 50-yard field goal attempt as time expired. Baldwin set a league record with a touchdown reception in seven consecutive games. Chicago outgained Buffalo 305-193 in total yards.

Buffalo Bills	7	0	0	7–14
Chicago Hornets	0	14	0	3–17

1 Buff—Baldwin 18 pass from Still (Adams kick)
2 Chi—Ramsey 63 pass from Hoernschemeyer (McCarthy kick)
 Chi—Patterson 30 pass from Clement (McCarthy kick)
4 Buff—Mutryn 13 run (Adams kick)
 Chi—FG McCarthy 21

Sunday, August 28, at San Francisco
Kezar Stadium. Attendance—29,095

In perfect football weather Frankie Albert (14 of 33 for 131 yards) sparked the 49ers to victory as they opened their fourth bid for the AAFC championship. The 49ers breezed to a 17-0 halftime lead on Joe Vetrano's field goal and Albert's touchdown passes to Eddie Carr and Alyn Beals. In the third quarter the Colts came to life on Y. A. Tittle's (13 of 28 for 132 yards) passing. Harry Jagade registered two touchdowns, the second one set up by John North's fumble recovery, and Rex Grossman's field goal knotted the score. The 49ers rebounded as Norm Standlee capped a 72-yard drive with a touchdown run. Aided by a roughing penalty, Albert pitched a scoring toss to Verl Lillywhite in the closing minutes. San Francisco's Paul Salata had nine catches for 78 yards.

Baltimore Colts	0	0	17	0–17
San Francisco 49ers	10	7	0	14–31

1 SF—FG Vetrano 28
 SF—Carr 21 pass from Albert (Vetrano kick)
2 SF—Beals 1 pass from Albert (Vetrano kick)
3 Balt—Jagade 45 run (Grossman kick)
 Balt—Jagade 1 run (Grossman kick)
 Balt—FG Grossman 29
4 SF—Standlee 9 run (Vetrano kick)
 SF—Lillywhite 10 pass from Albert (Vetrano kick)

Week Two

Bye: New York
Friday Night, September 2, at Los Angeles
Memorial Coliseum. Attendance—20,211

An ailing Glenn Dobbs (7 of 11 for 123 yards) ran, passed and punted the Dons to three touchdowns as Los Angeles swamped Baltimore to jump start their 1949 campaign. Earl Howell and Dobbs staked the Dons to a 14-0 lead. The Colts rebounded in the second quarter with Y. A. Tittle (12 of 25 for 207 yards) pitching touchdown passes to Bus Mertes and Bill Stone (4 catches for 132 yards). The Dons took the lead for good on Hosea Rodgers' (15 carries for 94 yards) touchdown. Dobbs left early in the third quarter with a shoulder injury, and George Taliaferro (5 of 8 for 101 yards) piloted Los Angeles to four more touchdowns, including passes to Dick Wilkins and Billy Grimes. The Dons outgained the Colts 518-328 in total yards.

Baltimore Colts	0	17	0	0–17
Los Angeles Dons	14	7	7	21–49

1 LA—Howell 8 run (Nelson kick)
  LA—Dobbs 7 run (Nelson kick)
2 Balt—Mertes 18 pass from Tittle (Grossman kick)
  Balt—Stone 64 pass from Tittle (Grossman kick)
  Balt—FG Grossman 37
  LA—Rodgers 1 run (Nelson kick)
3 LA—Wilkins 7 pass from Taliaferro (Nelson kick)
4 LA—Davis 4 run (Nelson kick)
  LA—Grimes 29 pass from Taliaferro (Nelson kick)
  LA—Grimes 9 run (Nelson kick)

Sunday, September 4, at San Francisco
Kezar Stadium. Attendance—28,311

Eddie Carr intercepted two passes and John Strzykalski scored two touchdowns as the 49ers routed the Hornets in a bruising battle. Carr returned his first one for a touchdown and his second one set up Strzykalski's first touchdown. Hal Shoener blocked a punt to set up Joe Perry's touchdown, and Frankie Albert capped a 62-yard drive with a touchdown. Strzykalski's second touchdown ended an 88-yard drive, and Len Eshmont's interception set up Norm Standlee's touchdown. Chicago's Bob Jensen recovered a fumble that led to Bob Hoernschemeyer's touchdown to avoid the shutout. Three Hornets were taken to the hospital: Ted Hazelwood with a broken nose, Walt McDonald with a dislocated shoulder and Martin Wendell with a mild concussion.

Chicago Hornets	0	7	0	0–7
San Francisco 49ers	28	0	7	7–42

1 SF—Perry 3 run (Vetrano kick)
  SF—Albert 22 run (Vetrano kick)
  SF—Carr 40 interception return (Vetrano kick)
  SF—Strzykalski 44 run (Vetrano kick)
2 Chi—Hoernschemeyer 1 run (McCarthy kick)
3 SF—Strzykalski 22 run (Beals pass from Albert)
4 SF—Standlee 1 run (Vetrano kick)

Monday Night, September 5, at Buffalo
Civic Stadium. Attendance—31,839

Otto Graham's (27 of 40 for 330 yards) touchdown pass to Mac Speedie (10 catches for 113 yards) with two minutes left capped a 48-yard drive and a furious comeback as the Browns tied the Bills. Ollie Cline (18 carries for 76 yards) matched Edgar Jones' first touchdown for a 7–7 halftime score. Joe Sutton recovered a fumble on Cleveland's 2-yard line to set up George Ratterman's first touchdown run, and Vince Mazza recovered Graham's fumble that led to Chet Mutryn's touchdown as Buffalo forged a 28–7 lead entering the fourth period. Graham, who completed 15 of his last 17 passes, capped 77 and 43-yard drives with touchdown passes to Jones. Cleveland's Lou Saban handled the kicking chores as Lou Groza was out with an injured right leg.

Cleveland Browns	7	0	0	21–28
Buffalo Bills	0	7	21	0–28

1 Cle—E. Jones 12 pass from Graham (Saban kick)
2 Buff—Cline 6 run (Adams kick)
3 Buff—Ratterman 2 run (Adams kick)
  Buff—Ratterman 1 run (Adams kick)
  Buff—Mutryn 2 run (Adams kick)
4 Cle—E. Jones 7 pass from Graham (Saban kick)
  Cle—E. Jones 38 pass from Graham (Saban kick)
  Cle—Speedie 2 pass from Graham (Saban kick)

WEEK THREE
Bye: San Francisco
Friday Night, September 9, at Los Angeles
Memorial Coliseum. Attendance—30,193

Jim McCarthy's field goal with 1:30 left gave the Hornets a surprising upset of the sluggish Dons. Chicago drew first blood on Bob Hoernschemeyer's touchdown pass to Dan Edwards. In the second period Fred Negus scooped up a fumble and raced to the Hornet's second touchdown, but McCarthy's extra point attempt was blocked. John Clement's touchdown gave Chicago a 20–0 lead. The Dons rallied on George Taliaferro's (6 of 9 for 179 yards) touchdown pass to Dick Wilkins (3 catches for 122 yards) and a pair of scoring runs by Billy Grimes and Glenn Dobbs. With 10 seconds left and the partisan crowd in an uproar, Dobbs' last pass from the Chicago 20-yard line fell incomplete and the game ended.

Chicago Hornets	7	13	0	3–23
Los Angeles Dons	0	7	7	7–21

1 Chi—Edwards 9 pass from Hoernschemeyer (McCarthy kick)
2 Chi—Negus 63 fumble return (kick blocked)
  Chi—Clement 2 run (McCarthy kick)
  LA—Wilkins 57 pass from Taliaferro (Nelson kick)
3 LA—Grimes 7 run (Nelson kick)
4 LA—Dobbs 7 run (Nelson kick)
  Chi—FG McCarthy 31

Sunday, September 11, at Cleveland
Municipal Stadium. Attendance—21,621

The Browns used a powerful mix of rushing and passing to whitewash the Colts for their first victory of the season. Warren Lahr intercepted a Y. A. Tittle pass on the Baltimore 42-yard line and six plays later Edgar Jones scored. Bill Boedeker (7 carries for 62 yards) returned the opening kickoff of the second half to the Cleveland 38-yard line, and then ran 32 yards to set up Otto Graham's (14 of 30 for 234 yards) touchdown pass to Dante Lavelli (5 catches for 77 yards). On the Browns' next possession Graham hit four passes to set up Jones' second touchdown. In the first period the Colts' Jake Leicht returned a missed field goal 74 yards to the Browns' 26-yard line. Baltimore moved to Cleveland's 1-yard line, but could not get it over.

Baltimore Colts	0	0	0	0–0	
Cleveland Browns	7	0	14	0–21	

1 Cle—E. Jones 3 run (Saban kick)
3 Cle—Lavelli 24 pass from Graham (Saban kick)
   Cle—E. Jones 7 run (Saban kick)

Sunday, September 11, at Buffalo Civic Stadium. Attendance—30,410

Harvey Johnson's field goal with 1:10 left lifted the Yankees over the Bills. Buffalo scored on its first two possessions. George Ratterman (13 of 23 for 173 yards) completed three passes to set up Chet Mutryn's score, ending a 68-yard advance, and Ratterman followed that with a pitch to Al Baldwin for a 14–0 lead. Marty Ruby then stole a deflected Ratterman pass for New York's first touchdown. In a 76-yard drive, Don Panciera's (6 of 24 for 142 yards) 35-yard pass to Tom Landry helped set up Lowell Tew's (14 carries for 65 yards) touchdown run. The Yankees were stopped on Buffalo's 5, 7, 4, 14 and 1-yard lines without scoring as they took advantage of interceptions, blocked punts and fumbles.

New York Yankees	7	0	0	10–17	
Buffalo Bills	14	0	0	0–14	

1 Buff—Mutryn 19 run (Adams kick)
   Buff—Baldwin 23 pass from Ratterman (Adams kick)
   NY—Ruby 19 interception return (H. Johnson kick)
4 NY—Tew 8 run (H. Johnson kick)
   NY—FG H. Johnson 21

Week Four

Bye: Buffalo
Friday Night, September 16, at Chicago Soldier Field. Attendance—18,483

Five Hornets flew into the end zone as Chicago gained its third victory and handed the Colts their fourth loss. John Clement capped a 71-yard drive with a touchdown run and then ended an 88-yard march with a scoring toss to Paul Patterson. Bob Hoernschemeyer's (15 carries for 97 yards) 66-yard pass to Dan Edwards (4 catches for 130 yards) set up Ernie Lewis' touchdown, capping another 88-yard drive. Hoernschemeyer and Edwards hooked up again for Chicago's fourth touchdown. A fumble recovery set up Clement's touchdown pass to Lafayette King. Late in the second quarter Y. A. Tittle (15 of 25 for 233 yards) threw a scoring toss to Lamar Davis (8 catches for 166 yards). Chicago forced seven turnovers. The next day the Colts accepted the resignation of Coach Cecil Isbell.

Baltimore Colts	0	7	0	0–7	
Chicago Hornets	7	14	7	7–35	

1 Chi—Clement 11 run (McCarthy kick)
2 Chi—Patterson 48 pass from Clement (McCarthy kick)
   Chi—Lewis 4 run (McCarthy kick)
   Balt—Davis 37 pass from Tittle (Grossman kick)
3 Chi—Edwards 49 pass from Hoernschemeyer (McCarthy kick)
4 Chi—King 27 pass from Clement (McCarthy kick)

Sunday, September 18, at Cleveland Municipal Stadium. Attendance—26,312

Playing in intermittent heavy showers, the Browns used a staunch defense and two defensive scores to hand the Yankees yet another frustrating defeat. On their first possession New York went 60 yards to the Cleveland 12-yard line, only to have Bruce Alford drop a fourth-down pass in the end zone. On their next possession Buddy Young fumbled and Les Horvath picked up the ball and raced down the sideline for a touchdown. Barney Poole stole an Otto Graham pass to set up Harvey Johnson's field goal. In the final minute Tommy James intercepted Don Panciera for Cleveland's second score. The Yankees had nary a touchdown to show for 17 plays launched inside Cleveland's 20-yard line, while the Browns crossed midfield only once. New York's Bob Kennedy had 12 carries for 88 yards.

New York Yankees	3	0	0	0–3	
Cleveland Browns	7	0	0	7–14	

1 Cle—Horvath 84 fumble return (Saban kick)
   NY—FG H. Johnson 25
4 Cle—James 27 interception return (Saban kick)

Sunday, September 18, at San Francisco Kezar Stadium. Attendance—31,960

The 49ers exploded for six consecutive touchdowns to lay waste to the Dons in a sloppy game. Frankie Albert (4 of 12 for 164 yards) scored on a bootleg, Joe Perry (7 carries for 85 yards) burst through the middle for a score and Albert threw a bomb to Eddie Carr for a 21–7 halftime lead. Interceptions set up touchdown runs by Norm Standlee and Verl Lillywhite, and a fumble recovery led to Albert's touchdown pass to Alyn Beals. Interceptions produced both Los Angeles touchdowns, as Dick Woodward stole an Albert pass and Bob Kennedy's 33-yard return set up Glenn Dobbs' (15 of 36 for 159 yards) touchdown pass to Joe Aguirre early in the fourth quarter. Each squad committed six turnovers, and fans began leaving in the third quarter.

Los Angeles Dons	7	0	0	7–14	
San Francisco 49ers	0	21	21	0–42	

1 LA—Woodward 33 interception return (Nelson kick)
2 SF—Albert 7 run (Vetrano kick)
   SF—Perry 59 run (Vetrano kick)
   SF—Carr 75 pass from Albert (Vetrano kick)
3 SF—Standlee 23 run (Vetrano kick)
   SF—Lillywhite 24 run (Vetrano kick)
   SF—Beals 39 pass from Albert (Vetrano kick)
4 LA—Aguirre 7 pass from Dobbs (Nelson kick)

Week Five

Bye: Chicago
Thursday Night, September 22, at Bronx, NY
Yankee Stadium. Attendance—14,437

In the rain and mud, Harvey Johnson's field goal with 0:21 left gave the Yankees a hard-fought victory over the Dons. Midway in the first quarter Bud Tinsley recovered Don Panciera's fumble to set up Glenn Dobbs' touchdown pass to Earl Howell two plays later. Late in the third quarter New York's Sherman Howard (7 carries for 93 yards) raced 79 yards, being ruled out at the Los Angeles 1-yard line. Two plays later Eddie Prokop crashed over for the touchdown on the first play of the fourth quarter. Late in the second quarter the Dons blocked a punt and moved the ball to New York's 1-foot line, but time ran out. Dobbs set a league record with 11 punts, and Howard's 79-yard run was the longest non-scoring run in league history.

Los Angeles Dons	7	0	0	0–7
New York Yankees	0	0	0	10–10

1 LA—Howell 8 pass from Dobbs (Nelson kick)
4 NY—Prokop 1 run (H. Johnson kick)
   NY—FG H. Johnson 31

Sunday, September 25, at Baltimore
Babe Ruth Stadium. Attendance—34,879

Capitalizing on three miscues, the Browns erased a double-digit deficit for the second time this season to avoid a defeat. Y. A. Tittle (7 of 18 for 95 yards) capped an 85-yard drive with a touchdown pass to Windell Williams and Rex Grossman booted two field goals for a 13–0 Colt lead. A partially blocked punt set up Otto Graham's (9 of 24 for 104 yards) touchdown run. A deflected pass fell into the hands of Cleveland's Bill Willis, and Marion Motley scored on the next play. Tittle hit Bill Stone (3 catches for 75 yards) with a touchdown pass with six minutes left. With two minutes left the Colts tried a fourth-down pass from their 14-yard line, but it failed. Moments later Edgar Jones scored his second touchdown to ice the game. Baltimore's Lou Gambino had 11 carries for 83 yards.

Cleveland Browns	0	0	7	21–28
Baltimore Colts	0	13	0	7–20

2 Balt—Williams 6 pass from Tittle (Grossman kick)
   Balt—FG Grossman 33
   Balt—FG Grossman 39
3 Cle—E. Jones 16 run (Groza kick)
4 Cle—Graham 6 run (Groza kick)
   Cle—Motley 1 run (Groza kick)
   Balt—Stone 49 pass from Tittle (Grossman kick)
   Cle—E. Jones 3 run (Groza kick)

Sunday, September 25, at Buffalo
Civic Stadium. Attendance—32,097

George Ratterman's (15 of 20 for 224 yards) pinpoint passing led the Bills to their first victory of the season, toppling the previously unbeaten 49ers. Ratterman capped an 80-yard drive with a touchdown pass to Rex Bumgardner, and followed that with a touchdown pass to Al Baldwin (6 catches for 106 yards). Lou Tomasetti's touchdown plunge ended a 69-yard drive. The 49ers rallied on Frankie Albert's (9 of 22 for 97 yards) scoring toss to Joe Perry (8 carries for 70 yards) and Eddie Carr's fumble return off of Chet Mutryn (16 carries for 84 yards). The Bills then marched 78 yards to Ollie Cline's game-clinching touchdown. Buffalo outgained San Francisco 445–230 in total yards.

San Francisco 49ers	3	0	14	0–17
Buffalo Bills	7	7	7	7–28

1 SF—FG Vetrano 23
   Buff—Bumgardner 39 pass from Ratterman (Adams kick)
2 Buff—Baldwin 6 pass from Ratterman (Adams kick)
3 Buff—Tomasetti 1 run (Adams kick)
   SF—Perry 23 pass from Albert (Vetrano kick)
   SF—Carr 35 fumble return (Vetrano kick)
4 Buff—Cline 2 run (Adams kick)

Week Six

Bye: New York
Friday Night, September 30, at Chicago
Soldier Field. Attendance—31,561

Frankie Albert (7 of 18 for 98 yards) passed for three touchdowns and Joe Perry (11 carries for 142 yards) led a 357-yard rushing attack as the 49ers got back to their winning ways by whipping the Hornets. Albert threw two scoring passes to Alyn Beals (5 catches for 106 yards), and flipped a lateral to Jim Cason who tossed Beals his third touchdown reception. Perry ran 57 yards to set up Eddie Carr's touchdown and later scored for a 35–17 San Francisco lead. Chicago's Bob Hoernschemeyer (6 of 15 for 209 yards) threw two touchdown passes, including one to Ray Ramsey on the Hornets' first play from scrimmage. Paul Patterson had two receptions, both for touchdowns. San Francisco outgained Chicago 493–365 in total yards.

San Francisco 49ers	14	14	7	7–42
Chicago Hornets	10	7	0	7–24

1 SF—Beals 3 pass from Albert (Vetrano kick)
   Chi—Ramsey 77 pass from Hoernschemeyer (McCarthy kick)
   Chi—FG McCarthy 30
   SF—Carr 27 run (Vetrano kick)
2 SF—Beals 44 pass from Albert (Vetrano kick)
   Chi—Patterson 20 pass from Clement (McCarthy kick)
   SF—Beals 38 pass from Cason (Vetrano kick)

3 SF—Perry 4 run (Vetrano kick)
4 Chi—Patterson 68 pass from Hoernschemeyer (McCarthy kick)
   SF—Lillywhite 23 pass from Albert (Vetrano kick)

Sunday, October 2, at Cleveland
Municipal Stadium. Attendance—30,465

Otto Graham (17 of 28 for 279 yards) passed for two touchdowns and Marion Motley (17 carries for 139 yards) scored on two trap plays as the Browns ripped the Dons. Graham opened with a touchdown bomb to Bill Boedeker and Motley capped a 77-yard drive with his first touchdown. On the first play of the third quarter Lou Saban intercepted George Taliaferro's pass for Cleveland's third score, and later Motley added his second touchdown. Graham added a scoring toss to Mac Speedie (9 catches for 135 yards) and Ed Susteric registered the Browns' final tally. Keyed by Glenn Dobbs' 37-yard pass to Len Ford, the Dons went 84 yards to score, capped by John Brown's recovery of teammate Earl Howell's fumble in the end zone.

Los Angeles Dons	0	0	0	7–7
Cleveland Browns	0	14	14	14–42

2 Cle—Boedeker 74 pass from Graham (Groza kick)
   Cle—Motley 2 run (Groza kick)
3 Cle—Saban 25 interception return (Groza kick)
   Cle—Motley 33 run (Groza kick)
4 Cle—Speedie 3 pass from Graham (Groza kick)
   LA—Brown fumble recovery in end zone (Nelson kick)
   Cle—Susteric 39 run (Groza kick)

Sunday, October 2, at Buffalo
Civic Stadium. Attendance—25,692

Y. A. Tittle's (12 of 19 for 276 yards) touchdown pass to Bill Stone (3 catches for 93 yards) with 0:24 left capped a 73-yard drive and gave the Colts their first victory of the season. Baltimore built a 21–7 lead on two Bob Pfohl runs and Tittle's scoring toss to Lou Gambino, which was set up by Stone's 39-yard catch. Buffalo's George Ratterman (16 of 28 for 165 yards) capped 84 and 66-yard drives with touchdown plunges to tie the score. Tittle answered with a touchdown bomb to John North (4 catches for 119 yards). With two minutes left Ratterman countered with a touchdown pass to Al Baldwin, who caught the ball near the goal line and rolled into the end zone for the score. Buffalo's Ollie Cline had 18 carries for 91 yards.

Baltimore Colts	0	14	7	14–35
Buffalo Bills	7	0	7	14–28

1 Buff—Bumgardner 23 pass from Ratterman (Adams kick)
2 Balt—Pfohl 12 run (Grossman kick)
   Balt—Gambino 11 pass from Tittle (Grossman kick)
3 Balt—Pfohl 1 run (Grossman kick)
   Buff—Ratterman 1 run (Adams kick)
4 Buff—Ratterman 1 run (Adams kick)
   Balt—North 79 pass from Tittle (Grossman kick)
   Buff—Baldwin 34 pass from Ratterman (Adams kick)
   Balt—Stone 47 pass from Tittle (Grossman kick)

Week Seven
Bye: Baltimore
Friday Night, October 7, at Chicago
Soldier Field. Attendance–17,098

Buddy Young (12 carries for 123 yards) and Don Panciera (9 of 12 for 164 yards) swept on the ground and in the air to pace the Yankees past the Hornets. Young scored three touchdowns, the first one on the first play from scrimmage, and Panciera hit three passes to set up Young's second touchdown. Chicago's Bob Hoernschemeyer (13 of 20 for 155 yards) tried to keep pace with a touchdown pass to Ray Ramsey (5 catches for 92 yards) and a touchdown plunge. After Panciera's touchdown pass to Bob Kennedy, Ramsey and Dan Edwards combined on a kickoff return. In a 65-yard drive Panciera completed three passes for 54 yards to set up Eddie Prokop's touchdown. The Yankees outgained the Hornets 422–208 in total yards.

New York Yankees	10	7	14	7–38
Chicago Hornets	7	3	7	7–24

1 NY—Young 71 run (H. Johnson kick)
   Chi—Ramsey 51 pass from Hoernschemeyer (McCarthy kick)
   NY—FG H. Johnson 18
2 Chi—FG McCarthy 23
   NY—Young 5 run (H. Johnson kick)
3 NY—Young 19 run (H. Johnson kick)
   Chi—Hoernschemeyer 1 run (McCarthy kick)
   NY—Kennedy 22 pass from Panciera (H. Johnson kick)
4 Chi—Edwards 17 lateral from Ramsey after 81 kickoff return (McCarthy kick)
   NY—Prokop 11 run (H. Johnson kick)

Sunday, October 9, at San Francisco
Kezar Stadium. Attendance—59,720

With AAFC Commissioner O. O. Kessing in attendance, Frankie Albert (16 of 27 for 222 yards) set a league record with five touchdown passes as the 49ers snapped the Browns' 30-game unbeaten streak in a rough game. In a wild first half Albert threw touchdown passes to John Strzykalski, Joe Perry (16 carries for 155 yards), Alyn Beals (6 catches for 100 yards) and Nick Susoeff. Cleveland's Otto Graham (12 of 26 for 281 yards) countered with two scoring tosses to Mac Speedie (6 catches for 125 yards) and one to Dante Lavelli. Albert's record-setter was a payoff pitch to Eddie Carr. Marion Motley (13 carries for 80 yards) scored early in the fourth stanza, but touchdown runs by Perry and Carr put the game on ice. The 49ers outgained the Browns 507–367 in total yards. After the game fans tried to tear down the goal posts, but police restrained them.

Cleveland Browns	7	14	0	7	–28
San Francisco 49ers	21	14	7	14	–56

1 SF—Strzykalski 16 pass from Albert (Vetrano kick)
   SF—Strzykalski 1 run (Vetrano kick)
   SF—Perry 27 pass from Albert (Vetrano kick)
   Cle—Speedie 39 pass from Graham (Groza kick)
2 Cle—Lavelli 25 pass from Graham (Groza kick)
   SF—Beals 15 pass from Albert (Vetrano kick)
   Cle—Speedie 13 pass from Graham (Groza kick)
   SF—Susoeff 8 pass from Albert (Vetrano kick)
3 SF—Carr 24 pass from Albert (Vetrano kick)
4 Cle—Motley 12 run (Groza kick)
   SF—Perry 49 run (Vetrano kick)
   SF—Carr 5 run (Vetrano kick)

Sunday, October 9, at Los Angeles Memorial Coliseum. Attendance—16,575

Glenn Dobbs (18 of 27 for 283 yards) accounted for three touchdowns as the Dons upset the Bills in an air battle. The teams fought to a 21–21 halftime tie. Dobbs hit Billy Grimes for a touchdown, and then Grimes and Dobbs added scoring runs. Buffalo countered with touchdown runs by Ollie Cline (11 carries for 89 yards) and Chet Mutryn, and George Ratterman's (17 of 34 for 305 yards) touchdown pass to Al Baldwin (5 catches for 108 yards). The Bills took their final lead on Ratterman's touchdown pass to Jim Lukens (5 catches for 92 yards). The Dons answered with Dobbs' touchdown pass to Dick Wilkins (6 catches for 124 yards), Hosea Rodgers' scoring plunge and Abner Wimberly's fumble return midway through the fourth quarter. The Dons forced six turnovers.

Buffalo Bills	7	14	7	0	–28
Los Angeles Dons	0	21	14	7	–42

1 Buff—Cline 35 run (Adams kick)
2 LA—Grimes 12 pass from Dobbs (Nelson kick)
   Buff—Mutryn 4 run (Adams kick)
   LA—Grimes 12 run (Nelson kick)
   LA—Dobbs 3 run (Nelson kick)
   Buff—Baldwin 8 pass from Ratterman (Adams kick)
3 Buff—Lukens 10 pass from Ratterman (Adams kick)
   LA—Wilkins 32 pass from Dobbs (Nelson kick)
   LA—Rodgers 1 run (Nelson kick)
4 LA—Wimberly 30 fumble return (Nelson kick)

WEEK EIGHT

Bye: Chicago
Friday Night, October 14, at Los Angeles Memorial Coliseum. Attendance—27,427

Otto Graham (15 of 24 for 362 yards) set a league record with six touchdown passes as the Browns took out their frustration of the humiliating loss to San Francisco on the hapless Dons. Dub Jones and Mac Speedie (6 catches for 99 yards) each caught one from Graham, and Dante Lavelli (7 catches) set league records with four touchdown receptions and 209 receiving yards. Cliff Lewis replaced Graham and threw a touchdown pass to Speedie. Two fourth quarter touchdowns completed the slaughter. The Dons' Hosea Rodgers and George Taliaferro scored after drives of 67 and 70 yards. The Browns' rage was also reflected in the fact that they set league records with 16 penalties and 195 penalty yards.

Cleveland Browns	14	20	14	13	–61
Los Angeles Dons	7	0	0	7	–14

1 Cle—Lavelli 46 pass from Graham (Groza kick)
   LA—Rodgers 1 run (Nelson kick)
   Cle—D. Jones 42 pass from Graham (Groza kick)
2 Cle—Lavelli 31 pass from Graham (Groza kick)
   Cle—Lavelli 67 pass from Graham (Groza kick)
   Cle—Lavelli 2 pass from Graham (kick failed)
3 Cle—Speedie 12 pass from Graham (Groza kick)
   Cle—Speedie 27 pass from Lewis (Groza kick)
4 LA—Taliaferro 9 run (Nelson kick)
   Cle—Lahr 2 run (kick failed)
   Cle—Lewis 2 run (Groza kick)

Sunday, October 16, at San Francisco Kezar Stadium. Attendance—35,476

On a fog-blanketed field Frankie Albert (9 of 20 for 140 yards) passed for three touchdowns and Joe Perry (13 carries for 88 yards) tallied three touchdowns as the 49ers avenged their only loss of the season. Perry staked the 49ers to a 14–0 lead with a pair of runs. Buffalo's George Ratterman (21 of 36 for 167 yards) answered with a touchdown pass to Joe Sutton. Albert then pitched scoring tosses to Alyn Beals and Paul Salata, and a safety and Perry's third touchdown built a 37–7 halftime lead. In the second half Albert found Salata for another touchdown and Bev Wallace capped a 60-yard drive with a touchdown plunge. The victory was costly for the 49ers as halfback John Strzykalski was lost for season with a broken ankle in the first quarter.

Buffalo Bills	7	0	0	0	–7
San Francisco 49ers	14	23	7	7	–51

1 SF—Perry 14 run (Vetrano kick)
   SF—Perry 3 run (Vetrano kick)
   Buff—Sutton 21 pass from Ratterman (Adams kick)
2 SF—Beals 33 pass from Albert (Vetrano kick)
   SF—Salata 20 pass from Albert (Vetrano kick)
   SF—Safety, Wizbicki tackled in end zone
   SF—Perry 24 run (Vetrano kick)
3 SF—Salata 17 pass from Albert (Vetrano kick)
4 SF—Wallace 1 run (Vetrano kick)

Sunday, October 16, at Baltimore Babe Ruth Stadium. Attendance—32,645

The Yankees converted two second-half interceptions into touchdowns to shade the Colts in a see-saw battle. Baltimore struck late in the first quarter on Y. A. Tittle's (15 of 30 for 325 yards) touchdown pass to Bill Stone (4 catches for 98 yards). New York went 57 yards to Bob Kennedy's first touchdown, and then added a Harvey Johnson field goal. Tittle drove the Colts 60 yards, capped by his touchdown pass to John North (6 catches for 123 yards). Early in the third period Pete Layden stole a Tittle pass for a touchdown. The Colts then swept 77 yards to Stone's second touchdown. In the fourth quarter Ed Sharkey stole a Tittle pass at the Colt 3-yard line, and on fourth down Kennedy had the game-winning touchdown. Harmon Rowe intercepted Tittle late in the fourth quarter to ice game.

```
New York Yankees      0   10   7   7–24
Baltimore Colts       7    7   7   0–21
```

1 Balt—Stone 37 pass from Tittle (Vacanti kick)
2 NY—Kennedy 5 run (H. Johnson kick)
   NY—FG H. Johnson 34
   Balt—North 8 pass from Tittle (Vacanti kick)
3 NY—Layden 30 interception return (H. Johnson kick)
   Balt—Stone 7 run (Vacanti kick)
4 NY—Kennedy 3 run (H. Johnson kick)

WEEK NINE

Bye: Cleveland
Sunday, October 23, at Bronx, NY
Yankee Stadium. Attendance—38,187

Seven turnovers and two touchdowns by Buddy Young led the Yankees to an upset of the 49ers, who were held without a touchdown for the first time ever. Frankie Albert's (13 of 30 for 137 yards) passing bedeviled the Yankees in the first half, but a Joe Vetrano field goal was all they could show for their efforts. In the third quarter Ed Sharkey's fumble recovery set up Harvey Johnson's field goal, Jack Russell's interception set up Young's first score, and Young capped a 51-yard drive with his second touchdown. Late in the fourth period the 49ers lost the ball on downs, and Sherman Howard scored on a sweep with 0:41 left. An interception and a fumble recovery by Otto Schnellbacher sabotaged efforts of the 49ers, who failed to make a first down in the second half.

```
San Francisco 49ers   0   3    0   0–3
New York Yankees      0   0   17   7–24
```

2 SF—FG Vetrano 28
3 NY—FG H. Johnson 40
   NY—Young 20 run (H. Johnson kick)
   NY—Young 8 pass from Panciera (H. Johnson kick)
4 NY—Howard 10 run (H. Johnson kick)

Sunday, October 23, at Buffalo
Civic Stadium. Attendance—21,310

The Bills withstood a late rally to avenge an earlier loss to the Dons in a rough contest. Lou Tomasetti (19 carries for 118 yards) capped a 71-yard drive with a touchdown burst. Alex Wizbicki stole a Glenn Dobbs' pass to set up George Ratterman's touchdown pass to Al Baldwin. When the Dons' defense held at their 2-yard line, Chet Adams kicked a field goal. Paul Crowe picked up Vito Kissell's fumble for the first Los Angeles score, and early in the fourth quarter Billy Grimes' 26-yard pass to Dick Wilkins set up Hosea Rodgers' touchdown. Buffalo's Chet Mutryn had 13 carries for 107 yards. Players had to be separated on several occasions when fights threatened. Early in the second period the Bills were set back 15 yards for unnecessary roughness, and then another 15 yards for protesting the roughness call.

```
Los Angeles Dons      0   0   7   7–14
Buffalo Bills        14   3   0   0–17
```

1 Buff—Tomasetti 1 run (Adams kick)
   Buff—Baldwin 16 pass from Ratterman (Adams kick)
2 Buff—FG Adams 11
3 LA—Crowe 56 fumble return (Nelson kick)
4 LA—Rodgers 2 run (Nelson kick)

Sunday, October 23, at Baltimore
Babe Ruth Stadium. Attendance–23,107

In warm, sunny weather John Clement, a refugee from the NFL's Steelers, guided the Hornets to a pair of touchdowns to topple the butter-fingered Colts. Jim McCarthy opened the scoring with a long field goal. Clement completed a 59-yard pass to Albin Collins (4 catches for 112 yards) to set up George Buksar's touchdown plunge. Ray Ramsey then scooped up a Colt fumble and raced 43 yards to the Baltimore 34-yard line. From there Clement passed to Collins at the 3-yard line, and took it over on the next play. The Colts finally scored with six minutes left on Y. A. Tittle's quarterback sneak. The Hornets intercepted two passes and recovered five of Baltimore's six fumbles, with Bob Jensen falling on two of them.

```
Chicago Hornets       3   14   0   0–17
Baltimore Colts       0    0   0   7–7
```

1 Chi—FG McCarthy 42
2 Chi—Buksar 1 run (McCarthy kick)
   Chi—Clement 3 run (McCarthy kick)
4 Balt—Tittle 1 run (Grossman kick)

WEEK TEN

Bye: Buffalo
Friday Night, October 28, at Chicago
Soldier Field. Attendance—11,249

In a game featuring a dozen turnovers, George Taliaferro (12 of 24 for 215 yards) registered a pair of touchdowns as the Dons virtually ended the Hornets' hopes of reaching the playoffs. Midway through the first period Abner Wimberly intercepted a Bob Hoernschemeyer pass for the first Los Angeles touchdown.

Chicago's John Clement knotted the score with a touchdown plunge. Taliaferro's 36-yard pass to Len Ford (8 catches for 126 yards) set up his first touchdown run. In the fourth quarter Clement rallied the Hornets with a touchdown pass to Dan Edwards, but Taliaferro sprinted around left end for his second touchdown with 0:12 left. The Dons' Dick Wilkins added five catches for 100 yards, and each team committed six turnovers.

Los Angeles Dons	7	7	0	10–24
Chicago Hornets	7	0	0	7–14

1 LA—Wimberly 16 interception return (Nelson kick)
   Chi—Clement 1 run (McCarthy kick)
2 LA—Taliaferro 2 run (Nelson kick)
4 LA—FG Nelson 18
   Chi—Edwards 2 pass from Clement (McCarthy kick)
   LA—Taliaferro 10 run (Nelson kick)

Sunday, October 30, at Cleveland Municipal Stadium. Attendance—72,189

Otto Graham (14 of 25 for 271 yards) passed for two scores and ran for another as the Browns avenged their loss to the 49ers. The teams set a blistering pace in the second quarter, scoring four touchdowns within seven minutes. San Francisco's Frankie Albert (14 of 27 for 253 yards) threw a touchdown pass to Len Eshmont and completed a 72-yard pass to Sam Cathcart (11 carries for 116 yards; 5 catches for 88 yards) to set up Verl Lillywhite's score. Cleveland countered with Graham's scoring toss to Dante Lavelli and Dub Jones' touchdown, which ended an 80-yard drive. Graham's scoring run was answered by Albert's touchdown pass to Alyn Beals. The Browns took a 10-point lead on Graham's touchdown pass to Mac Speedie (6 catches for 99 yards), and Albert concluded the scoring with a quarterback sneak with 0:11 left. Neither team committed a turnover.

San Francisco 49ers	0	14	0	14–28
Cleveland Browns	0	14	7	9–30

2 SF—Eshmont 48 pass from Albert (Vetrano kick)
   Cle—Lavelli 9 pass from Graham (Groza kick)
   SF—Lillywhite 8 run (Vetrano kick)
   Cle—D. Jones 6 run (Groza kick)
3 Cle—Graham 20 run (Groza kick)
4 SF—Beals 22 pass from Albert (Vetrano kick)
   Cle—FG Groza 38
   Cle—Speedie 11 pass from Graham (kick failed)
   SF—Albert 1 run (Vetrano kick)

Sunday, October 30, at Bronx, NY Yankee Stadium. Attendance—10,692

On a dark and damp afternoon the Yankees forged a 3-touchdown lead and then held off a late scare by the Colts for their fifth consecutive victory. Late in the first period Sherman Howard (15 carries for 102 yards) broke through on a trap play to score, and Bob Kennedy (20 carries for 79 yards) scored after a 40-yard march. Don Panciera then hit Jack Russell with a touchdown pass. Baltimore's Y. A. Tittle (17 of 28 for 216 yards) capped a 92-yard drive with a touchdown pass to Bill Stone, and the Colts recovered Tom Landry's fumble to set up John North's touchdown. In the fourth quarter the Colts threatened constantly, while New York's Buddy Young had a 79-yard touchdown run nullified by an illegal motion penalty.

Baltimore Colts	0	0	14	0–14
New York Yankees	7	14	0	0–21

1 NY—Howard 52 run (H. Johnson kick)
2 NY—Kennedy 1 run (H. Johnson kick)
   NY—Russell 42 pass from Panciera (H. Johnson kick)
3 Balt—Stone 19 pass from Tittle (Grossman kick)
   Balt—North 12 pass from Tittle (Grossman kick)

Week Eleven

Bye: Los Angeles
Sunday, November 6, at Cleveland Municipal Stadium. Attendance—16,506

Marion Motley (14 carries for 118 yards) and Les Horvath each scored two touchdowns as the Browns trounced the Hornets and moved into first place in the league standings. Motley's 34-yard reception from Otto Graham (13 of 19 for 242 yards) set up Dub Jones' touchdown, and Horvath's first touchdown capped a 77-yard drive. After a shanked Hornet punt, Cliff Lewis ended the scoring with a touchdown pass to Horvath. The Hornets scored when Jim McCarthy blocked Horace Gillom's (6 catches for 93 yards) punt out of the end zone. Chicago's Bob Hoernschemeyer was 12 of 26 for 184 yards. Tempers flared up in the third quarter between Chicago's Nate Johnson and Cleveland's Lou Groza. They started slugging away and officials tossed them both out of the game.

Chicago Hornets	0	0	0	2–2
Cleveland Browns	7	7	7	14–35

1 Cle—D. Jones 4 run (Groza kick)
2 Cle—Horvath 2 run (Groza kick)
3 Cle—Motley 49 run (Groza kick)
4 Chi—Safety, punt blocked out of end zone
   Cle—Motley 3 run (Saban kick)
   Cle—Horvath 54 pass from Lewis (Saban kick)

Sunday, November 6, at Bronx, NY Yankee Stadium. Attendance—16,758

George Ratterman (15 of 26 for 190 yards) passed for two scores and completed a 43-yard pass to Chet Mutryn to set up Chet Adams' game-clinching field goal as the Bills rallied to tumble the Yankees out of a first place tie with the Browns. Buddy Young (7 carries for 86 yards) scored on the first play from scrimmage and less than three minutes later Don Panciera passed to Bruce Alford for a 14–0 New York lead. Ratterman's scoring toss to Al Baldwin (6 catches for 74 yards) came on the last play of the first quarter, and early in the fourth period Ratterman hit Rex Bumgardner for the game-tying touchdown. New York's Harvey Johnson missed field goal tries from 40, 30 and 36 yards, and the Yankees' poor passing was a key factor in the defeat.

| Buffalo Bills | 7 | 0 | 0 | 10–17 |
| New York Yankees | 14 | 0 | 0 | 0–14 |

1 NY—Young 57 run (H. Johnson kick)
  NY—Alford 28 pass from Panciera (H. Johnson kick)
  Buff—Baldwin 16 pass from Ratterman (Adams kick)
4 Buff—Bumgardner 45 pass from Ratterman (Adams kick)
  Buff—FG Adams 12

Sunday, November 6, at Baltimore
Babe Ruth Stadium. Attendance–23,704

Frankie Albert (9 of 19 for 120 yards) passed for two touchdowns as the 49ers rallied twice to avoid an embarrassing loss to the last place Colts. After Rex Grossman's field midway in the first quarter, Albert capped a 64-yard drive with a touchdown pass to Paul Salata. Early in the third quarter Baltimore's Bob Kelly intercepted a Tittle pass and returned it 20 yards to set up Y. A. Tittle's (13 of 26 for 109 yards) touchdown plunge. Sparked by Joe Perry's 37-yards run, Norm Standlee's touchdown ended a 79-yard drive, and Standlee's 35-yard run set up Sam Cathcart's (10 carries for 108 yards) touchdown run. Albert then concluded a 71-yard advance with a touchdown pass to Alyn Beals. The 49ers outgained the Colts 415–227 in total yards.

| San Francisco 49ers | 0 | 7 | 7 | 14–28 |
| Baltimore Colts | 3 | 0 | 7 | 0–10 |

1 Balt—FG Grossman 26
2 SF—Salata 10 pass from Albert (Vetrano kick)
3 Balt—Tittle 3 run (Grossman kick)
  SF—Standlee 9 run (Vetrano kick)
4 SF—Cathcart 1 run (Vetrano kick)
  SF—Beals 12 pass from Albert (Vetrano kick)

Week Twelve
Bye: Baltimore
Sunday, November 13, at Cleveland
Municipal Stadium. Attendance–22,511

For the second time this season the Bills battled the Browns to a tie. On Buffalo's first play from scrimmage, Cleveland's Tony Adamle stole a George Ratterman pass to set up Otto Graham's (11 of 26 for 176 yards) score on a sneak from the 1-inch line. Late in the first quarter Cleveland's Cliff Lewis signaled for a fair catch of a punt, and then fumbled. Buffalo's Odell Stautzenberger recovered at the Browns' 24-yard line. Chet Mutryn (17 carries for 87 yards) then scooted around right end for the touchdown early in the second period. The Browns then swept to Buffalo's 4-yard line, but Ed King fell on Dub Jones' fumble. Light rain in the first half turned into a downpour in the second, and players sloshed around the field the rest of the game. Cleveland's Lou Groza missed a 51-yard field goal try on the final play.

| Buffalo Bills | 0 | 7 | 0 | 0–7 |
| Cleveland Browns | 7 | 0 | 0 | 0–7 |

1 Cle—Graham 1 run (Groza kick)
2 Buff—Mutryn 4 run (Adams kick)

Sunday, November 13, at Los Angeles
Memorial Coliseum. Attendance—17,880

In 89-degree heat Frankie Albert (14 of 19 for 220 yards) passed for four touchdowns as the 49ers eventually wore down the Dons. Albert pitched two to Alyn Beals and one to Joe Perry, while Len Eshmont and Paul Salata collaborated on the fourth one as the 49ers built a 41–17 lead. Perry capped a 71-yard drive with his first touchdown, but it was Don Garlin's slant around left end midway through the third period that broke the Dons' sturdy backs and gave San Francisco a 28–17 lead entering the fourth quarter. Los Angeles was competitive in the first half, with Len Ford and Billy Grimes scoring touchdowns, and Bob Nelson booting a field goal as the halftime gun sounded. The Dons added a late touchdown as John Brown and Bob Reinhard orchestrated a fumble return.

| San Francisco 49ers | 7 | 14 | 7 | 13–41 |
| Los Angeles Dons | 0 | 17 | 0 | 7–24 |

1 SF—Perry 3 run (Vetrano kick)
2 LA—Ford 21 pass from Taliaferro (Nelson kick)
  SF—Beals 12 pass from Albert (Vetrano kick)
  LA—Grimes 7 run (Nelson kick)
  SF—Perry 58 pass from Albert (Vetrano kick)
  LA—FG Nelson 43
3 SF—Garlin 60 run (Vetrano kick)
4 SF—Beals 12 pass from Albert (pass failed)
  SF—Eshmont 30 lateral from Salata after 8 pass from Albert (Vetrano kick)
  LA—Brown 27 lateral from Reinhard after 44 fumble return (Nelson kick)

Sunday, November 13, at Bronx, NY
Yankee Stadium. Attendance—9,091

The mistake-prone Yankees hung up a pair of early touchdowns and then hung on to defeat Chicago to clinch a playoff berth. The Hornets were offside on the opening kickoff, so Buddy Young fielded George Buksar's second kickoff and raced for a touchdown. Young was knocked down on the New York 35-yard line, but the Hornets neglected to pin him, and Young got up and continued into the end zone. Midway in the first period Sherman Howard crashed over right guard for a touchdown. Chicago converted two fumbles into Jim McCarthy's field goal and John Clement's (12 of 24 for 165 yards) scoring toss to Ray Ramsey. In the fourth period the Hornets, who forced seven turnovers, were stopped at New York's 9 and 14-yard lines.

| Chicago Hornets | 0 | 10 | 0 | 0–10 |
| New York Yankees | 14 | 0 | 0 | 0–14 |

1 NY—Young 91 kickoff return (H. Johnson kick)
   NY—Howard 6 run (H. Johnson kick)
2 Chi—FG McCarthy 27
   Chi—Ramsey 28 pass from Clement (McCarthy kick)

Week Thirteen

Bye: San Francisco
Sunday, November 20, at Bronx, NY
Yankee Stadium. Attendance—50,711

Otto Graham completed 19 of 34 passes for 382 yards and Mac Speedie set league records with 11 receptions and 228 receiving yards as the Browns smothered the Yankees and clinched a first place finish. Graham capped a 75-yard drive with a scoring toss to Bill Boedeker, and George Young recovered Don Panciera's fumble to set up Dub Jones' first touchdown. Second-period touchdown plunges by Jones and Marion Motley turned the game into a rout. In the second half the Yankees were stopped three times at the Browns' 1-yard line, and Buddy Young (6 carries for 66 yards), their lone threat, left early in the third quarter with an injury. Cleveland's John Yonakor made a farce of the New York offense, time after time spilling ball carriers and knocking down would-be passers.

| Cleveland Browns | 17 | 14 | 0 | 0–31 |
| New York Yankees | 0 | 0 | 0 | 0–0 |

1 Cle—Boedeker 23 pass from Graham (Groza kick)
   Cle—D. Jones 1 run (Groza kick)
   Cle—FG Groza 30
2 Cle—D. Jones 1 run (Groza kick)
   Cle—Motley 2 run (Groza kick)

Sunday, November 20, at Buffalo
Civic Stadium. Attendance—18,494

On a field ankle-deep in mud, ex–Hornet Bob Livingstone hurdled two Chicago defenders, slithered past several others and scored on a spectacular punt return as the Bills grabbed fourth place in the league standings. Paul Gibson and Bob Oristaglio threw key blocks on the return, and the running of Chet Mutryn (15 carries for 85 yards) and Rex Bumgardner set up Chet Adams' game-clinching field goal. Bob Hoernschemeyer returned the ensuing kickoff 61 yards, but Jim McCarthy missed a 44-yard field goal attempt. In the first quarter Adams missed a 26-yard field goal try. In the second period Paul Patterson intercepted a George Ratterman pass and returned it 55 yards to the Bills' 8-yard line, but the Hornets were stuffed at Buffalo's 1-yard line.

| Chicago Hornets | 0 | 0 | 0 | 0–0 |
| Buffalo Bills | 0 | 7 | 0 | 3–10 |

2 Buff—Livingstone 79 punt return (Adams kick)
4 Buff—FG Adams 17

Sunday, November 20, at Baltimore
Babe Ruth Stadium. Attendance—19,503

George Taliaferro scored a pair of touchdowns to lead the Dons past the lowly Colts. A poor punt by the Colts' Herman Wedemeyer sailed out of bounds at the Baltimore 35-yard line. Four plays later Taliaferro went around right end for the tally. The Colts evened it up when Bill Stone scored on a pitch-out around his left end. A weird play covering 67 yards gave the Dons their second touchdown. Dick Wilkins took a pass from Billy Grimes, but fumbled. Teammate Taliaferro picked up the ball and high-tailed it to the end zone. Wilkins suffered a broken collar bone on the play. Taliaferro's 24-yard pass to Len Ford set up Hosea Rodgers' touchdown. Rex Grossman ended the scoring with the season's longest field goal. Baltimore's Y. A. Tittle was 15 of 29 for 180 yards.

| Los Angeles Dons | 14 | 7 | 0 | 0–21 |
| Baltimore Colts | 7 | 3 | 0 | 0–10 |

1 LA—Taliaferro 14 run (Nelson kick)
   Balt—Stone 33 run (Grossman kick)
   LA—Taliaferro 42 fumble return (Nelson kick)
2 LA—Rodgers 1 run (Nelson kick)
   Balt—FG Grossman 44

Week Fourteen

Thursday, November 24, at Chicago
Soldier Field. Attendance—5,031

Despite snow and a slippery field, the Browns scored two touchdowns within the first ten minutes to hand the Hornets their fifth consecutive loss. Chicago's Bob Hoernschemeyer (23 carries for 91 yards) had trouble with the opening kickoff and was tackled on the 1-yard line. On the next play he fumbled and Cleveland's Cliff Lewis recovered at the 6-yard line, and Bill Boedeker crashed over from there. Marion Motley capped a 63-yard drive with the second score. Early in the second quarter Hardy Brown recovered Warren Lahr's fumble that led to John Clement's touchdown plunge. Late in the game Chicago recovered a fumble and moved to Cleveland's 4-yard line. But Clement was sacked twice for big losses and the Browns took over at their 20-yard line.

| Cleveland Browns | 14 | 0 | 0 | 0–14 |
| Chicago Hornets | 0 | 6 | 0 | 0–6 |

1 Cle—Boedeker 6 run (Groza kick)
   Cle—Motley 6 run (Groza kick)
2 Chi—Clement 1 run (kick failed)

Thursday, November 24, at Los Angeles Memorial Coliseum. Attendance—20,096

In the final seconds Yankee linemen Van Davis and Jack Russell crashed through and blocked Bob Nelson's extra point attempt as New York eliminated Los Angeles from the playoff chase. The Dons struck first on George Taliaferro's (14 carries for 112 yards) touchdown sprint on an off-tackle play. Early in the fourth period Ed Sharkey fell on Billy Grimes fumble, and the Yankees drove 52 yards to Bob Kennedy's first score. Another Grimes fumble, recovered by Otto Schnellbacher, set up Harvey Johnson's field goal. After Nelson's field goal, Los Angeles attempted an onside kick. But New York recovered on the Dons' 47-yard line and laboriously drove to Kennedy's second touchdown. With 0:30 left, fans roared as Taliaferro fielded a punt and streaked to the end zone.

New York Yankees	0	0	0	17–17
Los Angeles Dons	7	0	0	9–16

1 LA—Taliaferro 44 run (Nelson kick)
4 NY—Kennedy 1 run (H. Johnson kick)
   NY—FG H. Johnson 16
   LA—FG Nelson 26
   NY—Kennedy 1 run (H. Johnson kick)
   LA—Taliaferro 52 punt return (kick blocked)

Sunday, November 27, at San Francisco Kezar Stadium. Attendance—44,828

On a fog-covered field Frankie Albert (16 of 28 for 238 yards) passed for two scores and the 49ers scored on two interceptions as San Francisco took second place and forced a playoff game with the Yankees. Albert pitched touchdown passes to Alyn Beals (8 catches for 100 yards) and Paul Salata, while Lowell Wagner and Bill Johnson stole Don Panciera passes for two more touchdowns. The Yankees tallied on Panciera's touchdown pass to Buddy Young, and early in the third quarter took their only lead when Jack Russell picked up Sam Cathcart's fumble and sped to the end zone. Late in the game Jim Cason intercepted a Gil Johnson pass to set up his touchdown run, capping a 61-yard drive. New York's Harvey Johnson missed field goals in the second and third periods, both from 35 yards out.

New York Yankees	7	0	7	0–14
San Francisco 49ers	7	0	21	7–35

1 SF—Wagner 66 interception return (Vetrano kick)
   NY—Young 20 pass from Panciera (H. Johnson kick)
3 NY—Russell 26 fumble return (H. Johnson kick)
   SF—Beals 23 pass from Albert (Vetrano kick)
   SF—W. Johnson 15 interception return (Vetrano kick)
   SF—Salata 49 pass from Albert (Vetrano kick)
4 SF—Cason 14 run (Vetrano kick)

Sunday, November 27, at Baltimore Babe Ruth Stadium. Attendance–16,323

George Ratterman (21 of 30 for 218 yards) threw three touchdown passes as the Bills routed the Colts in preparation for their playoff showdown with the Browns. Ratterman threw scoring tosses to Rex Bumgardner (9 carries for 74 yards), Jim Lukens and Lou Tomasetti as Buffalo rolled to a 24–7 lead. Touchdown runs by Chet Mutryn (13 carries for 70 yards; 5 catches for 59 yards) and Wilbur Volz bloated the lead to 38–7 early in the fourth quarter. Baltimore's Y. A. Tittle (12 of 25 for 235 yards) threw for a pair of touchdowns. The first went to John North (2 catches for 88 yards) for the longest of the season. The second was a desperation heave to Bill Stone (5 catches for 84 yards) in the final minutes. The Bills outgained the Colts 461–277 in total yards.

Buffalo Bills	7	10	14	7–38
Baltimore Colts	0	7	0	7–14

1 Buff—Bumgardner 29 pass from Ratterman (Adams kick)
2 Buff—FG Adams 20
   Balt—North 80 pass from Tittle (Grossman kick)
   Buff—Lukens 14 pass from Ratterman (Adams kick)
3 Buff—Tomasetti 9 pass from Ratterman (Adams kick)
   Buff—Mutryn 3 run (Adams kick)
4 Buff—Volz 1 run (Adams kick)
   Balt—Stone 52 pass from Tittle (Grossman kick)

AAFC Playoffs

Sunday, December 4, at Cleveland Municipal Stadium. Attendance—17,270

With the AAFC down to seven teams for 1949, the Eastern and Western Divisions were dispensed with in favor of a single, league-wide race. That also called for a new playoff format. In the first round, the first-place team played the fourth-place team while the teams finishing second and third squared off against each other.

The Browns had more trouble than expected from the Bills. Buffalo's George Ratterman (21 of 39 for 293 yards) had a hot hand and threw three touchdown passes, but ultimately Cleveland's Otto Graham (22 of 43 for 326 yards) won the day. Graham put the Browns in front in the opening quarter with a touchdown pass to Dante Lavelli (5 catches for 96 yards). Lou Groza widened the lead to ten with a field goal. The Bills came roaring back, Ratterman threw four yards to Lou Tomasetti for a touchdown in the second period and then added a scoring toss to Chet Mutryn (6 catches for 81 yards) to put the Bills in front at the half. Ratterman's third touchdown throw wasn't enough to keep up with the Jones.' First Edgar Jones plunged for one Browns' touchdown. Then Dub Jones put Cleveland in front to stay by catching a touchdown pass from Graham. In the final stanza Warren Lahr picked off a Ratterman pass for the wrap-up touchdown. Cleveland's Mac Speedie had seven catches for 113 yards.

Buffalo Bills	0	14	7	0–21
Cleveland Browns	10	0	14	7–31

1 Cle—Lavelli 51 pass from Graham (Groza kick)
  Cle—FG Groza 31
2 Buff—Tomasetti 4 pass from Ratterman (Adams kick)
  Buff—Mutryn 8 pass from Ratterman (Adams kick)
3 Cle—E. Jones 2 run (Groza kick)
  Buff—Mutryn 30 pass from Ratterman (Adams kick)
  Cle—D. Jones 49 pass from Graham (Groza kick)
4 Cle—Lahr 52 interception return (Groza kick)

Team Statistics	Cle	Buff
First Downs	15	19
Rushing Yards	72	80
Passing Yards	326	293
Passes	22–43–2	21–42–2
Fumbles Lost	0	1
Punts	4–41	2–40
Penalty Yards	58	20

Sunday, December 4, at San Francisco
Kezar Stadium. Attendance—41,393

The second-place 49ers and third-place Yankees struggled through a defensive battle with San Francisco—better known for their ability to score—coming out ahead of the visitors. The 49ers scored a touchdown in the opening quarter when halfback Verl Lillywhite broke through right tackle and ran 40 yards for the score. New York bounced back in the second quarter with a 64-yard drive to Sherman Howard's touchdown. A few minutes later San Francisco broke the deadlock on Joe Vetrano's 38-yard field goal. The only score of the second half was a Frankie Albert pass to Don Garlin. Albert kept the Yankees back on their heels all day, deftly mixing passes and runs. He and New York's Tom Landry put on a spectacular punting duel. Landry averaged 55 yards per kick, including one of 75 yards; Albert had two of 60 yards, including one that rolled out at the Yankee 1-yard line early in the second period.

New York Yankees	0	7	0	0–7
San Francisco 49ers	7	3	7	0–17

1 SF—Lillywhite 40 run (Vetrano kick)
2 NY—Howard 1 run (H. Johnson kick)
  SF—FG Vetrano 38
3 SF—Garlin 10 pass from Albert (Vetrano kick)

Team Statistics	SF	NY
First Downs	10	9
Rushing Yards	164	64
Passing Yards	96	116
Passes	8–17–2	7–25–2
Fumbles Lost	1	0
Punts	9–46.6	10–55
Penalty Yards	10	35

AAFC Championship
Sunday, December 11, at Cleveland
Municipal Stadium. Attendance—22,550

The fourth and final AAFC Championship game took place only a few days after word leaked out that a merger agreement had been reached with the NFL, one that would close the AAFC forever. That this was a lame duck championship dampened the crowd. The field was a mixture of mud and slush, but surprisingly neither team committed a turnover. Only one penalty was walked off all afternoon, a mere five yards against the Browns. Cleveland's Edgar Jones scored the only touchdown of the first half on a 2-yard plunge midway through the first quarter. Marion Motley, Cleveland's big fullback, scored the Browns' second touchdown on the game's most spectacular play in the third quarter. He burst up the middle on a trap play for 63 yards.

The 49ers responded with a 74-yard drive culminating in a Frankie Albert-to-Paul Salata touchdown toss. That allowed little Joe Vetrano to kick his 107th consecutive extra point and preserve his record of having scored in every San Francisco game since they began. With the score narrowed to 14–7, the Browns began a march of their own to clinch the victory. It ended successfully 69 yards later on Dub Jones' 4-yard smash for a touchdown. Lou Groza, who had kicked the first extra point in AAFC history on 9/6/1946 on this very field, kicked the final extra point to conclude the scoring.

San Francisco 49ers	0	0	0	7–7
Cleveland Browns	7	0	7	7–21

1 Cle—E. Jones 2 run (Groza kick)
3 Cle—Motley 63 run (Groza kick)
4 SF—Salata 23 pass from Albert (Vetrano kick)
  Cle—D. Jones 4 run (Groza kick)

Team Statistics	Cle	SF
First Downs	16	14
Rushing	11	7
Passing	5	7
Penalty	0	0
Total Yardage	345	230
Net Rushing Yardage	217	122
Net Passing Yardage	128	108
Passes att.-comp.-had int	17–7–0	25–9–0

Rushing

Cle—Motley 8 for 75, 1 TD; E. Jones 16 for 63, 1 TD; Graham 9 for 62; Lahr 1 for 7; James 2 for 7; D. Jones 4 for 2, 1 TD; Lewis 1 for 1

SF—Albert 8 for 41; Perry 6 for 36; Standlee 10 for 21; Garlin 3 for 13; Cathcart 9 for 11

Passing

Cle—Graham 7 of 17 for 128
SF—Albert 9 of 24 for 108, 1 TD; Lillywhite 0 of 1

Receiving

Cle—Lavelli 4 for 56; Speedie 1 for 37; D. Jones 1 for 25; E. Jones 1 for 10

SF—Salata 3 for 47, 1 TD; Beals 3 for 26; Shoener 2 for 25; Garlin 1 for 10

Shamrock Charity Bowl All-Star Game
Saturday, December 17, 1949
Rice Stadium. Attendance—12,000

In the final game for the AAFC, the AAFC All-Stars defeated the champion Cleveland Browns 12–7 in one of the first racially integrated sports events in Houston. The Shamrock Bowl was a charity event to benefit three charities: Hally Hall Home for the Aged, the Damon Runyon Cancer Fund and National Kids Day Foundation. The organizer, Glenn McCarthy, had tried to purchase an AAFC franchise before the league folded. This was the only all-star game in the Conference's history.

George Ratterman started the game at quarterback for the All-Stars, but was benched after the second offensive series. He was replaced by San Francisco quarterback Frankie Albert, who was able to provide the necessary spark for the offense. Toward the end of the first quarter, Buffalo halfback Chet Mutryn crossed the line for the first score. Early in the second quarter, the Browns took the lead when Dub Jones pulled in an Otto Graham pass for a 40-yard gain and the touchdown. Later in the quarter, Buffalo end Al Baldwin caught a pass from Albert and took it in for the final score of the game.

All-Stars	6	6	0	0–12
Cleveland Browns	0	7	0	0–7

AAFC—Mutryn 2 Run (Albert Missed Kick)
CLE—Dub Jones 40 Pass From Graham (Groza Kick)
AAFC—Baldwin 23 Pass From Albert (Albert Missed Kick)

Part 7: The Draft

History of the AAFC Draft *(by Kenneth R. Crippen)*

1947

The All-America Football Conference held their first draft from December 20 through December 21, 1946. The owners were in Cleveland, Ohio, in preparation for their first championship game: the Cleveland Browns versus the New York Yankees. However, before the draft, the Miami Seahawks were expelled from the Conference for failure to meet contractual obligations. A replacement franchise was not announced, but Baltimore was the leader. Potential owner Robert R. Rodenberg was in town to discuss a franchise with the owners. He had also obtained a lease to play at Municipal Stadium in Baltimore in 1947. On December 28, 1946, Rodenberg and four associates were awarded a franchise.

The draft was similar to the National Football League in that teams drafted in reverse order of their finish. The Buffalo Bisons and Brooklyn Dodgers finished with the same record, but Buffalo won the tie-breaker and drafted ahead of Brooklyn. However, one difference is that a pre-draft draft was held. It is not known why this draft was held, but each team had two selections (except for Buffalo, which had four). San Francisco and Los Angeles each traded a selection to Buffalo. The first 15 rounds were held normally. Then, a supplemental draft was held. Rounds 16 through 20 had selections from all teams except for the top two teams in the standings: Cleveland and New York. The remaining rounds did not include Cleveland, New York, San Francisco and Los Angeles, the top four teams in the standings.

Even though Miami was expelled, they were still able to draft players. Their picks were later given to the new Baltimore Colts franchise. Their first pick was future College and Pro Football Hall of Famer Charley Trippi, a fullback out of Georgia. That pick was immediately swapped with the New York Yankees for three signed players (the identity of those players was not immediately revealed). Trippi was also picked by the NFL's Chicago Cardinals the previous week. He eventually signed with Chicago and began his Hall of Fame career.

Of note in the draft—beyond Trippi—was the selection of Charlie Conerly in the second round by the Brooklyn Dodgers. Conerly, who was drafted by the NFL's Washington Redskins in 1945, spurned both clubs and signed with the New York Giants and started to play in the 1948 season. Conerly propelled the Giants to a 47–7 win over the Chicago Bears for the 1956 NFL Championship and was named to two Pro Bowls.

1948

The 1948 draft was held December 17, 1947, in New York. The draft increased to 30 rounds, but not all teams selected in each round. For example, the Baltimore Colts and Chicago Rockets were the only teams to select in the second round. However, the weaker teams received more picks in the earlier part of the draft. The Chicago Rockets, Brooklyn Dodgers and Baltimore Colts had five selections in the first five rounds, while the Cleveland Browns and New York Yankees each had two. This was an attempt by the Conference to equalize the teams.

An interesting sidenote to this draft was that teams were relatively silent on releasing the names of their draft picks. The Bills, 49ers, Browns and Los Angeles Dons all refused to announce their picks. Chicago and Baltimore only released the name of their first round picks (Tony Minisi and Bobby Layne, respectively). Brooklyn announced the drafting of Harry Gilmer (first round) and Dan Edwards (third round). Only the New York Yankees announced their entire draft after the conclusion of the meeting.

As mentioned previously, Bobby Layne was drafted in the first round by the Baltimore Colts. He was also drafted by the Chicago Bears. He played one season for the Bears, one season for the New York Bulldogs, then started his nine-year tenure with the Lions, before finishing with the Pittsburgh Steelers. Layne was inducted into the Pro Football Hall of Fame in 1967.

Tom Landry, the Pro Football Hall of Fame coach for the Dallas Cowboys was selected by the New York Yankees in the 19th round. Landry played one season for the Yankees and six for the New York Giants. During his time with the Giants, he started as an assistant coach, before eventually taking the head coaching position with Dallas in 1960.

The Los Angeles Dons selected two future Hall of Famers in Len Ford (third round) and Lou Creekmur (28th round). Only Ford played for the Dons as Creekmur did not start his professional career until 1950 and played his entire career with the Detroit Lions. Ford played two seasons with Los Angeles before continuing with Cleveland and finally Green Bay.

1949

The All-America Football Conference held two drafts in 1949. The first was a secret draft, held on July 8, 1948. The second was on December 21, 1948.

The secret draft was a two-round draft held before the start of the college football season. This was designed to give the AAFC a leg up on signing players over the rival NFL.

For the first time in Conference history, teams traded draft picks. In the secret draft, New York traded their first round pick to the Chicago Rockets, who selected Pete Elliott, a back out of Michigan. The Brooklyn Dodgers sent their second round pick to the New York Yankees, who then selected Lou Kusserow, back out of Columbia. In the third round of the regular draft, the Chicago Hornets traded their pick to Buffalo, who selected Hugh Keeney, a back out of Rice.

On December 20, 1948, the All-America Football Conference and the National Football League met to discuss ending the war between the leagues. Negotiations ended in a stalemate with neither side agreeing to terms. The following day, the leagues held independent drafts.

While the 1948 AAFC draft saw four future Hall of Famers drafted, 1949 had five. Chuck Bednarik, a lineman out of the University of Pennsylvania, was selected by both the Brooklyn Dodgers of the AAFC and the Philadelphia Eagles of the NFL. He chose to sign with the Eagles. Of the remaining four future Hall of Famers: George Blanda, Norm Van Brocklin, Art Donovan and Doak Walker, none played in the AAFC. Donovan and Walker did not start their playing careers until 1950. Blanda signed with the Chicago Bears and Brocklin with the Los Angeles Rams. Both played the 1949 season.

Allocation Draft

When the All-America Football Conference dissolved in 1950, the NFL put together a draft to assign players from the Buffalo Bills, Chicago Hornets and Los Angeles Dons. The draft order was determined by the order of finish in the 1949 season. Therefore, the draft order was: Baltimore, New York Yanks, Green Bay, Detroit, Washington, New York Giants, Pittsburgh, Chicago Cardinals (Tied with Pittsburgh), Chicago Bears, San Francisco 49ers (Tied with Chicago Bears), Los Angeles, Cleveland and Philadelphia. Since Baltimore and Green Bay were the weakest teams, they were given five extra draft picks each.

1947

			Special Draft	
No.	Player	Position	College	Drafted By
—	Ernie Case	B	UCLA	Baltimore Colts*
—	Arnold Tucker	QB	Army	Baltimore Colts*
—	Doc Blanchard	FB	Army	Brooklyn Dodgers
—	Gene Roberts	HB-FB	Kansas, Tennessee-Chattanooga	Brooklyn Dodgers
—	Frank Aschenbrenner	RB	Marquette, North Carolina, Northwestern	Buffalo Bills
—	Red Cochran	QB-FB-HB	Wake Forest	Buffalo Bills
—	Bob Fenimore	B	Oklahoma State	Buffalo Bills
—	Cal Richardson	E	Tulsa	Buffalo Bills
—	Bernie Gallagher	T	Pennsylvania	Chicago Rockets
—	Johnny Lujack	QB	Notre Dame	Chicago Rockets
—	Dick Hoemer	FB	Iowa	Cleveland Browns
—	Larry Rice	C	Tulane	Cleveland Browns
—	Herm Wedemeyer	B	St. Mary's (CA)	Los Angeles Dons
—	Charlie Trippi	HB-QB-DB	Georgia	New York Yankees
—	Buddy Young	HB-FB-DB	Illinois	New York Yankees
—	Glenn Davis	B	Army	San Francisco 49ers

Round 1

No.	Player	Position	College	Drafted By
1	Elmer Madar	E	Michigan	Baltimore Colts*
2	Al Baldwin	E-DB	Arkansas	Buffalo Bills
3	Neill Armstrong	E-DB	Oklahoma State	Brooklyn Dodgers
4	George Sullivan	E	Notre Dame	Chicago Rockets
5	Burr Baldwin	E-DE	UCLA	Los Angeles Dons
6	Clyde LeForce	QB	Tulsa	San Francisco 49ers
7	Ben Raimondi	TB	Indiana, William & Mary	New York Yankees
8	Bob Chappuis	TB-DB	Michigan	Cleveland Browns

Round 2

No.	Player	Position	College	Drafted By
9	Hub Bechtol	E	Texas	Baltimore Colts*
10	Bob T. Davis	T	Georgia Tech	Buffalo Bills
11	Charlie Conerly	QB	Mississippi	Brooklyn Dodgers
12	Ray Manieri	B	Wake Forest	Chicago Rockets
13	Jerry Shipkey	LB-FB-DB	UCLA, USC	Los Angeles Dons
14	Bob Weise	B	Michigan	San Francisco 49ers
15	Monte Moncrief	T	Texas A&M	New York Yankees
16	Gerry Cowhig	LB-FB-DB	Notre Dame	Cleveland Browns

Round 3

No.	Player	Position	College	Drafted By
17	Tommy Mont	B	Maryland	Baltimore Colts*
18	Ray Kuffel	E	Marquette, Notre Dame	Buffalo Bills
19	Fritz Barzilauskas	G	Holy Cross, Yale	Brooklyn Dodgers
20	Robert Derleth	T	Michigan	Chicago Rockets
21	Lloyd Merriman	B	Stanford	Los Angeles Dons
22	Paul Duke	C-LB	Georgia Tech	San Francisco 49ers
23	Bill Collins	G	Southwestern (TX), Texas	New York Yankees
24	Jack Carpenter	T	Columbia, Michigan, Missouri	Cleveland Browns

Round 4

No.	Player	Position	College	Drafted By
25	Weldon Humble	G	Rice	Baltimore Colts*
26	Joe Andrejco	B	Fordham	Buffalo Bills
27	Jim Wright	G	SMU, Texas-Arlington	Brooklyn Dodgers
28	Johnny Reagan	B	Montana	Chicago Rockets
29	Cal Rossi	B	UCLA	Los Angeles Dons
30	Don Samuel	DB-HB	Oregon State	San Francisco 49ers
31	Joe Tereshinski	DE-E-LB	Georgia	New York Yankees
32	Bob Cowan	B	Indiana	Cleveland Browns

Round 5

No.	Player	Position	College	Drafted By
33	Russ Deal	T	Indiana	Baltimore Colts*
34	John Mastrangelo	T-G	Notre Dame	Buffalo Bills
35	Harlan Wetz	T	Texas	Brooklyn Dodgers
36	Jim Pharr	C	Auburn	Chicago Rockets
37	Boyd Clement	T	Oregon State	Los Angeles Dons
38	Al Satterfield	T	Vanderbuilt	San Francisco 49ers
39	Jack Durishan	T-G	Pittsburgh	New York Yankees
40	Bill Griffin	T	Kentucky	Cleveland Browns

Round 6

No.	Player	Position	College	Drafted By
41	Don Malmberg	T	UCLA	Baltimore Colts*
42	Bert Corley	C	Mississippi State	Buffalo Bills
43	Binks Bushmiaer	B	Vanderbilt	Brooklyn Dodgers
44	Bob Sandberg	B	Minnesota	Chicago Rockets
45	Willie Zapalac	B	Texas A&M	Los Angeles Dons
46	Jack Zilly	DE-E	Notre Dame	San Francisco 49ers
47	Walt Dropo	E	Connecticut	New York Yankees
48	Jack Bush	T	Georgia	Cleveland Browns

Round 7

No.	Player	Position	College	Drafted By
49	Vic Schwall	B	Northwestern	Baltimore Colts*
50	Ernie Knotts	G	Duke	Buffalo Bills
51	Garland Williams	T	Duke, Georgia	Brooklyn Dodgers
52	Eddie Allen	FB-LB	Pennsylvania	Chicago Rockets
53	George Savitsky	T	Pennsylvania	Los Angeles Dons
54	Gene Knight	B	Louisiana State	San Francisco 49ers
55	Roland Nabors	LB-C	Texas Tech	New York Yankees
56	John Rapacz	C-LB	Oklahoma, Western Michigan	Cleveland Browns

Round 8

No.	Player	Position	College	Drafted By
57	Howie Turner	B	North Carolina State	Baltimore Colts*
58	Joe Watt	HB-DB	Syracuse	Buffalo Bills
59	Jim Hefti	B	St. Lawrence	Brooklyn Dodgers
60	Matt Bolger	E	Notre Dame	Chicago Rockets
61	Don Paul	LB-G-C	UCLA	Los Angeles Dons
62	Charley Malmberg	T	Rice	San Francisco 49ers
63	George Strohmeyer	C-LB	Notre Dame, Texas A&M	New York Yankees
64	Robert Hazelhurst	HB	Denver	Cleveland Browns

Round 9

No.	Player	Position	College	Drafted By
65	Frank Hubbell	E	Tennessee	Baltimore Colts*
66	Paul Gibson	E-QB-DB-DE	North Carolina State	Buffalo Bills
67	Buddy Burris	G-LB	Oklahoma, Tulsa	Brooklyn Dodgers
68	Charlie Eikenberg	QB	La-Lafayette, Rice	Chicago Rockets
69	Paul Hart	B	Delaware	Los Angeles Dons
70	Bob Leonetti	G	Wake Forest	San Francisco 49ers
71	Ted Ossowski	T	Oregon State, USC	New York Yankees
72	Ralph Ellsworth	B	Texas	Cleveland Browns

Round 10

No.	Player	Position	College	Drafted By
73	Gaston Bourgeois	G	Tulane	Baltimore Colts*
74	John Maskas	G-T	Virginia Tech	Buffalo Bills
75	Bill Milner	LB-G-DE	Duke, South Carolina	Brooklyn Dodgers
76	Ermal Allen	QB-DB	Kentucky	Chicago Rockets
77	Walt Heap	B	Texas	Los Angeles Dons
78	Frank Broyles	QB	Georgia Tech	San Francisco 49ers
79	Dick Werder	G	Georgetown	New York Yankees
80	Jim Dewar	B	Indiana	Cleveland Browns

Round 11

No.	Player	Position	College	Drafted By
81	Jim Brieske	C	Michigan	Baltimore Colts*
82	Baxter Jarrell	T	North Carolina	Buffalo Bills
83	Jim Smith	DB-HB-WB	Iowa, Tulsa	Brooklyn Dodgers
84	Marty Chaves	G	Oregon State	Chicago Rockets
85	Mike Dimitro	G	UCLA	Los Angeles Dons
86	Jim Tyree	E-DE	Oklahoma	San Francisco 49ers
87	Bill Healy	G	Georgia Tech	New York Yankees
88	Bill Huber	E	Illinois	Cleveland Browns

Round 12

No.	Player	Position	College	Drafted By
89	Rudy Mobley	B	Hardin-Simmons	Baltimore Colts*
90	Chet Lipka	T	Boston College	Buffalo Bills
91	Marv Goodman	E	Willamette	Brooklyn Dodgers
92	George Jernigan	G	Georgia	Chicago Rockets
93	Red Moore	G	Penn State	Los Angeles Dons
94	Ed Robnett	FB-LB	Texas A&M, Texas Tech	San Francisco 49ers
95	Ed Sikorski	B	Muhlenberg	New York Yankees
96	Mario Giannelli	G	Boston College	Cleveland Browns

Round 13

No.	Player	Position	College	Drafted By
97	Gerry Doherty	B	Delaware	Baltimore Colts*
98	Joe Sowinski	G	Indiana	Buffalo Bills
99	Ted Scruggs	E	Rice	Brooklyn Dodgers
100	R.J. Jordan	E	Georgia Tech	Chicago Rockets
101	Joe Martin	B	Cornell	Los Angeles Dons
102	Walt Slater	TB	Tennessee	San Francisco 49ers
103	Bill Miklich	LB-BB-C	Idaho	New York Yankees
104	Marshall Shurnas	E-DE	Missouri	Cleveland Browns

Round 14

No.	Player	Position	College	Drafted By
105	Bill Baumgartner	E	Minnesota	Baltimore Colts*
106	Bill Chipley	E-DB	Clemson, Washington & Lee	Buffalo Bills
107	Reed Nilsen	C	BYU	Brooklyn Dodgers
108	Bob Livingstone	HB-DB	Notre Dame	Chicago Rockets
109	Gene Wilson	E	SMU	Los Angeles Dons
110	Earl Wheeler	C	Arkansas	San Francisco 49ers
111	Charlie Elliott	T	Oregon	New York Yankees
112	Joe Signaigo	G	Notre Dame	Cleveland Browns

Round 15

No.	Player	Position	College	Drafted By
113	Jim Kekeris	T	Missouri	Baltimore Colts*
114	Bronco Kosanovich	C	Penn State	Buffalo Bills
115	Gus Shannon	G	Colorado	Brooklyn Dodgers
116	Bill Ivy	T	Northwestern	Chicago Rockets
117	Frank Muehlheuser	FB-LB	Colgate	Los Angeles Dons
118	Les Proctor	G	Texas	San Francisco 49ers
119	Ed Grain	G	Pennsylvania	New York Yankees
120	Dean Widseth	T	Bemidji State	Cleveland Browns

Round 16

No.	Player	Position	College	Drafted By
121	John North	E	Vanderbilt	Baltimore Colts*
122	Frank Kosikowski	DE	Marquette, Notre Dame	Buffalo Bills
123	Joe Cook	B	Hardin-Simmons	Brooklyn Dodgers
124	Bruno Miedziela	T	Iowa	Chicago Rockets
125	Ed Cody	FB	Boston College, Purdue	Los Angeles Dons
126	Al DeRogatis	DT-T	Duke	San Francisco 49ers

Round 17

No.	Player	Position	College	Drafted By
127	Jim Canady	B	Texas	Baltimore Colts*
128	Wash Serini	DG-G-T	Kentucky	Buffalo Bills
129	Francis Laurinaitis	LB	Richmond	Brooklyn Dodgers
130	Bill Mackrides	QB	Nevada-Reno	Chicago Rockets
131	Bob G. Sullivan	HB	Holy Cross, Iowa	Los Angeles Dons
132	Earl Tullos	T	Louisiana State	San Francisco 49ers

Round 18

No.	Player	Position	College	Drafted By
133	Howie Brown	G	Indiana	Baltimore Colts*
134	Vinnie Yablonski	FB-LB	Columbia, Fordham	Buffalo Bills
135	Ed Gustafson	C-LB	Dartmouth, George Washington	Brooklyn Dodgers
136	Mac Wenskunas	C	Illinois	Chicago Rockets
137	Lou Cullen	B	New Mexico	Los Angeles Dons
138	Bryant Meeks	C-LB	Georgia, South Carolina	San Francisco 49ers

Round 19

No.	Player	Position	College	Drafted By
139	Johnny Simms	B	Tulane	Baltimore Colts*
140	Chuck Compton	T	Alabama	Buffalo Bills
141	Dick Hagen	E	Washington	Brooklyn Dodgers
142	Tony Graham	C	St. Mary's	Chicago Rockets
143	John Killilea	B	Boston College	Los Angeles Dons
144	Ed Royston	G	Wake Forest	San Francisco 49ers

Round 20

No.	Player	Position	College	Drafted By
145	Burt VanderClute	G	Wesleyan	Baltimore Colts*
146	Bill Swiacki	E	Columbia, Holy Cross	Buffalo Bills
147	Hank Foldberg	E	Army, Texas A&M	Brooklyn Dodgers
148	Russ Benda	G	Iowa	Chicago Rockets
149	Plato Andros	G-T-DG	Oklahoma	Los Angeles Dons
150	Max Bumgardner	DE	Texas	San Francisco 49ers

Round 21

No.	Player	Position	College	Drafted By
151	Tony Stalloni	T	Delaware	Baltimore Colts*
152	Hamilton Nichols	G-LB	Rice	Buffalo Bills
153	Harry Furman	T	Cornell	Brooklyn Dodgers
154	George Watkins	T	Texas	Chicago Rockets

Round 22

No.	Player	Position	College	Drafted By
155	Jean Lamoure	G	Fresno State	Baltimore Colts*
156	John Furey	T	Boston College	Buffalo Bills
157	Walt Kretz	B	Cornell	Brooklyn Dodgers
158	Sam Vacanti	QB	Iowa, Nebraska, Purdue	Chicago Rockets

Round 23

No.	Player	Position	College	Drafted By
159	Leo Daniels	B	Texas A&M	Baltimore Colts*
160	Don Schneider	HB	Pennsylvania	Buffalo Bills
161	John Monahan	E	Dartmouth	Brooklyn Dodgers
162	Len Zenkevitch	T	Idaho	Chicago Rockets

Round 24

No.	Player	Position	College	Drafted By
163	Tex Reilly	B	Colorado	Baltimore Colts*
164	Chan Highsmith	C	North Carolina	Buffalo Bills
165	Bruce Bailey	B	Virginia	Brooklyn Dodgers
166	Dave Day	G	Iowa	Chicago Rockets

Round 25

No.	Player	Position	College	Drafted By
167	Jim Landrigan	T	Dartmouth	Baltimore Colts*
168	Frank Wydo	T-DT	Cornell, Duquesne	Buffalo Bills
169	Ray L. Evans	G-T	Texas-El Paso	Brooklyn Dodgers
170	Bill Franks	T	Illinois	Chicago Rockets

*Selections were made by the Miami Seahawks and given to the Baltimore Colts when their franchise was awarded.

1948

Round 1

No.	Player	Position	College	Drafted By
1	Tony Manisi	HB	Pennsylvania	Chicago Rockets
2	Bobby Layne	QB	Texas	Baltimore Colts
3	Harry Gilmer	QB-HB	Alabama	Brooklyn Dodgers
4	Vaughan Mancha	C-LB	Alabama	Los Angeles Dons
5	Joe Scott	HB-DB-E	San Francisco, Texas A&M	San Francisco 49ers
6	Clyde Scott	B	Arkansas	Buffalo Bills
7	Lowell Tew	FB	Alabama	New York Yankees
8	Jeff Durkota	HB	Penn State	Cleveland Browns

Round 2

No.	Player	Position	College	Drafted By
9	Carl Samuelson	DT-T	Nebraska	Chicago Rockets
10	Dub Garrett	G-DT	Mississippi State	Baltimore Colts

Round 3

No.	Player	Position	College	Drafted By
11	John Nolan	T	Holy Cross, Penn State	Chicago Rockets
12	Earl Cooke	G	Southern Methodist	Baltimore Colts
13	Dan Edwards	E	Georgia	Brooklyn Dodgers
14	Len Ford	DE-E	Michigan, Morgan State	Los Angeles Dons
15	Jim Cason	DB-HB	LSU	San Francisco 49ers
16	Bill Gompers	HB	Notre Dame	Buffalo Bills
17	Otto Schnellbacher	DB-E	Kansas	New York Yankees
18	Ollie Cline	FB	Ohio State	Cleveland Browns

Round 4

No.	Player	Position	College	Drafted By
19	Paul Cleary	E-DE	USC	Chicago Rockets
20	Dan Sandifer	DB-HB	LSU	Baltimore Colts
21	Joe Spencer	T-DT	Oklahoma State	Brooklyn Dodgers
22	John Novitsky	T	Oklahoma City	Los Angeles Dons
23	Walter McCormick*	C-LB	USC, Washington	San Francisco 49ers
24	Zeke O'Connor	E-DE	Notre Dame	Buffalo Bills

Round 5

No.	Player	Position	College	Drafted By
25	William H. (John) Walsh*	C	Notre Dame	Chicago Rockets
26	Joe Smith	E-DB	Schreiner College, Texas Tech	Baltimore Colts
27	Les Bingaman	DG-G	Illinois	Brooklyn Dodgers

Round 6

No.	Player	Position	College	Drafted By
28	Vince DiFrancisca	G	Northwestern	Chicago Rockets
29	Gene Raczkowski	T	Ohio University	Baltimore Colts
30	William J. (Jim) Smith	E	Mississippi Southern	Brooklyn Dodgers
31	Lin Sexton	HB-DB	Wichita State	Los Angeles Dons
32	Fred Land	T-G	LSU	San Francisco 49ers
33	Martin Wendell	G	Notre Dame	Buffalo Bills

Round 7

No.	Player	Position	College	Drafted By
34	John Rhodemeyer	C-LB	Kentucky	Chicago Rockets
35	Jim Batchelor	HB	East Texas State	Baltimore Colts
36	Homer Paine	T	Oklahoma, Tulsa	Brooklyn Dodgers
37	Weldon Edwards	T	TCU, Texas–Arlington	Los Angeles Dons
38	Phil O'Reilly	T	Purdue	San Francisco 49ers
39	Robert Brugge	Halfback	Ohio State	Buffalo
40	Pete Stout	FB-LB	TCU, Texas–Arlington	New York Yankees
41	Tommy W. Thompson	LB-C	William & Mary	Cleveland Browns

154 Part 7: The Draft

Round 8

No.	Player	Position	College	Drafted By
42	Jim Turner	T	California	Chicago Rockets
43	Rex Olson	HB	Brigham Young	Baltimore Colts
44	Bruce Gehrke	E	Columbia	Brooklyn Dodgers
45	Jim Spavital	FB-LB	Oklahoma State	Los Angeles Dons

Round 9

No.	Player	Position	College	Drafted By
46	Myron Miller	C	Oklahoma A&M	Chicago Rockets
47	Aubrey Fowler	HB	Arkansas, Arkansas Tech	Baltimore Colts
48	Jim Minor	T	Arkansas	Brooklyn Dodgers
49	Knox Ramsey	G	William & Mary	Los Angeles Dons
50	William Luongo	FB	Pennsylvania	San Francisco 49ers
51	Louis King	HB	Iowa	Buffalo Bills
52	Barney Poole	DE-E	Army, Mississippi, North Carolina	New York Yankees
53	Bill Smith	T	North Carolina	Cleveland Browns

Round 10

No.	Player	Position	College	Drafted By
54	Phil Schlosburg	HB	Temple	Chicago Rockets
55	Jack Fitch	B	North Carolina	Baltimore Colts
56	Herb St. John	G	Georgia	Brooklyn Dodgers
57	Malechi Mills	G	VMI	Los Angeles Dons

Round 11

No.	Player	Position	College	Drafted By
58	Jack Swaner	B	California	Chicago Rockets
59	Don Ettinger	LB-G	Kansas	Baltimore Colts
60	Charles Borey Newman	E	Louisiana Tech	Brooklyn Dodgers
61	Lou Mihailovich	DE	Indiana	Los Angeles Dons
62	Robert Steckroth	E	William & Mary	San Francisco 49ers
63	John Finney	HB	Compton Jr. College	Buffalo Bills
64	Jack Weisenberger	B	Michigan	New York Yankees
65	Ralph Maughan	C	Utah State	Cleveland Browns

Round 12

No.	Player	Position	College	Drafted By
66	Thurman Gay	T	Oklahoma A&M	Chicago Rockets
67	Paul Redfield	T	Colgate	Baltimore Colts
68	Jim Camp	QB	North Carolina, Randolph-Macon	Brooklyn Dodgers
69	Harper Davis	DB	Mississippi State	Los Angeles Dons
70	Gene Malinowski	B	Detroit Mercy, Georgia	San Francisco 49ers
71	Richard Johnson	G	Baylor	Buffalo Bills
72	Bob Hendren	T-DT-DE	Culver-Stockton, USC	New York Yankees
73	Dean Sensanbaugher	HB-DB	Army, Ohio State	Cleveland Browns

Round 13

No.	Player	Position	College	Drafted By
74	Francis Parker*	T	Holy Cross	Chicago Rockets
75	Stan Madgziak	B	William & Mary	Baltimore Colts
76	Bob Koch	B	Oregon	Brooklyn Dodgers
77	Mike Graham	B	Cincinnati	Los Angeles Dons
78	Leonard Modzelski	T	Scranton Univ.	San Francisco 49ers
79	George Grimes	DB-WB	North Carolina, Virginia	Buffalo Bills
80	Dick Ottele	BB-DB	Washington	New York Yankees
81	Mike Rubish	E	North Carolina	Cleveland Browns

Round 14

No.	Player	Position	College	Drafted By
82	Lou Agase	T	Illinois	Chicago Rockets
83	Dick Deranek	B	Indiana	Baltimore Colts
84	John White	C	Michigan	Brooklyn Dodgers
85	Bernie Winkler	T	Millsaps, Texas Tech	Los Angeles Dons
86	Les Rideout	T	Bowling Green	San Francisco 49ers
87	Larry Joe	B	Penn State	Buffalo Bills
88	Dick McKissack*	DB	SMU	New York Yankees
89	Alex Sarkesian	C	Northwestern	Cleveland Browns

Round 15

No.	Player	Position	College	Drafted By
90	J.F. McCarthy	E	Pennsylvania	Chicago Rockets
91	Robert Norman	B	Washington & Lee	Baltimore Colts
92	Robert Terry*	T	Texas A&M	Brooklyn Dodgers
93	Bill Erickson	G	Mississippi, North Carolina	Los Angeles Dons
94	Larry Olsonoski*	G	Minnesota	San Francisco 49ers
95	Frank Ballard	G	V.P.I.	Buffalo Bills
96	Joe Magliolo	LB	Texas	New York Yankees
97	Dan Dworsky*	FB	Michigan	Cleveland Browns

Round 16

No.	Player	Position	College	Drafted By
98	Rudy Krall	B	New Mexico	Chicago Rockets
99	Charles (Dick) Working	B	Washington & Lee	Baltimore Colts
100	John Wozniak	G-LB	Alabama	Brooklyn Dodgers
101	Shorty McWilliams	DB-HB	Army, Mississippi State	Los Angeles Dons
102	Wallace Matulich	B	Mississippi State	San Francisco 49ers
103	James H. Walthall	HB	West Virginia	Buffalo Bills
104	Bob Ramsey	B	S.M.U.	New York Yankees
105	Scott Beasley	E	Nevada	Cleveland Browns

Round 17

No.	Player	Position	College	Drafted By
106	Dick Flanagan	LB-G-C	Ohio State	Chicago Rockets
107	George Sparter	C	North Carolina	Baltimore Colts
108	Bob Jensen	DE-E	Iowa State	Brooklyn Dodgers
109	Bob Levenhagen	G	Washington	Los Angeles Dons
110	Bob Ravensberg	E	Indiana	San Francisco 49ers
111	Ray Coates	HB-DB	LSU	Buffalo Bills
112	Charles Wright	E	Texas A&M	New York Yankees
113	Russ Steger	FB	Illinois	Cleveland Browns

Round 18

No.	Player	Position	College	Drafted By
114	Ed Ryan	E-DE	British Columbia, St. Mary's (CA)	Chicago Rockets
115	Rollin W. Prather*	E	Kansas State	Baltimore Colts
116	Joseph E. Jurich	E	West Chester State	Brooklyn Dodgers
117	Wayman Sellers	E	Georgia	Los Angeles Dons
118	William Pritula	T	Michigan	San Francisco 49ers
119	Dud Waybright	E	Notre Dame	Buffalo Bills
120	Marion Shirley	T	Oklahoma City, Oklahoma State	New York Yankees
121	Lou Hoistma	E	William & Mary	Cleveland Browns

Round 19

No.	Player	Position	College	Drafted By
122	Byron Gillory*	B	Texas	Chicago Rockets
123	Norm Mosley	TB	Alabama	Baltimore Colts
124	Bill Cromer	B	North Texas State	Brooklyn Dodgers
125	Ab Wimberly	DE-E	LSU	Los Angeles Dons
126	Art Fitzgerald	B	Yale	San Francisco 49ers
127	Wade Walker	T	Oklahoma	Buffalo Bills
128	Tom Landry	DB-HB-QB	Texas	New York Yankees
129	Pete Ashbaugh	B	Notre Dame	Cleveland Browns

Round 20

No.	Player	Position	College	Drafted By
130	Don Doll	DB	USC	Chicago Rockets
131	Carmen Ragonese	B	New Hampshire	Baltimore Colts
132	Richard U. Scott	C	Navy	Brooklyn Dodgers
133	Frank Ziegler	HB-DB	Georgia Tech	Los Angeles Dons
134	Pete Barbolak	T	Purdue	San Francisco 49ers
135	Roger Stephens	HB	Cincinnati	Buffalo Bills
136	Bobby Forbes	B	Florida	New York Yankees
137	Dave Templeton	G	Ohio State	Cleveland Browns

Round 21

No.	Player	Position	College	Drafted By
138	Fred Provo	HB	Washington	Chicago Rockets
139	Bob Walker	B	Colorado Mines	Baltimore Colts
140	Walt Marusa	G	Delaware	Brooklyn Dodgers
141	Ed Smith	HB-DB	Texas-El Paso	Los Angeles Dons
142	Dick Loepfe	T	Wisconsin	San Francisco 49ers
143	Howard Duncan	C	Ohio State	Buffalo Bills
144	Carl Russ	B	Rice	New York Yankees
145	Dwight Eddleman	HB	Illinois	Cleveland Browns

Round 22

No.	Player	Position	College	Drafted By
146	Phil Tinsley	E	UCLA	Chicago Rockets
147	Ray Borneman	B	Texas	Baltimore Colts
148	Knute Dobkins	E	Butler	Brooklyn Dodgers
149	Paul Mortelello	G	Florida	Los Angeles Dons
150	Bob Heck	DE-E	Purdue	San Francisco 49ers
151	Ralph Sazio	T	William & Mary	Buffalo Bills
152	Fred Enke*	QB	Arizona	New York Yankees
153	Lu Gambino	FB	Indiana, Maryland	Cleveland Browns

Round 23

No.	Player	Position	College	Drafted By
154	Glen Treichler	B	Colgate	Chicago Rockets
155	Pete Tillman	C-LB	Oklahoma, Southwest Oklahoma State	Baltimore Colts
156	Frederick Westphal	E	Cornell	Brooklyn Dodgers
157	Ted Kenfield	B	California	Los Angeles Dons
158	Floyd Lanhorne	G	Texas Tech	San Francisco 49ers
159	George Bloomquist	E	North Carolina State	Buffalo Bills
160	John Cunningham	E	California	New York Yankees
161	Jim McDowell	G	William & Mary	Cleveland Browns

Round 24

No.	Player	Position	College	Drafted By
162	Ike Owens	DE	Illinois	Chicago Rockets
163	Bob Pfohl	B	Kings Point, Purdue	Baltimore Colts
164	Merle Dinkins	E	Oklahoma	Brooklyn Dodgers
165	Buddy Mulligan	HB	Duke	Los Angeles Dons
166	Goble W. Bryant	T	West Point	San Francisco 49ers
167	J.D. Cheek	T	Oklahoma A&M	Buffalo Bills
168	Nick Ognovich	B	Wake Forest	New York Yankees
169	Heywood Fowle	T	North Carolina	Cleveland Browns

Round 25

No.	Player	Position	College	Drafted By
170	Ron Sockalov	T	California	Chicago Rockets
171	Lou Levanti	C-LB	Illinois	Baltimore Colts
172	Walt Pupa	FB	North Carolina	Brooklyn Dodgers
173	George Lambert	T	Mississippi	Los Angeles Dons
174	Bill Talarico	FB	Pennsylvania	San Francisco 49ers
175	Robert Rennebohm	E	Wisconsin	Buffalo Bills
176	Mike Zelezanak	B	Kansas State	New York Yankees
177	Ara Parseghian	HB	Akron, Miami (OH)	Cleveland Browns

Round 26

No.	Player	Position	College	Drafted By
178	Earl Eugene Corum	G	West Virginia	Chicago Rockets
179	Sam Zatkoff*	E	Illinois	Baltimore Colts
180	Ray Richeson	G	Alabama	Brooklyn Dodgers
181	Jim Still	B	Georgia Tech	Los Angeles Dons
182	Everett Marshall	T	Pennsylvania	San Francisco 49ers
183	Ted Andrus	G	SW Louisiana	Buffalo Bills
184	John Panelli*	HB	Notre Dame	New York Yankees
185	Horace (Todd) Saylor	E	Lafayette	Cleveland Browns

Round 27

No.	Player	Position	College	Drafted By
186	John Daniels	C	Santa Barbara	Chicago Rockets
187	Chick Jagade	FB	Indiana	Baltimore Colts
188	Ott Hurrle	C	Butler	Brooklyn Dodgers
189	Charles Tatom	G	Texas	Los Angeles Dons
190	Perry Moss	QB	Illinois, Tulsa	San Francisco 49ers
191	Ray Brown	HB	Virginia	Buffalo Bills
192	Jug Girard	E-HB-QB-DB	Wisconsin	New York Yankees
193	Harry W. Caughron	T	William & Mary	Cleveland Browns

Round 28

No.	Player	Position	College	Drafted By
194	Al Hoisch	B	UCLA	Chicago Rockets
195	Ben Bendrick*	B	Wisconsin	Baltimore Colts
196	Warren Lowans	T	West Chester	Brooklyn Dodgers
197	Lou Creekmur	T-G-DG-DT	William & Mary	Los Angeles Dons
198	Harold William Bell	QB	Muhlenberg	San Francisco 49ers
199	Lou Corriere	HB	Buffalo	Buffalo Bills
200	Rip Collins*	B	LSU	New York Yankees
201	Pete Lanzi	E	Youngstown State	Cleveland Browns

Round 29

No.	Player	Position	College	Drafted By
202	Dick Wedel	G	Wake Forest	Chicago Rockets
203	Rex Grossman	LB-FB	Indiana	Baltimore Colts
204	Art Littleton	E	Pennsylvania	Brooklyn Dodgers
205	Leon McLaughlin	C	UCLA	Los Angeles Dons
206	Herb Siegert	G-LB	Illinois	San Francisco 49ers
207	John Wosloski	C	Penn State	Buffalo Bills
208	Frank Nelson	B	Utah	New York Yankees
209	George Roman	T	Case Western Reserve	Cleveland Browns

Round 30

No.	Player	Position	College	Drafted By
210	Thomas N. Finical	E	Princeton	Chicago Rockets
211	Dick Reinking	E	SMU	Baltimore Colts
212	Clarence McGeary	DT	Minnesota, North Dakota State	Brooklyn Dodgers
213	A.B. Kitchens*	T	Tulsa	Los Angeles Dons
214	Frank Williams	FB-LB	Utah State	San Francisco 49ers
215	Talley Stevens*	E	Utah State	Buffalo Bills
216	Bill Clements	E	UCAL	New York Yankees
217	Mel Sheehan	E	Missouri	Cleveland Browns

Signed a player contract before the draft
**Declared ineligible*

1949

Secret Draft

Baltimore Colts

No.	Player	Pos	College	Drafted By
1	Dick Harris	C	Texas	Baltimore Colts
2	Levi Jackson*	B	Yale	Baltimore Colts

Brooklyn Dodgers

No.	Player	Pos	College	Drafted By
1	Chuck Bednarik	C	Pennsylvania	Brooklyn Dodgers
2	*Choice to the New York Yankees*			

Buffalo Bills

No.	Player	Pos	College	Drafted By
1	Abe Gibron	G	Purdue	Buffalo Bills
2	Frank Tripucka	QB	Notre Dame	Buffalo Bills

Chicago Rockets

No.	Player	Pos	College	Drafted By
1	Terry Brennan	B	Notre Dame	Chicago Rockets
1	Pete Elliott	B	Michigan	*From N.Y. Yankees*
2	Bill Fischer	G	Notre Dame	Chicago Rockets

Cleveland Browns

No.	Player	Pos	College	Drafted By
1	Gene Derricotte	B	Michigan	Cleveland Browns
2	Dick Kempthorn	B	Michigan	Cleveland Browns

Los Angeles Dons

No.	Player	Pos	College	Drafted By
1	Dan Dworsky	C	Michigan	Los Angeles Dons
2	Jack Price	B	Baylor	Los Angeles Dons

New York Yankees

No.	Player	Pos	College	Drafted By
1	*Choice to Chicago Rockets*			
2	Lou Kusserow	B	Columbia	*From Brooklyn Dodgers*
2	Johnny Rauch	QB	Georgia	New York Yankees

San Francisco 49ers

No.	Player	Pos	College	Drafted By
1	Ernie Stautner*	T	Bsoton College	San Francisco 49ers
2	Jim Winkler	T	Texas A&M	San Francisco 49ers

*Assigned to Cleveland / **Declared ineligible*

Draft

Round 1

No.	Player	Position	College	Drafted By
1	Stan Heath	QB	Nevada-Reno	Chicago Hornets
2	Joe Sullivan	B	Dartmouth	Brooklyn Dodgers
3	Bobby Thomason	QB	Virginia Military	New York Yankees
4	George Sims	B	Baylor	Baltimore Colts
5	George Taliaferro	B	Indiana	Los Angeles Dons
6	Bill Kay	T	Iowa	Buffalo Bills
7	Chester Fritz	T	Missouri	San Francisco 49ers
8	Jack Mitchell	QB	Oklahoma	Cleveland Browns

Round 2

No.	Player	Position	College	Drafted By
9	George Blanda	QB	Kentucky	Chicago Hornets
10	Len Szafaryn	T	North Carolina	Brooklyn Dodgers
11	Bill Walsh	C	Notre Dame	Brooklyn Dodgers
12	Lou Ferry	T	Villanova	Brooklyn Dodgers
13	John Panelli	B	Notre Dame	New York Yankees
14	Bobby Gage	B	Clemson	Baltimore Colts
15	Hugh Keeney	B	Rice	Buffalo Bills

Round 3

No.	Player	Position	College	Drafted By
16	Wally Tripplett	B	Penn State	Brooklyn Dodgers
17	Sherman Howard	B	Nevada-Reno	New York Yankees
18	Hosea Rogers	B	North Carolina	Los Angeles Dons
19	Vito Kissell	B	Holy Cross	Buffalo Bills
20	Frank Lovuolo	E	St. Bonaventure	San Francisco 49ers
21	Rip Collins	B	LSU	Cleveland Browns

Round 4

No.	Player	Position	College	Drafted By
22	Jim Finks	QB	Tulsa	Chicago Hornets
23	Dolph Tokarczyk	G	Pennsylvania	Brooklyn Dodgers
24	Dick Rifenburg	E	Michigan	New York Yankees
25	Ralph Kohl	T	Michigan	Baltimore Colts
26	Bob Meinert	B	Oklahoma State	Los Angeles Dons
27	Wilbur Volz	B	Missouri	Buffalo Bills
28	Mike DeNoia	B	Scranton	San Francisco 49ers
29	Bill McLellan	T	Brown	Cleveland Browns

Round 5

No.	Player	Position	College	Drafted By
30	Carmen Falcone	B	Pennsylvania	Chicago Hornets
31	Joe Quinn	G	Cornell	Brooklyn Dodgers
32	George Maddock	T	Northwestern	New York Yankees
33	Wally Jones	E	Kentucky	Baltimore Colts
34	Billy Grimes	B	Oklahoma State	Los Angeles Dons
35	Frank Gaul	G	Notre Dame	Buffalo Bills
36	George Brodnax	E	Georgia Tech	San Francisco 49ers
37	Ed McNeill	E	Michigan	Cleveland Browns

Round 6

No.	Player	Position	College	Drafted By
38	Sam Tamburo	B	Penn State	Chicago Hornets
39	Leo Skladany	E	Pittsburgh	Brooklyn Dodgers
40	Don Panciera	QB	San Francisco	New York Yankees
41	Frank Pattee	B	Kansas	Baltimore Colts
42	Joe Geri	B	Georgia	Los Angeles Dons
43	Frank Guess	B	Texas	Buffalo Bills
44	John Hamberger	T	SMU	San Francisco 49ers
45	Tom O'Malley	B	Cincinnati	Cleveland Browns

Round 7

No.	Player	Position	College	Drafted By
46	Ralph Hutchinson	T	Tenn-Chattanooga	Chicago Hornets
47	Lynn Chewing	B	Hampden-Sydney	Brooklyn Dodgers
48	Dan Garza	E	Oregon	New York Yankees
49	Frank Folger	B	Duke	Baltimore Colts
50	Bill Renna	C	Santa Clara	Los Angeles Dons
51	Harold Ensminger	QB	Missouri	Buffalo Bills
52	Dan Steigman	C	North Carolina	San Francisco 49ers
53	Phil Alexander	T	South Carolina	Cleveland Browns

Round 8

No.	Player	Position	College	Drafted By
54	Jim Cain	E	Alabama	Chicago Hornets
55	Bob McCurry	C	Michigan State	Brooklyn Dodgers
56	Brian Bell	B	Washington & Lee	New York Yankees
57	Bob Prymuski	T	Illinois	Baltimore Colts
58	Bill Austin	T	Oregon State	Los Angeles Dons
59	Vic Vasicek	G	Texas	Buffalo Bills
60	Bernie Reid	G	Georgia	San Francisco 49ers
61	Mike Cannevino	B	Ohio State	Cleveland Browns

Round 9

No.	Player	Position	College	Drafted By
62	Tino Sabucco	C	San Francisco	Chicago Hornets
63	Chuck Klemovitch	G	Columbia	Brooklyn Dodgers
64	Al Mastrangeli	C	Illinois	New York Yankees
65	Everett Faunce	B	Minnesota	Baltimore Colts
66	Mike Rubish	E	North Carolina	Los Angeles Dons
67	Alex Verdova	B	Ohio State	Buffalo Bills
68	Fred Wendt	B	Texas-El Paso	San Francisco 49ers
69	Doak Walker	B	SMU	Cleveland Browns

Round 10

No.	Player	Position	College	Drafted By
70	Warren Huey	E	Michigan State	Chicago Hornets
71	Bob Duncan	E	Duke	Brooklyn Dodgers
72	John Goldsberry	T	Indiana	New York Yankees
73	Kale Alexander	T	South Carolina	Baltimore Colts
74	Jerry Krall	B	Ohio State	Los Angeles Dons
75	Al Russas	E	Tennessee	Buffalo Bills
76	Dick Flowers	T	Alabama	San Francisco 49ers
77	Norb Adams	B	Purdue	Cleveland Browns

Round 11

No.	Player	Position	College	Drafted By
78	Norm Van Brocklin	QB	Oregon	Chicago Hornets
79	Hilary Chollet	B	Cornell	Brooklyn Dodgers
80	Ben Bendrick	B	Wisconsin	New York Yankees
81	Paul Page	B	SMU	Baltimore Colts
82	Chuck Drazenovich	B	Penn State	Los Angeles Dons
83	Ernie Settembre	T	Miami	Buffalo Bills
84	Bob Lund	B	Tennessee	San Francisco 49ers
85	Negley Norton	T	Penn State	Cleveland Browns

Round 12

No.	Player	Position	College	Drafted By
86	Jay Van Noy	B	Utah State	Chicago Hornets
87	Bill Davis	G	Duke	Brooklyn Dodgers
88	Frank Van Deren	E	California	New York Yankees
89	Jim Owens	E	Oklahoma	Baltimore Colts
90	Larry Klosterman	G	North Carolina	Los Angeles Dons
91	Milt Kormarnicki	C	Villanova	Buffalo Bills
92	Jon Baker	G	California	San Francisco 49ers
93	Frank Burns	B	Rutgers	Cleveland Browns

Round 13

No.	Player	Position	College	Drafted By
94	Tom Wham	E	Furman	Chicago Hornets
95	Roland Dale	T	Mississippi	Brooklyn Dodgers
96	Eddie Berrang	E	Villanova	New York Yankees
97	Warren Beson	C	Minnesota	Baltimore Colts
98	Tom Blake	G	Cincinnati	Los Angeles Dons
99	Butch Songin	QB	Boston College	Buffalo Bills
100	Jim Reichert	G	Arkansas	San Francisco 49ers
101	Clarence Self	B	Wisconsin	Cleveland Browns

Round 14

No.	Player	Position	College	Drafted By
102	Ivan Snowden	T	Texas A&I	Chicago Hornets
103	Murray Alexander	E	Mississippi State	Brooklyn Dodgers
104	Bob Doormink	T	Washington State	New York Yankees
105	David Moon	B	SMU	Baltimore Colts
106	Dick Lorenz	E	Oregon State	Los Angeles Dons
107	Leon Cooper	T	Hardin-Simmons	Buffalo Bills
108	Don Garlin	B	California	San Francisco 49ers
109	Walt Kersulis	E	Illinois	Cleveland Browns

Round 15

No.	Player	Position	College	Drafted By
110	Abbie Reynolds	B	Texas Tech	Chicago Hornets
111	Howard Derrick	B	Tenn-Chattanooga	Brooklyn Dodgers
112	Jack Glenn	T	Georgia Tech	New York Yankees
113	Jon Jenkins	T	Dartmouth	Baltimore Colts
114	Bob Bastian	G	USC	Los Angeles Dons
115	Clayton Tonnemaker	C	Minnesota	Buffalo Bills
116	Pete Wissman	C	St. Louis	San Francisco 49ers
117	Bobby Jack Stuart	B	Army	Cleveland Browns

Round 16

No.	Player	Position	College	Drafted By
118	Dick Monroe	C	Kansas	Chicago Hornets
119	Dale Armstrong	E	Dartmouth	Brooklyn Dodgers
120	Jack Bruce	B	William & Mary	New York Yankees
121	Johnny O'Quinn	E	Wake Forest	Baltimore Colts
122	Art Steffen	B	UCLA	Los Angeles Dons
123	Rob Goode	B	Texas A&M	Buffalo Bills
124	Homer Hobbs	G	Georgia	San Francisco 49ers
125	Dinky Bowen	B	Georgia Tech	Cleveland Browns

Round 17

No.	Player	Position	College	Drafted By
126	George Guerre	B	Michigan State	Chicago Hornets
127	Tank Younger	B	Grambling	Brooklyn Dodgers
128	Gil Johnson	B	SMU	New York Yankees
129	Clyde Geary	T	Connecticut Wes.	Baltimore Colts
130	Tom Gannon	B	Harvard	Los Angeles Dons
131	Art Donovan	G	Boston College	Buffalo Bills

Round 18

No.	Player	Position	College	Drafted By
132	John Phillips	B	Southern Mississippi	Chicago Hornets
133	Mitchell Holgren	T	Hartford	Brooklyn Dodgers
134	Barney Hafen	E	Utah	New York Yankees
135	Al Sanders	T	Southern Mississippi	Baltimore Colts
136	Larry Hatch	B	Washington	Los Angeles Dons
137	Jim Goodman	T	Maryland	Buffalo Bills

Round 19

No.	Player	Position	College	Drafted By
138	Verda Smith	B	Abilene Christian	Chicago Hornets
139	Frank Weaver	B	Moravian	Brooklyn Dodgers
140	Hal Jensen	B	San Francisco	New York Yankees
141	Guy Sundheim	C	Northwestern	Baltimore Colts
142	Jerry Tiblier	B	Mississippi	Los Angeles Dons
143	Merlin London	E	Oklahoma State	Buffalo Bills

Part 7: The Draft

Round 20

No.	Player	Position	College	Drafted By
144	Clayton Davis	C	Oklahoma State	Chicago Hornets
145	Eddie Price	B	Tulane	Brooklyn Dodgers
146	Tommy Kalmanir	B	Nevada	New York Yankees
147	Mernie Lazier	B	Illinois	Baltimore Colts
148	Gene Frasseto	T	California	Los Angeles Dons
149	Marty Breen	C	Canisius	Buffalo Bills

Round 21

No.	Player	Position	College	Drafted By
150	George Benigni	E	Georgetown	Chicago Hornets
151	John Geosits	T	Bucknell	Brooklyn Dodgers
152	Al Beasley	G	St. Mary's	New York Yankees
153	Harry Larche	T	Arkansas State	Baltimore Colts
154	Jim Clark	G	Mississippi	Los Angeles Dons
155	John Simon	G	Penn State	Buffalo Bills

Round 22

No.	Player	Position	College	Drafted By
156	R.M. Patterson	T	McMurry	Chicago Hornets
157	Tom Brennan	G	Boston College	Brooklyn Dodgers
158	Ernie Tolman	E	USC	New York Yankees

Round 23

No.	Player	Position	College	Drafted By
159	Bill Kemplin	E	North Texas State	Chicago Hornets
160	Jack McBride	E	Rice	Brooklyn Dodgers
161	Gerry Morrical	T	Indiana	New York Yankees

Round 24

No.	Player	Position	College	Drafted By
162	Bill Cadenhead	B	Alabama	Chicago Hornets
163	Bobby Folson	E	SMU	Brooklyn Dodgers
164	Bob Hood	E	Alabama	New York Yankees

Round 25

No.	Player	Position	College	Drafted By
165	Phil Poole	G	Mississippi	Chicago Hornets
166	Bill Long	E	Oklahoma State	Brooklyn Dodgers
167	Ross Nagel	T	St. Louis	New York Yankees
168	Joe Grothus	G	Iowa	Baltimore Colts
169	Ed Ralston	B	Richmond	Los Angeles Dons
170	Bernie Hanula	T	Wake Forest	Buffalo Bills
171	Paul Schoults	B	Miami (OH)	San Francisco 49ers
172	Larry Cooney	B	Penn State	Cleveland Browns

Round 26

No.	Player	Position	College	Drafted By
173	Byron Gillory	B	Texas	Baltimore Colts
174	John Donaldson	B	Georgia	Los Angeles Dons
175	Bobby Deuber	B	Pennsylvania	Buffalo Bills
176	Jack Kelly	T	Louisiana Tech	San Francisco 49ers
177	Jack Lininger	C	Ohio State	Cleveland Browns

Round 27

No.	Player	Position	College	Drafted By
178	Bob Cox	E	North Carolina	Baltimore Colts
179	Lloyd Eisenberg	T	Duke	Los Angeles Dons
180	Floyd Lewis	G	SMU	Buffalo Bills
181	Jasper Flanakin	E	Baylor	San Francisco 49ers
182	Verne Gagne	E	Minnesota	Cleveland Browns

Round 28

No.	Player	Position	College	Drafted By
183	Bob DeMoss	B	Purdue	Baltimore Colts
184	George Pastre	T	UCLA	Los Angeles Dons
185	Leon Cochran	B	Auburn	Buffalo Bills
186	Rudy Smith	T	Louisiana Tech	San Francisco 49ers
187	Jim Moran	B	John Carroll	Cleveland Browns

Round 29

No.	Player	Position	College	Drafted By
188	George Pryor	F	Wake Forest	Baltimore Colts
189	Joe Ethridge	G	SMU	Los Angeles Dons
190	Joe Leonard	T	Virginia	Buffalo Bills
191	Gordon Long	B	Arkansas	San Francisco 49ers
192	Joe Soboleski	T	Michigan	Cleveland Browns

*Declared ineligible

Allocation Draft

Round 1

No.	Player	Pos.	College	Drafted By	From (Reserve List Rights)	1950 Playing Status	Notes
1	Chet Mutryn	HB	Xavier	Baltimore Colts	Buffalo Bills	Baltimore Colts	
2	George Taliaferro	HB	Indiana	New York Yanks	LA Dons	New York Yanks	
3	Billy Grimes	HB	Oklahoma A&M	Green Bay Packers	LA Dons	Green Bay Packers	
4	Bob Hoernschemeyer	HB	Indiana	Det Lions	Chi Hornets	Detroit Lions	
5	Jim Spavital	FB	Oklahoma A&M	Wash. Redskins	LA Dons	Baltimore Colts[1]	
6	John Rapacz	C-T	Oklahoma	New York Giants	Chi Hornets	New York Giants	
7	Bud Tinsley	T	Baylor	Pittsburgh Steelers	LA Dons	Did Not Play	
8	Bob Reinhart	T	U. of California	Chicago Cardinals	LA Dons	Los Angeles Rams	Traded to Los Angeles Rams[2]
9	Harper Davis	HB	Mississippi State	Chicago Bears	LA Dons	Chicago Bears	
10	Knox Ramsey	G	William & Mary	SF 49ers	LA Dons	Chicago Cardinals	
11	Art Statuto	C	Notre Dame	Los Angeles Rams	Buffalo Bills	Los Angeles Rams	
12	Hal Herring	C	Auburn	Cleveland Browns	Buffalo Bills	Cleveland Browns	
13	Lindell Pearson	HB	Oklahoma	Philadelphia Eagles	N/A	Detroit Lions	Traded to Lions for 1st Round Pick[3]

Round 2

No.	Player	Pos.	College	Drafted By	From (Reserve List Rights)	1950 Playing Status	Notes
14	Bob Livingstone	HB	Notre Dame	Baltimore Colts	Buffalo Bills	Baltimore Colts	
15	Nate Johnson	T	Illinois	New York Yanks	Chic Hornets	New York Yanks	
16	Al Baldwin	E	Arkansas	Green Bay Packers	Buffalo Bills	GB Packers	
17	Lou Creekmur	T	William & Mary	Detroit Lions	William & Mary in 1949	Detroit Lions	Drafted in 1948 by Dons. Also on '48 Eagles Res. List.
18	Chuck Drazenovich	FB	Penn State	Wash. Redskins	Penn State in 1949	Wash. Redskins	Drafted by Dons in '49 and on '49 Lions Res. List.
19	Ollie Cline	FB	Ohio State	New York Giants[4]	Buffalo Bills	Detroit Lions	
20	Ray Richeson	G	Alabama	Pittsburgh Steelers	Chi Hornets	Did Not Play	
21	Martin Wendell	G	Notre Dame	Chicago Cardinals	Chi Hornets	Did Not Play	
22	Fred Negus	C	Wisconsin	Chicago Bears	Chi Hornets	Chicago Bears	
23	Ed Henke	T	USC	San Francisco 49ers	LA Dons	Did Not Play	Played for '51 49ers.
24	Vic Vasicek	G	USC	Los Angeles Rams	Buffalo Bills	LA Rams	
25	Len Ford	E	Michigan	Cleveland Browns	LA Dons	Cleveland Browns	
26	Jerry Krall	FB	Ohio State	Philadelphia Eagles	LA Dons	Detroit Lions	

Round 3

No.	Player	Pos.	College	Drafted By	From (Reserve List Rights)	1950 Playing Status	Notes
27	Rip Collins	HB	LSU	Baltimore Colts	Chi Hornets	Baltimore Colts	
28	Dan Edwards	E	Georgia	New York Yanks	Chi Hornets	New York Yanks	
29	Homer Paine	T	Oklahoma	Green Bay Packers	Chi Hornets	Did Not Play	
30	Bob Jensen	E	Iowa State	Detroit Lions	Chi Hornets	Baltimore Colts	
31	Roland Dale	T	Mississippi	Wash. Redskins	MS in 1949	Wash. Redskins	Drafted by Dodgers '49
32	Vince Mazza	E	(None)	New York Giants	Buffalo Bills	Did Not Play	Went to CFL
33	Tom McWilliams	HB	MS State	Pittsburgh Steelers	LA Dons	Pitts Steelers	
34	Ray Ramsey	HB	Bradley	Chicago Cardinals	Chi Hornets	Chi Cardinals	
35	James Clark	T	Mississippi	Chicago Bears	MS in 1949	Did Not Play	
36	Odell Stautzenberger	G	Texas A&M	SF 49ers	Buffalo Bills	Did Not Play	
37	Dick Wilkins	E	Oregon	Los Angeles Rams	LA Dons	Did Not Play[5]	Played '52 Dal. Texans
38	Bill Schroll	HB	LSU	Cleveland Browns	Buffalo Bills	Detroit Lions	Traded to Det Lions[6]
39	George Pastre	T	UCLA	Philadelphia Eagles	LA Dons	Did Not Play	Drafted by Dons in '49

Extra Picks

No.	Player	Pos.	College	Drafted By	From (Reserve List Rights)	1950 Playing Status	Notes
40	Art Donovan	G	Boston	Balt Colts	Buffalo Bills (Did Not Play)	Balt Colts	Drafted by Buffalo in 1949. On '47 Giants Reserve List.
41	Jim Lukens	E	Washington	GB Packers	Buffalo Bills	Did Not Play	
42	Ed King	G	Boston College	Balt Colts	Buffalo Bills	Balt Colts	
43	Ab Wimberly	E	LSU	GB Packers	LA Dons	GB Packers	

Round 4

No.	Player	Pos.	College	Drafted By	From (Reserve List Rights)	1950 Playing Status	Notes
44	George Buksar	FB	Purdue	Baltimore Colts	Chi Hornets	Balt Colts	
45	John Clowes	T	Wil. & Mary	New York Yanks	Chi Hornets	NY Yanks	
46	Wilbur E. Volz	HB	Missouri	Green Bay Packers	Buffalo Bills	Did Not Play	
47	William Kay	T	Iowa	Detroit Lions	Buffalo Bills (Did Not Play)	Did Not Play	Drafted by Bills in 1949. On Giants '49 Res. List
48	Lloyd Eisenberg	T	Duke	Wash. Redskins	LA Dons (Did Not Play)	Did Not Play	Drafted by Dons in '49. On Bears '49 Res. List
49	Alfred Schmid	E	Villanova	New York Giants	Villanova in '49	Did Not Play	
50	Dan Dworsky	C	Michigan	Pittsburgh Steelers	LA Dons	Did Not Play	
51	Ted Hazelwood	T	NC	Chicago Cardinals	Chi Hornets	Did Not Play	Played for 1953 Washington Redskins
52	Glenn Dobbs, Jr.	QB-HB	Tulsa	Chi Bears	LA Dons	Did Not Play	Went to CFL
53	Earl Howell	HB	MS	SF 49ers	LA Dons	Did Not Play	Drafted by Los Angeles Rams in 1949.
54	Wade Walker	T	Oklahoma	LA Rams	Buffalo Bills (Did Not Play)	Did Not Play	Drafted by Buffalo in '49. On '47 Chi. Cardinals Reserve List.
55	Alex Wizbicki	HB	Holy Cross	Cleveland Browns	Buffalo Bills	GB Packers	
56	Paul Gibson	E	NC State	Phil Eagles	Buffalo Bills	Did Not Play	

Round 5

No.	Player	Pos.	College	Drafted By	From (Reserve List Rights)	1950 Playing Status	Notes
57	Bob Oristaglio	E	Penn.	Balt Colts	Buffalo Bills	Baltimore Colts	
58	Bob H. Kennedy	FB	WA State	NY Yanks	NY Yankees	New York Yanks	Drafted by Pitt-Phila in '43.
59	John E. Kerns	T	Ohio	GB Packers	Buffalo Bills	Did Not Play	Went to CFL.
60	Richard Rifenberg	E	Michigan	Detroit Lions	NY Yankees	Detroit Lions (Did Not Play)	Drafted by Yankees in '49.
61	Hardy Brown	FB	Tulsa	WA Redskins	Chicago Hornets	Wash. Redskins[7]	
62	Joe Sullivan	QB	Dartmouth	NY Giants	N/A	Did Not Play	On '47 Lions Res. List.
63	Herb St. John	G	Georgia	Pitt. Steelers	Chicago Hornets	Did Not Play	
64	Jim Still	QB	GA Tech.	Chi Cardinals	Buffalo Bills	Did Not Play	

Allocation Draft

No.	Player	Pos.	College	Drafted By	From (Reserve List Rights)	1950 Playing Status	Notes
65	Al Beasley	G	St. Mary's	Chi Bears	New York Yankees (Did Not Play)	Did Not Play	Drafted by Yankees in '49.
66	John Brown	C	NC	SF 49ers	Los Angeles Dons	Did Not Play	
67	Ernest Williamson	T	NC	LA Rams	Los Angeles Dons	Did Not Play	
68	Walter Clay	FB	Colorado	Clev. Browns	Los Angeles Dons	Did Not Play	
69	Joe Sutton	HB	Temple	Phil. Eagles	Buffalo Bills	Philadelphia Eagles	

Extra Picks

No.	Player	Pos.	College	Drafted By	From (Reserve List Rights)	1950 Playing Status	Notes
70	Robert Deuber	HB	Penn.	Balt Colts	Penn. in 1949	Did Not Play	Drafted by Bills in 1949.
71	Ted Cook	E	Alabama	GB Packers	Green Bay Packers	GB Packers	Cut in 1949 and redrafted.

Round 6

No.	Player	Pos.	College	Drafted By	From (Reserve List Rights)	1950 Playing Status	Notes
72	Mike Perrotti	T	Cincinnati	Balt Colts	Los Angeles Dons	Did Not Play	
73	Chet Adams	T	Ohio	NY Yanks	Buffalo Bills	NY Yanks	
74	Jason A. Bailey	T	WV St.	GB Packers	Chicago Hornets	Did Not Play	
75	Joyce Pipkin	E	Arkansas	Detroit Lions	Los Angeles Dons	Did Not Play	
76	Buckets Hirsch	LB	NWern	WA Redskins	Buffalo Bills	Did Not Play	
77	Dick Woodard	C	Iowa	NY Giants	Los Angeles Dons	NY Giants	
78	George Grimes	HB	Virginia	Pitt. Steelers	Buffalo Bills (Did Not Play)	Did Not Play	Drafted by Bills in '48. On '48 Rams Res. List
79	Jim Turner	T	U of Cali.	Chi Cardinals	Chicago Hornets (Did Not Play)	Did Not Play	Drafted by Hornets in '48. On '47 Bears Res. List
80	John Cunningham	E	U of Cali.	Chicago Bears	N/A	Did Not Play	On '47 Bears Reserve List
81	George Murphy	QB	USC	SF 49ers	Los Angeles Dons	Did Not Play	
82	Bill Renna	C	Santa Clara	LA Rams	Los Angeles Dons (Did Not Play)	Did Not Play	Drafted by Dons in 1949. On '49 Rams Res. List
83	George Strohmeyer	C	Notre Dame	Clev Browns	Chi Hornets	Did Not Play	
84	Hosea Rodgers	FB	NC	Phil Eagles	Los Angeles Dons	Did Not Play	

Round 7

No.	Player	Pos.	College	Drafted By	From (Reserve List Rights)	1950 Playing Status	Notes
85	Bill Gompers	HB	Notre Dame	Balt Colts	Buffalo Bills	Did Not Play	Retired after '48 season
86	Paul Crowe	HB	St. Mary's	NY Yanks	LA Dons	Did Not Play	Played for '51 NY Yanks
87	Denver Crawford	T	TN	GB Packers	NY Yankees	Did Not Play	Retired after '48 season
88	George Benigni	E	Georgetown	Detroit Lions	Chi Hornets (Did Not Play)	Did Not Play	Drafted by Hornets in '49
89	Ed Smith	B	TX Mines	WA Redskins	N/A	Did Not Play	On '48 Packers Res. List
90	Henry Foldberg	E	Army	NY Giants	Chi Hornets	Did Not Play	
91	Ben Verick	FB	Wisconsin	Pitt. Steelers	N/A	Did Not Play	On 1949 Bears Res. List
92	Alex Sarkisian	C	NWern	Chi Cardinals	N/A	Did Not Play	On 1947 Eagles Res. List
93	John Donaldson	HB	Georgia	Chi Bears	LA Dons	Did Not Play	
94	John Maskas	T	VA Poly. Inst.	SF 49ers	Buffalo Bills	Did Not Play	
95	Jack Swaner	HB	U of Cali.	LA Rams	Chi Hornets (Did Not Play)	Did Not Play	Drafted by Hornets in '48. On '48 Eagles Res. List
96	Lynn Chewning	FB	Hampden-Sydney	Clev Browns	NY Yankees	Did Not Play	On '47 Boston Yanks Res. List
97	Don Panciera	QB	SF Univ.	Phil Eagles	NY Yankees	Detroit Lions	

Extra Picks

No.	Player	Pos.	College	Drafted By	From (Reserve List Rights)	1950 Playing Status	Notes
98	William Stanton	E	North Carolina St.	Baltimore Colts	Buffalo Bills	Did Not Play	
99	Carl Schuette	C	Marquette	Green Bay Packers	Buffalo Bills	Green Bay Packers	

Round 8

No.	Player	Pos.	College	Drafted By	From (Reserve List Rights)	1950 Playing Status	Notes
100	Vito Kissell	FB	Holy Cross	Balt Colts	Buffalo Bills	Balt Colts	
101	Mickey Colmer	FB	Miramonte Jr. Coll.	NY Yanks	NY Yankees	Did Not Play	
102	Ziggy Czarobski	T	Notre Dame	GB Packers	Chi Hornets	Did Not Play	
103	Gerald Morrical	T	Indiana	Det Lions	NY Yankees (Did Not Play)	Did Not Play	Drafted by Yankees in '49 On '49 Giants Res. List
104	Leon McLaughlin	C	UCLA	WA Redskins	LA Dons (Did Not Play)	Did Not Play	Drafted by Dons in '48. On '47 Rams Res. List. Played for 1951–6 Rams.
105	Bob Heck	E	Purdue	NY Giants	Chi Hornets	Did Not Play	Went to CFL.
106	Jim Pearcy	G	Marshall	Pitt Steelers	Chi Hornets	Did Not Play	
107	Phil O'Reilly	T	Purdue	Chi Cardinals	N/A	Did Not Play	On 1948 Steelers Res. List
108	George Maddock	T	Northwestern	Chi Bears	Chi Hornets	Did Not Play	On 1947 Cards Res. List
109	Paul Cleary	E	USC	SF 49ers	Chi Hornets	Did Not Play	
110	Richard Scott	C	Navy	LA Rams	Brklyn Dodgers (Did Not Play)	Did Not Play	Drafted by Dodgers in '48 On '48 Bears Res. List
111	Paul Patterson	HB	Illinois	Clev Browns	Chi Hornets	Did Not Play	
112	Tex Warrington	C	William & Mary	Phil Eagles	Brklyn Dodgers	Did Not Play	Retired after 1948 season

Round 9

No.	Player	Pos.	College	Drafted By	From (Reserve List Rights)	1950 Playing Status	Notes
113	Robert Hatch	QB-HB	Boston U	Balt Colts	N/A	Did Not Play	On '48 Giants Res. List
114	Spec Sanders	HB	Texas	NY Yanks	NY Yankees	NY Yanks	
115	Vic Schleich	T	Nebraska	GB Packers	Chi Rockets	Did Not Play	Retired after 1947 season.
116	Warren Huey	E	MI State	Detroit Lions	Chi Hornets	Did Not Play	Drafted by Hornets in '49. On '49 Eagles Res. List
117	Murray Alexander	E	MS State	WA Redskins	Brklyn Dodgers (Did Not Play)	Did Not Play	Drafted by Dodgers in '49.
118	Henry Kalver	T	OK City	NY Giants	N/A	Did Not Play	On '49 Eagles Res. List
119	Robert Forbes	HB	Florida	Pitt Steelers	N/A	Did Not Play	On '48 Boston Yanks Res. List
120	Ralph Sazio	T	Wil. & Mary	Chi Cardinals	Buffalo Bills (Did Not Play)	Did Not Play	Drafted by Bills in 1949
121	Bob Leonetti	G	Wake Forest	Chi Bears	Buffalo Bills	Did Not Play	Retired after 1948 season
122	Ernest Tolman	E	USC	SF 49ers	NY Yankees (Did Not Play)	Did Not Play	Drafted by Yankees in '49
123	Ed Kelley	T	Texas	LA Rams	LA Dons	Did Not Play	
124	Bill Reinhard	HB	U of Cali.	Clev Browns	LA Dons	Did Not Play	Retired after 1948 season
125	Carmen Falcone	QB	Pennsylvania	Phil Eagles	N/A	Did Not Play	

Extra Picks

No.	Player	Pos.	College	Drafted By	From (Reserve List Rights)	1950 Playing Status	Notes
126	Lou Tomasetti	FB	Bucknell	Baltimore Colts	Buffalo Bills	Did Not Play	
127	Paul Duke	C	Georgia Tech.	Green Bay Packers	NY Yankees	Did Not Play	Retired after 1947 season.

Round 10

No.	Player	Pos.	College	Drafted By	From (Reserve List Rights)	1950 Playing Status	Notes
128	Lou Agase	T	Illinois	Balt Colts	Chi Hornets	Did Not Play	On '48 Packers Res. List
129	Tom Colella	HB	Canisius	NY Yanks	Buffalo Bills	Did Not Play	
130	R.M. Patterson	T	McMurray, TX	GB Packers	Chi Hornets	Did Not Play	On '49 Lions Res. List
131	Ray Coates	HB	LSU	Det Lions	NY Giants	Did Not Play	Giants cut. Lions redrafted
132	Dewey Nelson	HB	Utah	WA Redskins	NY Bulldogs	Did Not Play	On '48 Boston Yanks Res. List
133	Dwight Eddleman	HB	Illinois	NY Giants	N/A	Did Not Play	On '47 Bears Reserve List
134	Robert Meinert	LB	OK A&M	Pitt Steelers	LA Dons (Did Not Play)	Did Not Play	Drafted by Dons in 1949. On '49 Lions Reserve List.

No.	Player	Pos.	College	Drafted By	From (Reserve List Rights)	1950 Playing Status	Notes
135	Vaughn Mancha	C	Alabama	Chi Cardinals	Boston Yanks	Did Not Play	Retired after 1948 season.
136	George Bernhardt	G	Illinois	Chi Bears	Chi Hornets	Did Not Play	
137	Dick Lorenz	E	Oregon State	SF 49ers	LA Dons (Did Not Play)	Did Not Play	Drafted by Dons in 1949. On 1946 Rams Res. List
138	Dale Armstrong	E	Dartmouth	LA Rams	Brklyn Dodgers (Did Not Play)	Did Not Play	Drafted by Dodgers in 1949. On '49 Eagles Reserve List
139	Lew Holder	E	Texas	Clev Browns	LA Dons	Did Not Play	
140	Gil Johnson	QB-HB	SMU	Phil Eagles	NY Yankees	Did Not Play	Given to Detroit

1. The Chicago Bears traded Walt Stickel to the Washington Redskins for John Adams (T) and the rights to Jim Spavital. The Bears then traded Spavital to the Baltimore Colts for a #1 draft pick in 1951. The Bears selected Bobby Williams (QB, Notre Dame).
2. Reinhart was traded to the Rams for Jim Hardy (QB), Bob Shaw (E), Jerry Cowhig (FB) and Tom Keane (DB).
3. The Eagles traded Lindell Pearson to the Lions for a #1 draft pick in 1951. With that pick, the Eagles drafted Chet Mutryn.
4. The Giants traded Ollie Cline to the Lions for end Kelly Mote (Duke).
5. Dick Wilkins was in the Marine Corps in 1950. He was part of the Les Ritcher trade with the Texans. Wilkins played for the 1952 Dallas Texans.
6. Schroll was traded to the Detroit Lions for a #12 draft pick in 1951. With that pick, the Browns selected Milan Sellers (HB, Florida State).
7. Hardy Brown was claimed on waivers by the Baltimore Colts from the Washington Redskins in 1950.

Part 8: Player Register

Editor's notes: The 1949 Brooklyn Dodgers—New York Yankees merged team is referred to as the 1949 New York Yankees in this list.

Items with an asterisk (*) designate statistics that are unavailable.

For players who also played in the NFL, their NFL statistics were added. Even through this is an AAFC encyclopedia, the editors felt that the addition of the NFL statistics for the players helped for a complete picture of their career.

Ken Pullis has done excellent work in correcting the statistics for the AAFC. Notations have been made where the corrected statistics have been added compared to the official statistics.

ADAMLE, Anthony (Tony)

Position: LB-FB
Height: 6'0"; Weight: 215
College: Ohio State
Born: May 15, 1924, Fairmont, WV
Deceased: October 7, 2000, Kent, OH

STATISTICS

Games		
	GP	GS
1947 Cleveland Browns	14	1
1948 Cleveland Browns	14	0
1949 Cleveland Browns	12	2
1950 Cleveland Browns	12	0
1951 Cleveland Browns	12	0
1954 Cleveland Browns	11	0
Total	75	3

Rushing			
	Rush	Yds	TD
1947 Cleveland Browns	23	95	1
1948 Cleveland Browns	17	88	1
1949 Cleveland Browns	17	64	0
1950 Cleveland Browns	3	8	0
Total	60	255	2

Receiving			
	Rec	Yds	TD
1947 Cleveland Browns	1	22	0
1949 Cleveland Browns	1	13	0
Total	2	35	0

Kick Returns			
	Ret	Yds	TD
1947 Cleveland Browns	1	22	0
1950 Cleveland Browns	4	53	0
Total	5	75	0

Interceptions			
	Int	Yds	TD
1947 Cleveland Browns	1	25	0
1949 Cleveland Browns	4	42	0
1950 Cleveland Browns	1	17	0
1951 Cleveland Browns	1	12	0
Total	7	96	0

Fumbles			
	Fum	Rec	Yds	TD
1950 Cleveland Browns	2	5	0	0
1951 Cleveland Browns	0	1	0	0
Total	2	6	0	0

ADAMS, Chester Frank (Chet)

Position: T-E-DT
Height: 6'3"; Weight: 233
College: Ohio
Born: October 24, 1915, Cleveland, OH
Deceased: October 28, 1990, Cleveland, OH

STATISTICS

Games		
	GP	GS
1939 Cleveland Rams	9	5
1940 Cleveland Rams	11	11
1941 Cleveland Rams	11	11
1942 Cleveland Rams	11	11
1943 Green Bay Packers	10	6
1946 Cleveland Browns	14	0
1947 Cleveland Browns	13	7
1948 Cleveland Browns	14	0
1949 Buffalo Bills	12	0
1950 New York Yanks	12	1
Total	117	52

Receiving			
	Rec	Yds	TD
1940 L.A. Rams	3	28	0
Total	3	28	0

Interceptions			
	Int	Yds	TD
1946 Cleveland Browns	1	4	1
Total	1	4	1

AGAJANIAN, Benjamin James (Ben)

Position: K
Height: 6'0"; Weight: 215
College: New Mexico
Born: August 28, 1919, Santa Ana, CA
Deceased:

STATISTICS

Games

	GP	GS
1945 Philadelphia Eagles	1	1
1945 Pittsburgh Steelers	5	1
1947 Los Angeles Dons	13	2
1948 Los Angeles Dons	13	1
1949 New York Giants	12	1
1953 Los Angeles Rams	10	0
1954 New York Giants	12	0
1955 New York Giants	12	0
1956 New York Giants	10	0
1957 New York Giants	12	0
1960 Los Angeles Chargers	14	0
1961 Dallas Texans	3	0
1961 Green Bay Packers	3	0
1962 Oakland Raiders	6	0
1964 San Diego Chargers	3	0
Total	129	6

Field Goals

	FGM	FGA
1940 Los Angeles Rams	1	5
1941 Los Angeles Rams	1	2
1942 Los Angeles Rams	3	6
1943 Green Bay Packers	1	6
1947 Cleveland Browns	1	1
1949 Buffalo Bills	4	11
1950 New York Yanks	2	9
Total	13	40

Field Goals

	FGM	FGA
1945 Pittsburgh Steelers	4	4
1947 Los Angeles Dons	15	24
1948 Los Angeles Dons	5	15
1949 New York Giants	8	13
1953 Los Angeles Rams	10	24
1954 New York Giants	13	25
1955 New York Giants	10	15
1956 New York Giants	5	13
1957 New York Giants	10	18
1960 Los Angeles Chargers	13	24
1961 Dallas Texans	3	9
1961 Green Bay Packers	1	2
1962 Oakland Raiders	5	14
1964 San Diego Chargers	2	4
Total	104	204

Point After Touchdown

	XPM	XPA
1939 Los Angeles Rams	5	5
1940 Los Angeles Rams	7	9
1941 Los Angeles Rams	13	14
1942 Los Angeles Rams	14	15
1946 Cleveland Browns	5	5
1947 Cleveland Browns	1	2
1949 Buffalo Bills	32	32
1950 New York Yanks	45	48
Total	122	130

Point After Touchdown

	XPM	XPA
1945 Pittsburgh Steelers	1	2
1947 Los Angeles Dons	39	40
1948 Los Angeles Dons	31	32
1949 New York Giants	35	36
1953 Los Angeles Rams	36	37
1954 New York Giants	35	35
1955 New York Giants	32	33
1956 New York Giants	23	23
1957 New York Giants	32	32
1960 Los Angeles Chargers	46	47
1961 Dallas Texans	7	7
1961 Green Bay Packers	8	8
1962 Oakland Raiders	10	11
1964 San Diego Chargers	8	8
Total	343	351

ADAMS, Howard O'Neal (Neal)

Position: E
Height: 6'3"; Weight: 195
College: Arkansas
Born: January 21, 1919, El Paso, AR
Deceased: October 27, 1998, Sand Springs, OK

STATISTICS

Games

	GP	GS
1942 New York Giants	11	11
1943 New York Giants	8	8
1944 New York Giants	10	10
1945 New York Giants	9	4
1946 Brooklyn Dodgers	13	2
1947 Brooklyn Dodgers	1	0
Total	52	35

Receiving

	Rec	Yds	TD
1942 New York Giants	6	87	3
1943 New York Giants	8	65	1
1944 New York Giants	14	342	1
1946 Brooklyn Dodgers	15	225	2
Total	43	719	7

Kick Returns

	Ret	Yds	TD
1943 New York Giants	1	8	0
1944 New York Giants	2	29	0
Total	3	37	0

Interceptions

	Int	Yds	TD
1942 New York Giants	1	66	1
Total	1	66	1

AGASE, Alexander Arrasi (Alex)

Position: LB-G
Height: 5'10"; Weight: 212
College: Illinois, Purdue
Born: March 27, 1922, Chicago, IL
Deceased: May 3, 2007, Tarpon Springs, FL

STATISTICS

Games

	GP	GS
1947 Chicago Rockets	11	11
1947 Los Angeles Dons	3	1
1948 Cleveland Browns	13	1
1949 Cleveland Browns	11	0
1950 Cleveland Browns	11	0
1951 Cleveland Browns	11	0
1953 Baltimore Colts	10	0
Total	70	13

Interceptions

	Int	Yds	TD
1947 Chicago Rockets	1	4	0
1949 Cleveland Browns	3	31	0
1950 Cleveland Browns	1	14	0
1951 Cleveland Browns	2	7	0
1953 Baltimore Colts	1	5	0
Total	8	61	0

Fumbles

	Fum	Rec	Yds	TD
1951 Cleveland Browns	0	1	0	0
Total	0	1	0	0

AGUIRRE, Joseph A. (Joe)

Position: E
Height: 6'4"; Weight: 225
College: St. Mary's (CA)
Born: October 17, 1918, Rock Springs, WV
Deceased: July 13, 1985, Grass Valley, CA

STATISTICS

Games

	GP	GS
1941 Washington Redskins	10	1
1943 Washington Redskins	10	10
1944 Washington Redskins	10	10
1945 Washington Redskins	10	9
1946 Los Angeles Dons	14	9
1947 Los Angeles Dons	12	6
1948 Los Angeles Dons	13	4
1949 Los Angeles Dons	4	0
Total	83	49

Rushing

	Rush	Yds	TD
1943 Wash. Redskins	1	21	0
1946 L.A. Dons	2	-5	0
Total	3	16	0

Receiving

	Rec	Yds	TD
1941 Wash. Redskins	10	103	2
1943 Wash. Redskins	37	420	7
1944 Wash. Redskins	34	410	4
1945 Wash. Redskins	16	189	0
1946 Los Angeles Dons	14	246	2
1947 Los Angeles Dons	11	219	5
1948 Los Angeles Dons	38	599	9
1949 Los Angeles Dons	3	37	1
Total	163	2223	30

Passing

	Comp	Att	Yds	TD	Int
1946 L.A. Dons	0	1	0	0	0
Total	0	1	0	0	0

Punting

	Punt	Yds	Blk
1944 Wash. Redskins	2	87	0
1946 Los Angeles Dons	2	91	0
Total	4	178	0

Kick Returns

	Ret	Yds	TD
1943 Wash. Redskins	3	21	0
1948 Los Angeles Dons	1	10	0
Total	4	31	0

Fumbles

	Fum	Rec	Yds	TD
1945 Wash. Redskins	1	1	0	0
Total	1	1	0	0

Field Goals

	FGM	FGA
1941 Wash. Redskins	2	5
1943 Wash. Redskins		2
1944 Wash. Redskins	4	8
1945 Wash. Redskins	7	13
1946 Los Angeles Dons	4	11
Total	17+	39

Point After Touchdown

	XPM	XPA
1941 Wash. Redskins	8	9
1943 Wash. Redskins	6	9
1944 Wash. Redskins	15	18
1945 Wash. Redskins	23	24
1946 Los Angeles Dons	31	32
1948 Los Angeles Dons	2	3
Total	85	95

*Joe Aguirre had three receptions for 61 yards and a touchdown credited to Bob Nelson in the official records. This reflects the corrected statistics. The error occurred in game one of the season.

AKINS, Albert George (Al)

Position: HB-DB
Height: 6'1"; Weight: 199
College: Washington, Washington State
Born: June 13, 1921, Spokane, WA
Deceased: August 29, 1995, Reno, NV

STATISTICS

Games

	GP	GS
1946 Cleveland Browns	4	0
1947 Brooklyn Dodgers	13	3
1948 Brooklyn Dodgers	3	1
1948 Buffalo Bills	5	0
Total	25	4

Rushing

	Rush	Yds	TD
1946 Cleveland Browns	5	42	1
1947 Brooklyn Dodgers	15	79	1
1948 Brooklyn Dodgers	4	−9	0
Total	24	112	2

Receiving

	Rec	Yds	TD
1947 Brooklyn Dodgers	6	101	1
1948 Brooklyn Dodgers	2	1	0
1949 Buffalo Bills	1	11	0
Total	9	113	1

Punt Returns

	Ret	Yds	TD
1947 Brooklyn Dodgers	1	17	0
Total	1	17	0

Kick Returns

	Ret	Yds	TD
1946 Cleveland Browns	2	74	0
1947 Brooklyn Dodgers	5	131	0
Total	7	205	0

Interceptions

	Int	Yds	TD
1946 Cleveland Browns	1	7	0
1947 Brooklyn Dodgers	1	31	0
Total	2	38	0

ALBERT, Frank Cullen (Frankie)

Position: QB-DB
Height: 5'10"; Weight: 166
College: Stanford
Born: January 27, 1920, Chicago, IL
Deceased: September 4, 2002, Palo Alto, CA

STATISTICS

Games

	GP	GS
1946 San Francisco 49ers	14	11
1947 San Francisco 49ers	14	9
1948 San Francisco 49ers	14	9
1949 San Francisco 49ers	12	9
1950 San Francisco 49ers	12	12
1951 San Francisco 49ers	12	11
1952 San Francisco 49ers	12	7
Total	90	68

Rushing

	Rush	Yds	TD
1946 S.F. 49ers	69	−10	4
1947 S.F. 49ers	46	179	5
1948 S.F. 49ers	69	349	8
1949 S.F. 49ers	35	249	3
1950 S.F. 49ers	53	272	3
1951 S.F. 49ers	35	146	3
1952 S.F. 49ers	22	87	1
Total	329	1272	27

Receiving

	Rec	Yds	TD
1948 SF 49ers	1	1	0
Total	1	1	0

Passing

	Comp	Att	Yds	TD	Int
1946 49ers	104	197	1404	14	14
1947 49ers	128	242	1692	18	15
1948 49ers	154	264	1990	29	10
1949 49ers	129	260	1862	27	16
1950 49ers	155	306	1767	14	23
1951 49ers	90	166	1116	5	10
1952 49ers	71	129	964	8	10
Total	831	1564	10795	115	98

Punt Returns

	Ret	Yds	TD
1946 SF 49ers	1	6	0
Total	1	6	0

Kick Returns

	Ret	Yds	TD
1946 SF 49ers	4	74	0
1947 SF 49ers	1	23	0
Total	5	97	0

Fumbles

	Fum	Rec	Yds	TD
1950 SF 49ers	4	3	0	0
1952 SF 49ers	3	0	0	0
Total	7	3	0	0

ALFORD, Herbert Bruce, Sr. (Bruce)

Position: E-DB
Height: 6'0"; Weight: 190
College: TCU
Born: September 12, 1922, Waco, TX
Deceased: May 8, 2010, Fort Worth, TX

STATISTICS

Games

	GP	GS
1946 New York Yankees	13	10
1947 New York Yankees	13	13
1948 New York Yankees	14	10
1949 New York Yankees	11	11
1950 New York Yanks	12	0
1951 New York Yanks	12	0
Total	75	44

Receiving

	Rec	Yds	TD
1946 New York Yankees	13	173	0
1947 New York Yankees	20	298	5
1948 New York Yankees	32	578	3
1949 New York Yankees	11	213	1
1950 New York Yanks	1	14	0
1951 New York Yanks	4	65	0
Total	**81**	**1341**	**9**

Punt Returns

	Ret	Yds	TD
1947 New York Yankees	1	34	1
Total	**1**	**34**	**1**

Kick Returns

	Ret	Yds	TD
1946 New York Yankees	1	62	0
1947 New York Yankees	2	90	1
1949 New York Yankees	2	31	0
Total	**5**	**183**	**1**

Interceptions

	Int	Yds	TD
1947 New York Yankees	1	1	0
Total	**1**	**1**	**0**

ALLEN, Carl Blanchard

Position: RB-DB
Height: 6'0"; Weight: 175
College: Ouachita Baptist
Born: June 25, 1920, Haskell, OK
Deceased: November 11, 2008, Benton, AR

STATISTICS

Games

	GP	GS
1948 Brooklyn Dodgers	13	0
Total	**13**	**0**

Rushing

	Rush	Yds	TD
1948 Brooklyn Dodgers	1	9	0
Total	**1**	**9**	**0**

Punt Returns

	Ret	Yds	TD
1948 Brooklyn Dodgers	1	17	0
Total	**1**	**17**	**0**

Interceptions

	Int	Yds	TD
1948 Brooklyn Dodgers	2	45	1
Total	**2**	**45**	**1**

ALLEN, Ermal Glen

Position: QB-DB
Height: 5'11"; Weight: 165
College: Kentucky
Born: December 25, 1918, Kyles Ford, TN
Deceased: February 9, 1988, Dallas, TX

STATISTICS

Games

	GP	GS
1947 Cleveland Browns	12	0
Total	**12**	**0**

Rushing

	Rush	Yds	TD
1947 Cleveland Browns	7	11	0
Total	**7**	**11**	**0**

Passing

	Comp	Att	Yds	TD	Int
1947 Browns	4	13	88	0	0
Total	**4**	**13**	**88**	**0**	**0**

Punting

	Punt	Yds	Blk
1947 Cleveland Browns	4	135	0
Total	**4**	**135**	**0**

Punt Returns

	Ret	Yds	TD
1947 Cleveland Browns	4	28	0
Total	**4**	**28**	**0**

Interceptions

	Int	Yds	TD
1947 Cleveland Browns	4	63	0
Total	**4**	**63**	**0**

ANDERSON, Ezzret (Sugarfoot)

Position: E
Height: 6'4"; Weight: 215
College: Kentucky State
Born: February 10, 1920, Nashville, AR
Deceased: March 8, 2017, Calgary, Alberta, Canada

STATISTICS

Games

	GP	GS
1947 Los Angeles Dons	13	3
Total	**13**	**3**

Rushing

	Rush	Yds	TD
1947 Los Angeles Dons	3	24	0
Total	**3**	**24**	**0**

Receiving

	Rec	Yds	TD
1947 Los Angeles Dons	11	126	1
Total	**11**	**126**	**1**

ARMSTRONG, Charles Andrew (Charlie)

Position: DB-TB
Height: 5'10"; Weight: 180
College: Mississippi College
Born: April 20, 1919, Hickory, MS
Deceased: July 20, 2001, Meridian, MS

STATISTICS

Games
	GP	GS
1946 Brooklyn Dodgers	10	2
Total		

Rushing
	Rush	Yds	TD
1946 Brooklyn Dodgers	22	78	0
Total	22	78	0

Passing
	Comp	Att	Yds	TD	Int
1946 Dodgers	9	21	126	1	2
Total	9	21	126	1	2

Punting
	Punt	Yds	Blk
1946 Brooklyn Dodgers	6	231	0
Total	6	231	0

Punt Returns
	Ret	Yds	TD
1946 Brooklyn Dodgers	6	97	0
Total	6	97	0

Kick Returns
	Ret	Yds	TD
1946 Brooklyn Dodgers	3	93	0
Total	3	93	0

Interceptions
	Int	Yds	TD
1946 Brooklyn Dodgers	2	54	0
Total	2	54	0

ARMSTRONG, Graham Leo

Position: T
Height: 6'4"; Weight: 230
College: John Carroll
Born: May 30, 1918, Cleveland, OH
Deceased: June 25, 1960, Cuyahoga County, OH

STATISTICS

Games
	GP	GS
1941 Cleveland Rams	7	0
1945 Cleveland Rams	1	0
1947 Buffalo Bills	14	8
1948 Buffalo Bills	13	13
Total	35	21

Receiving
	Rec	Yds	TD
1948 Buffalo Bills	1	0	0
Total	1	0	0

Kick Returns
	Ret	Yds	TD
1948 Buffalo Bills	1	9	0
Total	1	9	0

Point After Touchdown
	XPM	XPA
1947 Buffalo Bills	8	10
1948 Buffalo Bills	15	17
Total	23	27

ARTOE, Lee Robert Reno

Position: T
Height: 6'3"; Weight: 234
College: California, Santa Clara
Born: March 2, 1917, Tacoma, WA
Deceased: April 1, 2005, Wilmette, IL

STATISTICS

Games
	GP	GS
1940 Chicago Bears	11	7
1941 Chicago Bears	11	11
1942 Chicago Bears	11	11
1945 Chicago Bears	9	6
1946 Los Angeles Dons	14	13
1947 Los Angeles Dons	14	6
1948 Baltimore Colts	14	8
Total	84	62

Kick Returns
	Ret	Yds	TD
1946 Los Angeles Dons	1	13	0
1947 Los Angeles Dons	1	16	0
Total	2	29	0

Field Goals
	FGM	FGA
1940 Chicago Bears	1	1
1941 Chicago Bears	1	7
Total	2	8

Point After Touchdown
	XPM	XPA
1940 Chicago Bears	1	2
1941 Chicago Bears	3	4
1942 Chicago Bears	20	22
1946 Los Angeles Dons	1	2
Total	25	30

ASCHENBRENNER, Francis Xavier (Frank)

Position: RB
Height: 5'10"; Weight: 188
College: Marquette, North Carolina, Northwestern
Born: July 12, 1925, Heibuehl, Germany
Deceased: January 30, 2012, Fountain Hills, AZ

STATISTICS

Games
	GP	GS
1949 Chicago Hornets	6	0
Total	6	0

Rushing

	Rush	Yds	TD
1949 Chicago Hornets	8	14	0
Total	8	14	0

Receiving

	Rec	Yds	TD
1949 Chicago Hornets	2	−4	0
Total	2	−4	0

Kick Returns

	Ret	Yds	TD
1949 Chicago Hornets	2	35	0
Total	2	35	0

AUDET, Earl Toussaint

Position: T
Height: 6'2"; Weight: 252
College: Georgetown, USC
Born: May 14, 1921, Providence, RI
Deceased: December 18, 2002, Los Angeles, CA

Games

	GP	GS
1945 Washington Redskins	10	5
1946 Los Angeles Dons	13	0
1947 Los Angeles Dons	14	6
1948 Los Angeles Dons	14	14
Total	51	25

AVERY, Donald Lee (Don)

Position: T
Height: 6'4"; Weight: 254
College: Alabama, USC
Born: February 10, 1921, Los Angeles, CA
Deceased: August 8, 2006, Long Beach, CA

STATISTICS

Games

	GP	GS
1946 Washington Redskins	11	2
1947 Washington Redskins	10	4
1948 Los Angeles Dons	1	0
Total	22	6

Kick Returns

	Ret	Yds	TD
1947 Wash. Redskins	2	24	0
Total	2	24	0

BAILEY, James Arrelaus (Jim)

Position: G
Height: 6'2"; Weight: 215
College: West Virginia State
Born: March 22, 1927, Columbus, OH
Deceased: December 27, 1999, Atlanta, GA

BALATTI, Edward T. (Ed)

Position: E-DB
Height: 6'1"; Weight: 195
College: None
Born: April 8, 1924, Los Banos, CA
Deceased: August 27, 1990, Novato, CA

STATISTICS

Games

	GP	GS
1946 San Francisco 49ers	14	0
1947 San Francisco 49ers	14	3
1948 San Francisco 49ers	1	0
1948 New York Yankees	2	0
1948 Buffalo Bills	7	1
Total	38	4

Receiving

	Rec	Yds	TD
1946 SF 49ers	4	15	0
1947 SF 49ers	8	98	1
Total	12	113	1

Punt Returns

	Ret	Yds	TD
1947 SF 49ers	2	8	1
Total	2	8	1

Kick Returns

	Ret	Yds	TD
1947 SF 49ers	1	16	0
Total	1	16	0

Point After Touchdown

	XPM	XPA
1946 SF 49ers	2	2
1947 SF 49ers	1	1
Total	3	3

Note: *There are a few discrepancies between the actual statistics and the official records in 1946. The total receiving yards for the season for Len Eshmont, Joe Vetrano, Ed Balatti and Ken Roskie were not consistent. Eshmont had an extra six receiving yards, while Vetrano was missing six yards. Balatti had an extra seven receiving yards and Roskie was missing seven yards. Since the numbers could not be verified, the official statistics are listed.*

BALDWIN, Alton (Al)

Position: E-DB
Height: 6'2"; Weight: 201
College: Arkansas
Born: March 21, 1923, Hot Springs, AR
Deceased: May 23, 1994, Hot Springs, AR

STATISTICS

Games

	GP	GS
1947 Buffalo Bills	14	5
1948 Buffalo Bills	13	13
1949 Buffalo Bills	12	12
1950 Green Bay Packers	12	0
Total	51	30

Rushing

	Rush	Yds	TD
1949 Buffalo Bills	2	1	0
Total	2	1	0

Receiving

	Rec	Yds	TD
1946 Buffalo Bisons	25	468	7
1948 Buffalo Bills	54	916	8
1949 Buffalo Bills	53	719	7
1950 Green Bay Packers	28	555	3
Total	160	2658	25

Kick Returns

	Ret	Yds	TD
1947 Buffalo Bills	1	6	0
Total	1	6	0

Interceptions

	Int	Yds	TD
1947 Buffalo Bills	2	90	0
1950 Green Bay Packers	5	35	0
Total			

Fumbles

	Fum	Rec	Yds	TD
1950 GB Packers	3	1	-3	0
Total	3	1	-3	0

BALDWIN, Burr Browning

Position: E-DE
Height: 6'1"; Weight: 197
College: UCLA
Born: June 13, 1922, Bakersfield, CA
Deceased: August 20, 2007, Bakersfield, CA

STATISTICS

Games

	GP	GS
1947 Los Angeles Dons	13	3
1948 Los Angeles Dons	12	8
1949 Los Angeles Dons	9	8
Total	34	19

Rushing

	Rush	Yds	TD
1949 Los Angeles Dons	1	1	0
Total			

Receiving

	Rec	Yds	TD
1947 Los Angeles Dons	12	275	1
1948 Los Angeles Dons	10	96	0
1949 Los Angeles Dons	2	26	0
Total	24	397	1

Interceptions

	Int	Yds	TD
1949 Los Angeles Dons	2	4	0
Total	2	4	0

BALDWIN, John David (Jack)

Position: C-LB
Height: 6'3"; Weight: 223
College: Centenary
Born: July 31, 1921, Clyde, TX
Deceased: September 13, 1989, Kerrville, TX

STATISTICS

Games

	GP	GS
1946 New York Yankees	7	3
1947 New York Yankees	2	0
1947 San Francisco 49ers	3	0
1948 Buffalo Bills	3	0
Total	15	3

BANDUCCI, Bruno

Position: G
Height: 5'11"; Weight: 216
College: Stanford
Born: November 11, 1920, Tsingnano, Italy
Deceased: September 15, 1985, Sonoma, CA

STATISTICS

Games

	GP	GS
1944 Philadelphia Eagles	10	9
1945 Philadelphia Eagles	9	8
1946 San Francisco 49ers	14	14
1947 San Francisco 49ers	10	8
1948 San Francisco 49ers	8	0
1949 San Francisco 49ers	12	2
1950 San Francisco 49ers	12	0
1951 San Francisco 49ers	12	0
1952 San Francisco 49ers	12	0
1953 San Francisco 49ers	12	0
1954 San Francisco 49ers	11	0
Total	122	41

Receiving

	Rec	Yds	TD
1952 S.F. 49ers	1	-4	0
Total	1	-4	0

Punt Returns

	Ret	Yds	TD
1947 S.F. 49ers	1	19	0
Total	1	19	0

Kick Returns

	Ret	Yds	TD
1947 S.F. 49ers	1	27	0
1951 S.F. 49ers	1	3	0
Total	2	30	0

Fumbles				
	Fum	Rec	Yds	TD
1952 S.F. 49ers	0	2	0	0
1954 S.F. 49ers	0	2	0	0
Total	**0**	**4**	**0**	**0**

BARWEGAN, Richard James (Dick)

Position: G
Height: 6'1"; Weight: 227
College: Purdue
Born: December 25, 1921, Chicago, IL
Deceased: September 3, 1966, Baltimore, MD

STATISTICS

Games		
	GP	GS
1947 New York Yankees	14	14
1948 Baltimore Colts	12	12
1949 Baltimore Colts	12	10
1950 Chicago Bears	11	0
1951 Chicago Bears	12	0
1952 Chicago Bears	11	0
1953 Baltimore Colts	11	0
1954 Baltimore Colts	9	0
Total	**92**	**36**

Interceptions			
	Int	Yds	TD
1948 Baltimore Colts	1	0	0
Total	**1**	**0**	**0**

Fumbles				
	Fum	Rec	Yds	TD
1951 Chicago Bears	0	2	0	0
1953 Baltimore Colts	0	1	0	0
Total	**0**	**3**	**0**	**0**

BASS, William T. (Bill)

Position: B
Height: 5'10"; Weight: 180
College: Tennessee State, UNLV
Born: 1921, Greensboro, NC
Deceased: September 28, 1967, Tilsonburg, Canada

STATISTICS

Games		
	GP	GS
1947 Chicago Rockets	14	3
Total	**14**	**3**

Rushing			
	Rush	Yds	TD
1947 Chicago Rockets	28	44	0
Total	**28**	**44**	**0**

Receiving			
	Rec	Yds	TD
1947 Chicago Rockets	8	79	1
Total	**8**	**79**	**1**

Passing				
	Comp	Att	Yds	TD	Int
1947 Chi Rockets	1	1	14	0	0
Total	**1**	**1**	**14**	**0**	**0**

Punt Returns			
	Ret	Yds	TD
1947 Chicago Rockets	10	85	0
Total	**10**	**85**	**0**

Kick Returns			
	Ret	Yds	TD
1947 Chicago Rockets	12	264	0
Total	**12**	**264**	**0**

Interceptions			
	Int	Yds	TD
1947 Chicago Rockets	2	104	1
Total	**2**	**104**	**1**

BASSI, Richard Joseph (Dick)

Position: G
Height: 5'11"; Weight: 214
College: Santa Clara
Born: January 1, 1915, San Luis Obispo, CA
Deceased: August 12, 1973, San Francisco, CA

STATISTICS

Games		
	GP	GS
1938 Chicago Bears	9	0
1939 Chicago Bears	10	1
1940 Philadelphia Eagles	11	9
1941 Pittsburgh Steelers	11	11
1946 San Francisco 49ers	8	8
1947 San Francisco 49ers	8	0
Total	**57**	**29**

Receiving			
	Rec	Yds	TD
1941 Pittsburgh Steelers	1	6	0
Total	**1**	**6**	**0**

Interceptions			
	Int	Yds	TD
1946 SF 49ers	1	2	0
Total	**1**	**2**	**0**

BATORSKI, John Michael (Bat)

Position: E
Height: 6'2"; Weight: 238
College: Colgate
Born: September 27, 1920, Lackawanna, NY
Deceased: November 16, 1982, Old Field, NY

STATISTICS

Games		
	GP	GS
1946 Buffalo Bisons	8	2
Total	**8**	**2**

	Receiving		
	Rec	Yds	TD
1946 Buffalo Bisons	2	27	0
Total	2	27	0

BAUMAN, Alfred Ernest (Alf)

Position: DT-T
Height: 6'2"; Weight: 228
College: Northwestern
Born: January 3, 1920, Chicago, IL
Deceased: March 2, 1979, Pacifica, CA

STATISTICS

Games		
	GP	GS
1947 Philadelphia Eagles	2	0
1947 Chicago Rockets	3	0
1948 Chicago Bears	5	0
1949 Chicago Bears	12	1
1950 Chicago Bears	12	0
Total	34	1

Kick Returns			
	Ret	Yds	TD
1950 Chicago Bears	1	9	0
Total	1	9	0

Fumbles			
	Fum	Rec	Yds	TD
1949 Chicago Bears	0	1	0	0
Total	0	1	0	0

BAUMGARTNER, William R. (Bill)

Position: E
Height: 6'3"; Weight: 202
College: Minnesota
Born: April 17, 1921, Duluth, MN
Deceased: September 1981

Games		
	GP	GS
1947 Baltimore Colts	2	0
Total	2	0

BEALS, Alyn Richard

Position: E-DE
Height: 6'0"; Weight: 188
College: Santa Clara
Born: April 27, 1921, Marysville, CA
Deceased: August 11, 1993, Redwood City, CA

STATISTICS

Games		
	GP	GS
1946 San Francisco 49ers	14	1
1947 San Francisco 49ers	13	9
1948 San Francisco 49ers	14	13
1949 San Francisco 49ers	12	8
1950 San Francisco 49ers	12	0
1951 San Francisco 49ers	12	0
Total	77	31

Rushing		
	Rush	Yds	TD
1946 S.F. 49ers	2	−7	0
1947 S.F. 49ers	5	48	0
1949 S.F. 49ers	4	32	0
Total	11	73	0

Receiving			
	Rec	Yds	TD
1946 S.F. 49ers	40	586	10
1947 S.F. 49ers	47	655	10
1948 S.F. 49ers	46	591	14
1949 S.F. 49ers	44	678	12
1950 S.F. 49ers	22	315	3
1951 S.F. 49ers	12	126	0
Total	211	2951	49

Interceptions			
	Int	Yds	TD
1947 S.F. 49ers	1	0	0
Total	1	0	0

Point After Touchdown		
	XPM	XPA
1946 S.F. 49ers	1	1
1947 S.F. 49ers	1	1
Total	2	2

BECHTOL, Hubert Edwin (Hub)

Position: E
Height: 6'3"; Weight: 202
College: Texas, Texas Tech
Born: April 20, 1926, Amarillo, TX
Deceased: October 22, 2004, Austin, TX

STATISTICS

Games		
	GP	GS
1947 Baltimore Colts	14	12
1948 Baltimore Colts	12	0
1949 Baltimore Colts	12	2
Total	38	14

Rushing			
	Rush	Yds	TD
1947 Baltimore Colts	2	−1	0
Total	2	−1	0

Receiving			
	Rec	Yds	TD
1947 Baltimore Colts	17	167	1
1948 Baltimore Colts	2	25	0
Total	19	192	1

Kick Returns			
	Ret	Yds	TD
1947 Baltimore Colts	1	13	0
Total	1	13	0

Interceptions			
	Int	Yds	TD
1947 Baltimore Colts	1	7	0
1949 Baltimore Colts	1	6	0
Total	**2**	**13**	**0**

BELL, Edward (Ed)

Position: G-T
Height: 6'1"; Weight: 227
College: Indiana
Born: September 20, 1921, Chicago, IL
Deceased: December 6, 1990, South Bend, IN

STATISTICS

Games		
	GP	GS
1946 Miami Seahawks	7	0
1947 Green Bay Packers	11	1
1948 Green Bay Packers	12	0
1949 Green Bay Packers	12	0
Total	**42**	**1**

Fumbles			
	Fum	Rec	Yds	TD
1949 Green Bay Packers	0	1	0	0
Total	**0**	**1**	**0**	**0**

BENSON, George Nathan

Position: B
Height: 6'1"; Weight: 205
College: LSU, Northwestern
Born: May 7, 1919, Madison, IN
Deceased: August 24, 2001, Cape Coral, FL

STATISTICS

Games		
	GP	GS
1947 Brooklyn Dodgers	1	0
Total	**1**	**0**

Rushing			
	Rush	Yds	TD
1947 Brooklyn Dodgers	2	5	0
Total	**2**	**5**	**0**

BENTZ, Roman Walter

Position: G-T
Height: 6'2"; Weight: 230
College: Tulane
Born: September 1, 1919, Iron Ridge, WI
Deceased: June 24, 1996, Tomahawk, WI

STATISTICS

Games		
	GP	GS
1946 New York Yankees	12	3
1947 New York Yankees	13	13
1948 New York Yankees	5	3
1949 San Francisco 49ers	4	0
Total	**34**	**19**

BEREZNEY, Paul Lawrence

Position: T
Height: 6'2"; Weight: 220
College: Fordham
Born: September 25, 1915, Jersey City, NJ
Deceased: March 29, 1990, Columbus, GA

STATISTICS

Games		
	GP	GS
1942 Green Bay Packers	11	11
1943 Green Bay Packers	10	6
1944 Green Bay Packers	10	6
1946 Miami Seahawks	1	0
Total	**32**	**23**

Kick Returns			
	Ret	Yds	TD
1942 Green Bay Packers	1	7	0
Total	**1**	**7**	**0**

BEREZNEY, Peter John, Jr. (Pete)

Position: T
Height: 6'2"; Weight: 240
College: Notre Dame
Born: November 14, 1923, Jersey City, NJ
Deceased: October 13, 2008, Olean, NY

STATISTICS

Games		
	GP	GS
1947 Los Angeles Dons	12	3
1948 Baltimore Colts	13	0
Total	**25**	**3**

BERNHARDT, George W.

Position: G
Height: 5'10"; Weight: 213
College: Illinois
Born: June 15, 1920
Deceased: December 6, 1987

STATISTICS

Games		
	GP	GS
1946 Brooklyn Dodgers	14	12
1947 Brooklyn Dodgers	2	2
1948 Chicago Rockets	11	8
1948 Brooklyn Dodgers	3	2
Total	**30**	**24**

Kick Returns

	Ret	Yds	TD
1946 Brooklyn Dodgers	1	13	0
Total	**1**	**13**	**0**

BERRY, Connie Mack

Position: E
Height: 6'3"; Weight: 215
College: North Carolina State
Born: April 19, 1915, Spartanburg, SC
Deceased: June 24, 1980, Fayetteville, NC

STATISTICS

Games

	GP	GS
1939 Detroit Lions	3	0
1940 Cleveland Rams	3	0
1940 Green Bay Packers	1	0
1942 Chicago Bears	10	1
1943 Chicago Bears	10	2
1944 Chicago Bears	10	7
1945 Chicago Bears	7	3
1946 Chicago Bears	6	3
1947 Chicago Bears	1	0
Total	**51**	**16**

Receiving

	Rec	Yds	TD
1940 Green Bay Packers	1	17	0
1942 Chicago Bears	4	29	0
1943 Chicago Bears	4	99	2
1944 Chicago Bears	7	21	6
1945 Chicago Bears	12	202	0
1946 Chicago Bears	4	58	0
Total	**32**	**426**	**8**

Fumbles

	Fum	Rec	Yds	TD
1945 Chicago Bears	0	1	0	0
Total	**0**	**1**	**0**	**0**

BERTELLI, Angelo Bortolo

Position: QB
Height: 6'1"; Weight: 190
College: Notre Dame
Born: June 18, 1921, West Springfield, MA
Deceased: June 26, 1999, Clifton, NJ

STATISTICS

Games

	GP	GS
1946 Los Angeles Dons	12	3
1947 Chicago Rockets	1	0
1948 Chicago Rockets	3	2
Total	**16**	**5**

Rushing

	Rush	Yds	TD
1946 Los Angeles Dons	11	−16	1
1947 Chicago Rockets	1	2	0
1948 Chicago Rockets	2	−1	0
Total	**14**	**−15**	**1**

Passing

	Comp	Att	Yds	TD	Int
1946 L.A. Dons	67	127	917	7	14
1947 Rockets	2	7	−5	0	2
1948 Rockets	7	32	60	1	3
Total	**76**	**166**	**972**	**8**	**19**

Punting

	Punt	Yds	Blk
1946 Los Angeles Dons	2	76	0
Total	**2**	**76**	**0**

BESON, Warren Lawson

Position: C
Height: 6'0"; Weight: 205
College: Minnesota
Born: November 16, 1923, Minneapolis, MN
Deceased: October 25, 1959, Northfield, MN

STATISTICS

Games

	GP	GS
1949 Baltimore Colts	3	0
Total	**3**	**0**

BILLMAN, John Arthur

Position: G-LB-T
Height: 6'1"; Weight: 202
College: Minnesota
Born: December 1, 1919, Minneapolis, MN
Deceased: March 16, 2012, Plymouth, MA

STATISTICS

Games

	GP	GS
1946 Brooklyn Dodgers	3	0
1947 Chicago Rockets	2	1
Total	**5**	**1**

BLACK, John Thomas (Blondy)

Position: B
Height: 5'11"; Weight: 195
College: Mississippi State
Born: August 20, 1920, Philadelphia, MS
Deceased: May 4, 2000, Madison, MS

STATISTICS

Games

	GP	GS
1946 Buffalo Bisons	4	0
1947 Baltimore Colts	5	0
Total	**9**	**0**

Rushing

	Rush	Yds	TD
1946 Buffalo Bisons	1	10	0
1947 Baltimore Colts	5	39	0
Total	**6**	**49**	**0**

Receiving

	Rec	Yds	TD
1946 Buffalo Bisons	1	21	0
1947 Baltimore Colts	1	7	0
Total	**2**	**28**	**0**

Punt Returns

	Ret	Yds	TD
1946 Buffalo Bisons	2	58	0
Total	**2**	**58**	**0**

Interceptions

	Int	Yds	TD
1946 Buffalo Bisons	1	18	0
Total	**1**	**18**	**0**

BLANDIN, Ernest Elmer (Ernie)

Position: T-DT
Height: 6'4"; Weight: 248
College: Tulane
Born: June 21, 1919, Augusta, KS
Deceased: September 16, 1968, Randallstown, MD

STATISTICS

Games

	GP	GS
1946 Cleveland Browns	14	5
1947 Cleveland Browns	12	7
1948 Baltimore Colts	14	14
1949 Baltimore Colts	10	8
1950 Baltimore Colts	12	11
1953 Baltimore Colts	9	0
Total	**71**	**45**

Rushing

	Rush	Yds	TD
1947 Cleveland Browns	1	−6	0
Total	**1**	**−6**	**0**

Receiving

	Rec	Yds	TD
1948 Baltimore Colts	1	16	0
Total	**1**	**16**	**0**

Kick Returns

	Ret	Yds	TD
1950 Baltimore Colts	3	31	0
Total	**3**	**31**	**0**

Fumbles

	Fum	Rec	Yds	TD
1950 Baltimore Colts	2	2	0	0
Total	**2**	**2**	**0**	**0**

BLOUNT, Lloyd Lamar (Lamar)

Position: E-B
Height: 6'1"; Weight: 190
College: Duke, Mississippi State
Born: April 11, 1920, Decatur, MS
Deceased: August 6, 2007, Decatur, MS

STATISTICS

Games

	GP	GS
1946 Miami Seahawks	12	6
1947 Baltimore Colts	5	3
1947 Buffalo Bills	5	0
Total	**22**	**9**

Rushing

	Rush	Yds	TD
1947 Baltimore Colts	1	−2	0
1947 Buffalo Bills	3	7	0
Total	**4**	**5**	**0**

Receiving

	Rec	Yds	TD
1946 Buffalo Bisons	13	218	1
1947 Buffalo Bills	8	148	0
Total	**21**	**366**	**1**

BOEDEKER, William Henry (Bill)

Position: HB
Height: 5'11"; Weight: 192
College: DePaul
Born: March 7, 1924, Milwaukee, WI
Deceased: March 21, 2014, Fort Wayne, IN

STATISTICS

Games

	GP	GS
1946 Chicago Rockets	12	1
1947 Cleveland Browns	12	3
1948 Cleveland Browns	14	3
1949 Cleveland Browns	12	3
1950 Philadelphia Eagles	1	0
1950 Green Bay Packers	9	0
Total	**60**	**14**

Rushing

	Rush	Yds	TD
1946 Chicago Rockets	6	8	0
1947 Cleveland Browns	31	194	4
1948 Cleveland Browns	78	254	3
1949 Cleveland Browns	50	269	1
1950 Green Bay Packers	8	16	0
Total	**173**	**741**	**8**

Receiving

	Rec	Yds	TD
1946 Chicago Rockets	5	82	1
1947 Cleveland Browns	8	175	1
1948 Cleveland Browns	13	237	2
1949 Cleveland Browns	11	371	2
1950 Green Bay Packers	1	10	0
Total	**38**	**875**	**6**

Punt Returns

	Ret	Yds	TD
1946 Chicago Rockets	2	29	0
1947 Cleveland Browns	3	82	0
1948 Cleveland Browns	2	8	0
1950 Green Bay Packers	5	49	0
Total	**12**	**168**	**0**

Kick Returns

	Ret	Yds	TD
1946 Chicago Rockets	2	84	0
1947 Cleveland Browns	6	133	0
1948 Cleveland Browns	4	61	0
1949 Cleveland Browns	9	189	0
1950 Green Bay Packers	1	20	0
Total	**22**	**487**	**0**

Interceptions

	Int	Yds	TD
1946 Chicago Rockets	1	26	0
Total	**1**	**26**	**0**

BRAZINSKY, Samuel Joseph (Sam)

Position: C
Height: 6'1"; Weight: 215
College: Villanova
Born: January 9, 1921, Kulpmont, PA
Deceased: May 12, 2003, Manville, NJ

STATISTICS

Games

	GP	GS
1946 Buffalo Bisons	5	0
Total	**5**	**0**

Interceptions

	Int	Yds	TD
1946 Buffalo Bisons	2	7	0
Total	**2**	**7**	**0**

BROWN, George William

Position: G-DG
Height: 6'2"; Weight: 222
College: TCU
Born: September 23, 1923, Boyd, TX
Deceased: January 21, 2013, Roseville, CA

STATISTICS

Games

	GP	GS
1949 New York Yankees	8	0
1950 New York Yanks	12	0
Total	**20**	**0**

Fumbles

	Fum	Rec	Yds	TD
1950 New York Yanks	0	1	0	0
Total	**0**	**1**	**0**	**0**

BROWN, Hardy

Position: LB-DB-FB
Height: 6'0"; Weight: 193
College: SMU, Tulsa
Born: May 8, 1924, Quanah, TX
Deceased: November 8, 1991, Stockton, CA

STATISTICS

Games

	GP	GS
1948 Brooklyn Dodgers	11	4
1949 Chicago Hornets	12	1
1950 Baltimore Colts	4	0
1950 Washington Redskins	8	0
1951 San Francisco 49ers	12	0
1952 San Francisco 49ers	12	0
1953 San Francisco 49ers	12	0
1954 San Francisco 49ers	11	0
1955 San Francisco 49ers	12	0
1956 Chicago Cardinals	8	0
1960 Denver Broncos	13	0
Total	**115**	**5**

Rushing

	Rush	Yds	TD
1948 Brooklyn Dodgers	6	23	1
1949 Chicago Hornets	1	2	0
Total	**7**	**25**	**1**

Receiving

	Rec	Yds	TD
1948 Brooklyn Dodgers	3	36	1
1949 Chicago Hornets	1	10	0
Total	**4**	**46**	**1**

Punting

	Punt	Yds	Blk
1949 Chicago Hornets	10	397	0
Total	**10**	**397**	**0**

Kick Returns

	Ret	Yds	TD
1950 Baltimore Colts	2	15	0
1952 S.F. 49ers	2	31	0
1953 S.F. 49ers	1	3	0
Total	**5**	**49**	**0**

Interceptions

	Int	Yds	TD
1948 Brooklyn Dodgers	1	0	0
1949 Chicago Hornets	3	59	0
1950 Baltimore Colts	1	16	0
1951 S.F. 49ers	1	5	0
1952 S.F. 49ers	1	16	0
1953 S.F. 49ers	1	7	0
1954 S.F. 49ers	3	42	1
1955 S.F. 49ers	2	28	0
Total	13	173	1

Fumbles

	Fum	Rec	Yds	TD
1950 Baltimore Colts	1	0	0	0
1951 S.F. 49ers	0	1	0	0
1953 S.F. 49ers	0	1	0	0
1954 S.F. 49ers	0	2	0	0
1955 S.F. 49ers	0	1	0	0
Total	1	5	0	0

Point After Touchdown

	XPM	XPA
1948 Brooklyn Dodgers	25	29
Total	25	29

BROWN, John Edward

Position: LB-C
Height: 6'4"; Weight: 230
College: North Carolina Central
Born: April 9, 1922, Belen, MS
Deceased: June 1, 2009

STATISTICS

Games

	GP	GS
1947 Los Angeles Dons	14	2
1948 Los Angeles Dons	14	0
1949 Los Angeles Dons	12	3
Total	40	5

Interceptions

	Int	Yds	TD
1947 Los Angeles Dons	1	4	0
1948 Los Angeles Dons	1	1	0
1949 Los Angeles Dons	3	46	0
Total	5	51	0

BRUCE, Gail Robert

Position: DE-E
Height: 6'1"; Weight: 206
College: Washington
Born: September 29, 1923, Puyallup, PA
Deceased: August 23, 1998, Santa Maria, CA

STATISTICS

Games

	GP	GS
1948 San Francisco 49ers	14	0
1949 San Francisco 49ers	12	4
1950 San Francisco 49ers	12	0
1951 San Francisco 49ers	12	0
Total	50	4

Rushing

	Rush	Yds	TD
1948 S.F. 49ers	1	1	0
Total	1	1	0

Receiving

	Rec	Yds	TD
1948 S.F. 49ers	5	49	0
1949 S.F. 49ers	1	9	0
1950 S.F. 49ers	1	10	0
Total	7	68	0

Kick Returns

	Ret	Yds	TD
1949 S.F. 49ers	1	8	0
Total	1	8	0

Interceptions

	Int	Yds	TD
1949 S.F. 49ers	1	5	0
1950 S.F. 49ers	1	4	0
Total	2	9	0

Fumbles

	Fum	Rec	Yds	TD
1951 S.F. 49ers	0	2	0	0
Total	0	2	0	0

Point After Touchdown

	XPM	XPA
1951 S.F. 49ers	1	1
Total	1	1

BRUTZ, James Charles (Jim)

Position: T
Height: 6'0"; Weight: 230
College: Notre Dame
Born: February 12, 1919, Niles, OH
Deceased: November 5, 2000, Warren, OH

STATISTICS

Games

	GP	GS
1946 Chicago Rockets	14	3
1947 Chicago Rockets	9	8
Total	23	11

BRYANT, Robert R. (Bob)

Position: T
Height: 6'3"; Weight: 226
College: Texas Tech
Born: June 14, 1919, Frederick, OK
Deceased: November 3, 2000, Oklahoma City, OK

STATISTICS

Games

	GP	GS
1946 San Francisco 49ers	14	3
1947 San Francisco 49ers	14	14
1948 San Francisco 49ers	14	14
1949 San Francisco 49ers	5	5
Total	47	36

Punt Returns

	Ret	Yds	TD
1948 S.F. 49ers	1	14	0
Total	1	14	0

BUKSAR, George Benjamin

Position: LB-FB
Height: 6'0"; Weight: 206
College: Purdue, San Francisco
Born: August 12, 1926, St. Joseph, MI
Deceased: February 23, 2011, Solon, OH

STATISTICS

Games

	GP	GS
1949 Chicago Hornets	6	0
1950 Baltimore Colts	9	2
1951 Washington Redskins	11	0
1952 Washington Redskins	10	0
Total	36	2

Rushing

	Rush	Yds	TD
1949 Chicago Hornets	13	16	1
1950 Baltimore Colts	12	44	0
1952 Wash. Redskins	3	3	0
Total	28	63	1

Receiving

	Rec	Yds	TD
1950 Baltimore Colts	2	2	0
1952 Wash. Redskins	2	3	0
Total	4	5	0

Passing

	Comp	Att	Yds	TD	Int
1949 Hornets	0	1	0	0	0
Total	0	1	0	0	0

Punt Returns

	Ret	Yds	TD
1951 Wash. Redskins	1	0	0
Total	1	0	0

Kick Returns

	Ret	Yds	TD
1951 Wash. Redskins	4	56	0
1952 Wash. Redskins	4	43	0
Total	8	99	0

Interceptions

	Int	Yds	TD
1950 Baltimore Colts	6	79	0
1951 Wash. Redskins	1	20	0
Total	7	99	0

Fumbles

	Fum	Rec	Yds	TD
1950 Baltimore Colts	0	1	0	0
1951 Wash. Redskins	0	2	0	0
Total	0	3	0	0

Field Goals

	FGM	FGA
1952 Wash. Redskins	3	7
Total	3	7

Point After Touchdown

	XPM	XPA
1952 Wash. Redskins	15	18
Total	15	18

BUFFINGTON, Harry Webster

Position: G
Height: 6'0"; Weight: 206
College: Oklahoma State
Born: August 27, 1919, Pryor, OK
Deceased: November 19, 2003, Lubbock, TX

STATISTICS

Games

	GP	GS
1942 New York Giants	9	8
1946 Brooklyn Dodgers	12	10
1947 Brooklyn Dodgers	14	14
1948 Brooklyn Dodgers	10	1
Total	45	33

Interceptions

	Int	Yds	TD
1942 New York Giants	1	10	0
Total	1	10	0

BUMGARDNER, Rex Keith

Position: HB-DB
Height: 5'11"; Weight: 193
College: West Virginia
Born: September 6, 1923, Clarksburg, WV
Deceased: June 1, 1998, Clarksburg, WV

STATISTICS

Games

	GP	GS
1948 Buffalo Bills	13	3
1949 Buffalo Bills	10	8
1950 Cleveland Browns	10	0
1951 Cleveland Browns	10	0
1952 Cleveland Browns	11	0
Total	**54**	**11**

Rushing

	Rush	Yds	TD
1948 Buffalo Bills	14	82	0
1949 Buffalo Bills	101	391	1
1950 Cleveland Browns	67	231	2
1951 Cleveland Browns	45	126	1
1952 Cleveland Browns	9	38	0
Total	**236**	**868**	**4**

Receiving

	Rec	Yds	TD
1948 Buffalo Bills	1	63	0
1949 Buffalo Bills	7	168	4
1950 Cleveland Browns	9	112	1
1951 Cleveland Browns	5	61	1
Total	**22**	**404**	**6**

Punt Returns

	Ret	Yds	TD
1948 Buffalo Bills	16	336	2
1949 Buffalo Bills	4	35	0
1952 Cleveland Browns	4	24	0
Total	**24**	**395**	**2**

Kick Returns

	Ret	Yds	TD
1948 Buffalo Bills	9	141	0
1949 Buffalo Bills	9	163	0
1951 Cleveland Browns	3	75	0
1952 Cleveland Browns	5	89	0
Total	**26**	**468**	**0**

Interceptions

	Int	Yds	TD
1948 Buffalo Bills	2	7	0
1952 Cleveland Browns	2	33	0
Total	**4**	**40**	**0**

Fumbles

	Fum	Rec	Yds	TD
1950 Cleveland Browns	1	0	0	0
1951 Cleveland Browns	1	0	0	0
Total	**2**	**0**	**0**	**0**

BURRUS, Harry Clifton, Jr.

Position: B-E
Height: 6'1"; Weight: 195
College: Hardin-Simmons
Born: April 6, 1921, Slaton, TX
Deceased: September 20, 2004, Winter Haven, FL

STATISTICS

Games

	GP	GS
1946 New York Yankees	11	3
1947 New York Yankees	14	5
1948 Chicago Rockets	1	0
1948 Brooklyn Dodgers	12	1
Total	**38**	**9**

Rushing

	Rush	Yds	TD
1946 New York Yankees	1	3	0
1947 New York Yankees	1	5	0
1948 Brooklyn Dodgers	1	–3	0
Total	**3**	**5**	**0**

Receiving

	Rec	Yds	TD
1946 New York Yankees	10	251	1
1947 New York Yankees	8	192	2
1948 Chicago Rockets	2	60	0
1948 Brooklyn Dodgers	8	167	1
Total	**28**	**670**	**4**

Interceptions

	Int	Yds	TD
1946 New York Yankees	2	37	0
1947 New York Yankees	1	11	0
1948 Brooklyn Dodgers	3	82	0
Total	**6**	**130**	**0**

Point After Touchdown

	XPM	XPA
1948 Chicago Rockets	2	3
Total	**2**	**3**

BUTKUS, Carl John

Position: G-T
Height: 6'1"; Weight: 245
College: George Washington
Born: December 26, 1922, Scranton, PA
Deceased: August 3, 1978, Washington, DC

STATISTICS

Games

	GP	GS
1948 New York Yankees	4	1
1948 Washington Redskins	9	0
1949 New York Giants	11	7
Total	**24**	**8**

Fumbles

	Fum	Rec	Yds	TD
1948 Wash. Redskins	0	1	3	0
Total	**0**	**1**	**3**	**0**

CALLAHAN, Robert Francis (Bob)

Position: C-LB
Height: 6'0"; Weight: 205
College: Michigan, Missouri
Born: September 26, 1923, St. Louis, MO
Deceased:

STATISTICS

Games		
	GP	GS
1948 Buffalo Bills	7	0
Total	7	0

CALVELLI, Anthony T. (Tony)

Position: C-G
Height: 5'10"; Weight: 189
College: Stanford
Born: July 16, 1915, Stockton, CA
Deceased: May 17, 1979, San Mateo County, CA

STATISTICS

Games		
	GP	GS
1939 Detroit Lions	7	0
1940 Detroit Lions	11	6
1947 San Francisco 49ers	13	1
Total	31	7

Interceptions			
	Int	Yds	TD
1940 Detroit Lions	2	51	1
1947 S.F. 49ers	1	2	0
Total	3	53	1

CAMP, James Vernon (Jim)

Position: QB
Height: 6'0"; Weight: 162
College: North Carolina, Randolph-Macon
Born: August 8, 1924, Union, SC
Deceased: January 31, 2002, Durham, NC

STATISTICS

Games		
	GP	GS
1948 Brooklyn Dodgers	12	3
Total	12	3

Rushing			
	Rush	Yds	TD
1948 Brooklyn Dodgers	8	43	0
Total	8	43	0

Receiving			
	Rec	Yds	TD
1948 Brooklyn Dodgers	1	43	0
Total	1	43	0

Kick Returns			
	Ret	Yds	TD
1948 Brooklyn Dodgers	1	12	0
Total	1	12	0

Interceptions			
	Int	Yds	TD
1948 Brooklyn Dodgers	1	69	0
Total	1	69	0

CARDINAL, Frederick (Fred)

Position: B
Height: 5'11"; Weight: 220
College: Baldwin-Wallace, Notre Dame
Born: February 12, 1925, Dover, OH
Deceased: February 5, 2004, Barberton, OH

STATISTICS

Games		
	GP	GS
1947 New York Yankees	1	0
Total	1	0

CARPENTER, Jack Chrisman

Position: T
Height: 6'0"; Weight: 240
College: Columbia, Michigan, Missouri
Born: July 29, 1923, Kansas City, MO
Deceased: October 16, 2005, Honolulu, HI

STATISTICS

Games		
	GP	GS
1947 Buffalo Bills	13	2
1948 Buffalo Bills	12	5
1949 Buffalo Bills	8	7
1949 San Francisco 49ers	3	0
Total	36	14

Receiving			
	Rec	Yds	TD
1949 Buffalo Bills	2	20	0
Total	2	20	0

CARR, Edwin Forest (Eddie)

Position: DB-HB
Height: 6'0"; Weight: 185
College: None
Born: April 27, 1923
Deceased: January 7, 2011, Pasco, FL

STATISTICS

Games

	GP	GS
1947 San Francisco 49ers	10	0
1948 San Francisco 49ers	13	1
1949 San Francisco 49ers	7	2
Total	30	3

Rushing

	Rush	Yds	TD
1947 S.F. 49ers	11	42	0
1948 S.F. 49ers	14	121	1
1949 S.F. 49ers	19	120	2
Total	44	283	3

Receiving

	Rec	Yds	TD
1947 S.F. 49ers	4	41	0
1948 S.F. 49ers	3	40	0
1949 S.F. 49ers	7	165	3
Total	14	246	3

Punt Returns

	Ret	Yds	TD
1947 S.F. 49ers	1	20	0
1949 S.F. 49ers	1	6	0
Total	2	26	0

Kick Returns

	Ret	Yds	TD
1947 S.F. 49ers	2	42	0
1948 S.F. 49ers	1	16	0
Total	3	58	0

Interceptions

	Int	Yds	TD
1947 S.F. 49ers	2	59	0
1948 S.F. 49ers	7	144	1
1949 S.F. 49ers	7	87	1
Total	16	290	2

CASANEGA, Kenneth Thomas (Ken)

Position: QB-DB-HB
Height: 5'11"; Weight: 175
College: Santa Clara
Born: February 18, 1921, Alameda County, CA
Deceased:

STATISTICS

Games

	GP	GS
1946 San Francisco 49ers	14	5
1948 San Francisco 49ers	1	0
Total	15	5

Rushing

	Rush	Yds	TD
1946 S.F. 49ers	29	90	1
Total	29	90	1

Receiving

	Rec	Yds	TD
1946 S.F. 49ers	5	102	1
Total	5	102	1

Punt Returns

	Ret	Yds	TD
1946 S.F. 49ers	18	248	0
Total	18	248	0

Kick Returns

	Ret	Yds	TD
1946 S.F. 49ers	3	61	0
Total	3	61	0

Interceptions

	Int	Yds	TD
1946 S.F. 49ers	8	146	0
Total	8	146	0

CASE, Ernest Francis (Ernie)

Position: QB-DB
Height: 5'10"; Weight: 170
College: UCLA
Born: November 23, 1919, Case, TX
Deceased: December 13, 1995, Palos Verde Estates, CA

STATISTICS

Games

	GP	GS
1947 Baltimore Colts	14	10
Total	14	10

Rushing

	Rush	Yds	TD
1947 Baltimore Colts	1	0	0
Total	1	0	0

Passing

	Comp	Att	Yds	TD	Int
1947 Bal. Colts	4	11	49	0	1
Total	4	11	49	0	1

Punting

	Punt	Yds	Blk
1947 Baltimore Colts	5	152	1
Total	5	152	1

Punt Returns

	Ret	Yds	TD
1947 Baltimore Colts	2	18	0
Total	2	18	0

Kick Returns

	Ret	Yds	TD
1947 Baltimore Colts	4	104	0
Total	4	104	0

Interceptions

	Int	Yds	TD
1947 Baltimore Colts	2	56	0
Total	2	56	0

Field Goals

	FGM	FGA
1947 Baltimore Colts	1	1
Total	**1**	**1**

Point After Touchdown

	XPM	XPA
1947 Baltimore Colts	1	1
Total	**1**	**1**

CASEY, Thomas Ray (Tom)

Position: TB-DB
Height: 5'11"; Weight: 175
College: Hampton
Born: July 30, 1924, Wellsville, OH
Deceased: October 10, 2002, Winnipeg, Canada

STATISTICS

Games

	GP	GS
1948 New York Yankees	11	0
Total	**11**	**0**

Rushing

	Rush	Yds	TD
1948 New York Yankees	18	75	0
Total	**18**	**75**	**0**

Passing

	Comp	Att	Yds	TD	Int
1948 Yankees	2	5	31	1	0
Total	**2**	**5**	**31**	**1**	**0**

Punting

	Punt	Yds	Blk
1948 New York Yankees	6	242	0
Total	**6**	**242**	**0**

Punt Returns

	Ret	Yds	TD
1948 New York Yankees	9	229	1
Total	**9**	**229**	**1**

Kick Returns

	Ret	Yds	TD
1948 New York Yankees	7	170	0
Total	**7**	**170**	**0**

CASON, James Allnut, Jr. (Jim)

Position: DB-HB
Height: 6'0"; Weight: 171
College: LSU
Born: July 25, 1927, Sondheimer, LA
Deceased: November 24, 2013, Harlingen, TX

STATISTICS

Games

	GP	GS
1948 San Francisco 49ers	13	5
1949 San Francisco 49ers	12	6
1950 San Francisco 49ers	9	0
1951 San Francisco 49ers	12	0
1952 San Francisco 49ers	10	0
1954 San Francisco 49ers	9	0
1955 Los Angeles Rams	12	0
1956 Los Angeles Rams	12	0
Total	**89**	**11**

Rushing

	Rush	Yds	TD
1948 S.F. 49ers	20	146	2
1949 S.F. 49ers	21	70	1
1950 S.F. 49ers	38	129	1
1951 S.F. 49ers	1	5	0
1952 S.F. 49ers	2	1	0
Total	**82**	**351**	**4**

Receiving

	Rec	Yds	TD
1948 S.F. 49ers	4	99	1
1949 S.F. 49ers	5	38	0
1950 S.F. 49ers	30	374	3
1951 S.F. 49ers	1	8	0
Total	**40**	**519**	**4**

Passing

	Comp	Att	Yds	Td	Int
1949 S.F. 49ers	1	2	38	1	0
1954 S.F. 49ers	7	13	40	0	1
Total	**8**	**15**	**78**	**1**	**1**

Punt Returns

	Ret	Yds	TD
1948 S.F. 49ers	22	309	0
1949 S.F. 49ers	21	351	0
1950 S.F. 49ers	11	173	0
1951 S.F. 49ers	13	115	0
Total	**67**	**948**	**0**

Kick Returns

	Ret	Yds	TD
1948 S.F. 49ers	10	212	0
1949 S.F. 49ers	11	247	0
1950 S.F. 49ers	2	48	0
1951 S.F. 49ers	10	196	0
Total	**33**	**703**	**0**

Interceptions

	Int	Yds	TD
1948 S.F. 49ers	5	46	0
1949 S.F. 49ers	9	152	0
1950 S.F. 49ers	1	22	0
1951 S.F. 49ers	8	147	1
1952 S.F. 49ers	2	4	0
1955 Los Angeles Rams	5	41	0
1956 Los Angeles Rams	4	63	0
Total	**34**	**475**	**2**

Fumbles (continued)

	Fum	Rec	Yds	TD
1950 S.F. 49ers	3	1	0	0
1951 S.F. 49ers	1	2	0	0
1954 S.F. 49ers	1	1	0	0
1955 Los Angeles Rams	0	1	0	0
Total	**5**	**5**	**0**	**0**

CASTIGLIA, James Vincent (Jim)

Position: FB
Height: 5'11"; Weight: 208
College: Georgetown
Born: September 30, 1918, Passaic, NJ
Deceased: December 26, 2007, Rockville, MD

STATISTICS

Games

	GP	GS
1941 Philadelphia Eagles	11	6
1945 Philadelphia Eagles	1	1
1946 Philadelphia Eagles	11	2
1947 Baltimore Colts	2	2
1947 Washington Redskins	7	0
1948 Washington Redskins	10	1
Total	**42**	**12**

Rushing

	Rush	Yds	TD
1941 Philadelphia Eagles	60	183	4
1945 Philadelphia Eagles	13	29	0
1946 Philadelphia Eagles	39	87	1
1947 Baltimore Colts	9	18	0
1947 Wash. Redskins	104	426	5
1948 Wash. Redskins	97	330	0
Total	**322**	**1073**	**10**

Receiving

	Rec	Yds	TD
1941 Philadelphia Eagles	4	24	0
1946 Philadelphia Eagles	11	51	0
1947 Baltimore Colts	1	10	0
1947 Wash. Redskins	11	88	0
1948 Wash. Redskins	7	73	2
Total	**34**	**246**	**2**

Passing

	Comp	Att	Yds	TD	Int
1941 Eagles	0	7	0	0	1
Total	**0**	**7**	**0**	**0**	**1**

Kick Returns

	Ret	Yds	TD
1941 Philadelphia Eagles	7	199	0
1946 Philadelphia Eagles	1	17	0
1947 Wash. Redskins	1	10	0
1948 Wash. Redskins	1	18	0
Total	**10**	**244**	**0**

Interceptions

	Int	Yds	TD
1941 Philadelphia Eagles	1	0	0
Total	**1**	**0**	**0**

Fumbles

	Fum	Rec	Yds	TD
1946 Philadelphia Eagles	2	0	0	0
1947 Wash. Redskins	1	0	0	0
1948 Wash. Redskins	2	1	-3	0
Total	**5**	**1**	**-3**	**0**

CATHCART, Samuel Woodrow (Sam)

Position: DB-HB
Height: 6'0"; Weight: 175
College: California—Santa Barbara
Born: July 7, 1924, Canute, OK
Deceased: April 3, 2015, Santa Barbara, CA

STATISTICS

Games

	GP	GS
1949 San Francisco 49ers	12	0
1950 San Francisco 49ers	12	0
1952 San Francisco 49ers	12	0
Total	**36**	**0**

Rushing

	Rush	Yds	TD
1949 S.F. 49ers	69	412	1
1950 S.F. 49ers	33	76	0
1952 S.F. 49ers	6	21	0
Total	**108**	**509**	**1**

Receiving

	Rec	Yds	TD
1949 S.F. 49ers	12	182	0
1950 S.F. 49ers	7	99	0
1952 S.F. 49ers	2	15	0
Total	**21**	**296**	**0**

Passing

	Comp	Att	Yds	TD	Int
1952 S.F. 49ers	0	1	0	0	1
Total	**0**	**1**	**0**	**0**	**1**

Punt Returns

	Ret	Yds	TD
1949 S.F. 49ers	18	306	0
1950 S.F. 49ers	16	185	0
1952 S.F. 49ers	1	23	0
Total	**35**	**514**	**0**

Kick Returns

	Ret	Yds	TD
1949 S.F. 49ers	7	138	0
1950 S.F. 49ers	13	311	0
1952 S.F. 49ers	1	20	0
Total	**24**	**469**	**0**

Interceptions

	Int	Yds	TD
1949 S.F. 49ers	1	0	0
1950 S.F. 49ers	3	58	0
1952 S.F. 49ers	3	64	0
Total	**7**	**122**	**0**

CATO, Ralph Daryl (Daryl)

Position: C-LB
Height: 6'2"; Weight: 195
College: Arkansas
Born: January 8, 1920, Lonoke, AR
Deceased: October 3, 1970, Earle, AR

STATISTICS

Games		
	GP	GS
1946 Miami Seahawks	12	3
Total	12	3

Interceptions			
	Int	Yds	TD
1946 Miami Seahawks	1	29	0
Total	1	29	0

CHAPPIUS, Robert Richard (Bob)

Position: TB-DB
Height: 6'0"; Weight: 190
College: Michigan
Born: February 24, 1923, Toledo, OH
Deceased: June 14, 2012, Ann Arbor, MI

STATISTICS

Games		
	GP	GS
1948 Brooklyn Dodgers	13	6
1949 Chicago Hornets	6	0
Total	19	6

Rushing			
	Rush	Yds	TD
1948 Brooklyn Dodgers	52	310	1
1949 Chicago Hornets	4	13	0
Total	56	323	1

Passing					
	Comp	Att	Yds	TD	Int
1948 Dodgers	100	213	1402	8	15
1949 Hornets	2	14	40	0	4
Total	102	227	1442	8	19

Punt Returns			
	Ret	Yds	TD
1948 Dodgers	1	8	0
Total	1	8	0

Kick Returns			
	Ret	Yds	TD
1948 Dodgers	3	55	0
Total	3	55	0

CHEATHAM, Hilliard Lloyd (Lloyd)

Position: B
Height: 6'2"; Weight: 211
College: Auburn
Born: March 20, 1919, Nantes, OK
Deceased: June 11, 1989, Charlotte, NC

STATISTICS

Games		
	GP	GS
1942 Chicago Cardinals	11	3
1946 New York Yankees	13	7
1947 New York Yankees	14	10
1948 New York Yankees	7	76
Total	50	29

Rushing			
	Rush	Yds	TD
1942 Chicago Cardinals	1	1	0
1946 New York Yankees	3	2	0
1947 New York Yankees	1	-2	0
1948 New York Yankees	2	1	0
Total	7	2	0

Receiving			
	Rec	Yds	TD
1942 Chicago Cardinals	6	29	1
1946 New York Yankees	4	54	1
1947 New York Yankees	4	124	2
1948 New York Yankees	7	76	0
Total	21	283	4

Punt Returns			
	Ret	Yds	TD
1942 Chicago Cardinals	3	32	0
1946 New York Yankees	1	26	0
Total	4	58	0

Kick Returns			
	Ret	Yds	TD
1942 Chicago Cardinals	2	37	0
1946 New York Yankees	1	7	0
1948 New York Yankees	1	18	0
Total	4	62	0

Interceptions			
	Int	Yds	TD
1942 Chicago Cardinals	1	4	0
1946 New York Yankees	1	3	0
Total	2	7	0

CHEROKE, George

Position: G
Height: 5'9"; Weight: 195
College: Ohio State
Born: January 2, 1921, Jenners, PA
Deceased: October 19, 1986, Pico Rivera, GA

STATISTICS

Games

	GP	GS
1946 Cleveland Browns	14	0
Total	**14**	**0**

CLARK, Donald Rex (Don)

Position: G-LB
Height: 5'11"; Weight: 197
College: USC
Born: December 22, 1923, Shurdan, IA
Deceased: August 6, 1989, Huntington Beach, CA

STATISTICS

Games

	GP	GS
1948 San Francisco 49ers	14	14
1949 San Francisco 49ers	12	10
Total	**26**	**24**

Interceptions

	Int	Yds	TD
1948 S.F. 49ers	1	12	0
1949 S.F. 49ers	1	16	0
Total	**2**	**28**	**0**

CLARKE, Harry Charles

Position: HB-DB
Height: 6'0"; Weight: 186
College: West Virginia
Born: December 1, 1916, Cumberland, MD
Deceased: December 31, 2005, Morgantown, WV

STATISTICS

Games

	GP	GS
1940 Chicago Bears	11	0
1941 Chicago Bears	10	3
1942 Chicago Bears	10	7
1943 Chicago Bears	10	10
1946 Los Angeles Dons	14	2
1947 Los Angeles Dons	12	3
1948 Los Angeles Dons	2	2
1948 Chicago Rockets	5	2
Total	**74**	**29**

Rushing

	Rush	Yds	TD
1940 Chicago Bears	56	258	2
1941 Chicago Bears	28	122	0
1942 Chicago Bears	58	273	4
1943 Chicago Bears	120	556	2
1946 Los Angeles Dons	62	250	0
1947 Los Angeles Dons	44	173	2
1948 Los Angeles Dons	6	22	0
1948 Chicago Rockets	16	57	0
Total	**390**	**1711**	**10**

Receiving

	Rec	Yds	TD
1940 Chicago Bears	3	80	0
1941 Chicago Bears	2	61	0
1942 Chicago Bears	6	131	2
1943 Chicago Bears	23	535	7
1946 Los Angeles Dons	10	123	2
1947 Los Angeles Dons	3	54	0
1948 Los Angeles Dons	3	19	0
1948 Chicago Rockets	1	19	0
Total	**51**	**1022**	**11**

Passing

	Comp	Att	Yds	TD	Int
1940 Bears	0	3	0	0	2
1943 Bears	0	1	0	0	1
Total	**0**	**4**	**0**	**0**	**3**

Punting

	Punt	Yds	Blk
1940 Chicago Bears	1	30	0
Total	**1**	**30**	**0**

Punt Returns

	Ret	Yds	TD
1941 Chicago Bears	4	56	0
1942 Chicago Bears	5	76	0
1943 Chicago Bears	10	158	0
1946 Los Angeles Dons	2	24	0
1947 Los Angeles Dons	3	38	0
1948 Los Angeles Dons	1	16	0
1949 Chicago Rockets	1	11	0
Total	**26**	**379**	**0**

Kick Returns

	Ret	Yds	TD
1941 Chicago Bears	5	158	0
1942 Chicago Bears	5	159	0
1943 Chicago Bears	13	326	0
1946 Los Angeles Dons	2	48	0
1947 Los Angeles Dons	8	225	0
1948 Los Angeles Dons	1	17	0
1949 Chicago Rockets	3	79	0
Total	**37**	**1012**	**0**

Interceptions

	Int	Yds	TD
1940 Chicago Bears	4	62	1
1941 Chicago Bears	2	62	0
1943 Chicago Bears	5	32	0
1946 Los Angeles Dons	2	7	0
Total	**13**	**163**	**1**

Point After Touchdown

	XPM	XPA
1941 Chicago Bears	1	1
Total	**1**	**1**

CLAY, Walter Earl (Walt)

Position: TB
Height: 5'11"; Weight: 196
College: Colorado
Born: January 8, 1924, Erie, CO
Deceased: May 3, 2013, Charlotte, NC

STATISTICS

Games

	GP	GS
1946 Chicago Rockets	13	2
1947 Chicago Rockets	3	0
1947 Los Angeles Dons	8	0
1948 Los Angeles Dons	13	8
1949 Los Angeles Dons	10	1
Total	47	11

Rushing

	Rush	Yds	TD
1946 Chicago Rockets	65	283	1
1947 Los Angeles Dons	9	42	0
1948 Los Angeles Dons	86	293	3
1949 Los Angeles Dons	1	9	34
Total	169	652	4

Receiving

	Rec	Yds	TD
1946 Chicago Rockets	4	48	0
1947 Los Angeles Dons	1	52	0
1948 Los Angeles Dons	10	118	1
Total	15	218	1

Passing

	Comp	Att	Yds	TD	Int
1946 Rockets	12	27	140	2	3
1949 L.A. Dons	1	1	8	0	0
Total	13	28	148	2	3

Punting

	Punt	Yds	Blk
1946 Chicago Rockets	1	45	0
Total	1	45	0

Punt Returns

	Ret	Yds	TD
1946 Chicago Rockets	8	70	0
Total	8	70	0

Kick Returns

	Ret	Yds	TD
1946 Chicago Rockets	2	43	0
1948 Los Angeles Dons	4	48	0
Total	6	91	0

Interceptions

	Int	Yds	TD
1946 Chicago Rockets	6	72	0
1947 Los Angeles Dons	1	20	0
1948 Los Angeles Dons	2	33	0
Total	9	125	0

CLEARY, Paul Hanson

Position: E-DE
Height: 6'1"; Weight: 196
College: USC
Born: February 7, 1922, North Loop, NE
Deceased: January 8, 1996, South Laguna, CA

STATISTICS

Games

	GP	GS
1948 New York Yankees	13	0
1949 Chicago Hornets	10	0
Total	23	0

Receiving

	Rec	Yds	TD
1948 New York Yankees	4	37	0
Total	4	37	0

Kick Returns

	Ret	Yds	TD
1948 New York Yankees	1	8	0
Total	1	8	0

CLEMENT, John Louis (Johnny)

Position: TB
Height: 6'0"; Weight: 189
College: SMU
Born: October 31, 1919, Stonebluff, OK
Deceased: December 11, 1969, Mountain City, TN

STATISTICS

Games

	GP	GS
1941 Chicago Cardinals	9	4
1946 Pittsburgh Steelers	11	0
1947 Pittsburgh Steelers	10	4
1948 Pittsburgh Steelers	5	1
1949 Chicago Hornets	12	0
Total	47	9

Rushing

	Rush	Yds	TD
1941 Chicago Cardinals	61	94	1
1946 Pittsburgh Steelers	43	60	1
1947 Pittsburgh Steelers	129	670	4
1948 Pittsburgh Steelers	67	261	2
1949 Chicago Hornets	106	388	5
Total	406	1473	13

Receiving

	Rec	Yds	TD
1946 Pittsburgh Steelers	1	22	0
1947 Pittsburgh Steelers	1	6	0
Total	2	28	0

Passing

	Comp	Att	Yds	TD	Int
1941 Cardinals	48	100	690	3	7
1946 Steelers	16	47	345	1	3
1947 Steelers	52	123	1004	7	9
1948 Steelers	18	58	281	3	7
1949 Hornets	58	114	906	6	13
Total	192	442	3226	20	39

Punting

	Punt	Yds	Blk
1941 Chicago Cardinals	4	125	0
1946 Pittsburgh Steelers	9	314	0
Total	13	439	0

Punt Returns

	Ret	Yds	TD
1941 Chicago Cardinals	13	113	0
1946 Pittsburgh Steelers	3	26	0
Total	16	1139	0

Kick Returns

	Ret	Yds	TD
1941 Chicago Cardinals	2	42	0
1946 Pittsburgh Steelers	3	66	0
1947 Pittsburgh Steelers	1	24	0
Total	6	132	0

Fumbles

	Fum	Rec	Yds	TD
1946 Pittsburgh Steelers	4	2	0	0
1947 Pittsburgh Steelers	7	1	0	0
1948 Pittsburgh Steelers	5	2	0	0
Total	16	5	0	0

CLINE, Oliver Monroe (Ollie)

Position: FB
Height: 6'0"; Weight: 200
College: Ohio State
Born: December 31, 1925, Mount Vernon, OH
Deceased: May 12, 2001, Springfield, OH

STATISTICS

Games

	GP	GS
1948 Cleveland Browns	11	0
1949 Buffalo Bills	11	11
1950 Detroit Lions	10	0
1951 Detroit Lions	12	0
1952 Detroit Lions	8	0
1953 Detroit Lions	12	0
Total	64	11

Rushing

	Rush	Yds	TD
1948 Cleveland Browns	29	129	0
1949 Buffalo Bills	125	518	3
1950 Detroit Lions	69	227	2
1951 Detroit Lions	3	15	0
1952 Detroit Lions	13	36	1
1953 Detroit Lions	42	169	0
Total	281	1094	6

Receiving

	Rec	Yds	TD
1949 Buffalo Bills	15	110	0
1950 Detroit Lions	7	18	0
1952 Detroit Lions	2	45	0
1953 Detroit Lions	10	126	1
Total	34	299	1

Kick Returns

	Ret	Yds	TD
1948 Cleveland Browns	3	55	0
1949 Buffalo Bills	1	21	0
1950 Detroit Lions	1	20	0
1951 Detroit Lions	3	48	0
1953 Detroit Lions	1	0	0
Total	9	144	0

Fumbles

	Fum	Rec	Yds	TD
1950 Detroit Lions	7	1	0	0
1953 Detroit Lions	1	0	0	0
Total	8	1	0	0

CLOWES, John Alexander

Position: T-G-DT
Height: 6'1"; Weight: 240
College: William & Mary
Born: December 15, 1921, Williamsburg, VA
Deceased: February 13, 1978, Norfolk, VA

STATISTICS

Games

	GP	GS
1948 Brooklyn Dodgers	14	8
1949 Chicago Hornets	12	0
1950 New York Yanks	11	0
1951 New York Yanks	12	0
Total	49	8

COLELLA, Thomas Anthony (Tom)

Position: HB-TB
Height: 6'0"; Weight: 187
College: Canisius
Born: July 3, 1918, Albion, NY
Deceased: May 15, 1992, Hamburg, NY

STATISTICS

Games

	GP	GS
1942 Detroit Lions	9	2
1943 Detroit Lions	8	0
1944 Cleveland Rams	10	8
1945 Cleveland Rams	10	1
1946 Cleveland Browns	14	2
1947 Cleveland Browns	14	7
1948 Cleveland Browns	13	2
1949 Buffalo Bills	11	0
Total	89	22

Rushing

	Rush	Yds	TD
1942 Detroit Lions	23	51	0
1943 Detroit Lions	15	24	0
1944 Cleveland Rams	53	208	2
1945 Cleveland Rams	46	224	2
1946 Cleveland Browns	30	118	2
1947 Cleveland Browns	11	77	1

	Rush	Yds	TD
1948 Cleveland Browns	14	60	1
1949 Buffalo Bills	7	-9	0
Total	**199**	**753**	**8**

Receiving

	Rec	Yds	TD
1943 Detroit Lions	1	-1	0
1944 Cleveland Rams	2	64	1
1945 Cleveland Rams	7	64	2
1946 Cleveland Browns	1	12	1
1947 Cleveland Browns	4	63	1
1948 Cleveland Browns	1	7	0
1949 Buffalo Bills	2	6	0
Total	**18**	**215**	**5**

Passing

	Comp	Att	Yds	TD	Int
1942 Lions	18	41	178	0	4
1943 Lions	11	31	103	0	4
1944 Rams	27	75	336	4	10
1945 Rams	0	1	0	0	0
Total	**56**	**148**	**617**	**4**	**18**

Punting

	Punt	Yds	Blk
1942 Detroit Lions	16	609	0
1943 Detroit Lions	7	315	0
1944 Cleveland Rams	33	1247	0
1946 Cleveland Browns	47	1895	0
1947 Cleveland Browns	1	36	0
1948 Cleveland Browns	49	1716	0
1949 Buffalo Bills	44	1554	1
Total	**197**	**7372**	**1**

Punt Returns

	Ret	Yds	TD
1942 Detroit Lions	2	14	0
1943 Detroit Lions	2	11	0
1944 Cleveland Rams	4	65	0
1945 Cleveland Rams	1	10	0
1946 Cleveland Browns	8	172	0
1947 Cleveland Browns	5	113	1
1948 Cleveland Browns	5	60	0
1949 Buffalo Bills	5	42	0
Total	**32**	**487**	**1**

Kick Returns

	Ret	Yds	TD
1942 Detroit Lions	4	74	0
1944 Cleveland Rams	10	241	0
1945 Cleveland Rams	3	79	0
1946 Cleveland Browns	1	29	0
1947 Cleveland Browns	1	13	0
1949 Buffalo Bills	7	107	0
Total	**26**	**543**	**0**

Interceptions

	Int	Yds	TD
1942 Detroit Lions	1	10	0
1944 Cleveland Rams	4	53	0
1946 Cleveland Browns	10	110	0
1947 Cleveland Browns	6	130	0
1948 Cleveland Browns	2	34	0
1949 Buffalo Bills	3	49	0
Total	**26**	**386**	**1**

Fumbles

	Fum	Rec	Yds	TD
1945 Cleveland Rams	4	1	0	0
Total	**4**	**1**	**0**	**0**

Field Goals

	FGM	FGA
1944 Cleveland Rams	1	1
Total	**1**	**1**

COLEMAN, Herbert Edward (Herb)

Position: C-G
Height: 6'0"; Weight: 200
College: Notre Dame
Born: June 18, 1923, Chester, WV
Deceased: January 1, 1985, Northville, MI

STATISTICS

Games

	GP	GS
1946 Chicago Rockets	14	12
1947 Chicago Rockets	13	4
1948 Chicago Rockets	9	8
1948 Baltimore Colts	1	0
Total	**37**	**24**

Kick Returns

	Ret	Yds	TD
1946 Chicago Rockets	1	20	0
Total	**1**	**20**	**0**

Interceptions

	Int	Yds	TD
1946 Chicago Rockets	1	25	0
Total	**1**	**25**	**0**

COLLIER, Floyd Lee

Position: T
Height: 6'1"; Weight: 215
College: Fresno State, San Jose State, USC
Born: May 10, 1924, Fresno, CA
Deceased: September 3, 2002, Laguna Hills, CA

STATISTICS

Games

	GP	GS
1948 San Francisco 49ers	12	0
Total	**12**	**0**

COLLINS, Albin Harrell (Rip)

Position: HB-FB
Height: 6'0"; Weight: 190
College: LSU
Born: November 9, 1926, Baton Rouge, LA
Deceased: April 9, 2006, Houston, TX

STATISTICS

Games

	GP	GS
1949 Chicago Hornets	12	6
1950 Baltimore Colts	12	9
1951 Green Bay Packers	7	0
Total	31	15

Rushing

	Rush	Yds	TD
1949 Chicago Hornets	28	88	0
1950 Baltimore Colts	69	101	0
1951 Green Bay Packers	5	4	0
Total	102	193	0

Receiving

	Rec	Yds	TD
1949 Chicago Hornets	6	161	0
1950 Baltimore Colts	19	295	0
1951 Green Bay Packers	1	5	0
Total	26	461	0

Passing

	Comp	Att	Yds	TD	Int
1949 Hornets	0	1	0	0	0
Total	0	1	0	0	0

Punting

	Punt	Yds	Blk
1949 Chicago Hornets	41	1725	0
1950 Baltimore Colts	2	91	1
1951 Green Bay Packers	2	81	0
Total	45	1897	1

Kick Returns

	Ret	Yds	TD
1949 Chicago Hornets	2	23	0
1950 Baltimore Colts	2	33	0
1951 Green Bay Packers	1	40	0
Total	5	96	0

Interceptions

	Int	Yds	TD
1949 Chicago Hornets	1	0	0
1950 Baltimore Colts	1	7	0
1951 Green Bay Packers	2	0	0
Total	4	7	0

Fumbles

	Fum	Rec	Yds	TD
1950 Baltimore Colts	4	0	0	0
Total	4	0	0	0

COLMER, John Francis (Mickey)

Position: B
Height: 6'2"; Weight: 219
College: Miramonte Junior College
Born: October 23, 1918, Redondo Beach, CA
Deceased: July 20, 2000, Redondo Beach, CA

STATISTICS

Games

	GP	GS
1946 Brooklyn Dodgers	12	6
1947 Brooklyn Dodgers	14	10
1948 Brooklyn Dodgers	14	11
1949 New York Yankees	8	2
Total	48	29

Rushing

	Rush	Yds	TD
1946 Brooklyn Dodgers	46	155	0
1947 Brooklyn Dodgers	152	578	9
1948 Brooklyn Dodgers	164	704	6
1949 New York Yankees	36	100	0
Total	398	1537	15

Receiving

	Rec	Yds	TD
1946 Brooklyn Dodgers	22	327	1
1947 Brooklyn Dodgers	18	190	1
1948 Brooklyn Dodgers	21	372	4
1949 New York Yankees	2	10	0
Total	63	899	6

Passing

	Comp	Att	Yds	TD	Int
1947 Dodgers	1	3	20	0	0
1948 Dodgers	0	1	0	0	0
1949 Yankees	0	1	0	0	0
Total	1	5	20	0	0

Punting

	Punt	Yds	Blk
1947 Brooklyn Dodgers	56	2504	0
1948 Brooklyn Dodgers	56	2382	2
1949 New York Yankees	5	232	0
Total	117	5118	2

Punt Returns

	Ret	Yds	TD
1946 Brooklyn Dodgers	1	9	0
Total	1	9	0

Kick Returns

	Ret	Yds	TD
1946 Brooklyn Dodgers	1	9	0
1947 Brooklyn Dodgers	3	77	0
1948 Brooklyn Dodgers	8	163	0
1949 New York Yankees	1	16	0
Total	13	265	0

Interceptions

	Int	Yds	TD
1946 Brooklyn Dodgers	1	0	0
Total	1	0	0

COMER, Martin F. (Marty)

Position: DE-E
Height: 6'0"; Weight: 203
College: Tulane
Born: October 28, 1917, Indianapolis, IN
Deceased: March 22, 1998, New Orleans, LA

STATISTICS

Games

	GP	GS
1946 Buffalo Bisons	6	3
1947 Buffalo Bills	14	2
1948 Buffalo Bills	7	4
Total	**27**	**9**

Receiving

	Rec	Yds	TD
1946 Buffalo Bisons	2	17	0
1947 Buffalo Bills	2	75	1
1948 Buffalo Bills	5	66	1
Total	**9**	**158**	**2**

CONGER, Melvin Reese (Mel)

Position: DE-E
Height: 6'2"; Weight: 225
College: Georgia
Born: June 4, 1919, Atlanta, GA
Deceased: July 21, 1996, Atlanta, GA

STATISTICS

Games

	GP	GS
1946 New York Yankees	7	0
1947 Brooklyn Dodgers	2	0
Total	**9**	**0**

Receiving

	Rec	Yds	TD
1946 New York Yankees	3	61	0
Total	**3**	**61**	**0**

CONLEE, Gerald Russell (Gerry)

Position: C
Height: 5'11"; Weight: 203
College: St. Mary's
Born: August 22, 1914, Porterville, CA
Deceased: July 16, 2005, El Cajon, CA

STATISTICS

Games

	GP	GS
1938 Cleveland Rams	8	2
1943 Detroit Lions	10	2
1946 San Francisco 49ers	10	2
1947 San Francisco 49ers	13	1
Total	**41**	**7**

Punt Returns

	Ret	Yds	TD
1947 S.F. 49ers	1	1	0
Total	**1**	**1**	**0**

Kick Returns

	Ret	Yds	TD
1947 S.F. 49ers	1	15	0
Total	**1**	**15**	**0**

Interceptions

	Int	Yds	TD
1943 Detroit Lions	1	2	0
Total	**1**	**2**	**0**

CONNOLLY, Harry William

Position: TB
Height: 5'11"; Weight: 190
College: Boston College
Born: July 16, 1920, Norwalk, CT
Deceased: January 14, 2006, New Bedford, MA

STATISTICS

Games

	GP	GS
1946 Brooklyn Dodgers	3	2
Total	**3**	**2**

Rushing

	Rush	Yds	TD
1946 Brooklyn Dodgers	8	18	0
Total	**8**	**18**	**0**

Passing

	Comp	Att	Yds	TD	Int
1946 Dodgers	2	8	29	0	1
Total	**2**	**8**	**29**	**0**	**1**

Punt Returns

	Ret	Yds	TD
1946 Brooklyn Dodgers	1	6	0
Total	**1**	**6**	**0**

Kick Returns

	Ret	Yds	TD
1946 Brooklyn Dodgers	2	41	0
Total	**2**	**41**	**0**

COOPER, James Paul (Jim)

Position: C-LB
Height: 6'0"; Weight: 205
College: North Texas, TCU
Born: June 28, 1924, Colorado City, TX
Deceased: November 1, 2010, Big Spring, TX

STATISTICS

Games

	GP	GS
1948 Brooklyn Dodgers	1	0
Total	**1**	**0**

COOPER, Kenneth Rousseau (Ken)

Position: G
Height: 6'1"; Weight: 205
College: Vanderbilt
Born: February 26, 1923, Rogersville, AL
Deceased: November 2, 1997, Bexar County, TX

STATISTICS
Games
	GP	GS
1949 Baltimore Colts	12	5
1950 Baltimore Colts	12	8
Total	**24**	**13**

COPPAGE, Alton Minor (Al)

Position: E
Height: 6'1"; Weight: 195
College: Oklahoma
Born: February 8, 1916, Pilot Point, TX
Deceased: January 9, 1992, Hollis, OK

STATISTICS
Games
	GP	GS
1940 Chicago Cardinals	11	7
1941 Chicago Cardinals	9	2
1942 Chicago Cardinals	11	5
1946 Cleveland Browns	14	1
1947 Buffalo Bills	13	10
Total	**58**	**25**

Receiving
	Rec	Yds	TD
1940 Chicago Cardinals	15	163	1
1941 Chicago Cardinals	8	117	0
1942 Chicago Cardinals	20	196	0
1946 Cleveland Browns	2	34	0
1947 Buffalo Bills	20	226	2
Total	**65**	**736**	**3**

Kick Returns
	Ret	Yds	TD
1942 Chicago Cardinals	1	11	0
1947 Buffalo Bills	2	28	0
Total	**3**	**39**	**0**

CORLEY, Elbert Ellis (Bert)

Position: C
Height: 6'2"; Weight: 210
College: Mississippi State
Born: September 9, 1920, Okolona, MS
Deceased: September 22, 1988, Tupelo, MS

STATISTICS
Games
	GP	GS
1947 Buffalo Bills	13	4
1948 Baltimore Colts	9	8
Total	**22**	**12**

Interceptions
	Int	Yds	TD
1947 Buffalo Bills	1	41	0
Total	**1**	**41**	**0**

COWAN, Robert George (Bob)

Position: B
Height: 5'11"; Weight: 185
College: Indiana
Born: January 2, 1923, Fort Wayne, IN
Deceased: January 20, 2004, Fort Wayne, IN

STATISTICS
Games
	GP	GS
1947 Cleveland Browns	10	1
1948 Cleveland Browns	14	11
1949 Baltimore Colts	9	0
Total	**33**	**12**

Rushing
	Rush	Yds	TD
1947 Cleveland Browns	38	181	2
1948 Cleveland Browns	33	99	1
1949 Baltimore Colts	1	0	0
Total	**72**	**280**	**3**

Receiving
	Rec	Yds	TD
1947 Cleveland Browns	5	60	1
1948 Cleveland Browns	15	265	4
1949 Baltimore Colts	1	26	0
Total	**21**	**351**	**5**

Kick Returns
	Ret	Yds	TD
1947 Cleveland Browns	3	55	0
1948 Cleveland Browns	3	53	0
Total	**6**	**108**	**0**

Interceptions
	Int	Yds	TD
1949 Baltimore Colts	3	17	0
Total	**3**	**17**	**0**

COX, James Ellingson (Jim)

Position: G-LB
Height: 6'1"; Weight: 208
College: California, Stanford
Born: September 6, 1920, St. Louis, MO
Deceased: July 29, 2014, Lafayette, CA

STATISTICS
Games
	GP	GS
1948 San Francisco 49ers	14	0
Total	**14**	**0**

COX, Norman Lawrence (Norm)

Position: QB-TB
Height: 6'2"; Weight: 210
College: TCU
Born: September 22, 1925, Stamford, TX
Deceased: April 28, 2008, Monahns, TX

STATISTICS

Games

	GP	GS
1946 Chicago Rockets	3	0
1947 Chicago Rockets	2	0
Total	5	0

Rushing

	Rush	Yds	TD
1946 Chicago Rockets	1	12	0
1947 Chicago Rockets	1	-3	0
Total	2	9	0

Passing

	Comp	Att	Yds	TD	Int
1947 Rockets	1	2	9	0	0
Total	1	2	9	0	0

CRAWFORD, Denver Junior (Denny)

Position: G-T
Height: 6'0"; Weight: 190
College: Tennessee
Born: June 16, 1921, Kingsport, TN
Deceased: August 14, 2005, Kingsport, TN

STATISTICS

Games

	GP	GS
1948 New York Yankees	8	6
Total	8	6

CROWE, Paul James

Position: B
Height: 6'1"; Weight: 190
College: St. Mary's
Born: October 23, 1924, Chino, CA
Deceased: December 13, 1989, Butte County, CA

STATISTICS

Games

	GP	GS
1948 San Francisco 49ers	14	0
1949 San Francisco 49ers	2	1
1949 Los Angeles Dons	7	0
1951 New York Yanks	9	0
Total	32	1

Rushing

	Rush	Yds	TD
1948 S.F. 49ers	12	65	0
1949 S.F. 49ers	2	0	0
1949 Los Angeles Dons	1	2	0
Total	15	67	0

Receiving

	Rec	Yds	TD
1951 New York Yanks	3	20	0
Total	3	20	0

Punt Returns

	Ret	Yds	TD
1948 S.F. 49ers	2	14	0
1949 Los Angeles Dons	6	96	0
Total	8	110	0

Kick Returns

	Ret	Yds	TD
1948 S.F. 49ers	2	18	0
Total	2	18	0

Interceptions

	Int	Yds	TD
1948 S.F. 49ers	5	69	1
1949 Los Angeles Dons	1	25	0
1951 New York Yanks	3	15	0
Total	9	109	1

CROWELL, Odis Leonard

Position: T
Height: 6'2"; Weight: 220
College: Hardin-Simmons
Born: October 7, 1914, Matador, TX
Deceased: June 5, 1997, Amarillo, TX

STATISTICS

Games

	GP	GS
1947 San Francisco 49ers	2	0
Total	2	0

CURE, Armand Arthur

Position: B
Height: 6'0"; Weight: 198
College: Rhode Island
Born: August 1, 1919, New Bedford, MA
Deceased: December 5, 2003, Long Beach, CA

STATISTICS

Games

	GP	GS
1947 Baltimore Colts	1	0
Total	1	0

Rushing

	Rush	Yds	TD
1947 Baltimore Colts	2	-1	0
Total	2	-1	0

CZAROBSKI, Zygmont Peter (Ziggy)

Position: T
Height: 6'0"; Weight: 230
College: Notre Dame
Born: September 13, 1922, Chicago, IL
Deceased: July 1, 1984, Chicago, IL

DADDIO, Louis William (Bill)

Position: E
Height: 5'11"; Weight: 207
College: Pittsburgh
Born: April 26, 1916, Meadville, PA
Deceased: July 5, 1989, Mount Lebanon, PA

STATISTICS

Games

	GP	GS
1941 Chicago Cardinals	11	3
1942 Chicago Cardinals	11	10
1946 Buffalo Bisons	3	1
Total	25	14

Receiving

	Rec	Yds	TD
1941 Chicago Cardinals	5	39	0
1942 Chicago Cardinals	11	108	1
Total	16	147	1

Interceptions

	Int	Yds	TD
1942 Chicago Cardinals	1	4	0
Total	1	4	0

Field Goals

	FGM	FGA
1941 Chicago Cardinals	4	8
1942 Chicago Cardinals	5	10
Total	9	18

Point After Touchdown

	XPM	XPA
1941 Chicago Cardinals	8	9
1942 Chicago Cardinals	8	8
1946 Buffalo Bisons	3	3
Total	19	20

DALEY, William Edward (Bill)*

Position: FB-DB-LB
Height: 6'2"; Weight: 210
College: Columbia, DePaul, Michigan, Minnesota
Born: September 16, 1919, Melrose, MN
Deceased: October 20, 2015, MN

STATISTICS

Games

	GP	GS
1946 Miami Seahawks	1	0
1946 Brooklyn Dodgers	2	1
1947 Chicago Rockets	14	12
1948 New York Yankees	7	0
Total	24	13

Rushing

	Rush	Yds	TD
1946 Miami Seahawks	7	38	0
1946 Brooklyn Dodgers	7	25	0
1947 Chicago Rockets	121	447	4
1948 New York Yankees	40	102	1
Total	175	612	5

Receiving

	Rec	Yds	TD
1946 Brooklyn Dodgers	2	−5	0
1947 Chicago Rockets	12	116	0
1948 New York Yankees	4	31	0
Total	18	142	0

Punting

	Punt	Yds	Blk
1948 New York Yankees	1	41	0
Total	1	41	0

Punt Returns

	Ret	Yds	TD
1947 Chicago Rockets	1	3	0
Total	1	3	0

Kick Returns

	Ret	Yds	TD
1946 Brooklyn Dodgers	1	10	0
1947 Chicago Rockets	7	145	0
1948 New York Yankees	4	88	0
Total	12	243	0

*Bill Daley had three pass completions out of six pass attempts for 70 yards, a touchdown and an interception in the official records. These statistics should have been for Al Dekdebrun. This reflects the corrected statistics. The error occurred in game seven of the season.

DANEHE, Richard Michael (Dick)

Position: T
Height: 6'2"; Weight: 235
College: USC
Born: September 10, 1920, Memphis, TN
Deceased:

STATISTICS

Games

	GP	GS
1947 Los Angeles Dons	11	4
1948 Los Angeles Dons	5	0
Total	16	4

DANIELL, James Laughlin (Jim)

Position: T
Height: 6'2"; Weight: 230
College: Ohio State
Born: April 10, 1918, Pittsburgh, PA
Deceased: December 13, 1983, Pittsburgh, PA

DADDIO

STATISTICS

Games

	GP	GS
1948 Chicago Rockets	14	3
1949 Chicago Hornets	12	12
Total	26	15

STATISTICS

Games

	GP	GS
1945 Chicago Bears	7	5
1946 Cleveland Browns	14	9
Total	21	14

Kick Returns

	Ret	Yds	TD
1945 Chicago Bears	1	14	0
Total	1	14	0

Fumbles

	Fum	Rec	Yds	TD
1945 Chicago Bears	1	1	0	0
Total	1	1	0	0

DAUKAS, Louis James (Lou)

Position: C
Height: 6'0"; Weight: 203
College: Cornell
Born: July 4, 1921, Nashua, NH
Deceased: December 22, 2005, Glastonbury, CT

STATISTICS

Games

	GP	GS
1947 Brooklyn Dodgers	4	0
Total	4	0

Kick Returns

	Ret	Yds	TD
1947 Brooklyn Dodgers	1	1	0
Total	1	1	0

Interceptions

	Int	Yds	TD
1947 Brooklyn Dodgers	1	1	0
Total	1	1	0

DAUKAS, Nicholas James (Nick)

Position: T
Height: 6'4"; Weight: 225
College: Dartmouth
Born: December 11, 1922, Nashua, NH
Deceased: February 25, 2003, Middletown, CT

STATISTICS

Games

	GP	GS
1946 Brooklyn Dodgers	8	1
1947 Brooklyn Dodgers	7	1
Total	15	2

Receiving

	Rec	Yds	TD
1946 Brooklyn Dodgers	2	19	0
Total	2	19	0

Interceptions

	Int	Yds	TD
1946 Brooklyn Dodgers	1	5	0
Total	1	5	0

DAVID, Robert Joseph (Bob)

Position: G
Height: 6'0"; Weight: 219
College: Notre Dame, Villanova
Born: January 15, 1921, Blue Island, FL
Deceased: July 4, 1997, Oak Lawn, IL

STATISTICS

Games

	GP	GS
1947 Los Angeles Rams	8	0
1948 Los Angeles Rams	3	1
1948 Chicago Rockets	4	0
Total	15	1

Fumbles

	Fum	Rec	Yds	TD
1948 Los Angeles Rams	0	1	0	0
Total	0	1	0	0

DAVIS, William Dorris (Bill)

Position: T
Height: 6'1"; Weight: 234
College: Texas Tech
Born: November 10, 1916, Grapevine, TX
Deceased: November 8, 1994, Addison, TX

STATISTICS

Games

	GP	GS
1940 Chicago Cardinals	10	3
1941 Chicago Cardinals	10	5
1943 Brooklyn Dodgers	8	1
1946 Miami Seahawks	12	5
Total	40	14

Interceptions

	Int	Yds	TD
1946 Miami Seahawks	4	40	0
Total	4	40	0

DAVIS, Julius Harper, Jr. (Harper)

Position: DB
Height: 5'11"; Weight: 173
College: Mississippi State
Born: December 11, 1925, Clarksdale, MS
Deceased:

STATISTICS

Games
	GP	GS
1949 Los Angeles Dons	11	0
1950 Chicago Bears	12	0
1951 Green Bay Packers	12	0
Total	35	0

Rushing
	Rush	Yds	TD
1949 Los Angeles Dons	13	33	1
1950 Chicago Bears	10	57	1
Total	23	90	2

Receiving
	Rec	Yds	TD
1949 Los Angeles Dons	2	13	0
1950 Chicago Bears	2	15	0
1951 Green Bay Packers	1	15	0
Total	5	43	0

Punt Returns
	Ret	Yds	TD
1949 Los Angeles Dons	2	37	0
1950 Chicago Bears	1	19	0
1951 Green Bay Packers	2	21	0
Total	5	77	0

Kick Returns
	Ret	Yds	TD
1949 Los Angeles Dons	4	87	0
Total	4	87	0

Interceptions
	Int	Yds	TD
1949 Los Angeles Dons	2	5	0
1950 Chicago Bears	5	59	0
1951 Green Bay Packers	4	37	0
Total	11	101	0

Fumbles
	Fum	Rec	Yds	TD
1951 Green Bay Packers	0	1	0	0
Total	0	1	0	0

DAVIS, Joseph Austin (Joe)

Position: E-DE
Height: 6'2"; Weight: 195
College: USC
Born: November 20, 1919, St. Anthony, ID
Deceased: May 26, 1992, Bakersfield, CA

STATISTICS

Games
	GP	GS
1946 Brooklyn Dodgers	14	12
Total	14	12

Receiving
	Rec	Yds	TD
1946 Brooklyn Dodgers	22	337	1
Total	22	337	1

Kick Returns
	Ret	Yds	TD
1946 Brooklyn Dodgers	2	32	0
Total	2	32	0

Point After Touchdown
	XPM	XPA
1946 Brooklyn Dodgers	1	1
Total	1	1

DAVIS, Raymond Lamar (Lamar) (Racehorse)

Position: E-DE
Height: 6'1"; Weight: 185
College: Georgia
Born: June 15, 1921, Brunswick, GA
Deceased: February 23, 2008

STATISTICS

Games
	GP	GS
1946 Miami Seahawks	14	8
1947 Baltimore Colts	13	2
1948 Baltimore Colts	14	9
1949 Baltimore Colts	12	9
Total	53	28

Rushing
	Rush	Yds	TD
1946 Miami Seahawks	14	64	0
1947 Baltimore Colts	3	14	0
Total	17	78	0

Receiving
	Rec	Yds	TD
1946 Miami Seahawks	22	275	2
1947 Baltimore Colts	46	515	2
1948 Baltimore Colts	41	765	7
1949 Baltimore Colts	38	548	1
Total	147	2103	12

Passing
	Comp	Att	Yds	TD	Int
1947 Bal. Colts	0	1	0	0	0
Total	0	1	0	0	0

Punt Returns
	Ret	Yds	TD
1946 Miami Seahawks	4	54	0
1947 Baltimore Colts	1	33	0
1948 Baltimore Colts	1	10	0
Total	6	97	0

Kick Returns
	Ret	Yds	TD
1946 Miami Seahawks	5	235	0
1947 Baltimore Colts	2	44	0
1949 Baltimore Colts	1	13	0
Total	8	292	0

Interceptions

	Int	Yds	TD
1947 Baltimore Colts	1	12	0
1948 Baltimore Colts	5	110	0
1949 Baltimore Colts	1	35	0
Total	**7**	**157**	**0**

DAVIS, Van Andrew, Jr.

Position: DE-E
Height: 6'2"; Weight: 215
College: Georgia
Born: October 5, 1921, Philomath, GA
Deceased: July 11, 1987, Carrolton, GA

STATISTICS

Games

	GP	GS
1947 New York Yankees	13	0
1948 New York Yankees	13	4
1949 New York Yankees	11	1
Total	**37**	**5**

Receiving

	Rec	Yds	TD
1947 New York Yankees	8	179	0
1948 New York Yankees	4	49	1
1949 New York Yankees	2	26	0
Total	**14**	**254**	**1**

Kick Returns

	Ret	Yds	TD
1947 New York Yankees	1	9	0
Total	**1**	**9**	**0**

Interceptions

	Int	Yds	TD
1948 New York Yankees	1	5	0
Total	**1**	**5**	**0**

DEKDEBRUN, Allen, Edward (Al)

Position: B
Height: 5'11"; Weight: 185
College: Columbia, Cornell
Born: May 11, 1921, Buffalo, NY
Deceased: March 29, 2005, Cape Coral, FL

STATISTICS

Games

	GP	GS
1946 Buffalo Bisons	14	8
1947 Chicago Rockets	12	5
1948 Boston Yanks	2	0
1948 New York Yankees	4	0
Total	**32**	**13**

Rushing

	Rush	Yds	TD
1946 Buffalo Bisons	25	−55	0
1947 Chicago Rockets	20	71	0
1948 Boston Yanks	2	14	0
1948 New York Yankees	7	24	0
Total	**54**	**54**	**0**

Passing

	Comp	Att	Yds	TD	Int
1946 Buffalo Bisons	28	66	517	8	8
1947 Chi Rockets	48	81	626	6	8
1948 Boston Yanks	1	3	2	0	1
1948 NY Yankees	10	20	149	0	2
Total	**87**	**170**	**1294**	**14**	**19**

Punt Returns

	Ret	Yds	TD
1948 New York Yankees	1	12	0
Total	**1**	**12**	**0**

Kick Returns

	Ret	Yds	TD
1946 Buffalo Bisons	6	116	0
1948 New York Yankees	1	15	0
Total	**7**	**131**	**0**

Interceptions

	Int	Yds	TD
1946 Buffalo Bisons	3	19	0
1948 New York Yankees	1	16	0
Total	**4**	**35**	**0**

*Bill Daley had three pass completions out of six pass attempts for 70 yards, a touchdown and an interception in the official records. These statistics should have been for Al Dekdebrun. This reflects the corrected statistics. The error occurred in game seven of the season.

DELLERBA, Spiro

Position: LB-FB
Height: 5'11"; Weight: 200
College: Ohio State
Born: January 25, 1923, Ashtabula, OH
Deceased: August 19, 1968, North Madison, OH

STATISTICS

Games

	GP	GS
1947 Cleveland Browns	8	0
1948 Baltimore Colts	14	2
1949 Baltimore Colts	9	2
Total	**31**	**4**

Rushing

	Rush	Yds	TD
1947 Cleveland Browns	29	176	0
1948 Baltimore Colts	2	0	0
Total	**31**	**176**	**0**

Receiving

	Rec	Yds	TD
1947 Cleveland Browns	1	14	0
Total	**1**	**14**	**0**

Kick Returns

	Ret	Yds	TD
1947 Cleveland Browns	1	34	0
1948 Baltimore Colts	1	12	0
Total	**2**	**46**	**0**

Interceptions

	Int	Yds	TD
1948 Baltimore Colts	2	18	0
Total	**2**	**18**	**0**

DEWAR, James Alexander, Jr. (Jim)

Position: B
Height: 6'1"; Weight: 190
College: Indiana
Born: June 17, 1922, Oak Park, IL
Deceased: June 30, 1989

STATISTICS

Games

	GP	GS
1947 Cleveland Browns	10	0
1948 Brooklyn Dodgers	1	0
Total	**11**	**0**

Rushing

	Rush	Yds	TD
1947 Cleveland Browns	14	64	1
Total	**14**	**64**	**1**

Punt Returns

	Ret	Yds	TD
1947 Cleveland Browns	1	2	0
Total	**1**	**2**	**0**

Kick Returns

	Ret	Yds	TD
1947 Cleveland Browns	1	25	0
Total	**1**	**25**	**0**

Interceptions

	Int	Yds	TD
1947 Cleveland Browns	1	50	0
Total	**1**	**50**	**0**

DOBBS, Glenn, Jr.

Position: TB-QB
Height: 6'4"; Weight: 210
College: Tulsa
Born: July 12, 1920, McKinney, TX
Deceased: November 12, 2002, Tulsa, OK

STATISTICS

Games

	GP	GS
1946 Brooklyn Dodgers	12	11
1947 Brooklyn Dodgers	2	0
1947 Los Angeles Dons	9	3
1948 Los Angeles Dons	14	10
1949 Los Angeles Dons	12	6
Total	**49**	**40**

Rushing

	Rush	Yds	TD
1946 Brooklyn Dodgers	95	208	4
1947 Brooklyn Dodgers	14	41	1
1947 Los Angeles Dons	28	90	0
1948 Los Angeles Dons	91	539	4
1949 Los Angeles Dons	34	161	3
Total	**262**	**1039**	**12**

Receiving

	Rec	Yds	TD
1946 Brooklyn Dodgers	1	−5	0
1947 Brooklyn Dodgers	2	21	0
1948 Los Angeles Dons	2	11	0
Total	**5**	**27**	**0**

Passing

	Comp	Att	Yds	TD	Int
1946 Dodgers	135	269	1886	13	15
1947 Dodgers	12	34	112	1	1
1947 L.A. Dons	49	109	650	6	7
1948 L.A. Dons	185	369	2403	21	20
1949 L.A. Dons	65	153	825	4	9
Total	**446**	**934**	**5876**	**45**	**52**

Punting

	Punt	Yds	Blk
1946 Brooklyn Dodgers	80	3826	2
1947 Brooklyn Dodgers	14	579	0
1947 Los Angeles Dons	30	1330	2
1948 Los Angeles Dons	68	3336	3
1949 Los Angeles Dons	39	1650	0
Total	**231**	**10721**	**7**

Punt Returns

	Ret	Yds	TD
1946 Brooklyn Dodgers	7	146	1
1947 Los Angeles Dons	19	215	0
Total	**26**	**361**	**1**

Kick Returns

	Ret	Yds	TD
1946 Brooklyn Dodgers	12	214	0
1947 Los Angeles Dons	5	119	0
1948 Los Angeles Dons	2	38	0
Total	**19**	**371**	**0**

Interceptions

	Int	Yds	TD
1946 Brooklyn Dodgers	2	44	0
1947 Los Angeles Dons	5	44	0
1948 Los Angeles Dons	1	32	0
Total	**8**	**120**	**0**

DOBELSTEIN, Robert Edward (Bob)

Position: G
Height: 5'1"; Weight: 214
College: Tennessee
Born: October 27, 1922, Bridgeport, CT
Deceased: November 13, 2009, Lake City, FL

STATISTICS

Games

	GP	GS
1946 New York Giants	10	9
1947 New York Giants	12	11
1948 New York Giants	11	9
1949 Los Angeles Dons	8	5
Total	41	34

Interceptions

	Int	Yds	TD
1948 New York Giants	1	20	1
Total	1	20	1

Fumbles

	Fum	Rec	Yds	TD
1946 New York Giants	0	2	0	0
1947 New York Giants	0	1	0	0
Total	0	3	0	0

DOHERTY, George Edward

Position: T-G
Height: 6'1"; Weight: 218
College: Louisiana Tech
Born: September 5, 1920, Camden, MS
Deceased: December 31, 1987, Natchitoches, LA

STATISTICS

Games

	GP	GS
1944 Brooklyn Dodgers	10	7
1945 Boston Yanks	9	7
1946 New York Yanks	1	0
1946 Buffalo Bisons	12	7
1947 Buffalo Bills	11	8
Total	43	29

Kick Returns

	Ret	Yds	TD
1947 Buffalo Bills	1	0	0
Total	1	0	0

DONALDSON, John Colvin

Position: DB-TB
Height: 5'10"; Weight: 180
College: Georgia
Born: August 22, 1925, Jesup, GA
Deceased:

STATISTICS

Games

	GP	GS
1949 Los Angeles Dons	1	0
1949 Chicago Hornets	7	0
Total	8	0

Rushing

	Rush	Yds	TD
1949 Chicago Hornets	1	-2	0
Total	1	-2	0

Passing

	Comp	Att	Yds	Td	Int
1949 Hornets	0	1	0	0	0
Total	0	1	0	0	0

Punt Returns

	Ret	Yds	TD
1949 Chicago Hornets	1	18	0
Total	1	18	0

Kick Returns

	Ret	Yds	TD
1949 Chicago Hornets	1	27	0
Total	1	27	0

DOSS, Noble Webster

Position: HB
Height: 6'0"; Weight: 186
College: Texas
Born: May 22, 1920, Temple, TX
Deceased: February 15, 2009, Austin, TX

STATISTICS

Games

	GP	GS
1947 Philadelphia Eagles	9	0
1948 Philadelphia Eagles	11	0
1949 New York Yankees	4	0
Total	24	0

Rushing

	Rush	Yds	TD
1947 Philadelphia Eagles	11	45	0
1948 Philadelphia Eagles	62	193	0
1949 New York Yankees	5	15	0
Total	78	253	0

Receiving

	Rec	Yds	TD
1947 Philadelphia Eagles	2	17	0
1948 Philadelphia Eagles	8	96	0
Total	10	113	0

Punt Returns

	Ret	Yds	TD
1948 Philadelphia Eagles	1	0	0
Total	1	0	0

Kick Returns

	Ret	Yds	TD
1948 Philadelphia Eagles	1	26	0
1949 New York Yankees	1	22	0
Total	2	48	0

Interceptions

	Int	Yds	TD
1947 Philadelphia Eagles	2	31	0
Total	2	31	0

Fumbles

	Fum	Rec	Yds	TD
1948 Philadelphia Eagles	4	0	0	0
Total	4	0	0	0

DOVE, Robert Leo Patrick (Bob)

Position: DE-E
Height: 6'2"; Weight: 222
College: Notre Dame
Born: February 21, 1921, Youngstown, OH
Deceased: April 19, 2006, Austintown, OH

STATISTICS

Games

	GP	GS
1946 Chicago Rockets	14	5
1947 Chicago Rockets	13	3
1948 Chicago Cardinals	12	0
1949 Chicago Cardinals	12	0
1950 Chicago Cardinals	12	0
1951 Chicago Cardinals	12	0
1952 Chicago Cardinals	11	0
1953 Chicago Cardinals	4	0
1953 Detroit Lions	4	0
1954 Detroit Lions	12	0
Total	106	8

Rushing

	Rush	Yds	TD
1948 Chicago Cardinals	1	−2	0
Total	1	−2	0

Receiving

	Rec	Yds	TD
1946 Chicago Rockets	7	67	1
1947 Chicago Rockets	6	61	1
Total	13	128	2

Kick Returns

	Ret	Yds	TD
1947 Chicago Rockets	1	16	0
Total	1	16	0

Interceptions

	Int	Yds	TD
1950 Chicago Cardinals	1	0	0
Total	1	0	0

Fumbles

	Fum	Rec	Yds	TD
1949 Chicago Cardinals	0	1	0	0
1950 Chicago Cardinals	0	1	0	0
1951 Chicago Cardinals	0	4	13	0
1952 Chicago Cardinals	0	3	0	0
1954 Detroit Lions	0	1	0	0
Total	0	10	13	0

DUDISH, Andrew Charles (Andy)

Position: HB
Height: 5'11"; Weight: 182
College: Georgia
Born: October 13, 1921, Wilkes-Barre, PA
Deceased: January 19, 2001, Lawrenceville, GA

STATISTICS

Games

	GP	GS
1946 Buffalo Bisons	11	2
1947 Baltimore Colts	14	4
1948 Detroit Lions	4	0
Total	29	6

Rushing

	Rush	Yds	TD
1946 Buffalo Bisons	30	106	0
1947 Baltimore Colts	28	30	1
1948 Detroit Lions	1	5	0
Total	59	141	1

Receiving

	Rec	Yds	TD
1946 Buffalo Bisons	2	33	0
1947 Baltimore Colts	7	130	1
Total	9	163	1

Punt Returns

	Ret	Yds	TD
1946 Buffalo Bisons	5	73	0
1947 Baltimore Colts	5	121	0
1948 Detroit Lions	2	10	0
Total	12	204	0

Kick Returns

	Ret	Yds	TD
1946 Buffalo Bisons	7	196	0
1947 Baltimore Colts	8	184	0
1948 Detroit Lions	2	38	0
Total	17	418	0

DUGGAN, Gilford Earl (Gil)

Position: T
Height: 6'3"; Weight: 229
College: Oklahoma
Born: December 26, 1914, Benton, AR
Deceased: October 18, 1974, Harrah, OK

STATISTICS

Games

	GP	GS
1940 New York Giants	10	0
1942 Chicago Cardinals	11	11
1943 Chicago Cardinals	10	10
1944 Chicago Cardinals	10	8
1945 Chicago Cardinals	8	5
1946 Los Angeles Dons	11	0
1947 Buffalo Bills	12	2
Total	72	36

Interceptions

	Int	Yds	TD
1942 Chicago Cardinals	1	0	0
Total	1	0	0

DUGGER, John Richard (Jack)

Position: T-DE
Height: 6'3"; Weight: 230
College: Ohio State
Born: January 13, 1923, Pittsburgh, PA
Deceased: February 23, 1988, Charlotte, NC

STATISTICS

Games
	GP	GS
1946 Buffalo Bisons	7	0
1947 Detroit Lions	12	3
1948 Detroit Lions	12	7
1949 Chicago Bears	6	2
Total	37	12

Receiving
	Rec	Yds	TD
1946 Buffalo Bisons	1	15	0
1949 Chicago Bears	1	11	0
Total	2	26	0

Kick Returns
	Ret	Yds	TD
1949 Chicago Bears	1	8	0
Total	1	8	0

Interceptions
	Int	Yds	TD
1947 Detroit Lions	1	6	0
Total	1	6	0

Fumbles
	Fum	Rec	Yds	TD
1947 Detroit Lions	0	1	0	0
Total	0	1	0	0

DUKE, Paul Anderson

Position: C-LB
Height: 6'1"; Weight: 210
College: Georgia Tech
Born: September 24, 1924, DeKalb County, GA
Deceased: March 24, 2009

STATISTICS

Games
	GP	GS
1947 New York Yankees	10	0
Total	10	0

DURDAN, Donald Edgar (Don)

Position: HB-DB
Height: 5'9"; Weight: 175
College: Oregon State
Born: September 21, 1920, Arcata, CA
Deceased: June 28, 1971, Corvallis, OR

STATISTICS

Games
	GP	GS
1946 San Francisco 49ers	12	1
1947 San Francisco 49ers	1	0
Total	13	1

Rushing
	Rush	Yds	TD
1946 S.F. 49ers	32	132	0
1947 S.F. 49ers	1	2	0
Total	33	134	0

Receiving
	Rec	Yds	TD
1946 S.F. 49ers	2	27	1
Total	2	27	1

Punting
	Punt	Yds	Blk
1946 S.F. 49ers	6	239	0
Total	6	239	0

Punt Returns
	Ret	Yds	TD
1946 S.F. 49ers	3	37	0
Total	3	37	0

Interceptions
	Int	Yds	TD
1946 S.F. 49ers	2	38	0
Total	2	38	0

DURISHAN, John Donald (Jack)

Position: T-G
Height: 6'2"; Weight: 230
College: Pittsburgh
Born: July 7, 1922
Deceased: May 13, 1977, Hazelton, PA

STATISTICS

Games
	GP	GS
1947 New York Yankees	6	1
Total	6	1

Kick Returns
	Ret	Yds	TD
1947 New York Yankees	1	3	0
Total	1	3	0

DURKOTA, Jeffrey George (Jeff)

Position: HB-LB
Height: 6'0"; Weight: 205
College: Penn State
Born: December 20, 1923, Pittsburgh, PA
Deceased: March 5, 2013, Lancaster, PA

DWORSKY, Daniel Leonard (Dan)

Position: LB
Height: 6'0"; Weight: 211
College: Michigan
Born: October 4, 1927, Minneapolis, MN
Deceased:

STATISTICS

Games
	GP	GS
1948 Los Angeles Dons	12	4
Total	**12**	**4**

Rushing
	Rush	Yds	TD
1948 Los Angeles Dons	14	66	0
Total	**14**	**66**	**0**

Receiving
	Rec	Yds	TD
1948 Los Angeles Dons	2	12	0
Total	**2**	**12**	**0**

Kick Returns
	Ret	Yds	TD
1948 Los Angeles Dons	9	198	0
Total	**9**	**198**	**0**

Interceptions
	Int	Yds	TD
1948 Los Angeles Dons	1	18	0
Total	**1**	**18**	**0**

DWORSKY, Daniel Leonard (Dan)

Position: LB
Height: 6'0"; Weight: 211
College: Michigan
Born: October 4, 1927, Minneapolis, MN
Deceased:

STATISTICS

Games
	GP	GS
1949 Los Angeles Dons	11	0
Total	**11**	**0**

Kick Returns
	Ret	Yds	TD
1949 Los Angeles Dons	1	14	0
Total	**1**	**14**	**0**

Interceptions
	Int	Yds	TD
1949 Los Angeles Dons	1	3	0
Total	**1**	**3**	**0**

EAKIN, Oliver Kay, Jr. (Kay)

Position: HB
Height: 6'0"; Weight: 180
College: Arkansas
Born: August 3, 1917, Atkins, AR
Deceased: February 15, 1993, Fort Smith, AR

STATISTICS

Games
	GP	GS
1940 New York Giants	7	1
1941 New York Giants	11	1
1946 Miami Seahawks	13	1
Total	**31**	**3**

Rushing
	Rush	Yds	TD
1940 New York Giants	14	20	0
1941 New York Giants	27	–5	0
1946 Miami Seahawks	15	–41	0
Total	**56**	**–26**	**0**

Receiving
	Rec	Yds	TD
1941 New York Giants	5	81	1
1946 Miami Seahawks	6	67	0
Total	**11**	**148**	**1**

Passing
	Comp	Att	Yds	TD	Int
1940 N.Y. Giants	17	43	199	0	3
1941 N.Y. Giants	5	19	71	1	4
1946 Seahawks	19	45	331	2	5
Total	**41**	**107**	**601**	**3**	**12**

Punting
	Punt	Yds	Blk
1940 New York Giants	11	454	0
1941 New York Giants	20	949	0
1946 Miami Seahawks	37	1530	1
Total	**68**	**2933**	**1**

Punt Returns
	Ret	Yds	TD
1946 Miami Seahawks	3	30	0
Total	**3**	**30**	**0**

Kick Returns
	Ret	Yds	TD
1946 Miami Seahawks	4	51	0
Total	**4**	**51**	**0**

Interceptions
	Int	Yds	TD
1941 New York Giants	2	33	0
1946 Miami Seahawks	2	31	0
Total	**4**	**64**	**0**

Field Goals
	FGM	FGA
1941 New York Giants	*	1
Total	*****	**1**

EBLI, Raymond Henry (Ray)

Position: E
Height: 6'3"; Weight: 210
College: Notre Dame
Born: October 6, 1919, Bessemer, MI
Deceased: January 19, 2005, Green Bay, WI

STATISTICS
Games

	GP	GS
1942 Chicago Cardinals	6	0
1946 Buffalo Bisons	9	7
1947 Chicago Rockets	5	2
Total	**20**	**9**

Receiving

	Rec	Yds	TD
1942 Chicago Cardinals	6	83	0
1946 Buffalo Bisons	2	15	1
1947 Chicago Rockets	4	38	1
Total	**12**	**136**	**2**

ECKER, Enrique Edward (Ed)

Position: DT-T
Height: 6'7"; Weight: 276
College: John Carroll
Born: January 21, 1923, Cleveland, OH
Deceased: January 4, 1990, Los Angeles, CA

STATISTICS
Games

	GP	GS
1947 Chicago Bears	12	0
1948 Chicago Rockets	8	2
1950 Green Bay Packers	12	0
1951 Green Bay Packers	7	0
1952 Washington Redskins	9	0
Total	**48**	**2**

Fumbles

	Fum	Rec	Yds	TD
1952 Wash. Redskins	0	1	0	0
Total	**0**	**1**	**0**	**0**

ECKLUND, Bradford Sterling (Brad)

Position: C-LB
Height: 6'3"; Weight: 215
College: Oregon
Born: May 9, 1922, Los Angeles, CA
Deceased: February 6, 2010, Mount Holly, NJ

STATISTICS
Games

	GP	GS
1949 New York Yankees	12	9
1950 New York Yanks	12	0
1951 New York Yanks	12	0
1952 Dallas Texans	12	12
1953 Baltimore Colts	12	0
Total	**60**	**21**

EDWARDS, Daniel Moody (Dan)

Position: E
Height: 6'1"; Weight: 197
College: Georgia
Born: July 18, 1926, Osage, TX
Deceased: August 7, 2001, Gatesville, TX

STATISTICS
Games

	GP	GS
1948 Brooklyn Dodgers	11	7
1949 Chicago Hornets	12	12
1950 New York Yanks	12	0
1951 New York Yanks	10	0
1952 Dallas Texans	1	1
1953 Baltimore Colts	12	0
1954 Baltimore Colts	12	0
Total	**70**	**20**

Receiving

	Rec	Yds	TD
1948 Brooklyn Dodgers	23	176	0
1949 Chicago Hornets	42	573	3
1950 New York Yanks	52	775	6
1951 New York Yanks	39	509	3
1952 Dallas Texans	3	22	0
1953 Baltimore Colts	35	312	3
1954 Baltimore Colts	40	531	1
Total	**234**	**2898**	**16**

Kick Returns

	Ret	Yds	TD
1948 Brooklyn Dodgers	1	21	0
1949 Chicago Hornets	2	29	1
Total	**3**	**50**	**1**

Fumbles

	Fum	Rec	Yds	TD
1950 New York Yanks	1	1	0	0
1954 Baltimore Colts	0	1	7	0
Total	**1**	**2**	**7**	**0**

ELLENSON, Eugene (Gene)

Position: T
Height: 6'1"; Weight: 210
College: Georgia
Born: March 24, 1921, Chippewa Falls, WI
Deceased: March 17, 1995, Gainesville, FL

STATISTICS
Games

	GP	GS
1946 Miami Seahawks	13	11
Total	**13**	**11**

ELLIOTT, Charles Junior (Charlie)

Position: T
Height: 6'2"; Weight: 240
College: Oregon
Born: December 30, 1921, Corvallis, OR
Deceased: September 16, 1980, Oregon City, OR

STATISTICS

Games

	GP	GS
1947 New York Yankees	10	0
1948 San Francisco 49ers	3	0
1948 Chicago Rockets	1	0
Total	**14**	**0**

ELSEY, Earl D.

Position: HB
Height: 5'8"; Weight: 175
College: Loyola Marymount
Born: June 23, 1920
Deceased: October 12, 1972, Los Angeles County, CA

STATISTICS

Games

	GP	GS
1946 Los Angeles Dons	13	3
Total	**13**	**3**

Rushing

	Rush	Yds	TD
1946 Los Angeles Dons	47	165	0
Total	**47**	**165**	**0**

Receiving

	Rec	Yds	TD
1946 Los Angeles Dons	14	179	0
Total	**14**	**179**	**0**

Punt Returns

	Ret	Yds	TD
1946 Los Angeles Dons	9	147	0
Total	**9**	**147**	**0**

Kick Returns

	Ret	Yds	TD
1946 Los Angeles Dons	15	335	0
Total	**15**	**335**	**0**

Interceptions

	Int	Yds	TD
1946 Los Angeles Dons	2	2	0
Total	**2**	**2**	**0**

ELSTON, Arthur Warren (Dutch)

Position: C-BB
Height: 5'11"; Weight: 190
College: South Carolina
Born: November 19, 1918, Texhoma, TX
Deceased: September 10, 1989, Daly City, CA

STATISTICS

Games

	GP	GS
1942 Cleveland Rams	11	8
1946 San Francisco 49ers	13	11
1947 San Francisco 49ers	9	3
1948 San Francisco 49ers	12	0
Total	**45**	**22**

Rushing

	Rush	Yds	TD
1942 Cleveland Rams	1	15	0
Total	**1**	**15**	**0**

Receiving

	Rec	Yds	TD
1942 Cleveland Rams	4	58	0
Total	**4**	**58**	**0**

Kick Returns

	Ret	Yds	TD
1942 Cleveland Rams	2	46	0
Total	**2**	**46**	**0**

Interceptions

	Int	Yds	TD
1946 S.F. 49ers	1	34	0
1947 S.F. 49ers	2	13	0
1948 S.F. 49ers	1	0	0
Total	**4**	**47**	**0**

ERDLITZ, Richard Alfred (Dick)

Position: HB
Height: 5'10"; Weight: 181
College: Northwestern
Born: February 16, 1920, Menomonie, MI
Deceased: April 3, 2006, Melbourne, FL

STATISTICS

Games

	GP	GS
1942 Philadelphia Eagles	10	1
1945 Philadelphia Eagles	7	0
1946 Miami Seahawks	14	7
Total	**31**	**8**

Rushing

	Rush	Yds	TD
1942 Philadelphia Eagles	21	69	1
1945 Philadelphia Eagles	6	24	0
1946 Miami Seahawks	26	38	1
Total	**53**	**131**	**2**

Receiving

	Rec	Yds	TD
1942 Philadelphia Eagles	5	78	0
1946 Miami Seahawks	7	31	0
Total	**12**	**109**	**0**

Eshmont (continued)

Passing

	Comp	Att	Yds	TD	Int
1946 Seahawks	1	1	10	0	0
Total	1	1	10	0	0

Kick Returns

	Ret	Yds	TD
1942 Philadelphia Eagles	1	25	0
1946 Miami Seahawks	6	104	0
Total	7	129	0

Interceptions

	Int	Yds	TD
1942 Philadelphia Eagles	1	0	0
1945 Philadelphia Eagles	1	3	0
1946 Miami Seahawks	1	12	0
Total	3	15	0

Field Goals

	FGM	FGA
1946 Miami Seahawks	2	7
Total	2	7

Point After Touchdown

	XPM	XPA
1942 Philadelphia Eagles	8	8
1946 Miami Seahawks	22	22
Total	30	30

ERICKSON, William Clarence (Bill) (Wild Bill)

Position: G
Height: 6'2"; Weight: 210
College: Mississippi, North Carolina
Born: December 4, 1921
Deceased: November 18, 2010, Parker, CO

STATISTICS

Games

	GP	GS
1948 New York Giants	9	3
1949 New York Yankees	6	1
Total	15	4

ESHMONT, Leonard Charles (Len)

Position: HB-FB
Height: 5'11"; Weight: 179
College: Fordham
Born: August 26, 1917, Mount Carmel, PA
Deceased: May 12, 1957, Charlottesville, VA

STATISTICS

Games

	GP	GS
1941 New York Giants	9	5
1946 San Francisco 49ers	10	9
1947 San Francisco 49ers	13	13
1948 San Francisco 49ers	13	8
1949 San Francisco 49ers	12	6
Total	57	41

Rushing

	Rush	Yds	TD
1941 New York Giants	50	164	0
1946 S.F. 49ers	73	340	6
1947 S.F. 49ers	84	381	0
1948 S.F. 49ers	50	296	1
1949 S.F. 49ers	25	164	0
Total	282	1345	7

Receiving

	Rec	Yds	TD
1941 New York Giants	1	4	0
1946 S.F. 49ers	17	287	2
1947 S.F. 49ers	19	303	2
1948 S.F. 49ers	14	214	0
1949 S.F. 49ers	3	107	2
Total	54	915	6

Passing

	Comp	Att	Yds	TD	Int
1941 N.Y. Giants	2	3	32	1	0
1946 S.F. 49ers	1	2	42	1	0
Total	3	5	74	2	0

Punting

	Punt	Yds	Blk
1941 New York Giants	11	433	0
Total	11	433	0

Punt Returns

	Ret	Yds	TD
1941 New York Giants	6	131	0
1946 S.F. 49ers	2	25	0
1947 S.F. 49ers	1	3	0
Total	9	159	0

Kick Returns

	Ret	Yds	TD
1941 New York Giants	2	54	0
1946 S.F. 49ers	10	264	0
1947 S.F. 49ers	9	177	0
1948 S.F. 49ers	1	32	0
1949 S.F. 49ers	1	13	0
Total	23	540	0

Interceptions

	Int	Yds	TD
1947 S.F. 49ers	6	72	0
1948 S.F. 49ers	1	0	0
1949 S.F. 49ers	3	56	0
Total	10	128	0

NOTE: *There are a few discrepancies between the actual statistics and the official records in 1946. The total receiving yards for the season for Len Eshmont, Joe Vetrano, Ed Balatti and Ken Roskie were not consistent. Eshmont had an extra six receiving yards, while Vetrano was missing six yards. Balatti had an extra seven receiving yards and Roskie was missing seven yards. Since the numbers could not be verified, the official statistics are listed.*

EVANS, Frederick Owen, Jr. (Fred) (Dippy)

Position: HB
Height: 5'11"; Weight: 185
College: Notre Dame
Born: May 23, 1921, Grand Rapids, MI
Deceased: June 21, 2007, Cleveland, OH

Statistics

Games

	GP	GS
1946 Cleveland Browns	6	0
1947 Chicago Rockets	9	6
1947 Buffalo Bills	4	0
1948 Chicago Bears	3	0
Total	22	6

Rushing

	Rush	Yds	TD
1946 Cleveland Browns	8	27	0
1947 Chicago Rockets	20	110	1
1947 Buffalo Bills	11	14	0
1948 Chicago Bears	10	15	0
Total	49	166	1

Receiving

	Rec	Yds	TD
1946 Cleveland Browns	1	7	0
1947 Chicago Rockets	4	53	0
1947 Buffalo Bills	1	31	0
1948 Chicago Bears	1	-2	0
Total	7	89	1

Passing

	Comp	Att	Yds	Td	Int
1947 Rockets	0	2	0	0	0
Total	0	2	0	0	0

Punting

	Punt	Yds	Blk
1946 Cleveland Browns	8	296	0
1947 Chicago Rockets	2	73	0
Total	10	369	0

Punt Returns

	Ret	Yds	TD
1946 Cleveland Browns	1	0	0
1947 Chicago Rockets	2	20	0
1947 Buffalo Bills	3	10	0
1948 Chicago Bears	1	15	0
Total	7	45	0

Kick Returns

	Ret	Yds	TD
1947 Chicago Rockets	8	159	0
1947 Buffalo Bills	1	0	0
Total	9	159	0

Interceptions

	Int	Yds	TD
1946 Cleveland Browns	1	21	0
Total	1	21	0

Fumbles

	Fum	Rec	Yds	TD
1948 Chicago Bears	0	2	26	2
Total	0	2	26	2

EVANS, Raymond L. (Ray)

Position: G-T
Height: 6'1"; Weight: 225
College: Texas-El Paso
Born: January 10, 1924, Electra, TX
Deceased: April 25, 2008, Stayton, OR

Statistics

Games

	GP	GS
1949 San Francisco 49ers	10	0
1950 San Francisco 49ers	12	0
Total	22	0

Kick Returns

	Ret	Yds	TD
1950 S.F. 49ers	1	2	0
Total	1	2	0

EVANSEN, Paul

Position: G
Height: 6'3"; Weight: 240
College: Oregon State
Born: May 10, 1922, San Francisco, CA
Deceased: July 13, 2002, Medford, OR

Statistics

Games

	GP	GS
1948 San Francisco 49ers	1	0
Total	1	0

FARRIS, Thomas George (Tom)

Position: QB
Height: 6'1"; Weight: 185
College: Wisconsin
Born: September 16, 1920, Casper, WY
Deceased: November 16, 2002, Citrus Heights, CA

Statistics

Games

	GP	GS
1946 Chicago Bears	11	3
1947 Chicago Bears	9	0
1948 Chicago Rockets	13	0
Total	33	3

Rushing

	Rush	Yds	TD
1946 Chicago Bears	12	-11	0
1947 Chicago Bears	1	-3	0
1948 Chicago Rockets	4	5	0
Total	17	-9	0

FENENBOCK

Receiving

	Rec	Yds	TD
1946 Chicago Bears	1	16	0
Total	1	16	0

Passing

	Comp	Att	Yds	TD	Int
1946 Chi. Bears	8	21	108	1	2
1947 Chi. Bears	0	2	0	0	0
1948 Chi. Rockets	3	9	24	0	3
Total	11	32	132	1	5

Punt Returns

	Ret	Yds	TD
1946 Chicago Bears	2	4	0
Total	2	4	0

Kick Returns

	Ret	Yds	TD
1946 Chicago Bears	1	27	0
Total	1	27	0

Interceptions

	Int	Yds	TD
1946 Chicago Bears	4	43	0
1947 Chicago Bears	1	2	0
Total	5	45	0

Fumbles

	Fum	Rec	Yds	TD
1946 Chicago Bears	2	1	−9	0
1947 Chicago Bears	0	1	0	0
Total	2	2	−9	0

FEKETE, Eugene H. (Gene)

Position: FB-LB
Height: 6'0"; Weight: 195
College: Ohio State
Born: August 31, 1922, Sugar Creek, OH
Deceased: April 28, 2011, Columbus, OH

STATISTICS

Games

	GP	GS
1946 Cleveland Browns	6	2
Total	6	2

Rushing

	Rush	Yds	TD
1946 Cleveland Browns	26	106	1
Total	26	106	1

Receiving

	Rec	Yds	TD
1946 Cleveland Browns	1	2	0
Total	1	2	0

Kick Returns

	Ret	Yds	TD
1946 Cleveland Browns	1	21	0
Total	1	21	0

FEKETE, John Michael

Position: HB-DB
Height: 5'11"; Weight: 200
College: Ohio
Born: October 28, 1919, Morgantown, WV
Deceased: July 26, 1988, Cleveland, OH

STATISTICS

Games

	GP	GS
1946 Buffalo Bisons	3	0
Total	3	0

Rushing

	Rush	Yds	TD
1946 Buffalo Bisons	1	−1	0
Total	1	−1	0

FENENBOCK, Charles Bernard (Chuck)

Position: HB-TB
Height: 5'9"; Weight: 174
College: UCLA
Born: August 28, 1917, Oakland, CA
Deceased: July 27, 1998, Santa Rosa, CA

STATISTICS

Games

	GP	GS
1943 Detroit Lions	10	6
1945 Detroit Lions	10	2
1946 Los Angeles Dons	13	7
1947 Los Angeles Dons	14	12
1948 Los Angeles Dons	1	0
1948 Chicago Rockets	13	5
Total	61	32

Rushing

	Rush	Yds	TD
1943 Detroit Lions	46	180	0
1945 Detroit Lions	72	143	1
1946 Los Angeles Dons	50	420	3
1947 Los Angeles Dons	58	185	3
1948 Chicago Rockets	43	174	0
Total	269	1102	7

Receiving

	Rec	Yds	TD
1943 Detroit Lions	5	45	1
1945 Detroit Lions	1	24	0
1946 Los Angeles Dons	11	67	0
1947 Los Angeles Dons	20	276	2
1948 Chicago Rockets	8	111	1
Total	45	523	4

Passing

	Comp	Att	Yds	TD	Int
1943 Detroit Lions	28	58	338	3	9
1945 Detroit Lions	45	110	754	7	11
1946 L.A. Dons	0	1	0	0	0
1947 L.A. Dons	1	7	7	0	2

	Comp	Att	Yds	TD	Int
1948 Chi. Rockets	4	15	136	2	1
Total	70	191	1235	12	23

Punting

	Punt	Yds	Blk
1943 Detroit Lions	4	184	0
1945 Detroit Lions	29	1081	0
Total	33	1265	0

Punt Returns

	Ret	Yds	TD
1943 Detroit Lions	6	54	0
1945 Detroit Lions	5	69	0
1946 Los Angeles Dons	16	299	0
1947 Los Angeles Dons	17	210	0
1948 Chicago Rockets	5	17	0
Total	61	801	0

Kick Returns

	Ret	Yds	TD
1943 Detroit Lions	11	224	0
1945 Detroit Lions	7	192	0
1946 Los Angeles Dons	17	479	1
1947 Los Angeles Dons	18	452	0
1948 Chicago Rockets	14	311	0
Total	67	1658	1

Interceptions

	Int	Yds	TD
1943 Detroit Lions	1	28	0
1945 Detroit Lions	1	10	0
Total	2	38	0

Fumbles

	Fum	Rec	Yds	TD
1945 Detroit Lions	4	4	37	1
Total	4	4	37	1

FISK, William G. (Bill)

Position: E-DE
Height: 6'0"; Weight: 200
College: USC
Born: November 5, 1916, Los Angeles, CA
Deceased: March 27, 2007, Corona Del Mar, CA

Statistics

Games

	GP	GS
1940 Detroit Lions	10	3
1941 Detroit Lions	11	8
1942 Detroit Lions	11	11
1943 Detroit Lions	10	9
1946 San Francisco 49ers	14	12
1947 San Francisco 49ers	14	1
1948 Los Angeles Dons	13	2
Total	83	46

Rushing

	Rush	Yds	TD
1940 Detroit Lions	2	0	0
Total	2	0	0

Receiving

	Rec	Yds	TD
1940 Detroit Lions	1	10	0
1941 Detroit Lions	9	140	2
1942 Detroit Lions	15	177	0
1943 Detroit Lions	11	137	0
1946 S.F. 49ers	19	186	1
1947 S.F. 49ers	5	39	0
1948 Los Angeles Dons	9	102	0
Total	69	791	3

Kick Returns

	Ret	Yds	TD
1942 Detroit Lions	1	10	0
1943 Detroit Lions	1	5	0
Total	2	15	0

FLAGERMAN, Jack Michael

Position: C-LB
Height: 6'0"; Weight: 218
College: St. Mary's
Born: March 27, 1922, San Francisco, CA
Deceased: June 12, 2005, Rohnert Park, CA

Statistics

Games

	GP	GS
1948 Los Angeles Dons	14	0
Total	14	0

FLETCHER, Oliver C.

Position: G
Height: 6'3"; Weight: 210
College: USC
Born: February 5, 1923, San Diego County, CA
Deceased: May 10, 1994, Bullhead City, AZ

Statistics

Games

	GP	GS
1949 Los Angeles Dons	3	0
Total	3	0

FOLDBERG, Henry Christian, Jr. (Hank)

Position: E
Height: 6'2"; Weight: 205
College: Army, Texas A&M
Born: March 12, 1923, Dallas, TX
Deceased: March 6, 2001, Bella Vista, AR

Statistics

Games

	GP	GS
1948 Brooklyn Dodgers	13	6
1949 Chicago Hornets	12	9
Total	25	15

Receiving

	Rec	Yds	TD
1948 Brooklyn Dodgers	16	129	0
1949 Chicago Hornets	15	202	0
Total	31	331	0

FORD, Leonard Guy, Jr. (Len)

Position: DE-E
Height: 6'4"; Weight: 245
College: Michigan, Morgan State
Born: February 18, 1926, Washington, D.C.
Deceased: March 13, 1972, Detroit, MI

STATISTICS

Games

	GP	GS
1948 Los Angeles Dons	14	10
1949 Los Angeles Dons	12	8
1950 Cleveland Browns	5	0
1951 Cleveland Browns	12	0
1952 Cleveland Browns	12	0
1953 Cleveland Browns	12	0
1954 Cleveland Browns	12	0
1955 Cleveland Browns	12	0
1956 Cleveland Browns	12	0
1957 Cleveland Browns	11	0
1958 Green Bay Packers	11	0
Total	125	18

Receiving

	Rec	Yds	TD
1948 Los Angeles Dons	31	598	7
1949 Los Angeles Dons	36	577	1
Total	67	1175	8

Kick Returns

	Ret	Yds	TD
1948 Los Angeles Dons	1	24	0
Total	1	24	0

Interceptions

	Int	Yds	TD
1948 Los Angeles Dons	1	0	0
1949 Los Angeles Dons	1	45	0
1953 Cleveland Browns	1	0	0
Total	3	45	0

Fumbles

	Fum	Rec	Yds	TD
1950 Cleveland Browns	0	1	0	0
1951 Cleveland Browns	0	4	16	0
1952 Cleveland Browns	0	2	0	1
1953 Cleveland Browns	0	3	0	0
1954 Cleveland Browns	0	5	0	0
1955 Cleveland Browns	0	1	54	0
1956 Cleveland Browns	0	2	0	0
1957 Cleveland Browns	0	1	4	0
1958 Green Bay Packers	0	1	5	0
Total	0	20	79	1

FORKOVITCH, Nicholas John (Nick)

Position: FB
Height: 5'11"; Weight: 195
College: William & Mary
Born: March 1, 1920, McKeesport, PA
Deceased: April 5, 1998, Harrisonburg, VA

STATISTICS

Games

	GP	GS
1948 Brooklyn Dodgers	9	0
Total	9	0

Rushing

	Rush	Yds	TD
1948 Brooklyn Dodgers	1	4	0
Total	1	4	0

FORREST, Edwin George (Eddie)

Position: G
Height: 5'11"; Weight: 210
College: Santa Clara
Born: June 12, 1921, San Francisco, CA
Deceased: May 29, 2001, Palo Alto, CA

STATISTICS

Games

	GP	GS
1946 San Francisco 49ers	11	0
1947 San Francisco 49ers	14	5
Total	25	5

FOWLER, Robert Aubey (Aubrey)

Position: HB
Height: 5'10"; Weight: 160
College: Arkansas, Arkansas Tech
Born: June 12, 1920, Hamburg, AR
Deceased: February 29, 1996, Dumas, AR

STATISTICS

Games

	GP	GS
1948 Baltimore Colts	13	0
Total	13	0

Rushing

	Rush	Yds	TD
1948 Baltimore Colts	6	30	0
Total	6	30	0

Punt Returns

	Ret	Yds	TD
1948 Baltimore Colts	4	41	0
Total	4	41	0

Kick Returns

	Ret	Yds	TD
1948 Baltimore Colts	2	16	0
Total	**2**	**16**	**0**

Interceptions

	Int	Yds	TD
1948 Baltimore Colts	3	0	0
Total	**3**	**0**	**0**

FOX, Terrence Patrick (Terry)

Position: FB-LB
Height: 6'1"; Weight: 208
College: Miami (FL)
Born: July 6, 1918, Newark, NJ
Deceased: April 1, 1981, Miami, FL

STATISTICS

Games

	GP	GS
1941 Philadelphia Eagles	11	2
1945 Philadelphia Eagles	2	0
1946 Miami Seahawks	8	2
Total	**21**	**4**

Rushing

	Rush	Yds	TD
1941 Philadelphia Eagles	21	97	0
1946 Miami Seahawks	12	26	0
Total	**33**	**123**	**0**

Receiving

	Rec	Yds	TD
1941 Philadelphia Eagles	6	71	0
1946 Miami Seahawks	3	27	0
Total	**9**	**98**	**0**

Punting

	Punt	Yds	Blk
1946 Miami Seahawks	2	88	0
Total	**2**	**88**	**0**

Kick Returns

	Ret	Yds	TD
1941 Philadelphia Eagles	1	16	0
1946 Miami Seahawks	1	24	0
Total	**2**	**40**	**0**

FRANCESCHI, Peter Louis (Pete)

Position: HB-DB
Height: 5'9"; Weight: 170
College: San Francisco
Born: September 28, 1919, San Francisco, CA
Deceased: July 22, 1989, San Francisco, CA

STATISTICS

Games

	GP	GS
1946 San Francisco 49ers	9	1
Total	**9**	**1**

Rushing

	Rush	Yds	TD
1946 S.F. 49ers	8	−5	1
Total	**8**	**−5**	**1**

Receiving

	Rec	Yds	TD
1946 S.F. 49ers	3	35	1
Total	**3**	**35**	**1**

Punt Returns

	Ret	Yds	TD
1946 S.F. 49ers	1	6	0
Total	**1**	**6**	**0**

FRANKOWSKI, Raymond William (Ray)

Position: G
Height: 5'11"; Weight: 223
College: Washington
Born: September 14, 1919, Chicago, IL
Deceased: November 27, 2001, Laguna Niguel, CA

STATISTICS

Games

	GP	GS
1945 Green Bay Packers	2	0
1946 Los Angeles Dons	12	2
1947 Los Angeles Dons	14	8
1948 Los Angeles Dons	14	3
Total	**42**	**13**

FREEMAN, Jack Leonard

Position: G
Height: 6'0"; Weight: 198
College: Texas
Born: January 20, 1922, Mexia, TX
Deceased: July 23, 1970, Houston, TX

STATISTICS

Games

	GP	GS
1946 Brooklyn Dodgers	12	3
Total	**12**	**3**

FREITAS, Jesse

Position: QB
Height: 5'10"; Weight: 170
College: Santa Clara
Born: February 7, 1921, Red Bluff, CA
Deceased:

STATISTICS

Games

	GP	GS
1946 San Francisco 49ers	10	0
1947 San Francisco 49ers	10	0

	GP	GS
1948 Chicago Rockets	10	9
1949 Buffalo Bills	1	0
Total	31	9

Rushing

	Rush	Yds	TD
1946 S.F. 49ers	6	−21	0
1947 S.F. 49ers	6	−9	0
1948 Chicago Rockets	24	25	0
1949 Buffalo Bills	3	13	0
Total	39	8	0

Passing

	Comp	Att	Yds	Td	Int
1946 S.F. 49ers	22	44	234	3	7
1947 S.F. 49ers	13	33	215	4	2
1948 Chi Rockets	84	167	1425	14	16
1949 Buffalo Bills	4	9	10	0	2
Total	123	253	1884	21	27

Punting

	Punt	Yds	Blk
1947 S.F. 49ers	8	336	0
Total	8	336	0

Punt Returns

	Ret	Yds	TD
1946 S.F. 49ers	1	10	0
Total	1	10	0

Interceptions

	Int	Yds	TD
1946 S.F. 49ers	2	40	0
1947 S.F. 49ers	1	11	0
Total	3	51	0

FRENCH, Barry Alden

Position: G-T
Height: 6'0"; Weight: 225
College: Purdue
Born: February 12, 1922, Chamberlain, SD
Deceased: March 16, 1990, Vero Beach, FL

STATISTICS

Games

	GP	GS
1947 Baltimore Colts	14	14
1949 Baltimore Colts	11	4
1950 Baltimore Colts	12	11
1951 Detroit Lions	12	0
Total	49	29

Kick Returns

	Ret	Yds	TD
1947 Baltimore Colts	1	8	0
1951 Detroit Lions	1	3	0
Total	2	11	0

GAFFORD, Roy Haynes, Jr. (Monk)

Position: B
Height: 5'11"; Weight: 195
College: Auburn
Born: October 1, 1920, Fort Deposit, AL
Deceased: February 19, 1987, Montgomery, AL

STATISTICS

Games

	GP	GS
1946 Miami Seahawks	11	8
1946 Brooklyn Dodgers	2	0
1947 Brooklyn Dodgers	14	13
1948 Brooklyn Dodgers	12	6
Total	39	27

Rushing

	Rush	Yds	TD
1946 Miami Seahawks	22	60	1
1946 Brooklyn Dodgers	2	6	0
1947 Brooklyn Dodgers	46	232	1
1948 Brooklyn Dodgers	30	51	1
Total	100	349	3

Receiving

	Rec	Yds	TD
1946 Miami Seahawks	14	270	4
1947 Brooklyn Dodgers	8	113	0
1948 Brooklyn Dodgers	15	274	4
Total	37	657	8

Passing

	Comp	Att	Yds	Td	Int
1946 Miami Seahawks	1	5	−3	0	2
1948 Dodgers	17	39	268	4	2
Total	18	44	265	4	4

Punting

	Punt	Yds	Blk
1946 Miami Seahawks	12	474	0
1946 Brooklyn Dodgers	1	49	0
Total	13	523	49

Punt Returns

	Ret	Yds	TD
1946 Miami Seahawks	9	117	0
1947 Brooklyn Dodgers	11	186	0
1948 Brooklyn Dodgers	14	130	0
Total	34	433	0

Kick Returns

	Ret	Yds	TD
1946 Miami Seahawks	10	305	0
1946 Brooklyn Dodgers	1	40	0
1947 Brooklyn Dodgers	21	565	0
1948 Brooklyn Dodgers	23	559	0
Total	55	1469	0

Interceptions

	Int	Yds	TD
1946 Miami Seahawks	3	37	0
1946 Brooklyn Dodgers	1	51	0
1947 Brooklyn Dodgers	3	16	0
Total	7	104	0

GALLAGHER, Bernard John, Jr. (Bernie)

Position: G
Height: 6'0"; Weight: 234
College: Pennsylvania, Princeton
Born: November 8, 1921, Philadelphia, PA
Deceased: November 17, 1988, East Lansdowne, PA

STATISTICS

Games		
	GP	GS
1947 Los Angeles Dons	8	0
Total	8	0

GALVIN, John E.

Position: QB
Height: 5'10"; Weight: 170
College: Purdue
Born: December 7, 1920, Chicago, IL
Deceased: December 23, 1998, Oak Lawn, IL

STATISTICS

Games		
	GP	GS
1947 Baltimore Colts	13	1
Total	13	1

Rushing			
	Rush	Yds	TD
1947 Baltimore Colts	1	–4	0
Total	1	–4	0

Passing					
	Comp	Att	Yds	TD	Int
1947 Colts	3	6	34	0	0
Total	3	6	34	0	0

Punting			
	Punt	Yds	Blk
1947 Baltimore Colts	66	2377	2
Total	66	2377	2

Kick Returns			
	Ret	Yds	TD
1947 Baltimore Colts	2	38	0
Total	2	38	0

GAMBINO, Lucien Anthony (Lu)

Position: FB
Height: 6'1"; Weight: 205
College: Indiana, Maryland
Born: September 21, 1923, Berwyn, IL
Deceased: July 16, 2003, Chicago, IL

STATISTICS

Games		
	GP	GS
1948 Baltimore Colts	9	1
1949 Baltimore Colts	10	6
Total	19	7

Rushing			
	Rush	Yds	TD
1948 Baltimore Colts	54	194	1
1949 Baltimore Colts	56	208	0
Total	110	402	1

Receiving			
	Rec	Yds	TD
1948 Baltimore Colts	6	28	0
1949 Baltimore Colts	10	67	1
Total	16	95	1

Kick Returns			
	Ret	Yds	TD
1948 Baltimore Colts	3	57	0
Total	3	57	0

GARLIN, Donald Arthur (Don)

Position: HB-DB
Height: 5'11"; Weight: 188
College: USC
Born: November 10, 1926, Porterville, CA
Deceased: July 29, 1999, Bodega Bay, CA

STATISTICS

Games		
	GP	GS
1949 San Francisco 49ers	11	0
1950 San Francisco 49ers	8	0
Total	19	0

Rushing			
	Rush	Yds	TD
1949 S.F. 49ers	21	113	1
1950 S.F. 49ers	3	3	0
Total	24	116	1

Receiving			
	Rec	Yds	TD
1949 S.F. 49ers	6	64	0
Total	6	64	0

Kick Returns			
	Ret	Yds	TD
1949 S.F. 49ers	1	21	0
1950 S.F. 49ers	1	24	0
Total	2	45	0

Interceptions			
	Int	Yds	TD
1949 S.F. 49ers	1	0	0
Total	1	0	0

GARRETT, William Davis, Jr. (Dub)

Position: G-DT
Height: 6'1"; Weight: 235
College: Mississippi State
Born: January 29, 1925, Dundee, MS
Deceased: July 24, 1976, Dundee, MS

STATISTICS

Games

	GP	GS
1948 Baltimore Colts	14	14
1949 Baltimore Colts	11	7
1950 Chicago Bears	3	0
Total	**28**	**21**

Kick Returns

	Ret	Yds	TD
1948 Baltimore Colts	1	6	0
Total	**1**	**6**	**0**

Fumbles

	Fum	Rec	Yds	TD
1950 Chicago Bears	0	3	62	1
Total	**0**	**3**	**62**	**1**

GARZA, Daniel Robert (Dan)

Position: E
Height: 6'3"; Weight: 203
College: Central Missouri State, North Texas, Oregon
Born: February 21, 1924, Anderson, SC
Deceased: March 6, 2002, Tucson, AZ

STATISTICS

Games

	GP	GS
1949 New York Yankees	12	0
1951 New York Yanks	11	0
Total	**23**	**0**

Receiving

	Rec	Yds	TD
1949 New York Yankees	9	193	0
1951 New York Yanks	31	470	4
Total	**40**	**663**	**4**

Kick Returns

	Ret	Yds	TD
1949 New York Yankees	1	21	0
Total	**1**	**21**	**0**

GATSKI, Frank

Position: C-LB
Height: 6'3"; Weight: 233
College: Auburn, Marshall
Born: March 18, 1922, Farmington, WV
Deceased: November 22, 2005, Morgantown, WV

STATISTICS

Games

	GP	GS
1946 Cleveland Browns	10	1
1947 Cleveland Browns	12	3
1948 Cleveland Browns	14	14
1949 Cleveland Browns	12	11
1950 Cleveland Browns	12	0
1951 Cleveland Browns	12	0
1952 Cleveland Browns	12	0
1953 Cleveland Browns	12	0
1954 Cleveland Browns	12	0
1955 Cleveland Browns	12	0
1956 Cleveland Browns	12	0
1957 Cleveland Browns	12	0
Total	**144**	**29**

Kick Returns

	Ret	Yds	TD
1947 Cleveland Browns	1	17	0
Total	**1**	**17**	**0**

Interceptions

	Int	Yds	TD
1946 Cleveland Browns	1	35	1
1947 Cleveland Browns	2	0	0
Total	**3**	**35**	**1**

Fumbles

	Fum	Rec	Yds	TD
1950 Cleveland Browns	0	1	−6	0
1955 Cleveland Browns	0	1	0	0
1956 Cleveland Browns	0	1	0	0
Total	**0**	**3**	**−6**	**0**

GAUDIO, Angelo Robert (Bob)

Position: G
Height: 5'10"; Weight: 219
College: Ohio State
Born: July 13, 1925, Ashtabula, OH
Deceased: May 10, 2003, Miami, FL

STATISTICS

Games

	GP	GS
1947 Cleveland Browns	14	1
1948 Cleveland Browns	13	12
1949 Cleveland Browns	12	0
1951 Cleveland Browns	12	0
Total	**51**	**13**

Rushing

	Rush	Yds	TD
1948 Cleveland Browns	1	2	0
1949 Cleveland Browns	1	−2	0
Total	**2**	**0**	**0**

Kick Returns

	Ret	Yds	TD
1951 Cleveland Browns	1	8	0
Total	**1**	**8**	**0**

GENTRY, Dale LuAuverene

Position: E
Height: 6'3"; Weight: 223
College: St. Mary's, Washington State
Born: July 2, 1917, Umapine, OR
Deceased: June 27, 1968, Portland, OR

STATISTICS

Games

	GP	GS
1946 Los Angeles Dons	14	9
1947 Los Angeles Dons	14	13
1948 Los Angeles Dons	14	5
Total	42	27

Rushing

	Rush	Yds	TD
1946 Los Angeles Dons	5	29	1
Total	5	29	1

Receiving

	Rec	Yds	TD
1946 Los Angeles Dons	24	341	3
1947 Los Angeles Dons	22	352	2
1948 Los Angeles Dons	28	308	0
Total	74	1001	5

Punt Returns

	Ret	Yds	TD
1946 Los Angeles Dons	1	14	0
Total	1	14	0

GETCHELL, Charles Gorham (Gorham)

Position: E-DE
Height: 6'4"; Weight: 225
College: Temple
Born: August 14, 1920, Abington, PA
Deceased: July 7, 1980, Manhattan Beach, CA

STATISTICS

Games

	GP	GS
1947 Baltimore Colts	8	1
Total	8	1

Receiving

	Rec	Yds	TD
1947 Baltimore Colts	2	17	0
Total	2	17	0

GIBRON, Abraham (Abe)

Position: G
Height: 5'11"; Weight: 243
College: Purdue, Valparaiso
Born: September 22, 1925, Michigan City, IN
Deceased: September 23, 1997, Belleair, FL

STATISTICS

Games

	GP	GS
1949 Buffalo Bills	10	9
1950 Cleveland Browns	12	0
1951 Cleveland Browns	12	0
1952 Cleveland Browns	12	0
1953 Cleveland Browns	10	0
1954 Cleveland Browns	12	0
1955 Cleveland Browns	12	0
1956 Cleveland Browns	7	0
1956 Philadelphia Eagles	2	0
1957 Philadelphia Eagles	12	0
1958 Chicago Bears	12	0
1959 Chicago Bears	12	0
Total	125	9

Kick Returns

	Ret	Yds	TD
1951 Cleveland Browns	1	0	0
1952 Cleveland Browns	1	0	0
1958 Chicago Bears	1	12	0
Total	3	12	0

Fumbles

	Fum	Rec	Yds	TD
1950 Cleveland Browns	0	1	0	0
1951 Cleveland Browns	0	2	3	0
Total	0	3	3	0

GIBSON, Billy Joe (Joe)

Position: C-E
Height: 6'3"; Weight: 213
College: Cameron, Tulsa
Born: June 28, 1919, Nocona, TX
Deceased: October 19, 2002, Sacramento, CA

STATISTICS

Games

	GP	GS
1942 Cleveland Rams	11	8
1943 Washington Redskins	5	0
1944 Cleveland Rams	10	1
1946 Brooklyn Dodgers	14	5
1947 Brooklyn Dodgers	14	4
Total	54	18

Receiving

	Rec	Yds	TD
1942 Cleveland Rams	6	79	0
Total	6	79	0

Interceptions

	Int	Yds	TD
1947 Brooklyn Dodgers	1	0	0
Total	1	0	0

GIBSON, Paul Edward

Position: E-QB-DB-DE
Height: 6'2"; Weight: 195
College: North Carolina State
Born: October 28, 1921, Winston-Salem, NC
Deceased: August 11, 1999, Charleston, SC

STATISTICS

Games

	GP	GS
1947 Buffalo Bills	14	8
1948 Buffalo Bills	7	5
1949 Buffalo Bills	9	2
Total	**30**	**15**

Receiving

	Rec	Yds	TD
1947 Buffalo Bills	8	154	0
1948 Buffalo Bills	11	216	0
1949 Buffalo Bills	3	32	0
Total	**22**	**402**	**0**

Interceptions

	Int	Yds	TD
1949 Buffalo Bills	1	9	0
Total	**1**	**9**	**0**

GILLOM, Horace Albert

Position: E-DE
Height: 6'1"; Weight: 221
College: Nevada-Reno, Ohio State
Born: March 3, 1921, Roanoke, AL
Deceased: October 28, 1985, Los Angeles, CA

STATISTICS

Games

	GP	GS
1947 Cleveland Browns	14	4
1948 Cleveland Browns	13	8
1949 Cleveland Browns	12	4
1950 Cleveland Browns	12	0
1951 Cleveland Browns	12	0
1952 Cleveland Browns	12	0
1953 Cleveland Browns	12	0
1954 Cleveland Browns	12	0
1955 Cleveland Browns	12	0
1956 Cleveland Browns	5	0
Total	**116**	**16**

Rushing

	Rush	Yds	TD
1949 Cleveland Browns	2	8	0
1955 Cleveland Browns	1	-15	0
Total	**3**	**-7**	**0**

Receiving

	Rec	Yds	TD
1947 Cleveland Browns	2	24	0
1948 Cleveland Browns	20	295	1
1949 Cleveland Browns	23	359	0
1950 Cleveland Browns	2	54	1
1951 Cleveland Browns	11	164	0
1952 Cleveland Browns	4	45	1
1953 Cleveland Browns	7	80	0
1954 Cleveland Browns	5	62	0
Total	**74**	**1083**	**3**

Passing

	Comp	Att	Yds	TD	Int
1950 Browns	1	1	3	0	0
Total	**1**	**1**	**3**	**0**	**0**

Punting

	Punt	Yds	Blk
1947 Cleveland Browns	47	2096	0
1948 Cleveland Browns	6	227	0
1949 Cleveland Browns	54	2011	1
1950 Cleveland Browns	66	2849	1
1951 Cleveland Browns	73	3321	0
1952 Cleveland Browns	61	2787	1
1953 Cleveland Browns	63	2760	0
1954 Cleveland Browns	52	2230	0
1955 Cleveland Browns	58	2389	3
1956 Cleveland Browns	12	536	0
Total	**492**	**21206**	**6**

Kick Returns

	Ret	Yds	TD
1948 Cleveland Browns	3	10	0
1950 Cleveland Browns	3	51	0
1951 Cleveland Browns	2	25	0
1952 Cleveland Browns	1	2	0
Total	**9**	**88**	**0**

Interceptions

	Int	Yds	TD
1947 Cleveland Browns	1	29	0
Total	**1**	**29**	**0**

Fumbles

	Fum	Rec	Yds	TD
1951 Cleveland Browns	1	1	38	1
1952 Cleveland Browns	1	2	7	0
1953 Cleveland Browns	1	1	0	0
Total	**3**	**4**	**45**	**1**

GLODEN, Frederick Jean, Jr. (Fred)

Position: HB
Height: 5'10"; Weight: 187
College: Tulane
Born: December 21, 1918, Dubuque, IA
Deceased:

STATISTICS

Games

	GP	GS
1941 Philadelphia Eagles	6	0
1946 Miami Seahawks	7	0
Total	**13**	**0**

Rushing

	Rush	Yds	TD
1941 Philadelphia Eagles	22	55	0
1946 Miami Seahawks	13	24	1
Total	**35**	**79**	**1**

Receiving

	Rec	Yds	TD
1941 Philadelphia Eagles	2	13	0
Total	**2**	**13**	**0**

Kick Returns

	Ret	Yds	TD
1946 Miami Seahawks	1	20	0
Total	**1**	**20**	**0**

GOMPERS, William George (Bill)

Position: HB
Height: 6'1"; Weight: 185
College: Notre Dame
Born: March 20, 1928, Wheeling, WV
Deceased:

STATISTICS

Games

	GP	GS
1948 Buffalo Bills	14	3
Total	**14**	**3**

Rushing

	Rush	Yds	TD
1948 Buffalo Bills	48	219	1
Total	**48**	**219**	**1**

Punt Returns

	Ret	Yds	TD
1948 Buffalo Bills	1	10	0
Total	**1**	**10**	**0**

Kick Returns

	Ret	Yds	TD
1948 Buffalo Bills	4	62	0
Total	**4**	**62**	**0**

Interceptions

	Int	Yds	TD
1948 Buffalo Bills	2	74	0
Total	**2**	**74**	**0**

GRABINSKI, Thaddeus (Ted)

Position: C-LB-G
Height: 6'2"; Weight: 270
College: Duquesne
Born: February 6, 1916, Pittsburgh, PA
Deceased: November 30, 2000, Sarasota, FL

STATISTICS

Games

	GP	GS
1939 Pittsburgh Steelers	10	2
1940 Pittsburgh Steelers	11	9
1946 Buffalo Bisons	1	0
Total	**22**	**11**

GRAHAM, Michael N. (Mike)

Position: B
Height: 6'0"; Weight: 198
College: Cincinnati
Born: April 3, 1923, Warren, OH
Deceased: July 7, 2003, Warren, OH

STATISTICS

Games

	GP	GS
1948 Los Angeles Dons	14	1
Total	**14**	**1**

Rushing

	Rush	Yds	TD
1948 Los Angeles Dons	19	69	1
Total	**19**	**69**	**1**

Kick Returns

	Ret	Yds	TD
1948 Los Angeles Dons	6	145	0
Total	**6**	**145**	**0**

Interceptions

	Int	Yds	TD
1948 Los Angeles Dons	1	20	0
Total	**1**	**20**	**0**

GRAHAM, Otto Everett, Jr.

Position: QB-DB
Height: 6'1"; Weight: 196
College: Northwestern
Born: December 6, 1921, Waukegan, IL
Deceased: December 17, 2003, Sarasota, FL

STATISTICS

Games

	GP	GS
1946 Cleveland Browns	14	9
1947 Cleveland Browns	14	9
1948 Cleveland Browns	14	14
1949 Cleveland Browns	12	11
1950 Cleveland Browns	12	12
1951 Cleveland Browns	12	12
1952 Cleveland Browns	12	12
1953 Cleveland Browns	12	11
1954 Cleveland Browns	12	12
1955 Cleveland Browns	12	12
Total	**126**	**114**

Rushing

	Rush	Yds	TD
1946 Cleveland Browns	30	−125	1
1947 Cleveland Browns	19	72	1
1948 Cleveland Browns	23	146	6
1949 Cleveland Browns	27	107	3
1950 Cleveland Browns	55	145	6
1951 Cleveland Browns	35	29	3
1952 Cleveland Browns	42	130	4
1953 Cleveland Browns	43	143	6
1954 Cleveland Browns	63	114	8
1955 Cleveland Browns	68	121	6
Total	**405**	**882**	**44**

Passing

	Comp	Att	Yds	TD	Int
1946 Cle. Browns	95	174	1834	17	5
1947 Cle. Browns	163	269	2753	25	11
1948 Cle. Browns	173	333	2713	25	15

	Comp	Att	Yds	TD	Int
1949 Cle. Browns	161	285	2785	19	10
1950 Cle. Browns	137	253	1943	14	20
1951 Cle. Browns	147	265	2205	17	16
1952 Cle. Browns	181	364	2816	20	24
1953 Cle. Browns	167	258	2722	11	9
1954 Cle. Browns	142	240	2092	11	17
1955 Cle. Browns	98	185	1721	15	8
Total	1464	2622	23584	174	135

Punt Returns

	Ret	Yds	TD
1946 Cleveland Browns	12	129	0
1947 Cleveland Browns	10	121	0
1948 Cleveland Browns	1	12	0
Total	23	262	0

Interceptions

	Int	Yds	TD
1946 Cleveland Browns	5	102	1
1947 Cleveland Browns	1	0	0
1948 Cleveland Browns	1	0	0
Total	7	102	1

Fumbles

	Fum	Rec	Yds	TD
1950 Cleveland Browns	6	0	0	0
1951 Cleveland Browns	7	2	2	1
1952 Cleveland Browns	4	0	0	0
1953 Cleveland Browns	8	5	0	0
1954 Cleveland Browns	3	2	11	0
1955 Cleveland Browns	7	3	0	0
Total	35	12	13	1

GRAIN, Edwin Elswin III, (Ed)

Position: G
Height: 6'0"; Weight: 230
College: Pennsylvania
Born: February 25, 1922, Baltimore, MD
Deceased: October 6, 1984, Evanston, IL

STATISTICS

Games

	GP	GS
1947 New York Yankees	2	0
1947 Baltimore Colts	10	2
1948 Baltimore Colts	11	1
Total	23	3

GREENE, Nelson R.

Position: T
Height: 6'2"; Weight: 235
College: Tulsa
Born: March 21, 1924, Houston, TX
Deceased: May 3, 1983, Houston, TX

STATISTICS

Games

	GP	GS
1948 New York Yankees	14	10
Total	14	10

GREENWOOD, Donald Adams (Don)

Position: B
Height: 6'0"; Weight: 190
College: Illinois, Missouri
Born: February 18, 1921, Detroit, MI
Deceased: March 21, 1983, Princeville, IL

STATISTICS

Games

	GP	GS
1945 Cleveland Rams	9	6
1946 Cleveland Browns	13	10
1947 Cleveland Browns	11	6
Total	33	22

Rushing

	Rush	Yds	TD
1945 Cleveland Rams	101	376	4
1946 Cleveland Browns	77	274	6
1947 Cleveland Browns	18	94	0
Total	196	744	10

Receiving

	Rec	Yds	TD
1945 Cleveland Rams	3	72	0
1946 Cleveland Browns	4	0	0
1947 Cleveland Browns	5	49	0
Total	12	121	0

Passing

	Comp	Att	Yds	Td	Int
1946 Cle. Browns	1	1	27	0	0
Total	1	1	27	0	0

Kick Returns

	Ret	Yds	TD
1945 Cleveland Rams	5	106	0
1946 Cleveland Browns	5	105	0
Total	10	211	0

Interceptions

	Int	Yds	TD
1946 Cleveland Browns	2	56	0
1947 Cleveland Browns	4	19	0
Total	6	75	0

Fumbles

	Fum	Rec	Yds	TD
1945 Cleveland Rams	6	1	0	0
Total	6	1	0	0

GREGORY, Garland D.

Position: G-LB
Height: 5'11"; Weight: 185
College: Louisiana Tech
Born: March 8, 1919, Columbia, LA
Deceased: April 28, 2011, Ruston, LA

STATISTICS

Games
	GP	GS
1946 San Francisco 49ers	13	6
1947 San Francisco 49ers	14	14
Total	27	20

Punt Returns
	Ret	Yds	TD
1947 S.F. 49ers	1	31	0
Total	1	31	0

Kick Returns
	Ret	Yds	TD
1946 S.F. 49ers	1	0	0
Total	1	0	0

GRGICH, Visco Gerald

Position: G-MG-T-LB
Height: 5'11"; Weight: 217
College: Santa Clara
Born: January 19, 1923, Zlarin, Yugoslavia
Deceased: December 26, 2005, Modesto, CA

STATISTICS

Games
	GP	GS
1946 San Francisco 49ers	12	0
1947 San Francisco 49ers	14	0
1948 San Francisco 49ers	14	14
1949 San Francisco 49ers	12	10
1950 San Francisco 49ers	12	0
1951 San Francisco 49ers	12	0
1952 San Francisco 49ers	2	0
Total	78	24

Kick Returns
	Ret	Yds	TD
1947 S.F. 49ers	1	21	0
Total	1	21	0

Interceptions
	Int	Yds	TD
1950 S.F. 49ers	1	37	0
Total	1	37	0

Fumbles
	Fum	Rec	Yds	TD
1950 S.F. 49ers	0	3	0	0
1951 S.F. 49ers	0	1	0	0
1952 S.F. 49ers	0	1	0	0
Total	0	5	0	0

GRIFFIN, Donald Dean (Don)

Position: HB-DB
Height: 5'11"; Weight: 190
College: Illinois
Born: October 15, 1922, Benton Harbor, MI
Deceased: January 17, 2005, Aurora, IL

STATISTICS

Games
	GP	GS
1946 Chicago Rockets	13	4
Total	13	4

Rushing
	Rush	Yds	TD
1946 Chicago Rockets	28	13	0
Total	28	13	0

Receiving
	Rec	Yds	TD
1946 Chicago Rockets	5	28	0
Total	5	28	0

Passing
	Comp	Att	Yds	TD	Int
1946 Rockets	0	1	0	0	1
Total	0	1	0	0	1

Kick Returns
	Ret	Yds	TD
1946 Chicago Rockets	2	31	0
Total	2	31	0

Interceptions
	Int	Yds	TD
1946 Chicago Rockets	1	19	0
Total	1	19	0

GRIGG, Forrest Porter, Jr. (Chubby)

Position: DT
Height: 6'2"; Weight: 294
College: Tulsa
Born: January 10, 1926, El Dorado, AR
Deceased: October 10, 1983, Ore City, TX

STATISTICS

Games
	GP	GS
1946 Buffalo Bisons	8	0
1947 Chicago Rockets	13	7
1948 Cleveland Browns	14	0
1949 Cleveland Browns	12	0
1950 Cleveland Browns	11	0
1951 Cleveland Browns	11	0
1952 Dallas Texans	10	0
Total	79	7

Fumbles
	Fum	Rec	Yds	TD
1950 Cleveland Browns	0	3	0	0
Total	0	3	0	0

Field Goals
	FGM	FGA
1950 Cleveland Browns	1	2
1952 Dallas Texans	*	3
Total	1	5

Point After Touchdown

	XPM	XPA
1950 Cleveland Browns	9	9
1952 Dallas Texans	9	12
Total	**18**	**21**

GRIMES, William Joseph (Billy)

Position: HB
Height: 6'1"; Weight: 195
College: Oklahoma State
Born: July 27, 1927, County Line, OK
Deceased: March 26, 2005, Oklahoma City, OK

STATISTICS

Games

	GP	GS
1949 Los Angeles Dons	12	7
1950 Green Bay Packers	12	0
1951 Green Bay Packers	12	0
1952 Green Bay Packers	12	0
Total	**48**	**7**

Rushing

	Rush	Yds	TD
1949 Los Angeles Dons	83	429	4
1950 Green Bay Packers	84	480	5
1951 Green Bay Packers	44	123	1
1952 Green Bay Packers	17	59	0
Total	**228**	**1091**	**10**

Receiving

	Rec	Yds	TD
1949 Los Angeles Dons	13	189	2
1950 Green Bay Packers	17	261	1
1951 Green Bay Packers	15	170	1
Total	**45**	**620**	**4**

Passing

	Comp	Att	Yds	TD	Int
1949 L.A. Dons	3	3	105	1	0
Total	**3**	**3**	**105**	**1**	**0**

Punt Returns

	Ret	Yds	TD
1949 Los Angeles Dons	5	67	0
1950 Green Bay Packers	29	555	2
1951 Green Bay Packers	16	100	0
1952 Green Bay Packers	18	179	0
Total	**68**	**901**	**2**

Kick Returns

	Ret	Yds	TD
1949 Los Angeles Dons	16	411	0
1950 Green Bay Packers	26	600	0
1951 Green Bay Packers	23	582	0
1952 Green Bay Packers	18	422	0
Total	**83**	**2015**	**0**

Fumbles

	Fum	Rec	Yds	TD
1950 Green Bay Packers	8	3	0	0
1951 Green Bay Packers	5	0	0	0
1952 Green Bay Packers	5	2	0	0
Total	**18**	**5**	**0**	**0**

GROSSMAN, Rex Daniel

Position: LB-FB
Height: 6'1"; Weight: 215
College: Indiana
Born: February 5, 1924, Huntington, IN
Deceased: June 13, 1980, Bloomington, IN

STATISTICS

Games

	GP	GS
1948 Baltimore Colts	14	1
1949 Baltimore Colts	11	0
1950 Baltimore Colts	8	0
1950 Detroit Lions	4	0
Total	**37**	**1**

Rushing

	Rush	Yds	TD
1948 Baltimore Colts	8	−3	0
Total			

Receiving

	Rec	Yds	TD
1950 Baltimore Colts	1	4	0
Total	**1**	**4**	**0**

Passing

	Comp	Att	Yds	TD	Int
1949 Colts	0	1	0	0	1
Total	**0**	**1**	**0**	**0**	**1**

Punting

	Punt	Yds	Blk
1949 Baltimore Colts	28	1087	0
Total			

Kick Returns

	Ret	Yds	TD
1950 Detroit Lions	1	15	0
Total	**1**	**15**	**0**

Interceptions

	Int	Yds	TD
1948 Baltimore Colts	2	13	0
Total	**2**	**13**	**0**

Field Goals

	FGM	FGA
1948 Baltimore Colts	10	18
1949 Baltimore Colts	6	11
1950 Baltimore Colts	*	3
Total	**16**	**32**

Point After Touchdown

	XPM	XPA
1948 Baltimore Colts	43	43
1949 Baltimore Colts	19	19
1950 Baltimore Colts	16	19
Total	**78**	**81**

GROVES, George Noah

Position: G-LB
Height: 5'1"; Weight: 195
College: Marquette
Born: June 10, 1921, Hammond, IN
Deceased: July 23, 2011, Mexico, MO

STATISTICS

Games

	GP	GS
1947 Buffalo Bills	7	0
1948 Baltimore Colts	2	0
Total	9	0

GROZA, Louis Roy (Lou)

Position: T-C-DT-K
Height: 6'3"; Weight: 240
College: Ohio State
Born: January 25, 1924, Martins Ferry, OH
Deceased: November 29, 2000, Middleburg Heights, OH

STATISTICS

Games

	GP	GS
1946 Cleveland Browns	14	5
1947 Cleveland Browns	12	5
1948 Cleveland Browns	14	14
1949 Cleveland Browns	12	0
1950 Cleveland Browns	10	0
1951 Cleveland Browns	12	0
1952 Cleveland Browns	12	0
1953 Cleveland Browns	12	0
1954 Cleveland Browns	12	0
1955 Cleveland Browns	12	0
1956 Cleveland Browns	12	0
1957 Cleveland Browns	12	0
1958 Cleveland Browns	12	0
1959 Cleveland Browns	12	0
1961 Cleveland Browns	14	0
1962 Cleveland Browns	14	0
1963 Cleveland Browns	14	0
1964 Cleveland Browns	14	0
1965 Cleveland Browns	14	0
1966 Cleveland Browns	14	0
1967 Cleveland Browns	14	0
Total	268	36

Receiving

	Rec	Yds	TD
1950 Cleveland Browns	1	23	1
Total	1	23	1

Passing

	Comp	Att	Yds	TD	Int
1950 Cle. Browns	0	1	0	0	0
1963 Cle. Browns	0	1	0	0	1
1965 Cle. Browns	0	1	0	0	0
1966 Cle. Browns	1	1	−7	0	0
Total	1	4	−7	0	1

Kick Returns

	Ret	Yds	TD
1949 Cleveland Browns	1	2	0
Total	1	2	0

Fumbles

	Fum	Rec	Yds	TD
1950 Cleveland Browns	0	1	−1	0
1951 Cleveland Browns	0	1	16	0
1952 Cleveland Browns	0	1	0	0
1953 Cleveland Browns	0	1	0	0
1958 Cleveland Browns	0	1	0	0
1961 Cleveland Browns	0	1	0	0
1965 Cleveland Browns	0	1	0	0
Total	0	7	15	0

Field Goals

	FGM	FGA
1946 Cleveland Browns	13	29
1947 Cleveland Browns	7	19
1948 Cleveland Browns	8	19
1949 Cleveland Browns	2	9
1950 Cleveland Browns	13	19
1951 Cleveland Browns	10	23
1952 Cleveland Browns	19	33
1953 Cleveland Browns	23	26
1954 Cleveland Browns	16	24
1955 Cleveland Browns	11	22
1956 Cleveland Browns	11	20
1957 Cleveland Browns	15	22
1958 Cleveland Browns	8	19
1959 Cleveland Browns	5	16
1961 Cleveland Browns	16	23
1962 Cleveland Browns	14	31
1963 Cleveland Browns	15	23
1964 Cleveland Browns	22	33
1965 Cleveland Browns	16	25
1966 Cleveland Browns	9	23
1967 Cleveland Browns	11	23
Total	264	481

Point After Touchdown

	XPM	XPA
1946 Cleveland Browns	45	47
1947 Cleveland Browns	39	42
1948 Cleveland Browns	51	52
1949 Cleveland Browns	34	35
1950 Cleveland Browns	29	29
1951 Cleveland Browns	43	43
1952 Cleveland Browns	32	32
1953 Cleveland Browns	39	40
1954 Cleveland Browns	37	38
1955 Cleveland Browns	44	45
1956 Cleveland Browns	18	18
1957 Cleveland Browns	32	32
1958 Cleveland Browns	36	38
1959 Cleveland Browns	33	37
1961 Cleveland Browns	37	38
1962 Cleveland Browns	33	35
1963 Cleveland Browns	40	43
1964 Cleveland Browns	49	49
1965 Cleveland Browns	45	45
1966 Cleveland Browns	51	52
1967 Cleveland Browns	43	43
Total	810	833

GUSTAFSON, Edsel Warren (Ed)

Position: C-LB
Height: 6'3"; Weight: 205
College: Dartmouth, George Washington
Born: April 4, 1922, Moline, IL
Deceased: November 28, 2012, Madison, WI

Statistics

Games

	GP	GS
1947 Brooklyn Dodgers	13	9
1948 Brooklyn Dodgers	14	8
Total	27	17

Rushing

	Rush	Yds	TD
1948 Brooklyn Dodgers	1	7	0
Total	1	7	0

HALL, Forrest J.

Position: B
Height: 5'8"; Weight: 155
College: Duquesne, San Francisco
Born: October 29, 1921, Oil City, PA
Deceased: February 14, 2001, Scottsdale, AZ

Statistics

Games

	GP	GS
1948 San Francisco 49ers	14	5
Total	14	5

Rushing

	Rush	Yds	TD
1948 S.F. 49ers	66	413	2
Total	66	413	2

Receiving

	Rec	Yds	TD
1948 S.F. 49ers	4	87	0
Total	4	87	0

Punt Returns

	Ret	Yds	TD
1948 S.F. 49ers	3	97	0
Total	3	97	0

Kick Returns

	Ret	Yds	TD
1948 S.F. 49ers	13	369	0
Total	13	369	0

HALL, Linus Parker (Parker)

Position: TB-HB
Height: 6'0"; Weight: 198
College: Mississippi
Born: December 10, 1916, Tunica, MS
Deceased: February 8, 2005, Vicksburg, MS

Statistics

Games

	GP	GS
1939 Cleveland Rams	11	11
1940 Cleveland Rams	11	7
1941 Cleveland Rams	10	8
1942 Cleveland Rams	10	8
1946 San Francisco 49ers	11	0
Total	53	34

Rushing

	Rush	Yds	TD
1939 Cleveland Rams	120	458	2
1940 Cleveland Rams	94	365	1
1941 Cleveland Rams	57	232	2
1942 Cleveland Rams	41	–3	1
1946 S.F. 49ers	17	31	0
Total	329	1083	6

Receiving

	Rec	Yds	TD
1939 Cleveland Rams	1	–16	0
1946 S.F. 49ers	2	25	0
Total	3	9	0

Passing

	Comp	Att	Yds	TD	Int
1939 Cle. Rams	106	208	1227	9	13
1940 Cle. Rams	77	183	1108	7	16
1941 Cle. Rams	84	190	863	7	19
1942 Cle. Rams	62	140	815	7	19
1946 S.F. 49ers	2	8	15	0	0
Total	331	729	4028	30	67

Punting

	Punt	Yds	Blk
1939 Cleveland Rams	58	2369	0
1940 Cleveland Rams	57	2489	0
1941 Cleveland Rams	49	1967	0
1942 Cleveland Rams	36	1397	0
Total	200	8222	0

Punt Returns

	Ret	Yds	TD
1941 Cleveland Rams	13	125	0
1942 Cleveland Rams	12	148	0
Total	25	273	0

Kick Returns

	Ret	Yds	TD
1941 Cleveland Rams	7	131	0
1942 Cleveland Rams	10	155	0
1946 S.F. 49ers	1	22	0
Total	18	308	0

Interceptions

	Int	Yds	TD
1940 Cleveland Rams	2	0	0
1941 Cleveland Rams	2	0	0
1942 Cleveland Rams	3	60	0
Total	7	60	0

HANDLEY, Richard H. (Dick)

Position: C-LB
Height: 6'1"; Weight: 215
College: Fresno State
Born: May 22, 1922, Tulare, CA
Deceased: February 8, 2012, Fresno, CA

STATISTICS

Games		
	GP	GS
1947 Baltimore Colts	14	3
Total	14	3

HARE, Raymond Lewis (Ray)

Position: B
Height: 6'1"; Weight: 204
College: Gonzaga
Born: November 21, 1917, North Battleford, Canada
Deceased: June 2, 1975, Chewelah, WA

STATISTICS

Games		
	GP	GS
1940 Washington Redskins	5	1
1941 Washington Redskins	11	0
1942 Washington Redskins	11	7
1943 Washington Redskins	10	10
1944 Brooklyn Dodgers	10	9
1946 New York Yankees	4	1
Total	51	28

Rushing			
	Rush	Yds	TD
1940 Wash. Redskins	1	2	0
1941 Wash. Redskins	12	51	1
1942 Wash. Redskins	27	197	1
1943 Wash. Redskins	21	96	0
1944 Brooklyn Dodgers	72	196	0
Total	133	542	2

Receiving			
	Rec	Yds	TD
1941 Wash. Redskins	12	87	0
1942 Wash. Redskins	5	57	0
1943 Wash. Redskins	2	9	0
1944 Brooklyn Dodgers	9	206	1
Total	28	359	1

Passing					
	Comp	Att	Yds	TD	Int
1944 Dodgers	0	1	0	0	0
Total	0	1	0	0	0

Punt Returns			
	Ret	Yds	TD
1942 Wash. Redskins	1	0	0
1943 Wash. Redskins	1	5	0
1944 Brooklyn Dodgers	2	5	0
Total	4	10	0

Kick Returns			
	Ret	Yds	TD
1941 Wash. Redskins	3	57	0
1942 Wash. Redskins	1	95	1
1943 Wash. Redskins	2	36	0
1944 Brooklyn Dodgers	4	120	0
Total	10	308	1

Interceptions			
	Int	Yds	TD
1942 Wash. Redskins	1	0	0
1943 Wash. Redskins	3	13	0
1944 Brooklyn Dodgers	1	12	0
Total	5	25	0

HARRINGTON, John Patrick

Position: E-DE
Height: 6'3"; Weight: 198
College: Marquette
Born: April 15, 1921, Reedsburg, WI
Deceased: January 8, 1992, Green Bay, WI

STATISTICS

Games		
	GP	GS
1946 Cleveland Browns	12	2
1947 Chicago Rockets	13	3
Total	25	5

Receiving			
	Rec	Yds	TD
1946 Cleveland Browns	8	136	0
1947 Chicago Rockets*	17	233	3
Total	25	369	3

Kick Returns			
	Ret	Yds	TD
1946 Cleveland Browns	2	16	0
Total	2	16	0

*John Harrington had an extra two receiving yards and Pat Lahey was missing two receiving yards for the season. Since these numbers could not be verified, the official statistics were used.

HARRIS, Elmore Thomas

Position: HB
Height: 5'11"; Weight: 175
College: Morgan State
Born: June 3, 1922, Huntsville, AL
Deceased: December 8, 1968, New York, NY

STATISTICS

Games		
	GP	GS
1947 Brooklyn Dodgers	10	2
Total	10	2

Rushing			
	Rush	Yds	TD
1947 Brooklyn Dodgers	3	–2	0
Total	3	-2	0

	Kick Returns		
	Ret	Yds	TD
1947 Brooklyn Dodgers	14	329	0
Total	14	329	0

HAYNES, Joseph H. (Joe)

Position: C-G
Height: 6'3"; Weight: 225
College: Oklahoma, Tulsa
Born: March 26, 1921, Barnsdall, OK
Deceased: March 9, 1994, Tupelo, MS

STATISTICS

	Games	
	GP	GS
1947 Buffalo Bills	9	0
Total	9	0

HAZELWOOD, Theodore Eugene (Ted)

Position: T-DT
Height: 6'1"; Weight: 235
College: North Carolina, Purdue
Born: April 24, 1924, Silverwood, IN
Deceased: February 27, 2005, Bellingham, WA

STATISTICS

	Games	
	GP	GS
1949 Chicago Hornets	9	2
1953 Washington Redskins	6	0
Total	15	2

HEAP, Walter Richmond, Jr. (Walt)

Position: B
Height: 6'1"; Weight: 210
College: Texas
Born: September 18, 1921, Taylor, TX
Deceased: May 20, 1989, Dallas, TX

STATISTICS

	Games	
	GP	GS
1947 Los Angeles Dons	13	2
1948 Los Angeles Dons	14	7
Total	27	9

	Rushing		
	Rush	Yds	TD
1947 Los Angeles Dons	5	3	0
1948 Los Angeles Dons	3	12	0
Total	8	15	0

	Receiving		
	Rec	Yds	TD
1947 Los Angeles Dons	2	0	1
1948 Los Angeles Dons	2	9	0
Total	4	9	1

	Interceptions		
	Int	Yds	TD
1947 Los Angeles Dons	5	107	1
1948 Los Angeles Dons	5	94	1
Total	10	201	2

HECHT, Alfred George (George)

Position: G
Height: 6'0"; Weight: 235
College: Alabama
Born: September 17, 1920, Chicago Heights, IL
Deceased: October 24, 1994, Collinsville, AL

STATISTICS

	Games	
	GP	GS
1947 Chicago Rockets	10	2
Total	10	2

HECK, Robert Elgin (Bob)

Position: DE-E
Height: 6'4"; Weight: 210
College: Purdue
Born: June 17, 1925, South Bend, IN
Deceased: April 17, 2013, Naples, FL

STATISTICS

	Games	
	GP	GS
1949 Chicago Hornets	4	0
Total	4	0

HEIN, Robert William (Bob)

Position: E
Height: 6'3"; Weight: 220
College: Kent State
Born: February 6, 1921, Cleveland, OH
Deceased: March 17, 1999, Louisville, KY

STATISTICS

	Games	
	GP	GS
1947 Brooklyn Dodgers	5	0
Total	5	0

	Receiving		
	Rec	Yds	TD
1947 Brooklyn Dodgers	1	7	0
Total	1	7	0

HEKKERS, George James

Position: T
Height: 6'4"; Weight: 241
College: Wisconsin
Born: February 18, 1923, Milwaukee, WI
Deceased: February 6, 2008, Waukesha, WI

HENKE, Edgar Edwin (Ed)

Position: DE-LB-G
Height: 6'3"; Weight: 227
College: USC
Born: December 13, 1927, Ontario, Canada
Deceased:

Statistics

Games

	GP	GS
1946 Miami Seahawks	8	4
1947 Baltimore Colts	3	0
1947 Detroit Lions	6	0
1948 Detroit Lions	12	4
1949 Detroit Lions	12	6
Total	**41**	**14**

HENKE, Edgar Edwin (Ed)

Position: DE-LB-G
Height: 6'3"; Weight: 227
College: USC
Born: December 13, 1927, Ontario, Canada
Deceased:

Statistics

Games

	GP	GS
1949 Los Angeles Dons	11	0
1951 San Francisco 49ers	12	0
1952 San Francisco 49ers	12	0
1956 San Francisco 49ers	12	0
1957 San Francisco 49ers	12	0
1958 San Francisco 49ers	12	0
1959 San Francisco 49ers	12	0
1960 San Francisco 49ers	8	6
1961 St. Louis Cardinals	14	0
1962 St. Louis Cardinals	8	0
1963 St. Louis Cardinals	10	0
Total	**123**	**6**

Receiving

	Rec	Yds	TD
1949 Los Angeles Dons	1	15	0
1952 S.F. 49ers	1	13	0
Total	**2**	**28**	**0**

Fumbles

	Fum	Rec	Yds	TD
1951 S.F. 49ers	0	1	0	0
1952 S.F. 49ers	0	3	0	0
1957 S.F. 49ers	0	2	0	0
1958 S.F. 49ers	0	2	0	0
1959 S.F. 49ers	0	4	0	0
Total	**0**	**12**	**0**	**0**

HERRING, Harold Moreland (Hal)

Position: LB-C
Height: 6'1"; Weight: 211
College: Auburn
Born: February 24, 1924, Lanett, AL
Deceased: February 9, 2014, Cumming, GA

Statistics

Games

	GP	GS
1949 Buffalo Bills	12	0
1950 Cleveland Browns	12	0
1951 Cleveland Browns	10	0
1952 Cleveland Browns	12	0
Total	**46**	**0**

Interceptions

	Int	Yds	TD
1949 Buffalo Bills	1	1	0
1950 Cleveland Browns	2	12	0
1951 Cleveland Browns	1	28	0
Total	**4**	**41**	**0**

Fumbles

	Fum	Rec	Yds	TD
1950 Cleveland Browns	0	2	0	0
1951 Cleveland Browns	0	3	0	0
1952 Cleveland Browns	0	1	0	0
Total	**0**	**6**	**0**	**0**

HEYWOOD, Ralph Alvin

Position: E-DE
Height: 6'2"; Weight: 203
College: USC
Born: September 11, 1921, Los Angeles, CA
Deceased: April 10, 2007, Bandera, TX

Statistics

Games

	GP	GS
1946 Chicago Rockets	14	8
1947 Detroit Lions	12	1
1948 Detroit Lions	2	0
1948 Boston Yanks	8	6
1949 New York Yankees	12	2
Total	**48**	**17**

Rushing

	Rush	Yds	TD
1948 Boston Yanks	1	11	0
1949 New York Yankees	3	–6	0
Total	**4**	**5**	**0**

Receiving

	Rec	Yds	TD
1946 Chicago Rockets	20	287	4
1947 Detroit Lions	13	198	2
1948 Detroit Lions	3	31	0
1948 Boston Yanks	11	177	1
1949 New York Yankees	37	499	3
Total	**84**	**1192**	**10**

Punting

	Punt	Yds	Blk
1946 Chicago Rockets	2	57	0
1948 Detroit Lions	11	372	0
1948 Boston Yanks	35	1396	0
1949 New York Yankees	20	697	0
Total	**68**	**2532**	**0**

Kick Returns

	Ret	Yds	TD
1948 Boston Yanks	1	8	0
Total	**1**	**8**	**0**

Fumbles

	Fum	Rec	Yds	TD
1947 Detroit Lions	2	1	0	0
1948 Boston Yanks	2	3	75	2
1949 New York Yankees	1	2	0	1
Total	5	6	75	3

HIGGINS, Luke Martin

Position: G
Height: 6'0"; Weight: 210
College: Notre Dame
Born: May 3, 1921, Edgewater, NJ
Deceased: October 11, 1991

Statistics

Games

	GP	GS
1947 Baltimore Colts	11	0
Total	11	0

HILLENBRAND, William Frank (Billy)

Position: HB-BB
Height: 6'0"; Weight: 188
College: Indiana
Born: March 29, 1922, Armstrong, IN
Deceased: July 17, 1994, Indianapolis, IN

Statistics

Games

	GP	GS
1946 Chicago Rockets	14	9
1947 Baltimore Colts	13	13
1948 Baltimore Colts	14	13
Total	41	35

Rushing

	Rush	Yds	TD
1946 Chicago Rockets	50	175	2
1947 Baltimore Colts	66	204	2
1948 Baltimore Colts	100	510	7
Total	216	889	11

Receiving

	Rec	Yds	TD
1946 Chicago Rockets	21	315	4
1947 Baltimore Colts	39	702	7
1948 Baltimore Colts	50	970	6
Total	110	1987	17

Passing

	Comp	Att	Yds	TD	Int
1946 Chicago Rockets	0	3	0	0	2
1947 Bal. Colts	0	1	0	0	1
Total	0	4	0	0	3

Punt Returns

	Ret	Yds	TD
1946 Chicago Rockets	13	180	1
1947 Baltimore Colts	13	201	0
1948 Baltimore Colts	18	231	0
Total	44	612	1

Kick Returns

	Ret	Yds	TD
1946 Chicago Rockets	8	220	1
1947 Baltimore Colts	18	466	1
1948 Baltimore Colts	16	356	0
Total	42	1042	2

Interceptions

	Int	Yds	TD
1946 Chicago Rockets	3	37	0
1947 Baltimore Colts	1	48	0
Total	4	85	0

HIRSCH, Edward Norman (Buckets)

Position: QB-FB
Height: 5'10"; Weight: 207
College: Northwestern
Born: March 26, 1921, Clarence, NY
Deceased: January 28, 2000, Irving, NY

Statistics

Games

	GP	GS
1947 Buffalo Bills	14	2
1948 Buffalo Bills	13	0
1949 Buffalo Bills	7	0
Total	34	2

Rushing

	Rush	Yds	TD
1947 Buffalo Bills	4	7	0
Total	4	7	0

Interceptions

	Int	Yds	TD
1947 Buffalo Bills	3	73	1
Total	3	73	1

HIRSCH, Elroy Leon (Crazy Legs)

Position: E-HB-DE
Height: 6'2"; Weight: 190
College: Michigan, Wisconsin
Born: June 17, 1923, Wausau, WI
Deceased: January 28, 2004, Madison, WI

Statistics

Games

	GP	GS
1946 Chicago Rockets	14	12
1947 Chicago Rockets	5	4
1948 Chicago Rockets	5	3
1949 Los Angeles Rams	12	3
1950 Los Angeles Rams	12	0
1951 Los Angeles Rams	12	0
1952 Los Angeles Rams	10	0
1953 Los Angeles Rams	12	0

	GP	GS
1954 Los Angeles Rams	12	0
1955 Los Angeles Rams	9	0
1956 Los Angeles Rams	12	0
1957 Los Angeles Rams	12	0
Total	127	22

Rushing

	Rush	Yds	TD
1946 Chicago Rockets	87	226	1
1947 Chicago Rockets	23	51	1
1948 Chicago Rockets	23	93	0
1949 Los Angeles Rams	68	287	1
1950 Los Angeles Rams	2	19	0
1951 Los Angeles Rams	1	3	0
1953 Los Angeles Rams	1	−6	0
1954 Los Angeles Rams	1	6	0
1957 Los Angeles Rams	1	8	0
Total	207	687	3

Receiving

	Rec	Yds	TD
1946 Chicago Rockets	27	347	3
1947 Chicago Rockets	10	282	3
1948 Chicago Rockets	7	101	1
1949 Los Angeles Rams	22	326	4
1950 Los Angeles Rams	42	687	7
1951 Los Angeles Rams	66	1495	17
1952 Los Angeles Rams	25	590	4
1953 Los Angeles Rams	61	941	4
1954 Los Angeles Rams	35	720	3
1955 Los Angeles Rams	25	460	2
1956 Los Angeles Rams	35	603	6
1957 Los Angeles Rams	32	477	6
Total	387	7029	60

Passing

	Comp	Att	Yds	TD	Int
1946 Chicago Rockets	12	20	156	1	2
1947 Chicago Rockets	0	1	0	0	0
1950 L.A. Rams	0	1	0	0	0
Total	12	22	156	1	2

Punt Returns

	Ret	Yds	TD
1946 Chicago Rockets	17	235	1
1947 Chicago Rockets	2	24	0
1948 Chicago Rockets	2	27	0
Total	21	286	1

Kick Returns

	Ret	Yds	TD
1946 Chicago Rockets	14	384	1
1947 Chicago Rockets	6	172	0
1948 Chicago Rockets	1	10	0
Total	21	566	1

Interceptions

	Int	Yds	TD
1946 Chicago Rockets	6	97	0
1948 Chicago Rockets	2	59	0
1949 Los Angeles Rams	2	55	0
1950 Los Angeles Rams	4	28	0
1954 Los Angeles Rams	1	12	0
Total	15	251	0

Fumbles

	Fum	Rec	Yds	TD
1949 Los Angeles Rams	4	0	0	0
1951 Los Angeles Rams	0	1	3	0
1953 Los Angeles Rams	2	1	0	0
1954 Los Angeles Rams	1	0	0	0
Total	7	2	3	0

Point After Touchdown

	XPM	XPA
1946 Chicago Rockets	*	1
1950 Los Angeles Rams	5	5
1951 Los Angeles Rams	*	1
1952 Los Angeles Rams	4	5
Total	9	11

HOBBS, Homer Brown

Position: G
Height: 5'11"; Weight: 210
College: Georgia
Born: February 13, 1923, Lexington, SC
Deceased: January 5, 1997, Austell, GA

STATISTICS

Games

	GP	GS
1949 San Francisco 49ers	12	2
1950 San Francisco 49ers	10	0
Total	22	2

HOERNSCHEMEYER, Robert James (Bob) (Hunchy)

Position: B
Height: 5'11"; Weight: 194
College: Indiana, Navy
Born: September 24, 1925, Cincinnati, OH
Deceased: June 17, 1980, Detroit, MI

STATISTICS

Games

	GP	GS
1946 Chicago Rockets	14	10
1947 Chicago Rockets	2	2
1947 Brooklyn Dodgers	12	5
1948 Brooklyn Dodgers	14	6
1949 Chicago Hornets	12	12
1950 Detroit Lions	10	0
1951 Detroit Lions	11	0
1952 Detroit Lions	10	0
1953 Detroit Lions	12	0
1954 Detroit Lions	11	0
1955 Detroit Lions	5	0
Total	113	35

Rushing

	Rush	Yds	TD
1946 Chicago Rockets	111	375	0
1947 Chicago Rockets	5	2	0
1947 Brooklyn Dodgers	147	702	5

	Rush	Yds	TD
1948 Brooklyn Dodgers	110	574	3
1949 Chicago Hornets	133	456	2
1950 Detroit Lions	84	471	1
1951 Detroit Lions	132	678	2
1952 Detroit Lions	106	457	4
1953 Detroit Lions	101	482	7
1954 Detroit Lions	94	242	2
1955 Detroit Lions	36	109	1
Total	1059	4548	27

Receiving

	Rec	Yds	TD
1946 Chicago Rockets	1	11	0
1947 Chicago Rockets	1	4	1
1948 Brooklyn Dodgers	11	173	3
1950 Detroit Lions	8	78	1
1951 Detroit Lions	23	263	3
1952 Detroit Lions	17	139	0
1953 Detroit Lions	23	282	2
1954 Detroit Lions	20	153	1
1955 Detroit Lions	5	36	0
Total	109	1139	11

Passing

	Comp	Att	Yds	TD	Int
1946 Chicago Rockets	95	193	1266	14	14
1947 Chicago Rockets	9	22	143	1	0
1947 Dodgers	64	151	783	3	11
1948 Dodgers	71	155	854	8	15
1949 Chicago Hornets	69	167	1063	6	11
1950 Detroit Lions	1	4	19	1	1
1951 Detroit Lions	2	4	46	2	0
1952 Detroit Lions	2	4	14	2	1
1953 Detroit Lions	2	5	16	1	1
1954 Detroit Lions	3	7	81	3	1
1955 Detroit Lions	1	2	17	1	1
Total	319	714	4302	42	56

Punting

	Punt	Yds	Blk
1946 Chicago Rockets	11	484	0
1947 Brooklyn Dodgers	2	56	1
1948 Brooklyn Dodgers	1	40	0
1949 Chicago Hornets	4	195	0
1950 Detroit Lions	4	147	0
Total	22	922	1

Punt Returns

	Ret	Yds	TD
1946 Chicago Rockets	6	91	0
1947 Brooklyn Dodgers	1	19	0
1948 Brooklyn Dodgers	1	3	0
1949 Chicago Hornets	1	4	0
1951 Detroit Lions	2	16	0
Total	11	133	0

Kick Returns

	Ret	Yds	TD
1946 Chicago Rockets	9	275	0
1947 Chicago Rockets	1	11	0
1948 Brooklyn Dodgers	6	138	0
1949 Chicago Hornets	14	373	0
1951 Detroit Lions	3	78	0
1952 Detroit Lions	1	23	0
1953 Detroit Lions	1	10	0
1954 Detroit Lions	4	73	0
Total	39	981	0

Interceptions

	Int	Yds	TD
1946 Chicago Rockets	1	10	0
1947 Brooklyn Dodgers	1	8	0
Total	2	18	0

Fumbles

	Fum	Rec	Yds	TD
1950 Detroit Lions	1	0	0	0
1951 Detroit Lions	3	2	0	0
1952 Detroit Lions	3	1	0	0
1953 Detroit Lions	3	1	0	0
1954 Detroit Lions	3	0	0	0
1955 Detroit Lions	1	0	0	0
Total	14	4	0	0

HOFFMAN, Wayne Robert (Bob)

Position: B
Height: 6'1"; Weight: 208
College: USC
Born: December 13, 1917, Star City, WV
Deceased: April 13, 2005, Bakersfield, CA

STATISTICS

Games

	GP	GS
1940 Washington Redskins	8	3
1941 Washington Redskins	3	2
1946 Los Angeles Rams	10	2
1947 Los Angeles Rams	10	4
1948 Los Angeles Rams	11	4
1949 Los Angeles Dons	12	5
Total	54	20

Rushing

	Rush	Yds	TD
1940 Wash. Redskins	3	7	0
1941 Wash. Redskins	1	2	0
1946 L.A. Rams	43	162	3
1947 L.A. Rams	42	159	3
1948 L.A. Rams	22	68	4
Total	111	398	10

Receiving

	Rec	Yds	TD
1947 L.A. Rams	2	22	0
1948 L.A. Rams	3	28	1
1949 L.A. Dons	2	21	0
Total	7	71	1

Kick Returns

	Ret	Yds	TD
1947 L.A. Rams	1	12	0
1948 L.A. Rams	2	19	0
1949 L.A. Dons	1	14	0
Total	4	45	0

Interceptions

	Int	Yds	TD
1940 Wash. Redskins	1	6	0
1947 L.A. Rams	1	14	0
1949 L.A. Dons	1	7	0
Total	**3**	**27**	**0**

Fumbles

	Fum	Rec	Yds	TD
1947 L.A. Rams	1	1	0	0
1948 L.A. Rams	1	0	0	0
Total	**2**	**1**	**0**	**0**

HOLDER, Lewis C. (Lew)

Position: E
Height: 6'0"; Weight: 191
College: Texas
Born: October 10, 1923, Dallas, TX
Deceased:

STATISTICS

Games

	GP	GS
1949 Los Angeles Dons	12	1
Total	**12**	**1**

Rushing

	Rush	Yds	TD
1949 Los Angeles Dons	1	−1	0
Total	**1**	**−1**	**0**

Receiving

	Rec	Yds	TD
1949 Los Angeles Dons	5	71	0
Total	**5**	**71**	**0**

HOLLEY, Kenneth Joseph (Ken)

Position: QB
Height: 5'10"; Weight: 185
College: Holy Cross
Born: October 9, 1919, Hartford, CT
Deceased: March 1, 1986, Livingston, NJ

STATISTICS

Games

	GP	GS
1946 Miami Seahawks	5	0
Total	**5**	**0**

Rushing

	Rush	Yds	TD
1946 Miami Seahawks	2	−22	0
Total	**2**	**−22**	**0**

Passing

	Comp	Att	Yds	TD	Int
1946 Miami Seahawks	3	11	36	0	4
Total	**3**	**11**	**36**	**0**	**4**

HOPP, Harry (Hippety)

Position: B
Height: 6'0"; Weight: 209
College: Nebraska
Born: December 13, 1918, Hastings, NE
Deceased: December 22, 1964, Hastings, NE

STATISTICS

Games

	GP	GS
1941 Detroit Lions	10	6
1942 Detroit Lions	10	5
1943 Detroit Lions	10	9
1946 Miami Seahawks	3	2
1946 Buffalo Bisons	9	2
1947 Los Angeles Dons	9	0
Total	**51**	**24**

Rushing

	Rush	Yds	TD
1941 Detroit Lions	69	202	1
1942 Detroit Lions	66	230	0
1943 Detroit Lions	56	99	3
1946 Miami Seahawks	16	89	2
1946 Buffalo Bisons	45	129	1
1947 Los Angeles Dons	10	52	0
Total	**262**	**801**	**7**

Receiving

	Rec	Yds	TD
1941 Detroit Lions	2	7	0
1943 Detroit Lions	17	229	3
1946 Buffalo Bisons	2	−1	0
1947 Los Angeles Dons	3	59	0
Total	**24**	**294**	**3**

Passing

	Comp	Att	Yds	TD	Int
1941 Detroit Lions	0	3	0	0	1
1942 Detroit Lions	20	68	258	0	13
1943 Detroit	5	8	60	0	0
1946 Buffalo	11	22	190	0	0
Total	**36**	**101**	**508**	**0**	**14**

Punting

	Punt	Yds	Blk
1941 Detroit Lions	2	84	0
1942 Detroit Lions	27	52	0
1943 Detroit Lions	42	1643	0
1946 Buf. Bisons	15	461	2
Total	**86**	**3286**	**2**

Punt Returns

	Ret	Yds	TD
1942 Detroit Lions	9	86	0
1943 Detroit Lions	1	−7	0
Total	**10**	**79**	**0**

Kick Returns

	Ret	Yds	TD
1942 Detroit Lions	5	108	0
1943 Detroit Lions	3	57	0
1946 Miami Seahawks	3	74	0

	Ret	Yds	TD
1946 Buffalo Bisons	3	39	0
1947 Los Angeles Dons	1	13	0
Total	15	291	0

Interceptions			
	Int	Yds	TD
1941 Detroit Lions	1	3	0
1942 Detroit Lions	1	0	0
1943 Detroit Lions	2	40	1
1947 Los Angeles Dons	1	16	0
Total	5	59	1

HORNE, Richard Courtland (Dick)

Position: E
Height: 6'2"; Weight: 214
College: Oregon
Born: September 4, 1918, Denver, CO
Deceased: November 1964, Ventura, CA

STATISTICS

Games		
	GP	GS
1941 New York Giants	2	0
1946 Miami Seahawks	10	3
1947 San Francisco 49ers	10	2
Total	22	5

Receiving			
	Rec	Yds	TD
1946 Miami Seahawks	5	48	0
1947 S.F. 49ers	3	69	0
Total	8	117	0

HORVATH, Leslie (Les)

Position: HB
Height: 5'10"; Weight: 173
College: Ohio State
Born: October 12, 1921, South Bend, IN
Deceased: November 14, 1995, Glendale, CA

STATISTICS

Games		
	GP	GS
1947 Los Angeles Rams	10	1
1948 Los Angeles Rams	12	2
1949 Cleveland Browns	12	0
Total	34	3

Rushing			
	Rush	Yds	TD
1947 Los Angeles Rams	18	68	0
1948 Los Angeles Rams	30	118	0
1949 Cleveland Browns	10	35	1
Total	58	221	1

Receiving			
	Rec	Yds	TD
1947 Los Angeles Rams	3	29	0
1948 Los Angeles Rams	4	42	0
1949 Cleveland Browns	2	71	1
Total	9	142	1

Punt Returns			
	Ret	Yds	TD
1947 Los Angeles Rams	4	29	0
1948 Los Angeles Rams	13	203	0
1949 Cleveland Browns	3	19	0
Total	20	251	0

Kick Returns			
	Ret	Yds	TD
1947 Los Angeles Rams	3	58	0
1948 Los Angeles Rams	2	31	0
Total	5	89	0

Interceptions			
	Int	Yds	TD
1948 Los Angeles Rams	2	14	0
1949 Cleveland Browns	2	4	0
Total	4	18	0

Fumbles				
	Fum	Rec	Yds	TD
1947 Los Angeles Rams	3	2	0	0
1948 Los Angeles Rams	2	3	4	0
Total	5	5	4	0

HOUSTON, Lindell Lee (Lin)

Position: G
Height: 6'0"; Weight: 213
College: Ohio State
Born: January 11, 1921, Carbondale, IL
Deceased: September 8, 1995, Canton, OH

STATISTICS

Games		
	GP	GS
1946 Cleveland Browns	12	5
1947 Cleveland Browns	14	1
1948 Cleveland Browns	13	2
1949 Cleveland Browns	12	11
1950 Cleveland Browns	12	0
1951 Cleveland Browns	11	0
1952 Cleveland Browns	12	0
1953 Cleveland Browns	12	0
Total	98	19

Fumbles				
	Fum	Rec	Yds	TD
1952 Cleveland Browns	0	1	0	0
Total	0	1	0	0

HOWARD, Sherman John

Position: HB-DB
Height: 5'11"; Weight: 193
College: Iowa, Nevada-Reno
Born: November 28, 1924, New Orleans, LA
Deceased:

HOWELL, John Clarence Maurice (Clarence)

Position: E
Height: 6'1"; Weight: 188
College: Texas A&M
Born: April 7, 1927
Deceased: October 6, 1981, Houston, TX

STATISTICS

Games

	GP	GS
1949 New York Yankees	12	6
1950 New York Yanks	12	0
1951 New York Yanks	12	0
1952 Cleveland Browns	5	0
1953 Cleveland Browns	12	0
Total	**53**	**6**

Rushing

	Rush	Yds	TD
1949 New York Yankees	117	459	3
1950 New York Yanks	71	362	3
1951 New York Yanks	94	343	4
1952 Cleveland Browns	34	95	0
1953 Cleveland Browns	7	42	0
Total	**323**	**1301**	**10**

Receiving

	Rec	Yds	TD
1949 New York Yankees	1	24	0
1950 New York Yanks	12	278	5
1951 New York Yanks	21	447	3
1952 Cleveland Browns	11	219	3
Total	**45**	**968**	**11**

Punt Returns

	Ret	Yds	TD
1950 New York Yanks	1	12	0
Total	**1**	**12**	**0**

Kick Returns

	Ret	Yds	TD
1949 New York Yankees	4	95	0
1950 New York Yanks	8	240	1
1952 Cleveland Browns	1	22	0
1953 Cleveland Browns	1	6	0
Total	**14**	**363**	**1**

Interceptions

	Int	Yds	TD
1949 New York Yankees	1	26	0
1953 Cleveland Browns	1	3	0
Total	**2**	**29**	**0**

Fumbles

	Fum	Rec	Yds	TD
1950 New York Yanks	3	4	0	0
1951 New York Yanks	4	2	0	0
Total	**7**	**6**	**0**	**0**

STATISTICS

Games

	GP	GS
1948 San Francisco 49ers	12	0
Total	**12**	**0**

Receiving

	Rec	Yds	TD
1948 S.F. 49ers	1	9	0
Total	**1**	**9**	**0**

Interceptions

	Int	Yds	TD
1948 S.F. 49ers	1	5	0
Total	**1**	**5**	**0**

HRABETIN, Frank George

Position: T
Height: 6'4"; Weight: 233
College: Loyola Marymount
Born: December 1, 1915, Cedar Rapids, IA
Deceased: March 27, 2004, Tucson, AZ

STATISTICS

Games

	GP	GS
1942 Philadelphia Eagles	7	1
1946 Miami Seahawks	2	0
1946 Brooklyn Dodgers	8	2
Total	**17**	**3**

Receiving

	Rec	Yds	TD
1946 Brooklyn Dodgers	1	17	0
Total	**1**	**17**	**0**

Kick Returns

	Ret	Yds	TD
1942 Philadelphia Eagles	1	7	0
Total	**1**	**7**	**0**

HUMBLE, Weldon Gaston

Position: G
Height: 6'1"; Weight: 221
College: La-Lafayette, Rice
Born: April 24, 1921, Nixon, TX
Deceased: April 14, 1998, Houston, TX

STATISTICS

Games

	GP	GS
1947 Cleveland Browns	12	9
1948 Cleveland Browns	13	0
1949 Cleveland Browns	10	2
1950 Cleveland Browns	12	0
1952 Dallas Texans	11	9
Total	**58**	**20**

Rushing

	Rush	Yds	TD
1947 Cleveland Browns	1	0	0
1950 Cleveland Browns	1	−10	0
Total	2	−10	0

Kick Returns

	Ret	Yds	TD
1952 Dallas Texans	1	17	0
Total	1	17	0

Interceptions

	Int	Yds	TD
1947 Cleveland Browns	2	31	0
1948 Cleveland Browns	1	11	0
1949 Cleveland Browns	2	55	0
Total	5	97	0

Fumbles

	Fum	Rec	Yds	TD
1950 Cleveland Browns	1	2	0	0
Total	1	2	0	0

HUNEKE, Charles Franklin (Charlie)

Position: T
Height: 6'3"; Weight: 225
College: Benedictine, St. Mary's, Wyoming
Born: January 1, 1921, Lincoln, IL
Deceased: September 5, 1990, Chesterfield, MO

STATISTICS

Games

	GP	GS
1946 Chicago Rockets	14	11
1947 Chicago Rockets	1	0
1947 Brooklyn Dodgers	12	0
1948 Brooklyn Dodgers	2	0
Total	29	11

IVERSEN, Christopher Arnold (Duke)

Position: B
Height: 6'2"; Weight: 208
College: Oregon
Born: February 26, 1920, Petaluma, CA
Deceased: May 20, 2011, Petaluma, CA

STATISTICS

Games

	GP	GS
1947 New York Giants	8	5
1948 New York Yankees	10	1
1949 New York Yankees	12	0
1950 New York Yanks	7	0
1951 New York Yanks	9	0
Total	46	6

Rushing

	Rush	Yds	TD
1949 New York Yankees	6	50	0
Total			

Receiving

	Rec	Yds	TD
1947 New York Giants	1	11	0
1948 New York Yankees	4	30	0
Total	5	41	0

Kick Returns

	Ret	Yds	TD
1947 New York Giants	1	16	0
1949 New York Yankees	2	18	0
1951 New York Yanks	1	14	0
Total	4	48	0

Interceptions

	Int	Yds	TD
1948 New York Yankees	1	1	0
1949 New York Yankees	1	8	0
1950 New York Yanks	3	26	1
Total	5	35	1

Fumbles

	Fum	Rec	Yds	TD
1947 New York Giants	0	3	16	0
Total	0	3	16	0

JAGADE, Harry Charles (Chick)

Position: FB
Height: 6'0"; Weight: 213
College: Indiana
Born: December 9, 1926, Chicago, IL
Deceased: November 24, 1968, Washington Island, WA

STATISTICS

Games

	GP	GS
1949 Baltimore Colts	10	3
1951 Cleveland Browns	11	0
1952 Cleveland Browns	12	0
1953 Cleveland Browns	12	0
1954 Cleveland Browns	11	0
1955 Chicago Bears	12	0
Total	68	3

Rushing

	Rush	Yds	TD
1949 Baltimore Colts	33	174	2
1951 Cleveland Browns	7	30	0
1952 Cleveland Browns	57	373	2
1953 Cleveland Browns	86	344	4
1954 Cleveland Browns	157	498	3
1955 Chicago Bears	72	309	2
Total	412	1728	13

Receiving

	Rec	Yds	TD
1949 Baltimore Colts	8	44	0
1952 Cleveland Browns	9	203	1
1953 Cleveland Browns	20	193	0
1954 Cleveland Browns	24	172	0
1955 Chicago Bears	7	16	0
Total	68	628	1

Kick Returns

	Ret	Yds	TD
1949 Baltimore Colts	6	75	0
1951 Cleveland Browns	2	36	0
1952 Cleveland Browns	3	58	0
1954 Cleveland Browns	11	195	0
1955 Chicago Bears	1	23	0
Total	**23**	**387**	**0**

Fumbles

	Fum	Rec	Yds	TD
1952 Cleveland Browns	1	0	0	0
1954 Cleveland Browns	12	3	0	0
1955 Chicago Bears	3	0	0	0
Total	**16**	**3**	**0**	**0**

JAMES, Thomas Laverne, Jr. (Tommy)

Position: DB-HB
Height: 5'10"; Weight: 185
College: Ohio State
Born: September 16, 1923, Canton, OH
Deceased: February 7, 2007, Massillon, OH

STATISTICS

Games

	GP	GS
1947 Detroit Lions	2	0
1948 Cleveland Browns	14	0
1949 Cleveland Browns	12	1
1950 Cleveland Browns	12	0
1951 Cleveland Browns	12	0
1952 Cleveland Browns	12	0
1953 Cleveland Browns	12	0
1954 Cleveland Browns	12	0
1955 Cleveland Browns	8	0
1956 Baltimore Colts	2	0
Total	**98**	**1**

Rushing

	Rush	Yds	TD
1947 Detroit Lions	2	-1	0
1948 Cleveland Browns	1	8	0
1949 Cleveland Browns	10	28	0
1950 Cleveland Browns	1	-1	0
1954 Cleveland Browns	1	-6	0
1955 Cleveland Browns	1	2	0
Total	**16**	**30**	**0**

Receiving

	Rec	Yds	TD
1948 Cleveland Browns	1	44	0
Total	**1**	**44**	**0**

Punt Returns

	Ret	Yds	TD
1947 Detroit Lions	1	2	0
1948 Cleveland Browns	5	47	0
Total	**6**	**49**	**0**

Interceptions

	Int	Yds	TD
1948 Cleveland Browns	4	37	0
1949 Cleveland Browns	4	64	1
1950 Cleveland Browns	9	69	0
1951 Cleveland Browns	2	1	0
1952 Cleveland Browns	4	40	0
1953 Cleveland Browns	5	21	0
1954 Cleveland Browns	4	57	0
1955 Cleveland Browns	2	20	0
Total	**34**	**309**	**1**

Fumbles

	Fum	Rec	Yds	TD
1950 Cleveland Browns	0	1	0	0
1953 Cleveland Browns	0	2	37	1
1954 Cleveland Browns	0	2	7	0
Total	**0**	**5**	**44**	**1**

JEFFERS, Edward Francis (Ed)

Position: G
Height: 6'3"; Weight: 215
College: Oklahoma, Oklahoma State
Born: November 6, 1921, Hartshorne, OK
Deceased: April 4, 2010, Hobbs, NM

STATISTICS

Games

	GP	GS
1947 Brooklyn Dodgers	14	0
Total	**14**	**0**

JENKINS, Jonathan, R. (Jon)

Position: T
Height: 6'2"; Weight: 225
College: Dartmouth
Born: June 17, 1926, Frostburg, MD
Deceased: June 30, 1999, Frostburg, MD

STATISTICS

Games

	GP	GS
1949 Baltimore Colts	11	3
1950 Baltimore Colts	3	0
1951 New York Yanks	1	0
Total	**15**	**3**

JENSEN, Robert Peter (Bob)

Position: DE-E
Height: 6'2"; Weight: 220
College: Iowa State
Born: December 29, 1925, Chicago, IL
Deceased: October 8, 2015, Rancho Mirage, CA

STATISTICS

Games

	GP	GS
1948 Chicago Rockets	14	3
1949 Chicago Hornets	11	0
1950 Baltimore Colts	9	0
Total	**34**	**3**

Receiving

	Rec	Yds	TD
1948 Chicago Rockets	20	276	1
1949 Chicago Hornets	2	14	0
Total	22	290	1

Kick Returns

	Ret	Yds	TD
1948 Chicago Rockets	1	10	0
Total	1	10	0

JOE, Lawrence Edward (Larry)

Position: B
Height: 5'9"; Weight: 190
College: Penn State
Born: July 6, 1923, New Derry, PA
Deceased: April 1985

STATISTICS

Games

	GP	GS
1949 Buffalo Bills	1	0
Total	1	0

Rushing

	Rush	Yds	TD
1949 Buffalo Bills	2	18	0
Total	2	18	0

Receiving

	Rec	Yds	TD
1949 Buffalo Bills	2	52	0
Total	2	52	0

Kick Returns

	Ret	Yds	TD
1949 Buffalo Bills	1	12	0
Total	1	12	0

JOHNSON, William Levi, Sr. (Bill) (Tiger)

Position: C-LB
Height: 6'3"; Weight: 228
College: Texas A&M
Born: July 14, 1926, Tyler, TX
Deceased: January 7, 2011, Fort Myers, FL

STATISTICS

Games

	GP	GS
1948 San Francisco 49ers	5	0
1949 San Francisco 49ers	12	10
1950 San Francisco 49ers	12	0
1951 San Francisco 49ers	12	0
1952 San Francisco 49ers	11	0
1953 San Francisco 49ers	12	0
1954 San Francisco 49ers	12	0
1955 San Francisco 49ers	12	0
1956 San Francisco 49ers	7	0
Total	95	10

Interceptions

	Int	Yds	TD
1948 S.F. 49ers	1	0	0
1949 S.F. 49ers	1	16	1
Total	2	16	1

JOHNSON, Clyde Elmer

Position: T
Height: 6'6"; Weight: 269
College: Kentucky
Born: August 22, 1917, Ashland, KY
Deceased: September 14, 1997, Irvine, CA

STATISTICS

Games

	GP	GS
1946 Los Angeles Rams	11	0
1947 Los Angeles Rams	12	1
1948 Los Angeles Dons	9	0
Total	32	1

JOHNSON, Farnham James

Position: T-DE
Height: 6'0"; Weight: 215
College: Michigan, Wisconsin
Born: June 23, 1924, St. Paul, MN
Deceased: December 12, 2001, Winfield, AL

STATISTICS

Games

	GP	GS
1948 Chicago Rockets	8	0
Total	8	0

Point After Touchdown

	XPM	XPA
1948 Chicago Rockets	2	2
Total	2	2

JOHNSON, Gilbert (Gil)

Position: QB
Height: 5'11"; Weight: 195
College: SMU
Born: December 4, 1923, Tyler, TX
Deceased: July 10, 1999, Dallas, TX

STATISTICS

Games

	GP	GS
1949 New York Yankees	9	0
Total	9	0

Rushing

	Rush	Yds	TD
1949 New York Yankees	3	21	0
Total	3	21	0

Passing

	Comp	Att	Yds	TD	Int
1949 Yankees	12	36	179	0	5
Total	12	36	179	0	5

JOHNSON, Glenn Murray

Position: T
Height: 6'4"; Weight: 263
College: Arizona State
Born: June 28, 1922, Mesa, AZ
Deceased: October 31, 2001, Kirkland, WA

Statistics

Games

	GP	GS
1948 New York Yankees	9	0
1949 Green Bay Packers	8	0
Total	17	0

JOHNSON, Harvey Paul

Position: T-LB-BB-FB-G
Height: 5'11"; Weight: 212
College: William & Mary
Born: June 22, 1919, Bridgeton, NJ
Deceased: August 8, 1983, Orchard Park, NY

Statistics

Games

	GP	GS
1946 New York Yankees	13	2
1947 New York Yankees	14	0
1948 New York Yankees	14	0
1949 New York Yankees	12	0
1951 New York Yanks	12	0
Total	65	2

Rushing

	Rush	Yds	TD
1946 New York Yankees	16	63	0
Total	16	63	0

Receiving

	Rec	Yds	TD
1946 New York Yankees	2	19	0
1948 New York Yankees	1	6	0
Total	3	25	0

Kick Returns

	Ret	Yds	TD
1951 New York Yanks	1	4	0
Total	1	4	0

Interceptions

	Int	Yds	TD
1949 New York Yankees	1	1	0
Total	1	1	0

Fumbles

	Fum	Rec	Yds	TD
1951 New York Yanks	1	1	0	0
Total	1	1	0	0

Field Goals

	FGM	FGA
1946 New York Yankees	6	8
1947 New York Yankees	7	8
1948 New York Yankees	2	7
1949 New York Yankees	7	15
1951 New York Yanks	6	14
Total	28	52

Point After Touchdown

	XPM	XPA
1946 New York Yankees	36	36
1947 New York Yankees	49	51
1948 New York Yankees	37	37
1949 New York Yankees	25	25
1951 New York Yanks	31	31
Total	178	180

JOHNSON, Nathaniel Elijah (Nate)

Position: T-DT
Height: 6'3"; Weight: 244
College: Illinois
Born: June 18, 1920, Dale, IL
Deceased: August 24, 2004, Freeport, IL

Statistics

Games

	GP	GS
1946 New York Yankees	14	12
1947 New York Yankees	14	14
1948 Chicago Rockets	14	12
1949 Chicago Hornets	12	0
1950 New York Yanks	11	0
Total	65	38

JOHNSTON, Luther Preston (Pres)

Position: HB-FB-LB
Height: 6'0"; Weight: 205
College: SMU
Born: October 12, 1921, Newcastle, TX
Deceased: January 15, 1979, Lubbock, TX

Statistics

Games

	GP	GS
1946 Miami Seahawks	3	2
1946 Buffalo Bisons	8	5
Total	11	7

Rushing

	Rush	Yds	TD
1946 Miami Seahawks	30	165	2
1946 Buffalo Bisons	15	53	0
Total	45	218	2

Receiving

	Rec	Yds	TD
1946 Miami Seahawks	4	35	0
1946 Buffalo Bisons	2	19	1
Total	6	54	1

Passing

	Comp	Att	Yds	TD	Int
1946 Miami Seahawks	1	1	9	0	0
Total	1	1	9	0	0

Punting

	Punt	Yds	Blk
1946 Miami Seahawks	7	328	0
1946 Buffalo Bisons	21	784	1
Total	28	1112	1

Kick Returns

	Ret	Yds	TD
1946 Buffalo Bisons	2	21	0
Total	2	21	0

Interceptions

	Int	Yds	TD
1946 Buffalo Bisons	1	15	0
Total	1	15	0

Point After Touchdown

	XPM	XPA
1946 Miami Seahawks	1	1
Total	1	1

JONES, William H., Jr. (Billy)

Position: G
Height: 6'0"; Weight: 220
College: Charleston (WV), West Virginia Wesleyan
Born: January 30, 1920, Mannington, WV
Deceased: February 1988, Lexington, NC

STATISTICS

Games

	GP	GS
1947 Brooklyn Dodgers	7	1
Total	7	1

JONES, William Augustus (Dub)

Position: HB-DB-WB-TB
Height: 6'4"; Weight: 202
College: LSU, Tulane
Born: December 29, 1924, Arcadia, LA
Deceased:

STATISTICS

Games

	GP	GS
1946 Miami Seahawks	9	3
1946 Brooklyn Dodgers	2	1
1947 Brooklyn Dodgers	8	2
1948 Cleveland Browns	12	2
1949 Cleveland Browns	11	9
1950 Cleveland Browns	12	0
1951 Cleveland Browns	12	0
1952 Cleveland Browns	12	0
1953 Cleveland Browns	12	0
1954 Cleveland Browns	12	0
1955 Cleveland Browns	12	0
Total	114	17

Rushing

	Rush	Yds	TD
1946 Miami Seahawks	24	102	0
1946 Brooklyn Dodgers	19	62	0
1947 Brooklyn Dodgers	43	136	1
1948 Cleveland Browns	33	149	1
1949 Cleveland Browns	77	312	4
1950 Cleveland Browns	83	384	6
1951 Cleveland Browns	104	492	7
1952 Cleveland Browns	65	270	2
1953 Cleveland Browns	31	28	0
1954 Cleveland Browns	51	231	0
1955 Cleveland Browns	10	44	0
Total	540	2210	21

Receiving

	Rec	Yds	TD
1948 Cleveland Browns	9	119	2
1949 Cleveland Browns	12	241	1
1950 Cleveland Browns	31	458	5
1951 Cleveland Browns	30	570	5
1952 Cleveland Browns	43	651	4
1953 Cleveland Browns	24	373	0
1954 Cleveland Browns	19	347	2
1955 Cleveland Browns	3	115	1
Total	171	2874	20

Passing

	Comp	Att	Yds	TD	Int
1946 Dodgers	1	2	0	0	1
1947 Dodgers	3	15	37	0	2
1952 Cleveland Browns	1	2	3	1	0
1953 Cleveland Browns	0	1	0	0	0
Total	5	20	40	1	3

Punt Returns

	Ret	Yds	TD
1946 Brooklyn Dodgers	1	6	0
1947 Brooklyn Dodgers	14	157	0
1953 Cleveland Browns	1	7	0
Total	16	170	0

Kick Returns

	Ret	Yds	TD
1946 Brooklyn Dodgers	6	91	0
1947 Brooklyn Dodgers	7	121	0
1948 Cleveland Browns	2	35	0
1949 Cleveland Browns	8	204	0
Total			

Interceptions

	Int	Yds	TD
1947 Brooklyn Dodgers	2	35	0
Total	2	35	0

Fumbles				
	Fum	Rec	Yds	TD
1950 Cleveland Browns	1	0	0	0
1951 Cleveland Browns	3	0	0	0
1952 Cleveland Browns	2	0	0	0
1953 Cleveland Browns	3	0	0	0
1954 Cleveland Browns	1	0	0	0
1955 Cleveland Browns	1	0	0	0
Total	**11**	**0**	**0**	**0**

JONES, Edgar Francis (Special Delivery)

Position: HB-DB
Height: 5'10"; Weight: 193
College: Pittsburgh
Born: May 6, 1920, Scranton, PA
Deceased: May 18, 2004, Scranton, PA

STATISTICS

Games		
	GP	GS
1945 Chicago Bears	1	0
1946 Cleveland Browns	14	13
1947 Cleveland Browns	9	5
1948 Cleveland Browns	13	9
1949 Cleveland Browns	7	5
Total	**44**	**32**

Rushing			
	Rush	Yds	TD
1945 Chicago Bears	8	41	0
1946 Cleveland Browns	77	539	4
1947 Cleveland Browns	69	443	5
1948 Cleveland Browns	100	400	5
1949 Cleveland Browns	43	127	4
Total	**297**	**1550**	**18**

Receiving			
	Rec	Yds	TD
1945 Chicago Bears	1	0	0
1946 Cleveland Browns	4	120	1
1947 Cleveland Browns	5	92	1
1948 Cleveland Browns	14	293	5
1949 Cleveland Browns	9	130	3
Total	**33**	**635**	**10**

Passing					
	Comp	Att	Yds	TD	Int
1945 Chicago Bears	0	1	0	0	0
1946 Cle. Browns	1	4	4	0	0
1947 Cle. Browns	2	3	79	0	0
1949 Cle. Browns	0	1	0	0	0
Total	**3**	**9**	**83**	**0**	**0**

Punt Returns			
	Ret	Yds	TD
1946 Cleveland Browns	7	73	0
1947 Cleveland Browns	2	37	0
Total	**9**	**110**	**0**

Kick Returns			
	Ret	Yds	TD
1945 Chicago Bears	2	72	0
1946 Cleveland Browns	12	307	1
1947 Cleveland Browns	2	48	0
1949 Cleveland Browns	1	15	0
Total	**17**	**442**	**1**

Interceptions			
	Int	Yds	TD
1946 Cleveland Browns	2	16	0
Total	**2**	**16**	**0**

JONES, Elmer John, Jr.

Position: G-LB
Height: 6'0"; Weight: 224
College: Franklin & Marshall, Wake Forest
Born: August 4, 1920, Buffalo, NY
Deceased: February 21, 1996, New Smyrna Beach, FL

STATISTICS

Games		
	GP	GS
1946 Buffalo Bisons	12	1
1947 Detroit Lions	10	2
1948 Detroit Lions	9	0
Total	**31**	**3**

Interceptions			
	Int	Yds	TD
1946 Buffalo Bisons	2	7	0
Total	**2**	**7**	**0**

JONES, Ralph Carroll

Position: E-DE
Height: 6'3"; Weight: 200
College: Alabama, Union (TN)
Born: February 14, 1922, Florence, AL
Deceased: February 18, 1995, Florence, AL

STATISTICS

Games		
	GP	GS
1946 Detroit Lions	11	0
1947 Baltimore Colts	6	1
Total	**17**	**1**

Receiving			
	Int	Yds	TD
1946 Detroit Lions	4	84	0
1947 Baltimore Colts	3	23	0
Total	**7**	**107**	**0**

JUDD, Saxon Thomas

Position: E
Height: 6'1"; Weight: 190
College: La-Lafayette, Tulsa
Born: November 29, 1919, Pottsboro, TX
Deceased: March 31, 1990, Tulsa, OK

STATISTICS

Games

	GP	GS
1946 Brooklyn Dodgers	13	2
1947 Brooklyn Dodgers	14	10
1948 Brooklyn Dodgers	14	5
Total	**41**	**17**

Receiving

	Rec	Yds	TD
1946 Brooklyn Dodgers	34	443	4
1947 Brooklyn Dodgers	18	240	1
1948 Brooklyn Dodgers	32	350	2
Total	**84**	**997**	**7**

Kick Returns

	Ret	Yds	TD
1946 Brooklyn Dodgers	3	54	0
1947 Brooklyn Dodgers	2	5	0
Total	**5**	**59**	**0**

JUNGMICHEL, Harold Neve (Buddy)

Position: G
Height: 5'9"; Weight: 200
College: Texas
Born: October 18, 1919, Gonzales, TX
Deceased: August 28, 1982, Austin, TX

STATISTICS

Games

	GP	GS
1946 Miami Seahawks	14	13
Total	**14**	**13**

Interceptions

	Int	Yds	TD
1946 Miami Seahawks	1	21	0
Total	**1**	**21**	**0**

JUZWIK, Stephen Robert (Steve)

Position: HB-FB
Height: 5'8"; Weight: 186
College: Notre Dame
Born: June 18, 1918, Gary, IN
Deceased: June 6, 1964, Chicago, IL

STATISTICS

Games

	GP	GS
1942 Washington Redskins	2	1
1946 Buffalo Bisons	13	9
1947 Buffalo Bills	10	3
1948 Chicago Rockets	4	1
Total	**29**	**14**

Rushing

	Rush	Yds	TD
1942 Wash. Redskins	15	75	2
1946 Buffalo Bisons	71	455	3
1947 Buffalo Bills	26	130	0
1948 Chicago Rockets	13	19	0
Total	**125**	**679**	**5**

Receiving

	Rec	Yds	TD
1946 Buffalo Bisons	23	357	3
1947 Buffalo Bills	5	35	1
1948 Chicago Rockets	1	5	0
Total	**29**	**397**	**4**

Punt Returns

	Ret	Yds	TD
1942 Wash. Redskins	3	33	0
1946 Buffalo Bisons	11	135	0
1947 Buffalo Bills	4	36	0
Total	**18**	**204**	**0**

Kick Returns

	Ret	Yds	TD
1942 Wash. Redskins	1	22	0
1946 Buffalo Bisons	21	452	0
1947 Buffalo Bills	1	20	0
Total	**23**	**494**	**0**

Interceptions

	Int	Yds	TD
1946 Buffalo Bisons	5	108	1
Total	**5**	**108**	**1**

Field Goals

	FGM	FGA
1947 Buffalo Bills	2	3
Total	**2**	**3**

Point After Touchdown

	XPM	XPA
1942 Washington Redskins	3	3
1947 Buffalo Bills	28	32
1948 Chicago Rockets	5	5
Total	**36**	**40**

KAPTER, Alexander Joe (Alex)

Position: G
Height: 6'0"; Weight: 205
College: Northwestern
Born: March 26, 1922, Waukegan, IL
Deceased: July 26, 2005, Thousand Oaks, CA

STATISTICS

Games

	GP	GS
1946 Cleveland Browns	6	0
Total	**6**	**0**

KARMAZIN, Michael Lawrence (Mike)

Position: G
Height: 5'11"; Weight: 210
College: Duke
Born: July 16, 1919, Manown, PA
Deceased: January 21, 2004, New Orleans, LA

STATISTICS

Games
	GP	GS
1946 New York Yankees	10	0
Total	10	0

KASAP, Michael E. (Mike)

Position: T
Height: 6'2"; Weight: 255
College: Illinois, Purdue
Born: November 20, 1922, Oglesby, IL
Deceased: October 20, 1994, La Salle, IL

STATISTICS

Games
	GP	GS
1947 Baltimore Colts	12	3
Total	12	3

KELLAGHER, William Michael (Bill)

Position: FB
Height: 5'11"; Weight: 205
College: Fordham
Born: August 13, 1920, Locust Gap, PA
Deceased: May 11, 2003, DeBary, FL

STATISTICS

Games
	GP	GS
1946 Chicago Rockets	12	2
1947 Chicago Rockets	14	2
1948 Chicago Rockets	12	5
Total	38	9

Rushing
	Rush	Yds	TD
1946 Chicago Rockets	49	178	3
1947 Chicago Rockets	42	243	0
1948 Chicago Rockets	33	97	1
Total	124	518	4

Receiving
	Rec	Yds	TD
1946 Chicago Rockets	2	36	0
1947 Chicago Rockets	3	22	0
Total	5	58	0

Passing
	Comp	Att	Yds	TD	Int
1946 Chicago Rockets	2	3	15	0	1
Total	2	3	15	0	1

Punting
	Punt	Yds	Blk
1946 Chicago Rockets	1	56	0
Total	1	56	0

Kick Returns
	Ret	Yds	TD
1946 Chicago Rockets	3	48	0
1948 Chicago Rockets	3	54	0
Total	6	102	0

Interceptions
	Int	Yds	TD
1947 Chicago Rockets	6	77	0
Total	6	77	0

KELLEY, Edward Allen (Ed)

Position: T
Height: 6'4"; Weight: 230
College: Texas
Born: February 18, 1924, Sugar Land, TX
Deceased: June 27, 2002, Harlingen, TX

STATISTICS

Games
	GP	GS
1949 Los Angeles Dons	12	2
Total	12	2

Rushing
	Rush	Yds	TD
1949 Los Angeles Dons	1	-2	0
Total	1	-2	0

KELLY, Robert Joseph (Bob)

Position: HB-DB
Height: 5'10"; Weight: 190
College: Navy, Notre Dame
Born: June 6, 1925, Chicago, IL
Deceased:

STATISTICS

Games
	GP	GS
1947 Los Angeles Dons	12	8
1948 Los Angeles Dons	4	1
1949 Baltimore Colts	10	2
Total	26	11

Rushing
	Rush	Yds	TD
1947 Los Angeles Dons	51	205	2
1948 Los Angeles Dons	3	10	0
1949 Baltimore Colts	9	17	0
Total	63	232	2

Receiving
	Rec	Yds	TD
1947 Los Angeles Dons	9	68	1
1949 Baltimore Colts	2	25	0
Total	11	93	1

KENNEDY, Robert Henry (Bob H.)

Position: B
Height: 5'11"; Weight: 195
College: Washington State
Born: June 29, 1921, Sandpoint, ID
Deceased: July 29, 2010, Boise, ID

STATISTICS

Games

	GP	GS
1946 New York Yankees	13	4
1947 New York Yankees	14	1
1948 New York Yankees	14	3
1949 New York Yankees	12	10
1950 New York Yanks	5	0
Total	58	18

Rushing

	Rush	Yds	TD
1946 New York Yankees	58	179	2
1947 New York Yankees	44	258	1
1948 New York Yankees	33	90	1
1949 New York Yankees	118	490	5
Total	253	1017	9

Receiving

	Rec	Yds	TD
1946 New York Yankees	11	59	0
1948 New York Yankees	5	23	0
1949 New York Yankees	7	55	1
Total	23	137	1

Passing

	Comp	Att	Yds	TD	Int
1946 Yankees	2	6	45	0	3
1947 Yankees	2	3	56	0	0
1948 Yankees	0	1	0	0	0
1949 Yankees	1	1	27	0	0
Total	5	11	128	0	3

Punting

	Punt	Yds	Blk
1946 New York Yankees	7	259	1
1947 New York Yankees	5	126	3
1948 New York Yankees	7	237	0
Total	19	622	4

Punt Returns

	Ret	Yds	TD
1946 New York Yankees	3	20	0
1947 New York Yankees	6	44	0
1948 New York Yankees	1	14	0
Total	10	78	0

Kick Returns

	Ret	Yds	TD
1946 New York Yankees	4	105	0
1948 New York Yankees	2	20	0
1949 New York Yankees	1	15	0
1950 New York Yanks	1	15	0
Total	8	155	0

Interceptions

	Int	Yds	TD
1946 New York Yankees	3	35	0
1947 New York Yankees	2	66	0
1948 New York Yankees	4	49	0
1949 New York Yankees	2	2	0
1950 New York Yanks	1	11	0
Total	12	163	0

KENNEDY, Robert Michael (Bob M.)

Position: DB-HB
Height: 6'0"; Weight: 178
College: North Carolina
Born: September 16, 1928, Weehawken, NJ
Deceased: July 5, 1991, Richwood, NJ

STATISTICS

Games

	GP	GS
1949 Los Angeles Dons	10	1
Total	10	1

Rushing

	Rush	Yds	TD
1949 Los Angeles Dons	2	14	0
Total	2	14	0

Punt Returns

	Ret	Yds	TD
1947 Los Angeles Dons	4	69	0
Total	4	69	0

Kick Returns

	Ret	Yds	TD
1947 Los Angeles Dons	3	61	0
1949 Los Angeles Dons	2	31	0
Total	5	92	0

Interceptions

	Int	Yds	TD
1947 Los Angeles Dons	2	47	0
1948 Los Angeles Dons	3	14	0
1949 Baltimore Colts	3	24	0
Total	8	85	0

Interceptions

	Int	Yds	TD
1949 Los Angeles Dons	1	33	0
Total	1	33	0

KERNS, John Emery

Position: T
Height: 6'3"; Weight: 245
College: Duke, North Carolina, Ohio
Born: June 17, 1923, Ashtabula, OH
Deceased: June 1988, Leesburg, FL

STATISTICS

Games

	GP	GS
1947 Buffalo Bills	14	3
1948 Buffalo Bills	14	9
1949 Buffalo Bills	12	12
Total	**40**	**24**

KERR, William Howard (Bill)

Position: E
Height: 6'0"; Weight: 220
College: Notre Dame
Born: November 10, 1915, Tarrytown, NY
Deceased: April 9, 1964, San Mateo, CA

STATISTICS

Games

	GP	GS
1946 Los Angeles Dons	11	1
Total	**11**	**1**

Rushing

	Rush	Yds	TD
1946 Los Angeles Dons	1	10	0
Total	**1**	**10**	**0**

Receiving

	Rec	Yds	TD
1946 Los Angeles Dons	7	122	0
Total	**7**	**122**	**0**

Interceptions

	Int	Yds	TD
1946 Los Angeles Dons	1	34	0
Total	**1**	**34**	**0**

KIMBROUGH, John Alec

Position: FB
Height: 6'2"; Weight: 210
College: Texas A&M
Born: June 14, 1918, Haskell, TX
Deceased: May 9, 2006, Haskell, TX

STATISTICS

Games

	GP	GS
1946 Los Angeles Dons	14	7
1947 Los Angeles Dons	14	5
1948 Los Angeles Dons	10	3
Total	**38**	**15**

Rushing

	Rush	Yds	TD
1946 Los Angeles Dons	122	473	6
1947 Los Angeles Dons	131	562	8
1948 Los Angeles Dons	76	189	3
Total	**329**	**1224**	**17**

Receiving

	Rec	Yds	TD
1946 Los Angeles Dons	9	162	1
1947 Los Angeles Dons	16	281	3
1948 Los Angeles Dons	10	131	2
Total	**35**	**574**	**6**

Kick Returns

	Ret	Yds	TD
1946 Los Angeles Dons	5	111	0
1947 Los Angeles Dons	4	96	0
1948 Los Angeles Dons	5	54	0
Total	**13**	**261**	**0**

KINARD, Frank Manning (Bruiser)

Position: T
Height: 6'1"; Weight: 216
College: Mississippi
Born: October 23, 1914, Pelahatchie, MS
Deceased: September 7, 1985, Jackson, MS

STATISTICS

Games

	GP	GS
1938 Brooklyn Dodgers	11	11
1939 Brooklyn Dodgers	11	11
1940 Brooklyn Dodgers	9	8
1941 Brooklyn Dodgers	11	11
1942 Brooklyn Dodgers	11	11
1943 Brooklyn Dodgers	10	10
1944 Brooklyn Dodgers	10	10
1946 New York Yankees	14	14
1947 New York Yankees	14	3
Total	**101**	**89**

Receiving

	Rec	Yds	TD
1943 Brooklyn Dodgers	5	62	1
Total	**5**	**62**	**1**

Kick Returns

	Ret	Yds	TD
1941 Brooklyn Dodgers	1	14	0
1944 Brooklyn Dodgers	1	22	0
Total	**2**	**36**	**0**

Interceptions

	Int	Yds	TD
1944 Brooklyn Dodgers	1	26	0
Total	**1**	**26**	**0**

Field Goals

	FGM	FGA
1943 Brooklyn Dodgers	1	1
Total	**1**	**1**

Point After Touchdown

	XPM	XPA
1939 Brooklyn Dodgers	7	7
1941 Brooklyn Dodgers	3	5
1943 Brooklyn Dodgers	8	9
1944 Brooklyn Dodgers	9	9
Total	**27**	**30**

KINARD, George Truitt

Position: G
Height: 6'1"; Weight: 202
College: Mississippi
Born: October 9, 1916, Crystal Springs, MS
Deceased: March 23, 2000, Rankin, MS

Statistics

	Games	
	GP	GS
1941 Brooklyn Dodgers	11	0
1942 Brooklyn Dodgers	7	7
1946 New York Yankees	11	5
Total	**29**	**12**

KING, Edward Joseph (Ed)

Position: G-DE-DG
Height: 6'0"; Weight: 217
College: Boston College
Born: May 11, 1925, Chelsea, MA
Deceased: September 18, 2006, Burlington, MA

Statistics

	Games	
	GP	GS
1948 Buffalo Bills	14	1
1949 Buffalo Bills	5	0
1950 Baltimore Colts	12	0
Total	**31**	**1**

KING, Lafayette Henry (Fay) (Dolly)

Position: E
Height: 6'2"; Weight: 195
College: Georgia
Born: March 7, 1922, Dothan, AL
Deceased: June 5, 1983, Lincolnton, GA

Statistics

	Games	
	GP	GS
1946 Buffalo Bills	14	0
1947 Buffalo Bills	14	2
1948 Chicago Rockets	14	8
1949 Chicago Hornets	8	3
Total	**50**	**13**

	Receiving		
	Rec	Yds	TD
1946 Buffalo Bills	30	466	6
1947 Buffalo Bills	26	382	6
1948 Chicago Rockets	50	647	7
1949 Chicago Hornets	9	88	1
Total	**115**	**1583**	**20**

	Kick Returns		
	Ret	Yds	TD
1948 Chicago Rockets	1	11	0
1949 Chicago Hornets	1	13	0
Total	**2**	**24**	**0**

KINGERY, B. Wayne (Wayne)

Position: HB-DB
Height: 5'11"; Weight: 175
College: LSU, McNeese State
Born: June 5, 1927, Lake Charles, LA
Deceased: June 2, 2016, Lake Charles, LA

Statistics

	Games	
	GP	GS
1949 Baltimore Colts	9	0
Total	**9**	**0**

	Rushing		
	Rush	Yds	TD
1949 Baltimore Colts	3	3	0
Total	**3**	**3**	**0**

	Receiving		
	Rec	Yds	TD
1949 Baltimore Colts	1	-2	0
Total	**1**	**-2**	**0**

	Punting		
	Punt	Yds	Blk
1949 Baltimore Colts	3	109	0
Total	**3**	**109**	**0**

	Punt Returns		
	Ret	Yds	TD
1949 Baltimore Colts	2	19	0
Total	**2**	**19**	**0**

	Interceptions		
	Int	Yds	TD
1949 Baltimore Colts	1	0	0
Total	**1**	**0**	**0**

KISIDAY, George John

Position: E
Height: 5'11"; Weight: 210
College: Columbia, Duquesne
Born: April 16, 1923, Ambridge, PA
Deceased: November 9, 1970, Ambridge, PA

Statistics

	Games	
	GP	GS
1948 Buffalo Bills	14	0
Total	**14**	**0**

	Receiving		
	Rec	Yds	TD
1948 Buffalo Bills	1	20	0
Total	**1**	**20**	**0**

KISSELL, John Jay

Position: DT-T
Height: 6'3"; Weight: 245
College: Boston College
Born: May 14, 1923, Nashua, NH
Deceased: April 9, 1992, Nashua, NH

STATISTICS

Games

	GP	GS
1948 Buffalo Bills	14	1
1949 Buffalo Bills	12	0
1950 Cleveland Browns	12	0
1951 Cleveland Browns	12	0
1952 Cleveland Browns	12	0
1954 Cleveland Browns	12	0
1955 Cleveland Browns	12	0
1956 Cleveland Browns	12	0
Total	98	1

Fumbles

	Fum	Rec	Yds	TD
1950 Cleveland Browns	0	2	3	0
1951 Cleveland Browns	0	3	0	0
1952 Cleveland Browns	0	2	0	0
1954 Cleveland Browns	0	2	4	0
Total	0	9	7	0

KISSELL, Vito Joseph

Position: LB-FB
Height: 5'10"; Weight: 205
College: Holy Cross
Born: June 13, 1927, Nashua, NH
Deceased: March 19, 1997, Morris Plains, NJ

STATISTICS

Games

	GP	GS
1949 Buffalo Bills	9	0
1950 Baltimore Colts	11	0
Total	20	0

Rushing

	Rush	Yds	TD
1949 Buffalo Bills	10	19	0
1950 Baltimore Colts	2	6	0
Total	12	25	0

Receiving

	Rec	Yds	TD
1949 Buffalo Bills	3	37	0
Total	3	37	0

Kick Returns

	Ret	Yds	TD
1949 Buffalo Bills	1	1	0
1950 Baltimore Colts	2	19	0
Total	3	20	0

Interceptions

	Int	Yds	TD
1949 Buffalo Bills	1	14	0
1950 Baltimore Colts	2	7	0
Total	3	21	0

Fumbles

	Fum	Rec	Yds	TD
1950 Baltimore Colts	0	1	5	0
Total	0	1	5	0

Field Goals

	FGM	FGA
1950 Baltimore Colts	*	1
Total	*	1

Point After Touchdown

	XPM	XPA
1950 Baltimore Colts	11	11
Total	11	11

KLASNIC, John

Position: WB-DB
Height: 6'0"; Weight: 185
College: Auburn
Born: February 23, 1927, Port View, PA
Deceased: October 18, 2012, McKeesport, PA

STATISTICS

Games

	GP	GS
1948 Brooklyn Dodgers	1	0
Total	1	0

KLENK, Quentin Earl

Position: T
Height: 6'2"; Weight: 225
College: USC
Born: February 13, 1919, Long Beach, CA
Deceased: January 4, 1979, San Mateo, CA

STATISTICS

Games

	GP	GS
1946 Buffalo Bills	2	2
1946 Chicago Rockets	8	1
Total	10	3

KLUG, Alfred W. (Al)

Position: T-G
Height: 6'1"; Weight: 215
College: Marquette
Born: June 1, 1920, Milwaukee, WI
Deceased: June 14, 1957, Milwaukee, WI

STATISTICS

Games
	GP	GS
1946 Buffalo Bills	12	5
1947 Baltimore Colts	11	6
1948 Baltimore Colts	13	0
Total	**36**	**11**

KLUTKA, Nicholas (Nick)

Position: E
Height: 5'11"; Weight: 198
College: Florida
Born: January 21, 1921, New Brighton, PA
Deceased: April 2, 2003, Van Wert, OH

STATISTICS

Games
	GP	GS
1946 Buffalo Bills	11	4
Total	**11**	**4**

Receiving
	Rec	Yds	TD
1946 Buffalo Bills	1	9	0
Total	**1**	**9**	**0**

KOCH, George Theodore

Position: HB
Height: 6'0"; Weight: 200
College: Baylor, St. Mary's
Born: July 2, 1919, Temple, TX
Deceased: September 5, 1966, Temple, TX

STATISTICS

Games
	GP	GS
1945 Cleveland Rams	5	1
1947 Buffalo Bills	13	3
Total	**18**	**4**

Rushing
	Rush	Yds	TD
1945 Cleveland Rams	12	101	0
1947 Buffalo Bills	37	149	1
Total	**49**	**250**	**1**

Receiving
	Rec	Yds	TD
1947 Buffalo Bills	1	10	0
Total	**1**	**10**	**0**

Punt Returns
	Ret	Yds	TD
1947 Buffalo Bills	4	84	0
Total	**4**	**84**	**0**

Kick Returns
	Ret	Yds	TD
1945 Cleveland Rams	1	7	0
1947 Buffalo Bills	1	12	0
Total	**2**	**19**	**0**

Interceptions
	Int	Yds	TD
1947 Buffalo Bills	3	24	0
Total	**3**	**24**	**0**

KODBA, Joseph Stephen (Joe)

Position: C-LB
Height: 5'11"; Weight: 190
College: Butler, Purdue
Born: February 27, 1922
Deceased: September 7, 2005, Swartz Creek, MI

STATISTICS

Games
	GP	GS
1947 Baltimore Colts	13	3
Total	**13**	**3**

Interceptions
	Int	Yds	TD
1947 Baltimore Colts	1	2	0
Total	**1**	**2**	**0**

KOLESAR, Robert C. (Bob)

Position: G
Height: 5'10"; Weight: 200
College: Michigan
Born: April 5, 1921, Cleveland, OH
Deceased: January 13, 2004, Midland, MI

STATISTICS

Games
	GP	GS
1946 Cleveland Browns	2	0
Total	**2**	**0**

KONETSKY, Floyd Walter

Position: E
Height: 6'0"; Weight: 197
College: Florida
Born: May 26, 1920, Marianna, PA
Deceased: November 15, 1987, Cleveland, OH

STATISTICS

Games
	GP	GS
1944 Cleveland Rams	8	6
1945 Cleveland Rams	10	4
1947 Baltimore Colts	6	1
Total	**24**	**11**

KOSIKOWSKI, Frank Leon (continued)

Interceptions

	Int	Yds	TD
1947 Baltimore Colts	1	15	0
Total	**1**	**15**	**0**

KOSIKOWSKI, Frank Leon

Position: DE
Height: 6'1"; Weight: 200
College: Marquette, Notre Dame
Born: July 23, 1926, Cudahy, WI
Deceased: November 17, 1991

STATISTICS

Games

	GP	GS
1948 Cleveland Browns	12	0
Total	**12**	**0**

KOSTIUK, Michael (Mike)

Position: T
Height: 6'0"; Weight: 210
College: Detroit Tech
Born: August 1, 1919, Krydor, Canada
Deceased: July 26, 2015, Sterling Heights, MI

STATISTICS

Games

	GP	GS
1941 Cleveland Rams	1	0
1945 Detroit Lions	7	3
1946 Buffalo Bisons	2	0
Total	**10**	**3**

KOZEL, Chester Richard (Chet)

Position: T-G
Height: 6'2"; Weight: 211
College: Mississippi
Born: October 15, 1919, Kenosha, WI
Deceased: June 27, 1982, Kenosha, WI

STATISTICS

Games

	GP	GS
1947 Buffalo Bills	12	9
1948 Buffalo Bills	2	0
1948 Chicago Rockets	5	1
Total	**19**	**10**

Kick Returns

	Ret	Yds	TD
1947 Buffalo Bills	1	11	0
Total	**1**	**11**	**0**

KOZLOWSKI, Stanley J. (Stan)

Position: FB
Height: 6'1"; Weight: 200
College: Holy Cross, Notre Dame
Born: February 5, 1924, Rumford, RI
Deceased: August 23, 1972, Littleton, MA

STATISTICS

Games

	GP	GS
1946 Miami Seahawks	5	0
Total	**5**	**0**

Rushing

	Rush	Yds	TD
1946 Miami Seahawks	18	61	0
Total	**18**	**61**	**0**

Receiving

	Rec	Yds	TD
1946 Miami Seahawks	2	27	0
Total	**2**	**27**	**0**

Punt Returns

	Ret	Yds	TD
1946 Miami Seahawks	1	4	0
Total	**1**	**4**	**0**

Kick Returns

	Ret	Yds	TD
1946 Miami Seahawks	3	72	0
Total	**3**	**72**	**0**

KRAMER, John Francis (Jack)

Position: T
Height: 6'0"; Weight: 220
College: Marquette
Born: July 26, 1919, Milwaukee, WI
Deceased: December 15, 1978, Milwaukee, WI

STATISTICS

Games

	GP	GS
1946 Buffalo Bisons	13	2
Total	**13**	**2**

KRIVONAK, Joseph (Joe)

Position: G
Height: 6'2"; Weight: 230
College: South Carolina
Born:
Deceased: October 26, 1989, Phoenix, AZ

STATISTICS

Games

	GP	GS
1946 Miami Seahawks	4	0
Total	**4**	**0**

KRUEGER, Alvin John (Al)

Position: HB-E
Height: 6'0"; Weight: 190
College: USC
Born: April 3, 1919, Orange, CA
Deceased: February 20, 1999, Lancaster, CA

STATISTICS

Games

	GP	GS
1941 Washington Redskins	7	0
1942 Washington Redskins	11	0
1946 Los Angeles Dons	10	3
Total	28	3

Receiving

	Rec	Yds	TD
1941 Wash. Redskins	7	123	1
1942 Wash. Redskins	9	65	0
1946 Los Angeles Dons	19	213	1
Total	35	401	2

Kick Returns

	Ret	Yds	TD
1941 Wash. Redskins	1	23	0
1942 Wash. Redskins	1	19	0
Total	2	42	0

Interceptions

	Int	Yds	TD
1941 Wash. Redskins	1	12	0
Total	1	12	0

KUFFEL, Raymond Francis (Ray)

Position: E
Height: 6'3"; Weight: 213
College: Marquette, Notre Dame
Born: December 9, 1921, Milwaukee, WI
Deceased: December 22, 1974, Milwaukee, WI

STATISTICS

Games

	GP	GS
1947 Buffalo Bills	7	2
1948 Chicago Rockets	14	7
1949 Chicago Hornets	2	0
Total	23	9

Receiving

	Rec	Yds	TD
1947 Buffalo Bills	3	37	0
1948 Chicago Rockets	19	365	3
Total	22	402	3

Kick Returns

	Ret	Yds	TD
1948 Chicago Rockets	1	16	0
Total	1	16	0

KULBITSKI, Victor John (Vic)

Position: FB
Height: 5'10"; Weight: 205
College: Minnesota, Notre Dame
Born: June 15, 1921, Virginia, MN
Deceased: May 23, 1998, West St. Paul, MN

STATISTICS

Games

	GP	GS
1946 Buffalo Bisons	13	8
1947 Buffalo Bills	13	7
1948 Buffalo Bills	14	6
Total	40	21

Rushing

	Rush	Yds	TD
1946 Buffalo Bisons	97	605	2
1947 Buffalo Bills	56	249	1
1948 Buffalo Bills	40	152	0
Total	193	1006	3

Receiving

	Rec	Yds	TD
1946 Buffalo Bisons	1	0	0
1947 Buffalo Bills	9	117	4
1948 Buffalo Bills	3	37	0
Total	13	154	4

Punt Returns

	Ret	Yds	TD
1947 Buffalo Bills	1	13	0
Total	1	13	0

Kick Returns

	Ret	Yds	TD
1946 Buffalo Bisons	5	81	0
1947 Buffalo Bills	1	19	0
1948 Buffalo Bills	1	18	0
Total	7	118	0

Interceptions

	Int	Yds	TD
1946 Buffalo Bisons	1	20	0
1947 Buffalo Bills	1	14	0
Total	2	34	0

Point After Touchdown

	XPM	XPA
1947 Buffalo Bills	1	1
1948 Buffalo Bills	8	10
Total	9	11

KUSSEROW, Louis Joseph (Lou)

Position: LB-FB
Height: 6'1"; Weight: 200
College: Columbia
Born: September 6, 1927, Braddock, PA
Deceased: June 30, 2001, Rancho Mirage, CA

STATISTICS

Games

	GP	GS
1949 New York Yankees	11	4
1950 New York Yanks	11	0
Total	22	4

Rushing

	Rush	Yds	TD
1949 New York Yankees	39	136	0
1950 New York Yanks	1	6	0
Total	40	142	0

Passing

	Comp	Att	Yds	TD	Int
1949 Yankees	0	1	0	0	0
Total	0	1	0	0	0

Kick Returns

	Ret	Yds	TD
1949 New York Yankees	6	136	0
Total	6	136	0

KUZMAN, John N.

Position: T
Height: 6'1"; Weight: 232
College: Fordham
Born: June 29, 1915, Coaldale, PA
Deceased: January 29, 2008, Packanack Lake (Wayne), NJ

STATISTICS

Games

	GP	GS
1941 Chicago Cardinals	5	0
1946 San Francisco 49ers	11	1
1947 Chicago Rockets	13	7
Total	29	8

Kick Returns

	Ret	Yds	TD
1947 S.F. 49ers	1	7	0
Total	1	7	0

LAHAR, Harold Wade (Hal)

Position: G
Height: 6'0"; Weight: 225
College: Oklahoma
Born: July 14, 1919, Durant, OK
Deceased: October 20, 2003, Dallas, TX

STATISTICS

Games

	GP	GS
1941 Chicago Bears	8	0
1946 Buffalo Bisons	12	3
1947 Buffalo Bills	14	14
1948 Buffalo Bills	13	13
Total	47	30

Field Goals

	FGM	FGA
1941 Chicago Bears	1	1
Total	1	1

Point After Touchdown

	XPM	XPA
1941 Chicago Bears	1	3
Total	1	3

LAHEY, Thomas Patrick (Pat)

Position: E-DE
Height: 6'2"; Weight: 218
College: John Carroll
Born: October 21, 1919, Dunbridge, OH
Deceased: October 18, 2009, Northfield, IL

STATISTICS

Games

	GP	GS
1946 Chicago Rockets	13	10
1947 Chicago Rockets	13	4
Total	26	14

Rushing

	Rush	Yds	TD
1946 Chicago Rockets	1	−2	0
Total	1	−2	0

Receiving

	Rec	Yds	TD
1946 Chicago Rockets	17	203	0
1947 Chicago Rockets*	13	148	0
Total	30	351	0

Kick Returns

	Ret	Yds	TD
1946 Chicago Rockets	1	5	0
1947 Chicago Rockets	2	18	0
Total	3	23	0

Interceptions

	Int	Yds	TD
1946 Chicago Rockets	1	4	0
Total	1	4	0

*John Harrington had an extra two receiving yards and Pat Lahey was missing two receiving yards for the season. Since these numbers could not be verified, the official statistics were used.

LAHR, Warren Emmett

Position: DB
Height: 5'11"; Weight: 189
College: Case Western Reserve
Born: September 5, 1923, Mount Zion, PA
Deceased: January 13, 1975, Cleveland, OH

STATISTICS

Games

	GP	GS
1949 Cleveland Browns	11	0
1950 Cleveland Browns	12	0
1951 Cleveland Browns	12	0
1952 Cleveland Browns	12	0
1953 Cleveland Browns	12	0
1954 Cleveland Browns	12	0
1955 Cleveland Browns	12	0
1956 Cleveland Browns	12	0
1957 Cleveland Browns	11	0
1958 Cleveland Browns	7	0
1959 Cleveland Browns	12	0
Total	125	0

Rushing

	Rush	Yds	TD
1949 Cleveland Browns	9	36	1
1954 Cleveland Browns	3	18	0
Total	12	54	1

Receiving

	Rec	Yds	TD
1949 Cleveland Browns	1	20	0
Total	1	20	0

Passing

	Comp	Att	Yds	TD	Int
1954 Cle. Browns	0	1	0	0	1
Total	0	1	0	0	1

Punting

	Punt	Yds	Blk
1949 Cleveland Browns	4	125	1
Total	4	125	1

Punt Returns

	Ret	Yds	TD
1949 Cleveland Browns	6	83	0
Total	6	83	0

LAND, Frederick N. (Fred)

Position: T-G
Height: 6'1"; Weight: 220
College: LSU
Born: May 8, 1925, North Little Rock, AR
Deceased: March 19, 1992, Denham Springs, LA

STATISTICS

Games

	GP	GS
1948 San Francisco 49ers	2	0
Total	2	0

LANDRIGAN, James Montague (Jim)

Position: T
Height: 6'4"; Weight: 235
College: Dartmouth, Holy Cross
Born: May 31, 1923, Everett, MA
Deceased: June 24, 1974, San Diego, CA

STATISTICS

Games

	GP	GS
1947 Baltimore Colts	5	0
Total	5	0

LANDRY, Thomas Wade (Tom)

Position: DB-HB-QB
Height: 6'1"; Weight: 195
College: Texas
Born: September 11, 1924, Mission, TX
Deceased: February 12, 2000, Dallas, TX

STATISTICS

Games

	GP	GS
1949 New York Yankees	12	1
1950 New York Giants	10	0
1951 New York Giants	12	0
1952 New York Giants	12	0
1953 New York Giants	12	0
1954 New York Giants	12	0
1955 New York Giants	12	0
Total	82	1

Rushing

	Rush	Yds	TD
1949 New York Yankees	29	91	0
1952 New York Giants	7	40	1
Total	36	131	1

Receiving

	Rec	Yds	TD
1949 New York Yankees	6	109	0
Total	6	109	0

Passing

	Comp	Att	Yds	TD	Int
1952 N.Y. Giants	11	47	172	1	7
Total	11	47	172	1	7

Punting

	Punt	Yds	Blk
1949 New York Yankees	51	2249	2
1950 New York Giants	58	2136	1
1951 New York Giants	15	638	0
1952 New York Giants	82	3363	1
1953 New York Giants	44	1772	0
1954 New York Giants	64	2720	0
1955 New York Giants	75	3022	1
Total	389	15900	5

Punt Returns

	Ret	Yds	TD
1949 New York Yankees	3	52	0
1951 New York Giants	1	0	0
1952 New York Giants	10	88	0
1953 New York Giants	1	5	0
Total	15	145	0

LANDSBERG, Mortimer William, Jr. (Mort) (continued)

Kick Returns

	Ret	Yds	TD
1949 New York Yankees	2	39	0
1951 New York Giants	1	0	0
1952 New York Giants	1	20	0
1953 New York Giants	2	38	0
Total	6	97	0

Interceptions

	Int	Yds	TD
1949 New York Yankees	1	44	0
1950 New York Giants	2	0	0
1951 New York Giants	8	121	2
1952 New York Giants	8	99	1
1953 New York Giants	3	55	0
1954 New York Giants	8	71	0
1955 New York Giants	2	14	0
Total	32	404	3

Fumbles

	Fum	Rec	Yds	TD
1950 New York Giants	0	2	41	1
1951 New York Giants	0	1	9	1
1952 New York Giants	5	3	3	0
1953 New York Giants	1	1	0	0
1954 New York Giants	1	2	14	0
1955 New York Giants	0	1	0	0
Total	7	10	67	2

LANDSBERG, Mortimer William, Jr. (Mort)

Position: HB
Height: 5'11"; Weight: 180
College: Cornell
Born: July 25, 1919, New York, NY
Deceased: December 31, 1970, New York, NY

STATISTICS

Games

	GP	GS
1941 Philadelphia Eagles	11	7
1947 Los Angeles Dons	6	0
Total	17	7

Rushing

	Rush	Yds	TD
1941 Philadelphia Eagles	23	69	0
1947 Los Angeles Dons	2	-11	0
Total	25	58	0

Receiving

	Rec	Yds	TD
1941 Philadelphia Eagles	5	51	0
1947 Los Angeles Dons	1	0	0
Total	6	51	0

Punt Returns

	Ret	Yds	TD
1941 Philadelphia Eagles	2	15	0
Total	2	15	0

Kick Returns

	Ret	Yds	TD
1941 Philadelphia Eagles	2	49	0
Total	2	49	0

Interceptions

	Int	Yds	TD
1941 Philadelphia Eagles	2	45	0
Total	2	45	0

LANE, Clayton Harold

Position: T
Height: 6'0"; Weight: 215
College: New Hampshire
Born: November 23, 1922, Worcester, MA
Deceased: January 29, 2000, Wellsboro, NH

STATISTICS

Games

	GP	GS
1948 New York Yankees	1	0
Total	1	0

LAURINAITIS, Francis Ignatius

Position: LB
Height: 5'10"; Weight: 200
College: Richmond
Born: December 20, 1922, New Philadelphia, PA
Deceased: September 28, 2009, Wilkes-Bare, PA

STATISTICS

Games

	GP	GS
1947 Brooklyn Dodgers	8	0
Total	8	0

LAVELLI, Dante Bert Joseph

Position: E-DE
Height: 6'0"; Weight: 191
College: Ohio State
Born: February 23, 1923, Hudson, OH
Deceased: January 20, 2009, Westlake, OH

STATISTICS

Games

	GP	GS
1946 Cleveland Browns	14	8
1947 Cleveland Browns	13	6
1948 Cleveland Browns	8	7
1949 Cleveland Browns	9	7
1950 Cleveland Browns	12	0
1951 Cleveland Browns	12	0
1952 Cleveland Browns	8	0
1953 Cleveland Browns	12	0
1954 Cleveland Browns	12	0
1955 Cleveland Browns	12	0
1956 Cleveland Browns	11	0
Total	123	28

Rushing

	Rush	Yds	TD
1946 Cleveland Browns	1	14	0
1948 Cleveland Browns	1	9	0
Total	2	23	0

Receiving

	Rec	Yds	TD
1946 Cleveland Browns	40	843	8
1947 Cleveland Browns	49	799	9
1948 Cleveland Browns	25	463	5
1949 Cleveland Browns	28	475	7
1950 Cleveland Browns	37	565	5
1951 Cleveland Browns	43	586	6
1952 Cleveland Browns	21	336	4
1953 Cleveland Browns	45	783	6
1954 Cleveland Browns	47	802	7
1955 Cleveland Browns	31	492	4
1956 Cleveland Browns	20	344	1
Total	386	6488	62

Kick Returns

	Ret	Yds	TD
1947 Cleveland Browns	1	10	0
1948 Cleveland Browns	1	0	0
Total	2	10	0

Fumbles

	Fum	Rec	Yds	TD
1950 Cleveland Browns	2	0	0	0
1953 Cleveland Browns	1	1	0	0
1954 Cleveland Browns	0	1	0	0
1956 Cleveland Browns	1	0	0	0
Total	4	2	0	0

LAYDEN, John Peter, Jr. (Pete)

Position: B
Height: 5'11"; Weight: 192
College: Texas
Born: December 30, 1919, Dallas, TX
Deceased: July 18, 1982, Edna, TX

STATISTICS

Games

	GP	GS
1948 New York Yankees	9	4
1949 New York Yankees	12	0
1950 New York Yanks	10	0
Total	31	4

Rushing

	Rush	Yds	TD
1948 New York Yankees	95	576	3
1949 New York Yankees	19	96	0
Total	114	672	3

Receiving

	Rec	Yds	TD
1949 New York Yankees	1	0	0
Total	1	0	0

Passing

	Comp	Att	Yds	TD	Int
1948 Yankees	43	105	816	9	8
1949 Yankees	2	10	25	0	1
Total	45	115	841	9	9

Punting

	Punt	Yds	Blk
1948 New York Yankees	21	884	0
1949 New York Yankees	15	626	0
Total	36	1510	0

Punt Returns

	Ret	Yds	TD
1948 New York Yankees	7	64	0
1949 New York Yankees	29	287	0
Total	36	351	0

Kick Returns

	Ret	Yds	TD
1948 New York Yankees	8	211	0
1949 New York Yankees	1	28	0
Total	9	239	0

Interceptions

	Int	Yds	TD
1948 New York Yankees	3	63	0
1949 New York Yankees	7	137	1
1950 New York Yanks	3	40	0
Total	13	240	1

Point After Touchdown

	XPM	XPA
1950 New York Yanks	3	3
Total	3	3

LECTURE, James Wayne, Jr. (Jim)

Position: G
Height: 5'10"; Weight: 220
College: Northwestern, Washington (MO)
Born: October 29, 1924, Chicago, IL
Deceased: December 19, 1999, Cambridge, WI

STATISTICS

Games

	GP	GS
1946 Buffalo Bills	1	0
Total	1	0

LEICHT, Jacob (Jake)

Position: HB-DB
Height: 5'9"; Weight: 170
College: Oregon
Born: October 1, 1920, Jamestown, ND
Deceased: May 18, 1992, Medford, OR

STATISTICS

Games

	GP	GS
1948 Baltimore Colts	14	1
1949 Baltimore Colts	12	6
Total	**26**	**7**

Rushing

	Rush	Yds	TD
1948 Baltimore Colts	20	88	1
1949 Baltimore Colts	6	−7	0
Total	**26**	**81**	**1**

Receiving

	Rec	Yds	TD
1948 Baltimore Colts	12	134	1
1949 Baltimore Colts	1	12	0
Total	**13**	**146**	**1**

Punt Returns

	Ret	Yds	TD
1948 Baltimore Colts	8	139	0
1949 Baltimore Colts	9	109	0
Total	**17**	**248**	**0**

Kick Returns

	Ret	Yds	TD
1948 Baltimore Colts	4	83	0
1949 Baltimore Colts	8	171	0
Total	**12**	**254**	**0**

Interceptions

	Int	Yds	TD
1948 Baltimore Colts	5	91	0
Total	**5**	**91**	**0**

LENNON, Reid

Position: G
Height: 6'0"; Weight: 235
College: None
Born: August 17, 1920, Baltimore, MD
Deceased: February 10, 1979, Los Angeles County, CA

STATISTICS

Games

	GP	GS
1945 Washington Redskins	10	0
1947 Los Angeles Dons	7	2
Total	**17**	**2**

LEONARD, William George, Jr. (Bill)

Position: DE
Height: 6'2"; Weight: 200
College: Notre Dame
Born: April 27, 1927, Youngstown, OH
Deceased: July 20, 2006, Youngstown, OH

STATISTICS

Games

	GP	GS
1949 Baltimore Colts	11	2
Total	**11**	**2**

Kick Returns

	Ret	Yds	TD
1949 Baltimore Colts	1	25	0
Total	**1**	**25**	**0**

Interceptions

	Int	Yds	TD
1949 Baltimore Colts	1	7	0
Total	**1**	**7**	**0**

LEONETTI, Robert Phillip (Bob)

Position: G
Height: 6'0"; Weight: 230
College: Wake Forest
Born: January 1, 1923, Mount Carmel, PA
Deceased: August 16, 1973, Des Moines, IA

STATISTICS

Games

	GP	GS
1948 Brooklyn Dodgers	9	0
1948 Buffalo Bills	2	0
Total	**11**	**0**

LEVY, Leonard Bernard (Len)

Position: G
Height: 6'0"; Weight: 256
College: Minnesota
Born: February 19, 1921, Minneapolis, MN
Deceased: February 9, 1999, Minneapolis, MN

STATISTICS

Games

	GP	GS
1945 Cleveland Rams	7	1
1946 Los Angeles Rams	10	2
1947 Los Angeles Dons	11	8
1948 Los Angeles Dons	14	14
Total	**42**	**25**

LEWIS, Clifford Allen (Cliff)

Position: DB-QB
Height: 5'11"; Weight: 167
College: Duke
Born: March 22, 1923, Lakewood, OH
Deceased: July 25, 2002, Tampa, FL

STATISTICS

Games

	GP	GS
1946 Cleveland Browns	10	2
1947 Cleveland Browns	13	5
1948 Cleveland Browns	14	0
1949 Cleveland Browns	11	1
1950 Cleveland Browns	11	0
1951 Cleveland Browns	12	0
Total	71	8

Rushing

	Rush	Yds	TD
1946 Cleveland Browns	24	−34	0
1947 Cleveland Browns	11	66	0
1948 Cleveland Browns	5	44	0
1949 Cleveland Browns	9	−17	1
1950 Cleveland Browns	2	−1	0
1951 Cleveland Browns	3	−10	0
Total	54	48	1

Passing

	Comp	Att	Yds	TD	Int
1946 Cle. Browns	11	30	125	1	1
1947 Cle. Browns	5	11	70	1	1
1948 Cle. Browns	4	8	69	1	0
1949 Cle. Browns	5	10	144	2	2
1950 Cle. Browns	1	4	38	1	0
1951 Cle. Browns	4	6	68	1	1
Total	30	69	514	7	5

Punting

	Punt	Yds	Blk
1948 Cleveland Browns	1	18	0
Total	1	18	0

Punt Returns

	Ret	Yds	TD
1946 Cleveland Browns	8	133	0
1947 Cleveland Browns	7	84	0
1948 Cleveland Browns	26	258	0
1949 Cleveland Browns	20	174	0
1950 Cleveland Browns	2	13	0
1951 Cleveland Browns	14	48	0
Total	77	710	0

Kick Returns

	Ret	Yds	TD
1946 Cleveland Browns	3	70	0
1947 Cleveland Browns	4	71	0
1948 Cleveland Browns	7	147	0
Total	14	288	0

Interceptions

	Int	Yds	TD
1946 Cleveland Browns	5	41	0
1947 Cleveland Browns	4	19	0
1948 Cleveland Browns	9	103	0
1949 Cleveland Browns	6	53	0
1950 Cleveland Browns	1	4	0
1951 Cleveland Browns	5	46	0
Total	30	266	0

Fumbles

	Fum	Rec	Yds	TD
1951 Cleveland Browns	3	2	0	0
Total	3	2	0	0

LEWIS, Ernest Clayton (Ernie)

Position: FB-LB
Height: 6'1"; Weight: 211
College: Colorado
Born: November 20, 1923, Boonville, MO
Deceased: May 28, 1995, Denver, CO

STATISTICS

Games

	GP	GS
1946 Chicago Rockets	12	9
1947 Chicago Rockets	14	0
1948 Chicago Rockets	14	1
1949 Chicago Hornets	6	5
Total	46	15

Rushing

	Rush	Yds	TD
1946 Chicago Rockets	57	164	1
1947 Chicago Rockets	13	47	0
1948 Chicago Rockets	13	54	0
1949 Chicago Hornets	11	43	1
Total	94	308	2

Receiving

	Rec	Yds	TD
1946 Chicago Rockets	2	26	0
1948 Chicago Rockets	1	6	0
Total	3	32	0

Passing

	Comp	Att	Yds	TD	Int
1946 Chicago Rockets	4	8	17	0	1
Total	4	8	17	0	1

Punting

	Punt	Yds	Blk
1946 Chicago Rockets	50	2085	1
1947 Chicago Rockets	65	2549	4
1948 Chicago Rockets	60	2680	0
1949 Chicago Hornets	16	680	1
Total	191	7994	6

Kick Returns

	Ret	Yds	TD
1946 Chicago Rockets	2	22	0
Total	2	22	0

Interceptions

	Int	Yds	TD
1946 Chicago Rockets	1	10	0
Total	1	10	0

LILLYWHITE, Verl Thomas

Position: HB-LB
Height: 5'10"; Weight: 185
College: USC
Born: December 5, 1926, Garland, UT
Deceased: July 14, 2007, Mesa, AZ

STATISTICS

Games

	GP	GS
1948 San Francisco 49ers	14	1
1949 San Francisco 49ers	12	3
1950 San Francisco 49ers	9	0
1951 San Francisco 49ers	12	0
Total	47	4

Rushing

	Rush	Yds	TD
1948 S.F. 49ers	53	340	3
1949 S.F. 49ers	69	263	2
1950 S.F. 49ers	7	4	0
1951 S.F. 49ers	67	397	1
Total	196	1004	6

Receiving

	Rec	Yds	TD
1948 S.F. 49ers	1	−1	0
1949 S.F. 49ers	8	82	2
1950 S.F. 49ers	1	6	0
1951 S.F. 49ers	11	125	0
Total	21	212	3

Passing

	Comp	Att	Yds	TD	Int
1948 S.F. 49ers	0	1	0	0	1
Total	0	1	0	0	1

Punting

	Punt	Yds	Blk
1948 S.F. 49ers	3	76	0
1949 S.F. 49ers	4	202	0
1950 S.F. 49ers	26	1016	0
1951 S.F. 49ers	20	847	0
Total	53	2141	75

Punt Returns

	Ret	Yds	TD
1948 S.F. 49ers	3	41	0
Total	3	41	0

Kick Returns

	Ret	Yds	TD
1949 S.F. 49ers	1	16	0
1950 S.F. 49ers	2	36	0
Total	3	52	0

Interceptions

	Int	Yds	TD
1948 S.F. 49ers	3	26	0
1949 S.F. 49ers	1	9	0
1950 S.F. 49ers	1	11	0
1951 S.F. 49ers	3	47	0
Total	8	93	0

Fumbles

	Fum	Rec	Yds	TD
1950 S.F. 49ers	1	0	0	0
1951 S.F. 49ers	3	0	0	0
Total	4	0	0	0

LIO, Agostino Salvatore (Augie)

Position: G-T
Height: 6'0"; Weight: 234
College: Georgetown
Born: April 30, 1918, East Boston, MA
Deceased: September 3, 1989, Clifton, NJ

STATISTICS

Games

	GP	GS
1941 Detroit Lions	11	7
1942 Detroit Lions	10	8
1943 Detroit Lions	10	9
1944 Boston Yanks	10	10
1945 Boston Yanks	10	10
1946 Philadelphia Eagles	11	5
1947 Baltimore Colts	10	9
Total	72	58

Rushing

	Rush	Yds	TD
1941 Detroit Lions	1	−4	0
Total	1	−4	0

Punting

	Punt	Yds	Blk
1941 Detroit Lions	1	28	0
Total	1	28	0

Kick Returns

	Ret	Yds	TD
1941 Detroit Lions	1	7	0
1942 Detroit Lions	1	4	0
Total	2	11	0

Interceptions

	Int	Yds	TD
1941 Detroit Lions	3	12	0
1942 Detroit Lions	1	9	0
1943 Detroit Lions	1	−2	0
1944 Boston Yanks	2	13	0
1945 Boston Yanks	3	42	0
Total	10	74	0

Fumbles

	Fum	Rec	Yds	TD
1945 Boston Yanks	0	2	0	0
1946 Philadelphia Eagles	0	3	0	0
Total	0	5	0	0

Field Goals

	FGM	FGA
1941 Detroit Lions	*	5
1942 Detroit Lions	*	4
1943 Detroit Lions	2	11
1944 Boston Yanks	2	8

	FGM	FGA
1945 Boston Yanks	4	5
1946 Philadelphia Eagles	6	11
1947 Baltimore Colts	3	8
Total	17	52

Point After Touchdown

	XPM	XPA
1941 Detroit Lions	12	13
1942 Detroit Lions	5	5
1943 Detroit Lions	21	23
1944 Boston Yanks	10	11
1945 Boston Yanks	15	16
1946 Philadelphia Eagles	27	27
1947 Baltimore Colts	19	20
Total	109	115

LIVINGSTONE, Robert Edward (Bob)

Position: HB-DB
Height: 6'0"; Weight: 173
College: Notre Dame
Born: May 11, 1922, Hammond, IN
Deceased: August 1, 2013, Munster, IN

Statistics

Games

	GP	GS
1948 Chicago Rockets	13	5
1949 Chicago Hornets	6	0
1949 Buffalo Bills	5	0
1950 Baltimore Colts	11	0
Total	35	5

Rushing

	Rush	Yds	TD
1948 Chicago Rockets	55	174	0
1949 Buffalo Bills	1	0	0
1950 Baltimore Colts	1	-3	0
Total	57	171	0

Receiving

	Rec	Yds	TD
1948 Chicago Rockets	15	240	2
1949 Chicago Hornets	3	80	0
Total	18	320	2

Punt Returns

	Ret	Yds	TD
1948 Chicago Rockets	3	24	0
1949 Chicago Hornets	7	121	0
1949 Buffalo Bills	10	171	1
1950 Baltimore Colts	3	33	0
Total	23	349	1

Kick Returns

	Ret	Yds	TD
1948 Chicago Rockets	9	211	0
1949 Chicago Hornets	4	50	0
1949 Buffalo Bills	2	35	0
1950 Baltimore Colts	1	11	0
Total	16	307	0

Interceptions

	Int	Yds	TD
1949 Buffalo Bills	1	6	0
1950 Baltimore Colts	3	61	0
Total			

Fumbles

	Fum	Rec	Yds	TD
1950 Baltimore Colts	1	1	5	0
Total	1	1	5	0

LOGEL, Robert James (Bob)

Position: E
Height: 6'3"; Weight: 210
College: (None)
Born: July 29, 1928, East Aurora, NY
Deceased: July 4, 2001, Holland, NY

Statistics

Games

	GP	GS
1949 Buffalo Bills	1	0
Total	1	0

LOLOTAI, Albert (Al)

Position: G
Height: 6'0"; Weight: 224
College: Weber Junior College
Born: June 22, 1920
Deceased: September 30, 1990, Pago Pago, American Samoa

Statistics

Games

	GP	GS
1945 Washington Redskins	10	8
1946 Los Angeles Dons	14	12
1947 Los Angeles Dons	13	6
1948 Los Angeles Dons	14	0
1949 Los Angeles Dons	8	6
Total	59	32

Kick Returns

	Ret	Yds	TD
1945 Wash. Redskins	1	15	0
Total	1	15	0

Interceptions

	Int	Yds	TD
1945 Wash. Redskins	1	0	0
Total	1	0	0

LUKENS, James Willie, Jr. (Jim)

Position: E
Height: 6'4"; Weight: 205
College: Washington & Lee
Born: September 6, 1924, Chester, PA
Deceased: October 21, 2002, Wernersville, VA

STATISTICS

Games

	GP	GS
1949 Buffalo Bills	11	10
Total	11	10

Receiving

	Rec	Yds	TD
1949 Buffalo Bills	24	249	2
Total	24	249	2

LUND, William Harold (Bill)

Position: HB
Height: 5'10"; Weight: 180
College: Case Western Reserve
Born: October 27, 1924, Akron, OH
Deceased: September 27, 2008, Chagrin Falls, OH

STATISTICS

Games

	GP	GS
1946 Cleveland Browns	10	2
1947 Cleveland Browns	8	0
Total	18	2

Rushing

	Rush	Yds	TD
1946 Cleveland Browns	23	72	1
1947 Cleveland Browns	14	105	1
Total	37	197	2

Receiving

	Rec	Yds	TD
1946 Cleveland Browns	4	64	2
1947 Cleveland Browns	6	110	1
Total	10	174	3

Punt Returns

	Ret	Yds	TD
1946 Cleveland Browns	2	30	0
Total	2	30	0

Kick Returns

	Ret	Yds	TD
1946 Cleveland Browns	1	32	0
1947 Cleveland Browns	2	37	0
Total	3	69	0

Interceptions

	Int	Yds	TD
1946 Cleveland Browns	1	12	0
1947 Cleveland Browns	2	36	1
Total	3	48	1

MACEAU, Melvin Anthony (Mel)

Position: C
Height: 6'0"; Weight: 203
College: Marquette
Born: December 25, 1921, Milwaukee, WI
Deceased: February 1981, Bowling Green, OH

STATISTICS

Games

	GP	GS
1946 Cleveland Browns	12	0
1947 Cleveland Browns	14	0
1948 Cleveland Browns	11	0
Total	37	0

MADAR, Elmer F.

Position: E
Height: 5'11"; Weight: 185
College: Michigan
Born: November 28, 1920, Sykesville, PA
Deceased: February 9, 1972, Detroit, MI

STATISTICS

Games

	GP	GS
1947 Baltimore Colts	9	6
Total	9	6

Receiving

	Rec	Yds	TD
1947 Baltimore Colts	8	53	0
Total	8	53	0

Kick Returns

	Ret	Yds	TD
1947 Baltimore Colts	1	14	0
Total	1	14	0

MAGGIOLI, Achille Fred (Chick)

Position: DB-HB
Height: 5'11"; Weight: 178
College: Illinois, Indiana, Notre Dame
Born: May 17, 1922, Mishawaka, IN
Deceased:

STATISTICS

Games

	GP	GS
1948 Buffalo Bills	7	0
1949 Detroit Lions	12	0
1950 Baltimore Colts	8	0
Total	27	0

Rushing

	Rush	Yds	TD
1948 Buffalo Bills	11	27	0
Total	11	27	0

Receiving

	Rec	Yds	TD
1948 Buffalo Bills	3	23	0
1949 Detroit Lions	1	9	0
Total	4	32	0

Passing

	Comp	Att	Yds	TD	Int
1948 Buffalo Bills	1	1	0	0	0
Total	**1**	**1**	**0**	**0**	**0**

Punting

	Punt	Yds	Blk
1948 Buffalo Bills	2	95	0
Total	**2**	**95**	**0**

Punt Returns

	Ret	Yds	TD
1948 Buffalo Bills	1	0	0
Total	**1**	**0**	**0**

Kick Returns

	Ret	Yds	TD
1948 Buffalo Bills	2	38	0
Total	**2**	**38**	**0**

Interceptions

	Int	Yds	TD
1948 Buffalo Bills	1	7	0
1949 Detroit Lions	3	46	0
1950 Baltimore Colts	8	165	0
Total	**12**	**218**	**0**

Fumbles

	Fum	Rec	Yds	TD
1949 Detroit Lions	0	4	8	1
Total	**0**	**4**	**8**	**1**

MAGLIOLO, Joseph S., Jr. (Joe)

Position: LB
Height: 6'0"; Weight: 210
College: Texas
Born: October 17, 1922, Galveston, TX
Deceased: July 31, 2008, Houston, TX

STATISTICS

Games

	GP	GS
1948 New York Yankees	13	0
Total	**13**	**0**

Interceptions

	Int	Yds	TD
1948 New York Yankees	1	12	0
Total	**1**	**12**	**0**

MALONEY, Norman Edward (Ned)

Position: E
Height: 6'1"; Weight: 190
College: Purdue
Born: April 21, 1923, Chicago, IL
Deceased: October 7, 2011, West Lafayette, IN

STATISTICS

Games

	GP	GS
1948 San Francisco 49ers	14	1
1949 San Francisco 49ers	12	0
Total	**26**	**1**

Receiving

	Rec	Yds	TD
1948 S.F. 49ers	1	29	1
Total	**1**	**29**	**1**

Punt Returns

	Ret	Yds	TD
1949 S.F. 49ers	1	5	0
Total	**1**	**5**	**0**

Point After Touchdown

	XPM	XPA
1948 S.F. 49ers	1	1
Total	**1**	**1**

MANDERS, Clarence Edward (Pug)

Position: FB-HB
Height: 6'0"; Weight: 200
College: Drake
Born: May 5, 1913, Milbank, SD
Deceased: January 20, 1985, Des Moines, IA

STATISTICS

Games

	GP	GS
1939 Brooklyn Dodgers	11	9
1940 Brooklyn Dodgers	11	11
1941 Brooklyn Dodgers	11	11
1942 Brooklyn Dodgers	11	11
1943 Brooklyn Dodgers	10	9
1944 Brooklyn Dodgers	10	9
1945 Boston Yanks	10	10
1946 New York Yankees	13	4
1947 Buffalo Bills	3	0
Total	**90**	**74**

Rushing

	Rush	Yds	TD
1939 Brooklyn Dodgers	114	482	2
1940 Brooklyn Dodgers	80	311	5
1941 Brooklyn Dodgers	111	486	5
1942 Brooklyn Dodgers	93	316	6
1943 Brooklyn Dodgers	89	266	3
1944 Brooklyn Dodgers	127	430	5
1945 Boston Yanks	76	238	6
1946 New York Yankees	49	168	3
1947 Buffalo Bills	3	15	0
Total	**742**	**2712**	**35**

Receiving

	Rec	Yds	TD
1939 Brooklyn Dodgers	3	22	0
1940 Brooklyn Dodgers	1	38	1
1941 Brooklyn Dodgers	6	67	0

Part 8: Player Register

	Rec	Yds	TD	
1942 Brooklyn Dodgers	4	53	0	
1943 Brooklyn Dodgers	5	68	1	
1944 Brooklyn Dodgers	6	78	0	
1946 New York Yankees	3	49	0	
Total	28	375	2	

Passing

	Comp	Att	Yds	TD	Int
1940 Dodgers	0	1	0	0	0
1942 Dodgers	0	1	0	0	0
1943 Dodgers	4	5	31	1	0
1944 Dodgers	9	34	96	0	4
1945 Bos. Yanks	5	9	42	0	1
1946 Yankees	2	3	14	0	0
Total	20	53	183	1	5

Kick Returns

	Ret	Yds	TD
1941 Brooklyn Dodgers	7	128	0
1942 Brooklyn Dodgers	9	210	0
1943 Brooklyn Dodgers	1	19	0
1944 Brooklyn Dodgers	11	227	0
1945 Boston Yanks	2	10	0
1946 New York Yankees	1	26	0
Total	31	620	0

Interceptions

	Int	Yds	TD
1940 Brooklyn Dodgers	1	15	0
1941 Brooklyn Dodgers	4	73	1
1942 Brooklyn Dodgers	2	23	0
1944 Brooklyn Dodgers	1	4	0
1946 New York Yankees	3	5	0
Total	11	120	1

Fumbles

	Fum	Rec	Yds	TD
1945 Boston Yanks	6	4	−12	0
Total	6	4	−12	0

Field Goals

	FGM	FGA
1944 Brooklyn Dodgers	*	1
Total	*	1

MARCOLINI, Hugo Francis

Position: B
Height: 6'0"; Weight: 204
College: St. Bonaventure
Born: April 7, 1923, Brooklyn, NY
Deceased: September 22, 1963, Saddle River, NJ

STATISTICS

Games

	GP	GS
1948 Brooklyn Dodgers	10	0
Total	10	0

Rushing

	Rush	Yds	TD
1948 Brooklyn Dodgers	5	11	0
Total	5	11	0

Receiving

	Rec	Yds	TD
1948 Brooklyn Dodgers	2	38	0
Total	2	38	0

Kick Returns

	Ret	Yds	TD
1948 Brooklyn Dodgers	2	33	0
Total	2	33	0

MAREFOS, Andrew Gust (Andy)

Position: FB-HB
Height: 6'0"; Weight: 223
College: St. Mary's
Born: July 16, 1917, San Francisco, CA
Deceased: February 18, 1996, Marysville, CA

STATISTICS

Games

	GP	GS
1941 New York Giants	10	0
1942 New York Giants	11	4
1946 Los Angeles Dons	13	4
Total	34	8

Rushing

	Rush	Yds	TD
1941 New York Giants	60	153	2
1942 New York Giants	48	138	1
1946 Los Angeles Dons	30	93	4
Total	138	384	7

Receiving

	Rec	Yds	TD
1941 New York Giants	1	5	0
1946 Los Angeles Dons	1	13	0
Total	2	18	0

Passing

	Comp	Att	Yds	TD	Int
1941 N.Y. Giants	2	8	69	1	1
1942 N.Y. Giants	11	29	176	1	5
Total	13	37	245	2	6

Interceptions

	Int	Yds	TD
1941 New York Giants	2	48	0
1942 New York Giants	1	11	0
Total	3	59	0

Field Goals

	FGM	FGA
1941 New York Giants	4	5
1942 New York Giants	*	2
Total	4	7

Point After Touchdown

	XPM	XPA
1941 New York Giants	6	6
1946 Los Angeles Dons	2	2
Total	8	8

MARINO, Victor Irving (Vic)

Position: G
Height: 5'8"; Weight: 205
College: Ohio State
Born: October 2, 1918, Columbus, OH
Deceased: January 7, 2006, Worthington, OH

STATISTICS

Games		
	GP	GS
1947 Baltimore Colts	13	4
Total	13	4

MARTINELLI, Pasquale Joseph (Patsy)

Position: C
Height: 6'0"; Weight: 227
College: Scranton
Born: July 27, 1919
Deceased: September 7, 1992, Rockville, MD

STATISTICS

Games		
	GP	GS
1946 Buffalo Bisons	3	0
Total	3	0

MARTINOVICH, Philip Joseph (Phil)

Position: FB-G
Height: 5'10"; Weight: 220
College: Pacific
Born: February 9, 1915, Diamond Springs, CA
Deceased: September 22, 1964, West Sacramento, CA

STATISTICS

Games		
	GP	GS
1939 Detroit Lions	4	0
1940 Chicago Bears	2	0
1946 Brooklyn Dodgers	10	6
1947 Brooklyn Dodgers	14	5
Total	30	11

Field Goals		
	FGM	FGA
1939 Detroit Lions	3	6
1940 Chicago Bears	2	2
1946 Brooklyn Dodgers	5	10
1947 Brooklyn Dodgers	3	20
Total	13	38

Point After Touchdown		
	XPM	XPA
1946 Brooklyn Dodgers	21	22
1947 Brooklyn Dodgers	22	25
Total	43	47

MASINI, Leonard Leroy (Len)

Position: BB-FB-LB
Height: 6'0"; Weight: 225
College: Fresno State
Born: October 6, 1922, Firebaugh, CA
Deceased: September 27, 2000, Santa Cruz, CA

STATISTICS

Games		
	GP	GS
1947 San Francisco 49ers	11	0
1948 San Francisco 49ers	2	0
1949 Los Angeles Dons	11	5
Total	24	5

Rushing			
	Rush	Yds	TD
1947 S.F. 49ers	38	167	2
1948 S.F. 49ers	3	12	0
Total	41	179	2

Receiving			
	Rec	Yds	TD
1948 Los Angeles Dons	1	−1	0
Total	1	−1	0

Interceptions			
	Int	Yds	TD
1947 S.F. 49ers	1	0	0
Total	1	0	0

MASKAS, John J.

Position: G-T
Height: 5'11"; Weight: 212
College: Virginia Tech
Born: August 15, 1920, Chios, Greece
Deceased: February 9, 1983, Manahawkin, NJ

STATISTICS

Games		
	GP	GS
1947 Buffalo Bills	7	0
1949 Buffalo Bills	11	0
Total	18	0

MASTERSON, Robert Patrick (Bob)

Position: E
Height: 6'1"; Weight: 213
College: Miami
Born: January 5, 1915, North Branch, NJ
Deceased: June 29, 1994, Broward County, FL

STATISTICS

Games		
	GP	GS
1938 Washington Redskins	11	1
1939 Washington Redskins	10	3

	GP	GS
1940 Washington Redskins	11	1
1941 Washington Redskins	11	9
1942 Washington Redskins	11	11
1943 Washington Redskins	10	8
1944 Brooklyn Dodgers	10	9
1945 Boston Yanks	10	5
1946 New York Yankees	14	8
Total		

Rushing

	Rush	Yds	TD
1938 Wash. Redskins	3	89	0
1940 Wash. Redskins	1	0	0
1941 Wash. Redskins	1	3	0
1942 Wash. Redskins	3	12	0
Total	8	104	0

Receiving

	Rec	Yds	TD
1938 Wash. Redskins	10	213	1
1939 Wash. Redskins	10	114	1
1940 Wash. Redskins	18	283	4
1941 Wash. Redskins	11	135	1
1942 Wash. Redskins	22	308	2
1943 Wash. Redskins	16	200	3
1944 Brooklyn Dodgers	24	258	1
1945 Boston Yanks	15	186	0
1946 New York Yankees	10	119	0
Total	136	1816	13

Passing

	Comp	Att	Yds	TD	Int
1942 Redskins	0	1	0	0	0
1944 Dodgers	1	1	1	0	0
Total	1	2	1	0	0

Punting

	Punt	Yds	Blk
1944 Brooklyn Dodgers	4	136	0
Total	4	136	0

Kick Returns

	Ret	Yds	TD
1941 Wash. Redskins	2	20	0
1942 Wash. Redskins	3	45	0
1943 Wash. Redskins	2	66	0
1946 New York Yankees	5	55	0
Total	12	186	0

Interceptions

	Int	Yds	TD
1941 Wash. Redskins	1	0	0
1946 New York Yankees	1	0	0
Total	2	0	0

Field Goals

	FGM	FGA
1938 Wash. Redskins	1	1
1939 Wash. Redskins	1	6
1940 Wash. Redskins	1	2
1941 Wash. Redskins	3	6
1942 Wash. Redskins	1	5
1943 Wash. Redskins	1	5
1944 Brooklyn Dodgers	*	5
1945 Boston Yanks	*	1
1946 New York Yankees	*	1
Total	8	32

Point After Touchdown

	XPM	XPA
1938 Wash. Redskins	5	6
1939 Wash. Redskins	6	8
1940 Wash. Redskins	15	16
1941 Wash. Redskins	8	8
1942 Wash. Redskins	17	19
1943 Wash. Redskins	20	21
Total	71	78

MASTRANGELO, John Battista

Position: T-G
Height: 6'1"; Weight: 228
College: Notre Dame
Born: March 10, 1926, Vandergrift, PA
Deceased: October 2, 1987, Vandergriff, PA

STATISTICS

Games

	GP	GS
1947 Pittsburgh Steelers	11	5
1948 Pittsburgh Steelers	12	7
1949 New York Yankees	12	0
1950 New York Giants	9	0
Total	44	12

Fumbles

	Fum	Rec	Yds	TD
1947 Pittsburgh Steelers	0	2	0	0
Total	0	2	0	0

MATHESON, Riley

Position: G
Height: 6'2"; Weight: 207
College: Cameron, Texas-El Paso
Born: December 12, 1914, Shannon, TX
Deceased: June 1987, Paraguay

STATISTICS

Games

	GP	GS
1939 Cleveland Rams	2	2
1940 Cleveland Rams	11	0
1941 Cleveland Rams	9	6
1942 Cleveland Rams	10	8
1943 Detroit Lions	10	9
1944 Cleveland Rams	9	8
1945 Cleveland Rams	10	9
1946 Los Angeles Rams	11	7
1947 Los Angeles Rams	11	9
1948 San Francisco 49ers	14	0
Total	97	58

Punt Returns

	Ret	Yds	TD
1945 Cleveland Rams	1	5	0
Total	1	5	0

Interceptions

	Int	Yds	TD
1941 Cleveland Rams	1	1	0
1942 Cleveland Rams	1	13	0
1944 Cleveland Rams	3	12	0
1945 Cleveland Rams	2	49	0
1946 Los Angeles Rams	4	21	0
1947 Los Angeles Rams	1	5	0
1948 S.F. 49ers	2	4	0
Total	14	105	0

Fumbles

	Fum	Rec	Yds	TD
1945 Cleveland Rams	0	1	0	0
1946 Los Angeles Rams	0	1	0	0
1947 Los Angeles Rams	0	1	0	0
Total	0	3	0	0

MATHEWS, Ned Alfred

Position: WB-HB
Height: 5'10"; Weight: 187
College: UCLA
Born: August 11, 1918, Provo, UT
Deceased: September 18, 2002, Los Angeles, CA

STATISTICS

Games

	GP	GS
1941 Detroit Lions	9	1
1942 Detroit Lions	9	6
1943 Detroit Lions	10	4
1945 Boston Yanks	9	0
1946 Chicago Rockets	8	2
1946 San Francisco 49ers	6	1
1947 San Francisco 49ers	12	0
Total	63	14

Rushing

	Rush	Yds	TD
1941 Detroit Lions	31	56	0
1942 Detroit Lions	21	79	0
1943 Detroit Lions	38	124	1
1945 Boston Yanks	27	146	0
1946 Chicago Rockets	18	94	0
1946 S.F. 49ers	12	15	1
1947 S.F. 49ers	39	238	2
Total	186	752	4

Receiving

	Rec	Yds	TD
1941 Detroit Lions	6	56	0
1942 Detroit Lions	3	38	0
1943 Detroit Lions	9	193	1
1945 Boston Yanks	4	56	1
1946 Chicago Rockets	6	100	0
1947 S.F. 49ers	6	51	2
Total	34	494	6

Passing

	Comp	Att	Yds	TD	Int
1941 Detroit Lions	3	8	59	1	0
1942 Detroit Lions	6	22	53	1	2
1943 Detroit Lions	4	12	76	1	0
1945 Boston Yanks	0	1	0	0	0
1946 S.F. 49ers	1	1	26	0	0
1947 S.F. 49ers	0	2	0	0	0
Total	14	46	214	3	2

Punting

	Punt	Yds	Blk
1941 Detroit Lions	1	26	0
Total	1	26	0

Punt Returns

	Ret	Yds	TD
1941 Detroit Lions	1	3	0
1942 Detroit Lions	7	82	0
1943 Detroit Lions	4	37	0
1947 S.F. 49ers	4	44	0
Total	16	166	0

Kick Returns

	Ret	Yds	TD
1941 Detroit Lions	9	233	0
1942 Detroit Lions	5	97	0
1943 Detroit Lions	7	246	1
1945 Boston Yanks	4	108	0
1946 Chicago Rockets	5	110	0
1946 S.F. 49ers	1	8	0
1947 S.F. 49ers	2	46	0
Total	33	848	1

Interceptions

	Int	Yds	TD
1941 Detroit Lions	5	128	1
1943 Detroit Lions	4	44	0
1945 Boston Yanks	3	42	0
1946 Chicago Rockets	2	8	0
1947 S.F. 49ers	4	149	1
Total	18	371	2

Fumbles

	Fum	Rec	Yds	TD
1945 Boston Yanks	3	2	0	0
Total	3	2	0	0

MATISI, John Bernard

Position: T
Height: 6'2"; Weight: 221
College: Duquesne
Born: November 2, 1920, New York, NY
Deceased: April 29, 1997, Youngstown, OH

STATISTICS

Games

	GP	GS
1943 Brooklyn Dodgers	4	1
1946 Buffalo Bisons	12	0
Total	16	1

Interceptions

	Int	Yds	TD
1943 Brooklyn Dodgers	1	13	0
Total	1	13	0

MATTINGLY, Francis Edward (Fran)

Position: G-LB
Height: 5'11"; Weight: 212
College: exas A&M, Texas A&M-Kingsville
Born: December 4, 1919
Deceased: September 1988, Sand Springs, OK

STATISTICS

Games
	GP	GS
1947 Chicago Rockets	1	0
Total	1	0

Interceptions
	Int	Yds	TD
1947 Chicago Rockets	1	1	0
Total	1	1	0

MAYNE, Lewis Elwood (Lew)

Position: HB
Height: 6'1"; Weight: 190
College: Texas
Born: March 21, 1920, Cuero, TX
Deceased: October 26, 2013, Daingerfield, TX

STATISTICS

Games
	GP	GS
1946 Brooklyn Dodgers	13	2
1947 Cleveland Browns	13	4
1948 Baltimore Colts	8	0
Total	34	6

Rushing
	Rush	Yds	TD
1946 Brooklyn Dodgers	70	191	1
1947 Cleveland Browns	41	75	0
1948 Baltimore Colts	14	26	0
Total	125	292	1

Receiving
	Rec	Yds	TD
1946 Brooklyn Dodgers	5	9	0
1947 Cleveland Browns	6	238	3
1948 Baltimore Colts	2	33	0
Total	13	280	3

Passing
	Comp	Att	Yds	TD	Int
1946 Dodgers	14	25	219	3	4
Total	14	25	219	3	4

Punting
	Punt	Yds	Blk
1946 Baltimore Colts	3	79	0
Total	3	79	0

Punt Returns
	Ret	Yds	TD
1946 Brooklyn Dodgers	6	47	0
1948 Baltimore Colts	2	24	0
Total	8	71	0

Kick Returns
	Ret	Yds	TD
1946 Brooklyn Dodgers	4	90	0
1947 Cleveland Browns	5	102	0
1948 Baltimore Colts	3	61	0
Total	12	253	0

MAZZA, Vincent L. (Vince)

Position: E
Height: 6'1"; Weight: 216
College: (None)
Born: March 25, 1925, Niagara Falls, NY
Deceased: December 5, 1993, Winona, Canada

STATISTICS

Games
	GP	GS
1945 Detroit Lions	5	1
1946 Detroit Lions	1	0
1947 Buffalo Bills	13	2
1948 Buffalo Bills	14	1
1949 Buffalo Bills	12	0
Total	45	4

Receiving
	Rec	Yds	TD
1947 Buffalo Bills	2	11	0
Total	2	11	0

Interceptions
	Int	Yds	TD
1947 Buffalo Bills	1	26	0
Total	1	26	0

MCCAIN, Robert Floyd (Bob)

Position: E
Height: 5'11"; Weight: 195
College: Mississippi
Born: August 15, 1922, Stewart, MS
Deceased: September 30, 2001, Pasadena, TX

STATISTICS

Games
	GP	GS
1946 Brooklyn Dodgers	11	0
Total	11	0

Receiving
	Rec	Yds	TD
1946 Brooklyn Dodgers	3	27	0
Total	3	27	0

MCCARTHY, James Patrick (Jim)

Position: E
Height: 6'1"; Weight: 205
College: Illinois
Born: November 28, 1920, Lockport, IL
Deceased: November 22, 2007, Downers Grove, IL

STATISTICS

Games

	GP	GS
1946 Brooklyn Dodgers	14	12
1947 Brooklyn Dodgers	14	13
1948 Chicago Rockets	14	10
1949 Chicago Hornets	12	0
Total	54	35

Receiving

	Rec	Yds	TD
1946 Brooklyn Dodgers	11	296	3
1947 Brooklyn Dodgers	10	147	0
1948 Chicago Rockets	3	30	0
1949 Chicago Hornets	4	58	0
Total	28	531	3

Passing

	Comp	Att	Yds	TD	Int
1947 Dodgers	1	2	17	0	1
Total	1	2	17	0	1

Kick Returns

	Ret	Yds	TD
1946 Brooklyn Dodgers	1	8	0
Total	1	8	0

Interceptions

	Int	Yds	TD
1946 Brooklyn Dodgers	1	3	0
Total	1	3	0

Field Goals

	FGM	FGA
1946 Brooklyn Dodgers	*	1
1948 Chicago Rockets	2	3
1949 Chicago Hornets	6	13
Total	8	17

Point After Touchdown

	XPM	XPA
1946 Brooklyn Dodgers	5	7
1948 Chicago Rockets	21	21
1949 Chicago Hornets	21	23
Total	47	51

MCCOLLUM, Harley Raymond

Position: T
Height: 6'4"; Weight: 245
College: Tulane
Born: February 28, 1916
Deceased: June 1984, Palm Springs, CA

STATISTICS

Games

	GP	GS
1946 New York Yankees	10	0
1947 Chicago Rockets	13	9
Total	23	9

Kick Returns

	Ret	Yds	TD
1947 Chicago Rockets	1	9	0
Total	1	9	0

MCCORMICK, Gardner Len (Len)

Position: C-LB
Height: 6'3"; Weight: 232
College: Baylor, Schreiner College, Southwestern
Born: October 28, 1922, Eldorado, TX
Deceased: August 20, 2012, Eldorado, TX

STATISTICS

Games

	GP	GS
1948 Baltimore Colts	11	5
Total	11	5

Interceptions

	Int	Yds	TD
1948 Baltimore Colts	1	5	0
Total	1	5	0

MCCORMICK, Walter Kendell

Position: C-LB
Height: 6'1"; Weight: 215
College: USC, Washington
Born: September 4, 1926, Visalia, CA
Deceased: April 3, 2005, Visalia, CA

STATISTICS

Games

	GP	GS
1948 San Francisco 49ers	9	0
Total	9	0

MCDONALD, Donald Gene (Flip)

Position: E
Height: 6'2"; Weight: 200
College: Oklahoma
Born: February 12, 1921, Webb City, MO
Deceased: February 12, 2002, Quapaw, OK

STATISTICS

Games

	GP	GS
1944 Brooklyn Dodgers	2	0
1944 Philadelphia Eagles	5	0

	GP	GS
1945 Philadelphia Eagles	9	2
1946 Philadelphia Eagles	1	0
1948 New York Yankees	2	0
Total	19	2

Receiving			
	Rec	Yds	TD
1944 Philadelphia Eagles	4	26	1
1945 Philadelphia Eagles	8	75	1
1948 New York Yankees	3	30	0
Total	15	131	2

Interceptions			
	Int	Yds	TD
1944 Philadelphia Eagles	1	14	0
Total	1	14	0

MCDONALD, Walter Vincent (Walt)

Position: B
Height: 6'1"; Weight: 210
College: Tulane
Born: November 5, 1920, Lowellville, OH
Deceased: April 16, 2012, Flagstaff, AZ

STATISTICS

Games		
	GP	GS
1946 Miami Seahawks	4	0
1946 Brooklyn Dodgers	9	8
1947 Brooklyn Dodgers	12	10
1948 Brooklyn Dodgers	12	6
1949 Chicago Hornets	9	2
Total	46	26

Rushing			
	Rush	Yds	TD
1946 Miami Seahawks	1	−4	0
1946 Brooklyn Dodgers	3	−7	0
1947 Brooklyn Dodgers	1	1	0
1948 Brooklyn Dodgers	6	15	0
1949 Chicago Hornets	1	0	0
Total	12	5	0

Receiving			
	Rec	Yds	TD
1946 Miami Seahawks	4	55	0
1946 Brooklyn Dodgers	8	71	0
1947 Brooklyn Dodgers	3	30	0
1948 Brooklyn Dodgers	7	41	1
Total	22	197	1

Passing				
	Comp	Att	Yds	TD	Int
1946 Miami Seahawks	1	3	24	0	1
Total	1	3	24	0	1

Punt Returns			
	Ret	Yds	TD
1947 Brooklyn Dodgers	1	19	0
Total	1	19	0

Kick Returns			
	Ret	Yds	TD
1946 Brooklyn Dodgers	3	32	0
Total	3	32	0

Interceptions			
	Int	Yds	TD
1946 Brooklyn Dodgers	2	31	0
1948 Brooklyn Dodgers	3	21	0
Total	5	52	0

MCQUARY, John Edward (Jack)

Position: HB-DB
Height: 6'1"; Weight: 208
College: California
Born: June 20, 1920, Tacoma, WA
Deceased: December 20, 1986, Monterey, CA

STATISTICS

Games		
	GP	GS
1946 Los Angeles Dons	1	0
Total	1	0

MCWILLIAMS, Thomas Edward (Shorty)

Position: DB-HB
Height: 5'11"; Weight: 185
College: Army, Mississippi State
Born: May 12, 1926, Newton, MS
Deceased: January 9, 1997, Meridian, MS

STATISTICS

Games		
	GP	GS
1949 Los Angeles Dons	12	2
1950 Pittsburgh Steelers	10	0
Total	22	2

Rushing			
	Rush	Yds	TD
1949 Los Angeles Dons	3	15	0
1950 Pittsburgh Steelers	10	39	0
Total	13	54	0

Passing				
	Comp	Att	Yds	TD	Int
1949 L.A. Dons	0	2	0	0	0
1950 Pittsburgh Steelers	5	8	113	0	1
Total	5	10	113	0	1

Punting			
	Punt	Yds	Blk
1950 Pittsburgh Steelers	3	135	0
Total	3	135	0

Punt Returns			
	Ret	Yds	TD
1950 Pittsburgh Steelers	8	112	0
Total	19	251	0

MELLO, James Anthony (Jim)

Position: DB-FB-LB
Height: 5'10"; Weight: 190
College: Notre Dame
Born: November 8, 1920, Warwick, RI
Deceased: May 27, 2006, Mesa, AZ

STATISTICS

Games

	GP	GS
1947 Boston Yanks	9	4
1948 Chicago Rockets	6	2
1948 Los Angeles Rams	3	0
1949 Detroit Lions	10	0
Total	28	6

Rushing

	Rush	Yds	TD
1947 Boston Yanks	33	62	0
1948 Chicago Rockets	50	243	1
1948 Los Angeles Rams	7	3	0
Total	90	308	1

Receiving

	Rec	Yds	TD
1947 Boston Yanks	2	26	0
1948 Chicago Rockets	3	38	0
1948 Los Angeles Rams	1	17	0
Total	6	81	0

Kick Returns

	Ret	Yds	TD
1949 Los Angeles Dons	2	47	0
1950 Pittsburgh Steelers			
Total	2	47	0

Interceptions

	Int	Yds	TD
1949 Los Angeles Dons	2	35	0
1950 Pittsburgh Steelers	2	31	0
Total	4	66	0

Fumbles

	Fum	Rec	Yds	TD
1950 Pittsburgh Steelers	1	0	0	0
Total	1	0	0	0

MELLO, James Anthony (Jim)

Position: DB-FB-LB
Height: 5'10"; Weight: 190
College: Notre Dame
Born: November 8, 1920, Warwick, RI
Deceased: May 27, 2006, Mesa, AZ

STATISTICS

Games

	GP	GS
1947 Boston Yanks	9	4
1948 Chicago Rockets	6	2
1948 Los Angeles Rams	3	0
1949 Detroit Lions	10	0
Total	28	6

Rushing

	Rush	Yds	TD
1947 Boston Yanks	33	62	0
1948 Chicago Rockets	50	243	1
1948 Los Angeles Rams	7	3	0
Total	90	308	1

Receiving

	Rec	Yds	TD
1947 Boston Yanks	2	26	0
1948 Chicago Rockets	3	38	0
1948 Los Angeles Rams	1	17	0
Total	6	81	0

Kick Returns

	Ret	Yds	TD
1948 Chicago Rockets	2	30	0
1949 Detroit Lions	3	37	0
Total	5	67	0

Interceptions

	Int	Yds	TD
1947 Boston Yanks	1	0	0
1949 Detroit Lions	3	61	0
Total	4	61	0

Fumbles

	Fum	Rec	Yds	TD
1947 Boston Yanks	1	0	0	0
1949 Detroit Lions	0	3	25	0
Total	1	3	25	0

MELLUS, John G.

Position: T
Height: 6'0"; Weight: 214
College: Villanova
Born: June 16, 1917, Plymouth, PA
Deceased: November 28, 2005, Plymouth, PA

STATISTICS

Games

	GP	GS
1938 New York Giants	11	0
1939 New York Giants	11	8
1940 New York Giants	8	8
1941 New York Giants	11	11
1946 San Francisco 49ers	14	10
1947 Baltimore Colts	14	9
1948 Baltimore Colts	14	0
1949 Baltimore Colts	12	1
Total	95	47

Field Goals

	FGM	FGA
1946 S.F. 49ers	*	1
Total	*	1

Point After Touchdown

	XPM	XPA
1946 S.F. 49ers	1	2
Total	1	2

MERTES, Bernard James (Bus)

Position: B
Height: 6'0"; Weight: 201
College: Iowa
Born: October 6, 1921, Chicago, IL
Deceased: January 17, 2002, St. Louis Park, MN

STATISTICS

Games

	GP	GS
1945 Chicago Cardinals	8	3
1946 Los Angeles Dons	9	3
1947 Baltimore Colts	14	10
1948 Baltimore Colts	14	12
1949 Baltimore Colts	2	2
1949 New York Giants	8	1
Total	55	31

Rushing

	Rush	Yds	TD
1945 Chicago Cardinals	24	111	0
1946 Los Angeles Dons	40	111	0
1947 Baltimore Colts	95	321	2
1948 Baltimore Colts	155	680	4
1949 Baltimore Colts	16	46	0
1949 New York Giants	11	8	0
Total	341	1277	6

Receiving

	Rec	Yds	TD
1945 Chicago Cardinals	2	1	0
1946 Los Angeles Dons	5	61	1
1947 Baltimore Colts	2	28	0
1948 Baltimore Colts	6	56	0
1949 Baltimore Colts	2	22	1
1949 New York Giants	2	14	1
Total	**19**	**182**	**2**

Punt Returns

	Ret	Yds	TD
1945 Chicago Cardinals	1	7	0
Total	**1**	**7**	**0**

Kick Returns

	Ret	Yds	TD
1945 Chicago Cardinals	1	12	0
1946 Los Angeles Dons	2	35	0
1948 Baltimore Colts	1	15	0
Total	**4**	**62**	**0**

Interceptions

	Int	Yds	TD
1946 Los Angeles Dons	1	14	0
Total	**1**	**14**	**0**

Fumbles

	Fum	Rec	Yds	TD
1945 Chicago Cardinals	1	0	0	0
1949 New York Giants	3	0	0	0
Total	**4**	**0**	**0**	**0**

MIESZKOWSKI, Edward Thomas (Ed)

Position: T
Height: 6'3"; Weight: 220
College: Notre Dame
Born: October 14, 1925, Chicago, IL
Deceased: February 15, 2004, Lombard, IL

Statistics

Games

	GP	GS
1946 Brooklyn Dodgers	13	7
1947 Brooklyn Dodgers	10	0
Total	**23**	**7**

MIHAL, Joseph (Joe)

Position: T
Height: 6'2"; Weight: 234
College: Purdue
Born: April 2, 1916, Homestead, PA
Deceased: September 19, 1979, Dallas County, TX

Statistics

Games

	GP	GS
1940 Chicago Bears	11	1
1941 Chicago Bears	9	0
1946 Los Angeles Dons	12	0
1947 Chicago Rockets	1	0
Total	**33**	**1**

MIKULA, Thomas Michael (Tom)

Position: FB-LB
Height: 5'10"; Weight: 200
College: William & Mary
Born: September 26, 1926, Johnstown, PA
Deceased: March 24, 2014, Williamsburg, VA

Statistics

Games

	GP	GS
1948 Brooklyn Dodgers	1	0
Total	**1**	**0**

MITCHELL, Fondren Lack

Position: HB
Height: 6'0"; Weight: 185
College: Florida
Born: June 19, 1921, Tallahassee, FL
Deceased: September 24, 1952, Tampa, FL

Statistics

Games

	GP	GS
1946 Miami Seahawks	7	0
Total	**7**	**0**

Rushing

	Rush	Yds	TD
1946 Miami Seahawks	5	17	0
Total	**5**	**17**	**0**

Receiving

	Rec	Yds	TD
1946 Miami Seahawks	8	131	0
Total	**8**	**131**	**0**

Kick Returns

	Ret	Yds	TD
1946 Miami Seahawks	4	52	0
Total	**4**	**52**	**0**

Interceptions

	Int	Yds	TD
1946 Miami Seahawks	1	2	0
Total	**1**	**2**	**0**

MITCHELL, Paul Anthony

Position: DT-T
Height: 6'3"; Weight: 235
College: Minnesota
Born: August 10, 1920, Minneapolis, MN
Deceased: March 11, 2017, Palos Verdes Peninsula, CA

STATISTICS

Games

	GP	GS
1946 Los Angeles Dons	10	3
1947 Los Angeles Dons	11	4
1948 Los Angeles Dons	4	0
1948 New York Yankees	8	0
1949 New York Yankees	12	0
1950 New York Yanks	12	0
1951 New York Yanks	12	0
Total	**69**	**7**

Punt Returns

	Ret	Yds	TD
1949 New York Yankees	1	15	0
Total	**1**	**15**	**0**

Kick Returns

	Ret	Yds	TD
1951 New York Yanks	1	11	0
Total	**1**	**11**	**0**

Fumbles

	Fum	Rec	Yds	TD
1950 New York Yanks	0	1	0	0
Total	**0**	**1**	**0**	**0**

MITCHELL, Robert Stanley (Bob)

Position: HB-QB-DB
Height: 5'11"; Weight: 195
College: Stanford
Born: January 27, 1921, Turlock, CA
Deceased: July 17, 1997

STATISTICS

Games

	GP	GS
1946 Los Angeles Dons	11	3
1947 Los Angeles Dons	12	3
1948 Los Angeles Dons	14	1
Total	**37**	**7**

Rushing

	Rush	Yds	TD
1946 Los Angeles Dons	8	−12	0
1947 Los Angeles Dons	32	85	0
1948 Los Angeles Dons	2	−2	0
Total	**42**	**71**	**0**

Receiving

	Rec	Yds	TD
1946 Los Angeles Dons	1	1	0
1947 Los Angeles Dons	3	36	1
Total	**4**	**37**	**1**

Passing

	Comp	Att	Yds	TD	Int
1946 L.A. Dons	3	10	19	0	2
1948 L.A. Dons	1	2	15	0	1
Total	**4**	**12**	**34**	**0**	**3**

Punting

	Punt	Yds	Blk
1946 Los Angeles Dons	1	44	0
Total	**1**	**44**	**0**

Kick Returns

	Ret	Yds	TD
1947 Los Angeles Dons	6	119	0
Total	**6**	**119**	**0**

Interceptions

	Int	Yds	TD
1946 Los Angeles Dons	1	32	0
1947 Los Angeles Dons	2	24	0
1948 Los Angeles Dons	3	1	0
Total	**6**	**57**	**0**

MORGAN, Joe Winfred

Position: T
Height: 6'1"; Weight: 245
College: McNeese State, Southern Miss
Born: October 23, 1928, De Ridder, LA
Deceased: November 26, 2008, Ormond Beach, FL

STATISTICS

Games

	GP	GS
1949 San Francisco 49ers	8	0
Total	**8**	**0**

MORRIS, Glen Max (Max)

Position: E-DE
Height: 6'2"; Weight: 200
College: Illinois, Northwestern
Born: March 13, 1925, Norris City, IL
Deceased: January 8, 1998, Reno, NV

STATISTICS

Games

	GP	GS
1946 Chicago Rockets	11	1
1947 Chicago Rockets	14	8
1948 Brooklyn Dodgers	13	7
Total	**38**	**16**

Rushing

	Rush	Yds	TD
1946 Chicago Rockets	1	20	0
Total	**1**	**20**	**0**

Receiving

	Rec	Yds	TD
1946 Chicago Rockets	3	66	0
1947 Chicago Rockets	22	239	1
1948 Brooklyn Dodgers	28	372	1
Total	**53**	**677**	**2**

Kick Returns

	Ret	Yds	TD
1947 Chicago Rockets	1	13	0
1948 Brooklyn Dodgers	1	14	0
Total	**2**	**27**	**0**

MORROW, Robert Edward (Bob)

Position: B
Height: 6'0"; Weight: 222
College: Illinois Wesleyan
Born: May 5, 1918, Madison, WI
Deceased: July 9, 2003, Stuart, FL

STATISTICS

Games

	GP	GS
1941 Chicago Cardinals	9	0
1942 Chicago Cardinals	10	1
1943 Chicago Cardinals	10	4
1945 New York Giants	1	0
1946 New York Yankees	13	6
Total	**43**	**11**

Rushing

	Rush	Yds	TD
1941 Chicago Cardinals	37	128	1
1942 Chicago Cardinals	45	145	1
1943 Chicago Cardinals	38	129	2
1946 New York Yankees	8	54	0
Total	**128**	**456**	**4**

Receiving

	Rec	Yds	TD
1943 Chicago Cardinals	3	20	0
1946 New York Yankees	1	6	0
Total	**4**	**26**	**0**

Kick Returns

	Ret	Yds	TD
1943 Chicago Cardinals	3	66	0
Total	**3**	**66**	**0**

Interceptions

	Int	Yds	TD
1941 Chicago Cardinals	1	0	0
1943 Chicago Cardinals	2	49	0
Total	**3**	**49**	**0**

MORROW, Russell Lee (Russ)

Position: C
Height: 6'7"; Weight: 210
College: Tennessee
Born: September 7, 1924, St. Louis, MO
Deceased: May 2, 2004, Smoke Rise, AL

STATISTICS

Games

	GP	GS
1946 Brooklyn Dodgers	9	2
1947 Brooklyn Dodgers	1	0
Total	**10**	**2**

Receiving

	Rec	Yds	TD
1946 Brooklyn Dodgers	1	8	1
Total	**1**	**8**	**1**

MORTON, John Joseph (Jack)

Position: E-DE-DB
Height: 6'0"; Weight: 197
College: Missouri, Purdue
Born: July 22, 1922, East St. Louis, IL
Deceased: December 17, 1983, Manteno, IL

STATISTICS

Games

	GP	GS
1945 Chicago Bears	8	1
1946 Los Angeles Dons	12	1
1947 Buffalo Bills	2	0
Total	**22**	**2**

Receiving

	Rec	Yds	TD
1945 Chicago Bears	1	18	0
1946 Los Angeles Dons	4	44	0
Total	**5**	**62**	**1**

Interceptions

	Int	Yds	TD
1946 Los Angeles Dons	1	11	0
Total	**1**	**11**	**0**

Fumbles

	Fum	Rec	Yds	TD
1945 Chicago Bears	0	2	37	0
Total	**0**	**2**	**37**	**0**

MOTLEY, Marion

Position: FB-LB
Height: 6'1"; Weight: 232
College: Nevada-Reno, South Carolina State
Born: June 5, 1920, Leesburg, GA
Deceased: June 27, 1999, Cleveland, OH

STATISTICS

Games

	GP	GS
1946 Cleveland Browns	13	10
1947 Cleveland Browns	14	12
1948 Cleveland Browns	14	14
1949 Cleveland Browns	11	10
1950 Cleveland Browns	12	0
1951 Cleveland Browns	11	0
1952 Cleveland Browns	12	0
1953 Cleveland Browns	12	0
1955 Pittsburgh Steelers	7	0
Total	**106**	**46**

MUTRYN, Chester A. (Chet)

Rushing

	Rush	Yds	TD
1946 Cleveland Browns	73	601	5
1947 Cleveland Browns	146	889	8
1948 Cleveland Browns	157	964	5
1949 Cleveland Browns	113	570	8
1950 Cleveland Browns	140	810	3
1951 Cleveland Browns	61	273	1
1952 Cleveland Browns	104	444	1
1953 Cleveland Browns	32	161	0
1955 Pittsburgh Steelers	2	8	0
Total	828	4720	31

Receiving

	Rec	Yds	TD
1946 Cleveland Browns	10	188	1
1947 Cleveland Browns	7	73	1
1948 Cleveland Browns	13	192	2
1949 Cleveland Browns	15	191	0
1950 Cleveland Browns	11	151	1
1951 Cleveland Browns	10	52	0
1952 Cleveland Browns	13	213	2
1953 Cleveland Browns	6	47	0
Total	85	1107	7

Passing

	Comp	Att	Yds	TD	Int
1948 Cleveland Browns	0	1	0	0	0
1952 Cleveland Browns	0	2	0	0	0
Total	0	3	0	0	0

Punt Returns

	Ret	Yds	TD
1946 Cleveland Browns	1	0	0
Total	1	0	0

Kick Returns

	Ret	Yds	TD
1946 Cleveland Browns	3	53	0
1947 Cleveland Browns	13	322	0
1948 Cleveland Browns	14	337	0
1949 Cleveland Browns	12	262	0
1952 Cleveland Browns	3	88	0
1953 Cleveland Browns	3	60	0
Total	48	1122	0

Interceptions

	Int	Yds	TD
1946 Cleveland Browns	1	0	0
1947 Cleveland Browns	1	48	1
Total	2	48	1

Fumbles

	Fum	Rec	Yds	TD
1950 Cleveland Browns	5	3	0	0
1951 Cleveland Browns	1	0	0	0
1952 Cleveland Browns	2	1	0	0
1953 Cleveland Browns	1	0	0	0
Total	9	4	0	0

MULREADY, John Jerome (Jerry)

Position: E-DE
Height: 6'1"; Weight: 205
College: Minnesota, North Dakota State
Born: January 5, 1923, Fargo, ND
Deceased: June 3, 1976, Fargo, ND

STATISTICS

Games

	GP	GS
1947 Chicago Rockets	9	6
Total	9	6

Receiving

	Rec	Yds	TD
1947 Chicago Rockets	7	108	0
Total	7	108	0

MURPHY, George Patrick, Jr.

Position: BB
Height: 6'0"; Weight: 200
College: USC
Born: May 10, 1926, Santa Monica, CA
Deceased: August 25, 1987, Chula Vista, CA

STATISTICS

Games

	GP	GS
1949 Los Angeles Dons	11	7
Total	11	7

Rushing

	Rush	Yds	TD
1949 Los Angeles Dons	1	0	0
Total	1	0	0

Receiving

	Rec	Yds	TD
1949 Los Angeles Dons	1	17	0
Total	1	17	0

MUTRYN, Chester A. (Chet)

Position: HB-DB
Height: 5'9"; Weight: 179
College: Xavier
Born: March 12, 1921, Cleveland, OH
Deceased: March 24, 1995, Cleveland, OH

STATISTICS

Games

	GP	GS
1946 Buffalo Bisons	14	8
1947 Buffalo Bills	14	14
1948 Buffalo Bills	14	14
1949 Buffalo Bills	11	11
1950 Baltimore Colts	12	0
Total	65	47

Rushing

	Rush	Yds	TD
1946 Buffalo Bisons	57	289	1
1947 Buffalo Bills	140	868	9
1948 Buffalo Bills	147	823	10
1949 Buffalo Bills	131	696	5
1950 Baltimore Colts	108	355	2
Total	**583**	**3031**	**27**

Receiving

	Rec	Yds	TD
1946 Buffalo Bisons	7	168	3
1947 Buffalo Bills	10	176	2
1948 Buffalo Bills	39	794	5
1949 Buffalo Bills	29	333	0
1950 Baltimore Colts	36	379	2
Total	**121**	**1850**	**12**

Passing

	Comp	Att	Yds	TD	Int
1948 Buffalo Bills	2	6	21	0	0
1950 Bal. Colts	1	1	4	0	0
Total	**3**	**7**	**25**	**0**	**0**

Punt Returns

	Ret	Yds	TD
1946 Buffalo Bisons	5	57	0
1947 Buffalo Bills	13	187	0
1948 Buffalo Bills	10	171	1
1949 Buffalo Bills	7	77	0
1950 Baltimore Colts	6	45	0
Total	**41**	**537**	**1**

Kick Returns

	Ret	Yds	TD
1946 Buffalo Bisons	4	79	0
1947 Buffalo Bills	21	691	1
1948 Buffalo Bills	19	500	0
1949 Buffalo Bills	10	224	0
1950 Baltimore Colts	19	408	0
Total	**73**	**1902**	**1**

Interceptions

	Int	Yds	TD
1947 Buffalo Bills	1	11	0
Total	**1**	**11**	**0**

Fumbles

	Fum	Rec	Yds	TD
1950 Baltimore Colts	5	3	0	0
Total	**5**	**3**	**0**	**0**

Point After Touchdown

	XPM	XPA
1947 Buffalo Bills	1	2
Total	**1**	**2**

NABORS, Roland Richard

Position: LB-C
Height: 6'2"; Weight: 200
College: Texas Tech
Born: July 22, 1924, Meadow, TX
Deceased: December 3, 1999, Beaumont, TX

Statistics

Games

	GP	GS
1948 New York Yankees	10	0
Total	**10**	**0**

Interceptions

	Int	Yds	TD
1948 New York Yankees	1	10	0
Total	**1**	**10**	**0**

NAUMU, John Punualli (Johnny)

Position: HB
Height: 5'8"; Weight: 175
College: Hawaii, USC
Born: September 30, 1919, Hooevha, HI
Deceased: September 23, 1982

Statistics

Games

	GP	GS
1948 Los Angeles Dons	9	0
Total	**9**	**0**

Rushing

	Rush	Yds	TD
1948 Los Angeles Dons	1	0	0
Total	**1**	**0**	**0**

Punting

	Punt	Yds	Blk
1948 Los Angeles Dons	1	34	0
Total	**1**	**34**	**0**

Kick Returns

	Ret	Yds	TD
1948 Los Angeles Dons	6	131	0
Total	**6**	**131**	**0**

NEGUS, Frederick Wilson (Fred)

Position: C-LB
Height: 6'1"; Weight: 208
College: Michigan, Wisconsin
Born: November 7, 1923, Colerain, OH
Deceased: April 18, 2005, Fort Atkinson, WI

Statistics

Games

	GP	GS
1947 Chicago Rockets	12	9
1948 Chicago Rockets	14	5
1949 Chicago Hornets	12	5
1950 Chicago Bears	11	0
Total	**49**	**19**

Interceptions

	Int	Yds	TD
1948 Chicago Rockets	5	30	0
1949 Chicago Hornets	2	28	0
Total	**7**	**58**	**0**

NIEDZIELA, Bruno Joseph

Position: T
Height: 6'2"; Weight: 225
College: Iowa
Born: April 12, 1923, Chicago, IL
Deceased: May 1, 1991

STATISTICS

Games		
	GP	GS
1947 Chicago Rockets	12	9
Total	**12**	**9**

NELSON, Herbert Russell (Herb)

Position: E-T
Height: 6'4"; Weight: 219
College: Pennsylvania
Born: April 25, 1921, Hartford, CT
Deceased: July 18, 2004, Westwood, MA

STATISTICS

Games		
	GP	GS
1946 Buffalo Bisons	12	7
1947 Brooklyn Dodgers	14	4
1948 Brooklyn Dodgers	4	1
Total	**30**	**12**

Rushing		
	Rush	Yds	TD
1946 Buffalo Bisons	1	1	0
Total	**1**	**1**	**0**

Receiving		
	Rec	Yds	TD
1946 Buffalo Bisons	4	47	0
1947 Brooklyn Dodgers	2	17	0
Total	**6**	**64**	**0**

NELSON, Jimmy Guess

Position: B
Height: 5'11"; Weight: 180
College: Alabama
Born: July 26, 1919, Live Oak, FL
Deceased: December 24, 1986, Encinitas, CA

STATISTICS

Games		
	GP	GS
1946 Miami Seahawks	14	5
Total	**14**	**5**

Rushing		
	Rush	Yds	TD
1946 Miami Seahawks	39	163	1
Total	**39**	**163**	**1**

Receiving		
	Rec	Yds	TD
1946 Miami Seahawks	4	20	0
Total	**4**	**20**	**0**

Passing				
	Comp	Att	Yds	TD	Int
1946 Seahawks	8	24	135	0	4
Total	**8**	**24**	**135**	**0**	**4**

Punting		
	Punt	Yds	Blk
1946 Miami Seahawks	16	635	0
Total	**16**	**635**	**0**

Punt Returns		
	Ret	Yds	TD
1946 Miami Seahawks	7	71	0
Total	**7**	**71**	**0**

Kick Returns		
	Ret	Yds	TD
1946 Miami Seahawks	10	192	0
Total	**10**	**192**	**0**

Interceptions		
	Int	Yds	TD
1946 Miami Seahawks	2	8	0
Total	**2**	**8**	**0**

NELSON, Robert Cole (Bob)*

Position: C-T-DT-LB
Height: 6'1"; Weight: 214
College: Baylor
Born: January 30, 1920, Paris, TX
Deceased: November 3, 1986, Tarrant County, TX

STATISTICS

Games		
	GP	GS
1941 Detroit Lions	9	2
1945 Detroit Lions	9	7
1946 Los Angeles Dons	10	6
1947 Los Angeles Dons	14	12
1948 Los Angeles Dons	14	14
1949 Los Angeles Dons	12	11
1950 Baltimore Colts	3	0
Total	**71**	**52**

Rushing		
	Rush	Yds	TD
1948 Los Angeles Dons	1	−7	0
Total	**1**	**−7**	**0**

Kick Returns		
	Ret	Yds	TD
1946 Los Angeles Dons	1	0	0
Total	**1**	**0**	**0**

Interceptions

	Int	Yds	TD
1941 Detroit Lions	1	41	0
1945 Detroit Lions	1	0	0
1946 Los Angeles Dons	1	5	0
1947 Los Angeles Dons	2	52	0
1948 Los Angeles Dons	1	0	0
Total	6	98	1

Fumbles

	Fum	Rec	Yds	TD
1945 Detroit Lions	0	1	0	0
Total	0	1	0	0

Field Goals

	FGM	FGA
1945 Detroit Lions	1	4
1946 Los Angeles Dons	2	6
1949 Los Angeles Dons	3	6
Total	6	16

Point After Touchdown

	XPM	XPA
1946 Los Angeles Dons	3	5
1949 Los Angeles Dons	34	35
Total	37	40

Joe Aguirre had three receptions for 61 yards and a touchdown credited to Bob Nelson in the official records. This reflects the corrected statistics. The error occurred in game one of the season.

NEMETH, Steve Joseph

Position: QB-HB
Height: 5'10"; Weight: 174
College: Notre Dame
Born: December 10, 1922, South Bend, IN
Deceased: March 27, 1998, South Bend, IN

Statistics

Games

	GP	GS
1945 Cleveland Rams	9	4
1946 Chicago Rockets	13	1
1947 Baltimore Colts	4	1
Total	26	6

Rushing

	Rush	Yds	TD
1946 Chicago Rockets	4	10	0
1947 Baltimore Colts	1	1	0
Total	5	11	0

Passing

	Comp	Att	Yds	TD	Int
1945 Cle. Rams	0	1	0	0	0
1946 Chicago Rockets	5	23	68	0	0
1947 Bal. Colts	2	6	18	0	2
Total	7	30	86	0	2

Punting

	Punt	Yds	Blk
1946 Chicago Rockets	2	92	0
1947 Baltimore Colts	3	126	0
Total	5	218	0

Punt Returns

	Ret	Yds	TD
1946 Chicago Rockets	1	14	0
Total	1	14	0

Field Goals

	FGM	FGA
1946 Chicago Rockets	9	12
1947 Baltimore Colts	*	1
Total	9	13

Point After Touchdown

	XPM	XPA
1946 Chicago Rockets	32	33
1947 Baltimore Colts	1	1
Total	33	34

NOLANDER, Donald Austin (Don)

Position: C
Height: 6'1"; Weight: 210
College: Minnesota
Born: September 14, 1921, Minneapolis, MN
Deceased: April 24, 1999, Bonita Springs, FL

Statistics

Games

	GP	GS
1946 Los Angeles Dons	11	7
Total	11	7

Interceptions

	Int	Yds	TD
1946 Los Angeles Dons	1	13	0
Total	1	13	0

NORBERG, Henry Francis, Jr. (Hank)

Position: E
Height: 6'2"; Weight: 225
College: Stanford
Born: December 22, 1920, Oakland, CA
Deceased: December 4, 1974, Mountain View, CA

Statistics

Games

	GP	GS
1946 San Francisco 49ers	14	0
1947 San Francisco 49ers	11	0
1948 Chicago Rockets	10	0
Total	35	0

Receiving

	Rec	Yds	TD
1946 S.F. 49ers	3	29	0
1947 S.F. 49ers	2	31	0
1948 Chicago Rockets	1	4	0
Total	6	64	0

	Interceptions		
	Int	Yds	TD
1946 S.F. 49ers	1	22	0
Total	1	22	0

NORTH, John Puckett

Position: E-DB
Height: 6'2"; Weight: 199
College: Vanderbilt
Born: June 17, 1921, Gilliam, LA
Deceased: July 6, 2010, Mandeville, LA

STATISTICS

	Games	
	GP	GS
1948 Baltimore Colts	14	13
1949 Baltimore Colts	11	6
1950 Baltimore Colts	4	3
Total	29	22

	Receiving		
	Rec	Yds	TD
1948 Baltimore Colts	8	204	1
1949 Baltimore Colts	25	490	4
1950 Baltimore Colts	5	90	0
Total	38	784	5

	Interceptions		
	Int	Yds	TD
1948 Baltimore Colts	1	25	0
Total	1	25	0

NOWASKEY, Robert John (Bob)

Position: E-DE
Height: 6'0"; Weight: 205
College: George Washington
Born: February 3, 1918, Everson, PA
Deceased: March 21, 1971, Arlington Heights, IL

STATISTICS

	Games	
	GP	GS
1940 Chicago Bears	10	2
1941 Chicago Bears	11	5
1942 Chicago Bears	11	6
1946 Los Angeles Dons	14	5
1947 Los Angeles Dons	14	1
1948 Los Angeles Dons	1	0
1948 Baltimore Colts	13	3
1949 Baltimore Colts	12	2
1950 Baltimore Colts	9	0
Total	95	24

	Rushing		
	Rush	Yds	TD
1940 Chicago Bears	1	4	0
1941 Chicago Bears	3	5	0
1942 Chicago Bears	1	3	0
1946 Los Angeles Dons	3	14	0
Total	8	26	0

	Receiving		
	Rec	Yds	TD
1940 Chicago Bears	5	105	2
1941 Chicago Bears	12	199	1
1942 Chicago Bears	6	128	0
1946 Los Angeles Dons	19	198	3
1947 Los Angeles Dons	8	106	0
1948 Baltimore Colts	1	31	0
Total	51	767	6

	Punt Returns		
	Ret	Yds	TD
1946 Los Angeles Dons	1	5	0
1947 Los Angeles Dons	1	22	0
Total	2	27	0

	Interceptions		
	Int	Yds	TD
1946 Los Angeles Dons	1	35	1
1947 Los Angeles Dons	2	15	0
1949 Baltimore Colts	1	9	0
Total	4	59	1

	Point After Touchdown	
	XPM	XPA
1941 Chicago Bears	1	2
Total	1	2

NYGREN, Bernard Clifford (Bernie)

Position: HB-DB
Height: 5'9"; Weight: 193
College: Gustavus Adolphus, San Jose State
Born: November 14, 1918, Minneapolis, MN
Deceased: December 26, 1984, San Jose, CA

STATISTICS

	Games	
	GP	GS
1946 Los Angeles Dons	14	5
1947 Brooklyn Dodgers	1	0
Total	15	5

	Rushing		
	Rush	Yds	TD
1946 Los Angeles Dons	26	111	0
Total	26	111	0

	Receiving		
	Rec	Yds	TD
1946 Los Angeles Dons	13	170	1
Total	13	170	1

	Kick Returns		
	Ret	Yds	TD
1946 Los Angeles Dons	4	88	0
Total	4	88	0

	Interceptions		
	Int	Yds	TD
1946 Los Angeles Dons	2	30	0
Total	2	30	0

OBECK, Victor Francis Joseph

Position: G
Height: 6'0"; Weight: 225
College: Springfield
Born: March 28, 1917, Audubon, NJ
Deceased: April 21, 1979, New York, NY

STATISTICS

Games		
	GP	GS
1945 Chicago Cardinals	10	3
1946 Brooklyn Dodgers	12	0
Total	22	3

Punt Returns			
	Ret	Yds	TD
1946 Brooklyn Dodgers	1	3	0
Total	1	3	0

O'CONNOR, William Francis, Jr. (Bill) (Zeke)

Position: E-DE
Height: 6'4"; Weight: 220
College: Notre Dame
Born: May 2, 1926, New York, NY
Deceased:

STATISTICS

Games		
	GP	GS
1948 Buffalo Bills	14	4
1949 Cleveland Browns	9	1
1951 New York Yanks	12	0
Total	35	5

Receiving			
	Rec	Yds	TD
1948 Buffalo Bills	31	301	2
1951 New York Yanks	14	192	0
Total			

Kick Returns			
	Ret	Yds	TD
1948 Buffalo Bills	1	0	0
1951 New York Yanks	1	10	0
Total	2	10	0

OLENSKI, Mitchell Joseph (Mitch)

Position: T
Height: 6'3"; Weight: 222
College: Alabama
Born: January 13, 1921, Benton, IL
Deceased: June 13, 2000, Vestal, NY

STATISTICS

Games		
	GP	GS
1946 Miami Seahawks	14	10
1947 Detroit Lions	12	8
Total	26	18

Kick Returns			
	Ret	Yds	TD
1946 Miami Seahawks	1	2	0
Total	1	2	0

O'NEAL, James C. Summer (Jim)

Position: G
Height: 6'1"; Weight: 230
College: Southwestern (TX), TCU, Texas-El Paso
Born: February 13, 1924, Anna, TX
Deceased: October 13, 1959, Waller, TX

STATISTICS

Games		
	GP	GS
1946 Chicago Rockets	12	5
1947 Chicago Rockets	12	2
Total	24	7

ORISTAGLIO, Robert Peter (Bob)

Position: DE-E
Height: 6'2"; Weight: 214
College: Pennsylvania
Born: April 6, 1924, Philadelphia, PA
Deceased: February 14, 1995, York, PA

STATISTICS

Games		
	GP	GS
1949 Buffalo Bills	12	0
1950 Baltimore Colts	12	3
1951 Cleveland Browns	12	0
1952 Philadelphia Eagles	4	0
Total	40	3

Receiving			
	Rec	Yds	TD
1949 Buffalo Bills	1	14	0
1950 Baltimore Colts	14	134	0
1951 Cleveland Browns	1	20	1
Total	16	168	1

Kick Returns			
	Ret	Yds	TD
1950 Baltimore Colts	2	32	0
Total	2	32	0

Fumbles			
	Fum	Rec	Yds	TD
1950 Baltimore Colts	0	1	0	0
1952 Philadelphia Eagles	0	1	0	0
Total	0	2	0	0

O'ROURKE, Charles Christopher (Charlie)

Position: QB
Height: 5'11"; Weight: 175
College: Boston College
Born: May 10, 1917, Montreal, Canada
Deceased: April 14, 2000, Brockton, MA

STATISTICS

Games

	GP	GS
1942 Chicago Bears	11	1
1946 Los Angeles Dons	14	8
1947 Los Angeles Dons	14	9
1948 Baltimore Colts	14	1
1949 Baltimore Colts	5	0
Total	58	19

Rushing

	Rush	Yds	TD
1942 Chicago Bears	18	−17	1
1946 Los Angeles Dons	47	50	1
1947 Los Angeles Dons	24	55	1
1948 Baltimore Colts	7	15	1
Total	96	103	4

Passing

	Comp	Att	Yds	TD	Int
1942 Chi. Bears	37	88	951	11	16
1946 L.A. Dons	105	182	1250	12	14
1947 L.A. Dons	89	178	1449	13	16
1948 Bal. Colts	24	51	377	3	4
1949 Bal. Colts	1	7	12	0	1
Total	256	506	4039	39	51

Punting

	Punt	Yds	Blk
1942 Chicago Bears	23	817	0
1946 Los Angeles Dons	8	312	0
1948 Baltimore Colts	66	2546	1
1949 Baltimore Colts	28	1098	0
Total	125	4773	1

Punt Returns

	Ret	Yds	TD
1942 Chicago Bears	2	8	0
Total	2	8	0

Kick Returns

	Ret	Yds	TD
1946 Los Angeles Dons	1	28	0
1947 Los Angeles Dons	1	24	0
Total	2	52	0

Interceptions

	Int	Yds	TD
1942 Chicago Bears	3	15	0
Total	3	15	0

OSSOWSKI, Theodore Leroy (Ted)

Position: T
Height: 6'0"; Weight: 218
College: Oregon State, USC
Born: May 12, 1922, Beatrice, NE
Deceased: August 21, 1965, Contra Costa, CA

STATISTICS

Games

	GP	GS
1947 New York Yankees	3	0
Total	3	0

OTTELE, Richard G. (Dick)

Position: BB-DB
Height: 6'3"; Weight: 210
College: Washington
Born: December 8, 1926, Yuma, CO
Deceased: September 20, 1985, Bremerton, WA

STATISTICS

Games

	GP	GS
1948 Los Angeles Dons	8	0
Total	8	0

Rushing

	Rush	Yds	TD
1948 Los Angeles Dons	2	11	0
Total	2	11	0

Kick Returns

	Ret	Yds	TD
1948 Los Angeles Dons	3	47	0
Total	3	47	0

OWENS, Isiah Hudson (Ike)

Position: DE
Height: 6'1"; Weight: 190
College: Illinois
Born: January 8, 1920, Columbus, GA
Deceased: June 1980, Gary, IN

STATISTICS

Games

	GP	GS
1948 Chicago Rockets	8	0
Total	8	0

PAFFRATH, Robert William (Bob)

Position: B
Height: 5'8"; Weight: 190
College: Minnesota
Born: July 13, 1918, Mankato, MN
Deceased: May 21, 2005, Beaverton, OR

PAGE, Paul Eugene

Position: HB-DB
Height: 6'0"; Weight: 180
College: SMU
Born: September 16, 1927, Eldorado, TX
Deceased: February 15, 1997, Tom Green County, TX

STATISTICS

Games

	GP	GS
1946 Miami Seahawks	7	2
1946 Brooklyn Dodgers	5	0
Total	12	2

Rushing

	Rush	Yds	TD
1946 Miami Seahawks	23	81	1
1946 Brooklyn Dodgers	8	19	1
Total	31	100	2

Receiving

	Rec	Yds	TD
1946 Miami Seahawks	2	−3	0
1946 Brooklyn Dodgers	2	−3	—
Total	4	−6	0

Passing

	Comp	Att	Yds	TD	Int
1946 Dodgers	0	1	0	0	0
Total	0	1	0	0	0

Punting

	Punt	Yds	Blk
1946 Miami Seahawks	1	50	0
Total	1	50	0

Punt Returns

	Ret	Yds	TD
1946 Miami Seahawks	1	1	0
Total	1	1	0

Kick Returns

	Ret	Yds	TD
1946 Miami Seahawks	4	76	0
Total	4	76	0

PAGE, Paul Eugene

Position: HB-DB
Height: 6'0"; Weight: 180
College: SMU
Born: September 16, 1927, Eldorado, TX
Deceased: February 15, 1997, Tom Green County, TX

STATISTICS

Games

	GP	GS
1949 Baltimore Colts	8	2
Total	8	2

Rushing

	Rush	Yds	TD
1949 Baltimore Colts	25	81	0
Total	25	81	0

Receiving

	Rec	Yds	TD
1949 Baltimore Colts	4	62	0
Total	4	62	0

Punt Returns

	Ret	Yds	TD
1949 Baltimore Colts	1	16	0
Total	1	16	0

Kick Returns

	Ret	Yds	TD
1949 Baltimore Colts	4	108	0
Total	4	108	0

PAINE, Homer

Position: T
Height: 6'0"; Weight: 235
College: Oklahoma, Tulsa
Born: September 20, 1923, Hennessey, OK
Deceased: July 5, 2010, Enid, OK

STATISTICS

Games

	GP	GS
1949 Chicago Hornets	12	10
Total	12	10

PALMER, Derrell Franklin

Position: DT-T
Height: 6'2"; Weight: 240
College: TCU
Born: August 27, 1922, Breckenridge, TX
Deceased: February 22, 2009, Cleburne, TX

STATISTICS

Games

	GP	GS
1946 New York Yankees	13	1
1947 New York Yankees	14	11
1948 New York Yankees	14	10
1949 Cleveland Browns	11	1
1950 Cleveland Browns	12	0
1951 Cleveland Browns	10	0
1952 Cleveland Browns	11	0
1953 Cleveland Browns	11	0
Total	96	23

Fumbles

	Fum	Rec	Yds	TD
1951 Cleveland Browns	0	2	0	0
Total	0	2	0	0

PANCIERA, Donald Matthew (Don)

Position: QB-DB
Height: 6'1"; Weight: 192
College: Boston College, San Francisco
Born: June 23, 1927, Westerly, RI
Deceased: February 9, 2012, Westerly, RI

STATISTICS

Games

	GP	GS
1949 New York Yankees	12	12
1950 Detroit Lions	4	0
1952 Chicago Cardinals	10	1
Total	**26**	**13**

Rushing

	Rush	Yds	TD
1949 New York Yankees	10	−4	0
1952 Chicago Cardinals	4	6	0
Total	**14**	**2**	**0**

Passing

	Comp	Att	Yds	TD	Int
1949 Yankees	51	150	801	5	16
1952 Cardinals	35	96	582	5	9
Total	**86**	**246**	**1383**	**10**	**25**

Interceptions

	Int	Yds	TD
1950 Detroit Lions	1	1	0
Total	**1**	**1**	**0**

Fumbles

	Fum	Rec	Yds	TD
1952 Chicago Cardinals	4	2	−2	0
Total	**4**	**2**	**−2**	**0**

PARKER, Clarence McKay (Ace)

Position: TB-DB-QB
Height: 6'0"; Weight: 178
College: Duke
Born: May 17, 1912, Portsmouth, VA
Deceased: November 6, 2013, Portsmouth, VA

STATISTICS

Games

	GP	GS
1937 Brooklyn Dodgers	4	4
1938 Brooklyn Dodgers	11	11
1939 Brooklyn Dodgers	11	10
1940 Brooklyn Dodgers	11	10
1941 Brooklyn Dodgers	11	9
1945 Boston Yanks	8	1
1946 New York Yankees	12	4
Total	**68**	**49**

Rushing

	Rush	Yds	TD
1937 Brooklyn Dodgers	34	26	1
1938 Brooklyn Dodgers	93	253	2
1939 Brooklyn Dodgers	104	271	5
1940 Brooklyn Dodgers	89	306	2
1941 Brooklyn Dodgers	85	301	0
1945 Boston Yanks	18	−49	0
1946 New York Yankees	75	184	3
Total	**498**	**1292**	**13**

Receiving

	Rec	Yds	TD
1938 Brooklyn Dodgers	1	19	1
1939 Brooklyn Dodgers	1	5	0
1940 Brooklyn Dodgers	3	139	2
1941 Brooklyn Dodgers	3	66	0
Total	**8**	**229**	**3**

Passing

	Comp	Att	Yds	TD	Int
1937 Dodgers	28	61	514	1	7
1938 Dodgers	63	148	865	5	7
1939 Dodgers	72	157	977	4	13
1940 Dodgers	49	111	817	10	7
1941 Dodgers	51	102	639	2	8
1945 Yanks	10	24	123	0	5
1946 Yankees	62	115	763	8	3
Total	**335**	**718**	**4698**	**30**	**50**

Punting

	Punt	Yds	Blk
1939 Brooklyn Dodgers	40	1678	0
1940 Brooklyn Dodgers	49	1875	0
1941 Brooklyn Dodgers	27	1079	0
1945 Boston Yanks	7	224	0
1946 New York Yankees	27	911	2
Total	**150**	**5767**	**2**

Punt Returns

	Ret	Yds	TD
1941 Brooklyn Dodgers	16	153	0
1946 New York Yankees	8	85	0
Total	**24**	**238**	**0**

Kick Returns

	Ret	Yds	TD
1941 Brooklyn Dodgers	3	71	0
1946 New York Yankees	2	27	0
Total	**5**	**98**	**0**

Interceptions

	Int	Yds	TD
1940 Brooklyn Dodgers	6	146	1
1941 Brooklyn Dodgers	1	5	0
Total	**7**	**151**	**1**

Fumbles

	Fum	Rec	Yds	TD
1945 Boston Yanks	2	1	−4	0
Total	**2**	**1**	**−4**	**0**

PARKER, Howard Ingram (Howie)

Position: BB
Height: 6'2"; Weight: 220
College: SMU
Born: August 23, 1926, Greenville, TX
Deceased: December 8, 2009

STATISTICS

Games

	GP	GS
1948 New York Yankees	3	0
Total	**3**	**0**

Receiving

	Rec	Yds	TD
1948 New York Yankees	1	17	0
Total	**1**	**17**	**0**

PARKS, Edward Harry (Mickey)

Position: C-LB
Height: 6'0"; Weight: 225
College: Oklahoma
Born: December 4, 1915, Shawnee, OK
Deceased: September 27, 1976, Yountville, CA

STATISTICS

Games

	GP	GS
1938 Washington Redskins	8	3
1939 Washington Redskins	10	8
1940 Washington Redskins	6	0
1946 Chicago Rockets	13	2
Total	**37**	**13**

Point After Touchdown

	XPM	XPA
1939 Washington Redskins	*	1
Total	*****	**1**

PARSEGHIAN, Ara Raoul

Position: HB
Height: 5'10"; Weight: 194
College: Akron, Miami (OH)
Born: May 21, 1923, Akron, OH
Deceased: August 2, 2017, Granger, IN

STATISTICS

Games

	GP	GS
1948 Cleveland Browns	12	1
1949 Cleveland Browns	2	1
Total	**14**	**2**

Rushing

	Rush	Yds	TD
1948 Cleveland Browns	32	135	1
1949 Cleveland Browns	12	31	0
Total	**44**	**166**	**1**

Receiving

	Rec	Yds	TD
1948 Cleveland Browns	2	31	1
1949 Cleveland Browns	1	2	0
Total	**3**	**33**	**1**

Kick Returns

	Ret	Yds	TD
1948 Cleveland Browns	2	41	0
Total	**2**	**41**	**0**

Interceptions

	Int	Yds	TD
1948 Cleveland Browns	1	56	0
Total	**1**	**56**	**0**

PARSONS, Earle O., Jr.

Position: HB
Height: 6'0"; Weight: 180
College: USC
Born: September 16, 1921, Helena, MT
Deceased:

STATISTICS

Games

	GP	GS
1946 San Francisco 49ers	10	2
1947 San Francisco 49ers	11	0
Total	**21**	**2**

Rushing

	Rush	Yds	TD
1946 S.F. 49ers	74	362	2
1947 S.F. 49ers	33	125	0
Total	**107**	**487**	**2**

Receiving

	Rec	Yds	TD
1946 S.F. 49ers	8	52	0
1947 S.F. 49ers	9	163	2
Total	**17**	**215**	**2**

Punt Returns

	Ret	Yds	TD
1946 S.F. 49ers	15	198	0
1947 S.F. 49ers	10	106	0
Total	**25**	**304**	**0**

Kick Returns

	Ret	Yds	TD
1946 S.F. 49ers	4	94	9
1947 S.F. 49ers	4	99	0
Total	**8**	**193**	**0**

PATANELLI, Michael Joseph (Mike)

Position: DE
Height: 6'2"; Weight: 218
College: Ball State, Bowling Green, Manchester
Born: August 12, 1922, Elkhart, IN
Deceased: October 22, 2010

STATISTICS

Games

	GP	GS
1947 Brooklyn Dodgers	2	0
Total	**2**	**0**

PATTERSON, Paul L.

Position: WB-DB
Height: 5'9"; Weight: 185
College: Illinois
Born: February 16, 1927, Aurora, IL
Deceased: June 11, 1982, Chicago, IL

STATISTICS

Games

	GP	GS
1949 Chicago Hornets	12	0
Total	12	0

Rushing

	Rush	Yds	TD
1949 Chicago Hornets	2	0	0
Total	2	0	0

Receiving

	Rec	Yds	TD
1949 Chicago Hornets	16	304	4
Total	16	304	4

Punt Returns

	Ret	Yds	TD
1949 Chicago Hornets	4	33	0
Total	4	33	0

Interceptions

	Int	Yds	TD
1949 Chicago Hornets	3	104	0
Total	3	104	0

PAVLICH, Charles J.

Position: G-T
Height: 6'2"; Weight: 210
College: (None)
Born: May 18, 1921, Muskegon, MI
Deceased: February 6, 2011, Los Angeles, CA

STATISTICS

Games

	GP	GS
1946 San Francisco 49ers	10	0
Total	10	0

PEARCY, James Wheeler (Jim)

Position: G
Height: 5'11"; Weight: 210
College: Marshall
Born: July 26, 1918, Harrisville, WV
Deceased: March 15, 2005, Hendersonville, NC

STATISTICS

Games

	GP	GS
1946 Chicago Rockets	13	3
1947 Chicago Rockets	14	11
1948 Chicago Rockets	14	13
1949 Chicago Hornets	8	3
Total	49	30

PERANTONI, Joseph Francis (Frank)

Position: C
Height: 6'0"; Weight: 220
College: Princeton
Born: September 13, 1923, Raritan, NJ
Deceased: September 11, 1991, Somerville, NJ

STATISTICS

Games

	GP	GS
1948 New York Yankees	14	3
1949 New York Yankees	12	1
Total	26	4

PERDUE, Charles Willard (Bolo)

Position: DE-E
Height: 5'10"; Weight: 170
College: Arkansas, Duke
Born: May 10, 1916, Thomasville, NC
Deceased: March 31, 1988, Norfolk, VA

STATISTICS

Games

	GP	GS
1940 New York Giants	10	0
1946 Brooklyn Dodgers	10	1
Total	20	1

Receiving

	Rec	Yds	TD
1940 New York Giants	2	28	0
Total	2	28	0

PERINA, Robert Ian (Bob)

Position: DB-TB-HB
Height: 6'1"; Weight: 205
College: Princeton
Born: January 16, 1921, Irvington, NJ
Deceased: August 2, 1991, Madison, WI

STATISTICS

Games

	GP	GS
1946 New York Yankees	13	2
1947 Brooklyn Dodgers	14	4
1948 Chicago Rockets	13	1
1949 Chicago Bears	12	1
1950 Baltimore Colts	1	0
Total	53	8

Rushing

	Rush	Yds	TD
1946 New York Yankees	45	135	1
1947 Brooklyn Dodgers	67	116	3
1948 Chicago Rockets	6	1	0
1949 Chicago Bears	4	4	0
Total	122	256	4

Receiving

	Rec	Yds	TD
1947 Brooklyn Dodgers	9	67	1
1948 Chicago Rockets	2	13	0
1949 Chicago Bears	3	33	0
Total	14	113	1

Passing

	Comp	Att	Yds	TD	Int
1946 Yankees	21	48	279	1	4
1947 Dodgers	11	24	91	0	2
Total	32	72	370	1	6

Punting

	Punt	Yds	Blk
1946 New York Yankees	11	413	0
1947 Brooklyn Dodgers	7	209	2
Total	18	622	2

Punt Returns

	Ret	Yds	TD
1946 New York Yankees	15	205	0
1947 Brooklyn Dodgers	4	27	0
1948 Chicago Rockets	2	14	0
Total	21	246	0

Kick Returns

	Ret	Yds	TD
1946 New York Yankees	4	81	0
1947 Brooklyn Dodgers	3	67	0
1948 Chicago Rockets	3	52	0
1949 Chicago Bears	1	10	0
Total	11	210	0

Interceptions

	Int	Yds	TD
1946 New York Yankees	2	24	0
1947 Brooklyn Dodgers	4	40	0
1948 Chicago Rockets	6	87	0
1949 Chicago Bears	6	23	0
Total	18	174	0

Fumbles

	Fum	Rec	Yds	TD
1949 Chicago Bears	0	1	0	0
Total	0	1	0	0

PERKO, John Francis

Position: G
Height: 6'1"; Weight: 225
College: Minnesota, Notre Dame
Born: April 8, 1918, Ely, MN
Deceased: June 7, 1994, Hibbing, MN

STATISTICS

Games

	GP	GS
1946 Buffalo Bisons	14	10
Total	14	10

PERPICH, George Rudolph

Position: T
Height: 6'2"; Weight: 223
College: Georgetown
Born: June 22, 1920
Deceased: May 26, 1993, Hibbing, MN

STATISTICS

Games

	GP	GS
1946 Brooklyn Dodgers	13	0
1947 Baltimore Colts	14	10
Total	27	10

Punt Returns

	Ret	Yds	TD
1946 Brooklyn Dodgers	1	16	0
Total	1	16	0

PERROTTI, Michael Anthony (Mike)

Position: T
Height: 6'3"; Weight: 243
College: Cincinnati, Ohio State
Born: June 12, 1923, Cleveland, OH
Deceased: November 30, 1974, Montgomery, OH

STATISTICS

Games

	GP	GS
1948 Los Angeles Dons	14	0
1949 Los Angeles Dons	12	3
Total	26	3

PERRY, Fletcher Joseph (Joe)

Position: FB
Height: 6'0"; Weight: 200
College: Compton Community College
Born: January 22, 1927, Stevens, AR
Deceased: April 25, 2011, Chandler, AZ

STATISTICS

Games

	GP	GS
1948 San Francisco 49ers	14	0
1949 San Francisco 49ers	11	5
1950 San Francisco 49ers	12	0
1951 San Francisco 49ers	11	0
1952 San Francisco 49ers	12	0
1953 San Francisco 49ers	12	0
1954 San Francisco 49ers	12	0
1955 San Francisco 49ers	11	0
1956 San Francisco 49ers	11	0
1957 San Francisco 49ers	8	0
1958 San Francisco 49ers	12	0
1959 San Francisco 49ers	11	0
1960 San Francisco 49ers	10	0
1961 Baltimore Colts	13	0
1962 Baltimore Colts	12	0
1963 San Francisco 49ers	9	0
Total	181	5

Rushing

	Rush	Yds	TD
1948 S.F. 49ers	77	562	10
1949 S.F. 49ers	115	783	8
1950 S.F. 49ers	124	647	5
1951 S.F. 49ers	136	677	3
1952 S.F. 49ers	158	725	8
1953 S.F. 49ers	192	1018	10
1954 S.F. 49ers	173	1049	8
1955 S.F. 49ers	156	701	2
1956 S.F. 49ers	115	520	3
1957 S.F. 49ers	97	454	3
1958 S.F. 49ers	125	758	4
1959 S.F. 49ers	139	602	3
1960 S.F. 49ers	36	95	1
1961 Baltimore Colts	168	675	3
1962 Baltimore Colts	94	359	0
1963 S.F. 49ers	24	98	0
Total	1929	9723	71

Receiving

	Rec	Yds	TD
1948 S.F. 49ers	8	79	1
1949 S.F. 49ers	11	146	3
1950 S.F. 49ers	13	69	1
1951 S.F. 49ers	18	167	1
1952 S.F. 49ers	15	81	0
1953 S.F. 49ers	19	191	3
1954 S.F. 49ers	26	203	0
1955 S.F. 49ers	19	55	1
1956 S.F. 49ers	18	104	0
1957 S.F. 49ers	15	130	0
1958 S.F. 49ers	23	218	1
1959 S.F. 49ers	12	53	0
1960 S.F. 49ers	3	–3	0
1961 Baltimore Colts	34	322	1
1962 Baltimore Colts	22	194	0
1963 S.F. 49ers	4	12	0
Total	260	2021	12

Passing

	Comp	Att	Yds	TD	Int
1949 S.F. 49ers	0	2	0	0	0
1951 S.F. 49ers	1	1	31	1	0
1952 S.F. 49ers	0	2	0	0	0
1953 S.F. 49ers	1	1	14	0	0
1954 S.F. 49ers	1	1	34	0	0
1955 S.F. 49ers	0	2	0	0	0
1957 S.F. 49ers	0	1	0	0	0
1963 S.F. 49ers	0	1	0	0	0
Total	3	11	79	1	0

Kick Returns

	Ret	Yds	TD
1948 S.F. 49ers	4	145	1
1949 S.F. 49ers	14	337	0
1950 S.F. 49ers	12	223	0
1951 S.F. 49ers	1	32	0
1953 S.F. 49ers	2	21	0
Total	33	758	1

Interceptions

	Int	Yds	TD
1948 S.F. 49ers	1	24	0
Total	1	24	0

Fumbles

	Fum	Rec	Yds	TD
1950 S.F. 49ers	11	5	4	0
1951 S.F. 49ers	5	0	0	0
1952 S.F. 49ers	6	3	2	0
1953 S.F. 49ers	8	1	0	0
1954 S.F. 49ers	6	2	0	0
1955 S.F. 49ers	6	0	0	0
1956 S.F. 49ers	3	0	0	0
1957 S.F. 49ers	3	0	0	0
1958 S.F. 49ers	3	2	0	0
1959 S.F. 49ers	6	1	0	0
1960 S.F. 49ers	2	1	0	0
1961 Baltimore Colts	3	0	0	0
1962 Baltimore Colts	3	0	0	0
1963 S.F. 49ers	1	0	0	0
Total	66	15	6	0

Field Goals

	FGM	FGA
1953 S.F. 49ers	*	3
1954 S.F. 49ers	1	3
Total	1	6

Point After Touchdown

	XPM	XPA
1954 S.F. 49ers	6	7
Total	6	7

PFOHL, Robert Stormont (Bob)

Position: B
Height: 6'0"; Weight: 200
College: Kings Point, Purdue
Born: May 21, 1926, Vincennes, IN
Deceased: May 11, 1996, Lafayette, IN

STATISTICS

Games

	GP	GS
1948 Baltimore Colts	14	14
1949 Baltimore Colts	12	7
Total	26	21

Rushing

	Rush	Yds	TD
1948 Baltimore Colts	107	455	4
1949 Baltimore Colts	67	205	2
Total	174	660	6

Receiving

	Rec	Yds	TD
1948 Baltimore Colts	13	134	1
1949 Baltimore Colts	7	62	0
Total	20	196	1

Punt Returns

	Ret	Yds	TD
1948 Baltimore Colts	2	102	1
Total	2	102	1

PHILLIPS, Michael (Mike)

Position: C-LB
Height: 6'0"; Weight: 208
College: Western Maryland
Born: November 22, 1921, Clifton Heights, PA
Deceased: April 17, 1994, Midlothian, VA

Statistics

	Games	
	GP	GS
1947 Baltimore Colts	12	9
Total	**12**	**9**

	Kick Returns		
	Ret	Yds	TD
1948 Baltimore Colts	17	366	0
1949 Baltimore Colts	4	98	0
Total	**21**	**464**	**0**

PIGGOTT, Bert Coley

Position: RB
Height: 6'2"; Weight: 195
College: Illinois
Born: March 5, 1921, Hinsdale, IL
Deceased: January 10, 1999, Greensboro, NC

Statistics

	Games	
	GP	GS
1947 Los Angeles Dons	13	2
Total	**13**	**2**

	Rushing		
	Rush	Yds	TD
1947 Los Angeles Dons	46	161	0
Total	**46**	**161**	**0**

	Receiving		
	Rec	Yds	TD
1947 Los Angeles Dons	7	63	1
Total	**7**	**63**	**1**

	Punt Returns		
	Ret	Yds	TD
1947 Los Angeles Dons	1	7	0
Total	**1**	**7**	**0**

	Kick Returns		
	Ret	Yds	TD
1947 Los Angeles Dons	5	120	0
Total	**5**	**120**	**0**

	Interceptions		
	Int	Yds	TD
1947 Los Angeles Dons	1	9	0
Total	**1**	**9**	**0**

PIPKIN, Joyce Clarence

Position: E-DE-BB
Height: 6'1"; Weight: 204
College: Arkansas
Born: January 9, 1924, Lono, AR
Deceased: April 11, 2017, Bethlehem, PA

Statistics

	Games	
	GP	GS
1948 New York Giants	8	0
1949 Los Angeles Dons	11	0
Total	**19**	**0**

	Receiving		
	Rec	Yds	TD
1948 New York Giants	2	28	0
Total	**2**	**28**	**0**

	Fumbles			
	Fum	Rec	Yds	TD
1948 New York Giants	0	2	0	0
Total	**0**	**2**	**0**	**0**

PIRRO, Rocco A.

Position: G-B-T
Height: 6'0"; Weight: 226
College: Catholic
Born: June 30, 1916, Syracuse, NY
Deceased: January 26, 1995, Solvay, NY

Statistics

	Games	
	GP	GS
1940 Pittsburgh Steelers	9	0
1941 Pittsburgh Steelers	11	1
1946 Buffalo Bisons	13	11
1947 Buffalo Bills	13	12
1948 Buffalo Bills	14	14
1949 Buffalo Bills	11	11
Total	**71**	**49**

	Rushing		
	Rush	Yds	TD
1941 Pittsburgh Steelers	1	1	0
Total	**1**	**1**	**0**

	Receiving		
	Rec	Yds	TD
1941 Pittsburgh Steelers	2	31	0
Total	**2**	**31**	**0**

	Interceptions		
	Int	Yds	TD
1941 Pittsburgh Steelers	1	2	0
Total	**1**	**2**	**0**

PISKOR, Roman J. (Ray)

Position: G-T
Height: 6'0"; Weight: 245
College: Niagara
Born: August 9, 1917, North Tonawanda, NY
Deceased: August 1981, North Tonawanda, NY

Statistics

	Games	
	GP	GS
1946 New York Yankees	12	7
1947 Cleveland Browns	10	1
1948 Chicago Rockets	12	2
Total	34	10

POLANSKI, John B.

Position: FB
Height: 6'2"; Weight: 211
College: Wake Forest
Born: September 6, 1918, Buffalo, NY
Deceased: March 11, 1956, Detroit, MI

Statistics

	Games	
	GP	GS
1942 Detroit Lions	3	1
1946 Los Angeles Dons	13	3
Total	16	4

	Rushing		
	Rush	Yds	TD
1942 Detroit Lions	17	67	0
1946 Los Angeles Dons	28	77	1
Total	45	144	1

	Receiving		
	Rec	Yds	TD
1946 Los Angeles Dons	2	15	1
Total	2	15	1

	Kick Returns		
	Ret	Yds	TD
1942 Detroit Lions	2	49	0
Total	2	49	0

	Interceptions		
	Int	Yds	TD
1942 Detroit Lions	1	20	0
1946 Los Angeles Dons	1	50	0
Total	2	70	0

POOL, John Hampton (Hamp)

Position: E
Height: 6'3"; Weight: 221
College: Army, California, Stanford
Born: March 11, 1915, San Miguel, CA
Deceased: May 26, 2000, Mariposa, CA

Statistics

	Games	
	GP	GS
1940 Chicago Bears	5	4
1941 Chicago Bears	7	0
1942 Chicago Bears	11	0
1943 Chicago Bears	10	0
1946 Miami Seahawks	4	0
Total	37	4

	Receiving		
	Rec	Yds	TD
1940 Chicago Bears	2	55	0
1941 Chicago Bears	5	101	1
1942 Chicago Bears	10	321	5
1943 Chicago Bears	18	363	5
1946 Miami Seahawks	3	63	0
Total	38	903	11

POOLE, George Barney (Barney)

Position: DE-E
Height: 6'2"; Weight: 231
College: Army, Mississippi, North Carolina
Born: October 29, 1923, Gloster, MS
Deceased: April 12, 2005, Jackson, MS

Statistics

	Games	
	GP	GS
1949 New York Yankees	11	0
1950 New York Yanks	12	0
1951 New York Yanks	11	0
1952 Dallas Texans	12	0
1953 Baltimore Colts	12	0
1954 New York Giants	11	0
Total	69	0

	Receiving		
	Rec	Yds	TD
1949 New York Yankees	6	83	0
1950 New York Yanks	4	82	1
1952 Dallas Texans	2	23	0
Total	12	188	1

	Punt Returns		
	Ret	Yds	TD
1949 New York Yankees	1	6	0
Total	1	6	0

	Kick Returns		
	Ret	Yds	TD
1950 New York Yanks	2	8	0
1953 Baltimore Colts	2	24	0
Total	4	32	0

	Interceptions		
	Int	Yds	TD
1949 New York Yankees	1	0	0
Total	1	0	0

Fumbles

	Fum	Rec	Yds	TD
1950 New York Yanks	0	1	3	0
1951 New York Yanks	0	2	1	0
1953 Baltimore Colts	0	6	17	0
Total	0	9	21	0

POOLE, Oliver Lamar (Ollie)

Position: DE-E
Height: 6'3"; Weight: 220
College: Mississippi, North Carolina
Born: April 18, 1922, Gloster, MS
Deceased: June 27, 2009, Ruston, LA

STATISTICS

Games

	GP	GS
1947 New York Yankees	5	0
1948 Baltimore Colts	9	1
1949 Detroit Lions	8	0
Total	22	1

Receiving

	Rec	Yds	TD
1947 New York Yankees	1	19	0
1948 Baltimore Colts	1	2	0
Total	2	21	0

Punt Returns

	Ret	Yds	TD
1947 New York Yankees	1	5	0
Total	1	5	0

PREWITT, Felton Winters (Felto)

Position: C-LB
Height: 5'11"; Weight: 207
College: Tulsa
Born: May 17, 1924, Corsicana, TX
Deceased: March 15, 1998, Reno, NV

STATISTICS

Games

	GP	GS
1946 Buffalo Bisons	14	8
1947 Buffalo Bills	13	10
1948 Buffalo Bills	7	5
1949 Baltimore Colts	12	7
Total	46	30

Interceptions

	Int	Yds	TD
1946 Buffalo Bisons	4	89	0
1947 Buffalo Bills	2	20	0
Total	6	109	0

PRICE, Charles Walemon (Cotton)

Position: TB-DB-QB
Height: 6'1"; Weight: 180
College: Texas A&M
Born: May 31, 1918, Bridgeport, TX
Deceased: September 24, 2008, Lubbock, TX

STATISTICS

Games

	GP	GS
1940 Detroit Lions	9	1
1941 Detroit Lions	11	2
1945 Detroit Lions	8	3
1946 Miami Seahawks	7	2
Total	35	8

Rushing

	Rush	Yds	TD
1940 Detroit Lions	42	122	2
1941 Detroit Lions	16	36	0
1945 Detroit Lions	24	71	0
1946 Miami Seahawks	15	−55	0
Total	97	174	2

Receiving

	Rec	Yds	TD
1941 Detroit Lions	1	6	0
1946 Miami Seahawks	2	17	0
Total	3	23	0

Passing

	Comp	Att	Yds	TD	Int
1940 Detroit Lions	33	66	456	3	7
1941 Detroit Lions	9	33	118	0	4
1945 Detroit Lions	16	52	256	3	8
1946 Seahawks	36	74	484	2	5
Total	94	225	1314	8	24

Punting

	Punt	Yds	Blk
1940 Detroit Lions	9	374	0
1941 Detroit Lions	5	191	0
1945 Detroit Lions	4	148	0
1946 Miami Seahawks	4	105	1
Total	22	818	1

Punt Returns

	Ret	Yds	TD
1941 Detroit Lions	3	48	0
1945 Detroit Lions	3	32	0
Total	6	80	0

Kick Returns

	Ret	Yds	TD
1941 Detroit Lions	2	51	0
1945 Detroit Lions	4	79	0
1946 Miami Seahawks	2	32	0
Total	8	162	0

Interceptions

	Int	Yds	TD
1945 Detroit Lions	1	16	0
Total	1	16	0

Fumbles

	Fum	Rec	Yds	TD
1945 Detroit Lions	3	2	11	0
Total	**3**	**2**	**11**	**0**

Point After Touchdown

	XPM	XPA
1940 Detroit Lions	4	4
Total	**4**	**4**

PRINCIPE, Dominic Alfred (Dom)

Position: B-LB
Height: 6'0"; Weight: 205
College: Fordham
Born: February 9, 1917, Brockton, MA
Deceased: April 9, 2010, Jupiter, FL

STATISTICS

Games

	GP	GS
1940 New York Giants	6	1
1941 New York Giants	8	0
1942 New York Giants	11	1
1946 Brooklyn Dodgers	10	7
Total	**35**	**9**

Rushing

	Rush	Yds	TD
1940 New York Giants	11	8	0
1941 New York Giants	1	5	0
1946 Brooklyn Dodgers	39	139	2
Total	**51**	**152**	**2**

Receiving

	Rec	Yds	TD
1941 New York Giants	4	54	0
1942 New York Giants	2	33	0
1946 Brooklyn Dodgers	3	25	0
Total	**9**	**112**	**0**

Punting

	Punt	Yds	Blk
1942 New York Giants	1	32	0
Total	**1**	**32**	**0**

Kick Returns

	Ret	Yds	TD
1946 Brooklyn Dodgers	6	117	0
Total	**6**	**117**	**0**

Interceptions

	Int	Yds	TD
1940 New York Giants	1	12	0
Total	**1**	**12**	**0**

PROCTOR, Dewey Michael

Position: FB-LB
Height: 5'11"; Weight: 215
College: Furman
Born: July 1, 1921, Lake View, SC
Deceased: July 2, 2009, Mullins, SC

STATISTICS

Games

	GP	GS
1946 New York Yankees	4	0
1947 New York Yankees	11	1
1948 Chicago Rockets	9	4
1949 New York Yankees	1	0
Total	**25**	**5**

Rushing

	Rush	Yds	TD
1946 New York Yankees	23	76	1
1947 New York Yankees	15	15	1
1948 Chicago Rockets	47	190	1
1949 New York Yankees	1	−1	0
Total	**86**	**280**	**3**

Receiving

	Rec	Yds	TD
1946 New York Yankees	3	32	1
1947 New York Yankees	1	4	0
1948 Chicago Rockets	2	18	0
Total	**6**	**54**	**1**

Passing

	Comp	Att	Yds	TD	Int
1947 Yankees	0	1	0	0	0
Total	**0**	**1**	**0**	**0**	**0**

Kick Returns

	Ret	Yds	TD
1947 New York Yankees	1	15	0
Total	**1**	**15**	**0**

Interceptions

	Int	Yds	TD
1947 New York Yankees	1	32	0
Total	**1**	**32**	**0**

PROKOP, Edward Stanley (Eddie)

Position: B
Height: 5'11"; Weight: 200
College: Georgia Tech
Born: February 11, 1922, Cleveland, OH
Deceased: May 30, 1955, Cleveland, OH

STATISTICS

Games

	GP	GS
1946 New York Yankees	12	3
1947 New York Yankees	13	4
1948 Chicago Rockets	9	7
1949 New York Yankees	6	1
Total	**40**	**15**

Rushing

	Rush	Yds	TD
1946 New York Yankees	65	236	1
1947 New York Yankees	76	324	4
1948 Chicago Rockets	54	266	1
1949 New York Yankees	31	109	2
Total	**226**	**935**	**8**

Receiving

	Rec	Yds	TD
1946 New York Yankees	5	52	1
1947 New York Yankees	3	79	1
1948 Chicago Rockets	7	223	3
1949 New York Yankees	1	7	0
Total	**16**	**361**	**5**

Passing

	Comp	Att	Yds	TD	Int
1946 Yankees	4	11	72	0	0
1947 Yankees	4	8	137	2	1
1948 Chicago Rockets	0	1	0	0	0
Total	**8**	**20**	**209**	**2**	**1**

Punt Returns

	Ret	Yds	TD
1946 New York Yankees	4	116	1
1947 New York Yankees	7	78	0
1948 Chicago Rockets	6	80	0
Total	**17**	**274**	**1**

Kick Returns

	Ret	Yds	TD
1946 New York Yankees	2	47	0
1947 New York Yankees	7	188	0
1948 Chicago Rockets	15	323	0
1949 New York Yankees	3	62	0
Total	**27**	**620**	**0**

Interceptions

	Int	Yds	TD
1946 New York Yankees	1	14	0
1947 New York Yankees	3	57	0
Total	**4**	**71**	**0**

PUCCI, Benito Modesto (Ben)

Position: T
Height: 6'4"; Weight: 255
College: (None)
Born: January 26, 1925, St. Louis, MO
Deceased: July 8, 2013, San Antonio, TX

STATISTICS

Games

	GP	GS
1946 Buffalo Bisons	12	1
1947 Chicago Rockets	13	0
1948 Cleveland Browns	12	0
Total	**37**	**4**

PUDDY, Marvin Harold (Hal)

Position: T
Height: 6'3"; Weight: 220
College: Oregon State
Born: August 18, 1924, Hood River, OR
Deceased: January 31, 1975, Port Angeles, WA

STATISTICS

Games

	GP	GS
1948 San Francisco 49ers	4	0
Total	**4**	**0**

PUGH, Marion C.

Position: B
Height: 6'1"; Weight: 187
College: Texas A&M
Born: September 6, 1919, Fort Worth, TX
Deceased: November 20, 1976, College Station, TX

STATISTICS

Games

	GP	GS
1941 New York Giants	5	0
1945 New York Giants	5	2
1946 Miami Seahawks	14	10
Total	**24**	**12**

Rushing

	Rush	Yds	TD
1941 New York Giants	24	50	0
1945 New York Giants	24	−52	0
1946 Miami Seahawks	29	−125	0
Total	**77**	**−127**	**2**

Receiving

	Rec	Yds	TD
1946 Miami Seahawks	4	43	0
Total	**4**	**43**	**0**

Passing

	Comp	Att	Yds	TD	Int
1941 N.Y. Giants	12	24	161	1	0
1945 N.Y. Giants	27	58	390	3	3
1946 Seahawks	55	118	608	5	12
Total	**94**	**200**	**1159**	**9**	**15**

Punt Returns

	Ret	Yds	TD
1941 New York Giants	1	5	0
Total	**1**	**5**	**0**

Kick Returns

	Ret	Yds	TD
1946 Miami Seahawks	1	24	0
Total	**1**	**24**	**0**

Point After Touchdown

	XPM	XPA
1941 New York Giants	*	1
Total	*****	**1**

PURDIN, Calvin O'Neale (Cal)

Position: B
Height: 6'2"; Weight: 188
College: Tulsa
Born: February 22, 1921, Jefferson, OK
Deceased: December 29, 1982, Augusta, KS

STATISTICS

Games
	GP	GS
1943 Chicago Cardinals	4	2
1946 Miami Seahawks	2	1
1946 Brooklyn Dodgers	7	3
Total	13	6

Rushing
	Rush	Yds	TD
1943 Chicago Cardinals	9	20	0
1946 Miami Seahawks	2	1	0
1946 Brooklyn Dodgers	8	11	0
Total	19	32	0

Receiving
	Rec	Yds	TD
1943 Chicago Cardinals	3	35	0
1946 Miami Seahawks	2	1	0
1946 Brooklyn Dodgers	10	107	0
Total	15	143	0

Passing
	Comp	Att	Yds	TD	Int
1943 Chicago Cardinals	1	2	7	0	0
1946 Brooklyn Dodgers	1	1	-2	0	0
Total	2	3	5	0	0

Punting
	Punt	Yds	Blk
1943 Chicago Cardinals	8	341	0
Total	8	341	0

Punt Returns
	Ret	Yds	TD
1943 Chicago Cardinals	1	6	0
1946 Brooklyn Dodgers	4	52	0
Total	5	58	0

Kick Returns
	Ret	Yds	TD
1943 Chicago Cardinals	1	24	0
1946 Miami Seahawks	1	11	0
1946 Brooklyn Dodgers	3	66	0
Total	5	101	0

QUILLEN, Frank Harris

Position: E-DE
Height: 6'5"; Weight: 225
College: Pennsylvania
Born: December 18, 1920, Ridley Park, PA
Deceased: September 21, 1990, Hockessin, DE

STATISTICS

Games
	GP	GS
1946 Chicago Rockets	14	4
1947 Chicago Rockets	6	2
Total	20	6

Receiving
	Rec	Yds	TD
1946 Chicago Rockets	13	143	2
1947 Chicago Rockets	7	113	1
Total	20	256	3

Kick Returns
	Ret	Yds	TD
1946 Chicago Rockets	1	13	0
Total	1	13	0

Interceptions
	Int	Yds	TD
1946 Chicago Rockets	1	9	0
Total	1	9	0

QUILTER, Charles Rew (Charley)

Position: T-DT
Height: 6'1"; Weight: 240
College: Tyler Junior College
Born: May 8, 1926, Shreveport, LA
Deceased:

STATISTICS

Games
	GP	GS
1949 San Francisco 49ers	12	1
1950 San Francisco 49ers	8	0
Total	20	1

RADOVICH, William Alex (Bill)

Position: G
Height: 5'10"; Weight: 238
College: USC
Born: June 24, 1915, Chicago, IL
Deceased: March 6, 2002, Newport Beach, CA

STATISTICS

Games
	GP	GS
1938 Detroit Lions	10	4
1939 Detroit Lions	11	1
1940 Detroit Lions	10	2
1941 Detroit Lions	11	4
1945 Detroit Lions	9	8
1946 Los Angeles Dons	14	12
1947 Los Angeles Dons	14	3
Total	79	34

Fumbles
	Fum	Rec	Yds	TD
1945 Detroit Lions	0	1	0	0
Total	0	1	0	0

RAIMONDI, Benjamin Lewis (Ben)

Position: TB
Height: 5'10"; Weight: 175
College: Indiana, William & Mary
Born: January 23, 1925, Brooklyn, NY
Deceased:

STATISTICS

Games

	GP	GS
1947 New York Yankees	7	0
Total	**7**	**0**

Rushing

	Rush	Yds	TD
1947 New York Yankees	6	11	0
Total	**6**	**11**	**0**

Passing

	Comp	Att	Yds	TD	Int
1947 N.Y. Yankees	3	15	54	0	0
Total	**3**	**15**	**54**	**0**	**0**

RAMSEY, Knox Wagner

Position: G
Height: 6'1"; Weight: 216
College: William & Mary
Born: February 13, 1926, Speed, IN
Deceased: March 19, 2005, Richmond, VA

STATISTICS

Games

	GP	GS
1948 Los Angeles Dons	13	7
1949 Los Angeles Dons	12	8
1950 Chicago Cardinals	12	0
1951 Chicago Cardinals	10	0
1952 Philadelphia Eagles	3	0
1952 Washington Redskins	8	0
1953 Washington Redskins	11	0
Total	**69**	**15**

Kick Returns

	Ret	Yds	TD
1951 Chicago Cardinals	1	0	0
Total	**1**	**0**	**0**

Fumbles

	Fum	Rec	Yds	TD
1951 Chicago Cardinals	1	0	0	0
1952 Wash. Redskins	0	1	0	0
Total	**1**	**1**	**0**	**0**

RAMSEY, Raymond Leroy (Ray)

Position: B
Height: 6'2"; Weight: 166
College: Bradley
Born: July 18, 1921, Springfield, IL
Deceased: August 25, 2009, Springfield, IL

STATISTICS

Games

	GP	GS
1947 Chicago Rockets	14	10
1948 Brooklyn Dodgers	11	6
1949 Chicago Hornets	12	10
1950 Chicago Cardinals	6	0
1951 Chicago Cardinals	10	0
1952 Chicago Cardinals	9	0
1953 Chicago Cardinals	12	0
Total	**74**	**26**

Rushing

	Rush	Yds	TD
1947 Chicago Rockets	70	433	2
1948 Brooklyn Dodgers	22	48	0
1949 Chicago Hornets	32	43	0
Total	**124**	**524**	**2**

Receiving

	Rec	Yds	TD
1947 Chicago Rockets	35	768	8
1948 Brooklyn Dodgers	13	315	2
1949 Chicago Hornets	17	366	4
1951 Chicago Cardinals	8	135	0
1952 Chicago Cardinals	3	27	0
1953 Chicago Cardinals	12	118	0
Total	**88**	**1729**	**14**

Passing

	Comp	Att	Yds	TD	Int
1948 Dodgers	0	1	0	0	0
Total	**0**	**1**	**0**	**0**	**0**

Punt Returns

	Ret	Yds	TD
1947 Chicago Rockets	11	131	0
1948 Brooklyn Dodgers	5	82	1
1949 Chicago Hornets	8	64	0
Total	**24**	**277**	**1**

Kick Returns

	Ret	Yds	TD
1947 Chicago Rockets	16	406	0
1948 Brooklyn Dodgers	10	233	0
1949 Chicago Hornets	14	407	0
Total	**40**	**1046**	**0**

Interceptions

	Int	Yds	TD
1947 Chicago Rockets	5	66	0
1948 Brooklyn Dodgers	7	124	0
1949 Chicago Hornets	2	79	0
1950 Chicago Cardinals	1	0	0
1951 Chicago Cardinals	5	90	0
1952 Chicago Cardinals	5	67	0
1953 Chicago Cardinals	10	237	1
Total	**35**	**663**	**1**

Fumbles

	Fum	Rec	Yds	TD
1950 Chicago Cardinals	0	4	5	0
1952 Chicago Cardinals	1	0	0	0
1953 Chicago Cardinals	1	0	0	0
Total	**2**	**4**	**5**	**0**

RAPACZ, John Joseph

Position: C-LB
Height: 6'4"; Weight: 252
College: Oklahoma, Western Michigan
Born: April 25, 1924, Rosedale, OH
Deceased: January 2, 1991, Midwest City, OK

STATISTICS

Games

	GP	GS
1948 Chicago Rockets	10	3
1949 Chicago Hornets	12	7
1950 New York Giants	10	0
1951 New York Giants	12	0
1952 New York Giants	8	0
1953 New York Giants	12	0
1954 New York Giants	12	0
Total	76	10

Fumbles

	Fum	Rec	Yds	TD
1950 New York Giants	0	2	0	0
1952 New York Giants	0	1	0	0
Total	0	3	0	0

RATTERMAN, George William

Position: QB
Height: 6'0"; Weight: 192
College: Notre Dame
Born: November 12, 1926, Cincinnati, OH
Deceased: November 3, 2007, Centennial, CO

STATISTICS

Games

	GP	GS
1947 Buffalo Bills	14	4
1948 Buffalo Bills	14	13
1949 Buffalo Bills	11	11
1950 New York Yanks	12	12
1951 New York Yanks	6	1
1952 Cleveland Browns	6	0
1953 Cleveland Browns	9	1
1954 Cleveland Browns	6	0
1955 Cleveland Browns	10	0
1956 Cleveland Browns	4	4
Total	92	46

Rushing

	Rush	Yds	TD
1947 Buffalo Bills*	17	−49	1
1948 Buffalo Bills	12	−18	3
1949 Buffalo Bills	36	85	4
1950 New York Yanks	11	0	3
1951 New York Yanks	3	9	0
1952 Cleveland Browns	1	2	0
1953 Cleveland Browns	2	6	0
1954 Cleveland Browns	8	−13	1
1955 Cleveland Browns	6	8	1
1956 Cleveland Browns	10	19	1
Total	106	49	14

Passing

	Comp	Att	Yds	TD	Int
1947 Buffalo Bills	124	244	1840	22	20
1948 Buffalo Bills	168	335	2577	16	22
1949 Buffalo Bills	146	252	1777	14	13
1950 N.Y. Yanks	140	294	2251	22	24
1951 N.Y. Yanks	31	67	340	2	6
1952 Cleveland Browns	2	6	20	1	2
1953 Cleveland Browns	23	41	301	4	0
1954 Cleveland Browns	32	53	465	3	3
1955 Cleveland Browns	32	47	504	6	3
1956 Cleveland Browns	39	57	398	1	3
Total	737	1396	10473	91	96

Fumbles

	Fum	Rec	Yds	TD
1950 N.Y. Yanks	4	1	0	0
1951 N.Y. Yanks	1	0	0	0
1954 Cle. Browns	1	0	0	0
1955 Cle. Browns	2	0	0	0
1956 Cle. Browns	1	0	0	0
Total	9	1	0	0

Point After Touchdown

	XPM	XPA
1947 Buffalo Bills	*	1
Total	*	1

George Ratterman was credited with a rushing attempt for zero yards and a touchdown in the first game of the season. Since the numbers could not be verified, the official statistics were used.

REECE, Donald Miles (Don)

Position: FB-LB-T
Height: 6'1"; Weight: 230
College: Missouri
Born: December 1, 1919, Marysville, OH
Deceased: August 26, 1992, Maysville, MO

STATISTICS

Games

	GP	GS
1946 Miami Seahawks	13	4
Total	13	4

Rushing

	Rush	Yds	TD
1946 Miami Seahawks	30	109	2
Total	30	109	2

Receiving

	Rec	Yds	TD
1946 Miami Seahawks	1	5	0
Total	1	5	0

Interceptions

	Int	Yds	TD
1946 Miami Seahawks	1	17	0
Total	1	17	0

REINHARD, Robert Richard (Bob)

Position: T-FB
Height: 6'4"; Weight: 234
College: California
Born: October 17, 1920, Hollywood, CA
Deceased: August 2, 1996, Salem, OR

STATISTICS

Games

	GP	GS
1946 Los Angeles Dons	14	14
1947 Los Angeles Dons	14	11
1948 Los Angeles Dons	14	14
1949 Los Angeles Dons	12	12
1950 Los Angeles Rams	12	0
Total	66	51

Rushing

	Rush	Yds	TD
1946 Los Angeles Dons	1	−30	0
1947 Los Angeles Dons	41	150	0
1948 Los Angeles Dons	1	21	0
Total	43	141	0

Receiving

	Rec	Yds	TD
1947 Los Angeles Dons	3	34	1
1948 Los Angeles Dons	4	54	0
1949 Los Angeles Dons	1	2	0
1950 Los Angeles Rams	1	11	1
Total	9	101	2

Passing

	Comp	Att	Yds	TD	Int
1946 L.A. Dons	1	1	7	0	0
1947 L.A. Dons	2	4	21	0	0
Total	3	5	28	0	0

Punting

	Punt	Yds	Blk
1946 Los Angeles Dons	44	1996	1
1947 Los Angeles Dons	28	1279	1
1948 Los Angeles Dons	6	204	0
Total	78	3479	2

Punt Returns

	Ret	Yds	TD
1948 Los Angeles Dons	1	23	0
Total	1	23	0

Kick Returns

	Ret	Yds	TD
1947 Los Angeles Dons	3	42	0
1948 Los Angeles Dons	3	51	0
Total	6	93	0

Interceptions

	Int	Yds	TD
1947 Los Angeles Dons	1	0	0
Total	1	0	0

Fumbles

	Fum	Rec	Yds	TD
1950 Los Angeles Rams	0	2	0	0
Total	0	2	0	0

REINHARD, William Carl (Bill)

Position: B
Height: 5'10"; Weight: 168
College: California
Born: May 17, 1922, Los Angeles, CA
Deceased: January 30, 2017, Palm Desert, CA

STATISTICS

Games

	GP	GS
1947 Los Angeles Dons	8	0
1948 Los Angeles Dons	14	1
Total	22	1

Rushing

	Rush	Yds	TD
1947 Los Angeles Dons	1	2	1
1948 Los Angeles Dons	6	31	0
Total	7	33	1

Receiving

	Rec	Yds	TD
1948 Los Angeles Dons	5	48	0
Total	5	48	0

Passing

	Comp	Att	Yds	TD	Int
1947 L.A. Dons	0	2	0	0	0
1948 L.A. Dons	0	5	0	0	0
Total	0	7	0	0	0

Punt Returns

	Ret	Yds	TD
1947 Los Angeles Dons	2	22	0
1948 Los Angeles Dons	16	276	1
Total	18	298	1

Kick Returns

	Ret	Yds	TD
1948 Los Angeles Dons	2	41	0
Total	2	41	0

Interceptions

	Int	Yds	TD
1947 Los Angeles Dons	1	7	0
1948 Los Angeles Dons	4	52	1
Total	5	59	1

REISZ, Albert Harry (Albie)

Position: TB-HB-QB
Height: 5'10"; Weight: 175
College: Southeastern Louisiana
Born: November 29, 1917, Lorain, OH
Deceased: May 1, 1985, New Orleans, LA

STATISTICS

Games

	GP	GS
1944 Cleveland Rams	10	2
1945 Cleveland Rams	10	0
1946 Los Angeles Rams	2	1
1947 Buffalo Bills	13	0
Total	35	3

Rushing

	Rush	Yds	TD
1944 Cleveland Rams	69	134	2
1945 Cleveland Rams	12	–2	0
1947 Buffalo Bills	2	32	0
Total	83	164	2

Receiving

	Rec	Yds	TD
1945 Cleveland Rams	1	11	0
Total	1	11	0

Passing

	Comp	Att	Yds	TD	Int
1944 Cle. Rams	49	113	777	8	10
1945 Cle. Rams	8	21	146	2	3
Total	57	134	923	10	13

Punting

	Punt	Yds	Blk
1944 Cleveland Rams	24	959	0
1945 Cleveland Rams	7	258	0
1947 Buffalo Bills	57	2107	0
Total	88	3324	0

Punt Returns

	Ret	Yds	TD
1944 Cleveland Rams	5	68	0
1945 Cleveland Rams	8	78	0
Total	13	146	0

Kick Returns

	Ret	Yds	TD
1944 Cleveland Rams	12	285	0
Total	12	285	0

Interceptions

	Int	Yds	TD
1944 Cleveland Rams	3	72	0
1945 Cleveland Rams	2	55	0
Total	5	127	0

Fumbles

	Fum	Rec	Yds	TD
1945 Cleveland Rams	3	44	22	0
Total	3	44	22	0

REMINGTON, Joseph William (Bill)

Position: C-LB
Height: 6'1"; Weight: 185
College: Washington State
Born: November 2, 1920
Deceased: April 8, 2005, Bellevue, WA

STATISTICS

Games

	GP	GS
1946 San Francisco 49ers	9	1
Total	9	1

RENFRO, Golie Richard (Dick)

Position: FB-LB
Height: 5'10"; Weight: 200
College: Washington State
Born: January 25, 1919, Fort Worth, TX
Deceased: November 10, 1998, Eureka, CA

STATISTICS

Games

	GP	GS
1946 San Francisco 49ers	3	3
Total	3	3

Rushing

	Rush	Yds	TD
1946 S.F. 49ers	18	85	3
Total	18	85	3

Kick Returns

	Ret	Yds	TD
1946 S.F. 49ers	1	20	0
Total	1	20	0

REYNOLDS, James Albert (Jim)

Position: FB-LB
Height: 6'1"; Weight: 190
College: Auburn
Born: January 8, 1920, La Grange, GA
Deceased: January 30, 1985, Chatham County, GA

STATISTICS

Games

	GP	GS
1946 Miami Seahawks	7	2
Total	7	2

Rushing

	Rush	Yds	TD
1946 Miami Seahawks	32	96	0
Total	32	96	0

Receiving

	Rec	Yds	TD
1946 Miami Seahawks	1	32	0
Total	1	32	0

Punting

	Punt	Yds	Blk
1946 Miami Seahawks	1	39	0
Total	1	39	0

Kick Returns

	Ret	Yds	TD
1946 Miami Seahawks	1	13	0
Total	1	13	0

Interceptions

	Int	Yds	TD
1946 Miami Seahawks	2	33	0
Total	2	33	0

RICHESON, Thomas Ray (Ray)

Position: G
Height: 6'0"; Weight: 235
College: Alabama
Born: September 27, 1923, Russellville, AL
Deceased: April 1, 2003, Birmingham, AL

Statistics

Games

	GP	GS
1949 Chicago Hornets	12	1
Total	12	1

Kick Returns

	Ret	Yds	TD
1949 Chicago Hornets	1	0	0
Total	1	0	0

RIFFLE, Charles Francis (Charley)

Position: G
Height: 6'0"; Weight: 210
College: Notre Dame
Born: January 6, 1918, Dillonvale, OH
Deceased: February 28, 2002, Sun City West, AZ

Statistics

Games

	GP	GS
1944 Cleveland Rams	8	1
1946 New York Yankees	14	13
1947 New York Yankees	14	4
1948 New York Yankees	14	0
Total	50	18

Interceptions

	Int	Yds	TD
1948 New York Yankees	1	11	0
Total	1	11	0

ROBERTSON, Thomas Blane (Tom)

Position: C
Height: 6'0"; Weight: 199
College: Kansas, LSU, Tulsa
Born: July 25, 1917, Lawton, OK
Deceased: May 3, 1998, Tulsa, OK

Statistics

Games

	GP	GS
1941 Brooklyn Dodgers	11	0
1942 Brooklyn Dodgers	9	8
1946 New York Yankees	14	13
Total	34	21

Kick Returns

	Ret	Yds	TD
1942 Brooklyn Dodgers	1	9	0
Total	1	9	0

Interceptions

	Int	Yds	TD
1942 Brooklyn Dodgers	1	2	0
Total	1	2	0

ROBNETT, William Edward (Ed)

Position: FB-LB
Height: 5'8"; Weight: 205
College: Texas A&M, Texas Tech
Born: March 7, 1920, Klondike, TX
Deceased: September 20, 1990, Lubbock, TX

Statistics

Games

	GP	GS
1947 San Francisco 49ers	4	0
Total	4	0

Rushing

	Rush	Yds	TD
1947 S.F. 49ers	7	18	0
Total	7	18	0

ROCKWELL, Henry Albert (Hank)

Position: G
Height: 6'4"; Weight: 231
College: Arizona State
Born: February 10, 1917, Whittier, CA
Deceased: November 30, 1997, Okaloosa County, FL

Statistics

Games

	GP	GS
1940 Cleveland Rams	11	2
1941 Cleveland Rams	10	3
1942 Cleveland Rams	8	1
1946 Los Angeles Dons	13	1
1947 Los Angeles Dons	13	4
Total	55	11

Rushing

	Rush	Yds	TD
1940 Cleveland Rams	1	5	0
Total	1	5	0

Receiving

	Rec	Yds	TD
1940 Cleveland Rams	1	5	1
Total	1	5	1

Interceptions

	Int	Yds	TD
1940 Cleveland Rams	3	7	0
1941 Cleveland Rams	1	9	0
1942 Cleveland Rams	1	58	0
Total	5	74	0

RODGERS, Hosea Weaver

Position: FB
Height: 6'1"; Weight: 192
College: Alabama, North Carolina
Born: December 25, 1921, Brewton, AL
Deceased: April 9, 2001, Brewton, AL

STATISTICS

Games

	GP	GS
1949 Los Angeles Dons	12	9
Total	12	9

Rushing

	Rush	Yds	TD
1949 Los Angeles Dons	131	494	5
Total	131	494	5

Receiving

	Rec	Yds	TD
1949 Los Angeles Dons	7	97	0
Total	7	97	0

Passing

	Comp	Att	Yds	TD	Int
1949 L.A. Dons	0	1	0	0	0
Total	0	1	0	0	0

ROKISKY, John Joseph

Position: DE-E
Height: 6'2"; Weight: 202
College: Duquesne
Born: July 24, 1915, Mount Clare, WV
Deceased: November 28, 1993, Wintersville, OH

STATISTICS

Games

	GP	GS
1946 Cleveland Browns	5	0
1947 Chicago Rockets	14	1
1948 New York Yankees	6	0
Total	25	1

Receiving

	Rec	Yds	TD
1946 Cleveland Browns	1	13	0
1947 Chicago Rockets	1	8	0
Total	2	21	0

Field Goals

	FGM	FGA
1947 Chicago Rockets	4	8
Total	4	8

Point After Touchdown

	XPM	XPA
1946 Cleveland Browns	1	1
1947 Chicago Rockets	33	35
Total	34	36

ROSKIE, Kenneth (Ken)*

Position: FB
Height: 6'1"; Weight: 220
College: South Carolina
Born: November 29, 1920, Rockford, IL
Deceased: August 1986, Redmond, WA

STATISTICS

Games

	GP	GS
1946 San Francisco 49ers	8	0
1948 Green Bay Packers	6	0
1948 Detroit Lions	7	4
Total	21	4

Rushing

	Rush	Yds	TD
1946 S.F. 49ers	9	16	0
1948 Green Bay Packers	5	28	1
1948 Detroit Lions	1	1	0
Total	15	45	1

Kick Returns

	Ret	Yds	TD
1948 Detroit Lions	1	30	0
Total	1	30	0

Interceptions

	Int	Yds	TD
1948 Green Bay Packers	1	12	0
Total	1	12	0

Fumbles

	Fum	Rec	Yds	TD
1948 Detroit Lions	1	2	0	0
Total	1	2	0	0

NOTE: *There are a few discrepancies between the actual statistics and the official records in 1946. The total receiving yards for the season for Len Eshmont, Joe Vetrano, Ed Balatti and Ken Roskie were not consistent. Eshmont had an extra six receiving yards, while Vetrano was missing six yards. Balatti had an extra seven receiving yards and Roskie was missing seven yards. Since the numbers could not be verified, the official statistics are listed.*

ROTHROCK, Clifford Crossley (Cliff)

Position: C
Height: 5'10"; Weight: 190
College: North Dakota State
Born: January 10, 1922, Fargo, ND
Deceased: October 5, 2000, Anaheim, CA

STATISTICS

Games

	GP	GS
1947 Chicago Rockets	2	1
Total	**2**	**1**

ROWE, Harmon Beasley

Position: DB-HB
Height: 6'0"; Weight: 182
College: Baylor, San Francisco
Born: August 22, 1923, Livingston, TX
Deceased: January 26, 2002, Whitehouse, TX

STATISTICS

Games

	GP	GS
1947 New York Yankees	10	0
1948 New York Yankees	11	0
1949 New York Yankees	9	0
1950 New York Giants	7	0
1951 New York Giants	8	0
1952 New York Giants	12	0
Total	**57**	**0**

Rushing

	Rush	Yds	TD
1947 New York Yankees	2	−3	0
1949 New York Yankees	6	21	0
Total	**8**	**18**	**0**

Punt Returns

	Ret	Yds	TD
1948 New York Yankees	1	12	0
Total	**1**	**12**	**0**

Kick Returns

	Ret	Yds	TD
1947 New York Yankees	1	18	0
Total	**1**	**18**	**0**

Interceptions

	Int	Yds	TD
1947 New York Yankees	2	20	0
1949 New York Yankees	3	53	0
1950 New York Giants	3	48	0
1951 New York Giants	2	19	0
1952 New York Giants	1	22	0
Total	**11**	**162**	**0**

Fumbles

	Fum	Rec	Yds	TD
1950 New York Giants	1	0	0	0
Total	**1**	**0**	**0**	**0**

RUBY, Martin Owen

Position: T
Height: 6'4"; Weight: 249
College: Texas A&M
Born: June 9, 1922, Lubbock, TX
Deceased: January 3, 2002, Salmon Arm, Canada

STATISTICS

Games

	GP	GS
1946 Brooklyn Dodgers	14	13
1947 Brooklyn Dodgers	14	14
1948 Brooklyn Dodgers	14	5
1949 New York Yankees	11	11
1950 New York Yanks	12	0
Total	**65**	**43**

Receiving

	Rec	Yds	TD
1946 Brooklyn Dodgers	1	3	0
Total	**1**	**3**	**0**

Interceptions

	Int	Yds	TD
1949 New York Yankees	1	19	1
Total	**1**	**19**	**1**

Fumbles

	Fum	Rec	Yds	TD
1950 New York Yanks	0	2	0	0
Total	**0**	**2**	**0**	**0**

RUETZ, Joseph Hubert (Joe)

Position: G
Height: 6'0"; Weight: 200
College: Notre Dame
Born: October 21, 1916, Racine, WI
Deceased: January 2, 2003, Palo Alto, CA

STATISTICS

Games

	GP	GS
1946 Chicago Rockets	13	1
1948 Chicago Rockets	13	1
Total	**26**	**2**

Interceptions

	Int	Yds	TD
1946 Chicago Rockets	2	13	0
Total	**2**	**13**	**0**

RUSKUSKY, Roy J.

Position: E
Height: 6'3"; Weight: 200
College: St. Mary's
Born: April 6, 1921, Spring Valley, IL
Deceased: April 30, 2001, Peoria, IL

STATISTICS

Games

	GP	GS
1947 New York Yankees	11	1
Total	**11**	**1**

RUSSELL, James Monroe (Jack)

Position: E-DE
Height: 6'1"; Weight: 215
College: Baylor
Born: August 29, 1919, Nemo, TX
Deceased: January 16, 2006, Cleburne, TX

STATISTICS

Games
	GP	GS
1946 New York Yankees	14	6
1947 New York Yankees	14	14
1948 New York Yankees	14	13
1949 New York Yankees	12	12
1950 New York Yanks	11	0
Total	**65**	**45**

Receiving
	Rec	Yds	TD
1946 New York Yankees	23	223	4
1947 New York Yankees	20	368	2
1948 New York Yankees	23	433	6
1949 New York Yankees	7	130	1
1950 New York Yanks	10	177	2
Total	**83**	**1331**	**15**

Kick Returns
	Ret	Yds	TD
1947 New York Yankees	4	66	0
1950 New York Yanks	2	8	0
Total	**6**	**74**	**0**

Interceptions
	Int	Yds	TD
1947 New York Yankees	1	33	0
1948 New York Yankees	1	0	0
1949 New York Yankees	1	5	0
Total	**3**	**38**	**0**

Fumbles
	Fum	Rec	Yds	TD
1950 New York Yanks	0	3	8	1
Total	**0**	**3**	**8**	**1**

RUTHSTROM, Ralph David

Position: B
Height: 6'5"; Weight: 212
College: Sam Houston State, SMU
Born: July 12, 1921, Schenectady, NY
Deceased: March 29, 1962, Houston, TX

Interceptions
	Int	Yds	TD
1947 New York Yankees	1	8	0
Total	**1**	**8**	**0**

STATISTICS

Games
	GP	GS
1945 Cleveland Rams	6	1
1946 Los Angeles Rams	6	4
1947 Washington Redskins	2	1
1949 Baltimore Colts	4	0
Total	**18**	**6**

Rushing
	Rush	Yds	TD
1945 Cleveland Rams	10	74	0
1946 Los Angeles Rams	2	−4	0
1947 Wash. Redskins	2	5	0
Total	**14**	**75**	**0**

Receiving
	Rec	Yds	TD
1946 Los Angeles Rams	1	9	0
Total	**1**	**9**	**0**

Punt Returns
	Ret	Yds	TD
1945 Cleveland Rams	3	47	0
1946 Los Angeles Rams	1	2	0
Total	**4**	**49**	**0**

Kick Returns
	Ret	Yds	TD
1947 Wash. Redskins	1	5	0
Total	**1**	**5**	**0**

Interceptions
	Int	Yds	TD
1945 Cleveland Rams	1	46	0
1949 Baltimore Colts	1	15	0
Total	**2**	**61**	**0**

Fumbles
	Fum	Rec	Yds	TD
1945 Cleveland Rams	0	1	0	0
1946 Los Angeles Rams	2	0	0	0
Total	**2**	**1**	**0**	**0**

RYKOVICH, Julius Alphonsus (Julie)

Position: HB-DB
Height: 6'2"; Weight: 204
College: Illinois, Notre Dame
Born: April 6, 1923, Gary, IN
Deceased: December 22, 1974, Merrillville, IN

STATISTICS

Games
	GP	GS
1947 Buffalo Bills	12	9
1948 Buffalo Bills	6	2
1948 Chicago Rockets	6	4
1949 Chicago Bears	11	3
1950 Chicago Bears	12	0
1951 Chicago Bears	12	0
1952 Washington Redskins	11	0
1953 Washington Redskins	12	0
Total	**82**	**18**

Rushing

	Rush	Yds	TD
1947 Buffalo Bills	92	414	4
1948 Buffalo Bills	43	249	5
1948 Chicago Rockets	53	176	1
1949 Chicago Bears	88	340	6
1950 Chicago Bears	122	394	7
1951 Chicago Bears	83	399	4
1952 Wash. Redskins	94	361	1
1953 Wash. Redskins	73	251	0
Total	648	2584	28

Receiving

	Rec	Yds	TD
1947 Buffalo Bills	4	44	0
1948 Buffalo Bills	2	−7	0
1948 Chicago Rockets	3	78	0
1949 Chicago Bears	16	210	2
1950 Chicago Bears	21	344	0
1951 Chicago Bears	6	133	0
1952 Wash. Redskins	16	283	1
1953 Wash. Redskins	7	73	1
Total	75	1158	4

Passing

	Comp	Att	Yds	TD	Int
1948 Chicago Rockets	1	1	12	0	0
1951 Chicago Bears	0	3	0	0	1
Total	1	4	12	0	1

Punting

	Punt	Yds	Blk
1950 Chicago Bears	1	48	0
Total	1	48	0

Punt Returns

	Ret	Yds	TD
1947 Buffalo Bills	7	93	0
1948 Chicago Rockets	1	23	0
Total	8	116	0

Kick Returns

	Ret	Yds	TD
1947 Buffalo Bills	12	257	0
1948 Buffalo Bills	3	48	0
1948 Chicago Rockets	4	81	0
1953 Wash. Redskins	2	39	0
Total	21	425	0

Interceptions

	Int	Yds	TD
1947 Buffalo Bills	2	61	0
1948 Chicago Rockets	3	65	0
Total	5	126	0

Fumbles

	Fum	Rec	Yds	TD
1949 Chicago Bears	2	0	0	0
1950 Chicago Bears	2	0	0	0
1951 Chicago Bears	3	0	0	0
1952 Wash. Redskins	2	0	0	0
1953 Wash. Redskins	2	0	0	0
Total	11	0	0	0

Field Goals

	FGM	FGA
1948 Chicago Rockets	*	1
Total	*	1

Point After Touchdown

	XPM	XPA
1952 Wash. Redskins	1	1
Total	1	1

RYMKUS, Louis Joseph (Lou)

Position: T-DT
Height: 6'4"; Weight: 231
College: Notre Dame
Born: November 6, 1919, Royalton, IL
Deceased: October 31, 1998, Houston, TX

STATISTICS

Games

	GP	GS
1943 Washington Redskins	10	9
1946 Cleveland Browns	14	13
1947 Cleveland Browns	13	9
1948 Cleveland Browns	14	14
1949 Cleveland Browns	12	11
1950 Cleveland Browns	12	0
1951 Cleveland Browns	11	0
Total	86	56

Kick Returns

	Ret	Yds	TD
1949 Cleveland Browns	1	16	0
1950 Cleveland Browns	1	0	0
Total	2	16	0

Interceptions

	Int	Yds	TD
1943 Wash. Redskins	1	21	1
Total	1	21	1

Fumbles

	Fum	Rec	Yds	TD
1950 Cleveland Browns	0	1	5	0
Total	0	1	5	0

SABAN, Louis Henry (Lou)

Position: C-B
Height: 6'0"; Weight: 202
College: Indiana
Born: October 13, 1921, Brookfield, IL
Deceased: March 29, 2009, North Myrtle Beach, SC

STATISTICS

Games

	GP	GS
1946 Cleveland Browns	14	2
1947 Cleveland Browns	14	6
1948 Cleveland Browns	14	0
1949 Cleveland Browns	12	1
Total	54	9

Rushing

	Rush	Yds	TD
1946 Cleveland Browns	4	−4	0
Total	4	−4	0

Receiving

	Rec	Yds	TD
1946 Cleveland Browns	1	45	0
Total	1	45	0

Passing

	Comp	Att	Yds	TD	Int
1946 Cleveland Browns	0	3	0	0	1
Total	0	3	0	0	1

Interceptions

	Int	Yds	TD
1946 Cleveland Browns	4	32	0
1947 Cleveland Browns	2	2	0
1948 Cleveland Browns	5	41	0
1949 Cleveland Browns	2	35	1
Total	13	110	1

Field Goals

	FGM	FGA
1949 Cleveland Browns	*	2
Total	*	2

Point After Touchdown

	XPM	XPA
1947 Cleveland Browns	10	11
1949 Cleveland Browns	11	11
Total	21	22

SABUCO, Valentino (Tino)

Position: C
Height: 6'1"; Weight: 206
College: San Francisco, Wayne State (MI)
Born: December 20, 1926, Detroit, MI
Deceased: January 1, 2013, Sun Lakes, AZ

STATISTICS

Games

	GP	GS
1949 San Francisco 49ers	10	0
Total	10	0

SALATA, Paul Thomas

Position: E
Height: 6'2"; Weight: 191
College: USC
Born: October 17, 1926, Los Angeles, CA
Deceased:

STATISTICS

Games

	GP	GS
1949 San Francisco 49ers	12	1
1950 San Francisco 49ers	4	0
1950 Baltimore Colts	7	6
Total	23	7

Receiving

	Rec	Yds	TD
1949 S.F. 49ers	24	289	4
1950 S.F. 49ers	5	46	2
1950 Baltimore Colts	45	572	2
Total	74	907	8

Kick Returns

	Ret	Yds	TD
1950 Baltimore Colts	3	12	0
Total	3	12	0

SANDERS, Orban Eugene (Spec)

Position: TB-DB-HB
Height: 6'1"; Weight: 196
College: Texas
Born: January 26, 1918, Temple, OK
Deceased: July 6, 2003, Lawton, OK

STATISTICS

Games

	GP	GS
1946 New York Yankees	13	9
1947 New York Yankees	14	12
1948 New York Yankees	13	9
1950 New York Yanks	12	0
Total	52	30

Rushing

	Rush	Yds	TD
1946 New York Yankees	140	709	6
1947 New York Yankees	231	1432	18
1948 New York Yankees	169	759	9
Total	540	2900	33

Receiving

	Rec	Yds	TD
1946 New York Yankees	17	259	3
1947 New York Yankees	1	13	0
Total	18	272	3

Passing

	Comp	Att	Yds	TD	Int
1946 Yankees	33	79	411	4	9
1947 Yankees	93	171	1442	14	17
1948 Yankees	78	168	918	5	11
1950 Yanks	2	3	58	0	0
Total	206	421	2829	23	37

Punting

	Punt	Yds	Blk
1946 New York Yankees	33	1208	2
1947 New York Yankees	46	1938	2
1948 New York Yankees	42	1707	0
1950 New York Yanks	71	3001	2
Total	192	7854	6

Punt Returns

	Ret	Yds	TD
1946 New York Yankees	17	257	1
1947 New York Yankees	6	164	0
1948 New York Yankees	13	128	0
1950 New York Yanks	6	93	0
Total	42	642	1

Kick Returns

	Ret	Yds	TD
1946 New York Yankees	13	395	1
1947 New York Yankees	22	593	1
1948 New York Yankees	9	217	0
Total	**44**	**1205**	**2**

Interceptions

	Int	Yds	TD
1946 New York Yankees	2	71	1
1947 New York Yankees	3	63	0
1948 New York Yankees	1	24	0
1950 New York Yanks	13	199	0
Total	**19**	**357**	**1**

Fumbles

	Fum	Rec	Yds	TD
1950 New York Yanks	1	2	0	0
Total	**1**	**2**	**0**	**0**

SANDIG, Curtis Walter (Curt)

Position: HB
Height: 5'10"; Weight: 170
College: Baylor, St. Mary's
Born: July 12, 1918, Mart, TX
Deceased: February 13, 2006, San Antonio, TX

STATISTICS

Games

	GP	GS
1942 Pittsburgh Steelers	11	8
1946 Buffalo Bills	9	1
Total	**20**	**9**

Rushing

	Rush	Yds	TD
1942 Pittsburgh Steelers	50	116	3
1946 Buffalo Bills	22	52	1
Total	**72**	**168**	**4**

Receiving

	Rec	Yds	TD
1942 Pittsburgh Steelers	6	103	0
1946 Buffalo Bills	2	15	0
Total	**8**	**118**	**0**

Passing

	Comp	Att	Yds	TD	Int
1942 Pittsburgh Steelers	2	4	10	0	0
Total	**2**	**4**	**10**	**0**	**0**

Punting

	Punt	Yds	Blk
1942 Pittsburgh Steelers	37	1437	0
1946 Buffalo Bills	4	155	0
Total	**41**	**1592**	**0**

Punt Returns

	Ret	Yds	TD
1942 Pittsburgh Steelers	6	142	1
1946 Buffalo Bills	2	20	0
Total	**8**	**162**	**1**

Kick Returns

	Ret	Yds	TD
1942 Pittsburgh Steelers	7	168	0
1946 Buffalo Bills	2	43	0
Total	**9**	**211**	**0**

Interceptions

	Int	Yds	TD
1942 Pittsburgh Steelers	5	94	0
Total	**5**	**94**	**0**

SATTERFIELD, Alfred Neal (Al)

Position: T
Height: 6'3"; Weight: 225
College: Vanderbilt
Born: November 28, 1921, Belleville, AR
Deceased: October 28, 1989, Little Rock, AR

STATISTICS

Games

	GP	GS
1947 San Francisco 49ers	12	0
Total	**12**	**0**

SAZIO, Ralph Joseph

Position: T
Height: 6'1"; Weight: 250
College: William & Mary
Born: July 22, 1922, Avellino, Italy
Deceased: September 25, 2008, Burlington, Ontario

STATISTICS

Games

	GP	GS
1948 Brooklyn Dodgers	13	8
Total	**13**	**8**

SCARRY, Michael Joseph (Mike) (Mo)

Position: C-T
Height: 6'0"; Weight: 214
College: Waynesburg
Born: February 1, 1920, Duquesne, PA
Deceased: September 9, 2012, Duquesne, PA

STATISTICS

Games

	GP	GS
1944 Cleveland Rams	10	10
1945 Cleveland Rams	10	10
1946 Cleveland Browns	14	10
1947 Cleveland Browns	11	6
Total	**45**	**36**

Interceptions

	Int	Yds	TD
1944 Cleveland Rams	1	5	0
1945 Cleveland Rams	4	32	0
1946 Cleveland Browns	2	0	0
Total	7	37	0

SCHIECHL, John George

Position: C
Height: 6'3"; Weight: 244
College: Santa Clara
Born: August 22, 1917, San Francisco, CA
Deceased: February 1964, Dade County, FL

STATISTICS

Games

	GP	GS
1941 Pittsburgh Steelers	4	2
1942 Pittsburgh Steelers	2	0
1942 Detroit Lions	9	6
1945 Chicago Bears	9	5
1946 Chicago Bears	11	3
1947 San Francisco 49ers	14	11
Total	49	27

Interceptions

	Int	Yds	TD
1941 Pittsburgh Steelers	1	0	0
1946 Chicago Bears	3	26	0
1947 S.F. 49ers	2	45	0
Total	6	71	0

SCHILLING, Ralph Franklin

Position: DE-E
Height: 6'3"; Weight: 218
College: Oklahoma
Born: July 5, 1921, Morris, OK
Deceased: May 9, 1994, McAllen, TX

STATISTICS

Games

	GP	GS
1946 Washington Redskins	5	0
1946 Buffalo Bisons	2	0
Total	7	0

Receiving

	Rec	Yds	TD
1946 Wash. Redskins	1	14	0
Total	1	14	0

SCHLEICH, Victor (Vic)

Position: T
Height: 6'3"; Weight: 240
College: Nebraska
Born: April 26, 1920, Montrose, CO
Deceased: June 5, 2010, Lock Haven, PA

STATISTICS

Games

	GP	GS
1947 New York Yankees	11	0
Total	11	0

SCHNEIDER, Donald Paul (Don)

Position: HB
Height: 5'9"; Weight: 170
College: Pennsylvania
Born: April 4, 1924, Crafton, PA
Deceased: July 13, 2009, West Chester, PA

STATISTICS

Games

	GP	GS
1948 Buffalo Bills	9	0
Total	9	0

Rushing

	Rush	Yds	TD
1948 Buffalo Bills	15	70	0
Total	15	70	0

Receiving

	Rec	Yds	TD
1948 Buffalo Bills	1	14	0
Total	1	14	0

Punt Returns

	Ret	Yds	TD
1948 Buffalo Bills	1	4	0
Total	1	4	0

Kick Returns

	Ret	Yds	TD
1948 Buffalo Bills	4	77	0
Total	4	77	0

SCHNEIDER, Leroy

Position: T
Height: 5'11"; Weight: 237
College: Tulane
Born: July 16, 1923, Baltimore, MD
Deceased: July 14, 1999, Pompano Beach, FL

STATISTICS

Games

	GP	GS
1947 Brooklyn Dodgers	1	0
Total	1	0

SCHNELLBACHER, Otto Ole

Position: DB-E
Height: 6'4"; Weight: 188
College: Kansas
Born: April 15, 1923, Sublette, KS
Deceased: March 10, 2008, Topeka, KS

STATISTICS

Games

	GP	GS
1948 New York Yankees	14	1
1949 New York Yankees	12	0
1950 New York Giants	12	0
1951 New York Giants	12	0
Total	50	1

Receiving

	Rec	Yds	TD
1948 New York Yankees	5	72	0
1949 New York Yankees	1	11	0
Total	6	83	0

Punt Returns

	Ret	Yds	TD
1948 New York Yankees	5	45	0
1949 New York Yankees	4	31	0
1950 New York Giants	3	22	0
1951 New York Giants	7	32	0
Total	19	130	0

Interceptions

	Int	Yds	TD
1948 New York Yankees	11	239	1
1949 New York Yankees	4	26	0
1950 New York Giants	8	99	0
1951 New York Giants	11	194	2
Total	34	558	3

Fumbles

	Fum	Rec	Yds	TD
1950 New York Giants	1	2	0	0
1951 New York Giants	0	3	10	0
Total	1	5	10	0

SCHROEDER, William Henry (Bill)

Position: HB
Height: 6'0"; Weight: 190
College: Wisconsin
Born: April 11, 1923, Sheboygan, WI
Deceased: December 9, 2003, Sheboygan, WI

STATISTICS

Games

	GP	GS
1946 Chicago Rockets	14	3
1947 Chicago Rockets	12	3
Total	26	6

Rushing

	Rush	Yds	TD
1946 Chicago Rockets	12	42	0
1947 Chicago Rockets	11	45	0
Total	23	87	0

Receiving

	Rec	Yds	TD
1946 Chicago Rockets	1	9	0
1947 Chicago Rockets	2	19	1
Total	3	28	1

Passing

	Comp	Att	Yds	TD	Int
1946 Chicago Rockets	1	2	10	0	0
Total	1	2	10	0	0

Kick Returns

	Ret	Yds	TD
1946 Chicago Rockets	1	19	0
1947 Chicago Rockets	5	92	0
Total	6	111	0

Interceptions

	Int	Yds	TD
1946 Chicago Rockets	1	4	0
1947 Chicago Rockets	4	148	2
Total	5	152	2

SCHROLL, Charles William (Bill) (Bonk)

Position: FB-LB
Height: 6'0"; Weight: 214
College: Louisiana State
Born: January 24, 1926, Alexandria, LA
Deceased:

STATISTICS

Games

	GP	GS
1949 Buffalo Bills	11	0
1950 Detroit Lions	12	—
1951 Green Bay Packers	12	—
Total	35	—

Rushing

	Rush	Yds	TD
1950 Detroit Lions	1	1	0
Total	1	1	0

Interceptions

	Int	Yds	TD
1949 Buffalo Bills	1	4	0
1950 Detroit Lions	2	8	0
Total	3	12	0

Fumbles

	Fum	Rec	Yds	TD
1950 Detroit Lions	0	1	17	0
Total	0	1	17	0

SCHUETTE, Charles William (Carl)

Position: LB-C-DB
Height: 6'1"; Weight: 206
College: Marquette
Born: April 4, 1922, Sheboygan, WI
Deceased: December 9, 1975, Boston, MA

STATISTICS

Games

	GP	GS
1948 Buffalo Bills	14	0
1949 Buffalo Bills	10	0
1950 Green Bay Packers	12	0
1951 Green Bay Packers	12	0
Total	**48**	**0**

Interceptions

	Int	Yds	TD
1948 Buffalo Bills	4	97	1
1950 Green Bay Packers	1	0	0
Total	**5**	**97**	**1**

Fumbles

	Fum	Rec	Yds	TD
1950 Green Bay Packers	0	3	8	0
Total	**0**	**3**	**8**	**0**

SCHWARTZ, Perry

Position: E
Height: 6'2"; Weight: 199
College: California
Born: April 27, 1915, Chicago, IL
Deceased: January 4, 2001, Cloverdale, CA

STATISTICS

Games

	GP	GS
1938 Brooklyn Dodgers	10	9
1939 Brooklyn Dodgers	11	11
1940 Brooklyn Dodgers	11	11
1941 Brooklyn Dodgers	11	11
1942 Brooklyn Dodgers	11	10
1946 New York Yankees	14	1
Total	**68**	**53**

Rushing

	Rush	Yds	TD
1938 Brooklyn Dodgers	2	–3	0
1941 Brooklyn Dodgers	1	7	0
1942 Brooklyn Dodgers	2	20	0
Total	**5**	**24**	**0**

Receiving

	Rec	Yds	TD
1938 Brooklyn Dodgers	8	132	1
1939 Brooklyn Dodgers	33	550	3
1940 Brooklyn Dodgers	21	370	3
1941 Brooklyn Dodgers	25	362	2
1942 Brooklyn Dodgers	13	200	1
1946 New York Yankees	5	82	0
Total	**105**	**1696**	**10**

Kick Returns

	Ret	Yds	TD
1941 Brooklyn Dodgers	1	6	0
1942 Brooklyn Dodgers	2	25	0
1946 New York Yankees	2	23	0
Total	**5**	**54**	**0**

SCHWENK, Wilson Rutherford (Bud)

Position: QB-TB-HB
Height: 6'2"; Weight: 201
College: Washington (MO)
Born: August 26, 1918, St. Louis, MO
Deceased: October 1, 1980, St. Louis, MO

STATISTICS

Games

	GP	GS
1942 Chicago Cardinals	11	9
1946 Cleveland Browns	4	0
1947 Baltimore Colts	14	2
1948 New York Yankees	8	0
Total	**37**	**11**

Rushing

	Rush	Yds	TD
1942 Chicago Cardinals	111	313	2
1946 Cleveland Browns	6	–1	1
1947 Baltimore Colts	25	58	1
1948 New York Yankees	3	6	0
Total	**145**	**376**	**4**

Passing

	Comp	Att	Yds	TD	Int
1942 Chicago Cardinals	126	295	1360	6	27
1946 Cle. Browns	15	23	276	4	0
1947 Bal. Colts	168	327	2236	13	20
1948 Yankees	6	17	52	0	3
Total	**315**	**662**	**3924**	**23**	**50**

Punting

	Punt	Yds	Blk
1942 Chicago Cardinals	3	114	0
Total	**3**	**114**	**0**

Kick Returns

	Ret	Yds	TD
1942 Chicago Cardinals	2	24	0
Total	**2**	**24**	**0**

Interceptions

	Int	Yds	TD
1942 Chicago Cardinals	1	21	0
Total	**1**	**21**	**0**

SCOTT, Prince Arthur

Position: E-DB
Height: 6'1"; Weight: 190
College: Texas Tech
Born: June 30, 1917, Grapevine, TX
Deceased: April 13, 1993, Lindale, TX

STATISTICS

Games

	GP	GS
1946 Miami Seahawks	14	7
Total	**14**	**7**

Receiving

	Rec	Yds	TD
1946 Miami Seahawks	13	180	2
Total	**13**	**180**	**2**

Punt Returns

	Ret	Yds	TD
1946 Miami Seahawks	1	6	0
Total	**1**	**6**	**0**

Kick Returns

	Ret	Yds	TD
1946 Miami Seahawks	2	28	0
Total	**2**	**28**	**0**

Interceptions

	Int	Yds	TD
1946 Miami Seahawks	1	0	0
Total	**1**	**0**	**0**

SCOTT, Vincent Joseph (Vin)

Position: G
Height: 5'8"; Weight: 215
College: Notre Dame
Born: July 10, 1925, Le Roy, NY
Deceased: July 13, 1992, Hamilton, Canada

STATISTICS

Games

	GP	GS
1947 Buffalo Bills	14	0
1948 Buffalo Bills	14	0
Total	**28**	**0**

SCRUGGS, Edwin Theodore II (Ted)

Position: E
Height: 6'1"; Weight: 195
College: Rice
Born: April 18, 1923, Houston, TX
Deceased: November 30, 2000, Houston, TX

STATISTICS

Games

	GP	GS
1947 Brooklyn Dodgers	12	0
1948 Brooklyn Dodgers	14	2
Total	**26**	**2**

Receiving

	Rec	Yds	TD
1947 Brooklyn Dodgers	2	9	0
1948 Brooklyn Dodgers	1	8	0
Total	**3**	**17**	**0**

SENSANBAUGHER, Dean Sparks

Position: HB-DB
Height: 5'9"; Weight: 190
College: Army, Ohio State
Born: August 12, 1925, Midvale, OH
Deceased: November 8, 2005, Lakeland, FL

STATISTICS

Games

	GP	GS
1948 Cleveland Browns	11	0
1949 New York Yankees	4	2
Total	**15**	**2**

Rushing

	Rush	Yds	TD
1948 Cleveland Browns	18	59	1
1949 New York Yankees	20	36	1
Total	**38**	**95**	**2**

Punt Returns

	Ret	Yds	TD
1949 New York Yankees	1	9	0
Total	**1**	**9**	**0**

Kick Returns

	Ret	Yds	TD
1949 New York Yankees	3	81	0
Total	**3**	**81**	**0**

SERGIENKO, George, Jr.

Position: T
Height: 6'1"; Weight: 248
College: American International College
Born: May 22, 1918, Chicopee Falls, MA
Deceased: December 4, 1994, Springfield, MA

STATISTICS

Games

	GP	GS
1943 Brooklyn Dodgers	10	8
1944 Brooklyn Dodgers	10	3
1945 Boston Yanks	10	10
1946 Brooklyn Dodgers	7	3
Total	**37**	**24**

Fumbles

	Fum	Rec	Yds	TD
1945 Boston Yanks	0	1	0	0
Total	**0**	**1**	**0**	**0**

SEXTON, Linwood Bookard (Lin)

Position: HB-DB
Height: 6'0"; Weight: 180
College: Wichita State
Born: April 16, 1925, Wichita, KS
Deceased: March 29, 2017, Wichita, KS

STATISTICS

Games

	GP	GS
1948 Los Angeles Dons	11	1
Total	**11**	**1**

Rushing

	Rush	Yds	TD
1948 Los Angeles Dons	7	39	0
Total	**7**	**39**	**0**

Punt Returns

	Ret	Yds	TD
1948 Los Angeles Dons	3	47	0
Total	**3**	**47**	**0**

Kick Returns

	Ret	Yds	TD
1948 Los Angeles Dons	3	49	0
Total	**3**	**49**	**0**

Interceptions

	Int	Yds	TD
1948 Los Angeles Dons	1	30	0
Total	**1**	**30**	**0**

SEYMOUR, Robert Arnold (Bob)

Position: HB-FB
Height: 6'2"; Weight: 205
College: Oklahoma
Born: June 13, 1916, Wyandotte, OK
Deceased: May 1977, Golden, CO

STATISTICS

Games

	GP	GS
1940 Washington Redskins	9	0
1941 Washington Redskins	10	2
1942 Washington Redskins	11	1
1943 Washington Redskins	10	2
1944 Washington Redskins	10	7
1945 Washington Redskins	10	2
1946 Los Angeles Dons	13	8
Total	**73**	**22**

Rushing

	Rush	Yds	TD
1940 Wash. Redskins	57	170	4
1941 Wash. Redskins	62	137	2
1942 Wash. Redskins	54	190	1
1943 Wash. Redskins	65	232	0
1944 Wash. Redskins	92	315	3
1945 Wash. Redskins	30	102	2
1946 Los Angeles Dons	37	165	0
Total	**397**	**1311**	**12**

Receiving

	Rec	Yds	TD
1940 Wash. Redskins	2	3	0
1941 Wash. Redskins	6	85	2
1942 Wash. Redskins	3	20	0
1943 Wash. Redskins	17	167	2
1944 Wash. Redskins	19	263	3
1945 Wash. Redskins	8	91	1
1946 Los Angeles Dons	17	188	3
Total	**72**	**817**	**11**

Punting

	Punt	Yds	Blk
1944 Wash. Redskins	10	355	0
Total	**10**	**355**	**0**

Punt Returns

	Ret	Yds	TD
1941 Wash. Redskins	10	128	0
1942 Wash. Redskins	4	79	0
1943 Wash. Redskins	13	173	0
1944 Wash. Redskins	1	6	0
1946 Los Angeles Dons	18	211	0
Total	**46**	**597**	**0**

Kick Returns

	Ret	Yds	TD
1941 Wash. Redskins	3	96	0
1943 Wash. Redskins	2	34	0
1946 Los Angeles Dons	4	87	0
Total	**9**	**217**	**0**

Interceptions

	Int	Yds	TD
1940 Wash. Redskins	1	13	0
1941 Wash. Redskins	2	36	0
1942 Wash. Redskins	3	39	0
1943 Wash. Redskins	2	5	0
1944 Wash. Redskins	2	20	0
1945 Wash. Redskins	4	28	0
1946 Los Angeles Dons	4	34	0
Total	**18**	**175**	**0**

SHARKEY, Edward Joseph (Ed)

Position: LB-G-T-DG
Height: 6'3"; Weight: 229
College: Duke, Nevada-Reno
Born: July 6, 1927, Brooklyn, NY
Deceased:

STATISTICS

Games

	GP	GS
1947 New York Yankees	9	0
1948 New York Yankees	10	1
1949 New York Yankees	12	0
1950 New York Yanks	12	0
1952 Cleveland Browns	12	0
1953 Baltimore Colts	12	0
1954 Philadelphia Eagles	12	0
1955 Philadelphia Eagles	7	0
1955 San Francisco 49ers	5	0
1956 San Francisco 49ers	7	0
Total	**98**	**1**

Punt Returns

	Ret	Yds	TD
1954 Philadelphia Eagles	1	5	0
Total	1	5	0

Kick Returns

	Ret	Yds	TD
1952 Cleveland Browns	2	24	0
1955 Philadelphia Eagles	1	11	0
Total	3	35	0

Interceptions

	Int	Yds	TD
1949 New York Yankees	1	0	0
1950 New York Yanks	1	7	0
1954 Philadelphia Eagles	1	4	0
1956 S.F. 49ers	1	4	0
Total	4	15	0

Fumbles

	Fum	Rec	Yds	TD
1950 New York Yanks	0	3	0	0
1953 Baltimore Colts	0	1	0	0
1954 Philadelphia Eagles	0	2	0	0
Total	0	6	0	0

SHETLEY, Rhoten Nathan

Position: B
Height: 5'11"; Weight: 208
College: Furman
Born: February 7, 1918, Wolf Creek, TN
Deceased: January 7, 1993, Greenville, SC

STATISTICS

Games

	GP	GS
1940 Brooklyn Dodgers	11	8
1941 Brooklyn Dodgers	11	10
1942 Brooklyn Dodgers	3	3
1946 Brooklyn Dodgers	13	5
Total	38	26

Rushing

	Rush	Yds	TD
1940 Brooklyn Dodgers	7	30	0
1941 Brooklyn Dodgers	1	7	0
1946 Brooklyn Dodgers	9	21	0
Total	17	58	0

Receiving

	Rec	Yds	TD
1940 Brooklyn Dodgers	8	126	1
1941 Brooklyn Dodgers	4	41	0
1942 Brooklyn Dodgers	3	19	1
1946 Brooklyn Dodgers	1	10	0
Total	16	196	2

Passing

	Comp	Att	Yds	TD	Int
1940 Dodgers	1	4	2	0	1
1941 Dodgers	0	1	0	0	0
Total	1	5	2	0	1

Kick Returns

	Ret	Yds	TD
1941 Brooklyn Dodgers	4	80	0
Total	4	80	0

Interceptions

	Int	Yds	TD
1940 Brooklyn Dodgers	1	37	0
1941 Brooklyn Dodgers	1	22	0
1942 Brooklyn Dodgers	1	7	0
Total	3	66	0

SHIRLEY, Marion Vaughn

Position: T
Height: 6'4"; Weight: 260
College: Oklahoma City, Oklahoma State
Born: April 17, 1922, Denver, CO
Deceased: September 13, 1996, Stafford, TX

STATISTICS

Games

	GP	GS
1948 New York Yankees	13	1
1949 New York Yankees	7	0
Total	20	1

SHOENER, Harold Phillip (Hal)

Position: E-DE
Height: 6'3"; Weight: 200
College: Iowa
Born: January 2, 1923, Reedsville, WV
Deceased: December 13, 1983, Oakland, CA

STATISTICS

Games

	GP	GS
1948 San Francisco 49ers	14	1
1949 San Francisco 49ers	12	10
1950 San Francisco 49ers	12	0
Total	38	11

Rushing

	Rush	Yds	TD
1950 S.F. 49ers	1	1	0
Total	1	1	0

Receiving

	Rec	Yds	TD
1948 S.F. 49ers	15	76	3
1949 S.F. 49ers	7	84	0
Total	22	160	3

Punt Returns

	Ret	Yds	TD
1949 S.F. 49ers	1	8	0
Total	1	8	0

Kick Returns

	Ret	Yds	TD
1949 S.F. 49ers	1	17	0
1950 S.F. 49ers	4	53	0
Total	5	70	0

Interceptions

	Int	Yds	TD
1950 S.F. 49ers	1	14	0
Total	1	14	0

Fumbles

	Fum	Rec	Yds	TD
1950 S.F. 49ers	0	2	8	0
Total	0	2	8	0

SHURNAS, Marshall Kenneth

Position: E-DE
Height: 6'1"; Weight: 205
College: Missouri
Born: April 1, 1922, St. Louis, MO
Deceased: August 19, 2006, Columbia, MO

STATISTICS

Games

	GP	GS
1947 Cleveland Browns	11	1
Total	11	1

Receiving

	Rec	Yds	TD
1947 Cleveland Browns	2	30	0
Total	2	30	0

SIDORIK, Alexander Theodore (Alex)

Position: T
Height: 6'0"; Weight: 248
College: Mississippi State
Born: December 19, 1919, Hartford, CT
Deceased: April 12, 1980, Middletown, CT

STATISTICS

Games

	GP	GS
1947 Boston Yanks	12	0
1948 Baltimore Colts	9	1
1949 Baltimore Colts	12	0
Total	33	1

Fumbles

	Fum	Rec	Yds	TD
1947 Boston Yanks	0	1	0	0
Total	0	1	0	0

SIERADZKI, Stephen Henry

Position: DB
Height: 6'0"; Weight: 194
College: Michigan State
Born: April 7, 1924, NY
Deceased: May 2, 1968, Muskegon, MI

STATISTICS

Games

	GP	GS
1948 New York Yankees	2	0
Total	2	0

SIGNAIGO, Joseph Salvatore (Joe)

Position: G
Height: 6'1"; Weight: 220
College: Notre Dame
Born: February 9, 1923, Memphis, TN
Deceased: January 16, 2007, Memphis, TN

STATISTICS

Games

	GP	GS
1948 New York Yankees	14	9
1949 New York Yankees	12	12
1950 New York Yanks	12	0
Total	38	21

Fumbles

	Fum	Rec	Yds	TD
1950 New York Yanks	0	2	0	0
Total	0	2	0	0

SIGURDSON, Sigurd Frederick (Sig)

Position: E-DE
Height: 6'2"; Weight: 206
College: Pacific Lutheran
Born: November 27, 1918, Seattle, WA
Deceased: December 2, 2006, Seattle, WA

STATISTICS

Games

	GP	GS
1947 Baltimore Colts	8	3
Total	8	3

Receiving

	Rec	Yds	TD
1947 Baltimore Colts	8	104	0
Total	8	104	0

SIMMONS, John Charles (Jack)

Position: C-G-T
Height: 6'4"; Weight: 236
College: Detroit Mercy, Maryland
Born: October 8, 1924, Grosse Pointe, MI
Deceased: September 17, 1978, Royal Oak, MI

STATISTICS

Games

	GP	GS
1948 Baltimore Colts	10	0
1949 Detroit Lions	12	11
1950 Detroit Lions	12	0
1951 Chicago Cardinals	12	12
1952 Chicago Cardinals	12	12
1953 Chicago Cardinals	12	12
1954 Chicago Cardinals	12	12
1955 Chicago Cardinals	12	12
1956 Chicago Cardinals	12	0
Total	**106**	**71**

Punting

	Punt	Yds	Blk
1953 Chicago Cardinals	22	845	0
Total	**22**	**845**	**0**

Kick Returns

	Ret	Yds	TD
1955 Chicago Cardinals	1	7	0
Total	**1**	**7**	**0**

Fumbles

	Fum	Rec	Yds	TD
1949 Detroit Lions	0	1	0	0
1950 Detroit Lions	0	1	0	0
1954 Chicago Cardinals	0	1	3	0
1956 Chicago Cardinals	0	2	0	0
Total	**0**	**5**	**3**	**0**

SIMONETTI, Leonard Patrick (Lenny)

Position: T
Height: 5'11"; Weight: 225
College: Tennessee
Born: November 20, 1919, Roswell, OH
Deceased: August 14, 1973, Dennison, OH

STATISTICS

Games

	GP	GS
1947 Cleveland Browns	14	1
1948 Cleveland Browns	14	0
Total	**28**	**1**

Interceptions

	Int	Yds	TD
1947 Cleveland Browns	1	22	0
Total	**1**	**22**	**0**

SINKWICH, Francis Frank (Frankie)

Position: B
Height: 5'11"; Weight: 190
College: Georgia
Born: October 10, 1920, McKees Rocks, PA
Deceased: October 22, 1990, Athens, GA

STATISTICS

Games

	GP	GS
1943 Detroit Lions	10	4
1944 Detroit Lions	10	9
1946 New York Yankees	4	0
1947 New York Yankees	3	1
1947 Baltimore Colts	8	2
Total	**35**	**16**

Rushing

	Rush	Yds	TD
1943 Detroit Lions	93	266	1
1944 Detroit Lions	150	563	6
1946 New York Yankees	7	20	0
1947 New York Yankees	16	33	0
1947 Baltimore Colts	55	208	0
Total	**321**	**1090**	**7**

Receiving

	Rec	Yds	TD
1943 Detroit Lions	1	8	0
1947 Baltimore Colts	1	3	0
Total	**2**	**11**	**0**

Passing

	Comp	Att	Yds	TD	Int
1943 Detroit Lions	50	126	699	7	20
1944 Detroit Lions	58	148	1060	12	20
1946 Yankees	5	12	61	0	2
1947 Yankees	8	15	93	0	0
Total	**121**	**301**	**1913**	**19**	**42**

Punting

	Punt	Yds	Blk
1943 Detroit Lions	12	551	0
1944 Detroit Lions	45	1845	0
1947 New York Yankees	3	93	1
1947 Baltimore Colts	4	167	0
Total	**64**	**2656**	**1**

Punt Returns

	Ret	Yds	TD
1943 Detroit Lions	11	228	0
1944 Detroit Lions	11	148	0
1947 Baltimore Colts	1	15	0
Total	**23**	**391**	**0**

Kick Returns

	Ret	Yds	TD
1943 Detroit Lions	5	128	0
1944 Detroit Lions	6	144	0
1947 Baltimore Colts	5	118	0
Total	**16**	**390**	**0**

Interceptions

	Int	Yds	TD
1943 Detroit Lions	1	39	1
1944 Detroit Lions	3	28	0
Total	**4**	**67**	**1**

Field Goals

	FGM	FGA
1943 Detroit Lions	*	1
1944 Detroit Lions	2	8
Total	**2**	**9**

SIVELL, Ralph James (Jim)

Position: G
Height: 5'9"; Weight: 205
College: Auburn
Born: March 12, 1914, Chipley, GA
Deceased: March 16, 1997, Troup County, GA

STATISTICS

Games

	GP	GS
1938 Brooklyn Dodgers	11	5
1939 Brooklyn Dodgers	10	2
1940 Brooklyn Dodgers	11	11
1941 Brooklyn Dodgers	11	11
1942 Brooklyn Dodgers	8	8
1944 Brooklyn Dodgers	5	0
1944 New York Giants	5	5
1945 New York Giants	9	6
1946 Miami Seahawks	10	1
Total	80	49

Point After Touchdown

	XPM	XPA
1944 Detroit Lions	24	30
Total	24	30

Fumbles

	Fum	Rec	Yds	TD
1945 New York Giants	0	1	0	0
Total	0	1	0	0

SMITH, William Gerald (Bill) (Earthquake)

Position: T
Height: 6'2"; Weight: 250
College: North Carolina
Born: October 23, 1926, Lexington, NC
Deceased: September 6, 2009

STATISTICS

Games

	GP	GS
1948 Los Angeles Dons	10	0
1948 Chicago Rockets	2	0
Total	12	0

SMITH, James Robert (Bob)

Position: DB-HB-WB
Height: 6'1"; Weight: 191
College: Iowa, Tulsa
Born: August 20, 1925, Ranger, TX
Deceased: March 1, 2002, Flower Mound, TX

STATISTICS

Games

	GP	GS
1948 Brooklyn Dodgers	10	2
1948 Buffalo Bills	3	0
1949 Chicago Hornets	3	0
1949 Detroit Lions	12	2
1950 Detroit Lions	12	0
1951 Detroit Lions	12	0
1952 Detroit Lions	12	0
1953 Detroit Lions	12	0
1954 Detroit Lions	2	0
Total	78	4

Rushing

	Rush	Yds	TD
1948 Buffalo Bills	1	7	0
1949 Detroit Lions	33	162	0
1952 Detroit Lions	3	12	0
Total	37	181	0

Receiving

	Rec	Yds	TD
1949 Chicago Hornets	1	31	0
1949 Detroit Lions	2	16	0
1952 Detroit Lions	1	18	0
Total	4	65	0

Punting

	Punt	Yds	Blk
1948 Brooklyn Dodgers	1	58	0
1948 Buffalo Bills	13	480	1
1950 Detroit Lions	32	1310	0
1951 Detroit Lions	49	2082	1
1952 Detroit Lions	61	2729	0
1953 Detroit Lions	40	1647	0
Total	196	8306	2

Punt Returns

	Ret	Yds	TD
1948 Buffalo Bills	1	1	0
1949 Detroit Lions	2	25	0
Total	3	26	0

Kick Returns

	Ret	Yds	TD
1949 Detroit Lions	7	172	0
Total	7	172	0

Interceptions

	Int	Yds	TD
1948 Brooklyn Dodgers	3	11	0
1948 Buffalo Bills	1	18	0
1949 Detroit Lions	9	218	1
1950 Detroit Lions	5	128	1
1951 Detroit Lions	3	70	0
1952 Detroit Lions	9	184	1
1953 Detroit Lions	3	119	0
Total	33	748	3

Fumbles

	Fum	Rec	Yds	TD
1949 Detroit Lions	4	3	0	0
1950 Detroit Lions	0	3	30	0
1951 Detroit Lions	0	2	11	0
1952 Detroit Lions	1	1	0	0
Total	5	9	41	0

SMITH, Gaylon Wesley

Position: FB-WB-BB-DB-LB
Height: 5'11"; Weight: 202
College: Rhodes
Born: July 15, 1916, Lonoke, AR
Deceased: March 10, 1958, Cleveland, OH

STATISTICS

Games

	GP	GS
1939 Cleveland Rams	11	4
1940 Cleveland Rams	11	8
1941 Cleveland Rams	4	0
1942 Cleveland Rams	11	6
1946 Cleveland Browns	14	1
Total	51	19

Rushing

	Rush	Yds	TD
1939 Cleveland Rams	58	98	2
1940 Cleveland Rams	19	18	0
1941 Cleveland Rams	11	22	0
1942 Cleveland Rams	83	332	2
1946 Cleveland Browns	62	240	5
Total	233	710	9

Receiving

	Rec	Yds	TD
1939 Cleveland Rams	3	57	0
1940 Cleveland Rams	2	65	0
1942 Cleveland Rams	3	61	0
1946 Cleveland Browns	7	73	0
Total	15	256	0

Passing

	Comp	Att	Yds	TD	Int
1939 Cleveland Rams	4	5	3	0	0
1940 Cleveland Rams	10	18	150	2	2
1941 Cleveland Rams	0	2	0	0	1
1942 Cleveland Rams	2	12	49	0	1
Total	16	37	202	2	4

Punting

	Punt	Yds	Blk
1940 Cleveland Rams	11	391	0
1941 Cleveland Rams	1	23	0
Total	12	414	0

Punt Returns

	Ret	Yds	TD
1941 Cleveland Rams	1	33	0
1942 Cleveland Rams	6	62	0
Total	7	95	0

Kick Returns

	Ret	Yds	TD
1942 Cleveland Rams	6	109	0
Total	6	109	0

Interceptions

	Int	Yds	TD
1940 Cleveland Rams	3	48	0
1941 Cleveland Rams	1	16	0
1942 Cleveland Rams	4	20	0
1946 Cleveland Browns	1	0	0
Total	9	84	0

SMITH, George William

Position: C
Height: 6'2"; Weight: 220
College: California
Born: June 3, 1914, Los Angeles, CA
Deceased: March 5, 1986, Walnut Creek, CA

STATISTICS

Games

	GP	GS
1937 Washington Redskins	7	2
1941 Washington Redskins	9	6
1942 Washington Redskins	4	0
1943 Washington Redskins	9	8
1944 Brooklyn Dodgers	10	8
1945 Boston Yanks	10	8
1947 San Francisco 49ers	10	2
Total	59	34

Punting

	Punt	Yds	Blk
1944 Brooklyn Dodgers	6	223	0
1945 Boston Yanks	9	355	0
Total	15	578	0

Punt Returns

	Ret	Yds	TD
1943 Wash. Redskins	1	3	0
Total	1	3	0

Kick Returns

	Ret	Yds	TD
1945 Boston Yanks	1	0	0
Total	1	0	0

Interceptions

	Int	Yds	TD
1943 Wash. Redskins	2	40	0
1944 Brooklyn Dodgers	1	8	0
1945 Boston Yanks	2	23	0
1947 S.F. 49ers	1	10	0
Total	6	81	0

Fumbles

	Fum	Rec	Yds	TD
1945 Boston Yanks	1	0	0	0
Total	1	0	0	0

Field Goals

	FGM	FGA
1942 Wash. Redskins	*	1
Total	*	1

SMITH, James Dale (Jim)

Position: T
Height: 6'4"; Weight: 270
College: Colorado
Born: September 9, 1922, Alto, TX
Deceased: August 2, 1977, Rochester, MN

STATISTICS

Games
	GP	GS
1947 Los Angeles Dons	7	1
Total	7	1

SMITH, Joe H., Jr.

Position: E-DB
Height: 6'1"; Weight: 183
College: Schreiner College, Texas Tech
Born: July 23, 1922, Electra, TX
Deceased: April 8, 1978, Odessa, TX

STATISTICS

Games
	GP	GS
1948 Baltimore Colts	12	0
Total	12	0

Rushing
	Rush	Yds	TD
1948 Baltimore Colts	1	1	0
Total	1	1	0

Receiving
	Rec	Yds	TD
1948 Baltimore Colts	8	131	1
Total	8	131	1

Interceptions
	Int	Yds	TD
1948 Baltimore Colts	1	0	0
Total	1	0	0

SNEDDON, Robert Lee (Bob)

Position: DB-HB-WB
Height: 5'10"; Weight: 180
College: St. Mary's, Weber State
Born: July 9, 1921, Ogden, UT
Deceased:

STATISTICS

Games
	GP	GS
1944 Washington Redskins	10	0
1945 Detroit Lions	1	0
1946 Los Angeles Dons	11	0
Total	22	0

Rushing
	Rush	Yds	TD
1944 Wash. Redskins	14	30	0
1946 Los Angeles Dons	3	6	0
Total	17	36	0

Receiving
	Rec	Yds	TD
1944 Wash. Redskins	3	42	0
1946 Los Angeles Dons	2	11	0
Total	5	53	0

Interceptions
	Int	Yds	TD
1944 Wash. Redskins	1	20	0
1946 Los Angeles Dons	1	15	0
Total	2	35	0

SOBOLESKI, Joseph Robert, Jr. (Joe)

Position: G-T-DT
Height: 6'0"; Weight: 213
College: Michigan
Born: August 22, 1926, MI
Deceased:

STATISTICS

Games
	GP	GS
1949 Washington Redskins	7	1
1949 Chicago Hornets	5	0
1950 Detroit Lions	12	0
1951 New York Yanks	2	0
1952 Dallas Texans	1	0
Total	27	1

Fumbles
	Fum	Rec	Yds	TD
1949 Wash. Redskins	0	1	0	0
1952 Dallas Texans	0	1	3	0
Total	0	2	3	0

SOSSAMON, Louis Cody (Lou)

Position: C-LB
Height: 6'1"; Weight: 207
College: South Carolina
Born: June 2, 1921, Gaffney, SC
Deceased:

STATISTICS

Games
	GP	GS
1946 New York Yankees	14	1
1947 New York Yankees	14	14
1948 New York Yankees	14	11
Total	42	26

SPAVITAL, James J. (Jim)

Position: FB-LB
Height: 6'1"; Weight: 210
College: Oklahoma State
Born: September 15, 1926, Oklahoma City, OK
Deceased: March 7, 1993, Stillwater, OK

STATISTICS

Games
	GP	GS
1949 Los Angeles Dons	12	3
1950 Baltimore Colts	11	7
Total	23	10

Rushing	Rush	Yds	TD
1949 Los Angeles Dons	15	44	0
1950 Baltimore Colts	58	246	2
Total	**73**	**290**	**2**

Receiving	Rec	Yds	TD
1949 Los Angeles Dons	1	−1	0
1950 Baltimore Colts	21	238	1
Total	**22**	**237**	**1**

Punt Returns	Ret	Yds	TD
1949 Los Angeles Dons	6	58	0
Total	**6**	**58**	**0**

Kick Returns	Ret	Yds	TD
1949 Los Angeles Dons	1	32	0
Total	**1**	**32**	**0**

Interceptions	Int	Yds	TD
1949 Los Angeles Dons	4	58	0
Total	**4**	**58**	**0**

Fumbles	Fum	Rec	Yds	TD
1950 Baltimore Colts	3	0	0	0
Total	**3**	**0**	**0**	**0**

SPEEDIE, Mac Curtis

Position: E
Height: 6'3"; Weight: 203
College: Utah
Born: January 12, 1920, Odell, IL
Deceased: March 12, 1993, Laguna Hills, CA

Statistics

Games	GP	GS
1946 Cleveland Browns	14	10
1947 Cleveland Browns	14	9
1948 Cleveland Browns	12	11
1949 Cleveland Browns	12	11
1950 Cleveland Browns	12	0
1951 Cleveland Browns	10	0
1952 Cleveland Browns	12	0
Total	**86**	**41**

Rushing	Rush	Yds	TD
1947 Cleveland Browns	1	−7	0
1948 Cleveland Browns	1	7	0
Total	**2**	**0**	**0**

Receiving	Rec	Yds	TD
1946 Cleveland Browns	24	564	7
1947 Cleveland Browns	67	1146	6
1948 Cleveland Browns	58	816	4
1949 Cleveland Browns	62	1028	7
1950 Cleveland Browns	42	548	1
1951 Cleveland Browns	34	589	3
1952 Cleveland Browns	62	911	5
Total	**349**	**5602**	**33**

Punting	Punt	Yds	Blk
1946 Cleveland Browns	3	84	0
Total	**3**	**84**	**0**

Kick Returns	Ret	Yds	TD
1946 Cleveland Browns	1	1	0
1948 Cleveland Browns	1	13	0
Total	**2**	**14**	**0**

Point After Touchdown	XPM	XPA
1946 Cleveland Browns	1	1
Total	**1**	**1**

SPENCER, Joseph Emerson (Joe)

Position: T-DT
Height: 6'3"; Weight: 239
College: Oklahoma State
Born: August 15, 1923, Elk City, OK
Deceased: October 24, 1996, Houston, TX

Statistics

Games	GP	GS
1948 Brooklyn Dodgers	13	1
1949 Cleveland Browns	11	0
1950 Green Bay Packers	12	0
1951 Green Bay Packers	12	0
Total	**48**	**1**

Interceptions	Int	Yds	TD
1950 Green Bay Packers	1	0	0
Total	**1**	**0**	**0**

Fumbles	Fum	Rec	Yds	TD
1950 Green Bay Packers	0	2	0	0
Total	**0**	**2**	**0**	**0**

SPRUILL, James Winfred (Jim)

Position: T
Height: 6'3"; Weight: 225
College: Rice
Born: February 26, 1923, Dublin, TX
Deceased: January 8, 2006, Boulder City, NV

Statistics

Games	GP	GS
1948 Baltimore Colts	14	6
1949 Baltimore Colts	14	9
Total	**28**	**15**

STANDLEE, Norman S. (Norm)

Position: FB-LB
Height: 6'2"; Weight: 238
College: Stanford
Born: July 19, 1919, Downey, CA
Deceased: January 4, 1981, Mountain View, CA

STATISTICS

Games

	GP	GS
1941 Chicago Bears	10	3
1946 San Francisco 49ers	13	10
1947 San Francisco 49ers	14	12
1948 San Francisco 49ers	14	13
1949 San Francisco 49ers	12	8
1950 San Francisco 49ers	11	0
1951 San Francisco 49ers	11	0
1952 San Francisco 49ers	1	0
Total	86	46

Rushing

	Rush	Yds	TD
1941 Chicago Bears	81	414	5
1946 S.F. 49ers	134	651	2
1947 S.F. 49ers	145	585	8
1948 S.F. 49ers	52	261	3
1949 S.F. 49ers	44	237	4
1950 S.F. 49ers	12	23	1
1951 S.F. 49ers	16	65	0
1952 S.F. 49ers	2	8	0
Total	486	2244	23

Receiving

	Rec	Yds	TD
1941 Chicago Bears	2	-3	0
1946 S.F. 49ers	2	-5	0
1947 S.F. 49ers	2	22	0
1948 S.F. 49ers	1	1	0
Total	7	15	0

Punting

	Punt	Yds	Blk
1941 Chicago Bears	2	126	0
1946 S.F. 49ers	1	34	0
1949 S.F. 49ers	8	276	1
Total	11	436	1

Kick Returns

	Ret	Yds	TD
1941 Chicago Bears	2	32	0
1946 S.F. 49ers	1	33	0
1947 S.F. 49ers	3	24	0
1948 S.F. 49ers	1	31	0
1950 S.F. 49ers	1	17	0
Total	8	137	0

Interceptions

	Int	Yds	TD
1941 Chicago Bears	2	31	0
Total	2	31	0

Fumbles

	Fum	Rec	Yds	TD
1950 S.F. 49ers	1	1	0	0
1951 S.F. 49ers	1	0	0	0
Total	2	1	0	0

STANLEY, C.B.

Position: T
Height: 6'4"; Weight: 225
College: Tulsa
Born: January 25, 1919, Holdenville, OK
Deceased: April 1977, Tulsa, OK

STATISTICS

Games

	GP	GS
1946 Buffalo Bisons	13	11
Total	13	11

STANTON, William McKimmon (Bill)

Position: DE
Height: 6'2"; Weight: 210
College: North Carolina State
Born: April 21, 1924, Dillon, SC
Deceased: May 9, 2010, Garner, NC

STATISTICS

Games

	GP	GS
1949 Buffalo Bills	10	0
Total	10	0

STANTON, Henry R.

Position: E
Height: 6'2"; Weight: 200
College: Arizona
Born: August 24, 1920
Deceased: March 11, 1975, Phoenix AZ

STATISTICS

Games

	GP	GS
1946 New York Yankees	6	0
1947 New York Yankees	9	0
Total	15	0

Receiving

	Rec	Yds	TD
1946 New York Yankees	2	25	0
Total	2	25	0

STASICA, Stanley Joseph (Stan)

Position: HB-DB
Height: 5'10"; Weight: 175
College: Illinois, South Carolina
Born: June 24, 1919, Rockford, IL
Deceased: July 21, 2012, Arvada, CO

STATISTICS

Games

	GP	GS
1946 Miami Seahawks	1	0
Total	1	0

STATUTO, Arthur Gaetano (Art)

Position: C
Height: 6'2"; Weight: 221
College: Notre Dame
Born: July 17, 1925, Saugus, MA
Deceased: March 2, 2011, Carrolton, TX

STATISTICS

Games

	GP	GS
1948 Buffalo Bills	14	8
1949 Buffalo Bills	12	12
1950 Los Angeles Rams	12	0
Total	38	20

Fumbles

	Fum	Rec	Yds	TD
1950 Los Angeles Rams	0	1	0	0
Total	0	1	0	0

STAUTZENBERGER, Weldon Odell (Odell)

Position: G
Height: 6'0"; Weight: 218
College: Texas A&M
Born: October 23, 1924, San Antonio, TX
Deceased: May 5, 2002, Alexandria, LA

STATISTICS

Games

	GP	GS
1949 Buffalo Bills	9	6
Total	9	6

STEFIK, Robert Mathias (Bob)

Position: E
Height: 5'11"; Weight: 180
College: Niagara
Born: October 8, 1923, Madison, WI
Deceased: April 9, 2008, Lewiston, NY

STATISTICS

Games

	GP	GS
1948 Buffalo Bills	1	0
Total	1	0

Point After Touchdown

	XPM	XPA
1948 Buffalo Bills	*	1
Total	*	1

STEUBER, Robert James (Bob)

Position: HB
Height: 6'2"; Weight: 200
College: DePauw, Missouri
Born: October 25, 1921, Wenonah, NJ
Deceased: November 29, 1996, St. Louis, MO

STATISTICS

Games

	GP	GS
1943 Chicago Bears	1	0
1946 Cleveland Browns	6	1
1947 Los Angeles Dons	3	0
1948 Buffalo Bills	9	7
Total	19	8

Rushing

	Rush	Yds	TD
1943 Chicago Bears	1	3	0
1946 Cleveland Browns	8	19	0
1947 Los Angeles Dons	1	2	0
1948 Buffalo Bills	69	437	3
Total	79	461	3

Receiving

	Rec	Yds	TD
1946 Cleveland Browns	1	9	0
1948 Buffalo Bills	2	14	0
Total	3	23	0

Passing

	Comp	Att	Yds	TD	Int
1948 Buffalo Bills	1	2	−4	0	0
Total	1	2	−4	0	0

Punting

	Punt	Yds	Blk
1948 Buffalo Bills	1	40	0
Total	1	40	0

Kick Returns

	Ret	Yds	TD
1946 Cleveland Browns	2	53	0
1948 Buffalo Bills	6	123	0
Total	8	176	0

Field Goals

	FGM	FGA
1948 Buffalo Bills	1	2
Total	1	2

Point After Touchdown

	XPM	XPA
1948 Buffalo Bills	20	23
Total	20	23

STEWART, Ralph Edward

Position: C-LB
Height: 6'0"; Weight: 205
College: Missouri, Notre Dame
Born: December 10, 1925, St. Louis, MO
Deceased: July 30, 2016, Prairie Village, KS

STATISTICS

Games

	GP	GS
1947 New York Yankees	9	0
1948 New York Yankees	1	0
1948 Baltimore Colts	14	1
Total	24	1

STILL, James Edward, Jr. (Jim)

Position: B
Height: 6'3"; Weight: 193
College: Georgia Tech
Born: March 5, 1924, Columbia, SC
Deceased: January 3, 1999, Green Cove Springs, FL

STATISTICS

Games

	GP	GS
1948 Buffalo Bills	12	1
1949 Buffalo Bills	9	1
Total	21	2

Rushing

	Rush	Yds	TD
1948 Buffalo Bills	5	−26	0
1949 Buffalo Bills	2	6	0
Total	7	−20	0

Passing

	Comp	Att	Yds	TD	Int
1948 Buffalo Bills	5	14	89	1	3
1949 Buffalo Bills	6	12	86	1	1
Total	11	26	175	2	4

Punting

	Punt	Yds	Blk
1948 Buffalo Bills	47	1825	0
1949 Buffalo Bills	16	614	0
Total	63	2439	0

Interceptions

	Int	Yds	TD
1948 Buffalo Bills	1	37	0
Total	1	37	0

ST. JOHN, Herbert LaGrande (Herb)

Position: G
Height: 5'10"; Weight: 215
College: Georgia
Born: January 17, 1926, Perry, FL
Deceased: June 29, 2011, Perry, GA

STATISTICS

Games

	GP	GS
1948 Brooklyn Dodgers	10	3
1949 Chicago Hornets	11	11
Total	21	14

STOFER, Kenneth Lamont (Ken)

Position: QB-DB
Height: 5'9"; Weight: 188
College: Cornell
Born: August 10, 1919, Lakewood, OH
Deceased: May 4, 2006, Westlake, OH

STATISTICS

Games

	GP	GS
1946 Buffalo Bisons	11	1
Total	11	1

Rushing

	Rush	Yds	TD
1946 Buffalo Bisons	16	36	0
Total	16	36	0

Receiving

	Rec	Yds	TD
1946 Buffalo Bisons	1	14	0
Total	1	14	0

Passing

	Comp	Att	Yds	TD	Int
1946 Buffalo Bisons	9	26	86	1	1
Total	9	26	86	1	1

Punting

	Punt	Yds	Blk
1946 Buffalo Bisons	3	108	0
Total	3	108	0

Punt Returns

	Ret	Yds	TD
1946 Buffalo Bisons	5	53	0
Total	5	53	0

Kick Returns

	Ret	Yds	TD
1946 Buffalo Bisons	2	81	0
Total	2	81	0

STONE, William John (Billy)

Position: HB-DB
Height: 6'0"; Weight: 191
College: Bradley
Born: October 25, 1925, Peoria, IL
Deceased: May 16, 2004, Peoria, IL

STATISTICS

Games

	GP	GS
1949 Baltimore Colts	12	1
1950 Baltimore Colts	8	2
1951 Chicago Bears	12	0
1952 Chicago Bears	10	0
1953 Chicago Bears	12	0
1954 Chicago Bears	12	0
Total	66	33

Rushing

	Rush	Yds	TD
1949 Baltimore Colts	51	205	2
1950 Baltimore Colts	14	113	1
1951 Chicago Bears	30	123	1
1952 Chicago Bears	50	196	2
1953 Chicago Bears	72	169	2
1954 Chicago Bears	79	306	3
Total	296	1112	11

Receiving

	Rec	Yds	TD
1949 Baltimore Colts	31	621	6
1950 Baltimore Colts	12	324	4
1951 Chicago Bears	18	320	1
1952 Chicago Bears	13	283	2
1953 Chicago Bears	34	376	4
1954 Chicago Bears	35	395	3
Total	143	2319	20

Punt Returns

	Ret	Yds	TD
1950 Baltimore Colts	2	7	0
1951 Chicago Bears	14	120	0
1953 Chicago Bears	4	12	0
1954 Chicago Bears	14	40	0
Total	34	179	0

Kick Returns

	Ret	Yds	TD
1949 Baltimore Colts	1	25	0
1950 Baltimore Colts	2	35	0
1951 Chicago Bears	5	108	0
1952 Chicago Bears	2	40	0
1954 Chicago Bears	8	215	0
Total	18	423	0

Interceptions

	Int	Yds	TD
1950 Baltimore Colts	6	56	0
1951 Chicago Bears	4	20	0
1952 Chicago Bears	1	13	0
Total	11	89	0

Fumbles

	Fum	Rec	Yds	TD
1950 Baltimore Colts	2	1	0	0
1951 Chicago Bears	1	1	0	0
1952 Chicago Bears	3	2	0	0
1954 Chicago Bears	7	1	6	0
1950 Baltimore Colts	3	4	0	0
Total	16	9	6	0

STROHMEYER, George Ferdinand, Jr.

Position: C-LB
Height: 5'10"; Weight: 205
College: Notre Dame, Texas A&M
Born: January 27, 1924, Kansas City, MO
Deceased: January 12, 1992, Hidalgo County, TX

STATISTICS

Games

	GP	GS
1948 Brooklyn Dodgers	14	7
1949 Chicago Hornets	12	1
Total	26	8

Punt Returns

	Ret	Yds	TD
1948 Brooklyn Dodgers	1	5	0
Total	1	5	0

Interceptions

	Int	Yds	TD
1948 Brooklyn Dodgers	4	79	0
1949 Chicago Hornets	3	9	0
Total	7	88	0

STRZYKALSKI, John Raymond (Johnny)

Position: HB
Height: 5'9"; Weight: 190
College: Marquette
Born: December 14, 1921, Milwaukee, WI
Deceased: June 19, 2002, Hendersonville, NC

STATISTICS

Games

	GP	GS
1946 San Francisco 49ers	13	11
1947 San Francisco 49ers	14	13
1948 San Francisco 49ers	14	13
1949 San Francisco 49ers	7	4
1950 San Francisco 49ers	12	0
1951 San Francisco 49ers	11	0
1952 San Francisco 49ers	10	0
Total	81	41

Rushing

	Rush	Yds	TD
1946 S.F. 49ers	79	346	2
1947 S.F. 49ers	143	906	5
1948 S.F. 49ers	141	915	4
1949 S.F. 49ers	66	287	3
1950 S.F. 49ers	136	612	2
1951 S.F. 49ers	81	296	3
1952 S.F. 49ers	16	53	0
Total	662	3415	19

Receiving

	Rec	Yds	TD
1946 S.F. 49ers	9	80	0
1947 S.F. 49ers*	15	258	3
1948 S.F. 49ers	26	485	7
1949 S.F. 49ers	6	99	1
1950 S.F. 49ers	24	187	1
1951 S.F. 49ers	12	105	0
1952 S.F. 49ers	1	4	0
Total	93	1218	12

SULLIVAN

Passing
	Comp	Att	Yds	TD	Int
1947 49ers	1	4	38	0	0
1948 49ers	0	1	0	0	0
Total	1	5	38	0	0

Punt Returns
	Ret	Yds	TD
1946 S.F. 49ers	3	26	0
1947 S.F. 49ers	8	70	0
1948 S.F. 49ers	13	201	0
1949 S.F. 49ers	2	19	0
Total	26	316	0

Kick Returns
	Ret	Yds	TD
1946 S.F. 49ers	7	142	0
1947 S.F. 49ers	6	124	0
1948 S.F. 49ers	9	185	0
1949 S.F. 49ers	2	57	0
Total	24	508	0

Interceptions
	Int	Yds	TD
1946 S.F. 49ers	3	55	0
1947 S.F. 49ers	2	25	0
1948 S.F. 49ers	3	21	0
Total	8	101	0

Fumbles
	Fum	Rec	Yds	TD
1950 S.F. 49ers	2	0	0	0
Total	2	0	0	0

*John Strzykalski was credited with a receiving touchdown, but had zero receptions for zero yards. This happened in game one of the season. Since the numbers could not be verified, the official statistics were used.

STUART, Roy J., Jr.

Position: G-LB
Height: 5'8"; Weight: 188
College: Tulsa
Born: July 25, 1920, Shawnee, OK
Deceased: February 27, 2013, Tulsa, OK

STATISTICS

Games
	GP	GS
1942 Cleveland Rams	10	6
1943 Detroit Lions	6	0
1946 Buffalo Bisons	9	0
Total	25	6

Interceptions
	Int	Yds	TD
1942 Cleveland Rams	1	25	0
Total	1	25	0

SULLIVAN, Robert Gerard (Bob)

Position: HB
Height: 5'9"; Weight: 191
College: Holy Cross, Iowa
Born: December 24, 1924, Attleboro, MA
Deceased: November 12, 1992, Carmichael, CA

STATISTICS

Games
	GP	GS
1947 Pittsburgh Steelers	3	1
1948 Brooklyn Dodgers	2	1
Total	5	2

Rushing
	Rush	Yds	TD
1947 Pittsburgh Steelers	21	61	0
1948 Brooklyn Dodgers	2	−1	0
Total	23	60	0

Receiving
	Rec	Yds	TD
1947 Pittsburgh Steelers	4	72	1
Total	4	72	1

Passing
	Comp	Att	Yds	TD	Int
1947 Steelers	3	9	52	0	1
Total	3	9	52	0	1

Punt Returns
	Ret	Yds	TD
1947 Pittsburgh Steelers	1	10	0
Total	1	10	0

Kick Returns
	Ret	Yds	TD
1947 Pittsburgh Steelers	4	86	0
1948 Brooklyn Dodgers	1	22	0
Total	5	108	0

Fumbles
	Fum	Rec	Yds	TD
1947 Pittsburgh Steelers	2	1	7	0
Total	2	1	7	0

SULLIVAN, Robert Joseph (Bob)

Position: HB-DB
Height: 5'10"; Weight: 190
College: Holy Cross
Born: August 15, 1923, Lowell, MA
Deceased: June 19, 1981, North Andover, MA

STATISTICS

Games
	GP	GS
1948 San Francisco 49ers	13	0
Total	13	0

	Rushing		
	Rush	Yds	TD
1948 S.F. 49ers	33	121	0
Total	33	121	0

	Receiving		
	Rec	Yds	TD
1948 S.F. 49ers	4	58	1
Total	4	58	1

	Kick Returns		
	Ret	Yds	TD
1948 S.F. 49ers	2	40	0
Total	2	40	0

	Interceptions		
	Int	Yds	TD
1948 S.F. 49ers	1	6	0
Total	1	6	0

SUMPTER, Anthony B. (Tony)

Position: G
Height: 6'1"; Weight: 215
College: Cameron
Born: September 12, 1923, Fletcher, OK
Deceased:

STATISTICS

	Games	
	GP	GS
1946 Chicago Rockets	12	6
1947 Chicago Rockets	1	0
Total	13	6

SUSOEFF, Nicholas Peter (Nick)

Position: E
Height: 6'1"; Weight: 215
College: Washington State
Born: April 15, 1921, Umapine, OR
Deceased: January 31, 1967, Santa Clara County, CA

STATISTICS

	Games	
	GP	GS
1946 San Francisco 49ers	6	2
1947 San Francisco 49ers	14	13
1948 San Francisco 49ers	13	13
1949 San Francisco 49ers	11	1
Total	44	29

	Receiving		
	Rec	Yds	TD
1946 S.F. 49ers	5	98	0
1947 S.F. 49ers	24	223	2
1948 S.F. 49ers	27	237	1
1949 S.F. 49ers	5	52	1
Total	61	610	4

	Kick Returns		
	Ret	Yds	TD
1946 S.F. 49ers	1	10	0
1948 S.F. 49ers	1	12	0
Total	2	22	0

SUSTERIC, Edward J. (Ed)

Position: FB-LB
Height: 6'0"; Weight: 205
College: Findlay
Born: January 7, 1922, Cleveland, OH
Deceased: January 18, 1967, Brecksville, OH

STATISTICS

	Games	
	GP	GS
1949 Cleveland Browns	11	1
Total	11	1

	Rushing		
	Rush	Yds	TD
1949 Cleveland Browns	1	7	0
Total	23	114	1

	Kick Returns		
	Ret	Yds	TD
1949 Cleveland Browns	2	39	0
Total	2	39	0

SUTTON, Joseph Boyle (Joe)

Position: DB-HB
Height: 5'11"; Weight: 180
College: Temple
Born: April 26, 1924, Philadelphia, PA
Deceased: November 12, 2012, Bradenton, FL

STATISTICS

	Games	
	GP	GS
1949 Buffalo Bills	9	1
1950 Philadelphia Eagles	9	0
1951 Philadelphia Eagles	11	0
1952 Philadelphia Eagles	10	0
Total	39	1

	Rushing		
	Rush	Yds	TD
1949 Buffalo Bills	9	63	0
1950 Philadelphia Eagles	1	1	0
Total	10	64	0

	Receiving		
	Rec	Yds	TD
1949 Buffalo Bills	5	63	1
Total	5	63	1

Punt Returns

	Ret	Yds	TD
1949 Buffalo Bills	6	62	0
1950 Philadelphia Eagles	9	75	0
Total	15	137	0

Kick Returns

	Ret	Yds	TD
1949 Buffalo Bills	4	82	0
1950 Philadelphia Eagles	1	21	0
Total	5	103	0

Interceptions

	Int	Yds	TD
1950 Philadelphia Eagles	8	67	0
1951 Philadelphia Eagles	2	8	0
1952 Philadelphia Eagles	3	54	0
Total	13	129	0

Fumbles

	Fum	Rec	Yds	TD
1950 Philadelphia Eagles	2	0	0	0
1951 Philadelphia Eagles	0	3	0	0
1952 Philadelphia Eagles	0	1	0	0
Total	2	4	0	0

SWEIGER, Robert Michael (Bob)

Position: WB-BB-HB
Height: 6'0"; Weight: 209
College: Minnesota
Born: September 20, 1919, Minneapolis, MN
Deceased: November 1, 1975, Hennepin County, MN

STATISTICS

Games

	GP	GS
1946 New York Yankees	13	5
1947 New York Yankees	14	11
1948 New York Yankees	14	14
1949 Chicago Hornets	12	12
Total	53	42

Rushing

	Rush	Yds	TD
1946 New York Yankees	7	22	0
1947 New York Yankees	9	44	0
1948 New York Yankees	3	4	0
1949 Chicago Hornets	3	17	0
Total	22	87	0

Receiving

	Rec	Yds	TD
1946 New York Yankees	8	55	1
1947 New York Yankees	11	108	1
1948 New York Yankees	12	129	0
1949 Chicago Hornets	11	126	0
Total	42	418	2

Punting

	Punt	Yds	Blk
1946 New York Yankees	1	52	0
Total	1	52	0

Punt Returns

	Ret	Yds	TD
1946 New York Yankees	1	14	0
Total	1	14	0

Kick Returns

	Ret	Yds	TD
1946 New York Yankees	5	103	0
1947 New York Yankees	1	12	0
1948 New York Yankees	1	3	0
1949 Chicago Hornets	3	59	0
Total	10	177	0

Interceptions

	Int	Yds	TD
1946 New York Yankees	4	82	0
1947 New York Yankees	2	51	0
1949 Chicago Hornets	1	21	0
Total	7	154	1

SYLVESTER, John J.

Position: DB-HB
Height: 6'0"; Weight: 183
College: Temple
Born: January 14, 1923, Norristown, PA
Deceased: February 24, 2012, Royersford, PA

STATISTICS

Games

	GP	GS
1947 New York Yankees	7	0
1948 Baltimore Colts	12	0
Total	19	0

Rushing

	Rush	Yds	TD
1947 New York Yankees	17	101	0
Total	17	101	0

Receiving

	Rec	Yds	TD
1947 New York Yankees	1	5	0
Total	1	5	0

Passing

	Comp	Att	Yds	TD	Int
1947 Yankees	0	1	0	0	0
Total	0	1	0	0	0

Punting

	Punt	Yds	Blk
1947 New York Yankees	1	42	0
Total	1	42	0

Punt Returns

	Ret	Yds	TD
1947 New York Yankees	3	37	0
1948 Baltimore Colts	2	16	0
Total	5	53	0

Kick Returns

	Ret	Yds	TD
1947 New York Yankees	1	25	0
Total	**1**	**25**	**0**

Interceptions

	Int	Yds	TD
1948 Baltimore Colts	1	0	0
Total	**1**	**0**	**0**

TACKETT, Doyle Lee

Position: B
Height: 6'0"; Weight: 205
College: (None)
Born: August 22, 1923, Hector, AR
Deceased: September 7, 2002, Atkins, AR

STATISTICS

Games

	GP	GS
1946 Brooklyn Dodgers	14	3
1947 Brooklyn Dodgers	12	0
1948 Brooklyn Dodgers	1	0
Total	**27**	**5**

Rushing

	Rush	Yds	TD
1946 Brooklyn Dodgers	11	–6	0
Total	**11**	**–6**	**0**

Receiving

	Rec	Yds	TD
1946 Brooklyn Dodgers	10	191	2
Total	**10**	**191**	**2**

Punt Returns

	Ret	Yds	TD
1946 Brooklyn Dodgers	1	3	0
1948 Brooklyn Dodgers	1	10	0
Total	**2**	**13**	**0**

Kick Returns

	Ret	Yds	TD
1946 Brooklyn Dodgers	5	76	0
Total	**5**	**76**	**0**

Interceptions

	Int	Yds	TD
1946 Brooklyn Dodgers	1	16	0
1947 Brooklyn Dodgers	1	17	0
Total	**2**	**33**	**0**

TALIAFERRO, George

Position: HB-TB-QB-DB
Height: 5'11"; Weight: 196
College: Indiana
Born: January 8, 1927, Gates, TN
Deceased:

STATISTICS

Games

	GP	GS
1949 Los Angeles Dons	11	4
1950 New York Yankees	12	0
1951 New York Yankees	12	0
1952 Dallas Texans	12	12
1953 Baltimore Colts	11	11
1954 Baltimore Colts	11	0
1955 Philadelphia Eagles	3	0
Total	**72**	**27**

Rushing

	Rush	Yds	TD
1949 Los Angeles Dons	95	472	5
1950 New York Yankees	88	411	4
1951 New York Yankees	62	330	3
1952 Dallas Texans	100	419	1
1953 Baltimore Colts	102	479	2
1954 Baltimore Colts	48	157	0
1955 Philadelphia Eagles	3	–2	0
Total	**498**	**2266**	**15**

Receiving

	Rec	Yds	TD
1950 New York Yankees	21	299	5
1951 New York Yankees	16	230	2
1952 Dallas Texans	21	244	1
1953 Baltimore Colts	20	346	2
1954 Baltimore Colts	14	122	1
1955 Philadelphia Eagles	3	17	0
Total	**95**	**1300**	**12**

Passing

	Comp	Att	Yds	TD	Int
1949 L.A. Dons	45	124	790	4	14
1950 Yankees	3	7	83	1	0
1951 Yankees	13	33	251	1	3
1952 Texans	16	63	298	2	6
1953 Bal. Colts	15	55	211	2	5
1954 Bal. Colts	0	2	0	0	1
Total	**92**	**284**	**1633**	**10**	**29**

Punting

	Punt	Yds	Blk
1949 Los Angeles Dons	27	982	2
1950 New York Yankees	1	39	0
1951 New York Yankees	76	2881	1
1953 Baltimore Colts	65	2437	0
Total	**169**	**6339**	**3**

Punt Returns

	Ret	Yds	TD
1949 Los Angeles Dons	2	53	1
1950 New York Yankees	9	129	0
1951 New York Yankees	9	68	0
1952 Dallas Texans	1	4	0
1953 Baltimore Colts	10	31	0
1954 Baltimore Colts	5	34	0
Total	**36**	**319**	**1**

Kick Returns

	Ret	Yds	TD
1949 Los Angeles Dons	13	313	0
1950 New York Yankees	25	473	0
1951 New York Yankees	27	622	0
1952 Dallas Texans	6	146	0
1953 Baltimore Colts	16	331	0
1954 Baltimore Colts	7	134	0
1955 Philadelphia Eagles	1	16	0
Total	**95**	**2035**	**0**

Interceptions

	Int	Yds	TD
1951 New York Yankees	4	74	0
Total	**4**	**74**	**0**

Fumbles

	Fum	Rec	Yds	TD
1950 New York Yankees	11	5	0	0
1951 New York Yankees	5	3	0	0
1952 Dallas Texans	6	1	0	0
1953 Baltimore Colts	10	2	0	0
1954 Baltimore Colts	1	1	0	0
1955 Philadelphia Eagles	2	1	4	0
Total	**35**	**13**	**4**	**0**

TARRANT, James Robert, Jr. (Jimmy)

Position: QB
Height: 5'9"; Weight: 160
College: Samford, Tennessee
Born: February 18, 1921, Birmingham, AL
Deceased: May 17, 2010, Birmingham, AL

STATISTICS

Games

	GP	GS
1946 Miami Seahawks	4	1
Total	**4**	**1**

Rushing

	Rush	Yds	TD
1946 Miami Seahawks	5	–46	0
Total	**5**	**–46**	**0**

Passing

	Comp	Att	Yds	TD	Int
1946 Miami Seahawks	5	12	95	1	0
Total	**5**	**12**	**95**	**1**	**0**

TAVENER, John Harold

Position: C-LB
Height: 6'0"; Weight: 225
College: Indiana
Born: January 10, 1921, Newark, OH
Deceased: September 19, 1993, Johnstown, OH

STATISTICS

Games

	GP	GS
1946 Miami Seahawks	3	1
Total	**3**	**1**

TAYLOR, Charles Albert (Chuck)

Position: G
Height: 5'11"; Weight: 205
College: Stanford
Born: January 24, 1920, Portland, OR
Deceased: May 7, 1994, Stanford, CA

STATISTICS

Games

	GP	GS
1946 Miami Seahawks	14	13
Total	**14**	**13**

TERLEP, George Rudolph

Position: QB-DB
Height: 5'10"; Weight: 180
College: Notre Dame
Born: April 12, 1923, Elkhart, IN
Deceased: May 17, 2010, Springhill, FL

STATISTICS

Games

	GP	GS
1946 Buffalo Bisons	12	4
1947 Buffalo Bills	11	0
1948 Buffalo Bills	3	0
1949 Cleveland Browns	9	0
Total	**35**	**5**

Rushing

	Rush	Yds	TD
1946 Buffalo Bisons	36	29	1
1947 Buffalo Bills	4	11	0
1948 Cleveland Browns	1	4	0
Total	**41**	**44**	**1**

Passing

	Comp	Att	Yds	TD	Int
1946 Buf. Bisons	48	123	574	7	14
1947 Buffalo Bills	5	23	51	2	3
1948 Buffalo Bills	0	2	0	0	1
1949 Cle. Browns	1	2	27	0	1
Total	**54**	**150**	**652**	**9**	**19**

Punting

	Punt	Yds	Blk
1946 Buffalo Bisons	1	31	0
Total	**1**	**31**	**0**

Punt Returns

	Ret	Yds	TD
1947 Buffalo Bills	1	17	0
Total	**1**	**17**	**0**

Kick Returns

	Ret	Yds	TD
1946 Buffalo Bisons	1	23	0
Total	1	23	0

TERRELL, Raymond Willard (Ray)

Position: HB-DB
Height: 6'0"; Weight: 185
College: Mississippi
Born: June 29, 1919, Water Valley, MS
Deceased: February 11, 1997, Gulfport, MS

STATISTICS

Games

	GP	GS
1946 Cleveland Browns	9	4
1947 Cleveland Browns	3	1
1947 Baltimore Colts	10	5
Total	22	10

Rushing

	Rush	Yds	TD
1946 Cleveland Browns	39	117	0
1947 Cleveland Browns	5	28	0
1947 Baltimore Colts	21	20	0
Total	65	165	0

Receiving

	Rec	Yds	TD
1946 Cleveland Browns	4	21	0
1947 Baltimore Colts	6	21	0
Total	10	42	0

Passing

	Comp	Att	Yds	TD	Int
1946 Cleveland Browns	0	2	0	0	0
Total	0	2	0	0	0

Punt Returns

	Ret	Yds	TD
1947 Baltimore Colts	1	18	0
Total	1	18	0

Kick Returns

	Ret	Yds	TD
1946 Cleveland Browns	3	80	0
1947 Baltimore Colts	9	204	0
Total	12	284	0

Interceptions

	Int	Yds	TD
1946 Cleveland Browns	3	101	1
1947 Baltimore Colts	1	12	0
Total	4	113	1

TEVIS, Lee Kessler

Position: FB-LB
Height: 5'11"; Weight: 190
College: George Washington, Miami (OH)
Born: September 29, 1921
Deceased: August 23, 1992, Houston, TX

STATISTICS

Games

	GP	GS
1947 Brooklyn Dodgers	8	0
1948 Brooklyn Dodgers	14	4
Total	22	4

Rushing

	Rush	Yds	TD
1947 Brooklyn Dodgers	4	44	0
Total	4	44	0

Receiving

	Rec	Yds	TD
1948 Brooklyn Dodgers	1	−8	0
Total	1	−8	0

Passing

	Comp	Att	Yds	TD	Int
1947 Dodgers	0	3	0	0	0
1948 Dodgers	0	1	0	0	0
Total	0	4	0	0	0

Punting

	Punt	Yds	Blk
1947 Brooklyn Dodgers	5	246	0
1948 Brooklyn Dodgers	5	214	0
Total	10	460	0

Punt Returns

	Ret	Yds	TD
1948 Brooklyn Dodgers	6	59	0
Total	6	59	0

Kick Returns

	Ret	Yds	TD
1948 Brooklyn Dodgers	2	40	0
Total	2	40	0

Interceptions

	Int	Yds	TD
1947 Brooklyn Dodgers	2	9	0
Total	2	9	0

Field Goals

	FGM	FGA
1948 Brooklyn Dodgers	2	7
Total	2	7

Point After Touchdown

	XPM	XPA
1948 Brooklyn Dodgers	4	4
Total	4	4

TEW, Lowell William

Position: FB
Height: 5'11"; Weight: 195
College: Alabama
Born: January 2, 1927, Waynesboro, MS
Deceased: March 16, 1981, Laurel, MS

STATISTICS

Games

	GP	GS
1948 New York Yankees	14	2
1949 New York Yankees	1	1
Total	**15**	**3**

Rushing

	Rush	Yds	TD
1948 New York Yankees	24	95	5
1949 New York Yankees	14	65	1
Total	**38**	**160**	**6**

Receiving

	Rec	Yds	TD
1948 New York Yankees	7	97	0
Total	**7**	**97**	**0**

Kick Returns

	Ret	Yds	TD
1948 New York Yankees	3	75	0
1949 New York Yankees	1	17	0
Total	**4**	**92**	**0**

THIBAUT, James Pierre (Jim)

Position: FB-LB
Height: 5'11"; Weight: 205
College: Tulane
Born: August 31, 1919, New Orleans, LA
Deceased: April 5, 2006, Kenner, LA

STATISTICS

Games

	GP	GS
1946 Buffalo Bills	3	0
Total	**3**	**0**

Rushing

	Rush	Yds	TD
1946 Buffalo Bisons	10	48	1
Total	**10**	**48**	**1**

THOMPSON, Harold Charles (Hal)

Position: E-DE
Height: 6'1"; Weight: 205
College: Delaware
Born: October 18, 1922, Manasquan, NJ
Deceased: April 26, 2006, Rehoboth Beach, DE

STATISTICS

Games

	GP	GS
1947 Brooklyn Dodgers	12	1
1948 Brooklyn Dodgers	9	0
Total	**21**	**1**

Rushing

	Rush	Yds	TD
1947 Brooklyn Dodgers	1	4	0
Total	**1**	**4**	**0**

Receiving

	Rec	Yds	TD
1947 Brooklyn Dodgers	15	148	0
1948 Brooklyn Dodgers	4	37	1
Total	**19**	**185**	**1**

THOMPSON, Thomas Wright (Tommy)

Position: LB-C
Height: 6'1"; Weight: 221
College: William & Mary
Born: January 6, 1927, Jersey City, NJ
Deceased: October 1, 1990, Baltimore, MD

STATISTICS

Games

	GP	GS
1949 Cleveland Browns	9	0
1950 Cleveland Browns	12	0
1951 Cleveland Browns	12	0
1952 Cleveland Browns	12	0
1953 Cleveland Browns	9	0
Total	**54**	**0**

Interceptions

	Int	Yds	TD
1949 Cleveland Browns	1	9	0
1951 Cleveland Browns	2	23	0
1952 Cleveland Browns	1	21	0
1953 Cleveland Browns	2	13	0
Total	**6**	**66**	**0**

Fumbles

	Fum	Rec	Yds	TD
1950 Cleveland Browns	0	1	0	0
1951 Cleveland Browns	0	4	5	0
1952 Cleveland Browns	0	3	0	0
Total	**0**	**8**	**5**	**0**

THORNTON, Rupert Vance (Rupe)

Position: G-T
Height: 5'10"; Weight: 205
College: Santa Clara
Born: January 5, 1920, Denver, CO
Deceased: July 17, 1993, Burlingame, CA

STATISTICS

Games

	GP	GS
1946 San Francisco 49ers	11	0
1947 San Francisco 49ers	14	0
Total	**25**	**0**

Punt Returns

	Ret	Yds	TD
1947 S.F. 49ers	1	32	0
Total	**1**	**32**	**0**

THURBON, Robert William (Bob)

Position: HB
Height: 5'10"; Weight: 176
College: Pittsburgh
Born: February 22, 1918, Erie, PA
Deceased: September 20, 2000, Charlotte, NC

Statistics

Games

	GP	GS
1943 Philadelphia Eagles	10	1
1944 Chicago Cardinals	10	7
1946 Buffalo Bisons	2	0
Total	22	8

Rushing

	Rush	Yds	TD
1943 Philadelphia Eagles	71	291	5
1944 Chicago Cardinals	69	185	4
1946 Buffalo Bisons	3	2	0
Total	143	478	9

Receiving

	Rec	Yds	TD
1943 Philadelphia Eagles	6	100	1
1944 Chicago Cardinals	7	134	1
1946 Buffalo Bisons	1	−3	0
Total	14	231	2

Punting

	Punt	Yds	Blk
1944 Chicago Cardinals	15	450	0
Total	15	450	0

Punt Returns

	Ret	Yds	TD
1943 Philadelphia Eagles	2	19	0
1944 Chicago Cardinals	1	2	0
Total	3	21	0

Kick Returns

	Ret	Yds	TD
1943 Philadelphia Eagles	6	150	0
1944 Chicago Cardinals	12	291	0
1946 Buffalo Bisons	1	15	0
Total	19	456	0

Interceptions

	Int	Yds	TD
1943 Philadelphia Eagles	1	3	0
1944 Chicago Cardinals	2	14	0
Total	3	17	0

TILLMAN, Alonzo Monroe (Pete)

Position: C-LB
Height: 6'0"; Weight: 210
College: Oklahoma, Southwest Oklahoma State
Born: May 9, 1922, Mangum, OK
Deceased: March 31, 1998, Farmington, NM

Statistics

Games

	GP	GS
1949 Baltimore Colts	11	5
Total	11	5

TIMMONS, Charles Truman (Charlie)

Position: FB-LB
Height: 5'10"; Weight: 210
College: Clemson, Georgia
Born: February 8, 1917, Piedmont, SC
Deceased: March 27, 1996, Greenville, SC

Statistics

Games

	GP	GS
1946 Brooklyn Dodgers	13	1
Total	13	1

Rushing

	Rush	Yds	TD
1946 Brooklyn Dodgers	23	65	0
Total	23	65	0

Receiving

	Rec	Yds	TD
1946 Brooklyn Dodgers	1	4	0
Total	1	4	0

TINSLEY, Robert Porter, Jr. (Bud) (Buddy)

Position: T
Height: 6'4"; Weight: 245
College: Baylor
Born: August 16, 1924, Damon, TX
Deceased:

Statistics

Games

	GP	GS
1949 Los Angeles Dons	10	10
Total	10	10

TITCHENAL, Robert Alden (Bob)

Position: E-C-LB-DE
Height: 6'2"; Weight: 194
College: San Jose State
Born: October 17, 1917, Ventura, CA
Deceased: July 5, 2009, Santa Rosa, CA

Statistics

Games

	GP	GS
1940 Washington Redskins	11	7
1941 Washington Redskins	11	4
1942 Washington Redskins	10	1

TOMASETTI

	GP	GS
1946 San Francisco 49ers	14	13
1947 Los Angeles Dons	14	2
Total	**60**	**27**

Rushing

	Rush	Yds	TD
1946 S.F. 49ers	1	2	0
1947 Los Angeles Dons	1	0	0
Total	**2**	**2**	**0**

Receiving

	Rec	Yds	TD
1942 Wash. Redskins	1	7	0
1946 S.F. 49ers	7	160	2
1947 Los Angeles Dons	7	97	0
Total	**15**	**264**	**2**

Interceptions

	Int	Yds	TD
1941 Wash. Redskins	2	3	0
1942 Wash. Redskins	1	19	0
Total	**3**	**22**	**0**

TITTLE, Yelberton Abraham (Y.A.)

Position: QB
Height: 6'0"; Weight: 192
College: LSU
Born: October 24, 1926, Marshall, TX
Deceased: October 8, 2017, Stanford, CA

STATISTICS

Games

	GP	GS
1948 Baltimore Colts	14	12
1949 Baltimore Colts	11	7
1950 Baltimore Colts	12	9
1951 San Francisco 49ers	12	1
1952 San Francisco 49ers	12	5
1953 San Francisco 49ers	11	10
1954 San Francisco 49ers	12	11
1955 San Francisco 49ers	14	12
1956 San Francisco 49ers	14	10
1957 San Francisco 49ers	14	12
1958 San Francisco 49ers	14	11
1959 San Francisco 49ers	14	11
1960 San Francisco 49ers	14	9
1961 New York Giants	14	13
1962 New York Giants	14	14
1963 New York Giants	14	13
1964 New York Giants	14	14
Total	**203**	**154**

Rushing

	Rush	Yds	TD
1948 Baltimore Colts	52	157	4
1949 Baltimore Colts	29	89	2
1950 Baltimore Colts	20	77	2
1951 S.F. 49ers	13	18	1
1952 S.F. 49ers	11	−11	0
1953 S.F. 49ers	14	41	6
1954 S.F. 49ers	28	68	4
1955 S.F. 49ers	23	114	0
1956 S.F. 49ers	24	67	4
1957 S.F. 49ers	40	220	6
1958 S.F. 49ers	22	35	2
1959 S.F. 49ers	11	24	0
1960 S.F.49ers	10	61	0
1961 New York Giants	25	85	3
1962 New York Giants	17	108	2
1963 New York Giants	18	99	2
1964 New York Giants	15	−7	1
Total	**372**	**1245**	**39**

Receiving

	Rec	Yds	TD
1959 S.F. 49ers	1	4	0
Total	**1**	**4**	**0**

Passing

	Comp	Att	Yds	TD	Int
1948 Bal. Colts	161	289	2522	16	9
1949 Bal. Colts	148	289	2209	14	18
1950 Bal. Colts	161	315	1884	8	19
1951 S.F. 49ers	63	114	808	8	9
1952 S.F. 49ers	106	208	1407	11	12
1953 S.F. 49ers	149	259	2121	20	16
1954 S.F. 49ers	170	295	2205	9	9
1955 S.F. 49ers	147	287	2185	17	28
1956 S.F. 49ers	124	218	1641	7	12
1957 S.F. 49ers	176	279	2157	13	15
1958 S.F. 49ers	120	208	1467	9	15
1959 S.F. 49ers	102	199	1331	10	15
1960 S.F.49ers	69	127	694	4	3
1961 N.Y. Giants	163	285	2272	17	12
1962 N.Y. Giants	200	375	3224	33	20
1963 N.Y. Giants	221	367	3145	36	14
1964 N.Y. Giants	147	281	1798	10	22
Total	**2427**	**4395**	**33070**	**242**	**248**

Fumbles

	Fum	Rec	Yds	TD
1950 Baltimore Colts	2	0	0	0
1951 S.F. 49ers	3	1	0	0
1952 S.F. 49ers	3	1	0	0
1953 S.F. 49ers	3	2	0	0
1954 S.F. 49ers	4	2	0	0
1955 S.F. 49ers	2	0	0	0
1956 S.F. 49ers	3	1	0	0
1957 S.F. 49ers	0	1	0	0
1958 S.F. 49ers	5	1	0	0
1959 S.F. 49ers	7	3	0	0
1960 S.F.49ers	2	1	0	0
1961 New York Giants	0	1	0	0
1962 New York Giants	6	2	0	0
1963 New York Giants	5	4	0	0
1964 New York Giants	11	4	0	0
Total	**56**	**24**	**0**	**0**

TOMASETTI, Louis Vincent (Lou)

Position: FB-HB
Height: 6'0"; Weight: 198
College: Bucknell
Born: January 8, 1916, Old Forge, PA
Deceased: March 23, 2004, Doylestown, PA

STATISTICS

Games

	GP	GS
1939 Pittsburgh Steelers	11	6
1940 Pittsburgh Steelers	10	9
1941 Detroit Lions	4	2
1941 Philadelphia Eagles	6	3
1942 Philadelphia Eagles	10	5
1946 Buffalo Bisons	14	2
1947 Buffalo Bills	13	6
1948 Buffalo Bills	14	9
1949 Buffalo Bills	12	4
Total	94	46

Rushing

	Rush	Yds	TD
1939 Pittsburgh Steelers	49	86	1
1940 Pittsburgh Steelers	68	246	1
1941 Detroit Lions	6	4	0
1941 Philadelphia Eagles	10	37	0
1942 Philadelphia Eagles	45	102	0
1946 Buffalo Bisons	43	139	1
1947 Buffalo Bills	92	326	2
1948 Buffalo Bills	134	716	7
1949 Buffalo Bills	54	249	2
Total	501	1905	14

Receiving

	Rec	Yds	TD
1939 Pittsburgh Steelers	4	22	0
1940 Pittsburgh Steelers	6	129	1
1941 Philadelphia Eagles	5	54	1
1942 Philadelphia Eagles	4	22	0
1946 Buffalo Bisons	6	81	1
1947 Buffalo Bills	13	125	0
1948 Buffalo Bills	22	213	1
1949 Buffalo Bills	9	56	1
Total	69	702	5

Passing

	Comp	Att	Yds	TD	Int
1939 Pittsburgh Steelers	13	47	140	1	7
1940 Pittsburgh Steelers	3	6	30	0	2
Total	16	53	170	1	9

Punting

	Punt	Yds	Blk
1939 Pittsburgh Steelers	3	111	0
Total	3	111	0

Punt Returns

	Ret	Yds	TD
1941 Detroit Lions	1	18	0
1941 Philadelphia Eagles	2	30	0
1942 Philadelphia Eagles	3	37	0
1946 Buffalo Bisons	7	138	0
1949 Buffalo Bills	2	13	0
Total	15	236	0

Kick Returns

	Ret	Yds	TD
1941 Detroit Lions	1	18	0
1942 Philadelphia Eagles	4	90	0
1946 Buffalo Bisons	2	85	0
1947 Buffalo Bills	4	74	0
1948 Buffalo Bills	2	14	0
1949 Buffalo Bills	1	19	0
Total	14	300	0

Interceptions

	Int	Yds	TD
1941 Detroit Lions	1	13	0
1942 Philadelphia Eagles	1	23	0
1946 Buffalo Bisons	1	0	0
1947 Buffalo Bills	1	44	1
Total	4	80	1

TREBOTICH, Ivan Peter (Buzz)

Position: B
Height: 5'10"; Weight: 208
College: St. Mary's
Born: December 30, 1920, Oakland, CA
Deceased: August 4, 1992, Napa, CA

STATISTICS

Games

	GP	GS
1944 Detroit Lions	10	0
1945 Detroit Lions	9	5
1947 Baltimore Colts	2	0
Total	21	5

Rushing

	Rush	Yds	TD
1944 Detroit Lions	1	2	0
1945 Detroit Lions	3	3	0
1947 Baltimore Colts	3	–4	0
Total	7	1	0

Passing

	Comp	Att	Yds	TD	Int
1947 Bal. Colts	1	1	8	0	0
Total	1	1	8	0	0

Kick Returns

	Ret	Yds	TD
1947 Baltimore Colts	1	17	0
Total	1	17	0

Interceptions

	Int	Yds	TD
1945 Detroit Lions	3	46	0
Total	3	46	0

Fumbles

	Fum	Rec	Yds	TD
1945 Detroit Lions	1	1	0	0
Total	1	1	0	0

TRIGILIO, Frank J.

Position: FB
Height: 5'11"; Weight: 200
College: Alfred, Vermont
Born: January 19, 1919, NY
Deceased: March 5, 1992, Honolulu, HI

STATISTICS

Games

	GP	GS
1946 Miami Seahawks	7	1
1946 Los Angeles Dons	1	0
Total	8	1

Rushing

	Rush	Yds	TD
1946 Miami Seahawks	38	124	1
1946 Los Angeles Dons	3	2	0
Total	41	126	1

ULINSKI, Edward Franklin (Ed)

Position: G
Height: 5'11"; Weight: 203
College: Marshall
Born: December 7, 1919, Pittsburgh, P
Deceased: September 17, 2006, Munson Township, OH

STATISTICS

Games

	GP	GS
1946 Cleveland Browns	14	11
1947 Cleveland Browns	14	4
1948 Cleveland Browns	14	13
1949 Cleveland Browns	12	10
Total	54	38

Rushing

	Rush	Yds	TD
1946 Cleveland Browns	1	2	0
Total	1	2	0

ULRICH, Hubert J., Jr. (Hub)

Position: E-DE
Height: 6'0"; Weight: 205
College: Kansas
Born: December 12, 1920, Jennings, OK
Deceased: March 10, 1974, Topeka, KS

STATISTICS

Games

	GP	GS
1946 Miami Seahawks	14	6
Total	14	6

Receiving

	Rec	Yds	TD
1946 Miami Seahawks	4	75	1
Total	4	75	1

URBAN, Gasper George

Position: G-LB
Height: 6'1"; Weight: 215
College: Notre Dame
Born: March 18, 1923, Lynn, MA
Deceased: May 17, 1998, St. Augustine, FL

STATISTICS

Games

	GP	GS
1948 Chicago Rockets	14	1
Total	14	1

Interceptions

	Int	Yds	TD
1948 Chicago Rockets	1	5	0
Total	1	5	0

UREMOVICH, Emil P.

Position: T-DE-E
Height: 6'2"; Weight: 233
College: Indiana
Born: September 29, 1916, Gary, IN
Deceased: April 22, 1994, Knox, IN

STATISTICS

Games

	GP	GS
1941 Detroit Lions	10	1
1942 Detroit Lions	11	10
1945 Detroit Lions	8	8
1946 Detroit Lions	11	6
1948 Chicago Rockets	8	0
Total	48	25

Interceptions

	Int	Yds	TD
1948 Chicago Rockets	1	1	0
Total	1	1	0

Fumbles

	Fum	Rec	Yds	TD
1945 Detroit Lions	0	2	0	0
1946 Detroit Lions	0	4	24	0
Total	0	6	24	0

VACANTI, Samuel Filadelfo (Sam)

Position: QB
Height: 5'11"; Weight: 203
College: Iowa, Nebraska, Perdue
Born: March 20, 1922, Omaha, NE
Deceased: December 17, 1981, Omaha, NE

STATISTICS

Games

	GP	GS
1947 Chicago Rockets	13	8
1948 Chicago Rockets	9	3
1948 Baltimore Colts	5	0
1949 Baltimore Colts	12	5
Total	39	16

Rushing

	Rush	Yds	TD
1947 Chicago Rockets	11	-9	1
1948 Chicago Rockets	7	7	2
1949 Baltimore Colts	7	10	0
Total	25	8	3

Passing

	Comp	Att	Yds	TD	Int
1947 Chicago Rockets	96	225	1571	16	16
1948 Chicago Rockets	47	116	633	2	15
1949 Bal. Colts	11	27	134	0	1
Total	**154**	**368**	**2338**	**18**	**32**

Kick Returns

	Ret	Yds	TD
1949 Baltimore Colts	1	10	0
Total	**1**	**10**	**0**

Field Goals

	FGM	FGA
1949 Baltimore Colts	*	2
Total	*****	**2**

Point After Touchdown

	XPM	XPA
1949 Baltimore Colts	3	3
Total	**3**	**3**

VANDEWEGHE, Alfred Bernard (Al)

Position: E-DE
Height: 5'11"; Weight: 200
College: William & Mary
Born: October 25, 1920, Wyckoff, NJ
Deceased: February 2, 2014, Midlothian, VA

STATISTICS

Games

	GP	GS
1946 Buffalo Bisons	5	3
Total	**5**	**3**

Receiving

	Rec	Yds	TD
1946 Buffalo Bisons	6	67	1
Total	**6**	**67**	**1**

Kick Returns

	Ret	Yds	TD
1946 Buffalo Bisons	1	15	0
Total	**1**	**15**	**0**

VAN TONE, Arthur (Art)

Position: WB-DB
Height: 5'10"; Weight: 185
College: Southern Miss
Born: September 30, 1918, Ottawa, OH
Deceased: August 9, 1990, Conyers, GA

STATISTICS

Games

	GP	GS
1943 Detroit Lions	10	2
1944 Detroit Lions	10	8
1945 Detroit Lions	2	2
1946 Brooklyn Dodgers	9	3
Total	**31**	**15**

Rushing

	Rush	Yds	TD
1943 Detroit Lions	2	1	0
1944 Detroit Lions	25	30	1
1945 Detroit Lions	3	14	0
1946 Brooklyn Dodgers	4	10	0
Total	**34**	**55**	**1**

Receiving

	Rec	Yds	TD
1943 Detroit Lions	6	112	1
1944 Detroit Lions	9	237	4
1945 Detroit Lions	3	67	0
1946 Brooklyn Dodgers	7	152	3
Total	**25**	**568**	**8**

Passing

	Comp	Att	Yds	TD	Int
1943 Detroit Lions	1	3	7	0	1
1944 Detroit Lions	0	1	0	0	0
Total	**1**	**4**	**7**	**0**	**1**

Punting

	Punt	Yds	Blk
1944 Detroit Lions	2	94	0
Total	**2**	**94**	**0**

Punt Returns

	Ret	Yds	TD
1943 Detroit Lions	3	47	0
1944 Detroit Lions	5	70	0
1946 Brooklyn Dodgers	1	5	0
Total	**9**	**122**	**0**

Kick Returns

	Ret	Yds	TD
1944 Detroit Lions	9	227	1
1946 Brooklyn Dodgers	2	25	0
Total	**11**	**252**	**1**

Interceptions

	Int	Yds	TD
1943 Detroit Lions	2	29	0
1944 Detroit Lions	4	16	0
1946 Brooklyn Dodgers	1	5	0
Total	**7**	**50**	**0**

Fumbles

	Fum	Rec	Yds	TD
1945 Detroit Lions	1	0	0	0
Total	**1**	**0**	**0**	**0**

VARDIAN, John Joseph (Johnny)

Position: HB-DB
Height: 5'8"; Weight: 167
College: (None)
Born: September 25, 1921, Johnstown, PA
Deceased: August 8, 1989, Tampa, FL

VETRANO

STATISTICS

Games

	GP	GS
1946 Miami Seahawks	6	1
1947 Baltimore Colts	14	5
1948 Baltimore Colts	12	0
Total	32	6

Rushing

	Rush	Yds	TD
1946 Miami Seahawks	5	−8	0
1947 Baltimore Colts	35	57	0
1948 Baltimore Colts	6	13	0
Total	46	62	0

Receiving

	Rec	Yds	TD
1946 Miami Seahawks	7	108	0
1947 Baltimore Colts	16	280	1
1948 Baltimore Colts	3	26	0
Total	26	414	1

Passing

	Comp	Att	Yds	TD	Int
1946 Miami Seahawks	1	1	−4	0	0
Total	1	1	−4	0	0

Punt Returns

	Ret	Yds	TD
1947 Baltimore Colts	5	66	0
1948 Baltimore Colts	3	34	0
Total	8	100	0

Kick Returns

	Ret	Yds	TD
1946 Miami Seahawks	1	23	0
1947 Baltimore Colts	6	128	0
1948 Baltimore Colts	3	66	0
Total	10	217	0

Interceptions

	Int	Yds	TD
1947 Baltimore Colts	3	48	0
Total	3	48	0

VASICEK, Victor Frederick (Vic)

Position: LB-G-DG
Height: 5'11"; Weight: 223
College: Texas, USC
Born: May 5, 1926, El Campo, TX
Deceased: June 20, 2003, Midland, TX

STATISTICS

Games

	GP	GS
1949 Buffalo Bills	12	3
1950 Los Angeles Rams	12	0
Total	24	3

Kick Returns

	Ret	Yds	TD
1950 Los Angeles Rams	2	30	0
Total	2	30	0

Interceptions

	Int	Yds	TD
1950 Los Angeles Rams	1	52	0
Total	1	52	0

VERRY, David Norman (Norm)

Position: T
Height: 6'1"; Weight: 240
College: USC
Born: September 18, 1922, Hanford, CA
Deceased: October 12, 1961, Los Angeles, CA

STATISTICS

Games

	GP	GS
1946 Chicago Rockets	10	3
1947 Chicago Rockets	1	1
Total	11	4

VETRANO, Joseph George (Joe)

Position: HB-DB
Height: 5'9"; Weight: 170
College: Southern Miss
Born: October 15, 1918, Neptune, NJ
Deceased: May 10, 1995, Berkeley, CA

STATISTICS

Games

	GP	GS
1946 San Francisco 49ers	13	2
1947 San Francisco 49ers	14	2
1948 San Francisco 49ers	14	1
1949 San Francisco 49ers	12	0
Total	53	5

Rushing

	Rush	Yds	TD
1946 S.F. 49ers	23	69	1
1947 S.F. 49ers	10	11	0
1948 S.F. 49ers	12	71	1
1949 S.F. 49ers	11	50	0
Total	56	201	2

Receiving

	Rec	Yds	TD
1946 S.F. 49ers*	4	37	0
1948 S.F. 49ers	1	34	0
Total	5	71	0

Punting

	Punt	Yds	Blk
1946 S.F. 49ers	6	236	0
1948 S.F. 49ers	1	38	0
Total	7	274	0

Punt Returns

	Ret	Yds	TD
1946 S.F. 49ers	7	84	0
1947 S.F. 49ers	12	137	0
1949 S.F. 49ers	1	16	0
Total	20	237	0

Kick Returns

	Ret	Yds	TD
1946 S.F. 49ers	3	49	0
1947 S.F. 49ers	5	117	0
1948 S.F. 49ers	1	38	0
Total	9	204	0

Interceptions

	Int	Yds	TD
1946 S.F. 49ers	3	32	0
Total	3	32	0

Field Goals

	FGM	FGA
1946 S.F. 49ers	4	7
1947 S.F. 49ers	4	12
1948 S.F. 49ers	5	8
1949 S.F. 49ers	3	7
Total	16	34

Point After Touchdown

	XPM	XPA
1946 S.F. 49ers	31	38
1947 S.F. 49ers	38	43
1948 S.F. 49ers	62	66
1949 S.F. 49ers	56	56
Total	187	203

NOTE: *There are a few discrepancies between the actual statistics and the official records in 1946. The total receiving yards for the season for Len Eshmont, Joe Vetrano, Ed Balatti and Ken Roskie were not consistent. Eshmont had an extra six receiving yards, while Vetrano was missing six yards. Balatti had an extra seven receiving yards and Roskie was missing seven yards. Since the numbers could not be verified, the official statistics are listed.*

VINNOLA, Paul Peter

Position: HB-DB
Height: 5'10"; Weight: 180
College: Santa Clara
Born: August 24, 1922, Denver, CO
Deceased: October 23, 1994, Denver, CO

STATISTICS

Games

	GP	GS
1946 Los Angeles Dons	13	0
Total	13	0

Rushing

	Rush	Yds	TD
1946 Los Angeles Dons	23	36	0
Total	23	36	0

Receiving

	Rec	Yds	TD
1946 Los Angeles Dons	4	39	0
Total	4	39	0

Punt Returns

	Ret	Yds	TD
1946 Los Angeles Dons	2	24	0
Total	2	24	0

Kick Returns

	Ret	Yds	TD
1946 Los Angeles Dons	5	83	0
Total	5	83	0

Interceptions

	Int	Yds	TD
1946 Los Angeles Dons	1	4	0
Total	1	4	0

VOGDS, Evan Edward

Position: G
Height: 5'10"; Weight: 210
College: Wisconsin
Born: February 10, 1923, Johnsburg, WI
Deceased: August 6, 1994, Fond du Lac, WI

STATISTICS

Games

	GP	GS
1946 Chicago Rockets	14	11
1947 Chicago Rockets	13	0
1948 Green Bay Packers	12	12
1949 Green Bay Packers	12	10
Total	51	33

Kick Returns

	Ret	Yds	TD
1949 Green Bay Packers	1	0	0
Total	1	0	0

Fumbles

	Fum	Rec	Yds	TD
1949 Green Bay Packers	0	1	0	0
Total	0	1	0	0

VOGT, Alois, Jr. (Allie)

Position: B
Height: 6'0"; Weight: 185
College: Wisconsin
Born: June 20, 1921, Germany
Deceased: February 26, 2002, Milwaukee, WI

STATISTICS

Games

	GP	GS
1946 Buffalo Bisons	1	0
Total	1	0

VOLZ, Wilbur Edward

Position: HB-DB
Height: 6'0"; Weight: 192
College: Missouri
Born: January 1, 1924, Edwardsville, IL
Deceased: December 27, 2015, Sun City, AZ

STATISTICS

Games

	GP	GS
1949 Buffalo Bills	8	0
Total	**8**	**0**

Rushing

	Rush	Yds	TD
1949 Buffalo Bills	4	7	1
Total	**4**	**7**	**1**

Receiving

	Rec	Yds	TD
1949 Buffalo Bills	1	6	0
Total	**1**	**6**	**0**

Kick Returns

	Ret	Yds	TD
1949 Buffalo Bills	3	43	0
Total	**3**	**43**	**0**

WAGNER, Lowell R.

Position: B
Height: 6'0"; Weight: 194
College: USC
Born: August 21, 1924, Santa Monica, CA
Deceased: September 26, 2005, Kirkland, WA

STATISTICS

Games

	GP	GS
1946 New York Yankees	13	7
1947 New York Yankees	7	3
1948 New York Yankees	14	3
1949 San Francisco 49ers	10	3
1950 San Francisco 49ers	12	0
1951 San Francisco 49ers	12	0
1952 San Francisco 49ers	12	0
1953 San Francisco 49ers	10	0
1955 San Francisco 49ers	1	0
Total	**91**	**16**

Rushing

	Rush	Yds	TD
1946 New York Yankees	15	29	0
1949 S.F. 49ers	3	17	0
1950 S.F. 49ers	2	5	0
1953 S.F. 49ers	1	4	0
Total	**21**	**55**	**0**

Receiving

	Rec	Yds	TD
1946 New York Yankees	9	126	1
1947 New York Yankees	4	50	1
1948 New York Yankees	6	99	1
1952 S.F. 49ers	1	6	0
Total	**20**	**281**	**3**

Punt Returns

	Ret	Yds	TD
1946 New York Yankees	2	55	1
1949 S.F. 49ers	1	2	0
1950 S.F. 49ers	1	4	0
Total	**4**	**61**	**1**

Kick Returns

	Ret	Yds	TD
1946 New York Yankees	4	119	0
Total	**4**	**119**	**0**

Interceptions

	Int	Yds	TD
1948 New York Yankees	1	31	0
1949 S.F. 49ers	6	121	1
1950 S.F. 49ers	4	12	0
1951 S.F. 49ers	9	115	0
1952 S.F. 49ers	6	69	0
1953 S.F. 49ers	6	135	0
Total	**32**	**483**	**1**

Fumbles

	Fum	Rec	Yds	TD
1950 S.F. 49ers	1	3	7	0
1952 S.F. 49ers	0	1	0	0
1953 S.F. 49ers	0	1	0	0
Total	**1**	**5**	**7**	**0**

WALLACE, Beverly William (Bev)

Position: QB
Height: 6'2"; Weight: 180
College: Compton Community College
Born: March 7, 1923
Deceased: June 17, 1992, Newport Beach, CA

STATISTICS

Games

	GP	GS
1947 San Francisco 49ers	4	0
1948 San Francisco 49ers	10	0
1949 San Francisco 49ers	9	1
1951 New York Yanks	1	0
Total	**24**	**1**

Rushing

	Rush	Yds	TD
1948 S.F. 49ers	3	2	0
1949 S.F. 49ers	2	2	1
1951 New York Yanks	1	−8	0
Total	**6**	**−4**	**1**

Passing

	Comp	Att	Yds	TD	Int
1947 S.F. 49ers	5	16	48	0	2
1948 S.F. 49ers	8	22	114	1	3
1949 S.F. 49ers	9	23	95	0	4
1951 N.Y. Yanks	1	8	9	0	0
Total	**23**	**69**	**266**	**1**	**9**

Punting

	Punt	Yds	Blk
1947 S.F. 49ers	2	78	0
1948 S.F. 49ers	5	192	0
1949 S.F. 49ers	1	30	0
Total	**8**	**300**	**0**

Fumbles

	Fum	Rec	Yds	TD
1951 New York Yanks	1	1	0	0
Total	**1**	**1**	**0**	**0**

WARREN, Morrison Fulbright (Morrie)

Position: FB-LB
Height: 5'11"; Weight: 208
College: Arizona State
Born: December 6, 1923, Marlin, TX
Deceased: April 9, 2002, Tempe, AZ

STATISTICS

Games

	GP	GS
1948 Brooklyn Dodgers	2	0
Total	**2**	**0**

Rushing

	Rush	Yds	TD
1948 Brooklyn Dodgers	1	1	0
Total	**1**	**1**	**0**

Kick Returns

	Ret	Yds	TD
1948 Brooklyn Dodgers	1	36	0
Total	**1**	**36**	**0**

WARRINGTON, Caleb Van, Jr. (Tex)

Position: G-C-LB
Height: 6'2"; Weight: 210
College: Auburn, William & Mary
Born: March 21, 1921, Dover, DE
Deceased: September 20, 1983, Gifford, FL

STATISTICS

Games

	GP	GS
1946 Brooklyn Dodgers	12	6
1947 Brooklyn Dodgers	13	9
1948 Brooklyn Dodgers	14	11
Total	**39**	**26**

WASSERBACH, Lloyd George

Position: T
Height: 5'11"; Weight: 205
College: Wisconsin
Born: January 30, 1921, Baileys Harbor, WI
Deceased: February 1, 1949, Ripon, WI

STATISTICS

Games

	GP	GS
1946 Chicago Rockets	12	3
1947 Chicago Rockets	5	0
Total	**17**	**3**

Kick Returns

	Ret	Yds	TD
1946 Chicago Rockets	1	13	0
Total	**1**	**13**	**0**

Interceptions

	Int	Yds	TD
1946 Chicago Rockets	1	0	0
Total	**1**	**0**	**0**

WEDEMEYER, Herman John (Herm)

Position: B
Height: 5'10"; Weight: 178
College: St. Mary's
Born: May 20, 1924, Honolulu, HI
Deceased: January 25, 1999, Honolulu, HI

STATISTICS

Games

	GP	GS
1948 Los Angeles Dons	14	10
1949 Baltimore Colts	11	5
Total	**25**	**15**

Rushing

	Rush	Yds	TD
1948 Los Angeles Dons	79	249	0
1949 Baltimore Colts	64	291	0
Total	**143**	**540**	**0**

Receiving

	Rec	Yds	TD
1948 Los Angeles Dons	36	330	2
1949 Baltimore Colts	10	112	0
Total	**46**	**442**	**2**

Passing

	Comp	Att	Yds	TD	Int
1948 L.A. Dons	9	30	79	0	3
1949 Bal. Colts	0	1	0	0	1
Total	**9**	**31**	**79**	**0**	**4**

Punting

	Punt	Yds	Blk
1948 Los Angeles Dons	1	10	0
1949 Baltimore Colts	3	54	0
Total	**4**	**64**	**0**

Punt Returns

	Ret	Yds	TD
1948 Los Angeles Dons	23	368	0
1949 Baltimore Colts	16	221	0
Total	**39**	**589**	**0**

Kick Returns			
	Ret	Yds	TD
1948 Los Angeles Dons	11	240	0
1949 Baltimore Colts	30	602	0
Total	**41**	**842**	**0**

WEINMEISTER, Arnold George (Arnie)

Position: DT-T
Height: 6'4"; Weight: 235
College: Washington
Born: March 23, 1923, Rhein, Canada
Deceased: June 28, 2000, Seattle, WA

STATISTICS

Games		
	GP	GS
1948 New York Yankees	14	8
1949 New York Yankees	11	11
1950 New York Giants	10	0
1951 New York Giants	12	0
1952 New York Giants	12	0
1953 New York Giants	12	0
Total	**71**	**19**

Receiving			
	Rec	Yds	TD
1950 New York Giants	1	16	0
Total	**1**	**16**	**0**

Fumbles				
	Fum	Rec	Yds	TD
1950 New York Giants	0	2	0	0
1951 New York Giants	0	1	0	0
1952 New York Giants	0	1	0	0
1953 New York Giants	0	4	0	0
Total	**0**	**8**	**0**	**0**

WENDELL, Martin Peter

Position: G
Height: 5'10"; Weight: 215
College: Notre Dame
Born: November 22, 1926, Chicago, IL
Deceased: March 7, 2012, Wheeling, IL

STATISTICS

Games		
	GP	GS
1949 Chicago Hornets	10	8
Total	**10**	**8**

WERDER, Richard Irving (Dick)

Position: G
Height: 5'9"; Weight: 210
College: Georgetown
Born: July 31, 1922, Buffalo, NY
Deceased: February 14, 2002, Buffalo, NY

STATISTICS

Games		
	GP	GS
1948 New York Yankees	3	1
Total	**3**	**1**

WETZ, Harlan Henry

Position: T
Height: 6'5"; Weight: 265
College: Texas
Born: September 15, 1925, New Braunfels, TX
Deceased: November 14, 1983, San Antonio, TX

STATISTICS

Games		
	GP	GS
1947 Brooklyn Dodgers	11	0
Total	**11**	**0**

WHALEN, Gerald Cornelius (Jerry)

Position: C-G
Height: 6'1"; Weight: 235
College: Canisius
Born: April 23, 1928, Buffalo, NY
Deceased: November 1973, Buffalo, NY

STATISTICS

Games		
	GP	GS
1948 Buffalo Bills	7	0
Total	**7**	**0**

WHALEY, Benjamin Franklyn (Ben)

Position: G
Height: 5'11"; Weight: 210
College: Virginia State
Born: October 14, 1926, Richmond, VA
Deceased: November 4, 2001, Richmond, VA

STATISTICS

Games		
	GP	GS
1949 Los Angeles Dons	3	0
Total	**3**	**0**

WHITE, Eugene George (Gene)

Position: G
Height: 6'2"; Weight: 205
College: Indiana
Born: August 3, 1919, South Bend, IN
Deceased: April 24, 1989, South Bend, IN

STATISTICS

Games

	GP	GS
1946 Buffalo Bisons	1	0
Total		

WHITLOW, Kenneth Moody (Ken)

Position: C-LB
Height: 6'1"; Weight: 190
College: Rice
Born: November 30, 1917, Wichita Falls, TX
Deceased: November 12, 1969, Houston, TX

STATISTICS

Games

	GP	GS
1946 Miami Seahawks	13	7
Total	13	7

Interceptions

	Int	Yds	TD
1946 Miami Seahawks	2	20	0
Total	2	20	0

WILKIN, Wilbur B. (Willie)

Position: T
Height: 6'4"; Weight: 261
College: St. Mary's
Born: April 21, 1916, Bingham Canyon, UT
Deceased: May 16, 1973, Palo Alto, CA

STATISTICS

Games

	GP	GS
1938 Washington Redskins	11	3
1939 Washington Redskins	11	4
1940 Washington Redskins	11	9
1941 Washington Redskins	11	10
1942 Washington Redskins	11	8
1943 Washington Redskins	9	3
1946 Chicago Rockets	10	8
Total	74	45

Point After Touchdown

	XPM	XPA
1939 Wash. Redskins	*	1
Total	*	1

WILKINS, Richard Maurice (Dick)

Position: E
Height: 6'2"; Weight: 194
College: Oregon
Born: September 28, 1925, Portland, OR
Deceased: October 21, 1997, Lane County, OR

STATISTICS

Games

	GP	GS
1949 Los Angeles Dons	11	3
1952 Dallas Texans	12	11
1954 New York Giants	6	0
Total	29	14

Rushing

	Rush	Yds	TD
1949 Los Angeles Dons	8	28	0
Total	8	28	0

Receiving

	Rec	Yds	TD
1949 Los Angeles Dons	32	589	3
1952 Dallas Texans	32	416	3
1954 New York Giants	4	45	1
Total	68	1050	7

Passing

	Comp	Att	Yds	TD	Int
1949 L.A. Dons	0	1	0	0	0
Total	0	1	0	0	0

WILLIAMS, Joel Herschel

Position: C
Height: 6'1"; Weight: 220
College: Louisiana-Lafayette, Texas
Born: March 18, 1926, San Angelo, TX
Deceased: March 10, 1997, Ector County, TX

STATISTICS

Games

	GP	GS
1948 San Francisco 49ers	14	13
1950 Baltimore Colts	12	—
Total	26	—

Rushing

	Rush	Yds	TD
1950 Baltimore Colts	1	50	1
Total	1	50	1

Fumbles

	Fum	Rec	Yds	TD
1950 Baltimore Colts	1	1	0	0
Total	1	1	0	0

WILLIAMS, Jack Gressett (Tex)

Position: C-LB
Height: 5'11"; Weight: 193
College: Auburn
Born: August 20, 1918, Lancaster, PA
Deceased: April 25, 1989, Harris, TX

STATISTICS

Games

	GP	GS
1942 Philadelphia Eagles	5	0
1946 Miami Seahawks	6	0
Total	11	0

Interceptions

	Int	Yds	TD
1946 Miami Seahawks	1	3	0
Total	1	3	0

WILLIAMS, Walter L. (Walt)

Position: TB-DB-QB
Height: 6'1"; Weight: 194
College: Boston University
Born: February 12, 1919
Deceased: August 8, 1990, Jackson County, NC

STATISTICS

Games

	GP	GS
1946 Chicago Rockets	14	0
1947 Boston Yanks	11	3
Total	25	3

Rushing

	Rush	Yds	TD
1946 Chicago Rockets	21	19	1
Total	21	19	1

Receiving

	Rec	Yds	TD
1946 Chicago Rockets	1	3	0
1947 Boston Yanks	1	2	0
Total	2	5	0

Passing

	Comp	Att	Yds	TD	Int
1946 Chicago Rockets	13	30	226	1	5
1947 Boston Yanks	0	1	0	0	0
Total	13	31	226	1	5

Punting

	Punt	Yds	Blk
1946 Chicago Rockets	24	998	1
Total	24	998	1

Punt Returns

	Ret	Yds	TD
1946 Chicago Rockets	1	6	0
1947 Boston Yanks	1	14	0
Total	2	20	0

Kick Returns

	Ret	Yds	TD
1946 Chicago Rockets	1	18	0
Total			

WILLIAMS, Dale Windell (Windell)

Position: E
Height: 6'2"; Weight: 185
College: La-Lafayette, Rice
Born: March 10, 1923, Fort Towson, OK
Deceased: May 12, 1992, Houston, TX

STATISTICS

Games

	GP	GS
1948 Baltimore Colts	14	1
1949 Baltimore Colts	12	4
Total	26	5

Receiving

	Rec	Yds	TD
1948 Baltimore Colts	32	360	2
1949 Baltimore Colts	20	266	1
Total	52	626	3

Kick Returns

	Ret	Yds	TD
1948 Baltimore Colts	1	20	0
Total	1	20	0

WILLIAMSON, Ernest Warriner (Ernie)

Position: T
Height: 6'4"; Weight: 245
College: Apprentice, North Carolina
Born: September 9, 1922, Crewe, VA
Deceased: March 6, 2002, Chapel Hill, NC

STATISTICS

Games

	GP	GS
1947 Washington Redskins	9	3
1948 New York Giants	2	0
1949 Los Angeles Dons	12	0
Total	23	3

Kick Returns

	Ret	Yds	TD
1947 Wash. Redskins	1	28	0
Total	1	28	0

Fumbles

	Fum	Rec	Yds	TD
1947 Wash. Redskins	0	1	0	0
Total	0	1	0	0

WILLIS, William Karnet (Bill)

Position: DG-G
Height: 6'2"; Weight: 213
College: Ohio State
Born: October 5, 1921, Columbus, OH
Deceased: November 27, 2007, Columbus, OH

Statistics

Games

	GP	GS
1946 Cleveland Browns	13	9
1947 Cleveland Browns	13	12
1948 Cleveland Browns	14	0
1949 Cleveland Browns	12	1
1950 Cleveland Browns	12	0
1951 Cleveland Browns	12	0
1952 Cleveland Browns	12	0
1953 Cleveland Browns	11	0
Total	99	22

Interceptions

	Int	Yds	TD
1949 Cleveland Browns	1	6	0
Total	1	6	0

Fumbles

	Fum	Rec	Yds	TD
1951 Cleveland Browns	0	1	0	0
1953 Cleveland Browns	0	1	0	0
Total	0	2	0	0

WIMBERLY, Abner Perry (Ab)

Position: DE-E
Height: 6'1"; Weight: 213
College: LSU
Born: May 4, 1926, Oak Ridge, LA
Deceased: September 19, 1976, Oak Ridge, LA

Statistics

Games

	GP	GS
1949 Los Angeles Dons	12	4
1950 Green Bay Packers	11	0
1951 Green Bay Packers	12	0
1952 Green Bay Packers	12	0
Total	47	4

Receiving

	Rec	Yds	TD
1949 Los Angeles Dons	3	22	0
1950 Green Bay Packers	2	18	0
1951 Green Bay Packers	1	10	0
Total	6	50	0

Kick Returns

	Ret	Yds	TD
1951 Green Bay Packers	2	4	0
Total	2	4	0

Interceptions

	Int	Yds	TD
1949 Los Angeles Dons	1	16	1
1950 Green Bay Packers	1	0	0
1951 Green Bay Packers	1	5	0
Total	3	21	0

Fumbles

	Fum	Rec	Yds	TD
1950 Green Bay Packers	0	2	0	0
1951 Green Bay Packers	1	1	0	0
1952 Green Bay Packers	0	2	0	0
Total	2	5	0	0

WINKLER, Bernard Arthur (Bernie)

Position: T
Height: 6'1"; Weight: 232
College: Millsaps, Texas Tech
Born: December 5, 1925, The Grove, TX
Deceased: June 28, 1990, New Braunfels, TX

Statistics

Games

	GP	GS
1948 Los Angeles Dons	4	0
Total	4	0

WISSMAN, Lawrence Peter (Pete)

Position: LB-C
Height: 6'0"; Weight: 215
College: Miami (OH), St. Louis, Washington (MO)
Born: October 9, 1923, St. Louis, MO
Deceased:

Statistics

Games

	GP	GS
1949 San Francisco 49ers	12	2
1950 San Francisco 49ers	12	0
1951 San Francisco 49ers	9	0
1952 San Francisco 49ers	12	0
1954 San Francisco 49ers	3	0
Total	48	2

Interceptions

	Int	Yds	TD
1949 S.F. 49ers	1	12	0
1950 S.F. 49ers	1	5	0
1951 S.F. 49ers	2	12	0
Total	4	29	0

Fumbles

	Fum	Rec	Yds	TD
1950 S.F. 49ers	0	2	0	0
1951 S.F. 49ers	1	1	0	0
1952 S.F. 49ers	0	1	0	0
Total	1	4	0	0

WIZBICKI, Alexander John (Alex)

Position: DB-HB
Height: '11"; Weight: 188
College: Dartmouth, Holy Cross
Born: October 6, 1921, Brooklyn, NY
Deceased:

STATISTICS
Games
	GP	GS
1947 Buffalo Bills	13	2
1948 Buffalo Bills	9	1
1949 Buffalo Bills	12	1
1950 Green Bay Packers	11	0
Total	45	4

Rushing
	Rush	Yds	TD
1947 Buffalo Bills	9	44	0
1949 Buffalo Bills	5	-10	0
Total	14	34	0

Punt Returns
	Ret	Yds	TD
1947 Buffalo Bills	9	105	0
1948 Buffalo Bills	3	33	0
Total	12	138	0

Kick Returns
	Ret	Yds	TD
1947 Buffalo Bills	5	164	1
1949 Buffalo Bills	1	22	0
Total	6	186	1

Interceptions
	Int	Yds	TD
1948 Buffalo Bills	3	49	0
1949 Buffalo Bills	1	1	0
1950 Green Bay Packers	2	38	0
Total	6	88	0

Fumbles
	Fum	Rec	Yds	TD
1950 Green Bay Packers	0	2	12	0
Total	0	2	12	0

WOODARD, Richard Ernest (Dick)

Position: LB-C
Height: 6'2"; Weight: 224
College: Iowa
Born: July 26, 1926, Britt, IA
Deceased:

STATISTICS
Games
	GP	GS
1949 Los Angeles Dons	12	0
1950 New York Giants	12	0
1951 New York Giants	11	0
1952 Washington Redskins	12	0
1953 New York Giants	12	0
Total	59	0

Interceptions
	Int	Yds	TD
1949 Los Angeles Dons	2	39	1
1950 New York Giants	1	11	0
1951 New York Giants	2	13	0
1953 New York Giants	1	10	0
Total	6	73	1

Fumbles
	Fum	Rec	Yds	TD
1950 New York Giants	0	3	0	1
1951 New York Giants	1	0	0	0
1952 Wash. Redskins	0	1	6	0
Total	1	4	6	1

WOUDENBERG, John William, Jr.

Position: T
Height: 6'3"; Weight: 226
College: Denver, St. Mary's
Born: May 25, 1918, Denver, CO
Deceased: May 3, 2005, Southdale, AZ

STATISTICS
Games
	GP	GS
1940 Pittsburgh Steelers	7	0
1941 Pittsburgh Steelers	11	8
1942 Pittsburgh Steelers	11	11
1946 San Francisco 49ers	14	14
1947 San Francisco 49ers	14	14
1948 San Francisco 49ers	14	14
1949 San Francisco 49ers	12	10
Total	83	71

Receiving
	Rec	Yds	TD
1942 Pittsburgh Steelers	1	-1	0
Total	1	-1	0

Kick Returns
	Ret	Yds	TD
1947 S.F. 49ers	1	2	0
Total	1	2	0

WOZNIAK, John Edward

Position: G-LB
Height: 6'0"; Weight: 218
College: Alabama
Born: August 2, 1921, Arnold City, PA
Deceased: August 1982, Tuscaloosa, AL

STATISTICS
Games
	GP	GS
1948 Brooklyn Dodgers	14	9
1949 New York Yankees	12	12
1950 New York Yanks	12	0
1951 New York Yanks	12	0
1952 Dallas Texans	12	11
Total	62	32

Receiving
	Rec	Yds	TD
1951 New York Yanks	1	4	0
1952 Dallas Texans	1	-1	0
Total	2	3	0

Rushing
	Rush	Yds	Td
1948 Brooklyn Dodgers	10	13	0

Kick Returns

	Ret	Yds	TD
1952 Dallas Texans	1	4	0
Total	**1**	**4**	**0**

Interceptions

	Int	Yds	TD
1948 Brooklyn Dodgers	1	7	0
Total	**1**	**7**	**0**

Fumbles

	Fum	Rec	Yds	TD
1950 New York Yanks	0	1	1	0
1951 New York Yanks	1	1	0	0
1952 Dallas Texans	0	1	0	0
Total	**1**	**3**	**1**	**0**

WUKITS, Albert Robert (Al)

Position: C-LB-G
Height: 6'3"; Weight: 218
College: Duquesne
Born: December 16, 1917, Millvale, PA
Deceased: October 15, 1978, Pittsburgh, PA

STATISTICS

Games

	GP	GS
1943 Pittsburgh Steelers	10	1
1944 Chicago Cardinals	10	3
1945 Pittsburgh Steelers	3	1
1946 Miami Seahawks	7	2
1946 Buffalo Bisons	8	5
Total	**38**	**12**

Interceptions

	Int	Yds	TD
1943 Pittsburgh Steelers	1	7	0
1946 Miami Seahawks	2	26	0
Total	**3**	**33**	**0**

Fumbles

	Fum	Rec	Yds	TD
1945 Pittsburgh Steelers	2	0	0	0
Total	**2**	**0**	**0**	**0**

WYHONIC, John N.

Position: G
Height: 6'0"; Weight: 213
College: Alabama
Born: December 23, 1919, Tiltonsville, OH
Deceased: July 19, 1989, Arcadia, FL

STATISTICS

Games

	GP	GS
1946 Philadelphia Eagles	11	2
1947 Philadelphia Eagles	12	2
1948 Buffalo Bills	13	1
1949 Buffalo Bills	3	0
Total	**39**	**5**

Fumbles

	Fum	Rec	Yds	TD
1946 Philadelphia Eagles	0	1	0	0
Total	**0**	**1**	**0**	**0**

YACKANICH, Joseph Peter (Joe)

Position: G
Height: 5'10"; Weight: 205
College: Fordham
Born: March 31, 1922
Deceased: August 1969, Lansing, IL

STATISTICS

Games

	GP	GS
1946 New York Yankees	11	0
1947 New York Yankees	14	0
1948 New York Yankees	1	0
Total	**26**	**0**

YOKAS, Frank P.

Position: G
Height: 5'11"; Weight: 210
College: (None)
Born: February 27, 1924, Rock Island, IL
Deceased: May 12, 1994, Los Angeles, CA

STATISTICS

Games

	GP	GS
1946 Los Angeles Dons	12	0
1947 Baltimore Colts	13	2
Total	**25**	**2**

YONAKOR, John Joseph

Position: E-DE-DT
Height: 6'5"; Weight: 222
College: Notre Dame
Born: August 4, 1921, Boston, MA
Deceased: April 18, 2001, Euclid, OH

STATISTICS

Games

	GP	GS
1946 Cleveland Browns	14	5
1947 Cleveland Browns	14	7
1948 Cleveland Browns	14	2
1949 Cleveland Browns	12	1
1950 New York Yanks	8	0
1952 Washington Redskins	12	0
Total	**74**	**15**

Receiving

	Rec	Yds	TD
1946 Cleveland Browns	7	98	2
1947 Cleveland Browns	6	95	2
1948 Cleveland Browns	5	27	0
Total	**18**	**220**	**4**

Punt Returns

	Ret	Yds	TD
1949 Cleveland Browns	1	1	0
Total	**1**	**1**	**0**

Kick Returns

	Ret	Yds	TD
1947 Cleveland Browns	1	0	0
Total	**1**	**0**	**0**

Interceptions

	Int	Yds	TD
1948 Cleveland Browns	1	1	0
1950 New York Yanks	1	10	0
Total	**2**	**11**	**0**

Fumbles

	Fum	Rec	Yds	TD
1952 Wash. Redskins	0	2	0	0
Total	**0**	**2**	**0**	**0**

YONAMINE, Wallace K. (Wally)

Position: HB-DB
Height: 5'9"; Weight: 180
College: (None)
Born: June 24, 1925, Maui, HI
Deceased: February 28, 2011, Honolulu, HI

STATISTICS

Games

	GP	GS
1947 San Francisco 49ers	12	3
Total	**12**	**3**

Rushing

	Rush	Yds	TD
1947 S.F. 49ers	19	74	0
Total	**19**	**74**	**0**

Receiving

	Rec	Yds	TD
1947 S.F. 49ers	3	40	0
Total	**3**	**40**	**0**

Punt Returns

	Ret	Yds	TD
1947 S.F. 49ers	2	29	0
Total	**2**	**29**	**0**

Kick Returns

	Ret	Yds	TD
1947 S.F. 49ers	7	127	0
Total	**7**	**127**	**0**

Interceptions

	Int	Yds	TD
1947 S.F. 49ers	1	20	0
Total	**1**	**20**	**0**

YOUNG, Claude Henry K. (Buddy)

Position: HB-FB-DB
Height: 5'4"; Weight: 175
College: Illinois
Born: January 5, 1926, Chicago, IL
Deceased: September 4, 1983, Terrell, TX

STATISTICS

Games

	GP	GS
1947 New York Yankees	14	8
1948 New York Yankees	12	11
1949 New York Yankees	12	11
1950 New York Yanks	12	0
1951 New York Yanks	12	0
1952 Dallas Texans	12	11
1953 Baltimore Colts	10	0
1954 Baltimore Colts	10	0
1955 Baltimore Colts	11	0
Total	**105**	**41**

Rushing

	Rush	Yds	TD
1947 New York Yankees	116	712	3
1948 New York Yankees	70	245	1
1949 New York Yankees	76	495	5
1950 New York Yanks	76	334	1
1951 New York Yanks	46	165	1
1952 Dallas Texans	71	243	3
1953 Baltimore Colts	40	135	0
1954 Baltimore Colts	70	311	2
1955 Baltimore Colts	32	87	1
Total	**597**	**2727**	**17**

Receiving

	Rec	Yds	TD
1947 New York Yankees	27	303	2
1948 New York Yankees	21	259	4
1949 New York Yankees	12	171	2
1950 New York Yanks	20	302	1
1951 New York Yanks	31	508	3
1952 Dallas Texans	22	269	2
1953 Baltimore Colts	12	201	3
1954 Baltimore Colts	15	272	3
1955 Baltimore Colts	19	426	1
Total	**179**	**2711**	**21**

Passing

	Comp	Att	Yds	TD	Int
1947 Yankees	1	2	13	0	0
1952 Texans	0	3	0	0	1
Total	**1**	**5**	**13**	**0**	**1**

Punt Returns

	Ret	Yds	TD
1947 New York Yankees	8	127	1
1948 New York Yankees	2	11	0
1949 New York Yankees	9	171	0
1950 New York Yanks	9	54	0
1951 New York Yanks	12	231	1
1952 Dallas Texans	6	35	0
1953 Baltimore Colts	6	9	0
1954 Baltimore Colts	14	60	0
1955 Baltimore Colts	1	0	0
Total	**67**	**698**	**2**

YOUNG, George Donald (Kick Returns continued)

	Kick Returns		
	Ret	Yds	TD
1947 New York Yankees	12	332	1
1948 New York Yankees	12	303	0
1949 New York Yankees	11	316	1
1950 New York Yanks	20	536	0
1951 New York Yanks	14	427	1
1952 Dallas Texans	23	643	0
1953 Baltimore Colts	11	378	1
1954 Baltimore Colts	13	308	0
1955 Baltimore Colts	9	222	0
Total	**125**	**3465**	**4**

	Fumbles			
	Fum	Rec	Yds	TD
1950 New York Yanks	6	5	-8	0
1951 New York Yanks	3	0	0	0
1952 Dallas Texans	5	2	0	0
1953 Baltimore Colts	6	1	0	0
1954 Baltimore Colts	1	0	0	0
1955 Baltimore Colts	1	1	0	0
Total	**22**	**9**	**-8**	**0**

YOUNG, George Donald

Position: DE-E
Height: 6'3"; Weight: 214
College: Baldwin-Wallace, Georgia
Born: May 10, 1924, Wilkes-Barre, PA
Deceased: September 21, 1969, Chicago, IL

STATISTICS

	Games	
	GP	GS
1946 Cleveland Browns	13	2
1947 Cleveland Browns	13	2
1948 Cleveland Browns	14	0
1949 Cleveland Browns	9	0
1950 Cleveland Browns	12	0
1951 Cleveland Browns	12	0
1952 Cleveland Browns	12	0
1953 Cleveland Browns	12	0
Total	**97**	**4**

	Receiving		
	Rec	Yds	TD
1946 Cleveland Browns	3	37	0
1948 Cleveland Browns	2	20	0
Total	**5**	**57**	**0**

	Kick Returns		
	Ret	Yds	TD
1953 Cleveland Browns	1	0	0
Total	**1**	**0**	**0**

	Fumbles			
	Fum	Rec	Yds	TD
1950 Cleveland Browns	0	1	0	0
1951 Cleveland Browns	0	1	47	1
1952 Cleveland Browns	0	3	0	0
1953 Cleveland Browns	0	1	0	0
Total	**0**	**6**	**47**	**1**

ZONTINI, Louis Rogers

Position: B
Height: 5'9"; Weight: 189
College: Notre Dame
Born: August 30, 1917, Whitesville, WV
Deceased: August 6, 1986, Richmond Heights, OH

STATISTICS

	Games	
	GP	GS
1940 Chicago Cardinals	8	0
1941 Chicago Cardinals	8	1
1944 Cleveland Rams	10	0
1946 Buffalo Bisons	14	5
Total	**40**	**6**

	Rushing		
	Rush	Yds	TD
1940 Chicago Cardinals	1	1	0
1941 Chicago Cardinals	1	-9	0
1944 Los Angeles Rams	33	105	3
1946 Buffalo Bisons	13	36	0
Total	**48**	**133**	**3**

	Receiving		
	Rec	Yds	TD
1941 Chicago Cardinals	1	22	0
1944 Los Angeles Rams	3	88	1
Total	**4**	**110**	**1**

	Passing				
	Comp	Att	Yds	Td	Int
1944 L.A. Rams	2	2	18	0	0
1946 Buffalo Bisons	0	1	0	0	0
Total	**2**	**3**	**18**	**0**	**0**

	Punting		
	Punt	Yds	Blk
1940 Chicago Cardinals	2	92	0
1941 Chicago Cardinals	12	446	0
1946 Buffalo Bisons	44	1595	0
Total	**58**	**2133**	**0**

	Punt Returns		
	Ret	Yds	TD
1944 Los Angeles Rams	4	47	0
Total	**4**	**47**	**0**

	Kick Returns		
	Ret	Yds	TD
1944 Los Angeles Rams	3	66	0
1946 Buffalo Bisons	1	19	0
Total	**4**	**85**	**0**

	Interceptions		
	Int	Yds	TD
1940 Chicago Cardinals	1	20	0
1944 Los Angeles Rams	2	14	0
1946 Buffalo Bisons	1	2	0
Total	**4**	**36**	**0**

Field Goals

	FGM	FGA
1940 Chicago Cardinals	2	5
1941 Chicago Cardinals	*	4
1944 Los Angeles Rams	3	6
1946 Buffalo Bisons	4	8
Total	9+	23

Point After Touchdown

	XPM	XPA
1940 Chicago Cardinals	10	10
1941 Chicago Cardinals	5	7
1944 Los Angeles Rams	14	16
1946 Buffalo Bisons	30	31
Total	59	64

ZORICH, George

Position: G-LB
Height: 6'2"; Weight: 213
College: Northwestern
Born: November 24, 1915, Wakefield, MA
Deceased: October 14, 1962, Rensselaer, IN

STATISTICS

Games

	GP	GS
1944 Chicago Bears	10	10
1945 Chicago Bears	8	6
1946 Miami Seahawks	6	0
1947 Baltimore Colts	11	1
Total	35	17

Punt Returns

	Ret	Yds	TD
1946 Miami Seahawks	1	18	0
Total	1	18	0

Interceptions

	Int	Yds	TD
1944 Chicago Bears	1	4	0
Total	1	4	0

Part 9: Coach Register

by John Maxymuk

Excerpt from *The Coffin Corner*, Volume 35, Number 4: "Correcting the Coaching Record" by John Maxymuk.

Despite being listed in all but one of the standard football encyclopedias as the Brooklyn Dodgers' co-coach with Cliff Battles for the second half of the 1946 All America Football Conference season, Tom Scott actually was merely the interim coach of the team for just one game. NFLE (*The Official NFL Encyclopedia*, Beau Riffenburgh, 1986) is the only source to have this instance correct.

Scott was a 6'3" 215-pound Highland Falls, New York native, who played end on the freshman team at NYU in 1939 when Dr. Mal Stevens was head coach. He transferred to West Point in the next year and played for Army in 1942 before injuring his knee and helped out as a coach in 1943. During the War, Scott served in an anti-aircraft unit all across Europe.

Following his post–War discharge, Tom tried out for the Dodgers in the new AAFC, but when his knee problem flared up in training camp, he was added to the coaching staff by Coach Mal Stevens. Stevens soon found that coaching the dreadful Dodgers was interfering with his medical practice and abruptly resigned less than six hours before the team's seventh game on October 25th. All but NFLE credit this seventh game to Stevens, giving him a 2–4–1 record rather than the actual 1–4–1 one he deserves.

Scott was put in charge of the team that day, and the Dodgers knocked off feeble Miami 30–7. The team announced that Stevens' former assistant at NYU, Fred Linehan, would be taking over in a few days. However, Linehan withdrew from his appointment on the 29th, so Brooklyn had to scramble to hire Cliff Battles, who had coached at Columbia and in the Marines, as head coach on November 1st, one day prior to their next game against Chicago. Reporters questioned Scott whether he'd been offered the head coaching job, "No, I haven't been asked to take over on that basis. That would be silly. I'm only 26 and have had just one year of coaching experience, that in the service. Of course, someday I hope to qualify, but right now I know I'm not ripe for such a job. When the new man is named, I'll string along as assistant."

Scott continued as an assistant to Battles for the rest of 1946 and all of 1947. Battles was fired in 1948 and replaced by Carl Voyles. Scott never coached in the pros again and died at the age of 58 in 1978.

The other 1946 misallocation occurs with the AAFC's Chicago Rockets. Rockets' owner John Keeshin, a blustery trucking magnate, hired the prominent former Northwestern coach Dick Hanley as his head coach. During the War, Hanley had coached the powerful El Toro Marines team in California. Predictably, Dick stocked the Rockets with 17 players from El Toro, including Elroy Hirsch, Willie Wilkin and Bob Dove. From the outset, the prickly Hanley struggled to get along with the meddlesome Keeshin and either quit or was fired (they disagreed about that, too) on September 25th, the date of the Rockets' third game. Hanley and his two assistants watched from the stands as the Rockets, directed by the player-coach triumvirate of Bob Dove, Ned Mathews and Willie Wilkin, beat Buffalo for its first victory.

Dick told reporters, "For someone who knows nothing about football, Keeshin has more coaching advice than anybody I ever knew." And then it turned uglier. When Keeshin told the Chicago Tribune on September 27th that 32 of 33 Rocket players voted that Hanley should be fired, Hanley sued him for libel. The case dragged on for seven years, but in January 1953, Hanley was awarded $100,000 in damages for malicious libel when multiple players testified that there had been no vote and that several players indeed had a high regard for Hanley. By 1953, he was long out of football (so was Keeshin).

In 1946, Keeshin left the player-coach trio in charge for the next month, but kept Boland and Nevers on the payroll while he tried to persuade Sid Luckman to coach the team. On October 29th with the Rockets at 3-3-2, Keeshin brought back Boland as head coach with Nevers as his assistant, and Pat finished out the season. At that point, Mathews was waived, although Dove and Wilkin remained on the team. Mathews was claimed by the 49ers and even got to score a touchdown against his old team on November 30th when San Francisco beat Chicago 14–0.

The 5–6–3 record that year would prove to be the franchise's best, but of the 1946 ownership and coaching staff, only Bob Dove was still with the team a year later. Boland returned to the college ranks and worked for several years as a recruiter for Iowa and Miami before his death at age 64. All the reference sources credit Hanley with that third game victory when it truly belonged to the player-coach trio.

The following year, Keeshin sold the Rockets to a group headed by league boss Jim Crowley who then resigned as AAFC commissioner. After former Notre Dame coach Ed McKeever turned down the Rockets' coaching job, Jim stepped in, but nothing went right all year. The 1947 team was terrible, and Crowley was exposed. Halfback Elroy Hirsch later told Stuart Leuthner for *Iron Men,* "Sleepy Jim Crowley didn't know one of us from the other anyhow. He'd grab a tackle and send him into the backfield." After a 0–8 start, rumors circulated that Crowley would be fired by the majority owner and replaced by assistant coach Hampton Pool. Indeed, three football references list Crowley as having coached only the first 10 games of 1947 before being replaced by Pool, while NFLE and MG (*The Pro Football Encyclopedia*, Tod Maher and Bob Gill, 1997) record Pool as assuming control only for the season finale. However, contemporary news accounts continue to talk about Crowley as the coach until his resignation in Los Angeles after the Rockets last game in December. He was replaced in 1948 by Ed McKeever who also went 1–13 with the woebegone Rockets.

Contemporary newspaper accounts confirm Crowley was still in charge right to the club's closing trip to Los Angeles. In fact, Pool resigned as Crowley's assistant on the Rockets before Halloween when the team was 0–8. Crowley owns the full 1–13 record, while Pool's true tally reads 25–26–2 for half a season with the Miami Seahawks and three with the Rams.

Editor's Note: The records listed here reflect the research done by Mr. Maxymuk. This differs from the records seen elsewhere, as described in the article above.

AUSTIN, James Lawrence (Jim)

Born: August 11, 1913, Omaha, NE
Deceased: December 12, 1995, Dixon, CA

STATISTICS

Assistant Coach

	Position
1949 Los Angeles Dons	Ends

BABARTSKY, Albert John

Born: April 19, 1915, Shenandoah, PA
Deceased: December 29, 2002, Kettering, OH

STATISTICS

Assistant Coach

	Position
1947 Chicago Rockets	Assistant

BARBER, James R. (Jim)

Born: July 21, 1912, Murfreesboro, TN
Deceased: January 30, 1998, Spokane, WA

STATISTICS

Assistant Coach

	Position
1946 New York Yankees	Line
1947 New York Yankees	Line
1948 New York Yankees	Line
1949 Chicago Hornets	Line

BATTLES, Clifford Franklyn (Cliff)

Born: May 1, 1910, Akron, OH
Deceased: April 28, 1981, Clearwater, FL

STATISTICS

Head Coach

	W	L	T
1946 Brooklyn Dodgers	1	6	0
1947 Brooklyn Dodgers	3	10	1
Total	4	16	1

BOLAND, Patrick Henry (Pat)

Born: October 12, 1906, Duluth, MN
Deceased: July 2, 1971, Duluth, MN

STATISTICS

Head Coach

	W	L	T
1946 Chicago Rockets	1	5	0
Total	1	5	0

Assistant Coach

	Position
1946 Chicago Rockets	Line

BRICKELS, John L. (Stub)

Born: April 6, 1907, Newark, OH
Deceased: March 17, 1964, Oxford, OH

STATISTICS

Assistant Coach

	Position
1946 Cleveland Browns	Backfield
1947 Cleveland Browns	Backfield
1948 Cleveland Browns	Backfield

BROWN, Paul Eugene

Born: September 7, 1908, Norwalk, OH
Deceased: August 5, 1991, Cincinnati, OH

Statistics

Head Coach

	W	L	T
1946 Cleveland Browns	12	2	0
1947 Cleveland Browns	12	1	1
1948 Cleveland Browns	14	0	0
1949 Cleveland Browns	9	1	2
Total	47	4	3

CAMPOFREDA, Nicholas William (Nick)

Born: January 14, 1914, Baltimore, MD
Deceased: May 23, 1959, Baltimore, MD

Statistics

Assistant Coach

	Position
1947 Baltimore Colts	Assistant

CLARK, Earl Henry (Dutch)

Born: October 11, 1906, Fowler, CO
Deceased: August 5, 1978, Canon City, CO

Statistics

Assistant Coach

	Position
1949 Los Angeles Dons	Backfield

COLLIER, Blanton Long

Born: July 2, 1906, Millersburg, KY
Deceased: March 22, 1983, Houston, TX

Statistics

Assistant Coach

	Position
1946 Cleveland Browns	Backfield
1947 Cleveland Browns	Backfield
1948 Cleveland Browns	Backfield
1949 Cleveland Browns	Backfield

CONDIT, Merlyn Edwin (Merl)

Born: March 21, 1917, Belle Vernon, PA
Deceased: October 18, 1992, Wexford, PA

Statistics

Assistant Coach

	Position
1947 Los Angeles Dons	Ends

CONKRIGHT, William Franklin (Red)

Born: April 17, 1914, Beggs, OK
Deceased: October 27, 1980, Houston, TX

Statistics

Assistant Coach

	Position
1946 Cleveland Browns	Ends/Centers
1947 Buffalo Bills	Ends/Centers
1948 Buffalo Bills	Ends/Centers
1949 Baltimore Colts	Assistant

CRISP, Henry Gorham (Hank)

Born: December 10, 1896, Crisp, NC
Deceased: January 23, 1970, Birmingham, AL

Statistics

Head Coach (Co-Head Coach)*

	W	L	T
1946 Miami Seahawks	0	2	0
Total	0	2	0

Assistant Coach

	Position
1946 Miami Seahawks	Line

*According to research by John Maxymuk, when Jack Meagher quit the Miami Seahawks, Hank Crisp and Hamp Pool were named co-head coaches. After two losses, Pool was named the head coach for the remainder of the season.

CROWE, Clem Frederick

Born: October 18, 1903, Lafayette, IN
Deceased: April 13, 1983, Rochester, NY

Statistics

Head Coach

	W	L	T
1949 Buffalo Bills	4	1	1
Total	4	1	1

Assistant Coach

	Position
1946 Buffalo Bisons	Assistant
1947 Buffalo Bills	Line
1948 Buffalo Bills	Line
1949 Buffalo Bills	Line

CROWLEY, James Harold (Jim)

Born: September 10, 1902, Chicago, IL
Deceased: January 15, 1986, Scranton, PA

Statistics

Head Coach

	W	L	T
1947 Chicago Rockets	1	13	0
Total	1	13	0

DADDIO, Louis William (Bill)

Born: April 26, 1916, Meadville, PA
Deceased: July 5, 1989, Mount Lebanon, PA

STATISTICS

Assistant Coach

	Position
1946 Buffalo Bisons	Assistant

DAWSON, Lowell Potter (Red)

Born: December 20, 1906, Minneapolis, MN
Deceased: June 10, 1983, Ocala, FL

STATISTICS

Head Coach

	W	L	T
1946 Buffalo Bisons	3	10	1
1947 Buffalo Bills	8	4	2
1948 Buffalo Bills	7	7	0
1949 Buffalo Bills	1	4	1
Total	19	25	4

DEFLIPPO, Louis Phillip (Lou)

Born: August 28, 1916, East Haven, CT
Deceased: March 5, 2000, Miami, FL

STATISTICS

Assistant Coach

	Position
1948 Baltimore Colts	Assistant

DEGROOT, Dudley Sargent

Born: November 20, 1899, Chicago, IL
Deceased: May 5, 1970, El Cajon, CA

STATISTICS

Head Coach

	W	L	T
1946 Los Angeles Dons	7	5	2
1947 Los Angeles Dons	5	6	0
Total	12	11	2

DOVE, Robert Leo Patrick (Bob)

Born: February 21, 1921, Youngstown, OH
Deceased: April 19, 2006, Austintown, OH

STATISTICS

Head Coach (Co-Head Coach)

	W	L	T
1946 Chicago Rockets	3	2	1
Total	3	2	1

Assistant Coach

	Position
1946 Chicago Rockets	Assistant

DRISKILL, Walter Scott (Walt)

Born: September 20, 1913, Austin, TX
Deceased: July 25, 1998, Delray Beach, FL

STATISTICS

Head Coach

	W	L	T
1949 Baltimore Colts	1	7	0
Total	1	7	0

DUNNEY, Howard

Born: November 19, 1912, Brooklyn, NY
Deceased: January 31, 2004, Paramus, NJ

STATISTICS

Assistant Coach

	Position
1946 Brooklyn Dodgers	Guards/Tackles

EDMONDS, Otis Don

Born: September 2, 1909, Georgetown, IL
Deceased: May 26, 1996

STATISTICS

Assistant Coach

	Position
1947 Baltimore Colts	Backfield

EDWARDS, William Miller (Bill)

Born: June 21, 1905, Massillon, OH
Deceased: June 12, 1987, Springfield, OH

STATISTICS

Assistant Coach

	Position
1947 Cleveland Browns	Tackles
1948 Cleveland Browns	Tackles

ERDELATZ, Edward J. (Eddie)

Born: April 21, 1913, San Francisco, CA
Deceased: November 11, 1966, Burlingame, CA

STATISTICS

Assistant Coach

	Position
1948 San Francisco 49ers	Assistant
1949 San Francisco 49ers	Assistant

EWBANK, Wilbur Charles (Weeb)

Born: May 6, 1907, Richmond, IN
Deceased: November 17, 1998, Oxford, OH

STATISTICS

Assistant Coach

	Position
1949 Cleveland Browns	Tackles

FLAHERTY, Ray Paul

Born: September 1, 1903, Spokane, WA
Deceased: July 19, 1994, Coeur d'Alene, ID

STATISTICS

Head Coach

	W	L	T
1946 New York Yankees	10	3	1
1947 New York Yankees	11	2	1
1948 New York Yankees	1	3	0
1949 Chicago Hornets	4	8	0
Total	**26**	**16**	**2**

GALLAGHER, Richard F. (Dick)

Born: October 28, 1909, Ironton, OH
Deceased: March 29, 1995, North Canton, OH

STATISTICS

Assistant Coach

	Position
1947 Cleveland Browns	Ends
1948 Cleveland Browns	Ends
1949 Cleveland Browns	Ends

GIFT, Leland Wayne

Born: October 21, 1915, Medina, OH
Deceased: February 13, 1998, Louisville, KY

STATISTICS

Assistant Coach

	Position
1947 Brooklyn Dodgers	Assistant

HANLEY, Richard Edgar (Dick)

Born: November 19, 1894, Cloquet, MN
Deceased: December 16, 1970, Palo Alto, CA

STATISTICS

Head Coach

	W	L	T
1946 Chicago Rockets	0	1	1
Total	**0**	**1**	**1**

HEIN, Melvin Jack (Mel)

Born: August 22, 1909, Redding, CA
Deceased: January 31, 1992, San Clemente, CA

STATISTICS

Head Coach (Co-Head Coach)

	W	L	T
1947 Los Angeles Dons	2	1	0
Total	**2**	**1**	**0**

Assistant Coach

	Position
1947 Los Angeles Dons	Assistant
1948 Los Angeles Dons	Tackles/Centers
1949 New York Yankees	Line

HEISLER, Frederick K. (Fritz)

Born: May 18, 1915, Massillon, OH
Deceased: March 11, 1982, Cleveland, OH

STATISTICS

Assistant Coach

	Position
1946 Cleveland Browns	Guards
1947 Cleveland Browns	Guards
1948 Cleveland Browns	Guards
1949 Cleveland Browns	Guards

HENDRICKSON, Horace James

Born: August 24, 1910, Delphos, OH
Deceased: May 22, 2004, Raleigh, NC

STATISTICS

Assistant Coach

	Position
1948 Brooklyn Dodgers	Backfield

HEWLETT, Andrew Jackson (Andy)

Born: February 20, 1905
Deceased: May 8, 1998

STATISTICS

Assistant Coach

	Position
1947 Baltimore Colts	Backfield

HOKUF, Stephen Melvin (Steve)

Born: September 26, 1910, Wilber, NE
Deceased: July 1, 2000, Cockeysville, MD

1947 Brooklyn Dodgers	Assistant
1948 Brooklyn Dodgers	Ends

HUNT, Oliver Joel

Born: October 11, 1905, Texico, NM
Deceased: July 24, 1978, Teague, TX

STATISTICS
Assistant Coach

	Position
1949 Buffalo Bills	Backfield

ISBELL, Cecil Frank

Born: July 11, 1915, Houston, TX
Deceased: June 23, 1985, Hammond, IN

STATISTICS
Head Coach

	W	L	T
1947 Baltimore Colts	2	11	1
1948 Baltimore Colts	7	7	0
1949 Baltimore Colts	0	4	0
Total	9	22	1

JASKWHICH, Charles Joseph (Chuck)

Born: March 4, 1911, Kenosha, WI
Deceased: January 12, 1988

STATISTICS
Assistant Coach

	Position
1947 Buffalo Bills	Backfield
1948 Buffalo Bills	Backfield

JORDAN, Ralph (Shug)

Born: September 25, 1910, Selma, AL
Deceased: July 17, 1980, Auburn, AL

STATISTICS
Assistant Coach

	Position
1946 Miami Seahawks	Assistant

KORDICK, Martin Frank (Marty)

Born: June 9, 1914, Los Angeles, CA
Deceased: September 5, 2010, Las Vegas, NV

1948 Los Angeles Dons	Guards
1949 Los Angeles Dons	Line

LAWSON, James Willmer (Jim)

Born: March 11, 1902, Chelsea, IN
Deceased: January 3, 1989, Carmel-by-the-Sea, CA

STATISTICS
Assistant Coach

	Position
1946 San Francisco 49ers	Ends
1947 San Francisco 49ers	Ends/Backs
1948 San Francisco 49ers	Ends
1949 San Francisco 49ers	Ends

MADDOCK, Robert Charles (Bob)

Born: August 6, 1920, Santa Ana, CA
Deceased: October 24, 2003, Newport Beach, CA

STATISTICS
Assistant Coach

	Position
1948 Chicago Rockets	Guards/Centers

MARTINEAU, Earl T.

Born: August 30, 1896
Deceased: January 13, 1966, Menominee, WI

STATISTICS
Assistant Coach

	Position
1948 Los Angeles Dons	Backfield

MASTERSON, Bernard Edward (Bernie)

Born: August 10, 1911, Shenandoah, IA
Deceased: May 16, 1963, Chicago, IL

STATISTICS
Assistant Coach

	Position
1949 New York Yankees	Backfield

MASTERSON, Robert Patrick (Bob)

Born: January 5, 1915, North Branch, NJ
Deceased: June 29, 1994, Broward County, FL

STATISTICS
Assistant Coach

	Position
1946 New York Yankees	Ends

MATHEWS, Ned Alfred

Born: August 11, 1918, Provo, UT
Deceased: September 18, 2002, Los Angeles, CA

STATISTICS

Head Coach (Co-Head Coach)

	W	L	T
1946 Chicago Rockets	3	2	1
Total	3	2	1

Assistant Coach

	Position
1946 Chicago Rockets	Assistant

MCKEEVER, Edward Clark Timothy

Born: August 25, 1910, San Antonio, TX
Deceased: September 12, 1974, Baton Rouge, LA

STATISTICS

Head Coach

	W	L	T
1948 Chicago Rockets	1	13	0
Total	1	13	0

MCLEAN, Raymond Tuttle (Scooter)

Born: December 6, 1915, Lowell, MA
Deceased: March 4, 1964, Ann Arbor, MI

STATISTICS

Assistant Coach

	Position
1948 Chicago Rockets	Backfield

MCMULLEN, Daniel Edward (Danny)

Born: May 8, 1906, Belleville, KS
Deceased: August 22, 1983, St. Francis, KS

STATISTICS

Assistant Coach

	Position
1948 Brooklyn Dodgers	Assistant Line

MEAGHER, John Francis (Jack)

Born: July 5, 1894, Chicago, IL
Deceased: December 7, 1968, Miami, FL

STATISTICS

Head Coach

	W	L	T
Miami Seahawks	1	5	0
Total	1	5	0

MICHALSKE, August Michael (Mike)

Born: April 24, 1903, Cleveland, OH
Deceased: October 26, 1983, Green Bay, WI

STATISTICS

Assistant Coach

	Position
1949 Baltimore Colts	Assistant

MILLER, Creighton Eugene Duff

Born: September 26, 1922, Cleveland, OH
Deceased: May 20, 2002, Shaker Heights, OH

STATISTICS

Assistant Coach

	Position
1946 Cleveland Browns	Backfield

MILLNER, Wayne Vernal

Born: January 31, 1913, Boston, MA
Deceased: November 19, 1976, Arlington, VA

STATISTICS

Assistant Coach

	Position
1949 Chicago Hornets	Ends

MOLENDA, John Joseph (Bo)

Born: February 20, 1905, Oglesby, IL
Deceased: July 20, 1986, Banning, CA

STATISTICS

Assistant Coach

	Position
1949 Chicago Hornets	Backfield

MUSSO, George Francis

Born: April 8, 1910, Collinsville, IL
Deceased: September 5, 2000, Edwardsville, IL

STATISTICS

Assistant Coach

	Position
1948 Chicago Rockets	Tackles

NEVERS, Ernest Alonzo (Ernie)

Born: June 11, 1903, Willow River, MN
Deceased: May 3, 1976, San Rafael, CA

STATISTICS

Assistant Coach

	Position
1946 Chicago Rockets	Assistant

PECAROVICH, Michael Joseph

Born: September 23, 1898, OR
Deceased: March 22, 1965, Rolling Hills, CA

STATISTICS

Assistant Coach

	Position
1948 New York Yankees	Assistant

PHELAN, James Michael (Jimmy)

Born: December 5, 1893, Portland, OR
Deceased: November 14, 1974, Honolulu, HI

STATISTICS

Head Coach

	W	L	T
1948 Los Angeles Dons	7	7	0
1949 Los Angeles Dons	4	8	0
Total	11	15	0

POOL, John Hampton (Hamp)

Born: March 11, 1915, San Miguel, CA
Deceased: May 26, 2000, Mariposa, CA

STATISTICS

Head Coach

	W	L	T
1946 Miami Seahawks	2	6	0
Total	2	6	0

Assistant Coach

	Position
1946 Miami Seahawks	Backfield
1947 Chicago Rockets	Assistant

*According to research by John Maxymuk, when Jack Meagher quit the Miami Seahawks, Hank Crisp and Hamp Pool were named co-head coaches. After two losses, Pool was named the head coach for the remainder of the season.

REESE, Henry L. (Hank)

Born: October 24, 1909, Scranton, PA
Deceased: August 3, 1975, Ocean City, NJ

STATISTICS

Assistant Coach

	Position
1946 Brooklyn Dodgers	Line
1949 Buffalo Bills	Line

RUFFO, Albert John

Born: July 1, 1908
Deceased: February 10, 2003, San Jose, CA

STATISTICS

Assistant Coach

	Position
1946 San Francisco 49ers	Line
1947 San Francisco 49ers	Line

SCAFIDE, John Andrew

Born: June 21, 1911, Bay St. Louis, MS
Deceased: October 24, 1979, Bay St. Louis, MS

STATISTICS

Assistant Coach

	Position
1946 Buffalo Bisons	Assistant
1947 Buffalo Bills	Line/Chief Scout
1948 Buffalo Bills	Assistant Line
1949 Buffalo Bills	Assistant Line

SCOTT, Thomas P. (Tom)

Born: 1920
Deceased:

STATISTICS

Head Coach

	W	L	T
1946 Brooklyn Dodgers	1	0	0
Total	1	0	0

Assistant Coach

	Position
1946 Brooklyn Dodgers	Ends
1947 Brooklyn Dodgers	Assistant

SHAW, Lawrence Timothy (Buck)

Born: March 28, 1899, Mitchellville, IA
Deceased: March 19, 1977, Menlo Park, CA

STATISTICS

Head Coach

	W	L	T
1946 San Francisco 49ers	9	5	0
1947 San Francisco 49ers	8	4	2
1948 San Francisco 49ers	12	2	0
1949 San Francisco 49ers	9	3	0
Total	38	14	2

SHIPKEY, Theodore Edwin (Ted)

Born: September 23, 1904, Great Falls, MT
Deceased: July 18, 1978, Placentia, CA

STATISTICS

Head Coach (Co-Head Coach)

	W	L	T
1947 Los Angeles Dons	2	1	0
Total	2	1	0

Assistant Coach

	Position
1946 Los Angeles Dons	Backfield
1947 Los Angeles Dons	Backfield
1948 Los Angeles Dons	Ends

STEVENS, Marvin Allen (Mal)

Born: April 14, 1900, Stockton, KS
Deceased: December 6, 1979, New York, NY

STATISTICS

Head Coach

	W	L	T
1946 Brooklyn Dodgers	1	4	1
Total	1	4	1

STIDHAM, Thomas Edward (Tom)

Born: March 27, 1905, Checotah, OK
Deceased: January 29, 1964, Milwaukee, WI

STATISTICS

Assistant Coach

	Position
1946 Buffalo Bisons	Assistant
1947 Baltimore Colts	Line
1948 Baltimore Colts	Line

STRADER, Norman Parker (Red)

Born: December 21, 1902, Newton, NJ
Deceased: May 26, 1956, Berkeley, CA

STATISTICS

Head Coach

	W	L	T
1948 New York Yankees	5	5	0
1949 New York Yankees	8	4	0
Total	13	9	0

Assistant Coach

	Position
1946 New York Yankees	Backfield
1947 New York Yankees	Backfield
1948 New York Yankees	Backfield

SWEIGER, Robert Michael (Bob)

Born: September 20, 1919, Minneapolis, MN
Deceased: November 1, 1975, Hennepin County, MN

STATISTICS

Assistant Coach

	Position
1949 Chicago Hornets	Assistant Backfield

TAYLOR, John Lachlan (Tarzan)

Born: January 10, 1895, Superior, WI
Deceased: May 1, 1971, Green Bay, WI

STATISTICS

Assistant Coach

	Position
1947 Baltimore Colts	Assistant

VOIGTS, Werner Robert (Bob)

Born: March 29, 1916, Evanston, IL
Deceased: December 7, 2000, Wilmette, IL

STATISTICS

Assistant Coach

	Position
1946 Cleveland Browns	Tackles

VOYLES, Carl Marvin

Born: August 11, 1898, McLoud, OK
Deceased: January 11, 1982, Fort Myers, FL

STATISTICS

Head Coach

	W	L	T
1948 Brooklyn Dodgers	2	12	0
Total	2	12	0

WERNER, Albert Henry

Born: June 29, 1908, Lykens, PA
Deceased: December 21, 1981, Durham, NV

STATISTICS

Assistant Coach

	Position
1948 Brooklyn Dodgers	Line

WHITE, John Joseph (Jack)

Born: July 30, 1913, New Britain, CT
Deceased: September 26, 1997, Medford, OR

STATISTICS

Assistant Coach

	Position
1946 New York Yankees	Assistant
1947 New York Yankees	Assistant
1949 New York Yankees	Assistant

WILKIN, Wilbur B. (Willie)

Born: April 20, 1916, Bingham Canyon, UT
Deceased: May 16, 1973, Palo Alto, CA

STATISTICS

Head Coach (Co-Head Coach)

	W	L	T
1946 Chicago Rockets	3	2	1
Total	3	2	1

Assistant Coach

	Position
1946 Chicago Rockets	Assistant

WITUCKI, Bernard Francis (Bernie)

Born: February 25, 1911, Sound Bend, IN
Deceased: April 8, 2000, South Bend, IN

STATISTICS

Assistant Coach

	Position
1948 Chicago Rockets	Ends

Sources

Books

Bene, David A. *History of the All-American Football Conference*. N.p.: Amazon Digital Services, 2016.
Carroll, Bob, Michael Gershman, David Neft, and John Thorn. *Total Football: The Official Encyclopedia of the National Football League*. New York: Harper-Collins, 1997.
Crippen, Kenneth R. *The Original Buffalo Bills: A History of the All-America Football Conference Team, 1946–1949*. Jefferson, NC: McFarland, 2010.
Hogrogian, John, John Turney, and Paul Klatt. "The Best of Each Season: All-Pros." Professional Football Researchers Association. Unpublished manuscript.
Palmer, Pete, Ken Pullis, Sean Lahman, Tod Maher, Matthew Silverman, Christina Kahrl, and Gary Gillette. *The ESPN Pro Football Encyclopedia*. Second Edition. New York: Sterling, 2007.

Newspapers

December 21, 1946 *Milwaukee Journal*
December 21, 1946 *Milwaukee Sentinel*
December 22, 1946 *Milwaukee Journal*
February 1, 1947 *Milwaukee Journal*
December 17, 1947 *Milwaukee Sentinel*
December 17, 2009 *Houston Chronicle*

Magazine Articles

Bolding, Mark. "The Shamrock Bowl." *The Coffin Corner*, Volume 31, Number 3. The Professional Football Researchers Association. 2009.
Grosshandler, Stan. "All-America Football Conference." *The Coffin Corner*, Volume 2, Number 7. The Professional Football Researchers Association. 1980.
Maxymuk, John. "Correcting the Coaching Record." *The Coffin Corner*, Volume 35, Number 4. The Professional Football Researchers Association. 2013.
Piascik, Andy. "AAFC vs. NFL: The Attendance Battle." *The Coffin Corner*, Volume 29, Number 3. The Professional Football Researchers Association. 2007.

Websites

Pro Football Archives; http://www.profootballarchives.com
Pro Football Reference; http://www.pro-football-reference.com

Miscellaneous

1946 Information Booklet: Buffalo Bisons of the All-America Football Conference.
1946 Season Information Booklet: San Francisco 49ers.
1947 Press and Radio Information: Los Angeles Dons of the All-America Football Conference.
1948 Baltimore Colts Press and Radio Guide.
1948 Press and Radio Book: Buffalo Bills—Representing Western N.Y. in the AAFC.
1949 Baltimore Colts Press, Radio and Television Guide.
1949 Chicago Hornets Press, Radio and Television Guide.
1949 Los Angeles Dons Press, Radio, Television Guide.
1949 Press and Radio Book: Buffalo Bills—Representing Western N.Y. in the AAFC.
All-America Football Conference 1946 Information Booklet.
All-America Football Conference Record Manual: 1947.
All-America Football Conference Record Manual: 1948.
All-America Football Conference Record Manual: 1949.
All-America Football Conference: Supplement to 1949 Record Manual.
Baltimore Colts 1947 Press Guide.
Brooklyn Dodgers Press Brochure: 1948 Season.
Brooklyn—New York Football Sketch Book: 1949.
Brooklyn Professional Football Club of the All-America Football Conference: Press Brochure—1946 Season.
Brooklyn Professional Football Club of the All-America Football Conference: Press Brochure—1947 Season.
The Chicago Rockets 1947 Press and Radio Book.

The Chicago Rockets Training Camp Roster: July 28, 1946.
The Cleveland Browns Champions All-America Football Conference 1947 Press Book
Cleveland Browns 1946 Press Book.
Cleveland Browns 1948 Press-Radio Guide.
Cleveland Browns 1949 Press, Radio, Television Guide.
It's the Forty Niners in '49 Press, Radio and T.V. Guide.
L.A. Dons 1948 Press and Radio Guide.
The New Chicago Rockets 1948 Press and Radio Information Book.
New York Yankees Football Sketch Book: 1947.
New York Yankees Football Sketch Book: 1948.
Official Scoresheets of the All-America Football Conference.
San Francisco 49ers of the All-America Football Conference: 1947 Press and Radio Info.
San Francisco 49ers Press and Radio Information Booklet: 1948.

Game Films

September 25, 1946: Buffalo Bisons versus Chicago Rockets.
December 1, 1946: Buffalo Bisons versus Los Angeles Dons.
August 24, 1947: Los Angeles Dons versus San Francisco 49ers.
November 2, 1947: Buffalo Bills versus Cleveland Browns.
December 14, 1947: Cleveland Browns versus New York Yankees.
September 5, 1948: New York Yankees versus Baltimore Colts.
September 16, 1948: Baltimore Colts versus New York Yankees.
September 19, 1948: San Francisco 49ers versus Los Angeles Dons.
September 26, 1948: Chicago Rockets versus Cleveland Browns.
September 26, 1948: Brooklyn Dodgers versus Baltimore Colts.
October 15, 1948: Chicago Rockets versus Brooklyn Dodgers.
November 7, 1948: Baltimore Colts versus Cleveland Browns.
November 28, 1948: Buffalo Bills versus New York Yankees.
November 28, 1948: San Francisco 49ers versus Cleveland Browns.
December 5, 1948: Buffalo Bills versus Baltimore Colts.
December 12, 1948: Buffalo Bills versus Baltimore Colts.
December 18, 1948: Buffalo Bills versus Cleveland Browns.
August 28, 1949: Baltimore Colts versus San Francisco 49ers.
September 5, 1949: Buffalo Bills versus Cleveland Browns.
September 11, 1949: Baltimore Colts versus Cleveland Browns.
September 25, 1949: Cleveland Browns versus Baltimore Colts.
October 2, 1949: Buffalo Bills versus Baltimore Colts.
October 16, 1949: New York Yankees versus Baltimore Colts.
October 23, 1949: Los Angeles Dons versus Buffalo Bills.
October 23, 1949: Chicago Hornets versus Baltimore Colts.
October 30, 1949: Baltimore Colts versus New York Yankees.
October 30, 1949: San Francisco 49ers versus Cleveland Browns.
November 13, 1949: Cleveland Browns versus Buffalo Bills.
November 20, 1949: Chicago Hornets versus Buffalo Bills.
November 20, 1949: Los Angeles Dons versus Baltimore Colts.
November 27, 1949: Buffalo Bills versus Baltimore Colts.
December 4, 1949: Buffalo Bills versus Cleveland Browns.

Highlight Films

1946 Buffalo Bisons
1946 Cleveland Browns
1947 Buffalo Bills
1947 Los Angeles Dons
1949 Cleveland Browns

Index

Adamle, Tony 12–13, 19, 34, 36–38, 40–41, 47–50, 105, 114, 131–132, 134, 142, 168
Adams, Chet 12, 29, 31–32, 39–40, 52, 58, 86–87, 100, 114, 134–145, 165, 167–168
Adams, Neal 27, 32, 87, 95–97, 169
Agajanian, Ben 11, 39, 46, 54, 67–68, 101, 103–105, 107–112, 114, 116–122, 124–125, 127, 129–131, 133, 169
Agase, Alex 11, 37, 50, 57, 122, 155, 166, 170
Aguirre, Joe 2, 26–28, 31–33, 35–36, 39–40, 42, 45–46, 49, 52, 54, 57, 86–89, 91–92, 94–96, 98–101, 104–105, 107, 109, 111, 120, 122–123, 125, 127, 129–130, 133, 136, 170, 274
Akins, Al 26, 29–32, 34–38, 40–42, 86, 97, 109–110, 116, 170
Albert, Frankie 12–13, 20–21, 25–26, 28–34, 36, 38–41, 43, 46–49, 52–60, 64, 67–68, 84–85, 87–88, 90–91, 93–94, 97–99, 101–104, 106, 108–109, 112–117, 119–126, 128, 130, 132–142, 144–146, 171
Alford, Bruce 10–11, 27, 30–31, 35, 37–39, 42, 46, 49, 51–52, 57, 104, 110, 112–114, 118, 120, 124, 126, 129–130, 132, 136, 142, 171
Allen, Carl 41, 43–44, 46–47, 126–127, 172
Allen, Ermal 34, 36–38, 102, 150, 172
Anderson, Ezzret 34–35, 40, 111, 172
Armstrong, Charlie 25–26, 28–31, 100, 172
Armstrong, Graham 39–40, 43, 45–47, 110–113, 120–121, 123, 131–133, 173
Artoe, Lee 10, 30–33, 38–39, 56–58, 96, 98, 173
Aschenbrenner, Frank 48–49, 51, 148, 173
Audet, Earl 174
Austin, Jim 343
Avery, Don 174

Babartsky, Albert 343
Bailey, Jim 174
Balatti, Ed 25, 27, 29, 31–32, 35, 37–39, 98–99, 106, 115, 174, 209, 295, 330
Baldwin, Al 11–12, 35–36, 38–39, 42, 46, 48–49, 52–54, 56–59, 104–108, 113, 117, 120–121, 123, 126–127, 129, 131–134, 136–140, 142, 146, 149, 163, 174
Baldwin, Burr 35, 40, 42, 48–50, 105, 111–112, 116, 149, 175
Baldwin, Jack 175
Banducci, Bruno 10–11, 13, 15, 38, 55–58, 175
Barber, Jim 343
Barwegan, Dick
Bass, Bill 34–38, 40, 106, 113, 176
Bassi, Dick 29, 176
Batorski, Bat 27, 176
Battles, Cliff 55, 57, 93, 342–343
Bauman, Alf 177
Baumgartner, Bill 151, 177
Beals, Alyn 10, 12–14, 26–27, 31–32, 34–35, 37, 39, 42, 46, 48–49, 52–59, 64, 67–68, 87, 89–91, 93, 97, 99, 102–103, 106, 108–109, 112, 114–115, 117, 120, 122–125, 128, 130, 132–139, 141–142, 144, 146, 177
Bechtol, Hub 34–36, 38–40, 43, 45–46, 50, 103, 114–115, 149, 177
Bell, Ed 178
Benson, George 34, 178
Bentz, Roman 85, 178
Berezney, Paul 178
Berezney, Pete 178
Bernhardt, George 30–31, 167, 178
Berry, Connie 179
Bertelli, Angelo 6, 25–26, 28, 32, 34–35, 39–42, 86, 91, 95–96, 98–100, 104, 119, 122, 179
Beson, Warren 160, 179
Billman, John 179
Black, Blondy 26, 28–29, 31, 34, 36, 179
Blandin, Ernie 34, 58, 180
Blount, Lamar 27, 32, 34–35, 96, 117, 180
Boedeker, Bill 26–27, 29–31, 33–35, 37–39, 41–42, 44–49, 51–52, 64, 86, 104–106, 115, 120, 122–123, 125, 135, 138, 143, 180
Boland, Pat 342–343
Brazinsky, Sam 28, 181
Brickels, Stub 343
Brown, George 181
Brown, Hardy 41–42, 44, 46, 48–50, 123–127, 130–131, 133, 143, 164, 167, 181
Brown, John 37, 44, 50, 52, 103, 138, 142, 165, 182
Brown, Paul 4, 8–9, 14, 16, 21, 78, 84, 88, 94, 105, 119, 130, 132, 344
Bruce, Gail 41–42, 49–52, 182
Brutz, Jim 182
Bryant, Bob 44, 46, 57, 111, 122, 183
Buksar, George 48, 52, 140, 142, 164, 183
Buffington, Harry 103, 183
Bumgardner, Rex 12, 41, 43–45, 47–52, 54, 61, 127–128, 131, 133–134, 137–138, 142–144, 152, 183
Burrus, Harry 26–28, 32, 34–36, 40–43, 46–47, 61, 86, 100, 104, 107, 131–132, 184
Butkus, Carl 184

Callahan, Bob 185
Calvelli, Tony 37, 185
Camp, Jim 41, 43, 45–46, 154, 185
Campofreda, Nick 344
Cardinal, Fred 185
Carpenter, Jack 49, 115, 149, 185
Carr, Eddie 12, 34–38, 41–43, 45–50, 52–53, 115, 125, 134–139, 185
Casanega, Ken 10–11, 25, 27–30, 32, 93–94, 98–99, 186
Case, Ernie 34, 36–40, 103, 105, 148, 186
Casey, Tom 41–45, 47, 61, 67, 119, 122, 128, 187
Cason, Jim 12–13, 41–46, 48–54, 58, 61, 68, 120, 123, 137, 144, 153, 187
Castiglia, Jim 34, 36, 40, 103, 188
Cathcart, Sam 47–52, 141–142, 144–145, 188
Cato, Daryl 26, 29, 189
Chappius, Bob 189
Cheatham, Lloyd 26–27, 29–31, 33–35, 39, 41–42, 45–46, 85, 94, 107–108, 118, 189
Cheroke, George 189
Clark, Don 43, 50, 130, 190
Clark, Dutch 344
Clarke, Harry 25, 27–32, 34–35, 37–38, 40–42, 44–45, 86, 98–99, 111, 116, 190
Clay, Walt 25–31, 33–34, 36, 41–43, 45–46, 48, 85–86, 97, 100, 127, 129–131, 165, 190
Cleary, Paul 42, 45–46, 153, 166, 191
Clement, Johnny 47–48, 52, 58, 134–137, 140–141, 143, 191

356 Index

Cline, Ollie 41, 44–45, 47–49, 51–52, 59, 134–135, 137–139, 153, 163, 167, 192
Clowes, John 164, 192
Colella, Tom 10–11, 13, 19, 25, 28–32, 34–39, 41, 43–45, 47–51, 53–54, 58, 61, 68, 84, 86, 89–90, 94, 97, 100–101, 104–108, 114, 116, 119, 121, 130, 132, 134, 166, 192
Coleman, Herb 29–31, 100, 193
Collier, Blanton 344
Collier, Floyd 193
Collins, Rip 48–51, 134, 140, 149, 157, 159, 164, 193
Colmer, Mickey 11, 25, 27, 29–31, 33, 35–46, 48–54, 56–58, 60, 68, 87, 93, 98, 102, 107, 109, 111–114, 116, 119–120, 124–128, 130, 166, 194
Comer, Marty 27, 32, 35, 40, 42, 47, 93, 113, 115, 124–125, 194
Condit, Merl 344
Conger, Mel 27, 195
Conkright, Red 344
Conlee, Gerry 37, 39, 195
Connolly, Harry 26, 29–31, 195
Cooper, Jim 195
Cooper, Ken 195
Coppage, Al 27, 35, 38, 40, 89, 102, 112, 117, 196
Corley, Bert 36, 149, 196
Cowan, Bob 34–35, 38–39, 41–42, 44–46, 48–50, 106–108, 121–122, 127, 130–131, 149, 196
Cox, Jim 196
Cox, Norm 26, 34–35, 196
Crawford, Denny 165, 197
Crisp, Hank 344, 349
Crowe, Clem 344
Crowe, Paul 41, 43–45, 47–48, 50–52, 58, 122, 126, 128, 140, 165, 197
Crowell, Odis 197
Crowley, Jim 3–4, 6–7, 21–22, 84, 101, 117, 343–344
Cure, Armand 34, 197
Czarobski, Ziggy 166, 197

Daddio, Bill 31, 33, 84–85, 198, 345
Daley, Bill 2, 26, 28, 30–31, 33, 35, 37–45, 47, 101, 103, 107, 111, 120, 198, 201
Danehe, Dick 36, 198
Daniell, Jim 198
Daukas, Lou 37, 199
Daukas, Nick 27, 29, 38–39, 199
David, Bob 199
Davis, Bill 28, 160, 199
Davis, Harper 48–52, 135, 154, 163, 199
Davis, Joe 27, 30–32, 84, 90, 92–93, 200
Davis, Lamar 26–27, 29–32, 34–38, 40, 42–44, 46, 49–53, 57–58, 64, 67, 85–86, 99–100, 104, 108, 113, 119–122, 125, 129–132, 136, 200

Davis, Van 35, 38–39, 42, 44, 47, 49, 128, 144, 201
Dawson, Red 345
Deflippo, Lou 345
Degroot, Dudley 85, 345
Dekdebrun, Al 2, 25–26, 28, 30–31, 33–35, 40–45, 87, 89, 91, 93–96, 99, 101, 107, 109, 115, 117–118, 198, 201
Dellerba, Spiro 34, 36, 38, 40–41, 43, 45–46, 105–106, 121–122, 201
Dewar, Jim 34, 36–38, 40, 115, 150, 202
Dobbs, Glenn 10–13, 20, 25–26, 28–30, 32–38, 40–41, 43, 45–49, 52–54, 56–61, 63–64, 67–68, 84–85, 87, 89–100, 102–105, 111–112, 114, 116, 119–125, 127–131, 133–140, 164, 202
Dobelstein, Bob 202
Doherty, George 30–31, 151, 203
Donaldson, George 48–51, 162, 165, 203
Doss, Noble 48, 51, 203
Dove, Bob 27, 33, 35, 38–40, 88, 100, 106, 204, 342–343, 345
Driskill, Walt 345
Dudish, Andy 25, 27, 29–31, 34–35, 37–38, 40, 114–115, 204
Duggan, Gil 204
Dugger, Jack 28, 32, 93, 205
Duke, Paul 149, 166, 205
Durdan, Don 25, 27–29, 31, 33–34, 93, 205
Durishan, Jack 38–39, 149, 205
Durkota, Jeff 41, 43–45, 153, 205
Dworsky, Dan 50–52, 155, 158, 164, 206

Eakin, Kay 26–31, 86, 91, 94, 206
Ebli, Ray 27, 32, 35, 40, 95, 117–118, 206
Ecker, Ed 207
Ecklund, Brad 58, 207
Edmonds, Otis 345
Edwards, Bill 345
Edwards, Dan 42, 45–46, 49, 51–52, 58, 135–136, 138, 141, 147, 153, 164, 207
Ellenson, Gene 207
Elliott, Charlie 151, 208
Elsey, Earl 25, 27–30, 208
Elston, Dutch 29, 36, 44, 208
Erdelatz, Eddie 345
Erdlitz, Dick 26–27, 29–32, 86, 90–92, 94–96, 98, 100, 208
Erickson, Bill 155, 209
Eshmont, Len 11–13, 20, 25–27, 29–38, 40–42, 44–45, 47–54, 67, 84, 87–91, 93–94, 102, 104, 106, 114, 116, 121–122, 128, 141–142, 174, 209, 295, 330
Evans, Fred 26, 28–29, 31, 34–38, 40, 104, 113, 117, 210
Evans, Ray 152, 210

Evansen, Paul 210
Ewbank, Weeb 346

Farris, Tom 41–42, 119, 210
Fekete, Gene 25, 28, 30–31, 33, 99, 211
Fekete, John 26, 211
Fenenbock, Chuck 11, 25, 27, 29–30, 32, 34–35, 37–39, 41–42, 44–45, 47, 54, 61, 63, 68, 85, 94, 96, 99, 103, 105, 107–111, 116, 124, 131, 211
Fisk, Bill 27, 32, 35, 42, 97, 212
Flagerman, Jack 43, 212
Flaherty, Ray 21, 84, 88, 109, 118–119, 346
Fletcher, Oliver 212
Foldberg, Hank 42, 47, 49, 125, 152, 165, 212
Ford, Len 8, 22, 42, 44–46, 49–50, 52, 58, 121, 123–124, 127, 129, 133, 138, 141–143, 148, 153, 163, 213
Forkovitch, Nick 41, 213
Forrest, Eddie 213
Fowler, Aubrey 41, 43–45, 126–127, 154, 213
Fox, Terry 26–28, 30–31, 214
Franceschi, Pete 26–27, 29, 31–32, 99, 214
Frankowski, Ray 32, 98–99, 214
Freeman, Jack 214
Freitas, Jesse 26, 28–29, 31, 34, 36, 40–42, 48, 89–91, 97, 102, 106, 109, 115, 123–126, 128–129, 131–132, 214
French, Barry 38–39, 215

Gafford, Monk 11–12, 26–30, 32, 34–38, 40–42, 44–46, 54, 61, 68, 85–86, 89–91, 94, 96, 98, 113–114, 116, 123–124, 126–127, 131, 133, 215
Gallagher, Bernie 148, 216
Gallagher, Dick 346
Galvin, John 34–36, 38, 216
Gambino, Lu 41–42, 44–45, 47–49, 52, 125, 128, 130, 137–138, 156, 216
Garlin, Don 48–52, 142, 145–146, 161, 216
Garrett, Dub 15, 45–46, 153, 216
Garza, Dan 49, 51, 159, 217
Gatski, Frank 22, 29, 32, 36, 38–39, 95–96, 217
Gaudio, Bob 41, 48, 217
Gentry, Dale 10, 26–27, 29, 31–32, 35, 39, 42, 57, 89, 94, 98–100, 105, 117–118, 217
Getchell, Gorham 35, 218
Gibron, Abe 49, 158, 218
Gibson, Joe 37, 218
Gibson, Paul 35, 49, 49–50, 117, 121, 134, 143, 150, 164, 218
Gift, Leland 346
Gillom, Horace 11, 35–36, 42–43, 45–49, 53, 120, 132, 134, 141, 219
Gloden, Fred 26, 30–31, 33, 90, 92, 219
Gompers, Bill 41, 43–45, 47, 127, 133, 153, 165, 220

Grabinski, Ted 220
Graham, Mike 41, 43–45, 47, 154, 220
Graham, Otto 10–13, 15–16, 21, 25–26, 28–29, 31–34, 37–38, 40–41, 44, 46–48, 52–53, 55–60, 64, 66–68, 84–88, 90, 92–97, 99–102, 104–116, 118–139, 141–146, 220
Grain, Ed 151, 221
Greene, Nelson 120, 129, 221
Greenwood, Don 25–28, 30–32, 34–36, 84–85, 88–89, 93, 101, 221
Gregory, Garland 30–31, 37–38, 57, 221
Grgich, Visco 12–13, 18–19, 38–39, 57–58, 115, 222
Griffin, Don 26–27, 29–31, 222
Grigg, Chubby 132, 222
Grimes, Billy 47–52, 67, 134–135, 139–140, 142–144, 159, 163, 223
Grossman, Rex 12–13, 20, 41, 43, 46, 49, 52, 54, 68, 120–138, 140–144, 157, 223
Groves, George 224
Groza, Lou 11–12, 22, 31–32, 39, 46, 51–52, 54, 57–58, 67–68, 84–90, 92–97, 99–102, 104, 106–114, 116, 118–128, 130–133, 135, 137–139, 141–146, 224
Gustafson, Ed 41, 57, 151, 225

Hall, Forrest 12, 40–42, 44–45, 47, 125–126, 128, 130, 225
Hall, Parker 26–27, 30–31, 225
Handley, Dick 226
Hanley, Dick 87–88, 342–343, 346
Hare, Ray 226
Harrington, John 27, 30–31, 33, 35, 39, 107, 109, 117, 226, 250
Harris, Elmore 34, 37–38, 103, 226
Haynes, Joe 227
Hazelwood, Ted 135, 164, 227
Heap, Walt 34, 36, 40–41, 43, 47, 110–111, 114, 124, 129, 150, 227
Hecht, George 227
Heck, Bob 156, 166, 227
Hein, Bob 36, 227
Hein, Mel 346
Heisler, Fritz 346
Hekkers, George 227
Hendrickson, Horace 346
Henke, Ed 49, 163, 228
Herring, Hal 50, 163, 228
Hewlett, Andy 346
Heywood, Ralph 27–28, 32, 87–88, 90–91, 97, 228
Higgins, Luke 229
Hillenbrand, Billy 12, 25, 27–30, 32, 34–42, 44–46, 53–54, 56–58, 61, 85, 87, 89, 93, 97, 103, 105, 108, 110, 112–115, 117, 120, 122–132, 229
Hirsch, Buckets 12, 34, 36, 40, 107, 115, 133, 165, 229
Hirsch, Elroy 4, 22, 25–30, 32, 34–35, 37–39, 41–45, 47, 55, 87–88, 91, 93, 96, 101–103, 105, 110, 122, 229, 342–343
Hobbs, Homer 161, 230
Hoernschemeyer, Bob 12, 25–26, 28–30, 33–34, 36–48, 50–54, 56–58, 60, 67, 87–88, 90–91, 95–97, 100–105, 109–111, 113–114, 116, 118–126, 129–131, 133–138, 140–141, 143, 163, 230
Hoffman, Bob 49–52, 231
Hokuf, Steve 346
Holder, Lew 48–49, 167, 232
Holley, Ken 26, 232
Hopp, Harry 25–26, 28, 30–32, 34–36, 38–39, 84–86, 90, 100, 232
Horne, Dick 27, 35, 233
Horvath, Les 48–50, 52, 136, 141, 233
Houston, Lin 49, 58, 128, 233
Howard, Sherman 47–52, 58, 137, 140–141, 143, 145, 159, 233
Howell, Clarence 43–44, 234
Hrabetin, Frank 28, 234
Humble, Weldon 12, 34, 36, 43, 50, 57–58, 109, 123, 149, 234
Huneke, Charlie 235
Hunt, Oliver 347

Ingram, Jonas 7–8, 22–23, 108
Isbell, Cecil 103, 108, 122, 136, 347
Iversen, Duke 235

Jagade, Chick 48–49, 51–52, 134, 157, 235
James, Tommy 12, 41, 43–45, 48, 50, 52, 58, 124, 136, 145, 236
Jaskwhich, Chuck 347
Jeffers, Ed 236
Jenkins, Jon 161, 236
Jensen, Bob 15, 42, 45–47, 49, 128, 135, 140, 155, 164, 236
Joe, Larry 48–49, 51–52, 155, 237
Johnson, Bill 44, 50, 52, 58, 144, 237
Johnson, Clyde 237
Johnson, Farnham 46–47, 237
Johnson, Gil 48, 144, 161, 167, 237
Johnson, Glenn 238
Johnson, Harvey 26–27, 31–32, 39, 43, 46, 50, 52, 54, 59, 68, 84–86, 88–89, 91–92, 94–98, 100–104, 106–110, 112, 114–115, 117–120, 122–123, 125–132, 136–138, 140–145, 238
Johnson, Nate 11, 56–58, 141, 163, 238
Johnston, Pres 25–32, 86, 92–93, 95, 99, 238
Jones, Billy 239
Jones, Dub 25–26, 29–31, 34–38, 40–42, 45–49, 51–52, 59, 61, 107, 118, 123, 132, 134, 139, 141–146, 239
Jones, Edgar 25–30, 32–35, 37–42, 46, 48–49, 51–54, 59, 88, 95–97, 99–102, 110, 112, 118–119, 124–126, 128, 130, 132–137, 144–146, 240
Jones, Elmer 28, 240
Jones, Ralph 35, 240

Judd, Saxon 27, 30–32, 35, 38–40, 42, 47, 84–85, 99–100, 105, 114, 128, 130, 240
Jungmichel, Buddy 29, 56, 241
Juzwik, Steve 10, 25, 27–30, 32, 34–35, 37–39, 41, 43, 46–47, 56–57, 84, 86–87, 90, 92–96, 102, 104–108, 115, 117, 121–122, 241

Kapter, Alex 241
Karmazin, Mike 241
Kasap, Mike 242
Kellagher, Bill 11, 25–28, 30–32, 34–36, 41, 44–45, 47, 88, 95, 131, 242
Kelley, Ed 48, 166, 242
Kelly, Bob 34–39, 41, 43, 48–51, 103, 109, 112, 117–119, 142, 162, 167, 242
Kennedy, Bob H. 25–32, 34, 36–38, 40–45, 47–53, 88–89, 100, 103, 110, 121, 126, 129–130, 132, 136, 138, 140–141, 144, 164, 243
Kennedy, Bob M. 48, 50, 243
Kerns, John 44–46, 113, 164, 243
Kerr, Bill 26–27, 29, 88, 244
Kessing, Oliver 7–8, 22–23, 111, 138
Kimbrough, John 25, 27, 30–33, 35, 37–39, 41–42, 44–46, 53–54, 57, 85–86, 92, 94, 98–101, 103, 105, 109–111, 114, 116–120, 124–125, 133, 244
Kinard, Bruiser 10–11, 23, 55–57, 88, 244
Kinard, George 245
King, Ed 164, 245
King, Fay (Dolly) 27, 32, 35, 39, 42, 45–46, 49, 51–54, 87, 90–91, 93–94, 96–97, 102, 104–105, 107, 111, 117–118, 121, 124, 126, 128, 131, 136, 142, 245
Kingery, Wayne 48–51, 245
Kisiday, George 43, 245
Kissell, John 12, 58, 246
Kissell, Vito 48–52, 140, 159, 166, 246
Klasnic, John 246
Klenk, Quentin 246
Klug, Al 246
Klutka, Nick 28, 247
Koch, George 34, 36–38, 40, 102, 154, 247
Kodba, Joe 37, 247
Kolesar, Bob 247
Konetsky, Floyd 36, 247
Kordick, Marty 347
Kosikowski, Frank 151, 248
Kostiuk, Mike 248
Kozel, Chet 38–39, 248
Kozlowski, Stan 26–27, 29–31, 248
Kramer, Jack 248
Krivonak, Joe 248
Krueger, Al 27, 32, 86, 249
Kuffel, Ray 35, 42, 45–47, 124, 126, 129, 149, 249
Kulbitski, Vic 25, 28–32, 34–39, 41–42, 45–47, 53, 86–88, 95, 97, 104–

358 Index

105, 111, 113, 123–124, 129, 131, 134, 249
Kusserow, Lou 48–49, 51, 148, 158, 249
Kuzman, John 33, 38–39, 89–90, 250

Lahar, Hal 57, 93, 250
Lahey, Pat 26–27, 29–31, 33, 35, 38–39, 226, 250
Lahr, Warren 48–51, 53, 135, 139, 143–145, 250
Land, Fred 153, 251
Landrigan, Jim 152, 251
Landry, Tom 13, 23, 48–51, 136, 145, 147, 155, 251
Landsberg, Mort 34, 36, 252
Lane, Clayton 252
Laurinaitis, Francis 151, 252
Lavelli, Dante 10–11, 23, 26–27, 32, 35, 38–39, 41–42, 45–46, 49, 52–54, 56–58, 61, 67–68, 84, 88, 90, 92–97, 99–102, 104, 111–114, 118–119, 127, 131–132, 134–136, 138–139, 141, 144–146, 252
Lawson, Jim 347
Layden, Elmer 4–5, 21
Layden, Pete 40–46, 48–51, 53–54, 60, 64, 123, 127–130, 132, 140, 253
Lecture, Jim 253
Leicht, Jake 41–45, 47–51, 129, 131–132, 135, 253
Lennon, Reid 254
Leonard, Bill 50–51, 254
Leonetti, Bob 150, 166, 254
Levy, Len 56, 58, 254
Lewis, Cliff 10, 26, 28–31, 34, 36–38, 41–45, 48, 50–51, 53–54, 84, 89, 118–119, 122, 126, 130–131, 139, 141–143, 145, 254
Lewis, Ernie 25–31, 33–34, 36, 41, 43, 48–49, 53, 88, 91, 131, 136, 255
Lillywhite, Verl 41–52, 123, 125, 128, 134, 136, 138, 141, 145, 256
Lindheimer, Benjamin 7, 23, 78
Lio, Augie 39, 107–108, 110, 112–115, 117, 256
Livingstone, Bob 13, 41–42, 44–45, 47–51, 53–54, 129, 143, 151, 163, 257
Logel, Bob 257
Lolotai, Al 57, 257
Lukens, Jim 49, 52, 139, 144, 164, 257
Lund, Bill 26–27, 29–32, 34–36, 38–39, 94–96, 100, 104, 109, 118, 258

Maceau, Mel 258
Madar, Elmer 35, 38–39, 149, 258
Maddock, Bob 347
Maggioli, Chick 41–45, 258
Magliolo, Joe 43, 155, 259
Maloney, Ned 43, 46–47, 50, 52, 122, 125, 259
Manders, Pug 25–27, 30–32, 34, 85, 92, 95, 99–100, 131, 259

Marcolini, Hugo 41–42, 45, 260
Marefos, Andy 25, 28, 31–32, 85, 89, 91, 98, 260
Marino, Vic 261
Martineau, Earl 347
Martinelli, Patsy 29, 85, 261
Martinovich, Phil 31–32, 39, 89–93, 95–98, 100, 102–105, 107, 109–114, 116, 118, 261
Masini, Len 34, 37, 40–41, 43, 109, 115, 261
Maskas, John 150, 165, 261
Masterson, Bernie 347
Masterson, Bob 27, 29–33, 101, 261, 347
Mastrangelo, John 58, 149, 262
Matheson, Riley 43, 56, 58, 262
Mathews, Ned 25–28, 30–32, 34–39, 88, 90–91, 109, 112, 114, 117, 263, 342, 348
Matisi, John 263
Mattingly, Fran 37, 264
Mayne, Lew 25–32, 34–35, 37–39, 41–42, 44–45, 67, 84, 87, 89, 92, 113, 116, 118–119, 264
Mazza, Vince 35–36, 44, 47, 113, 128, 132, 135, 164, 264
McBride, Arthur 3, 23, 78
McCain, Bob 27, 264
McCarthy, Jim 27, 29–32, 35, 42, 46, 49, 52, 54, 67, 84–85, 87, 90, 92, 100, 123–124, 126, 128–129, 131–132, 134–138, 140–141, 143, 146, 265
McCollum, Harley 38–39, 265
McCormick, Len 44, 265
McCormick, Walter 153, 265
McDonald, Flip 265
McDonald, Walt 26–28, 30–31, 34–35, 37, 39, 41–43, 47–48, 58, 97, 121, 125, 266
McKeever, Edward 5, 343, 348
McLean, Scooter 348
McMullen, Danny 348
McQuary, Jack 266
McWilliams, Shorty 48–51, 155, 164, 266
Meagher, Jack 344, 348–349
Mello, Jim 41–42, 45, 47, 131–132, 267
Mellus, John 32–33, 36, 87, 267
Mertes, Bus 25, 27, 29–32, 34–35, 39–42, 45–46, 48–49, 53, 86, 107, 117, 125, 128–129, 131, 133–135, 267
Michalske, Mike 348
Mieszkowski, Ed 109, 268
Mihal, Joe 268
Mikula, Tom 268
Miller, Creighton 348
Millner, Wayne 348
Mitchell, Bob 26, 28–29, 34–38, 41–43, 104, 119, 269
Mitchell, Fondren 26–27, 29–31, 268
Mitchell, Paul 40, 50, 52, 268

Molenda, Bo 348
Morabito, Anthony 3–4, 23
Morgan, Joe 48, 269
Morris, Max 26–27, 35, 38–40, 42, 45–47, 104, 113, 126–127, 269
Morrow, Bob 26, 28, 270
Morrow, Russ 26, 28, 32, 67, 91, 270
Morton, Jack 27, 29, 32, 89, 270
Motley, Marion 10–13, 16, 19, 25, 27, 29–33, 35–42, 44–47, 49–58, 60–61, 66, 68, 85–87, 89, 92, 94, 97, 100–111, 114–116, 118–119, 121, 124–126, 128, 130, 132–134, 137–139, 141, 143, 145, 270
Mulready, Jerry 35, 271
Murphy, George 48–49, 165, 271
Musso, George 348
Mutryn, Chet 11–13, 16–17, 25, 27, 29–33, 35–42, 44–47, 49–54, 56–58, 64, 68, 88–89, 91, 93, 99, 102, 104–110, 113, 115, 120–121, 123–129, 131–132, 134–137, 139–146, 163, 167, 271

Nabors, Roland 43, 150, 272
National Football League 2–9, 14–18, 20–24, 55–56, 78–82, 84, 96, 99, 110, 112–113, 131, 140, 145, 147–148, 168, 342
Naumu, Johnny 41, 43–45, 272
Negus, Fred 43, 47, 50, 53, 57, 67, 115, 124, 129, 135, 163, 272
Nelson, Herb 26–27, 35, 273
Nelson, Jimmy 25–32, 100, 273
Nelson, Bob 2, 10–13, 15, 29–33, 36, 40–41, 44, 52, 55–58, 85–86, 92, 96, 105, 135–144, 170, 273–274
Nemeth, Steve 11, 26, 28–29, 31–32, 34–36, 39–40, 86–91, 93, 95–97, 100, 103, 274
Nevers, Ernie 342, 348–349
Niedziela, Bruno 273
Nolander, Don 29, 274
Norberg, Hank 27, 29, 35, 274–275
North, John 12, 42–43, 47, 49, 52, 120, 122, 134, 138, 140–141, 144, 151, 275
Nowaskey, Bob 26–27, 29, 31–32, 35–37, 39, 43, 50, 58, 86, 91–92, 98, 275
Nygren, Bernie 25, 27–28, 30–32, 85, 275

Obeck, Victor 29, 31, 276
O'Connor, Zeke 42, 45–47, 120, 127, 133–134, 153, 276
Olenski, Mitch 30–31, 90, 276
O'Neal, Jim 276
Oristaglio, Bob 49, 143, 164, 276
O'Rourke, Charlie 25–26, 28–31, 33–34, 38, 40–43, 47–49, 85–89, 91–92, 98–99, 101, 103–105, 107, 110, 112–113, 116, 118, 122–125, 127, 277
Ossowski, Ted 150, 277

Ottele, Dick 41, 45, 154, 277
Owens, Ike 156, 277

Paffrath, Bob 25, 27–32, 85, 100, 277–278
Page, Paul 48–51, 160, 278
Paine, Homer 153, 164, 278
Palmer, Derrell 114, 278
Panciera, Don 47–48, 136–138, 140–144, 159, 165, 278–279
Parker, Ace 23–26, 28–32, 55, 57, 64, 84, 91–92, 94–98, 101, 279
Parker, Howie 43, 279–280
Parks, Mickey 280
Parseghian, Ara 41–43, 45, 47–49, 120, 128, 130, 134, 156, 280
Parsons, Earle 25, 27, 29–32, 34–35, 37–38, 40, 89–91, 103, 108, 280
Patanelli, Mike 280
Patterson, Paul 48–52, 134, 136–138, 143, 166, 280–281
Pavlich, Charles 281
Pearcy, Jim 58, 166, 281
Pecarovich, Michael 349
Perantoni, Frank 281
Perina, Bob 15, 25–26, 28–31, 33–39, 41, 43–45, 54, 88, 91, 94, 96, 103, 105, 107, 112, 119, 123, 128, 281–282
Perko, John 282
Perpich, George 29, 31, 282
Perrotti, Mike 43, 165, 282
Perry, Joe 12, 24, 40–47, 49, 51–55, 57, 59–60, 66, 68, 120, 122–126, 128, 130, 132–133, 135–139, 142, 145, 282–283
Pfohl, Bob 40–42, 44–46, 48–49, 51–52, 67, 122–123, 125, 130, 138, 156, 283–284
Phelan, Jimmy 349
Phillips, Mike 108, 284
Piggott, Bert 34–38, 40, 112, 284
Pipkin, Joyce 165, 284
Pirro, Rocco 104, 284
Piskor, Ray 285
Polanski, John 25, 27–28, 32, 87–88, 99, 285
Pool, Hampton 4, 27, 85–86, 94, 285, 343, 344, 349
Poole, Barney 49–50, 52, 136, 154, 285–286
Poole, Ollie 36–37, 39, 43, 286
Prewitt, Felto 28, 36, 95, 113, 286
Price, Cotton 25–28, 30–31, 85–86, 94–95, 286–287
Principe, Dom 25, 27, 30–32, 84, 90, 92, 287
Proctor, Dewey 26–27, 32, 34–36, 38–41, 43, 47–48, 84–86, 103, 121, 125, 287
Prokop, Eddie 25–27, 29–39, 41–42, 44–46, 48–49, 51–52, 61, 95–97, 101–104, 106, 109, 114, 118–119, 121, 123–124, 132, 137–138, 287–288

Pucci, Ben 288
Puddy, Hal 288
Pugh, Marion 25–27, 30–32, 85–86, 95–96, 98–100, 288
Purdin, Cal 26–27, 29–31, 288–289
Purdue, Bolo 281

Quillen, Frank 27, 29–32, 35, 40, 100, 106, 289
Quilter, Charley 289

Radovich, Bill 10–11, 13, 56–57, 95, 289
Raimondi, Ben 34, 149, 290
Ramsey, Knox 58, 130, 154, 163, 290
Ramsey, Ray 13, 33, 35–39, 41–46, 48–54, 58–59, 61, 101, 104, 107, 109–110, 113, 115, 117–118, 125, 128, 130–131, 134, 137–138, 140, 143, 164, 290
Rapacz, John 57–58, 150, 163, 291
Ratterman, George 33–34, 39–41, 46–48, 52–53, 56–58, 64, 66–67, 102, 104–108, 111–113, 115, 117, 120–121, 123–127, 129, 131–146, 291
Reece, Don 25, 28–29, 32, 94, 291
Reese, Hank 349
Reinhard, Bill 34–37, 39–45, 47, 95, 116–118, 121, 124–125, 130, 166, 292
Reinhard, Bob 10, 12–14, 26, 28, 32, 34–38, 40–45, 49, 53, 55–58, 88, 103, 110, 127, 142, 292
Reisz, Albie 34, 36, 292–293
Remington, Bill 293
Renfro, Dick 25, 30–32, 60, 85–86, 293
Reynolds, Jim 25, 28, 30–31, 95, 293–294
Richeson, Ray 51–52, 157, 163, 294
Riffle, Charley 43, 57, 119, 294
Robertson, Tom 294
Robnett, Ed 34, 150, 294
Rockwell, Hank 43, 294–295
Rodgers, Hosea 47–49, 52, 134–135, 139–140, 143, 165, 295
Rokisky, John 28, 32–33, 36, 39, 93, 101, 103–107, 109–113, 115, 117–118, 295
Roskie, Ken 25–26, 28, 174, 209, 295, 330
Rothrock, Cliff 295–296
Rowe, Harmon 11, 34, 36, 38–39, 44, 46, 48, 50, 119, 140, 296
Ruby, Martin 10–13, 18, 28, 50, 53, 55–58, 89, 136, 296
Ruetz, Joe 28, 296
Ruffo, Albert 349
Ruskusky, Roy 36, 296–297
Russell, Jack 10–13, 17, 27, 32, 35–39, 42, 44, 46, 49–50, 52, 56–58, 88, 94, 97–98, 101, 103, 109, 113–114, 118–119, 126, 128–129, 131–132, 140–141, 144, 297
Ruthstrom, Ralph 50, 297

Rykovich, Julie 33, 35–46, 60, 106, 108, 110–111, 113, 115, 117, 121, 124, 128, 131, 297–298
Rymkus, Lou 4, 10–14, 51–52, 55–58, 89, 101, 298

Saban, Lou 11–13, 19, 26–28, 36, 39–40, 43, 50, 52–53, 56–59, 114–116, 130, 133, 135–136, 138, 141, 298–299
Sabuco, Tino 299
St. John, Herb 154, 315
Salata, Paul 49, 52, 134, 139, 142, 144–146, 299
Sanders, Spec 10–11, 13, 16–17, 25–30, 32–34, 36–46, 53–54, 56–58, 60, 63–64, 66–68, 84–86, 88–92, 94–95, 97–98, 100–104, 106–110, 112–115, 117–122, 124–126, 129, 131–132, 166, 299–300
Sandig, Curt 26, 28–31, 33, 84, 300
Satterfield, Al 149, 300
Sazio, Ralph 41, 156, 166, 300
Scafide, John 349
Scarry, Mo 28, 56–57, 88, 94, 102, 300–301
Schiechl, John 36, 102, 301
Schilling, Ralph 301
Schleich, Vic 166, 301
Schneider, Don 41, 43–45, 152, 301
Schneider, Leroy 301
Schnellbacher, Otto 12–13, 20, 42–45, 47, 49–51, 53, 58–59, 64, 67–68, 126–129, 132, 140, 144, 153, 301–302
Schroeder, Bill 26, 28–31, 34–36, 103–104, 109, 117, 302
Schroll, Bill 50, 164, 167, 302
Schuette, Carl 43, 47, 120–121, 128, 165, 302–303
Schwartz, Perry 27, 30–31, 101, 303
Schwenk, Bud 26, 32–34, 40–42, 57, 95–97, 99–100, 104–105, 107–108, 110, 112–115, 117–118, 303
Scott, Prince 27, 29–32, 85–86, 89–90, 95, 303–304
Scott, Tom 342, 349
Scott, Vin 304
Scruggs, Ted 43, 58, 151, 304
Sensanbaugher, Dean 41, 47, 154, 304
Sergienko, George 304
Sexton, Lin 41, 43–45, 127, 153, 304–305
Seymour, Bob 25, 27–30, 32, 87, 95–96, 98, 305
Sharkey, Ed 50, 140, 144, 305–306
Shaw, Buck 24, 84, 119, 128, 349
Shetley, Rhoten 26, 28, 306
Shipkey, Ted 349–350
Shirley, Marion 123, 155, 306
Shoener, Hal 12, 42, 46, 49–51, 120, 135, 146, 306–307
Shurnas, Marshall 35, 151, 307
Sidorik, Alex 307

Index

Sieradzki, Stephen 307
Signaigo, Joe 12, 57–58, 151, 307
Sigurdson, Sig 35, 307
Simmons, Jack 307–308
Simonetti, Lenny 36, 308
Sinkwich, Frankie 26, 33–34, 36–38, 102, 308–309
Sivell, Jim 309
Smith, Bill 154, 309
Smith, Bob 41, 43–44, 46, 49, 309
Smith, Gaylon 25, 27, 29, 32, 86–87, 93–94, 99–100, 310
Smith, George 36, 103, 310
Smith, Jim 310–311
Smith, Joe 41–42, 44, 47, 122–123, 153, 311
Sneddon, Bob 26, 28–29, 311
Soboleski, Joe 163, 311
Sossamon, Lou 40, 56–58, 117, 311
Spavital, Jim 48–51, 154, 163, 167, 311–312
Speedie, Mac 10–14, 27–28, 30–32, 34–35, 39, 41–42, 45–46, 49, 52–58, 61, 64, 67–68, 84, 88–89, 92–97, 100–101, 104–106, 108–112, 115–116, 118–119, 121, 123, 126–128, 134–135, 138–139, 141, 143, 145–146, 312
Spencer, Joe 153, 312
Spruill, Jim 312
Standlee, Norm 11, 13, 25, 28, 30–33, 35, 38–39, 41, 43, 45, 47–48, 50, 52–53, 56–58, 94, 97, 99, 103–106, 108–111, 114, 116, 120, 123–124, 128, 130, 134–136, 142, 145, 313
Stanley, C.B. 313
Stanton, Bill 165, 313
Stanton, Henry 27, 313
Stasica, Stan 313–314
Statuto, Art 43, 163, 314
Stautzenberger, Odell 142, 164, 314
Stefik, Bob 46–47, 314
Steuber, Bob 4, 26, 28, 30–31, 34, 40–46, 123–128, 314
Stevens, Mal 5, 92, 342, 350
Stewart, Ralph 314–315
Stidham, Tom 350
Still, Jim 41–43, 48–49, 121, 126, 133–134, 157, 164, 315
Stofer, Ken 26, 28–31, 84, 90, 315
Stone, Billy 48–49, 51–52, 59, 134–135, 137–138, 140–141, 143–144, 315–316
Strader, Red 350
Strohmeyer, George 43–44, 46, 50, 58, 126, 129, 134, 150, 165, 316
Strzykalski, John 25, 33–54, 56, 58–59, 67, 84, 96–98, 102, 106, 108–109, 111–112, 114–116, 120–126, 130, 132–133, 135, 138–139, 316–317
Stuart, Roy 317
Sullivan, Bob G. 41, 45–46, 151, 317
Sullivan, Bob J. 41–43, 45, 47, 122, 317–318

Sumpter, Tony 318
Susoeff, Nick 27, 30–31, 35, 39, 42, 45–47, 49, 53, 88, 112, 117, 126, 138–139, 318
Susteric, Ed 48–49, 51, 53, 138, 318
Sutton, Joe 48–51, 53, 135, 139, 165, 318–319
Sweiger, Bob 26–31, 33–36, 38–42, 45–46, 48–51, 57, 61, 97, 106–108, 119, 132, 319, 350
Sylvester, John 34–38, 44, 46, 319–320

Tackett, Doyle 26–27, 29–32, 36, 44, 46, 95–96, 105, 116, 320
Taliaferro, George 47–52, 57–58, 134–135, 138–144, 158, 163, 320–321
Tarrant, Jimmy 26, 89–90, 321
Tavener, John 321
Taylor, Chuck 321
Taylor, John 350
Terlep, George 25–26, 28, 30–31, 33–34, 37, 39, 41–42, 86–89, 93–94, 97, 99, 104, 113, 127, 134, 321–322
Terrell, Ray 25, 27–28, 30–32, 34–38, 84, 97, 101, 322
Tevis, Lee 34–36, 42–47, 118–119, 125, 127–129, 322
Tew, Lowell 41–42, 44–46, 48, 51–53, 128–129, 132, 136, 153, 322–323
Thibaut, Jim 26, 32, 92–93, 323
Thompson, Hal 34–35, 42, 47, 123, 323
Thompson, Tommy 50, 153, 323
Thornton, Rupe 37–38, 115, 323
Thurbon, Bob 26, 28, 30–31, 324
Tillman, Pete 156, 324
Timmons, Charlie 26, 28, 324
Tinsley, Bud 137, 163, 324
Titchenal, Bob 26–27, 34–35, 87, 93–94, 324–325
Tittle, Y.A. 24, 40–41, 46–48, 52–53, 55, 58, 66–67, 120–122, 124–144, 325
Tomasetti, Lou 25, 27, 29–42, 45–46, 48–53, 87–88, 102, 111, 121, 124, 126, 128, 131–132, 134, 137, 140, 144–145, 166, 325–326
Trebotich, Buzz 34, 38–39, 326
Trigilio, Frank 25, 32, 98, 326–327

Ulinski, Ed 10, 26, 56–58, 90, 327
Ulrich, Hub 27, 32, 95, 327
Urban, Gasper 44, 327
Uremovich, Emil 44, 327

Vacanti, Sam 33–34, 40–42, 47–48, 51–53, 104–107, 109–110, 117–118, 121, 126, 140, 152, 327–328
Vandeweghe, Al 27, 30–32, 67, 85, 88, 328
Van Tone, Art 26–27, 29–32, 93, 95, 100, 328
Vardian, Johnny 26–27, 30–31, 34–38, 40–42, 44–45, 90, 112, 328–329
Vasicek, Vic 49, 160, 163, 329
Verry, Norm 329
Vetrano, Joe 25–32, 34, 37–39, 41, 43, 45–46, 48, 50, 52, 54, 59, 68, 84, 86–88, 90–91, 93–94, 96–99, 102–103, 105–106, 108–109, 111–117, 120, 122–126, 128, 130, 132–142, 144–145, 174, 209, 295, 329–330
Vinnola, Paul 26–27, 29–31, 330
Vogds, Evan 330
Vogt, Allie 330
Voigts, Bob 350
Volz, Wilbur 48–49, 51, 53, 144, 159, 164, 331
Voyles, Carl 119, 342, 350

Wagner, Lowell 26–27, 29–32, 35, 40, 42–43, 47–48, 50, 52–53, 84, 89, 101, 103, 124–125, 144, 331
Wallace, Bev 34, 36, 41–43, 48, 50, 53, 125, 139, 331–332
Ward, Arch 3, 24, 78
Warren, Morrie 41, 45, 332
Warrington, Tex 36, 58, 84, 111, 130, 166, 332
Wasserbach, Lloyd 29–31, 332
Wedemeyer, Herm 13, 41–45, 47–51, 54, 58, 61, 64, 67–68, 121–125, 143, 148, 332–333
Weinmeister, Arnie 12–13, 18, 56, 58, 333
Wendell, Martin 58, 135, 153, 163, 333
Werder, Dick 150, 333
Werner, Albert 350
Wetz, Harlan 149, 333
Whalen, Jerry 333
Whaley, Ben 333
White, Gene 333–334
White, Jack 350–351
Whitlow, Ken 28, 98, 334
Wilkin, Willie 28–29, 334, 342, 351
Wilkins, Dick 48–49, 52, 134–135, 139–141, 143, 164, 167, 334
Williams, Joel 334
Williams, Tex 29, 334–335
Williams, Walt 26, 28–32, 61, 67, 86, 89, 93, 97, 335
Williams, Windell 42, 45–47, 49, 53, 125, 129, 137, 335
Williamson, Ernie 165, 335
Willis, Bill 10–13, 18, 50, 55–58, 130, 137, 335–336
Wimberly, Ab 49–50, 52, 139–141, 155, 164, 336
Winkler, Bernie 155, 336
Wissman, Pete 50, 161, 336
Witucki, Bernie 351
Wizbicki, Alex 34, 37–38, 40, 43–45, 48, 50–51, 109–110, 139–140, 164, 336–337

Woodard, Dick 50, 53, 165, 337
Woudenberg, John 11, 13, 38–39, 56–59, 337
Wozniak, John 41, 43, 58, 155, 337–338
Wukits, Al 28, 94, 338
Wyhonic, John 338

Yackanich, Joe 338
Yokas, Frank 338
Yonakor, John 13, 17, 27, 32, 35, 38–40, 42, 44, 50, 52, 58–59, 86–87, 100–101, 106, 112, 143, 338–339
Yonamine, Wally 34–38, 339
Young, Buddy 33, 35, 37–39, 41–42, 44–58, 60, 66, 80, 102–104, 107, 109–110, 112, 114–115, 117–120, 125, 127–129, 136, 138, 140–144, 148, 339–340

Young, George 27, 43, 47, 125, 133, 340

Zontini, Lou 26–32, 84–85, 87–91, 93–97, 99, 340–341
Zorich, George 29, 31, 341

www.ingramcontent.com/pod-product-compliance
Lightning Source LLC
Chambersburg PA
CBHW080756300426
44114CB00020B/2740